Beginning E-Commerce with Visual Basic, ASP, SQL Server 7.0 and MTS

Matthew Reynolds

Wrox Press Ltd. ®

Beginning E-Commerce
with Visual Basic, ASP,
SQL Server 7.0 and MTS

© 2000 Wrox Press

First Printed:	February 2000
Reprinted:	April 2000

Published by Wrox Press Ltd,
Arden House, 1102 Warwick Road, Acocks Green, Birmingham B27 6BH, UK.
Printed in Canada
3 4 5 TRI 04 03 02 01 00
ISBN 1-861003-9-86

Trademark Acknowledgements

Credits

Author
Matthew Reynolds

Additional Material
Jerry Ablan
Chris Ullman

Technical Reviewers
Elise Naomi G
Richard Harrison
John Kauffman
Juan T. Llibre
Kevin Lundy
Ruth Nantais
Steven C. Robertson
Salman Sheikh
Adrian Teasdale

Technical Editors
Ian Blackham
Kate Hall
Andrew Polshaw
Robin Smith
Chris Ullman

Managing Editors
Chris Hindley
Joanna Mason

Development Editor
Dominic Lowe

Project Manager
Tony Berry

Design/Layout
Tom Bartlett
Mark Burdett
Jonathan Jones
John McNulty

Figures
Tom Bartlett

Cover
Chris Morris

Index
Michael Brinkman

Proofreader
Christopher Smith

About the Author

Matthew Reynolds is an independent Internet consultant and evangelist specializing in building high-end Web sites based on the Windows DNA paradigm. He lives in the United Kingdom and divides his time equally between consulting work for established "dot coms" and donating time to help enthusiastic Internet startups get from idea to IPO. He can be reached at `matthewr@wrox.com`.

Acknowledgements

I'd like to thank pretty much everyone I know for his or her contribution to making this book possible! This includes: Alex, Darren, Edward, Vickie, Tim, Clare, Paul, Claire, Jenni, Niamh, Steve, Natasha, Mark, David, Tom, Ollie, Chris, Alex B, Chris C, Neil, Nick, Amir, Gretchen, Benjamin, Brandon, Denise, Rick, Steve, Mum, Dad and apologies to everyone else that I've shamefully omitted.

Much sincere appreciation has to go to the sterling efforts of the Wrox team, without whom this book would in no way have been possible. Ian and Kate – I'd like to extend special thanks for putting your life on hold these past few weeks to make this book a success. Thanks also go to Dominic, Chris, Tony, Sophie, and everyone else at Wrox.

Finally, thanks to Jo for kindly agreeing to be the subject of this book and being willing to become a geek icon the world over!

Table of Contents

Chapter 6: Building the Product Catalog   153

Chapter 7: The Shopping Basket   205

Chapter 9: Order Processing   321

Introduction

E-commerce is one of *the* major concerns playing on the minds of corporate executives the world over. In interview after interview, senior managers say one of the biggest challenges facing their organizations is how to effectively leverage the Internet, to give them a competitive advantage (or make sure they're not left behind!).

But e-commerce isn't just for the big multi-nationals – one of beauties of the Web is that anybody can establish themselves with a Web site that can be accessed by a world-wide consumer base. Increasingly, small and medium enterprises are realizing that, with a reasonable amount of computing skill, common sense, and the entrepreneurial enterprise that has kept them going in business they too can take part in this new marketing paradigm.

This book is aimed squarely at those who are wishing to become acquainted with e-business at the grass roots level, who do not have IT departments and computing gurus sitting at their elbows (and the spare cash to invest in serious consultancy). Through a book-long case study, we lead you through the steps needed to put a small, one-shop specialist retailer, up onto the Web with a site that can turn them from a retailer into an e-tailer.

During the study we'll show you the underlying computing models you need to understand to design an Internet based application, we'll give you a grasp of the software concepts we employ during the full coding of the solution. The software we develop in this book will be flexible enough to act as a basis for your own solutions. As a natural course of the project we'll discuss some of the marketing strategies you may wish to implement as part of your solution.

At the end of this book, you'll be in a position to know how to get your business on the Web and available to a world-wide audience.

Who Should Read this Book

This book is a *Beginning...*. series book and we aim to take you gently from knowing nothing about e-commerce, to a point where you'll be able to put up a Web site that will make money for your business. That's a tall order and we don't pretend that there aren't points in the book where you'll have to take some professional advice (after all we're going to show you how to take credit card orders so there's some pretty serious stuff in here!). We do signpost those points clearly though, and a careful reading of this book will help you to understand the questions you need to ask...and the answers you get.

To start this book we would expect you to have a certain knowledge of Visual Basic programming (say familiarity with the level reached by the end of *Beginning Visual Basic 6, ISBN 1861001053*). An acquaintance with ASP will help (if you've read *Beginning Active Server Pages 2.0, ISBN 1861001347* you'll be absolutely on top of the material), although if you haven't we have an ASP quick reference in Appendix C.

Apart from that the book is aimed at people who are looking to provide Web based e-commerce solutions for small and medium enterprises, who are *not* in a position to use high end Web solutions based on Microsoft Site Server.

How to Get the Most from this Book

The detailed software requirements for building the project are outlined in Chapter 2, but as a short list you'll need:

❑ Windows NT 4.0 Workstation is the suggested platform for this book. You'll also need the Windows NT Option Pack which can be ordered (or downloaded free) from Microsoft's web site at
   `http://www.microsoft.com/ntserver/nts/downloads/recommended/NT4OptPk/default.asp`.

❑ Microsoft Visual Basic 6.0

❑ Microsoft Visual InterDev 6.0

❑ Microsoft SQL Server (Desktop version)

What's Covered in this Book

The following is a brief roadmap of where this book is going to take us:

Chapter 1 gets you started off on the e-commerce road. We'll be looking at what e-commerce is and why it's going to be a big thing in business – as such we consider how offline and online business's differ. We also introduce Jo's Coffee; the small single-shop business that we're going convert from being a retailer to becoming an e-tailer over the course of the book.

Chapter 2 opens up with a look at the underlying concepts behind designing software solutions for the Internet. We look at the benefits of 3-tier development including the separation of business logic from presentation and data logic, and the flexibility and scalability such an approach offers. This is where we start out on the Jo's Coffee project by creating a database and opening the Visual InterDev project we'll use.

Chapter 3 is where we get stuck into the business tier of the application. Before we start coding the ActiveX DLL which will power the site, we firstly run through a quick overview of the software programming paradigms we'll be using (object and component-oriented programming). Secondly, we set about designing the object model, which we implement when we code the `WroxCommerce` project.

Presenting the online store is the focus of **Chapter 4**. We step back from the business tier and look at the aesthetics of web site design. We discuss how to use include files to produce reusable code, how to design an easily navigable site, and how to create a consistent style through the site.

In **Chapter 5** we consider how to structure the store. This involves addressing database and presentation tier issues to allow us to present information to the customer in a logical and engaging manner. Additionally, this is the point at which we start to construct the administration tools that will enable us to manage our site and keep the information it holds up-to-date.

Moving into **Chapter 6** we'll deal with all three tiers of the development architecture as we expand the database to store product information. Following on from this, we have to enhance the functionality of the object model to allow us to deal with these new tables and, of course, we have to modify our ASP pages to allow us to access the information.

In **Chapter 7** is where we start to build in the components that allow us to move from a display site to a commerce site. Here we'll build the code (in all 3 logical tiers) that gives us the functionality of a shopping basket on our site.

Once our customers have a full shopping basket the next stop is the checkout, which is what we construct in **Chapter 8** after we discuss how to keep track of the customers carrying that basket.

Chapter 9 involves some theory, as we consider the various steps along the order-processing route and develop the concept of a pipeline. Once we have our pipeline planned, we start a new project (`WroxProcessing`) that will enable us to take advantage of the transactional management capabilities of MTS. In this chapter, we discuss who to carry out online credit card transactions.

Chapter 10 moves slightly away from our project, but gives you important information on secure communications. Since you'll want sensitive credit card information from your customers – you need to make sure they are confident in dealing with you. This is one of the areas where you'll need professional advice to build on the content of the chapter.

With **Chapter 11** it's back once more to our project, as we see how we can add simple search functionality to the site to complement the existing navigation for moving around the store's departments.

Chapter 12, again strays away from coding and discusses deployment. Firstly, we examine the issues surrounding finding a suitable host for your site and secondly we look at how, practically, we move our code from our development server to the ISP production server.

Customer confidence in your site is built by a number of things (security we alluded to earlier), in **Chapter 13** we consider the issue of privacy, and our attitude to the data we collect on our customers while they shop with us.

In **Chapter 14** we move on to discuss the customer support strategies we want to put in place to enhance our reputation as a good organization to deal with.

This theme is continued in **Chapter 15** when we look at how we can set up a forum, where people can use the Web site to chat to each other about topics of mutual interest related to the theme of coffee (which coincidentally is being sold on a page only a click away).

This move to more sophisticated online marketing also involves advertising related items to those your customers have already selected, and showing featured items – a topic area that is covered in **Chapter 16**.

In **Chapter 17** we really expand our horizons and look at how we may set ourselves up for data interchange with our suppliers – to this end we're going to look at the technology of XML, and how it can be used in our site.

Finally, in **Chapter 18** we look at marketing our site so we can attract more people to Jo's Coffee.

Conventions Used

You are going to encounter different styles as you are reading through this book. This has been done to help you easily identify different types of information and to help you keep from missing any key points. These styles are:

> **Important information, key points, and additional explanations are displayed like this to make them stand out. Be sure to pay attention to these when you find them.**

General notes, background information, and brief asides look like this.

❑ Keys that you press on the keyboard, like *Ctrl* and *Delete*, are displayed in italics

❑ If you see something like, `BackupDB`, you'll know that it is a filename, object name or function name

❑ The first time you encounter an **important word**, it is displayed in bold text

❑ Words that appear on the screen, such as menu options, are in a similar font to the one used on screen, for example, the File menu

This is how code samples look the first time they are introduced:

```
Private Sub Command_Click
    MsgBox "Don't touch me"
End Sub
```

Whereas code that you've already seen or that doesn't relate directly to the point being made, looks like this:

```
Private Sub Command_Click
    MsgBox "Don't touch me"
End Sub
```

Customer Support

We want to know what you think about this book; what you liked, what you didn't like, and what you think we can do better next time. You can send your comments, either by returning the reply card in the back of the book, or by e-mail (to feedback@wrox.com). Please be sure to mention the book title in your message.

❑ **Source Code** – Source code for the examples used in this book, as well as the example source database script, can be downloaded from Wrox's web site at: http://www.wrox.com.

❑ **Errata** – We've made every effort to make sure that there are no errors in the text or the code. However, to err is human and as such we recognize the need to keep you informed of any mistakes as they're spotted and corrected. Errata sheets are available for all our books at www.wrox.com. If you find an error that hasn't already been reported, please let us know.

P2P.WROX.COM

For author and peer support join the Beginning E-Commerce and ASP mailing lists. Our unique system provides **programmer to programmer™ support** on mailing lists, forums and newsgroups all *in addition* to our one-to-one e-mail system. Be confident that your query is not just being examined by a support professional, but by the many Wrox authors and other industry experts present on our mailing lists. At p2p.wrox.com you'll find six different lists, each tailored to a specific subject area that will support you, not only while you read this book, but also as you start to develop your own applications. These lists are:

❑ **ASP ECommerce** – Heavily moderated list containing only queries dealing with E-commerce and ASP. This list deals with both general queries about E-commerce (concerning topics like personalization, security, and creation of shopping baskets) and specific queries relating to the Beginning E-Commerce book. Off topic queries will be directed to either How To? or Beginning ASP.

❑ **How To?** – A general discussion of ASP topics. If there's something ASP related you'd just like to know more about, or a completely baffling problem with no solution, then this is your forum.

❑ **Beginning ASP** – A heavily moderated list to make sure that questions that can stop you dead in your tracks at an early stage of learning are answered quickly.

❑ **Code Clinic** – For readers of Professional ASP and ASP Programmer's Reference who've read the books, and are developing their own applications.

❑ **ASP Databases** – A heavily moderated list containing only queries dealing with ASP and Databases.

❑ **ASP CDO** – A heavily moderated list containing only queries dealing with ASP and e-mail integration.

To enroll for support just follow this four-step system:

1. Go to p2p.wrox.com.

2. Click on the ASP button.

3. Click on the type of mailing list you wish to join.

4. Fill in your e-mail address and password (of at least 4 digits) and e-mail it to us.

Any queries about joining, leaving lists, or any query about the list itself should be sent to moderatorecommerce@wrox.com.

From Business to E-Business

E-commerce is the name given to the business process of selling your products, goods, and services over the Web. In its simplest form, it allows your company's product catalog to be hosted on a Web server so that customers and potential customers can visit your site, see what you have to sell and then place orders. The majority of e-commerce sites that sell to general consumers ask you to pay for the items you want using a credit card, and so they present forms that can safely and securely capture this information, and perform automatic credit card authorization without human intervention.

Any size business can have an e-commerce strategy, from a sports club selling T-shirts with their name on, to a medium-sized business selling widgets, through to a traditional retail behemoth like Wal-Mart. Like most things where business and information technology intersect, the e-commerce strategy you are able to implement is dependent on the money you have to invest. For example, a large e-commerce company will be able to directly place orders into a supplier's order processing system, negating the need to have a telephone operator marshalling the sales requests from merchant to supplier. A smaller e-commerce company may still have to phone in or fax their orders. A large e-commerce company may be able to afford to buy space for prime time television commercials; a small e-commerce company may only be able to buy adverts in the local paper or industry journals.

In this chapter, we're going to set the scene for the rest of the book. In particular, we'll discuss:

- ❏ What e-commerce is and why it's more than a passing trend
- ❏ The e-commerce company that we'll be using as an example throughout the book
- ❏ Business models, and how online models and those offline compare
- ❏ The importance of getting a strong brand

So let's get started!

E-Commerce is Not a Fad

I recently attended a TechNet session at Microsoft's Customer Briefing Center in the UK and the presenter asked, "How many people have heard of Brook's Books?" No one in the room raised their hands, myself included. He proceeded to tell us that Brooks Books have been in business for about a dozen years, have a number of stores and do pretty well.

He then asked the question, "How many people have heard of Amazon.com?" Along with every one of the hundred or so attendees, I raised my hand.

Amazon.com is the "granddaddy" of an industry that's only been around for a few years. It is famous for bringing the concept of e-commerce into the mainstream. It epitomizes e-commerce success and is, arguably, now one of the most famous retailers in the western world. Before Amazon, Barnes and Noble and Borders pretty much owned the US book selling market. Both of these companies now face eroding market share from a company that came from nowhere.

Whatever has happened or will happen to American book retail, one thing is for sure. The past two years have seen an incredible shift from doing business offline through tools such as voice mail, postal mail, faxes, and face-to-face meetings to doing business online. The online shift means that we lose faxes, we lose face-to-face meetings, and the postal services in several large countries are running scared. It also means we can do business 24 hours a day, 7 days a week, and have the capability sell our products or services anywhere in the world.

What I'm trying to say is that the Internet is not a casual occurrence. It is not a "faddish technology" or something that's just neat or cool. The Internet is a new communications platform. It can connect people and organizations together in any way the individual components require. It's something that brings us as individuals and organizations together in new and exciting ways. The Internet will twist, turn, re-evaluate, and re-engineer every single logistic process that affects our lives.

We know a major shift is happening, so all we have to do is work out how to make the most of this wealth of new opportunity!

E-Commerce vs. E-Business

You may have heard the term **e-business** being bantered around and you may be wondering what exactly it is.

Well, the difference is that e-commerce refers *only* to the process of selling goods and services online. To determine if a business is an e-business requires analysis of other aspects of that business.

For example, if I receive an order through my online store, but I then phone up my supplier to replenish and shout across the room to a colleague to pack the item, I am *not* an e-business. To be an e-business, our business model re-engineering must permeate throughout all aspects of my business.

However, if I receive the order and my site automatically e-mails my supplier with a replenishment order, and then prints shipping and packing notes in my warehouse while I sit back and do nothing, then I have an e-business. OK, so it's an oversimplification, but you get my point.

> **Basically, you're an e-business when you are using Internet technologies in the majority of your business operations.**

B2B vs. B2C

Business-to-Business (**B2B**) e-commerce is the process of selling items to another business. That too is an over-simplification. If I were to place an order with Buy.com for a new hard disk for the computer I use for my work, I have not directly been part of a B2B transaction. As far as Buy.com's concerned that was a **Business-to-Consumer** (**B2C**) transaction, even though it was selling an item to another business.

> **B2B e-commerce usually suggests that there is some form of negotiated relationship between supplier and company and it's mainly used for corporate procurement.**

Microsoft Market

Microsoft's internal B2B-based procurement site Microsoft Market is an excellent example of a B2B implementation. As Microsoft Market is Microsoft's internal procurement system, it's not a product, which is why you may not have heard of it.

Before Microsoft Market, Microsoft used to spend $60 per procurement transaction. This meant that if a member of staff purchased a $1 box of paper clips, Microsoft had to spend $60 to process that transaction. Over the last few years, Microsoft has been attempting to eradicate any paperwork or unnecessary administrative tasks from its global operations. All Microsoft employees are now able to visit the Microsoft Market site and browse a list of products from preferred suppliers, and then order online. They can order anything from office supplies to computers and even cars. With the system in place, the cost per transaction has dropped to $5.

If you're interested in learning more about Microsoft Market, you can find a case study on it at http://www.microsoft.com/dns/ecommerce/msmarket.htm.

Negotiated Agreements

The important difference between B2B and B2C is that purchases are not usually made through credit cards. Typically, credit relationships exist between a company and its suppliers so accounts are balanced at the end of the month. This means that there's an opportunity for employees to seriously abuse any procurement system by placing wild and unrealistic orders into the system. Imagine visiting Amazon.com and being able to get anything you wanted for free! This loophole is plugged in paper-based systems by placing a requirement for an employee's manager to authorize any transaction before it's committed. In B2B systems, the employee's manager will be e-mailed with a request to confirm the purchase. If the purchase is approved, the transaction goes through.

Another important aspect of B2B is the connectivity between supplier and customer. Rather than having to phone or fax an order, the negotiated nature of B2B relationships typically enables customers to drop orders directly into a supplier's computer system for fulfillment. It's mainly because of this reason that B2B transactions usually only exist in situations where both parties have negotiated the arrangement.

The Internet's role in B2B is two-fold. Firstly, the presence of the Internet makes us think about communicating differently, whether it is through e-mail or whatever. Secondly, it makes the physical connection between the two systems easier. If both are connected to the Internet, there's already a physically communication route. Before the Internet, a physical link would have to be established and this would be another barrier to successful negotiation.

9

B2B is an interesting subject in the whole e-business sphere. Industry experts reckon that the B2B market will be something like ten times *bigger* than the B2C market will be when it matures. However, today there are no really compelling solutions in this space, mainly because people are trying to figure how the whole deal will shakedown. When dealing with B2B transactions, there has to be this degree of negotiation between both the buyer and the seller that doesn't exist with B2C. B2C transactions are deemed OK when a valid credit card number is presented, and the majority of the time prices are fixed and non-negotiable. As I'm sure you're aware, pricing schedules between your company and your suppliers are often negotiated.

No one really knows how to solve these problems yet in an "off-the-shelf" manner, which is why if I ask you to take a piece of paper and write down 10 B2C companies and 10 B2B companies, unless you happen to be an expert on B2B, you'll most likely find that a problem. There is one technology, however, that will play a major role in connecting the distinct computer systems of buyer and seller together, and that's **eXtensible Markup Language**, or **XML**.

An Introduction to XML

We won't be talking too much about XML in this book, because it's not strictly relevant to the B2C solution we're laying out in the book. However, Chapter 17 does go into some examples of how XML can be used and runs you through a few of the concepts. To whet your appetite, here's a primer on what XML does; but first let's look at HTML.

What's Wrong with HTML?

When Tim Berners-Lee invented HTML, he designed a language that enabled documents to be understood by an unknown, remote system to a degree that the words and layout contained within could be rendered on the screen in an agreeable fashion.

Interpretation of the data an HTML documents contains is, however, down to the person reading it. For example, if you go to an online retailer and bring up a copy of an invoice, you know it's an invoice because the world-class pattern matching technology in your brain tells you that, based on past experience, it looks extremely similar to other documents that you know for a fact were invoices. Suddenly you know its context and can understand it. However, if you try to send that same HTML document representing an invoice over to your accountant's computer, it would have a very difficult job both identifying that document as an invoice, and extracting the data from it in such a way that it can do something useful with it, such as entering it into an accounting ledger.

The Advantages of XML

XML solves this problem by allowing companies to mark-up documents in such a way that computer systems that receive them can implicitly understand what they are (so they don't have to recognize the document based on experience, they just *know* it's an invoice), and then they can easily extract the relevant data from them.

XML documents contain sections (or **elements**) indicating the shipping address, number of lines in the order, quantities, prices, taxes, etc. This time when you send the XML document over to your accountant's computer, it will be able to determine it's an invoice, extract the data, and enter it into a ledger. The proviso here is that the XML document has to be set up to adhere to a common standard so that both the computer that generated the document and the company that receives it are talking the same language. That process of ratifying document standards is one of the things slowing down widespread adoption of XML right now. How all this works is beyond the scope of the discussion for this time, but if you want to learn more about XML, I suggest you refer to *Professional XML* (Wrox Press, ISBN 1-861003-11-0).

XML's relevance to B2B is that it will most likely provide a way to share documents. Imagine an independent body defined an XML document standard for marking up purchase orders. Any B2B system that wanted to submit a request to buy would build an XML document according to the purchase order standards and then fire it off to the supplier's B2B system that would understand how to read the same document. Embedded within the document would be the details of the items in the order, together with negotiated prices and contact information. The prices would be checked against the seller's price list to make sure they matched and, if OK, the goods would be shipped and an XML shipping notice document is sent back to the buyer indicating what was shipped, when, to whom, and for how much. It's this concept of sharing documents of a known, accepted form that will allow organizations to quickly set up deals to buy and sell from each other in a true business-to-business style.

The Aim of this Book

As each e-commerce site is different, each reader of this book will be aiming for a different goal. You could be a friend of a small business owner who wants a simple e-commerce site, or you could be a consultant trying to build the next big thing in an as-yet-untapped sector of the market.

Whoever you are, by the time you reach the end of the book, you will have a basic e-commerce site running on a Microsoft Windows NT Server 4, using Microsoft SQL Server 7 for the database, and with software comprising components written in Microsoft Visual Basic 6 and Active Server Pages. It will feature:

- ❑ Managing and presenting a product catalog of unlimited size, structured into a set of departments, also of unlimited size

- ❑ A product catalog that can hold dynamic sets of attributes against the different types of items you sell

- ❑ A shopping basket that customers can use to choose the products they want from the site

- ❑ Forms that provide a way for your customers to supply address and credit card information securely

- ❑ A database structure capable of holding an unlimited number of customers, and an unlimited number of addresses and credit card details per customer

- ❑ An order-processing pipeline that can be fully customized to integrate with whatever systems you already have in place, or systems your business partners have in place

- ❑ Customer service tools that allow customers to visit the site and examine the statuses of their orders

- ❑ Search facilities that make use of Microsoft Full-Text Indexing

- ❑ Up-sell and cross-sell capabilities to suggest additional and alternative purchases to your customers

- ❑ An open object model that can be leveraged by other applications capable of hosting ActiveX components

You will also have an understanding of:

- ❑ How to create a secure server based on Secure Socket Layer technology

❏ How to integrate your Web site with a payment-processing gateway to automatically validate and authorize credit card transactions

❏ How to choose a quality hosting provider for your Web site

❏ How to implement a high-availability hosting environment – should you require one

❏ How to market your site to your customers

What you will not have by the end of the project is a turnkey solution that you can drop into your company and have an e-commerce presence. You will, however, have the foundation for a site you can use and a thorough grounding in both the technology aspects and the business aspects of producing a quality e-commerce solution. As you move from business to business, the detailed requirements and environment of each one makes it impossible to generate a "one size fits all" solution.

This book provides a framework that you can use to build your own e-commerce solution by customizing the work we do in this book. The Visual Basic project, database schema, and ASP pages are all available from the Wrox Web site at www.wrox.com. Feel free to take this software and alter it to fit the exact needs of your business.

Although we can teach you a lot in this book, we can only teach you so much. If you haven't done so by now, buy something online before proceeding! (Why not buy a copy of this book for a friend?) There's really no alternative to raw experience when building e-commerce sites – it is essential you understand how people out there are currently doing it to make sure you deliver something close to what your customers expect to see.

Jo's Coffee

This book is an imaginary account of how a small specialist coffee retailer in the UK with one store moves her business online. Throughout the book, we'll see how Jo Bovingdon transforms her single-store business into a thriving online brand. We'll see that what she does, anyone can do.

Business Models

Throughout this discussion, we'll be talking about **business models** – specifically referring to offline and online models. We describe Jo's business today, before she puts her online strategy into play, as her "offline business model".

If you're unfamiliar with the term business model, it's simply a way of describing the separate procedures and processes that a business has. "Taking your business model online" is about analyzing your existing business processes and altering them so that they make the most of online technologies.

Jo's Online and Offline Business Models

The remainder of this book goes into great detail on how each part of Jo's offline model can be transformed into her online model. Here is a very brief summary of the kinds of things we can expect to see:

Offline Model	Online Model
Store open 9-5, Monday through Saturday.	Store open 24 hours a day, 7 days a week.
Sells mainly locally.	Sells nationally. Has the option to sell internationally.
Phone number for customers.	Phone number for customers, but this has to be a toll-free number for national customers. Also accessible through e-mail.
Sells about a dozen different machines, one or two held in stock.	Can sell any number of machines. She could, if she wanted, sell any machine from any manufacturer in the world. No need to hold any in stock as our suppliers ship directly to her customers.
Coffee, filters, etc. also sold and held in stock.	Now the same process as selling individual machines, which represents a simplification in day-to-day operations.
New stock ordered by phoning suppliers.	As items are not stocked by Jo, but are instead sent directly by suppliers to her customers, she can either phone orders in to the supplier, or have the site e-mail suppliers directly, or have the site communicate with the suppliers in some other manner.
New stock delivered two days after ordering.	Goods delivered to customers two days after ordering.
Promotion through "word-of-mouth", Yellow Pages, and occasional ads in the local press.	Promotion through word-of-mouth, search engines, occasional ads in the local or national press, links from manufacturers' sites, junk e-mail, banner ads on coffee information sites. Also, promotion through community features (more later).
Jo's time is spent talking to customers and performing administrative tasks.	Jo manages the Web site, updates the product list when new products are introduced or prices changed, manages community features of the site (more later).

Banner ads are the rectangular advertisements that appear at the top of many Web sites, in return for which the site owner receives a small amount of money for each one shown, or in some cases, clicked on.

The reason why we are using Jo's Coffee is that her existing model leads to three exciting online opportunities:

❏   Equipment Retail

❏   Consumables Retail

❏   Community Building

Once Jo manages to do this, she stops being just a retailer and becomes an **e-tailer**.

Equipment Retail

Presently, the majority of Jo's business comes in the form of equipment retail. By establishing a local reputation for stocking only the best coffee machines and having a knack for understanding buyers' requirements to make a good fit, Jo gets a lot of custom as a result of word-of-mouth recommendation by satisfied customers. Because most of her business comes through these sales, the location she chose for her store is away from the main shopping district and so she doesn't get a lot of people who were "just passing".

In the current model, Jo buys stock of machines she expects to sell and has a number on display. Additionally, she's also in a position to demonstrate each machine to each customer by letting them grind their own beans in different grinders, use each machine and sample the results from each.

Along with machines, Jo also sells books on making better coffee, metal jugs for frothing and steaming milk, mixing spoons and other associated merchandise.

When we go online with her model, Jo will be able to sell a greater range of machines; she will still be able to recommend and talk about her machines, but she will lose the ability to let her customers play with the machines and to sample the results. However, she will be able to sell to a national market and, if she chooses, an international one.

Consumables Retail

When someone buys a new machine, she can usually cross-sell a number of items like filters, syrups, and coffee. However, because her location is optimized towards people buying actual machines, they rarely revisit her store; choosing instead to purchase beans, filters, and other products from a supplier that's closer, like a supermarket. The issue here is that the machines she sells are of such high quality that people don't need to come back to the store to buy new machines. She rarely sees the same customer twice.

When we go online we not only have customers coming in to buy the expensive one-off equipment, but we can continue to cross-sell consumables to them for years to come. Rather than buying coffee at their local grocery store, her customers can now purchase the particular blend they enjoy online and have it delivered.

Community Building

After her online move, we can use tried and tested tools to build community features that bring together coffee lovers from around the world to chat, share ideas, and learn about new products. This new community will be housed under the umbrella of her new online brand.

The equipment and consumable retailing sections of the site are translations of her existing, offline business model. Taking those parts online is obvious – many people are doing this. Why then do we need to introduce the community section into the model?

Imagine that we take "community building" out of her online model. Her online and offline models are then very similar in nature. In her offline model, people only walk through her front door to buy or browse her wares. If we simply transfer her existing model online, people will still only walk through her virtual front door to buy or browse. However, going online affords us an extra opportunity.

Imagine I need to find out how to make a good mocha. I might visit Excite or Yahoo, enter "mocha recipes" as a search term, and see if anything looks good. Imagine then that one of the links I choose is an article that Jo's written called "The Perfect Mocha". I read the article, and I may even bookmark or print it. More importantly, imagine there is a link on the page advertising that on this site I can also buy a new machine, or buy imported Hershey's syrup from the United States that's ideal for the mocha recipe I'm reading about. There may also be a link to a discussion forum where I can chat with fellow aficionados about whether Cadbury's is better than Hershey's in mochas.

If we introduce these community features, Jo has an alternative route for customers to come into the site. Until the point they are converted to customers (by virtue of them making a purchase), we refer to them as **visitors**. We can liken this to Jo having a coffee appreciation day where she opens her store to people who want to chat about coffee. She may get one or two new customers through such a promotion.

In the online world, we can run the appreciation day all day, every day. See the strength of including it in the online model?

Creating the Brand

An integral part of a successful e-business is establishing a good online identity. For Jo, we're going to refer to her online brand as joscoffee.com. The use of the word **brand** is important here as part of our re-engineering process. When establishing her offline store Jo thought, "I'll rent a store and sell some coffee machines". There was no consideration of establishing a national brand, mainly because in the old economy it would not have been feasible to play in that market.

Now, Jo can think nationally and, moreover, if it all works as planned more opportunities will become available. (After establishing a strong online brand with joscoffee.co.uk, Jo might decide to use that brand to springboard into a national chain of Internet cafes.) When we work with Jo's online model, we're going to be thinking "national", but with an eye on "international".

The Importance of Being Different

Taking your company online is very easy. Truthfully, it is very easy in its most basic form. I can take any business online within an hour if you give me a digital camera and a copy of FrontPage. I can create a flat page, put some photos on it, add a phone number at the bottom, register it with search engines and ask you to put your new URL on your adverts and business cards.

Like any traditional business, you have to differentiate to survive. Jo's business has done well because people know that if you want a good coffee machine, you go and see Jo. If you just wanted *any* coffee machine, you could just go down your local mall and buy one at random.

When the Internet first started to become popular many people were saying, "One man in his apartment can compete with a $5bn multinational". Well, that's valid to an extent. They were referring to a time before that particular multinational got clued in to what was going on and decided to spend the equivalent of ten times your yearly revenue on consultants to work out how to crush the uprising among amateur e-tailers.

What's happening now is that even if I sat in my apartment for a very long time it's unlikely I'd have the founder of Amazon.com, Jeff Bezos, scared any time soon. Nevertheless, I can make a living and chances are I can make a lot of money if I do it right. If my chosen strategy is to clone Amazon.com I will lose, no question, but if I offer something that Amazon.com doesn't, I can win my own personal victory.

Offering Specialized Features

Fatbrain.com is an online retailer of technical books that, like any good business, continually re-evaluates the market it's in and its competition. It realizes that it only takes someone with a bit of cash to get set up as a retailer of computer books. You or I can go to a distributor, set up an account, build a Web site and get running. (In fact, a lot of this book shows you how easy it actually is!)

The employees at Fatbrain.com are betting it all on their ability to innovate and build new features into their site, and get it established before their competition mimic those new features. At the end of August 1999, they released an initiative called "eMatter". This initiative lets people publish and sell their own work through Fatbrain.com. Anyone can post a manuscript on the site. When people download it, they pay Fatbrain.com and then Fatbrain.com in turn cuts the author of the manuscript a commission check. That's a unique program, and one of the major functions of it is to increase awareness of the Fatbrain.com brand.

Getting to the Top of Customers' Internal Lists

Through the introduction of this feature, Fatbrain.com hopes that when we think about technical books, we'll think of them first. Through shopping history, and I include traditional **bricks-and-mortar stores** here (which have a physical location that customers physically visit and make purchases from), we each have an internal list of vendors for anything we need. Getting to the top spot on that list usually means we'll visit them first. The marketing industry is based on the principle of re-ordering people's internal lists so that we think about, say, one brand of washing powder before we think of another.

When we're shopping online, if the price looks good (and most of the time it will be cheaper than buying from the local bricks-and-mortar store), we click "Add to Cart" and we're away. But what happens to the site that's tenth on our mental rankings of "online technical book retailers"? Chances are we won't even look. This exemplifies how important it is for Fatbrain.com, Amazon.com and barnesandnoble.com to stay in the top three of our internal lists.

We introduce community features into our new model not only as an alternative method to gain customers, but also to ward off competition. If we establish the site as a portal for information about coffee, chances are we will remain at the top of our customers' internal "Coffee" list.

> *A portal is a site that usually connects a number of sites together as a common meeting place or starting point for people interested in a particular subject. Some portals are so large that they appear to have no associated subject, such as Yahoo or Excite, whereas others, like Fool.com clearly have specific goals.*

Balancing Features against Stability

I want to make one last point about features. The balancing between features on your site and the stability of your site is the hardest task you have to face.

When a company is in a development mode, it can reach a point where adding new functionality is detrimental to the performance of the site. A site that is unable to sell its products to a customer is doing absolutely nothing right (or, at least, anything they are doing right is relatively worthless). It's essential that you strike a good balance between building new features in order to make the site more visible to customers and getting service provision levels as high as possible, in terms of servers and bandwidth.

So, Who's Doing It Right?

As we've discussed, quite a few sites out there are doing really well with their online models. Let's wrap up this chapter by taking a good look at Amazon so that we know the kind of thing we're aiming for.

Although Amazon has yet to make a profit, it is a major online brand. Starting as just a book reseller, it has used that brand to successfully push into music and video and is now moving into auctions and other retail sectors. This is why people often believe that Amazon is getting it right, despite a balance sheet that would spell certain death in the offline business world.

Amazon.com is going through an interesting phase right now. (Although, really it's always going through an interesting phase.) When Jeff Bezos founded the company, he was already aware of the potential of the Internet and had deliberately set out something that would not only sell online, but would sell well. He chose books and, together, he and Amazon.com made a lot of money and, as we know, changed all our lives forever.

Jeff wants to make Amazon.com capable of selling anything to anyone, which is why you'll now find music, videos, toys, games, electronics, auctions, and e-cards available. Industry analysts are often drawing comparisons between him and Sam Walton, founder of the most successful retail venture of all time: Wal-Mart.

Look at Amazon.com's home page; notice the Search box in the top left-hand corner and the clear department label banner at the top of the page:

Studies have shown that, most of the time, when people visit an online store they already have a strong idea of an item they're interested in purchasing. What Amazon is trying to facilitate here is the ability to visit the site and type in a book's ISBN number, a movie's title, or "Palm IIIx". Either way, Amazon's mission is to present the price to the visitor as quickly as possible. We'll see that theme continued through the successful sites we see, and we'll be adopting it as we work through our site.

Auctions and E-cards

The adoption of auctions on Amazon's site deserves special mention. Noticing the sheer mass of traffic that eBay, the most popular auction site, was experiencing, Amazon believed that if it also did auctions, it would see more visitors come to the site.

This approach is the same as Jo's approach of putting communities into her online business model. When Amazon starts getting people visiting the site for reasons other than making purchases, it strengthens its online brand and provides opportunities to convert visitors into customers. Moreover, Amazon has some smart technology that can associate listed auction items with items in the store. So, if I visit Amazon Auctions and look for "Trainspotting", chances are Amazon will mention to me that the Trainspotting DVD is now available for sale at $19.99. This means that it can up-sell me from a used copy of Trainspotting on VHS that someone else is selling, to a new copy on DVD that it's selling. This is an interesting example of using an internal brand to publicize another brand. By linking videos and auctions together in this way, regular visitors to the video section are "sold" the fact that Amazon also does auctions.

The inclusion of electronic greeting cards (e-cards), popularized by Blue Mountain Arts and egreetings.com is something of a surprising anomaly. Again, it could be an attempt to strengthen their brand – someone sends me a birthday card from their site and when I pick up the card, I get their brand marketing.

Summary

I hope that you've now got a really good picture of the world of e-commerce. Having defined exactly what e-commerce is and how it is different from e-business, we studied two particular forms of e-commerce: Business-to-Business (B2B) and Business-to-Commerce (B2C). We then briefly discussed the importance of XML in B2B e-commerce.

We then looked at the Jo's Coffee scenario. We saw that by including three key features (equipment retail, consumables retail, and community building), Jo becomes a true e-tailer, with a strong online brand. We discussed how, on the Internet, it is vital to find a way of being different, to distinguish your brand from the many others.

Finally, we looked at Amazon.com, which has diversified into selling not only books, but also music, video, electronics, toys and games. With the recommendations that Amazon makes, one part of Amazon publicizes another. This makes it really easy to go on to Amazon's site to buy a book, but come out having bought not only that book, but also a video and a portable DVD player.

In the next chapter, we'll discuss distributed applications and the software we'll need to build the Jo's Coffee e-commerce site.

Starting Our Site

Now that we have a sound understanding of our offline and online business models, it's time to start considering the practical aspects of site construction. To begin, we're going to have to develop an appreciation of the issues concerned with designing applications for the Internet. This will naturally lead us into making decisions about the technologies we need to use in building our application, and from there the precise software we actually require. By the end of the chapter, we will have taken our first steps in constructing the application, which will allow the world to buy from Jo's Coffee.

So, in order we'll look at:

- ❑   Distributed applications
- ❑   Software requirements for the Jo's Coffee project
- ❑   Starting the Jo's Coffee project

> **Please note, all the files for Jo's Coffee project are available for download from www.wrox.com**

Distributed Applications

The **client/server** or **two-tier** application architecture, where tasks are divided between a *server* (which stores, manipulates and delivers data) and *clients* (that need it), has over time been replaced by **distributed applications**.

The *distributed* in distributed application simply means that the functionality that the software provides is shared or distributed between a number of different users. In a small business, an accounting application may be distributed between the owner and her assistant. In a large telesales organization, a call center application may be distributed between a hundred or so telephone operators.

In the traditional client/server architecture, the server and client are both custom written applications. For example, I might fire up Visual Basic and create an application, that runs on the server, which can send lunch orders down to a local restaurant by fax. Then I can create another Visual Basic project and write another application that is capable of connecting to that server. From there I can distribute this client application to my friends and colleagues in the office to allow them to choose their lunch order and pass the request back to the server.

With this approach, I still have to face the inevitable problem of how to deploy that client application to the rest of my department. I have to go away, create a setup program and then tell them where to find it on the network. After they've installed it, I get to wait for the phone to ring as one of my colleagues tells me that it didn't install properly, or won't open up.

What the Web lets us do is scrap the client application end of the puzzle. Basically, I can assume that everyone on my network has a Web browser. I can also assume that they can connect to a server in our office that runs a copy of Personal Web Server or Internet Information Server.

Now what I do is re-engineer the functionality of my server application into a set of **business objects** (we'll discuss these in more detail in Chapter 3) and create **Active Server Pages** (**ASP**) pages that use those objects to listen to lunch orders and fax them off. I'll probably have to play around with getting the application working 100% on the server, but now I can just drop e-mail to everyone telling them that their lunch orders can now be placed through a page on the intranet and the client side deployment hassles are no longer there.

In fact, there's more. Imagine the departmental server hosting the lunch application is accessible from the Internet. If Alex was at a client meeting in the morning, he can place his lunch order from the client's site using a Web browser. Most likely this would not be possible if our distributed application had a custom Visual Basic client. Now this is just an example of what a distributed application using Web browser clients is capable of – to make a fully viable online application there are issues such as security we'd have to worry about, but you get the idea.

We can describe our lunch application as a *distributed application using a Web browser as its presentation tier*, (tiers are considered in more detail below). What it means is that, providing we build our application in such a way that it uses a Web server as an **application server** (and this can be through Active Server Pages, or other similar technologies), any user having a Web browser can potentially use the application. We do not need them to have access to a custom-built client application.

Connecting to the Distributed Application

Now that we have an idea of what distributed applications are, let's take a look at where the users of joscoffee.com could reside (don't worry about the connection technicalities; we'll revisit those later):

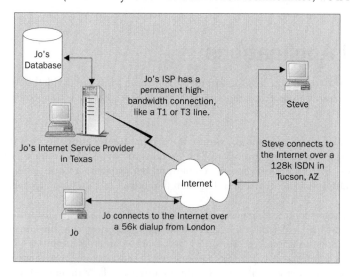

Before the Internet, an application with a server in Texas, a user in London and another user in Arizona would have been a fairly impressive achievement. Although the technology has been around for decades, it would not have been a practical proposition to build this kind of distributed application just for selling coffee to consumers.

Usually, the Internet is described as "a giant network of computers" or some such thing. The reason why the Internet is such a fabulous tool is that it enables systems to connect and coalesce in ways that previously would have been impossible or impractical.

Try this: open your browser and connect to Amazon.com and consider what's *really* happening. Although you could say, "I'm looking at a Web page", that's only half the story. In reality, you're extending the distributed computer system of Amazon.com by adding your PC into the mix. On some level, its computer system is not just the computers installed in its data center, but rather it's all that, *plus* the thousand or so other visitors, *plus* the computers that its suppliers use, the computers that their supplier's suppliers use and so on and so on.

The Internet enables businesses, organizations, and individuals to rapidly connect, disconnect and reconnect the computer they're currently using into a variety of Web-based distributed applications, such as e-commerce sites, auction sites or television guide sites.

For Jo, it means that Steve in Tucson, and herself in London can easily become part of the distributed application that's hosted and running at her ISP in Texas. Before, she'd have to make an international phone call or she'd have to negotiate a fixed link between British Telecom and AT&T to get a connection into that application. Today, the Internet operates like an unimaginably complex switch with billions upon billions of gates and nodes, capable of establishing and routing a connection between London and Texas in milliseconds, negating the boundaries that were previously in place.

So, next time you visit Amazon.com, consider that you're not just looking at a Web page. Rather, you're connected to a massive distributed application that's designed to sell you, and others like you, books, CDs, videos and more!

3-Tier Development

One architecture for building distributed applications is the 3-tier model, which has been found to be an extremely efficient development approach and is the one we'll be following as we build Jo's site.

In any application, complex or simple, we talk about **application services**. Each service has a particular role in the application and typically includes things like:

- ❏ **Database services** – let an application query and manipulate databases
- ❏ **User Interface services** – let an application present a user interface to the user
- ❏ **Mail services** – provide e-mail functionality to applications
- ❏ **Print services** – let an application print documents
- ❏ **Network services** – let servers and clients communicate
- ❏ **File services** – let an application manipulate files on disks
- ❏ **Help services** – provide application help to a user
- ❏ **Integration services** – let an application talk to other services and applications

The 3-tier client/server approach defines a way of dividing those application services into three distinct roles (concerning presentation, business rules, and data), which are arranged so that each can operate at the maximum efficiency. Here's what those roles look like, together with the services we've listed above spread across the tiers:

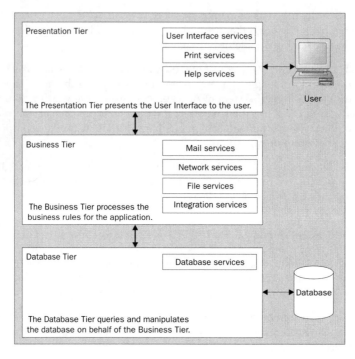

Let's explore each of these roles in more detail and see what it means for the development of Joscoffee.com.

Presentation Tier

The **presentation tier** is responsible for providing the services the application needs to allow the user to view and manipulate the application; in other words it presents a user interface to the user. In old-school distributed applications, this would be built using Visual Basic.

In our Web-oriented distributed application for Jo the presentation tier will be composed of a bundle of ASP pages that will use an ASP-enabled Web server (Microsoft Internet Information Server) to serve the *presentation* of the application down to the user's browser in HTML format. In this book we'll be using Visual InterDev 6.0 to aid us in our construction of these pages.

Before the Web, the client application was responsible for generating the entire user interface. A developer might place a button on a form and then the application would draw that button on the screen and keep track of when the user clicked it. Now, there's a partnership between the Web server and Web browser – the Web server generates the HTML that the browser uses to present the application and the browser itself keeps track of the users' activities.

Business Tier

The **business tier** is the most complicated to appreciate and, interestingly, isn't much different in traditional distributed applications than in Web-based ones.

To understand how the business tier works, we need to step way back so we can see the entire business as a whole. In essence, any business operates by following a set of procedures (or "rules") to accomplish any tasks. These rules can be something simple like *all employees must work 9 a.m. to 5 p.m.*, or complex like *on the third Thursday of each month, we need to take all sales records for the past four weeks and formulate them into reports according to a given spec.*

If it's true that all business operations follow specified procedures and rules, then it follows that all software that drives that business must also follow the exact same rules. For example, if we write some software for managing deliveries into a warehouse, the software must follow the business procedures governing what happens when a truck pulls up to the warehouse door with the stuff that we've purchased.

We refer to the software implementation of these procedures as either **business rules** or **business logic**. Because we live in an object-oriented world, we implement these business rules in **business objects** (a subject that we return to in Chapter 3).

In this book we're using Microsoft technology, and we're going to implement the business objects needed for Jo's Coffee as server-side ActiveX objects written in Visual Basic. Two sets of components are utilized; one set is built iteratively throughout the book, while in Chapter 9 a special set is constructed for order processing.

Database Tier

The **database tier** is the simplest one to understand; it's responsible for querying and manipulating the database under instruction from the business tier.

One of the most important tenets to follow when building 3-tier solutions is that the presentation tier must never talk to the database tier. This is deliberately done because of the importance placed on the business tier. If, as a developer, you accurately replicate the procedures and rules of the business into business objects, those business objects can never act in a way contrary to the rules of that business. However, if you allow the presentation tier to bypass the business tier and talk to the database directly, you're effectively granting the person building that tier the ability to circumvent the rules of that business.

In our application we'll be using a SQL Server database to provide the necessary data storage capabilities.

Scalability

Before we finish our discussion of 3-tier development, we have to talk a little about **scalability**.

Imagine your traditional non-Web-based distributed application has ten users. Chances are your application works just fine in this environment – responses to queries are fast, print jobs run on time, etc. Now imagine your company gets absorbed into a much, much larger one and now your distributed application has 10,000 users. Will your application run just as fast and will your users be just as happy?

Well, no. Not without, at the very least, hardware upgrades. But, even after you redo all the server hardware, will your application still perform to specification?

If it doesn't (and chances are it won't), we say that the application does not **scale** well; in other words the application is not capable of adapting itself to fit into a new environment where there are more users. If the application copes, then we say it does scale well.

Scalability is important in many areas, but the consequences of ignoring it can be particularly acutely felt if you suddenly find yourself with a successful Web-based distributed application, like an e-commerce site, where the original traffic of 1,000 visits a day suddenly jumps to 10,000,000. How do you design your application in such a way that increases of that magnitude are manageable?

Luckily, you're half way there. The first step in managing that kind of increase is to adopt a 3-tier architecture. In short, by separating the business tier away from presentation and database roles, you can build business objects that work smarter and scale better. The trick with managing scale is to think about the perceived number of users concurrently working on the system at any one time. Say you do have 10,000,000 visits a day. At any given second, 1,157 users are on that system. Imagine all of these users are using the same page. How many database connections do you need? The answer: 1,157. Now, how many database connections will be required *at the same time*? The answer: *less* than 1,157.

Designing for Scalability

The trick to designing business objects to scale well is to understand that the resources you have are limited. Say your installation of SQL Server can handle only 500 simultaneous connections. If a user needs a database connection and all 500 are in use, that user will have to wait in a queue for one to become available. That is why we often see such a reduction in performance when we start to increase the load on distributed applications – the demand for resources outstrips supply.

Imagine I write a business object that takes 5 seconds to walk through a list of 100 invoices and performs a complex calculation on each one. If I connect to the database as I enter the `CalculateRefund` method and close it just before I leave, chances are I've wasted a lot of the database's time as I read one record, process it for a little while, get the next record, and so on. If I, instead, design my object to open the database, read and cache all the records, and close the database, the database resource is being used efficiently. Now, as the resource is being used more efficiently, other pages servicing other users can obtain database connections more readily, reducing the performance lag we were previously feeling.

Coming back to our 10,000,000 visits example: if we can build our business objects to use the database efficiently, we may be able to reduce the number of simultaneous database connections required to always be below 500, and our application won't feel a performance hit when we scale.

You'll learn more about scalability as we work through the project.

Now that we understand the online business model we're after and we have an understanding of what a 3-tier distributed application is, we can move on to designing the software we'll need to make our site a reality.

WroxCommerce

If we look at Jo's business model for a moment, we can see that a lot of the problems she's trying to solve will be felt elsewhere in other businesses. In fact, one possible reason for you reading this book is that you have to solve your company's "e-commerce problem" and take your business online.

To make this book more useful to its readers, rather than building a site that just sells coffee, we're going to build an engine that can be used to manage the e-commerce part of the site and in this instance use it inside joscoffee.com to sell coffee.

> *Effectively, we'll be building the business tier of the application as reusable components that can be taken and deployed in other e-commerce sites.*

The ASP code will be specific to joscoffee.com, but we'll take care to ensure that the presentation tier can either be easily discarded, or adapted, to address the needs of your business.

Here's an overview of the general e-commerce tasks the engine will be able to do:

❑   Manage the product catalog – the list of items for sale on the site

❑   Manage visitors – keep track of who's on the site and what they're doing

❑   Manage the shopping cart – keep track of who wants to buy what

❑   Manage customers – handle the conversion from visitors to customers, along with all of the order capture information

❑   Process orders – take the cart and turn the contents into orders for fulfillment

We call this engine WroxCommerce, and you'll be able to download the source code for the engine we build in this book, and all of the ASP pages that go along with it, from www.wrox.com. You can then take the engine and build it into your own e-commerce solution!

Software Requirements

In Chapter 12, we're going to see how we can host our e-commerce solution at an Internet Service Provider running NT 4.0 and Microsoft Internet Information Server 4. The majority of the time, outsourcing management of your application servers to an ISP is a good move, especially if you want a lot of bandwidth, don't want to worry about setting up server hardware and you don't want to hire an around-the-clock administrative team.

In this book, we're focused towards developing the site on Windows NT 4.0 Workstation because it's closer to the environment in which we anticipate the site will run. If you're planning to develop on Windows 98 most of what you see here will work, but be advised the screenshots you see throughout this book are for Windows NT Workstation.

Additionally, from the **Windows NT 4.0 Option Pack** (available for download from the Microsoft site or from an MSDN or TechNet subscription) you'll require the following options to be installed:

❑   Microsoft Personal Web Server (PWS)

❑   Microsoft FrontPage 98 Server Extensions (needed for Visual InterDev operation)

❑   Microsoft Transaction Server (MTS)

Naturally, you can do your development work on a Windows NT 4.0 Server machine. If you choose to do this, however, some of our discussions of Personal Web Server won't be relevant, as you'll be using the full Internet Information Server (from the NT 4.0 Option Pack).

As the book went to press, no issues (other than those few documented) were discovered when the project was run on Windows 2000. Of course, if subsequent problems are found, the solutions will be posted on the support site for the book at www.wrox.com.

Running on Windows 2000 will avoid the requirement for installing options from the Windows NT 4.0 Option Pack, although you will need to ensure you've installed IIS 5.0 (an optional component of Windows 2000).

The application we build is going to be developed and deployed within a Microsoft environment, so to work through this book the additional software products you'll need to have installed are:

❑   **Microsoft SQL Server 7.0** – This database product, rather than Microsoft Access, was chosen since it's a great product for use in building both small, but scalable, solutions and in the development of large distributed applications, like an e-commerce site. We use this database both for development and on the production server.

On NT Workstation, it will only be possible to install the Desktop edition of SQL Server. Interestingly, the Desktop and Enterprise editions are, in fact, exactly the same. The difference is that the Enterprise edition is optimized towards server environments, whereas the other is for desktop and development use.

❑   **Microsoft Visual Basic 6.0** – This will be used for building our business objects for the business tier of our application.

❑   **Microsoft Visual InterDev 6.0** – This product will be used to provide the development environment in which we code our ASP pages.

Microsoft Visual InterDev 6.0 and Microsoft Visual Basic 6.0 can both either be purchased as a separate package, or you can find them in Microsoft Visual Studio 6.0 Professional or Enterprise editions. Of course to generate ASP pages you can use whatever tool you prefer; but all our steps are based around using Visual Interdev

Now we know what we're going to be working with, let's move onto setting up some of these software elements for our project.

Starting the Jo's Coffee Project

Before we can start coding we need to put some foundations in place; within this section we're going to look at setting up the database we'll be using for our data tier, and setting up the Visual InterDev project.

Try It Out - Creating the Database

1. Open the SQL Server 7 Enterprise Manager and drill down to the node that represents the SQL Server you want to create your database in (expand **Microsoft SQL Servers** then expand **SQL Server Group**). If this is the first time you've run Enterprise Manager and you want to create the database on your local computer, there will already be an entry in the list that represents your local computer.

    Now expand this node to get a screen that looks similar to that shown:

    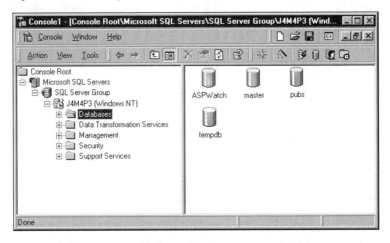

2. Now right-click on **Databases** and choose **New Database...** Enter the name of the database as JoCoffee and click **OK** (we're going to leave the other database options as they are):

    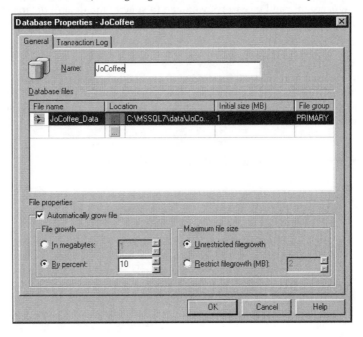

3. It will take a couple of seconds to create our new database. Once that's done, we need to create a login. Our site will connect to the database through this login. In Enterprise Manager, expand the **Security** node to reveal find the **Logins** object:

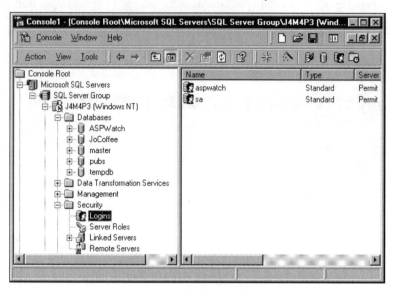

4. Next right-click **Logins** and choose **New Login...** The first thing we have to do is give our login user a name. We're going to call it **JoCoffeeWeb**. We also need a password. First of all, make sure **SQL Server Authentication** is checked on, and then enter *eermlate* for the password. You can choose your own, but we'll be using *eermlate* throughout this book. After you've entered the username and password, we need to specify the default database. This should be JoCoffee.

> **Although we've used quite a straightforward password here, a better method is to use a combination of alphanumeric characters. One suggestion is to take two short words and combine them, say, dogshed then substitute in some numbers leading to something like d0gsh3d.**

After you've done all that, you should have something that looks like:

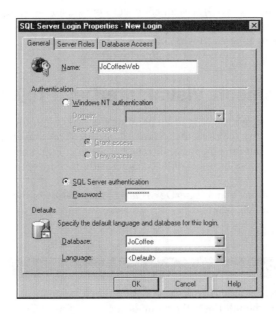

5. Before we press **OK**, we need to give our new login access to the database. Switch to the **Database Access** tab, check on **Permit** next to **JoCoffee** on the top list, and then check on **db_owner** in the roles list at the bottom. When you have something that looks like this, press **OK**. Enterprise Manager will ask you to re-confirm the password you entered earlier before you can proceed:

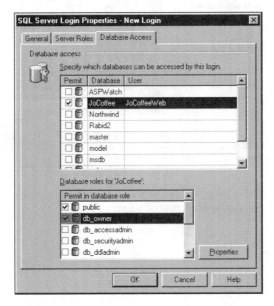

After those six steps have been completed, you'll be in a position where you have a new SQL Server database, which we will use to hold the product catalog, customer database, and order information. Additionally, we also have a login for the database called **JoCoffeeWeb**.

By using **ActiveX Data Objects (ADO)** we can connect to our database using either a **connection string** or a **data source name (DSN)**. Irrespective of which one is used, at some point we're going to have to tell our site where to find the database and what it needs to know to establish the connection. In this book, we're going to connect to the database via a connection string.

Creating the Microsoft Visual InterDev Project

As we've already mentioned, we're going to be building the ASP pages for our site in Visual InterDev. These ASP pages will make up the presentation tier of our site. The sole purpose of them is to create (or **instantiate**) and make calls into the business objects that we're going to build using Visual Basic. Chapter 3 introduces us to these business objects, along with the concept of an **object model**.

Remember, any work we do in Visual InterDev is *almost* disposable, in that it will be specifically aimed at creating a site for Jo's Coffee, whereas the `WroxCommerce` engine is designed to be easily re-used in other e-commerce sites.

Try It Out – Creating a Project

1. Open Visual Interdev; the New Project dialog should appear (if it doesn't choose File | New Project…from the menu). Enter the name of the project as JoCoffee and select a folder to store the local copy of the files in:

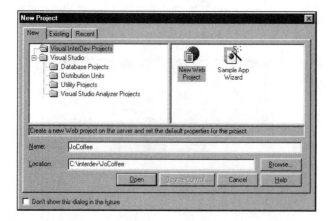

2. Click Open and, after a couple of seconds, the Web Project Wizard will appear asking you to specify a server you want to host your site on:

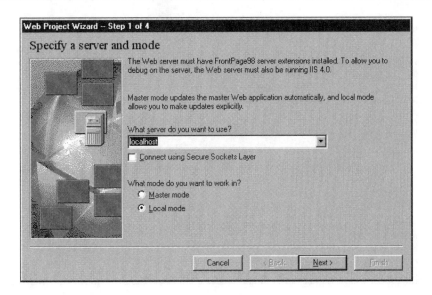

Visual InterDev does a very nice job of helping you deploy your site to other servers. As we've pointed out, we are going to use a commercial ISP to host our site and Visual InterDev makes it very easy for us to "push" our site onto its servers. After we've finished the development phase of the project on our local computer, all we have to do is give Visual InterDev the domain name joscoffee.com *and a username and password. Our ISP will take care of all the configuration stuff on its end. We'll be talking more about this deployment phase in Chapter 12.*

3. For now, we're going to leave the server name as localhost, as we want to use the local computer for development. If you are using another server on your network for hosting your development work, enter the name of the machine instead of localhost. We're assuming throughout this book that your development server is your local computer; failing that, we're assuming it's on the same network as your local computer.

We have noticed some inconsistencies in Visual InterDev – sometimes giving the server name as localhost doesn't work and you'll have to use your machine name instead.

4. Make sure Local Mode is checked on and click Next.

5. The next thing we need to input is the name of the Web application we want to create on our local machine. Accept the suggestion of JoCoffee, which is the name we want. Ensure Create search.htm to enable full text searching is *not* checked, as we won't be using the built-in search utility for this site – we'll build our own search utility in Chapter 11. We want to create a new Web application, so make sure Create a new Web application is checked:

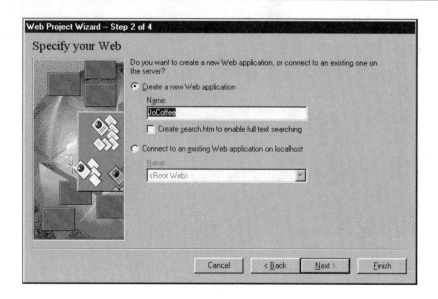

6. Although we have a **Next** button, we actually don't want to bother with the next two pages of this Wizard, so click **Finish**. (InterDev provides the functionality of letting us choose a layout and theme from a library of available options, much like FrontPage does. However, because we want to make our site as individual as possible, we're going to skip it and roll our own!)

7. After you click **Finish**, InterDev will go away and create some folders and files and configure Personal Web Server – remember, we're assuming you're using Personal Web Server for your development work. If you're actually developing on Windows NT Server, InterDev has gone way and configured IIS, not PWS.

In the next section we'll have a closer look at Visual InterDev and the way it manages projects.

A Quick Overview of Visual InterDev

One of the smart things about Visual InterDev is that it makes it easy for you to work on a local copy of the site. Imagine you're making changes to a Web site for your company. Chances are that during your development work, you don't want visitors to the main site to see the changes you're making. Asking InterDev to take a copy of the Web site from the server and installing it on your local machine means that other developers, or external visitors to the site, cannot see any changes you make.

We say that a live site that's up and running is called a **production** site. A site that's installed on your local computer for the purposes of development and testing is called a **staging** site.

InterDev's Master mode is used for when you know you're the only developer working on a site and that the site is going to have no visitors. What happens is, whenever a change is made to your local staging copy, that change is replicated up to the server.

The Local mode is used when you're working with other developers, or there may be a version of the site in production that may have visitors. It's good practice to always use the Local mode, as you get into the habit of checking and making sure that changes you make should be pushed up to production, and it also makes sure that things do not accidentally get updated when they shouldn't do.

Let's take a look now at what InterDev actually did when you created the project. In the following sections we'll quickly look at the folders and files InterDev creates and the locations where they are stored. We'll finish off with a look at what happens when a file is added to the project.

Project Explorer

Visual InterDev presents a project tree much like Visual Basic's. With a new project, this Project Explorer is a bit bare, but it looks like this:

A Visual InterDev solution can contain any number of projects, but here we can see our new JoCoffee solution contains just one project. That project is referred to as localhost/JoCoffee, which is actually the address of the virtual folder that holds the production files for this project. We'll be learning more about this in a little while.

The Project Explorer is telling us that our project contains three folders – _private and _ScriptLibrary are both used to hold certain InterDev files which we'll look at as the occasion arises; images is an empty folder provided by InterDev that we can use to hold our site's images in. Alongside these three folders, we also have one global.asa file. This is the standard ASP global.asa file, and we'll be looking at this later too.

Finding the Local Copy

The first thing InterDev does is to create a folder that holds the staging copy of our site. By default, changes made to this site can only be seen by us, which prevents us from making a catastrophic mistake that may ruin a co-workers work.

By default, InterDev will create the local version of the site in a subfolder below the one you asked it to create the project in. It will name this folder to be the same as the Web application (in our case JoCoffee) with _Local tacked on the end, like this:

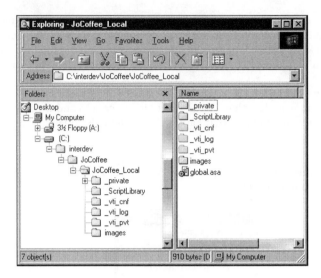

You'll notice that the _private, _ScriptLibrary and images folders that we first met in Project Explorer are represented, as is the global.asa file. InterDev also creates three hidden folders starting with _vti that are used by the FrontPage extensions.

Finding the Production Copy

Because we asked InterDev to host the production version of our site on the local machine, we should also be able to find the production folder too.

By default, Personal Web Server and Internet Information Server will configure themselves to use C:\InetPub\wwwroot as the default root folder for Web sites. Looking in this folder, we can see a JoCoffee folder:

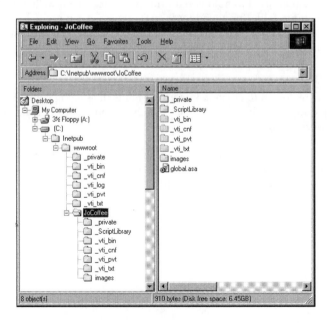

You can see that, at the moment, the staging folder (JoCoffee_Local) and production folder (Inetpub\wwwroot\JoCoffee) are identical. You can also see that the wwwroot folder itself contains a number of _vti folders too.

What Happened to the Web Server Configuration?

The last thing that InterDev did was to alter the configuration of the Personal Web Server. If we open the Personal Web Manager, and change to the Advanced Tab, we can see the existence of a /JoCoffee entry, as shown here:

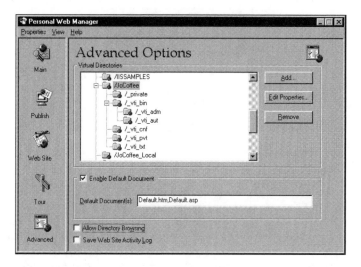

The /JoCoffee virtual folder points to C:\InetPub\wwwroot\JoCoffee, which means that any calls on our box to http://localhost/jocoffee will get routed to the production folder at C:\InetPub\wwwroot\JoCoffee.

Likewise, the /JoCoffee_Local virtual folder points to C:\interdev\JoCoffee\JoCoffee_Local, so any calls to http://localhost/jocoffee_local will get routed to the staging folder at C:\interdev\JoCoffee\JoCoffee_Local.

> **If you look at Personal Web Manager as soon as your InterDev project is created, you won't see an entry for /JoCoffee_Local. InterDev only creates this folder the first time you ask it to run the project.**

Try It Out – Working in Visual InterDev

Let's have a quick look at what happens when a file is added to the project and how we can work with it.

1. Create a new ASP page by right-clicking localhost/JoCoffee, select <u>A</u>dd | Acti<u>v</u>e Server Page.., and when prompted name it test.asp. When we do this Project Explorer will indicate we have a new file:

The icon to the left of the file name and the file type icon indicate the state of the file. The little flag next to test.asp means that the file is new and only exists on the staging site and not on the production site. The little padlock icon next to the global.asa file means that the copy on the staging server has been released and published up to the production server.

2. If we look now at the staging folder (in C:\Interdev\JoCoffee\JoCoffee_Local) we can see our new test.asp file. But, if we look at our production folder (in C:\Inetpub\wwwroot\JoCoffee) there is no test.asp file. Because we're working in Local mode, any changes made to the staging site are not automatically pushed to production.

3. If we right-click on test.asp in Project Explorer and choose View in <u>B</u>rowser, Internet Explorer will be launched and we can then see that the version opened by default is the staging version:

4. You can push test.asp up to the production server by right-clicking on it and choosing Add to <u>M</u>aster Web. After this has been done, you can look at the production site's folder and see the new folder.

Additionally, you'll notice that the icon next to test.asp has changed to the little padlock. If you want to change this file, you can right-click and choose Get Wor<u>k</u>ing Copy. This will download an up-to-date version of the file to your staging folder (we do this to make sure that, if any of our co-workers have made changes to the site, those changes will be reflected in our local copy too).

5. When we have a local working copy we can mess around with, the padlock icon changes to a little pencil. After we're happy with our changes, we can push the revised file back up to the production site by right-clicking and choosing Release Working Copy.

> **After we push files stored in our local staging folder up to the production folder, the local files are automatically set to be read-only.**

6. Lastly, as we don't need this file during our project building, let's tidy up by right-clicking on `test.asp` and selecting Delete.

We'll be using InterDev often as we work through this book, so we'll be practicing those techniques as we learn.

Summary

This is quite an involved chapter, so lets look at what we learned.

We started by taking at look at the client/server model, and the uses of that type of software application. We then looked at how the Web has created a new breed of distributed application and that, sometimes, when we visit a Web site like an e-commerce or an auction site, we're actually becoming part of a highly dispersed distributed application. We then discussed what is meant by the term 3-tier distributed application architecture, why that model is so useful, and how we'll be building our site based on that model.

Following a quick summary of the tools we'll be using during our project, we created the SQL Server database we'll be using (`JoCoffee`) and created a DSN connection. We then opened the Visual InterDev project we'll be using and had a quick look round the file structure Visual InterDev sets up to manage web projects.

So, now we've laid the foundations for the data tier and the presentation tier, in the next chapter we'll make a start on the business tier.

Building the Object Model

Most modern software can be controlled programmatically through its exposed **object models**. In fact, most of the applications you use everyday on your Windows PC have an object model, including Microsoft Word, Excel, and Internet Explorer.

The careful design of these object models is the key to building good software. We're now going to embark on the design, and start the construction, of the business tier for Jo's Coffee. This business tier will consist of a number of objects whose interrelationships are defined by their position in the object model. Implementing the object model will define what we can do within the application. During the course of the chapter we'll be discussing the object-oriented approach to programming as well as ActiveX and COM technology; all topics that directly influence the way we construct the application.

> **These topics merit whole books on themselves, and we are merely going to provide the background you need for our project. If you wish to know more try** *Beginning Visual Basic 6 Objects, ISBN 186100172x* **and** *VB COM, ISBN 1861002130.* **Both by** *Wrox Press*

There are going to be three basic parts to this chapter – we're going to start off with the theory (concepts behind object-oriented programming, COM and ActiveX) then we'll move onto see how that theory influences our design of the object model for Jo's Coffee. Finally we'll begin to implement the design in the `WroxCommerce` VB project.

More specifically our path through the chapter will involve:

- ❑ Looking at object-oriented programming
- ❑ Understanding a little about components
- ❑ Designing an object model for Jo's Coffee
- ❑ Creating a project in Visual Basic
- ❑ Building the `Visit` object
- ❑ Building the `Database` object
- ❑ Building the `Catalog` object

Let's start by looking at object-oriented programming.

Object-Oriented Programming

Object-oriented programming (**OOP**) is based on the idea that real-world entities or relationships can be represented in code as objects. These code objects have associated with them data and behave in certain ways when asked to. Objects can be linked together to form programs and applications.

*Objects may be regarded as **black-boxes** – the user of an object may know what information needs to be input to the object to get a certain result out, but does not need to know what process goes on inside the object.*

OK, let's step back from that rather terse summary and use the metaphor of a television set to explain this concept. We're all pretty conversant with televisions in so much as we know if we input a signal (from aerial, cable, video or wherever) and we use the control set properly we'll get sound and vision. Pushing the buttons allows us to vary the channel we watch, raise or lower the volume, alter the picture brightness, and so on. Most of us don't know the precise workings of the electronics that control the TV, and neither do we care, because we know enough to be able to control it.

Object Behavior

In the first paragraph we said that objects contain data and have behavior; in programming data is represented as **variables** while behavior is represented by terms familiar to all VB programmers; **properties**, **methods** and **events**. So to continue our TV analogy we could have a property called `channel` which you could query to discover what channel was being displayed, or alternatively you could set that property to actually change the channel. Note, a property is different to the underlying data – in the case of the `channel` property the underlying variable may be the actual frequency of the input signal that gives the picture corresponding to that channel number. Methods describe something the object can do, so our television may have `IncrementVolumeOneStep` or `SwitchToVideo` methods that are invoked in response to input from the control set. Events occur when an action or state occurs, so the event of pushing the **Increase Volume** button would fire the `IncrementVolumeOneStep` method.

Incidentally, the process of objects hiding their internal design and data from the outside world is termed **encapsulation**. It means an object can hide data and not allow it to be accessed. So on a TV there maybe a `TVMustNotBeOnForLongerThan` property that controls the maximum length of time a TV can be on before it automatically turns off to ensure it doesn't overheat.

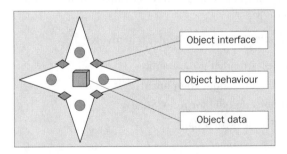

The properties, methods, and events an object has form the **interface** through which that object can be manipulated.

All this is very familiar in VB where a control like a **CommandButton** is an object and has, for example, a **Caption** property and a **Click** event to which you can attach a method. It acts as a black-box, as you the programmer do not have to worry how the button responds to the click input or how it looks – that has been sorted out for you.

Classes

A **class** is basically a template from which we stamp out objects (like a biscuit punch) with each created object being termed an **instance** of the class and the process of creating the object being termed **instantiation**. In Visual Basic, classes are defined using **class modules** (in C++, they are simply known as a class).

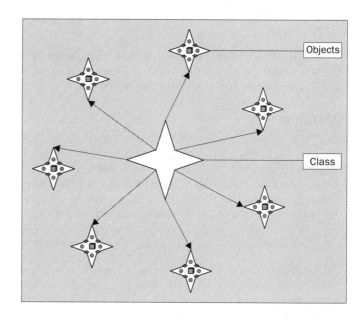

OOP in Action

The vast majority of object-oriented programming work is concerned with building objects that have no user interface. These objects provide some function to an application. Imagine you are working on a development project in a team and you need access to a billing system that your company owns. One of your colleagues has built a set of objects for talking to this billing system, but it is used on another application. In an object-oriented world, if your colleague has done their job properly, they can give you a copy of the objects, you can plug them into your application and now your application code has access to a billing system through those objects. You haven't had to learn anything about how the billing system works; you've just plugged the objects in.

Let's say our colleague gives us their class module called `BillingSystem`, (and provides us with information about its properties, methods, and events) in VB we can create instances of it like this:

```
Dim MyBillingSystem
Set MyBillingSystem = New BillingSystem
```

Once we've created a billing system object, we can use it:

```
MyBillingSystem.BillCustomer "Neil", "Mcevoy", "$500", "1/27/2000"
```

What's happening there is that we know that the BillingSystem object supports a method called BillCustomer. We also know that the code that drives the BillCustomer object is something that we don't understand the internals of – our colleague has been through all that hard work, so we are **reusing** their efforts. The term reuse is something that comes up time and time again in software development and is an important facet of object-oriented programming. It means that the cost of the time and money we put into developing something can be offset by the fact that whatever original work we come up with can be reused in other applications. This is one of the reasons why people actually sell objects for use in other applications.

Similarly the use of objects within large projects allows for easier maintenance and more flexibility and this is something we will see clearly exemplified when we come to Chapter 9 and talk about the order processing pipeline in the Jo's Coffee project.

Interfaces

We talked above about the interface that a class can present to the world being defined via the public properties, events, and methods it exposes – in fact classes can actually present multiple interfaces to the world via use of the Implements command. Let's say for an instance we develop a new black-box – one that will work as a TV and an Internet access device. When we are programming this device up we start a new class module say ClassInternetBrowser; now we know that this unit should have all the functionality of the TV, so we could add to our new module something like:

```
Implements ClassTelevision
```

This would mean that we have to use all the methods, properties, and events we used with a television then additionally we could add properties, methods, and events specifically related to Internet access which would then form a second interface. As an added benefit, although we have to use the same methods etc. for Television we could provide slightly different code, for instance changing the step size in the IncrementVolumeOneStep method.

Components

Building on the idea of object-oriented programming comes component-oriented design, which facilitates even better reuse of the objects we design and build.

Objects vs Components

Objects are created from classes and classes are made up of source code – which is language specific and thus can only be used, easily, in one environment. In contrast components are pre-compiled units of *binary* code – thus they are language independent.

>   *A component may consist of one object or a collection of objects.*

A component based approach to software design enhances the OO approach we first looked at – in the case that a component consists of a group of objects, we can actually define which objects are accessible outside the component (and hence keep some objects restricted to being accessed by other objects inside the component) by defining the *interface of the component*.

In our application we are going to see that we build a number of class modules that represent the objects we define in our object model; these objects will be tied together in the `WroxCommerce` ActiveX component. By carefully designing our object model and building a component interface we control how the whole component can be accessed by our presentation layer.

COM

Of course the above section rather glosses over at least one very important topic; how do we get all these components talking to each other? That's where the **Component Object Model (COM)** comes in – it's Microsoft's standard for allowing objects and components to interact irrespective of the language in which the components were first built. So, using COM technology we can call up a component, and providing we know what interface it has, we can get it to go away and do things for us.

We'll see this in action later this chapter when we build the database class module – we add a reference to the Microsoft ActiveX Data Objects 2.1 Library, which is a COM based library. Using the methods and properties exposed by the ADO 2.1 library we can communicate with a database without worrying about how it's done at the base level.

As part of the COM mechanism, components that we create in VB actually have a number of interfaces that are provided as part of the standard architecture in addition to any interfaces we define. We'll discuss this further at the appropriate time, but the important thing to note is that VB fits seamlessly into COM and as VB developers we are insulated from a great deal of complexity.

ActiveX

ActiveX technology is a wide-ranging term that has evolved alongside the development of distributed computing. It does not generally mean one thing; broadly one can say that the term ActiveX encompasses a set of technologies that each define interfaces between software components to implement some type of functionality. Within this book we are primarily concerned with **ActiveX components** and **Active Scripting** (discussed below).

An ActiveX component is an application that stands alone and lets other applications use the classes and objects it contains. The `WroxCommerce` object model is implemented as an ActiveX DLL and, as we'll see is controlled programmatically – it won't have a user interface itself.

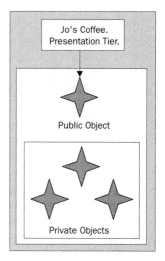

Jo's Coffee. Presentation Tier.

Public Object

Private Objects

Active Scripting

ASP pages are able to access ActiveX components through a technology called **Active Scripting**. We've skated over the previous general theory pretty quickly (as we alluded to, there are whole books written on the subject) but it's probably worth lingering over this particular aspect.

Active Scripting is a reusable scripting engine that, if you want, you can use in your own application. It can be found in use in **Active Server Pages** (**ASP**) and **Windows Script Host** (**WSH**).

Active Scripting is capable of supporting many languages by allowing developers to write supporting language plug-ins. Active Scripting ships with VBScript (a cut down version of Visual Basic) and JScript. Other vendors have developed PERL plug-ins, as well as support for other languages. Broadly, this means that you can write ASP code in whatever language plug-in you have available, as Active Scripting and the plug-in work together to make the call into the component and, through that call, tell Visual Basic to execute the code contained within the method or property.

ASP works (as illustrated below) by stripping out all of the VBScript code, creating an instance of Active Scripting, and asking it to execute the code on its behalf. ASP presents a set of its own ActiveX components to the **context** of the script (the environment that the script runs in). So, the `Response` object we call in ASP is actually an ActiveX component that ships with ASP, and when ASP fires up Active Scripting to run your code, it passes a reference to this component to Active Scripting and asks for it to be made available to your code as `Response`.

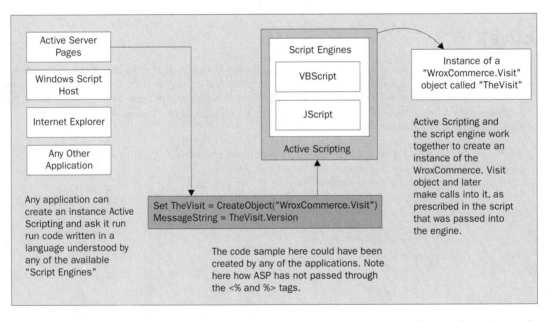

At this point we need to bring in the idea of a **type library**. A type library is a file that describes an object (here meaning component or control) in a standard format such that anything wanting to make use of that object can find out which classes are accessible (or **supported**). This type library is actually embedded into ActiveX DLL files created via Visual Basic; however, it's still available to programs interacting with it using COM.

So, when our ASP page attempts to call a method on the `Response` object, Active Scripting looks at the type information in the type library and determines if the method or property name is valid and, if it is valid, what parameters it takes (the type library is not just a list of the names of the methods and properties – it also includes the parameters that any call has and the possible types of value that can be returned). This inspection of the **published information** is part of the technology that makes up ActiveX, not Active Scripting.

Object Models

As we said back in Chapter 2, what we want to do is build a set of business objects (code objects that represent real-world entities, relationships, and concepts within a given business) that we can use in Jo's site as well as reuse in other sites. The business objects we build will be related to each other and arranged into an object model. If we design this correctly, it will provide a rich set of functionality that may be accessed through the ASP code contained in the presentation layer. Designing object models is not trivial, but it's outside the scope of this book to discuss object-oriented design methodologies; however, through reading this section you'll at least get an idea of how we've approached the problem of designing an application for Jo's Coffee.

Usually object models are in a hierarchical type of structure with one object at the **root**. The design of the object model defines how objects within that model can be accessed so let's get ahead of ourselves just slightly (we'll discuss how we arrived at that particular design below) and sneak a look at the object model for `WroxCommerce`:

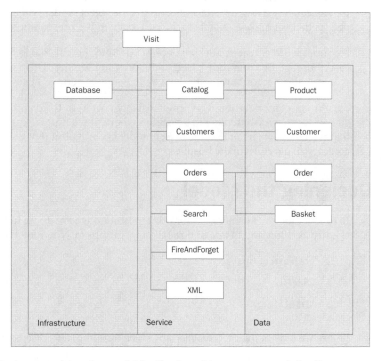

In our model the `Visit` object is the **root** object from which all other objects are created. So, if you want to create a `Customers` service object, you *can't* just use the code:

```
CreateObject("Customers")
```

Instead you specifically have to ask the `Visit` object to carry out that task. We'll go into more detail as to why that should be the case later in this discussion.

Linking the Theory and Implementation

When we make a call to the `Visit` object Active Scripting looks in the type library of the DLL containing the object to determine how the call should be made. Once it's validated the call, it runs some low-level code to pass the data we want in (as we'll usually pass in some parameters to a call like this), interpret the results, and present them back.

As we've alluded to, Visual Basic lets us build ActiveX component objects through a combination of **class modules** and **ActiveX DLL** projects. Class modules are available in all VB project types, but it's the specific project type that dictates how we can use the objects. If we created a Standard EXE project, any classes we created would not be created as ActiveX components and, therefore, they would not be available to an ActiveX component container, like Active Scripting.

By creating an ActiveX DLL project (as we will shortly), Visual Basic will do all the hard work of setting up the project so that the class modules ("objects") contained inside it adhere to ActiveX component standards and can therefore be contained by ActiveX component containers.

The root object `Visit` represents a single visit to the site. From this point on, we count a visit the same as a page view – in other words one request from the Browser to display a single page. We call the person controlling the Browser a **visitor**. We describe all the pages that a visitor requests in a period of time that they're actively using the site as a **session**. Our object model will, in effect, be the complete set of business objects that we make available to the ASP code in the presentation tier.

As you'll see later, careful design of our object model will enable us to restrict the types of activities we can carry out directly from code based in the presentation tier. This will help us to build an application that will operate in accordance with the way Jo wants to run her business.

So, our object model should comprehensively represent the complete set of functionality available on our site. In short, we want to get to a position where, if we find we can't perform a task through the ASP code that we want to, it's not that the object model is wrong but that we're trying to achieve a task that is contrary to the rules of the business.

Designing the Model

In developing the business tier for our application we are going to build a series of objects that we can classify as belonging to one of three distinct groups (as you may have noticed on our diagram):

❑ **Infrastructure**

❑ **Service**

❑ **Data**

Before we look at the precise objects we'll be building, let's discuss these general groupings.

Infrastructure Objects

Infrastructure objects provide access to the resources that an application will use. In our case, we only need to actively manage one resource – the connection to the database. The application will use more resources, like memory, disk drives, and so on, but the application framework provided by Visual Basic and the Web server (either PWS or IIS) will do this for us.

One sure way of ensuring the presentation layer code is not allowed to circumvent the business rules is to never allow the ASP code direct access to any of the infrastructure objects. In our case, we do this by creating an object that is only accessible to objects in the model. In other words, this object is private to the model as a whole and the ASP code will not be able to directly access or call methods on it.

Service Objects

Service objects provide access to **application services**. An application service is defined to be anything that an application can actually do. So, in our case we might have an object that can carry out operations like creating customers, deleting customers, viewing orders placed by a customer, etc. The activities outlined (for example the operation of creating a new customer) will have to conform to certain criteria – **business rules**.

We may decide that any object in our model can create a customer by calling the appropriate object; additionally we may decide that not only can another object call this object to create a customer but ASP code can as well. It is through these service objects that the presentation layer code can get to the business rules. We'll see more service objects in a little while.

Data Objects

Data objects define single instances of some entity in the system somewhere. This is a deliberately broad description, but in our case it nearly always refers to rows in the database. So, we may have an object to describe a single customer, or a single order, and so on. The advantage of this approach is that it lets you add a great degree of detail to the data objects.

Now we've seen the classifications, let's move on to see how we choose the actual objects we are going to put into our object model.

Choosing the Objects

Now we know what kinds of objects we are going to have in our model, we need to decide what objects will actually make up that model. To do this, we have to go through a process of deciding how the various users of the system will flow through the application. By that we mean that a user on the system will create some form of event (not the Visual Basic type) – they will do something that requires some action.

Scenarios

To think through various events leading to actions it is useful to consider actual scenarios; imagine a user opens the home page of the site. In response to that event, we have to extract a list of items that we particularly want to sell to the user and add them to the HTML that makes up the page. By conceptually following that event from inception through to conclusion, we can grasp an understanding of what objects our application needs. Remember, we're talking about object-oriented programming, so each part of the resulting activity will be encapsulated in an object of some form. When we decide which object implements the activity, we can decide which methods and properties are needed on that object to instruct the object to perform that activity. In this discussion, we won't be going deeply into the methods and properties of the objects we decide to build, as that's the work of later chapters.

> As with a spookily large number of things in life, the 80:20 rule applies to the object design we're about to see here. We only need to consider 20% of the possible number of events in order to do 80% of the things people will want to do with our site. In order to keep the discussion in this book manageable, we're only going to look at 20% of the scenarios, so our object model will not be absolutely complete. Our goal is to create a site that can sell coffee products to Jo's customers and let Jo manage those sales. In real-world situations, you will most likely find need to implement objects to cover other, less often used, functionality.

Let's start to work through some different events in order and see where that gets us. Our starting point is the example of a visitor opening the home page of the site.

1. User opens home page.

When this event occurs we need to get a list of products from the database that we particularly want to sell. These are our *featured items* (a topic that we cover in depth in Chapter 16). These products then have to be added to the HTML.

We've already decided that an object called `Visit` will represent a single visit to the site and will be our root object. This is the entry point into the model and it's through this that we gain access to other objects in the model.

Secondly, we've identified the need to query data in the database. Therefore, we need an object capable of talking to the database, and we'll call that `Database` (this will be an *infrastructure* object – it provides services that should only be visible to the business tier). However, that `Database` object won't actually do anything unless something asks it to do something. We need, then, an object capable of asking the database object to return items from the product catalog. We'll call this object `Catalog` (this will be a *service* object because it provides a service to whoever called it). We've also identified a method that this `Catalog` object could have – `GetFeaturedProducts`. It's important at this point to ignore the bit of code that actually adds the featured items to the HTML that makes up the page. The activity of adding to the HTML is very much a function of the presentation tier. Our object model is concerned only with the business tier.

So at this point we've identified three objects: `Visit`, `Database` and `Catalog` and our fledgling object model has the appearance:

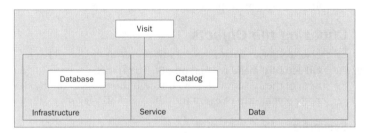

2. User wants product information

Let's now consider the scenario of the user wanting more information on a product presented on the home page. We'll need to gain access to the information on that product and present it through HTML. To gain access to the information about the product, a neat way to do this is to create an object specifically for extracting a row from the database and presenting that row as a object, rich in properties and methods that we can use to manipulate the object. We'll call this object `Product`. It's a *data* object because it represents a single row in the database and its main activity is not to provide services to other objects. The `Product` object will use the `Database` object to extract the data from the database. The `Catalog` object will create `Product` objects on demand through a method called `GetProductObject`. The `Product` object itself will be able to return details of the product through properties such as `Name` and `Price`.

Since the first scenario, we've only added one additional object: `Product`. Notice how we can add additional methods and properties to other objects in the model to create a rich set of functionality, but without bloating the number of objects in the model. Reducing the amount of objects in the model makes it easier for developers using the model to understand both how to use and how to maintain the model. We now have:

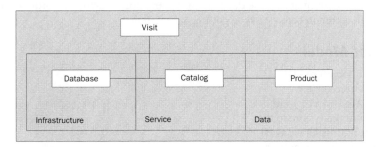

3. User adds product to basket

Now let's look at what happens when a user adds a product to her basket (or cart as it's otherwise termed). To do this, we need an object that both represents the basket as stored in the database, and can modify the basket. So, the distinction between data object and service object on this `Basket` object is fuzzy. We're going to put it into the model as a data object. We're also going to create these objects through a service object called `Orders` – and we'll talk about that in a moment.

The most complicated thing our site can do is turning the products in the basket into an order. This has impact on a number of different aspects of the system:

❑   Firstly, we need to transform the `Basket` into an order, and we use a method on the `Orders` object called `SplitBasket` (all of this will make more sense when we get to it in Chapter 8).

❑   Secondly, we'll need an object to represent an order – we'll call this `Order` (a data object).

❑   Thirdly, the concept of an order doesn't make much sense without a customer behind it, so we create a service object called `Customers` to create new customers through `CreateCustomer`. We also then create a data object called `Customer` to represent an object in the database.

This has considerably expanded our model, giving us:

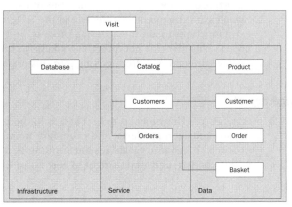

Although we've only seen a few different scenarios, it becomes easier to understand how each object can be expanded to make it very easy for the developer to get at the data that she needs. For example, if we add a method called `GetOrdersForCustomer` to the `Orders` object, we make is possible for a developer to query any of the orders that a customer has placed. If we add a property to the `Customer` object called `Orders`, we can rig that property to call into `GetOrdersForCustomer`. We only have to write the actual code for querying the database and extracting a customer's orders once, yet we instantly have two logical, common-sense ways of getting at that data.

The Full Object Model

To recap, our full object model (including the service objects `Search`, `FireAndForget`, and `XML` which are not really core to the design we've built thus far, so we'll discuss these as we add them to the model) can be represented as:

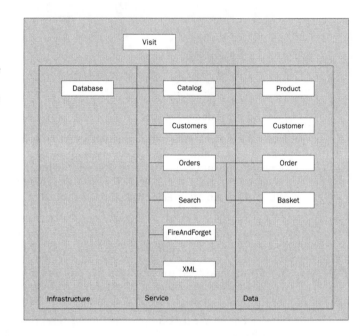

Apart from the root object `Visit`, which we've already talked about, here's a summary of the other objects, that you will build over the course of the book, and some elaboration on their tasks:

Infrastructure objects

❑ `Database` – This object has a number of uses; it simplifies our database communications (which are subsequently achieved via the ADO `Connection` object) it provides a couple of extra functions to aid the ordering process, and allows direct access to the ADO `Connection` object. This object is not directly available to the ASP code. We build this object and detail how we prevent ASP from calling into this object in this chapter.

Service objects

❑ `Catalog` – This object provides access to the product catalogue. It enables creation of departments and products, and can query manufacturers, suppliers, departments, and products. It can also create instances of the `Product` data object. We start building this object in this chapter, and start using it in earnest in Chapter 5.

- ❑ Customers – This object manages customers. It can log a customer into the *customers only* areas of the site and can create new customers in the database and manage their address and credit card information. We start building this object in Chapter 8.

- ❑ Orders – This object manages orders. It can take a shopping basket and turn it into an order, and it can move an order through the order-processing pipeline (Chapter 9). It can also return audit trail information.

- ❑ Search – This object provides a way of searching the product catalogue. We build this object in Chapter 11.

- ❑ FireAndForget – This object provides a way of sending e-mails to customers and visitors at a given date and time. It is part of our customer service strategy and we build this object in Chapter 14.

- ❑ XML – This object provides a way of publishing data in our database as XML, and importing XML data into our system. This object is discussed in more detail in Chapter 17.

Data objects

- ❑ Product – This object represents a single product stored in the database. It can return information about itself, get and set dynamic attribute data, and add and return up-sell/cross-sell recommendations.

- ❑ Customer – This object represents a single customer stored in the database. It can return information about itself, along with stored address and credit card information and orders that have been placed.

- ❑ Order – This object represents a single order stored in the database. It can return all of its information, including customer, addresses and credit cards, and the data that makes up the order.

- ❑ Basket – This object represents a single cart (basket) stored in the database. Most often, this object is used to represent the current visitor's basket. It can return its contents and summary information (total price and total quantity), and it can add and remove items from itself.

Building a Scalable Application

Now we've discussed the composition of our object model, we should quickly talk about how we intend to employ it to build a scalable application.

Two of the basic principles of highly scalable applications (based on the concept that objects take up memory and you should use as little memory as possible to aid scalability) are:

- ❑ Create objects only when you need to (also called **Just-In-Time Activation**)
- ❑ Create as few instances as possible

As you'll soon learn, we're going to create an instance of the Visit object each time a page is requested from the server. We will only create a single Visit object per page, as the object is designed so there is no requirement to have many of them accessible. This Visit object will then be used to create other service objects that provide access to the business rules, and with it, instances of data objects.

Although we may require more than one of the same kind of data object on a page (we might want to compare two customers, for example), we will never require more than one instance of the same kind of service object. If we want to use the `Customers` object, the same `Customers` object will be able to provide everything we need until the end of the page.

As we build the `Visit` object throughout this book, we'll be adding properties to it that will return instances of service objects. Later in this chapter, we'll build the `Visit.Catalog` property. The first time this is called, the property will create exactly once instance of the `Catalog` object and keep it **cached** as a member of the `Visit` object. The next time the property is called, the cached version will be returned.

This means two things:

❏ Only one instance of the `Catalog` object can ever exist per instance of the `Visit` object. As there is only one Visit instance per page, we can either have zero or one **Catalog** objects on that same page.

❏ We only create the `Catalog` object when it's needed.

This neatly ties up with the principles we expounded at the top of the section. Let's consider what this could mean in practice for us. If the `Visit` object creates instances of all six service objects on initialisation, a session would take up seven objects (remember to add `Visit`), so 1,000 sessions would take up 7,000 objects. However, creating the objects **on demand** means that your object count fluctuates between 1,000 and 7,000 objects depending on the usage of the page. Realistically, it's unusual a page would require more than two or three service objects, so your usage snapshot would most likely vary between 1,000 in the best case, and 3,000 in the worst. This approach minimises the **resource footprint** (the amount of resources required) for the application and enhances its scalability.

Now we've gained an overview of the background to the technology we're using and the object model we're going to build, let's dive in and start programming.

Starting the WroxCommerce Project

As we start our project the first thing we're going to look at is creating the root object of our model – the `Visit` object – and adding some basic configuration code to the `Visit` class module we build. We'll then move on to deal with the `Database` object via the `Database` class module.

Try It Out – Starting the Project

1. Start Visual Basic 6.0 and choose **ActiveX DLL** from the list of available projects:

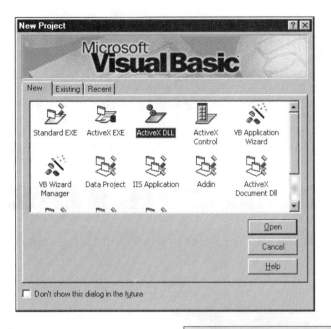

2. When the project appears, use the Project Explorer and Properties window to rename the project to WroxCommerce and the object itself (called Class1) to Visit:

Thanks to the wonder of VB, we're now in a position where we could run our project and create and use instances of the Visit ActiveX object inside ASP! Revisiting our earlier ActiveX discussion, Active Scripting is now able, at the behest of ASP, to look at the properties and methods on that object from the type library and determine how to make the calls. But, we're not going to start using the object inside ASP just yet. Rather, for the remainder of this chapter we're going to continue putting the framework of our model together.

Adding the Configure Method

As we stated earlier, when we build our ASP pages, we're going to create an instance of the `Visit` object in code at the top of the page and add code to delete it at the bottom. This means that an instance of the `Visit` object will only exist for as long as the page is running. When the object is created it needs to have some information about the environment it exists in (mainly so it can connect to the database) and we're going to supply this information via the `Configure` method. As we want to be able to reuse this `Visit` object in other sites, we're going to tell it some other useful information, like the site name and the mail domain.

1. First of all, double-click on the **Visit** class in **Project Explorer** and enter the following code into the code window:

```
Option Explicit

' these variables hold the things about the site, like the name and mail domain. We'll ' use
' these later on...
Private m_strSiteName as String
Private m_strMailDomain as String

' this variable holds the connection string needed to connect to the database...
Private m_strDBString as String

' Configure - tells the Visit object a little about the site...
Public Sub Configure(ByVal strSiteName As String, ByVal strMailDomain As String, _
   ByVal strDBString As String)

   ' copy the site name, etc...
   m_strSiteName = strSiteName
   m_strMailDomain = strMailDomain

   ' copy the database details...
   m_strDBString = strDBString

End Sub
```

2. Next we want to create a `Shutdown` method. So, add this code to `Visit`:

```
' Shutdown - releases any resources we may have open...
Public Sub Shutdown()

   ' we've got nothing to clean up yet, so we'll leave it blank...

End Sub
```

3. Then using the two drop-down lists at the top of the code editor window, select Class and Terminate and add the following:

```
' Called when the object is deleted...
Private Sub Class_Terminate()

   ' Make a call to Shutdown just to be sure...
   Shutdown

End Sub
```

4. Save the work you've done so far, saving the class as `Visit.cls` and the project as `WroxCommerce.vbp`.

5. Then select **Make WroxCommerce.dll** from the File menu to create the library.

6. Although we're jumping ahead of ourselves, we can now call a `Visit` object from a sample ASP page. Open Visual InterDev, right-click on the **JoCoffee** project and select Add | Active Server Page. Name the page `WroxCommerceTest.asp` and type in the following code:

```
<% option explicit %>
<HTML>
<HEAD>
<TITLE>WroxCommerce Test Page</TITLE>
</HEAD>
<BODY>

<%
' create the visit object...
Dim objVisit
Set objVisit = Server.CreateObject("WroxCommerce.Visit")

' configure the visit object...
objVisit.Configure "Jo's Coffee", "joscoffee.com", "driver=SQL " & _
"Server;DATABASE=JoCoffee;UID=JoCoffeeWeb;PWD=eermlate;SERVER=localhost"

%>

<b>Interesting HTML here!</b>

<%
' now we've finished shut down and clean up the object...
objVisit.Shutdown
Set objVisit = Nothing
%>

</BODY>
</HTML>
```

7. Right-click in the code area and select **View In Browser**; save when prompted and hopefully you should see:

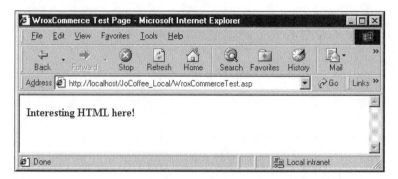

It doesn't do anything yet, but it shows that at least our object has been successfully created. We're not really interested in how the ASP works, as it won't form part of our final application, but we do need to look at the code we used to create the `Configure` and `Shutdown` methods.

How It Works

Let's take a look at the code we've just entered and see what it does. The first line is `Option Explicit`, which is located in the General Declaration section of the code:

```
Option Explicit
```

For those unfamiliar with `Option Explicit`, it's the number one recommendation I make when talking to developers about making their code manageable. Simply, it tells VB that before you can refer to a variable name in your code, you must have already defined it using a `Dim` statement. Using the `Option Explicit` command means that Visual Basic will automatically alert you when the program runs if you have misspelled a variable name by throwing up an error message stating **Variable not defined**.

The failure of procedures and functions due to misspelled variables is one of the most common, and difficult to find, bugs in VB programs and hence experienced programmers often have the statement automatically inserted into the declaration section of forms and modules. This is easily achieved by clicking on **Tools | Options…**, then the **Editor** tab, and placing a check mark in the **Require Variable Declaration** box.

Next, we defined several variables in the class module. We'll be using these variables to hold so called **environmental information**, such as the name of the site, the default domain for mail and the database connection information. We are using the term environmental information to describe the data that the object can use to determine what state the system is in, and discover metrics about the system.

```
' these variables hold the things about the site, like the name and mail domain.
' We'll ' use these later on...
Private m_strSiteName as String
Private m_strMailDomain as String

' this variable holds the connection string needed to connect to the database...
Private m_strDBString as String
```

Then we defined the `Configure` method. As we alluded to earlier, we are going to define a convention that this method must be called from ASP immediately after we create an instance of the `Visit` object. You'll see this in action in a little while (in fact, we can use this `Configure` method in other scripting environments like Windows Script Host, not just in ASP).

```
' configure the visit object...
objVisit.Configure "Jo's Coffee", "joscoffee.com", "driver=SQL " & _
"Server;DATABASE=JoCoffee;UID=JoCoffeeWeb;PWD=eermlate;SERVER=localhost"

  ' copy the site name, etc...
  m_strSiteName = strSiteName
  m_strMailDomain = strMailDomain

' copy the database details...
  m_strDBString = strDBString

End Sub
```

Finally, we created a `Shutdown` method that will be called at the bottom of the page:

```
' Called when the object is deleted...
Private Sub Class_Terminate()

  ' Make a call to Shutdown just to be sure...
  Shutdown

End Sub
```

It's good practice to explicitly close any resources that we use in our page, rather than relying on any housekeeping functionality built into Active Scripting and VBScript. For example, when the ASP page has finished, any objects we created during the life of that page will automatically be released by Active Scripting. What we want to do is explicitly tell the `Visit` object that we've finished with it and that it's OK for it to go ahead and release any resources it's using. Releasing objects and resources as early as possible helps increase the scalability of any system we put together (just-in-time activation and as-soon-as possible deactivation).

This is all good programming practice and, as the architect of this object model, it's a good idea to ensure that we put checks in place so that if we (or perhaps a future developer working with our code – good code should be maintainable), make a mistake the effects will be contained and managed. What we want to do is make sure that `Shutdown` always gets called. To ensure this, happens when our object is finally deleted, we created a `Class_Terminate` Sub, which made a call to `Shutdown`.

Now that we've prepared the foundations of the `Visit` class, we should start examining how we are going to make the connection to the database.

Connecting to the Database

Our chosen technology for connecting to our database is going to be **ActiveX Data Objects**, or **ADO**. ADO is a set of objects that can connect to any ODBC or OLE DB database. To further my earlier point about object models, ADO is arranged into an object model (we're not going to go into the model in detail here as it's a big subject – if you want to know more, try looking at *ADO 2.1 Programmer's Reference ISBN 1861002688* also by *Wrox Press*). In this case, the root object is typically the `Connection` object.

Linking to the ADO Library

When we want to access external components in Visual Basic, it's good practice to include a reference to those components. Here we'll be linking to the ADO library (as we see shortly). By including references we experience a huge performance increase versus not including references.

As an example of low performance code, consider the following, where an ADO `Connection` object is created in ASP:

```
<%
  Dim Connection
  Set Connection = CreateObject("ADODB.Connection")
%>
```

Once we have a `Connection` object around we can run queries on the database using the `Execute` method, like this:

```
<%
  Dim Query
  Set Query = Connection.Execute("select * from customers")
%>
```

In this case Active Scripting (the Microsoft technology that interprets and runs the VBScript code embedded in your ASP scripts) goes away and asks the `Connection` object if it supports the `Execute` method. After it's determined it does, it then needs to ask the `Connection` object what parameters the `Execute` method supports.

That operation is very expensive (since it requires a lot of processor cycles) and happens whenever you call a method or property on an ActiveX object created inside ASP, irrespective of the language you're using. Similarly it happens in Visual Basic whenever you call methods on objects that Visual Basic doesn't understand. Paradoxically, although this technology costs a lot of **processor cycles** (the unit of work that the processor is capable of doing) when it runs, it's the very essence of ActiveX.

Reference Benefits

Including references in our Visual Basic project, tells VB where to go to find the methods and properties the object supports, ahead of time. As we mentioned before, when an ActiveX DLL is compiled a type library is added to the file. When requested, the DLL can give that type library to whatever wants to contain that ActiveX control – and in this case Visual Basic is the thing that wants to contain your control.

Visual Basic is much smarter at executing code than the VBScript/Active Scripting combination. Once VB has loaded and understood the type information in the library it can make a much faster, lower-level, call into the ActiveX object than the route VBScript/Active Scripting takes. Without getting into too much detail, what VB is able to do is to make the call into the ActiveX control in one hop, as it is a compiled language. Essentially, this takes a few processor cycles. VBScript/Active Scripting cripples itself because it cannot make calls in this fashion, as it is an interpreted language. Instead, it has to move through a higher-level architecture that takes between 10 and 20 times as many cycles.

We'll be learning a little more about this later, but as we know we are using ADO in our project we'll be including a reference to the ADO DLL in our project. This will mean that whenever we call `Connection.Execute` from our objects we'll be calling it between 10 and 20 times faster than if we made the same call from ASP without the library reference.

Providing Data Services

Our next task in the construction of our object model is to create another class module (`Database`) that will provide *data services* to the remainder of the objects in the model (thus `Database` is an infrastructure object). The term data services encompasses any database activity, such as selecting rows, inserts or deletes, schema manipulation, etc. Although ADO provides a rich set of database functionality, we are going to build our own object, so that we can build a smaller set of very useful functions that leverage the ADO functionality. This makes our writing objects in our model a little easier (the motives for doing this will become clear in later chapters).

We'll use the `Database` object to connect to the database and, after we have created it, the other objects in our model can then use this object to get a connection to the database without having to worry about the details of creating the connection.

Try It Out – Creating the Database Class Module

1. Our first task is to include a reference to the ADO DLL. Select Project | References from the menu and when the list of objects appears, locate and check on the Microsoft ActiveX Data Objects 2.1 Library as shown here:

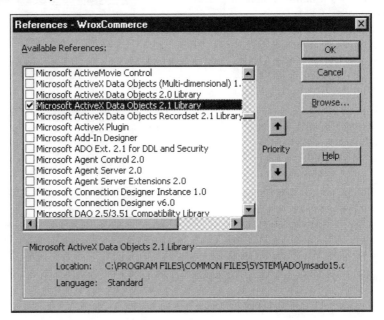

> If you do not have ActiveX Data Objects 2.1 installed on your computer, it can be downloaded from http://www.microsoft.com/data/.

2. Using the Project Explorer window, right-click Class Modules and select Add | Class Module. Select Class Module from the New tab and click Open:

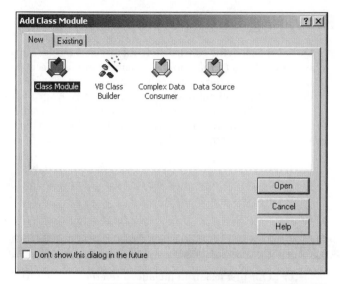

3. After the class has been created, use the Properties window to name the class Database:

4. In the code window, type in the following code:

```
Option Explicit

' this variable holds the connection string needed to connect to the database...
Private m_strDBString As String

' this variable is used to hold the database connection...
Private m_db As ADODB.Connection

' Configure - tells the Database object about the database
Public Sub Configure(ByVal strDBString As String)
```

```
' copy the database details...
  m_strDBString = strDBString

End Sub

' DB - property to return an ADO Connection back...
Public Property Get DB() As Connection

' do we have a connection?
  If m_db Is Nothing Then

    ' create the connection object...
    Set m_db = New Connection

      ' connect to the database based on what was passed
      ' to the Configure method...
    m_db.Open m_strDBString

  End If

' return it back to the caller...
Set DB = m_db

End Property

' Shutdown - releases any resources we may have open...
Public Sub Shutdown()

  ' do we have a database connection?
  ' If m_db is not "Nothing" then we assume we do...
  If Not m_db Is Nothing Then

    ' close the connection...
    m_db.Close
    Set m_db = Nothing

  End If

End Sub
```

5. Then, once again using the two drop-down lists at the top of the code editor window, select **Class** and **Terminate** and add the following:

```
' Called when the object is deleted...
Private Sub Class_Terminate()

  ' Make a call to Shutdown just to be sure...
  Shutdown

End Sub
```

6. We're not going to test the code we've created here, because once again there is nothing to see at the moment; however, we can save it as `Database.cls`.

How It Works

We saw before, when we started building the `Visit` class module, how we can use a `Configure` method to supply environmental information to an object. Environmental information in the WroxCommerce module refers mainly to the database connection parameters, as well as the site name and mail domain name and here we're now going to provide a way for the `Database` object to get that information.

As before the opening lines of code specify `Option Explicit` and a private variable to hold the database connection string.

```
Option Explicit

' this variable holds the connection string needed to connect to the database...
Private m_strDBString As String
```

We then create a private member variable to hold a database connection:

```
' this variable is used to hold the database connection...
Private m_db As ADODB.Connection
```

Then, like before, we created a `Configure` method:

```
' Configure - tells the Database object about the database
Public Sub Configure(ByVal strDBString As String)

  ' copy the database details...
  m_strDBString = strDBString

End Sub
```

It might be tempting to create a connection to the database inside the `Configure` method itself. After all, we know everything about the database at that point, so why not? Well, when we're trying to build a scalable distributed application, as we previously discussed, we must always think about resource use. Hence, we'll create the database connection *on demand*, just before we want to use it for the first time, so the scarce resource is preserved until the exact moment it's required.

The objects in our model are going to obtain access to the database through the DB property of this `Database` object. What we want to do is create a `Connection` object and open that connection only on the first call to this property. To do this, we'll check to make sure the `Connection` object hasn't been set to anything, and if it hasn't, we establish the connection:

```
' DB - property to return an ADO Connection back...
Public Property Get DB() As Connection

' do we have a connection?
  If m_db Is Nothing Then

    ' create the connection object...
    Set m_db = New Connection

    ' connect to the database based on what was passed
    ' to the Configure method...
    m_db.Open m_strDBString
```

```
    End If

    ' return it back to the caller...
    Set DB = m_db

    End Property
```

In our `Visit` object, we had a `Shutdown` method to clear out any resources we may be using. Here we do the same to disconnect from the database:

```
    ' Shutdown - releases any resources we may have open...
    Public Sub Shutdown()

        ' do we have a database connection?
        ' If m_db is not "Nothing" then we assume we do...
        If Not m_db Is Nothing Then

            ' close the connection...
            m_db.Close
            Set m_db = Nothing

        End If

    End Sub
```

Again in a similar manner to the `Visit` object, we finish this section of code building by adding a `Class_Terminate` method to double-check `Shutdown` had been called.

Accessing the Database

The `Database` object is an infrastructure object, and its sole purpose is to provide data services to the `Visit` object and other objects in the model. In order to do that, we need to provide a mechanism that allows these objects to get hold of a correctly configured database object.

To enforce adherence to business rules, we absolutely do *not* want to provide direct access to the data services to ASP code. This means we somehow need to expose methods and properties that create and manage these database services to objects in the model, but prevent these methods and properties from being exposed to calls coming in from outside the object model (for example from ASP). We're going to learn how to do that next.

To start with, though, we need to put in place some way of monitoring our development of the site.

Versioning

When we make the site available to visitors we'll **deploy** (copy across the ASP code and ActiveX components) the application to a Web server at a remote location. At this point one of the things that can cause a lot of hassle is not knowing for certain whether the software components we're running are the correct ones.

Put it this way – say you identify a problem with a component on your site. During a round of testing and development you create a new component that addresses the problem that you duly deploy to the remote server. Now when you come to test, the bug appears to still be there. The question that runs through most developers' heads at this point is "Is the code the correct version?"

Well, Microsoft does a really neat job of hiding most of the internals of ActiveX away from us, so in order to determine if IIS (the Server we intend to deploy to) is loading the right component we have to start digging through the Registry. Even if all that appears to be in order, we still can't see inside IIS to determine if it's doing something odd. We then can't be confident that our next step in solving the problem is the correct one.

One of the quickest and easiest ways to address this problem is through versioning. Since the beginning, Windows has put functionality into its development tools that lets developers tack version numbers onto the end of any DLL, EXE or OCX.

For example, if you open up Windows Explorer and find a DLL or EXE on your system, then right-click on it, choose **Properties**, and change to the **Version** tab, you should see something like:

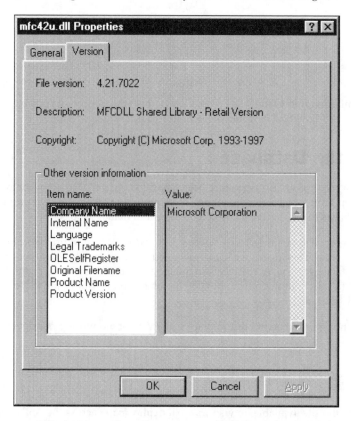

In this example, which is one of Microsoft's MFC runtime DLLs, we can see the version number that the developers tacked onto the end of the file to identify it; in this case it's 4.21.7022.

The three parts making up this number are, in order, termed:

- **Major Number**
- **Minor Number**
- **Revision**

Thus in our example the major number is 4, the minor 21 and it's revision 7022. The major and minor numbers usually stay fixed throughout a development project. So, if six months after we've deployed Jo's Coffee we need to do some maintenance work, we will probably choose to increase the minor number. If we need to do a serious overhaul of the code, we will probably choose to increase the major number.

For day-to-day deployment and testing, we'll usually increase the revision number (sometimes called **build** number). The very first component we deploy will have a revision number of 0. The second will be 1, and so on.

> It's a good idea to do include versioning information with our DLLs, but we should make sure that each time we compile a new version of the DLL for deployment we have to change the version number.

Try It Out – Setting the Original Version Number

1. You can use VB's Project Properties dialog to set the original version number of the project. Select Project | WroxCommerce Properties and change to the Make tab:

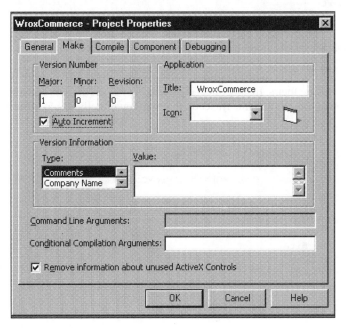

You can see on the dialog that there are three boxes, one for each of minor, major and revision. There's also a **Version Information** box that you can use to set other information on the DLL, like copyright information, product information and such like. Referring back to the MFC DLL Properties screenshot, you can guess that, if we change that information here, users of Windows Explorer will be able to see the values we set when they bring up the file's properties.

We can ask VB to automatically increment this revision number for us each time we make (or compile) the DLL by ensuring **Auto Increment** is checked on.

2. As we are just starting out on our project set **Major** to **1**, **Minor** to **0**, and **Revision** to **0** and close the dialog.

An Aside – Obtaining the Version Number

Once we're confident in our versioning strategy, we can make our business object DLLs tell us their version number by querying a property on the root object in the model.

Programmatically checking the version number of DLLs on your system is actually quite tricky. For this reason, we're going to build properties into our `Visit` object that we can use to quickly find the version number of our business object DLLs.

To do this, all you have to do is ask the `Visit` object for it's Major, Minor, and Revision numbers, like this:

```
' Version - returns the version number back...
Public Property Get Version() As String
 Version = App.Major & "." & App.Minor & "." & App.Revision
End Property
```

In our `Version` property, all we've done is taken those three numbers and mangled them into a string, like this: 1.0.0. We'll see this approach in action later on.

As you'll see later, we can, when required, build a very simple ASP page that lets us keep our head while all around are losing theirs. Just by querying a single page on the server, we can see if we are using the correct version of the component. The code that we'll eventually use to achieve this aim is:

```
<%
   ' create an instance of the site...
   Dim Visit
   Set Visit = Server.CreateObject("WroxCommerce.Visit")

   ' get the version number...
   Response.Write "Version: " & Visit.Version

   ' stop the site...
   Visit.ShutDown
   Set Visit = Nothing
%>
```

Compiling the File

Although we won't talk about registering components and deployment to production servers at this point in time (this will be covered in Chapter 12), it is perhaps worth mentioning a useful naming convention associated with versioning.

One of the worst gotchas a typical developer goes through when they deploy components to a remote site is when the set of business objects put up there doesn't work as planned and the site is broken. If it's a production site that's being deployed to (and it usually is), the site must be reset to its previous state as quickly as possible.

A neat technique that can be used here is, when replacing an existing DLL, rename the DLL installed on the server to a different filename based on the version number. As shown above, use Windows Explorer to get the version number of the existing DLL and rename the file as shown:

Version Number	File Name
Version 1.0.0	WroxCommerce_1_0_0.dll
Version 1.1.1	WroxCommerce_1_1_1.dll
Version 1.1.2	WroxCommerce_1_1_2.dll

Now copy the freshly compiled DLL and register it as normal. If it appears that something is wrong, stop IIS to release the lock on the DLL (stopping Web servers is a topic covered in some detail in Chapter 12), un-register the new DLL, rename the old DLL back to WroxCommerce.dll and register it again. Finally, restart IIS. The system should be back to its original state.

Permissions

Furthermore, Internet Information Server (the Web server that we will be deploying to) is tightly integrated with the Windows NT security subsystem. This means that it's possible to use NT security to control access either to all, or to parts of, any Web site. For most publicly accessible sites, IIS uses a special user account on the domain. When a user accesses the site, the IIS process pretends to be, or more correctly, **impersonates** this user to determine the access rights to various system resources. This anonymous user is created on installation and typically takes the name IUSR_machinename, so on my computer my anonymous user is called IUSR_BEETLE.

When you try and create an ActiveX component, the permissions set on the actual DLL that contains the components are checked to ensure that the IIS anonymous user has access. If that user doesn't, the file cannot be opened, and you'll see an error like this:

```
Microsoft VBScript runtime error '800a01ad'
ActiveX component can't create object
/site.asp, line 75
```

The 800a01ad is the key thing to look for here, as this is the error code for a permissions failure. If you're debugging the object from within Visual Basic, you won't usually see this error. The reason for this is the DLL that handles ActiveX object debugging (VB6Debug.dll which can be found in the Visual Basic directory) has no specific permissions set on installation and so by default it is always accessible to all users.

However, if you copy the DLL over to another server, depending on how your security is set up and how you are logged on to the remote server, you may see this error. This will only happen if the new file is installed with permissions that do not include the IIS anonymous user.

To resolve the problem, you just have to:

1. Use Windows Explorer to locate the file.

2. Right-click on the file, select Properties, change to the Security tab, and select Permissions.

3. Click Add...

4. Find the IIS anonymous user in the list, select it, make sure Type of Access: is set to Full Control, and click OK.

Here's what the permissions look like for the WroxCommerce.dll file with my IIS anonymous user in place:

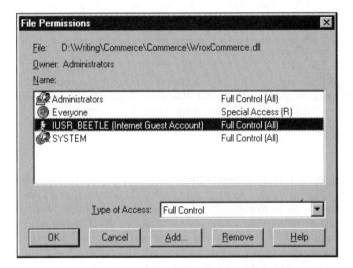

Interfaces in the WroxCommerce Project

As we indicated previously, when we create an ActiveX object in Visual Basic, VB does all the hard work of putting the correct interfaces in place so that it can plug itself into Active Scripting, and by association, ASP, Windows Script Host, or anything else that acts as an ActiveX component container. Additionally, VB also creates an interface that just contains the methods and properties that are public on that object. This allows VB to call into that object highly efficiently.

Try It Out – Using the OLE/COM Viewer

Let's try to illustrate the presence of interfaces by using the OLE/COM Viewer utility that comes with Visual C++ to inspect our recently built ActiveX objects. If you don't have Visual C++ or the Visual C++ tools installed on your machine, you can download the tool from http://www.microsoft.com/com/resources/oleview.asp. If you can't get hold of it, don't worry. This is the best tool to illustrate the interfaces on our object, but you should be able to follow the discussion through the screenshots.

1. Run the OLE/COM Viewer. Expand **Object Classes** then expand **All Objects**.

2. Scroll down until you find **WroxCommerce.Visit**. (You may have to scroll down quite a long way.) Expand the object. This is what our `WroxCommerce.Visit` object looks like inside this utility:

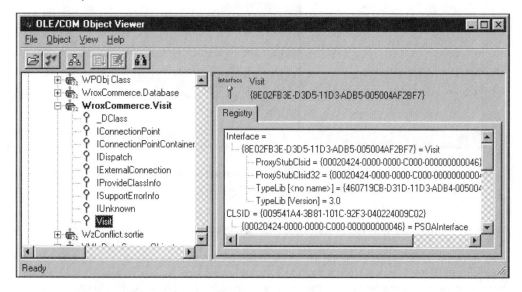

Look at the list of interfaces shown in the screenshot. The highlighted `Visit` interface shows the existence of the interface VB builds that just features the methods and properties on our object.

Note, although this is called `Visit`, it is an interface, not a class.

3. Let's look now at what's inside the `Visit` interface. To do this, double-click on the **Visit** object. This will display a little dialog with a button labeled **View Type Info**. Click this button and you'll see something like this:

```
ITypeInfo Viewer                                                    _ □ ×
File  View

 □  □  ?

 ⊟─ Visit                          [
    ⊟─ m Methods                       uuid(8E02FB3E-D3D5-11D3-ADB5-005004AF2BF7),
       ─ m Configure                   version(1.0),
       └─ m Shutdown                   hidden,
    ⊞─ ? Inherited Interfaces          dual,
                                       nonextensible
                                   ]
                                   dispinterface _Visit {
                                       properties:
                                       methods:
                                           [id(0x60030000)]
                                           void Configure(
                                                       [in] BSTR strSiteName,
                                                       [in] BSTR strMailDomain,
                                                       [in] BSTR strDataSource,
                                                       [in] BSTR strUsername,
                                                       [in] BSTR strPassword);
                                           [id(0x60030001)]
                                           void Shutdown();
                                   };

Ready
```

4. Lastly, close down the **ITypeInfo Viewer** and then close down OLE/COM Viewer as well, otherwise we'll prevent later examples from working.

When we examine the interface, we can see that this object contains only the methods we created on it. Note also that VB has defined these methods as having the parameters we defined against them. COM uses the term `BSTR` to represent the `As String` directive that you're familiar with. Notice that the `Class_Terminate` method has not made it into this interface. As you've probably guessed, that's because it's a private method and is therefore not accessible from outside the object.

This discussion is leading up to how we build another interface on our VB objects that lets us create public methods accessible to other objects in the model, but prevents those methods from being accessible to ASP.

Creating our own Interface

To achieve our aim of creating public methods for access by other objects, but not by ASP, we're going to create an interface definition of our own and then tell the `Visit` object that it supports that alternative interface. We can then pass that alternative interface through to other objects in the model when they're created.

Try It Out – Creating an Interface in the WroxCommerce Project

1. To kick off, return to the VB Project, add a new class module, and call it `IUtility`. We use the "I" to signify that it's an interface, in accordance with the COM standards.

2. When you create interface definitions, you simply define the methods and properties. You do *not* under any circumstances enter code into the methods and properties that are defined in the interface class module. So, it's OK to use the Public Property and Public Function constructs, but no methods or properties can contain any code. The next task is to enter the following:

```
' DB - property to return a populated and configured database object...
Public Property Get DB() As Database
End Property

' Visit - property to return the Visit object back again...
Public Property Get Visit() As Visit
End Property
```

To clarify the earlier point about where you can and can't put code, the above code is fine; however, the following two segments of code are both *not* acceptable:

```
' DB - property to return a populated and configured database object...
Public Property Get DB() As Database
  MsgBox "There's code here. There shouldn't be!"
End Property


Dim Buf As String
Buf = "There's code here. There shouldn't be!"

' DB - property to return a populated and configured database object...
Public Property Get DB() As Database
End Property
```

> **Literally, the only things that can be in an interface class module are lines that are blank lines, lines that are comments, lines that start `Public Property` or `Public Function`, and lines that start `End Property` or `End Function`.**

3. Our next job is to tell the `Visit` object that it **implements** (in other words – supports) that interface. So make the following addition to the `Visit` class module:

```
' this variable holds the connection string needed to connect to the database...
Private m_strDBString as String
```

```
' tell it what interfaces it supports...
Implements IUtility
```

> When we tell an object that it implements an interface we enter into a contract with
> VB that we will add functions in order for the object to handle each of the methods
> and properties in the interface.

4. In the object drop-down list box in the top left of the code window, you should now be able to
find the IUtility interface. Selecting that will display a list of the methods and properties
on the interface, as shown here:

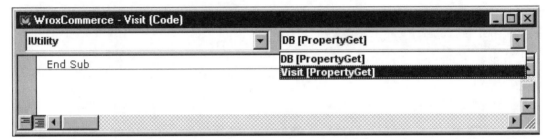

Our next tasks are to implement the Visit and DB properties contained in our interface definition.

Try It Out – Implementing the Visit Property

At present, our Visit object implements two interfaces: Visit and IUtility. When we create other
objects in the model we're going to pass them an IUtility interface, mainly to provide access to the data
services. Additionally, they may want access back to the public Visit interface that our ASP code will be
using.

1. Add this code to the bottom of the Visit object:

```
' Called when the object is deleted...
Private Sub Class_Terminate()

  ' Make a call to Shutdown just to be sure...
  ShutDown

End Sub
```

```
' Visit - returns the public visit interface back to the caller...
Private Property Get IUtility_Visit() As Visit
  Set IUtility_Visit = Me
End Property
```

How It Works

When we defined the `Visit` property on the `IUtility` interface, we indicated that it would be returning a `Visit` object back to the caller. As we said, the `Visit` object implements two interfaces: `Visit` and `IUtility`. If we indicated that the `IUtility.Visit` property returned an Object or a Variant datatype, Visual Basic would not reliably know which interface the caller actually wants, which is why we clearly state the intentions of this call through the `As Visit` directive at the end of the definition.

The only line in this property:

```
Set IUtility_Visit = Me
```

looks simple, but what happens is pretty smart. VB is expecting `IUtility_Visit` to be set to an object that implements the `Visit` interface. The object `Me` represents the current object and implements both the `Visit` and the `IUtility` interfaces. This object is a COM object, so VB is able to specifically query it for the known `Visit` interface. This technique ensures that there is no ambiguity in the calls.

Try It Out – Implementing the "DB" Property

The first time the `DB` property is called, we want to create an instance of a new `Database` object and properly configure it so it's able to connect to the database. As we saw before, that `Database` object will not establish a physical database connection until the first time its `DB` property is called.

1. Firstly, we need to add some code to the `Visit` object – create a private member variable to hold the database object:

```
' this variable holds the connection string needed to connect to the database...
Private m_strDBString As String

' variable to hold database object
Private m_db As Database
```

2. Then, we need to implement the `DB` property of the `IUtility` interface, again on the `Visit` object itself. Firstly, we check to see if the object has been created. If not, we create it and configure it based on what was passed to `Visit.Configure` from ASP. Either way, we pass a `Database` object back to the caller:

```
' Visit - returns the public visit interface back to the caller...
Private Property Get IUtility_Visit() As Visit
  Set IUtility_Visit = Me
End Property

Private Property Get IUtility_DB() As Database

  ' do we have a connection?
  If m_db Is Nothing Then

    ' create the object...
    Set m_db = New Database

    ' configure it...
    m_db.Configure m_strDBString
```

```
      End If

      ' pass the connection back...
      Set IUtility_DB = m_db

End Property
```

3. With the `Visit` object now able to create instances of `Database` objects, we need to tweak our `Shutdown` code to properly cleanup the database connection. Recall how the `Shutdown` method of the `Database` physically closes and removes the ADO `Connection` object? Well, we'll now use the `Shutdown` method of the `Visit` object to call the `Shutdown` method of `Database`, by changing the existing `Shutdown` method that we added to the `Visit` object previously.

So to the `Visit` object add:

```
' Shutdown - releases any resources we may have open...
Public Sub Shutdown()

      ' do we have a database?
      If Not m_db Is Nothing Then

      ' shutdown the database...
      m_db.Shutdown
      Set m_db = Nothing

      End If

End Sub
```

4. Finally save the project, including all class modules as prompted, and select File | Make WroxCommerce.dll. If at this point you're hit with a dialog saying Permission Denied C:\inetpub\wwwroot\JoCoffee_Local\WroxCommerce.dll or some similar message, then we need to do one last thing to get it to work. When you create a component in Visual Basic and view it in a web page, then you can sometimes find that IIS still holds a lock on the DLL, and won't let anyone else use it. To get IIS to release the lock, you need to bring up the Services Dialog and physically stop and start the IIS Admin Service, taking care to also restart the World Wide Web Publishing Service before attempting to make the DLL again. If it's still not letting you in, then check that OLE/COM viewer has been shut down, as instructed in the last Try It Out.

We'll discuss this further when we look at code testing transactions in Chapter 9.

Looking at the Results

We can now use the OLE/COM Object Viewer once more to take a look at what our object looks like to anyone who wants to use it now all that's in place. Again if you haven't the appropriate tools installed, you can follow along in the screenshots.

Again run the OLE/COM Viewer, expand **Object Classes** then expand **All Objects** and scroll down until you find WroxCommerce.Visit. Expanding the object should give something like:

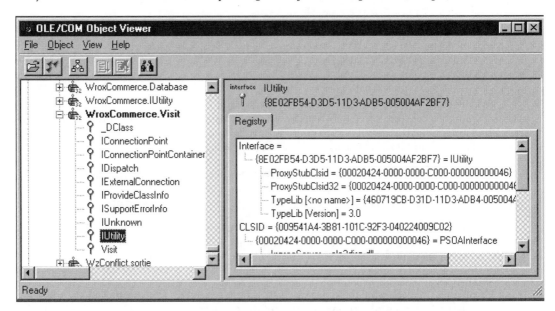

We can now see that our `Visit` object implements the `IUtility` interface. As before, we can drill further in and have a look at the methods that that interface supports by double-clicking on `IUtility` and selecting **View Type Info** as appropriate:

We've done a lot of work so far, but we still haven't done anything practical! Well, fear not, we're now at a point where we can start building the object model and start building the database for our store.

77

Building the Catalog Object

In Chapter 5, we're going to look in earnest at the **product catalog** – the tables, code and business logic that make up the list of products and services we'll be providing through our e-commerce initiative. At this point though we'll build the framework for the `Catalog` object – this will give us a good start for further work and will also let us get something working after all the hard preparation we've done in this chapter.

Creating the Object

The `Catalog` object is the object that we use when we want to access the list of products and services that we sell. It will enable ASP developers to query the available departments, get data on individual products, and facilitate changes to the catalog as it appears in the database.

When we want to access the catalog, we won't create instances of `WroxCommerce.Catalog` from ASP. Our preferred technique is to create a property on the `Visit` object that's capable of returning a properly configured `Catalog` object back to the caller. There are two main reasons for doing this:

❑ Firstly, we don't want to have to provide environment information (the database connection details, main domain, and site name) to the other objects in the model each time we create them. At the moment, we give the `Visit` object the environmental information, and so this object should pass that information down to the other objects without our intervention.

❑ Secondly, we can cache the object the first time it's created. This means that we only have either no instances, or just one instance, of the `Catalog` object each time the `Visit` object is created. Remember, the `Visit` object only gets created one time per page too, so this means the total number of open objects taking up scarce resources on the system is minimized, aiding scalability.

In order for the `Catalog` object to get to the database, it needs to access the `Database` object. Just now, we created a mechanism to provide a properly configured `Database` object through the `IUtility` interface. The trick now is to supply an `IUtility` interface to the `Catalog` object.

Try It Out – Creating the Catalog Object

1. Using the Project Explorer, create a new class module and use the Properties window to rename it to Catalog.

2. If you haven't already got it automatically added, ensure the first line is the `Option Explicit` command; then, let's create somewhere to put the `IUtility` interface:

```
Option Explicit

' use IUtility to call back into the Visit and Database objects...
Private m_utility As IUtility
```

3. Now, let's create a `Configure` method that will store the `IUtility` interface:

```
' Configure - set up IUtility...
Public Sub Configure(ByVal utility As IUtility)

    ' hold the utility object...
    Set m_utility = utility

End Sub
```

Let's see how we can use this method.

Try It Out – Implementing the Catalog Property on the Visit Object

We want ASP developers to be able to access the `Catalog` property directly through a call similar to:

```
<%
    Dim catalog
    Set catalog = visit.Catalog
%>
```

So, obviously, we need to build a `Catalog` property on the `Visit` object that is capable of creating and configuring a `Catalog` object, in much the same way as we did with the database object.

1. First off, let's create somewhere to hold the `Catalog` object. Add this code to the `Visit` object:

```
    ' this variable holds the connection string needed to connect to the
    ' database...

Private m_strDBString as String
```

```
    ' these variables hold the objects that are in the next hierarchical
    ' level in our object model...
Private m_catalog As Catalog
```

2. Then, let's look at creating an appropriate property on the `Visit` object – so make the following addition after the `Shutdown` subroutine:

```
' Shutdown - releases any resources we may have open...
Public Sub Shutdown()

    ' do we have a database?
    If Not m_db Is Nothing Then

        ' shutdown the database...
        m_db.Shutdown
        Set m_db = Nothing

    End If


End Sub
```

```
' Catalog - returns an instance of a Catalog object...
Public Property Get Catalog() As Catalog

    ' do we have one already?
    If m_catalog Is Nothing Then

        ' create and configure
        Set m_catalog = New Catalog
        m_catalog.Configure Me

    End If

    ' return the catalog...
    Set Catalog = m_catalog

End Property
```

The `Configure` call:

```
m_catalog.Configure Me
```

is responsible for passing a reference to the `IUtility` interface implemented on the `Visit` object through to the new `Catalog` object. In a moment, we'll see how the `Catalog` object can keep a handle to this object around so that it can obtain a connection to the database (through the `DB` property), and access to the greater `WroxCommerce` object model (through the `Visit` property).

3. As we learned before, it's good practice to make sure things get cleaned up properly, so let's get the `Shutdown` method to release the `Catalog` object that we may have created. Add this code to the `Shutdown` method on the `Visit` object:

```
' Shutdown - releases any resources we may have open...
Public Sub Shutdown()

    ' do we have a database?
    If Not m_db Is Nothing Then

        ' shutdown the database...
        m_db.Shutdown
        Set m_db = Nothing

    End If

    ' clean up any other objects...
    Set m_catalog = Nothing

End Sub
```

Well, we're still not at a point where we can do anything practical with our objects, but we can make it do something to prove that it works!

Let's test all our hard work (and the foundations for our later code building) by creating a simple ASP page that creates an instance of the `Visit` object, configures it with the database connection details and site name, and then renders the internal names of the visit objects:

1. Firstly, we need to add a Version property to the `Visit` object, which will return the Major, Minor, and Revision numbers. We came across this code before when we talked about obtaining the versioning number earlier:

```
' Configure - tells the Visit object a little about the site...
Public Sub Configure(ByVal strSiteName As String, ByVal strMailDomain As String, _
  ByVal strDBString As String)

  ' copy the site name, etc...
  m_strSiteName = strSiteName
  m_strMailDomain = strMailDomain

  ' copy the database details...
  m_strDBString = strDBString

End Sub
```

```
' Version - returns the version number back...
Public Property Get Version() As String
  Version = App.Major & "." & App.Minor & "." & App.Revision
End Property
```

2. Next, open Visual InterDev, right-click on the **JoCoffee** project and select <u>A</u>dd I Acti<u>v</u>e Server Page. Name the page `WroxCommerceTest2.asp` and type in the following code:

```
<% option explicit %>
<HTML>
<HEAD>
  <TITLE>WroxCommerce Test Page</TITLE>
</HEAD>
<BODY>

  <%
  ' create the visit object...
  Dim visit
  Set visit = Server.CreateObject("WroxCommerce.Visit")

  ' configure the visit object with the name of the site, the mail domain
  ' and the database connection details...
  Visit.Configure "Jo's Coffee", "joscoffee.com", "driver=SQL " & _
"Server;DATABASE=JoCoffee;UID=JoCoffeeWeb;PWD=eermlate;SERVER=localhost"

  ' what's the version number of the DLL?
  Response.Write "Version Number: " & visit.Version & "<br><br>"

  ' let's write out the names of some of the objects...
  Response.Write "Visit object: " & typename(visit) & "<br>"
  Response.Write "Catalog object: " & typename(visit.Catalog) & "<br>"

  ' now we've finished shut down and clean up the object...
  visit.Shutdown
```

```
        Set visit = Nothing
    %>

</BODY>
</HTML>
```

3. Before we can run the page, we need to save the project before telling VB to run the project. Select **Run | Start** and when prompted make sure **Wait for components to be created** is selected.

4. Now return to Visual InterDev, right-click on the `WroxCommerceTest2.asp` page, and select **View In Browser** – you should see the following:

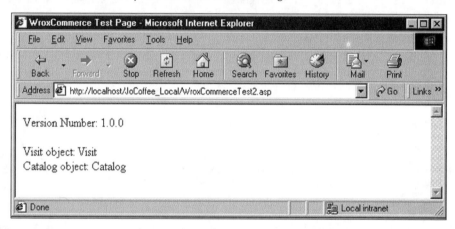

How It Works

Let's have a look at the ASP code – the first thing we do is to create a new instance of the `Visit` object:

```
' create the visit object...
Dim visit
Set visit = Server.CreateObject("WroxCommerce.Visit")
```

After we've created the `Visit` object, we can set up the environmental information. Here, we're passing in the site name, mail domain, OLE DB connection string, and the username and password for that data source. Ultimately, this connection information will be passed through to the `Database` object and used to establish a connection.

```
' configure the visit object with the name of the site, the mail domain
    ' and the database connection details...
    Visit.Configure "Jo's Coffee", "joscoffee.com", "driver=SQL " & _
"Server;DATABASE=JoCoffee;UID=JoCoffeeWeb;PWD=eermlate;SERVER=localhost"
```

We can then write out the version number of the object using the `Version` property, and then write out the type name of the `Visit` object itself. Next, we use the `Catalog` property to create a cached instance of the `Catalog` object and then write out its type name:

```
' what's the version number of the DLL?
   Response.Write "Version Number: " & visit.Version & "<br><br>"

   ' let's write out the names of some of the objects...
   Response.Write "Visit object: " & typename(visit) & "<br>"
   Response.Write "Catalog object: " & typename(visit.Catalog) & "<br>"
```

Finally, we call the Shutdown method. If we had created a database connection, this would be closed now. It's at this point where we release the reference to the cached Catalog object, causing it to be deleted.

```
' now we've finished shut down and clean up the object...
   visit.Shutdown
   Set visit = Nothing
```

An Aside Concerning Component Registration

Running the Visual Basic project before attempting to view the Web page avoids the necessity to go through the routine of registering components on our machine before trying to access them. When the project is run Visual Basic instantly registers entries for all the classes that make up the project and references them back to file called Vb6debug.dll that gets installed along with the rest of VB.

This then acts as a proxy back into the Visual Basic process. So, when Active Scripting creates an instance of an object implemented inside the project VB is running, the COM subsystem (the bit of Windows that actually implements the core COM functionality) actually asks Vb6debug to create the object. Vb6Debug intercepts this call and routes it all the way into Visual Basic, which basically runs the code that makes up the object in an interpreted fashion. Essentially, this creates an object in the Visual Basic process, a reference to which is passed back to the original caller. When you stop running the project, VB undoes the changes it made to the registry.

> **Windows 2000 users might also find a further pitfall at this point. If you experience either an ASP 0178 error, or a 'Version' not found error, then you'll need to give the IUSR account permissions using the DCOMCNFG.EXE utility, taking care to add Default Access Permissions and Default Launch Permissions for IUSR under the Debugging tab in this utility. If needed, you can find more detailed instructions at the following URL:**
> **http://support.microsoft.com/support/kb/articles/Q192/1/52.asp**

If you find, on code testing, error messages are thrown up saying that your newly added methods aren't being recognized, this maybe because application is using a previously compiled version of the WroxCommerce.dll. In this case, you have two options:

❑   Unregister (using regsvr32 pathname/WroxCommerce.dll \u) the DLL and delete it, or

❑   Continually remake the WroxCommerce.dll as you work through the project (in this case you may like to look forward to Chapter 9 – when we discuss code testing of transactions – for more details of how to do this effectively).

Summary

This has been a pretty heavy chapter. We've tried to give you a quick overview of a lot of theory; we've then used this theory as a basis for the design of our project and from there moved on to start implementing the design.

Our starting point was to get a feel for object-oriented programming concepts. We developed our understanding of the beauty of objects by moving forwards in complexity to component-oriented design. In this area we looked at the topics of COM, ActiveX and Active Scripting.

With that under our belts we then stepped back a little bit and looked at the idea of hierarchical object models and then developed an object model that encompassed much of the functionality that we feel the Jo's Project will need to contain in the business tier. At this point, we learnt a little about the need to think about what the site visitor needs from the application as well as the site owner.

During the design stage we alluded to the importance of isolating potentially dangerous functionality from the presentation tier by encapsulating business rules in objects and forcing the ASP code to access the object model in defined ways. This concept was carried through to the implementation stage of the chapter, where we learned how we can build our own private interfaces in our code that let objects in the model leverage functionality while preventing access from external sources.

We started to implement our object model design by beginning the coding of the `WroxCommerce` project. Within this section of coding we started on coding the following class modules:

❑   `Visit`

❑   `Database`

❑   `Catalog`

Additionally we created the `IUtility` Interface.

During the coding of these modules we looked at the performance benefits of using references in VB, and coded general methods for configuring objects as they are created and connecting to the database.

Presenting Our Online Store

Now that we're in a position where we've started to build the objects that comprise the business tier of our site, we can turn our attention to the presentation tier.

In Chapter 2, we discussed how to make our Web application more scalable and we chose to split the business code and presentation code apart. We mentioned that we would develop our presentation tier using Active Server Pages – and that's what this section is about.

However, one thing you won't see by the time we get to the end of this chapter is anything that we can present to customers. We still haven't built the business functionality that drives our product catalogs and shopping cart, so really this chapter is about building a framework into which we can then fit all of this stuff.

In this chapter, we will cover:

- ❑ Rules for good Web site design. We want our online store to be accessible to as many people as possible, so we must consider factors such as display size, number of colors used, browsers used and Web site size.

- ❑ We will then move on to cover include files, which enable us to produce reusable and maintainable HTML and ASP code.

- ❑ Next, we'll discuss the key properties of a good home page and the necessity of being able to navigate back to the home page from anywhere in the site.

- ❑ The last major topic we will cover is Cascading Style Sheets, which enable us to create a consistent and easily maintainable style throughout our site.

Designing a Layout

The biggest difficulty most Web developers face when building sites is that the mental processes involved in writing code, and designing graphics and layout are worlds apart. Developers who can not only write really tight, maintainable code but can also hold their own when it comes to designing company logos and laying out text are white tiger rare. In fact, personally, this is my number one frustration when I build a site. I've been developing software for a long time, and the code I write to drive sites such as joscoffee.com is pretty good, but ask me to come up with a color scheme for the site and I fall apart!

Fortunately for us, there are two schools of thought for the actual design work on a site:

Plan A – Get a Graphic Designer

When the Web first started to become popular, people were generally interested in building "flat" sites. These are what I refer to as **Web sites**. Simply, they're a collection of HTML pages, GIF, and JPG files, and they perform one function. They are, more or less, just a book, catalog, or brochure that's been taken online. (We often refer to sites that are just an online catalog or brochure as **brochureware**.)

Back then, several graphic designers who were aware of the Web figured that this Web thingy might be something lucrative to get involved with and so they started honing their skills in developing HTML and designing graphics that looked good across all platforms. Today, we find that most graphic designers are willing and able to put together flat Web sites that look pretty good.

Recruiting from Outside

Today, we find ourselves in a situation where graphic designers market themselves as experts in building Web sites. What you must be *really* careful of when you're looking for a graphic designer is you want one that will work with you, rather than someone who wants to take over the whole project.

Just as developers who can design logos are white tiger rare, graphic designers who understand 3-tier distributed application architectures are equally scarce.

When sourcing a company to help you with logo design, color palettes, fonts, and layout, explain to it clearly that you will be building all of the ASP and HTML pages that make up the site.

All graphic designers that work on the Web will have an online portfolio of their work. Take a look at a number of these and see if you think they can come up with the goods you need. You can find graphic designers by searching Yahoo for "graphic designers", or by looking in your local Yellow Pages. One way that I find graphic designers is to look for a site that I like and then approach the owners of the site for the contact details of the company they used.

Recruiting from Inside

If you work for a large company, chances are there will be someone in your organization that is a graphic designer. This person may be employed in that capacity at the company (such as someone who puts together brochures, in-house magazines, etc.), or may have training or experience in the field, in which case you'll have to negotiate rates with them just like a professional graphic design firm.

Check to make sure that person has experience at Web design. If they don't, run (don't walk!) to a training company and get them booked on a course to learn the specific skills involved. For one thing, they'll love you for it because people like to learn new skills, and secondly you'll actually get a good job.

At the very least, make sure they read the section *What You Need to Know about Web Site Design* below!

Plan B – Do Nothing

Because hiring a graphic designer isn't cheap, Plan B is to ignore the issue altogether. While it's essential for some sites to have slick graphic design (the brochureware sites that car manufacturers operate are particularly good examples), if your site actually does something, there's very little need.

My favorite example of a site that does rather well, despite the fact it looks like no graphic designer has ever been anywhere near it (although that doesn't mean that was the case) is Yahoo. Yahoo operates a number of services in addition to its search engine, such as television and movie listings, car buying services and e-mail services. Take a look at a page taken from its movie listings:

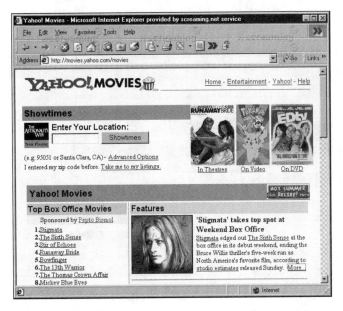

Looking at this page, you can see that it's easy to read and understand, but it doesn't look flashy. There are very few graphics, the page is tiny (just 12k), and it works.

> *Graphic designers may well have been involved in the creation of Yahoo – keeping it simple is part of good design.*

Research has shown that if the site *does* something, like sell you stuff, search for a vacation, etc., visitors are not turned off by a lack of Shockwave animations or ActiveX widgets. What makes the average visitor happy is the ability to get into the site, find the information they want and move around the site quickly. In short, "layout" is the magic word when designing e-commerce sites.

What You Need to Know about Web Site Design

When I first started building Web sites, there were a few things I got wrong. Here's a list of what they were:

Not Everyone Works at 1024x768 Resolution...

This was the first thing I got wrong.

> **Just because you've been using 1024x768 resolution on your desktop for the past six years, that doesn't mean other people don't use 640x480 screens.**

Designing Web pages that look good at 1024x768 and 640x480 is an extremely difficult art. In short, you have to make the layout stretch and shrink in order to accommodate the user's browser size. Most public sites design for 640x480 resolution, which is why many sites seem to only take up a small region of the page, like this:

In order to design for 640x480, don't make the elements that make up your page take more than 600 pixels total width. Intranets and private sites tend to have wider pages because they have a good idea of what their audience will be using. Public sites, like Jo's, typically stick to the 640x480 layout.

The magic number of 600 leaves space for the side of the browser and the scrollbars. Also, make sure that the important elements of the page fit into the first 400 pixels that make up the height. Allow 125 to 150 pixels for the left navigation bar (if you have one), leaving 450 pixels for the width content. Remember, you're building pages for iMacs and Linux boxes too.

There's a bit of a move now towards designing sites for 800x600 resolution. To do this, fit your elements into a width of 760, and a height of 520. However, for Jo's site, we'll be designing for 640x480.

Not Everyone Has 16 Million Colors...

> **You must design your graphics so they look good in 256 colors. In addition, graphics for logos and buttons, etc., should be in GIF format.**

In fact, the 256-color limit is not even true. When designing for the Web, you only have available to you 216 separate colors that you know will be there. This is known as the **Webmaster Safety Palette** and most graphic design programs, like Adobe PhotoShop and JASC's Paint Shop Pro come with a palette that you can import into your graphics to ensure you're using the correct color spread.

You can find an excellent online color resource at http://www.visibone.com/colorlab/

Not only do you need to be careful about the colors you use in GIF files, but you also have to watch the colors you use in the rest of the layout, on table backgrounds, fonts etc. Make sure you only use colors specified in the Webmaster Safety Palette and things will look equally good for people who only have 256 color displays as for those with 16 million.

Not Everyone Uses Internet Explorer 5...

This is the one that, to this day, *still* regularly puts me into the Hall of Shame!

There are a lot of people who use Netscape. There's also a fair difference between Netscape and Internet Explorer, enough to make me have nightmares and spend hours re-engineering presentation code to make a site look cool in both.

> **In order to reach the maximum audience, you have to make sure that your site not only works great in IE5 and Netscape 4, but that it works great in IE3, Netscape 3, Web TV, Opera, and so on. This means that the decision to use style sheets, JavaScript, VBScript, ActiveX controls, etc. on your site is not one to be taken lightly.**

Amazon.com, for example, has *not one line* of JavaScript code on the public portion of the site. They recognize that in order to cover the biggest audience, they have to forgo some of the cool functionality that these technologies afford. It's usually non-technical audiences that have older browsers.

In Jo's site, we will be building for IE4/Netscape 4 because we want to use **Cascading Style Sheets** (**CSS**) to keep our code samples easier to read. For a real world site, we would probably design for IE3, Netscape 3 and avoid CSS as we assume our audience is a non-technical one.

You can download copies of older browsers from http://browsers.evolt.org/

Not Everyone Has a T1...

Luckily, I'm not alone on this one! Many Web developers forget that just because they have a high-bandwidth Internet connection, that doesn't mean everyone else does too. The issue is that if the site is not responsive, visitors to the site will grow frustrated and click out of the site and onto a competitor. If all of the developers on the site enjoy daily access over a fast Internet connection, like a T1, cable modem, or DSL/ADSL, the developers will not see the site as the customer sees it. Effectively, they could be living under a false sense of security believing that the site is performing quickly, whereas from the visitors' perspective, pages take an age to load.

There are five tricks to enhancing the performance of your site:

❑ Minimal use of graphics. Make sure you use just the right amount of graphics, and make sure that these graphics are as optimized as possible.

❑ Make pages smaller. Convey just the right amount of information on a page. Don't keep the user waiting around to get all the information he or she needs. If necessary, spread information over a number of pages.

However, there is a caveat here. It's important not to expect the visitor to hunt around for information or to go through too many clicks to find the information they want. Ideally, keep the vast majority of information accessible within three clicks of the home page. (This includes using a search box, which typically counts as one click. So, if you sold CDs, a visitor might enter the search terms of "Tori Amos" which counts as the first click, and then click on the particular CD they were interested in which counts as the second click.)

❑ Keep URLs short. In dynamic sites, this is an interesting one. If you ever look at the URLs on Yahoo, you'll notice that instead of calling a folder "images", they'll call it just "i". The logic behind this is sound – there's no need to write "images" in full if the browser can understand "i". Wherever possible, keep the names of ASP pages and folders as short as possible.

❑ Avoid the use of ActiveX controls or Java applets. Additional components that need to be downloaded and installed in order for your visitors to get the full benefit of site functionality can frustrate users both through the speed it takes to download the components, and possible problems they may encounter once they have been downloaded.

❑ Cascading Style Sheets (CSS) can reduce the amount of repetition used when delivering formatting information to the browser. We'll see more of CSS later in this chapter.

Not Everyone is "Just Looking"...

Research has shown that most people visit e-commerce sites to buy something specific. Rarely do people come across a site and browse around. For this reason, make sure that visitors to the site have ready access to a Search box, and keep the navigation simple yet clear.

When we build our site, we'll go into more detail on how we make it easy for our visitors to find what they need.

Designing the Layout

Typically, when we look at a site we find that all of the pages have a common layout and theme. This common layout makes it easy for visitors to always find tools on the site, like the navigation bars, search boxes, etc.

In this chapter, we'll show how we go about building the layout that we'll use on every page on Jo's site.

Picking a Theme

Although Visual InterDev and FrontPage both come with a number of themes that we can use on our site, we're going to use our own to give the site a sense of individuality.

To choose a theme that works, we have to step back and take a look at what the company is and what it stands for. This is, in fact, the same process that happens when we choose a look for our traditional offline store – we examine the business and try to design a theme that keys into the cultural expectations of our customers. If we want a Victorian-style tearoom, for example, we might choose lots of wood, old style typefaces, and have the serving staff dress in costumes from that era. If we want a trendy wine bar in the center of a metropolis, we might choose lots of glass and chrome.

The same applies here, and the look we're after should convey quality, professionalism, and appeal to both old-school coffee lovers and, because we're online, geeks who enjoy caffeine.

> *You may want to get a professional graphics firm involved here to make sure the theme is consistent with your marketing message and audience.*

The Prototype

When creating a Web site, I first make a prototype of the site layout in a graphics package such as Paint Shop Pro, which I convert into an ASP template that I can use throughout the site.

The steps required to build a prototype of joscoffee.com are:

1. Create a document that's 600x400 pixels.

2. The name of the site (Jo's Coffee) implies that there's a person running the show. We want to use Jo's reputation as a coffee aficionado and so in some manner present her presence in our online store, in the same way that her presence is felt in her offline store. To achieve this, we put a picture of Jo looking cool and professional on each page in the site.

3. Next, we need to turn our attention to navigation. In e-commerce sites, it's critically important that we get this right. Like we've mentioned a number of times, visitors to our site know what they want and they want to get to the product information as fast as possible. The two methods people typically expect to see are:

❏   Search box

❏   Clear buttons and links indicating the separate "departments" in the store

As our online business model is in three parts, it makes sense to provide one button for each of those departments, which we'll place along the top of the prototype.

4. The last element of the layout is the navigation bar. Traditionally, sites position a navigation bar down the left-hand side of the page, and this is exactly what we're going to do. This bar is usually used for second level navigation, so we'd see the main options for the site along the top, and then different options down the left-hand side, depending on which main option we selected.

To clarify, if we were in the "Coffee Equipment" section of the site, the left navigation bar would offer options on manufacturers, machine types, etc. We're also going to be using the left navigation bar to host the Search box. (Although we won't be implementing the Search box until later in this book.)

In keeping with engineering for 640x480 resolution, we usually make the left navigation bar around 125 pixels wide. In our example here, our left bar is actually 110 pixels wide because we want some white space between the page content and the navigation bars.

At the end of those four steps, we're left with the following design:

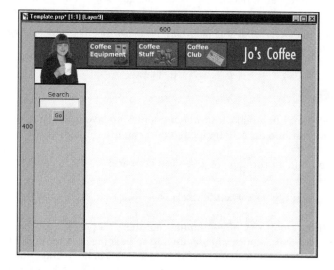

Building the Framework

Our next job is to take the Paint Shop Pro layout and turn it into a set of ASP pages that we can use as a template for each of the ASP pages that will make up our site.

Making Tables

We will now look at how we could break up our layout into a set of HTML tables, making it easy to lay out our fairly complex design.

The lines in the following figure show where we expect to see the table data cells. The cells along the top contain mostly graphic content, so we'll just be cutting GIF images out of the layout and placing these directly into the cells. The left navigation bar will be another table embedded into its hosting cell, and we'll set the background image of this table to be a thin, green GIF with a black line on the right hand side, which should give the desired effect. The remainder of the page is left for content:

By convention, we'll be placing the images that make up the structure of our site into a subfolder called `i`, immediately below the root folder (`localhost/JoCoffee`) of the Web site. Rather than calling this folder `images` or `pics`, we use the name `i` because it's only one byte. As we've discussed earlier, it's often the case that people who are Web site developers make very long script and folder names when they don't need to. On a site like this, we'll most likely only see one- or two-dozen scripts and four or five folders. We might as well refer to our images folder in a shorthand manner, because during development we're unlikely to get confused. After deployment, the benefits are substantial.

Imagine you have a Web site that gets 100,000 page views a day. Imagine each page has at least 10 graphics on it. If you call your images folder `images`, you're sending down 4.8MB more each day than if you just referred to your images folder as `i`. Repeat that technique on all the script names and all of the folder names throughout your site, and you can make significant bandwidth savings.

However, I once took this to extremes and referred to each script as `a.asp`, `b.asp`, etc. – the site turned out to be unmanageable. Stick to the middle ground! Use names like `info.asp`, rather than `information.asp`, `db.asp` rather than `database.asp` and so on.

Finally, remember that when breaking up a layout into tables, we want to be careful that we do not make it too complicated. The simpler the table structure, the more likely our site will look cool on older browsers.

Adding GIFs to Our Visual InterDev Project

Before we get started on building the presentation code for joscoffee.com, let's add all the GIFs that we determined were needed in the previous section. All of the GIFs can be downloaded from the Wrox Press Web site at www.wrox.com.

Try It Out – Adding Images to Our Project

1. Change the name of the `Images` directory in your Visual InterDev project to `i`.

2. Place the site images for joscoffee.com into the `i` folder.

3. Right-click on i in the Project Explorer of Visual Interdev and select <u>A</u>dd | Add <u>I</u>tem. Then select the Existing tab:

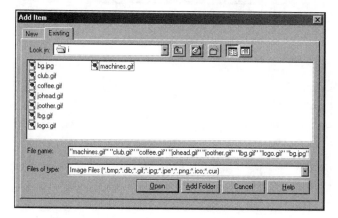

4. Select all of the images from the i folder and click on <u>O</u>pen.

Include Files

We are going to build our template out of a set of **include files** that we can use on the dozen or so ASP pages that will actually make up our site.

If you've never used include files before, simply speaking they let you write some code (ASP, HTML or even plain text) and then use that code in other ASP pages. Include files make maintenance easier as you only have to make one change in one place.

Using the Include Files

The rest of this section covers how to build the three include files (site.asp, start.asp, and end.asp) that make up the template for our site, which features the logo, the search box and the navigation bars:

❑   The purpose of site.asp is to provide the ASP code with access to the business objects, so we put this in the <HEAD> section of the page as it doesn't contain any HTML code to be sent to the client.

❑   start.asp will be used to build the tables that define the layout of the site. This will effectively build a "sub-page" into which everything between the start.asp and end.asp include files will be placed.

❑   Finally, end.asp will be used to close off the layout of the site; it will add a footer to the page containing copyright and version information, and it will also be responsible for closing the connection to the business objects.

We'll be using the site.asp page as what's sometimes called an environment page. The other pages in the site will use it to determine the environment in which they're running. In our case, this usually means providing access in some way to the WroxCommerce components that power the site. However, this page will also contain presentation functions that are needed by a number of pages on the site, such as functions for rendering text in a certain way. We'll be seeing these as we work through the site.

A trick that traditional Windows developers have been doing for some time involves language strings. Usually, these are used to "localize" an application, or rather to "port an application over to another language". Rather than entering literal strings onto buttons that say, "Click here", they instruct the application to go and get the value from a lookup table that in English says, "Click here", but in French says "Cliquez ici". The advantage of this is when they want to move the application to another language they just have to replace the table and there's no need to hunt around the application changing strings.

Although we'll be learning all about Web site localization in Chapter 12, this concept of centrally locating strings rather than using literal values has merit. We can centrally control elements of the site, such as its name, database connection, etc., through globally defined variables in site.asp.

Try It Out – Referencing the Include Files in default.asp

1.   In Visual InterDev, right-click on localhost/JoCoffee and select <u>A</u>dd | Acti<u>v</u>e Server Page. When prompted, enter the name as default.asp and click <u>O</u>pen.

2.   Make the following changes to default.asp:

```
<% option explicit %>
<HTML>
<HEAD>
    <!-- #include file="site.asp" -->
    <TITLE>WroxCommerce Test Page</TITLE>
</HEAD>
<BODY>
```

```
    <!-- #include file="start.asp" -->

    Welcome to Jo's Coffee!

    <!-- #include file="end.asp" -->
</BODY>
</HTML>
```

How It Works

The `#include file` statement allows us to specify a file to be included:

```
    <!-- #include file="site.asp" -->
...
    <!-- #include file="start.asp" -->
...
    <!-- #include file="end.asp" -->
```

As `site.asp`, `start.asp`, and `end.asp` are in the same directory as `default.asp`, we just need to provide the file name.

> *The include files may be placed in a subdirectory, in which case you supply the path and file name. The include files cannot be placed in a directory above that of the page that references it.*

Next, we will create the `site.asp` page.

Try It Out – Creating site.asp

1. Right-click on localhost/JoCoffee and select <u>A</u>dd | Acti<u>v</u>e Server Page. When prompted, enter the name as site.asp and click <u>O</u>pen.

2. As this is an include file, the default code that Visual InterDev adds for us isn't valid, especially the `<@ Language=VBScript @>` line, which will actually cause a runtime error because the ASP parser will not consider the first line of `site.asp` to be the first line of the overall script that defines the page. Select and delete all of the code that Visual InterDev has added to this file.

3. Next add this code to `site.asp`:

```
<%
    ' Globally define certain site metrics, such as its name and domain...
    const g_sitename = "Jo's Coffee"
    const g_domainname = "joscoffee.com"

    ' g_bodytag is used to set elements of the style sheet that don't work
    ' 100% in all browsers.
    const g_bodytag = _
        "bgcolor=#ffffff leftmargin=0 topmargin=0 marginleft=0 margintop=0"
%>
```

4. Now change `default.asp` to this:

```
<% option explicit %>
<HTML>
<HEAD>
    <!-- #include file="site.asp" -->
    <TITLE><%=g_sitename%></TITLE>
</HEAD>
<BODY <%=g_bodytag%>>
    <!-- #include file="start.asp" -->

    Welcome to Jo's Coffee!

    <!-- #include file="end.asp" -->
</BODY>
</HTML>
```

5. The main purpose of the `site.asp` page is to let ASP code access a configured instance of the `WroxCommerce.Visit` object. So add this code to `site.asp`:

```
const g_bodytag = _
        "bgcolor=#ffffff leftmargin=0 topmargin=0 marginleft=0 margintop=0"

' Create somewhere to hold the Visit object as we process the page...
Dim m_visit

' Visit - this function returns an instance of the Visit back to the caller.
' If one doesn't exist, it will create one...
Function Visit

    ' Do we have one?
    If IsEmpty(m_visit) Then

        ' Create an instance of a Visit object...
        Set m_visit = Server.CreateObject("WroxCommerce.Visit")

        m_visit.Configure g_sitename, g_domainname, "driver=SQL Server;" & _
                        "DATABASE=JoCoffee; UID=JoCoffeeWeb;PWD=eermlate;" & _
                        "SERVER=localhost"

    End If

    ' Return the Visit object back...
    Set Visit = m_visit

End Function

%>
```

99

How It Works

The first part of `site.asp` allows us to change the site name, domain name, and body tag in `default.asp` from one central location if the need ever arose:

```
' Globally define certain site metrics, such as its name and domain...
const g_sitename = "Jo's Coffee"
const g_domainname = "joscoffee.com"

' g_bodytag is used to set elements of the style sheet that don't work
' 100% in all browsers...
const g_bodytag = "bgcolor=#ffffff leftmargin=0 topmargin=0 "
                  marginleft=0 margintop=0"
```

Remember in Chapter 3 we talked about how exactly one instance of the `Visit` object would be created for each page view on the site? To achieve this, we add a variable to `site.asp` called `m_visit`, which holds an instance of a `Visit` object:

```
Dim m_visit
```

The `Visit` function examines the `m_visit` variable to see if it contains a Visit object. If it doesn't we create a new instance of the object and then tell that object the name, mail domain, and database connection information for the site through the `Configure` method:

```
' Do we have one?
If IsEmpty(m_visit) Then

   m_visit.Configure g_sitename, g_domainname, "driver=SQL Server;" & _
                     "DATABASE=JoCoffee; UID=JoCoffeeWeb;PWD=eermlate;" & _
                     "SERVER=localhost"

End If
```

Finally, we return the `Visit` object back to the caller:

```
Set Visit = m_visit
```

Now let's build `start.asp`.

Try It Out – Creating start.asp

1. In Visual InterDev, right-click on localhost/JoCoffee and select Add | Active Server Page. When prompted, enter the name as start.asp and click Open.

2. As before with `site.asp`, select and delete all of the code that Visual InterDev has added to this file.

3. Now add this code to `start.asp`:

```
<!-- We already have BODY/HTML tags, etc., so want to get started with the main
table. Remember, we design this table to be 600 pixels wide to accommodate 640x480
displays... -->
<table cellspacing=0 cellpadding=0 width=600 border=0>

    <!-- Now we need to look at the first line in the layout.
    This comprises Jo's head, the three site section buttons,
    and the "Jo's Coffee" logo... -->
    <tr>
        <td><img src="i/johead.gif"></td>    <!-- Jo's head -->
        <td><img src="i/machines.gif"></td> <!-- "Coffee Equipment" button -->
        <td><img src="i/coffee.gif"></td>    <!-- "Coffee Stuff" button -->
        <td><img src="i/club.gif"></td>      <!-- "Coffee Club" button -->
        <td><img src="i/logo.gif"></td>      <!-- "Jo's Coffee" logo -->
    </tr>

    <!-- The next line in the layout comprises the other bit of Jo that
    was cut off, and a blank space -->
    <tr>
        <td><img src="i/joother.gif"></td>    <!-- the other bit of Jo -->
        <td colspan=4> </td>             <!-- blank space -->
    </tr>

    <!-- the third line hosts the left navigation bar,
    and the site content itself -->
    <tr>
        <td bgcolor="#ccff99" background="i/lbg.gif" width="112" valign=top>
        <!-- In here is where we'll be adding the left navigation bar -->
        </td>
        <td colspan=4>

            <!-- Start another table that will be used for the
            actual content of each page -->
            <table cellspacing=0 cellpadding=5 width=100% border=0>
                <tr>

                <!-- First, add a blank column to move the content away
                from the left bar... -->
                <td> </td>

                <!-- Then, the column that will contain the content -->
                <td>
```

How It Works

Note that we don't begin `start.asp` with `<BODY>` or `<HTML>` as we already have these in the page that this code will be dropped into, `default.asp`.

When we split the layout designed in Paint Shop Pro into tables we decided to make the table 600 pixels wide so it could fit into a 640x480 display:

```
<table cellspacing=0 cellpadding=0 width=600 border=0>
```

The first row in our table holds the top part of Jo's picture and the bar along the top, which allows customers to access departments within our online store:

```
<tr>
    <td><img src="i/johead.gif"></td>    <!-- Jo's head -->
    <td><img src="i/machines.gif"></td>  <!-- "Coffee Equipment" button -->
    <td><img src="i/coffee.gif"></td>    <!-- "Coffee Stuff" button -->
    <td><img src="i/club.gif"></td>      <!-- "Coffee Club" button -->
    <td><img src="i/logo.gif"></td>      <!-- "Jo's Coffee" logo -->
</tr>
```

The second row in the table holds the lower part of Jo's picture and some white space:

```
<tr>
    <td><img src="i/joother.gif"></td>   <!-- the other bit of Jo -->
    <td colspan=4> </td>            <!-- blank space -->
</tr>
```

The third row contains the navigation bar on the left-hand side and the actual content of the page. Here's the code for the green background of the navigation bar:

```
<td bgcolor="#ccff99" background="i/lbg.gif" width="112" valign=top>
```

Only Internet Explorer supports the `background` attribute (which contains our narrow, green GIF with the thin black line). So for cross-browser support we've also specified that a `bgcolor` of `#ccff99` (which is a pale green) can be used, as this attribute is supported by Netscape.

The content is held within a second table:

```
<table cellspacing=0 cellpadding=5 width=100% border=0>
```

The first cell of the new table is a blank column. This moves our content away from the navigation bar and stops the page from looking too tightly packed:

```
<td> </td>
```

The second cell contains our content. We stop `start.asp` abruptly after the last `<TD>` tag because we want to get to a point where any pages using this template can just start writing their content out and they'll be confident that the layout of the page fits a common format. Effectively, we write the presentation code in a sub-page that `start.asp` and `end.asp` generate.

The big advantage of using this approach when building sites is that if we need to re-engineer the look of the site (move navigation bars around, introduce more buttons, etc.), we change `start.asp`, `end.asp`, and the style sheets, and the job's done. We don't have to re-engineer any of the pages to take advantage of the new look.

1. Right-click on localhost/JoCoffee and select <u>A</u>dd | Acti<u>v</u>e Server Page. Enter the name as end.asp and click <u>O</u>pen.

2. Once more, select and delete all of the code that Visual InterDev has automatically added to this file.

3. Add the following code to end.asp:

```
            <!-- Stop the main content cell and row -->
            </td></tr>
            <!-- Add a row to make sure the content always
            takes up the full available width... -->
            <tr>
                <!-- Ignore the first column, it's a spacer -->
                <td>
                </td>

                <!-- Now add a load of white dashes to fill up the
                alloted space -->
                <td>
                    <font color=#ffffff>
                        --------- --------- --------- ---------
                        --------- --------- --------- ---------
                        --------- --------- --------- ---------
                    </font>
                </td>
            </tr>
        </table>

        <!-- Stop the third line in the layout that hosted
        the content table and the left navigation bar -->
        </td>
    </tr>

    <!-- Add a row that looks like a line... -->
    <tr>
    <td colspan=5 bgcolor=#000000><img src="i/bd.gif" width=1 height=3></td>
    </tr>

    <!-- Add a row that acts like a spacer... -->
    <tr>
        <td colspan=5>
            <br>
        </td>
    </tr>

    <!-- Add a footer containing a copyright message -->
    <tr>
        <td colspan=5 align=center>
            Copyright &copy; Jo's Coffee <%=Year(Now)%>
```

```
            <br>
            Powered by WroxCommerce <%=Visit.Version%>
        </td>
    </tr>

<!-- Close the master table that contained it all -->
</table>
<%
    ' Do we have a Visit object to close?
    If Not IsEmpty(m_visit) Then
        m_visit.ShutDown
        Set m_visit = Nothing
    End If
%>
```

How It Works

end.asp begins by closing the cell and row that contained our main content:

```
</td></tr>
```

To make sure the content table takes up all the available space, we use this kludge to make the browser think it always contains enough text to justify the 100% it has been allotted. We add a new row, in which the second cell is full of white dashes:

```
<!-- Add a row to make sure the content always
takes up the full available width... -->
<tr>
    <!-- Ignore the first column, it's a spacer -->
    <td>
    </td>

    <!-- Now add a load of white dashes to fill up the
    alloted space -->
    <td>
        <font color=#ffffff>
        --------- --------- --------- ---------
        --------- --------- --------- ---------
        --------- --------- --------- ---------
        </font>
    </td>
</tr>
```

If we don't do this and the sub-page only contains a few words, IE will stretch out the left-hand navigation bar so that it's wider than was intended in the original design.

After finishing the table that contained the content and its associated row in the main table, we add a line that rules off the end of the content section of the page and delimits the footer:

```
<td colspan=5 bgcolor=#000000><img src="i/bd.gif" width=1 height=3></td>
```

It's important *not* to add a carriage return between the `<td>` and `</td>` tags as the browser will interpret this as a space and make the row much taller than the three pixels deep it needs to be. Also, notice how we've used `bd.gif` in our IMG tag. `bd.gif` is a very useful tool for Web designers to have. It's a 1 by 1 pixel GIF file containing a single black dot. After placing the dot in a Web page, you can use the `WIDTH` and `HEIGHT` attributes of the `IMG` tag to stretch it to the size you want. Here, we're using it to create a three pixel deep image. The `BGCOLOR` attribute of the `td` tag makes sure that, even though our image is only 1 pixel wide, the black color appears across the whole length of the row.

We then add a space between the end of the content table and the page footer so that our page is not squashed up:

```
<tr>
    <td colspan=5>
        <br>
    </td>
</tr>
```

Recall our discussion on adding a `Version` property to the `Visit` object. By adding this code to `end.asp`, each page on our site will report the version number of the `Visit` object each time it runs:

```
Powered by WroxCommerce <%=Visit.Version%>
```

What happens here is that the `Visit` function will look to see if `m_visit` has been set to anything. If it hasn't, it creates a new one; but either way the `Visit` function will always return a `Visit` object. Once we have the object, we can ask it for its version number through the `Version` property.

The last, but very important, function of `end.asp` is to close out the resources that may have been used by the `Visit` object during the page execution:

```
<%
    ' Do we have a Visit object to close?
    If Not IsEmpty(m_visit) Then
        m_visit.ShutDown
        Set m_visit = Nothing
    End If
%>
```

Let's see what we've got:

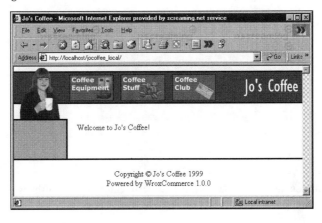

Our Web page looks similar to the design created earlier in the chapter, so I guess we've won! We haven't coded anything on the left navigation bar yet and none of the buttons does anything. Nevertheless, we can see that the interaction between the site and the `WroxCommerce` object model is working by virtue of the fact that we can see the version number of the components in the footer.

We can't wire in the top bar either at this point because we haven't written any of scripts that run the three site sections yet, but what we should do is sort out the Home Navigation.

Home Navigation

Home Navigation is the term given to the click that takes you back to the site's home page, and is one of those innocent sounding things that's actually critically important to get right.

Over the years, positioning a site's name or logo in the top left-hand corner has become standard practice, as has wiring this logo back through to the home page of the site. The reason for this is simple – the home page of a site is the equivalent of a reset. If a visitor to your site becomes lost and confused, they will have a natural tendency to jump back to the last thing they understood clearly. (Much like a student flicking backwards through a textbook trying to find the last part of the discussion he followed.) The vast majority of the time this is the site's home page, and we'll be learning more about why people naturally gravitate there in the next section.

For now, we need to wire in links to jump back to `default.asp`. On our site, we have a picture of Jo in the top left-hand corner and the logo in the right. To satisfy everyone, we need to make both Jo's picture and the Jo's Coffee logo link to `default.asp`.

Try It Out – Navigating Back to the Home Page

1. In the `start.asp` template page add the following lines of code:

```
<!-- Now we need to look at the first line in the layout.
This comprises Jo's head, the three site section buttons,
and the "Jo's Coffee" logo... -->
<tr>
    <td><a href="default.asp"><img src="i/johead.gif" border=0></a></td>
    <td><img src="i/machines.gif"></td>   <!-- "Coffee Equipment" button -->
    <td><img src="i/coffee.gif"></td>    <!-- "Coffee Stuff" button -->
    <td><img src="i/club.gif"></td>     <!-- "Coffee Club" button -->
    <td><a href="default.asp"><img src="i/logo.gif" border=0></a></td>
</tr>

<!-- The next line in the layout comprises the other bit of Jo that
was cut off, and a blank space-->
<tr>
    <td><a href="default.asp"><img src="i/joother.gif" border=0></a></td>
    <td colspan=4> </td>                <!-- blank space -->
</tr>
```

> Make sure that you set the **BORDER=0** attribute in the **IMG** tags; otherwise your graphics will have "tasteful" chunky borders around them!

The Home Page

The **home page** on a Web site that works well is something of a paradox. It's the *most often hit* page, but it should be the *least used* page.

As we've noted before, when someone comes to an e-commerce site, they're looking for something specific. The moment they have their foot in the door, so to speak, they want access to some tool or link that carries them off to the area of the store they want. The only purpose of the front page then, is that it must clearly and quickly route the visitor off to the part of the site he or she wants.

One of the most frustrating things commonly found in bad Web design is when a company feels it necessary to make the first page into the site a **splash page**. These pages are similar to the splash screens featured on desktop applications such as Microsoft Word that tell the user what package is being loaded. Although acceptable for desktop applications (mainly because parts of the application are still being loaded), this is simply not acceptable for Web design as it makes the visitor click through unnecessarily and adds to download time.

The visitor to the site only remembers the domain name of the site, in this case joscoffee.com. If she happens to be looking for a Gaggia Automatica espresso machine, she can't accurately guess the location of this product from outside of the site. (Just as she can't climb onto the roof of Wal-Mart, cut a hole in the roof and drop down into the specific aisle she wants.) So, she remembers the front door (joscoffee.com), and then quickly follows the link to "Espresso Machines", then to "Manufacturer: Gaggia" and hopefully within three clicks she's learned all she needs to know about our ability to sell her the Gaggia Automatica.

A well-designed home page is another reason why it operates like a "reset button" in the site. If the user has experienced a home page that whisks them off to the part of the site they actually want quickly, they'll intuitively remember that they understood that bit of the site if they get lost somewhere else. Once they hit a point where they say, "Ah, I'm stuck", if they can get back to a bit they did understand (the home page), chances are they won't click out of your site and go to another vendor. As most sites feature a link back to the home page in the top left-hand corner, we make sure ours features a link there too.

Cascading Style Sheets

A **Cascading Style Sheet** (**CSS**) is a separate file containing style rules, to which our Web pages can link. CSS either alters the default actions of existing HTML tags, or contains definitions of your own CSS **classes** (which are not the same as those in Visual Basic). By using style sheets, we can be sure that our pages have a consistent appearance throughout the site. If Jo decides to change the color of her site from green to blue, she does not have to laboriously search through each page for references to green, she just needs to alter the style sheet.

Let's look at two samples of code – they both perform exactly the same action, but one is written without the use of style sheets:

```
<font size=3 face="Arial" color=#000080><b>This is my font!</b></font>
```

Whereas this code sample uses a CSS:

```
<style>
.myStyle { font-size: 12pt;
           font-weight:bold;
           color:#000080;
           font-family: "Arial" }
</style>

<font class=myStyle>This is my font!</font>
```

In our example, we've used the STYLE tags to define a group of display attributes including the font size, weight, color, and typeface. When we start the FONT tag, we set its class to the one defined in the style sheet. Notice how when defining the classes we precede the class name with a period, but when we use it we do not.

There are two main advantages with CSS:

❑   We define the way we want things in the document to look and behave centrally, with the result that we don't have to repeat ourselves whenever we want to use them. Without CSS, wherever we want our font to be 12 point, bold, red, and Arial, we have to explicitly specify each attribute every time. On the other hand, with CSS, all we do is define all of that first and then reference it whenever we want to use it. This keeps the size of the HTML code down, which is beneficial, as when building Web sites it's important to keep the size of the pages as small as possible.

❑   The other big advantage is that it makes it easy to actually write the code. This technique of code reuse is by no means new and if you've done any sort of programming at all, you'll recognize the benefits of having a basic set of definitions with references throughout the project. In this example, if we want every 12 point font to be 10 point, we only have to change it in one place and the changes effectively cascade through without any more work. It also makes the code much more readable, which is typically a good thing for all concerned.

As we mentioned earlier in the chapter, we're going to use CSS to format the text on our site, as this will make the code examples in this book as simple as possible. However, in the real world, this still isn't the right technology to use on a site like this, because it relies on modern browsers. To achieve complete audience coverage, it's a much better plan to use code that doesn't make use of CSS. So, it's a tradeoff – use CSS to make the site smaller, make the code more manageable, and take advantage of the other plus-points of this technology and risk alienating a percentage of your customer base.

We don't have space to go into the machinations of Cascading Style Sheets here, but if you would like to learn more then I recommend you refer to *Professional Style Sheets for HTML and XML* (Wrox Press, ISBN 1-861001-65-7) and the CSS specification at http://www.w3.org/style/css/.

Cascading Style Sheets and Visual InterDev

Visual InterDev comes with tools to help you build style sheets. Technically, style sheets are just blocks of text, put together in a similar style to what you'd expect from HTML or ASP code. To start with, we'll take a look at using the Visual InterDev tools and then do a quick run-through of the code that the tools created.

Try It Out – Creating a Cascading Style Sheet in Visual InterDev

1. To start the Visual InterDev style sheet editor, right-click on localhost/JoCoffee in the Project Explorer and select Add | Style Sheet. When prompted, enter the name as style.css. This will start the Visual InterDev Style Sheet Editor:

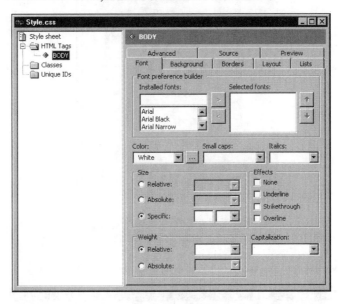

2. By default, a new editor will start with a BODY tag selected. This means that you're currently configuring the settings for the BODY tag, and you can consider this as effectively changing the default values for that BODY tag. The editor is quite intimidating in terms of the number of tabs and options. As style sheets allow you to programatically control every display attribute of every possible HTML tag, we have options to change the background color, change the default font, change the border of the page and so on. We won't be covering every single option here, as it's a big topic!

3. For our style sheet, one thing we want to do is change the default operation of the A tag. We want links to become highlighted only when the mouse is hovering over them, and we want them to be the same color whether they have been visited before or not. To do this, right-click on HTML Tags, select Insert HTML Tag and in the dialog that follows, select A from the drop-down box:

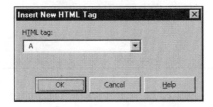

4. A new object will appear in the tag list allowing you to edit the attributes for the A tag. In the dialog for the A tag, click on the ellipsis button (...) to the right of the Color drop-down box. Select Navy from the Basic list:

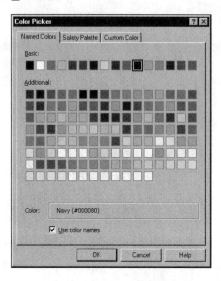

5. After you've selected the color, select None from the Effects group:

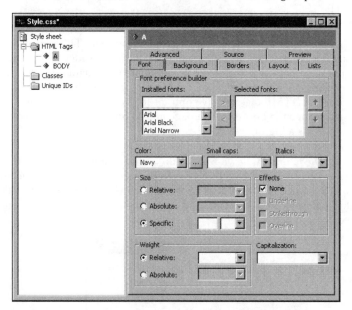

6. To complete this operation, we also want to make tags appear to have an underline when the mouse is floated over them. Right-click on HTML Tags and select Insert HTML Tag again, and enter A:hover into the dialog box. When the editor for this tag appears, check on the Underline option in the Effects frame:

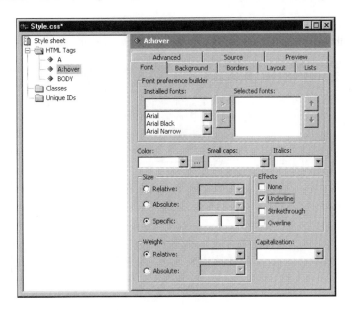

7. We're going to define a convention now that states that whenever we need a specific block of text to have a certain appearance, we'll use a class. We use classes in Cascading Style Sheets to group together different attributes in such a way that when applied to another element, that element adopts the attributes. So, we can build a class that has an eight-point font and by setting the CLASS attribute of the FONT tag to the name of the class, that FONT tag will adopt an eight-point font in order to adhere to the class.

To create a new class, right-click on **Classes** and select **Insert Class**. Enter the name of the new class as small:

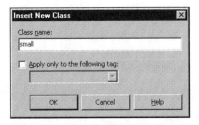

8. Click **OK** and you'll see that the editor will open, select the new class, and bring up the same dialogs for attribute editing that we saw before. One important point – you may notice that small has a period before it. This is deliberate and you didn't mistype anything! By convention, CSS looks for a period at the start of an identifier name to determine if it's an alteration of a known tag (BODY, FONT, etc.) or a new class definition.

9. To define our new class, use the controls at the top of the Font tab to set the font for the small class to Tahoma. When you've finished there, set the Specific size of the font to eight-points:

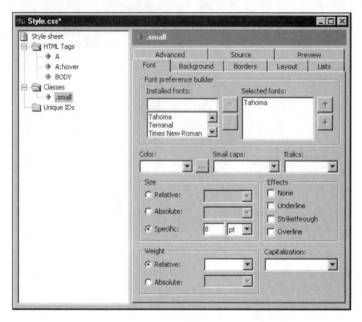

10. We need to create another few classes in our style sheet, but rather than using the editor we're going to do them manually so you can understand better how style sheets work.

Close the Style Sheet Editor. When prompted, save the changes to the file.

11. Right-click on style.css in Project Explorer and select Open With. By default, Visual InterDev will open style sheets in the editor, so we want to give it a little kick and open it as a plain text editor so we can better see the code and manually add our three other classes.

12. Select Source Code (Text) Editor and click Open:

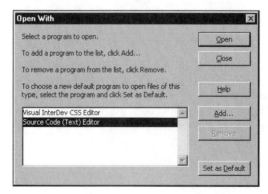

Here's what the "raw" style sheet looks like:

```
A
{
    COLOR: navy;
    TEXT-DECORATION: none
}
A:hover
{
    TEXT-DECORATION: underline
}
.small
{
    FONT-FAMILY: Tahoma;
    FONT-SIZE: 8pt
}
```

13. You can see from the code that only the changes we made to the default attributes for each tag or class have been stored in the style sheet. To create a new class called .std (for standard), all we have to do is copy the definition for .small, change the name and change the font-size, like this:

```
.small
{
    FONT-FAMILY: Tahoma;
    FONT-SIZE: 8pt
}
.std
{
    FONT-FAMILY: Tahoma;
    FONT-SIZE: 10pt
}
```

14. Add these three other classes now:

```
.small
{
    FONT-FAMILY: Tahoma;
    FONT-SIZE: 8pt
}
.std
{
    FONT-FAMILY: Tahoma;
    FONT-SIZE: 10pt
}
.heading
{
    FONT-FAMILY: Tahoma;
    FONT-SIZE: 10pt;
    FONT-WEIGHT: BOLD;
```

```
}
.bigheading
{
    FONT-FAMILY: Tahoma;
    FONT-SIZE: 14pt;
    FONT-WEIGHT: BOLD;
    COLOR: #800000;
}
.tableRed
{
    FONT-SIZE:10pt;
    FONT-FAMILY:verdana;
    FONT-WEIGHT:bold;
    COLOR:#ffffff;
    BACKGROUND-COLOR:#ff0000;
}
```

15. Save the style sheet, close it and reopen it again. By default, InterDev will open the style sheet in the editor. Here's what it looks like:

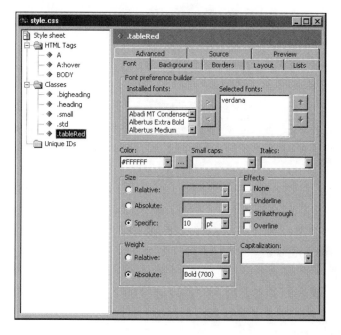

16. After you've created the style sheet, open `default.asp` and drag `style.css` from the Project Explorer and drop it into the <HEAD> tag of the page, like this:

```
<% option explicit %>
<HTML>
<HEAD>
```

```
<!-- #include file="site.asp" -->
<TITLE><%=g_sitename%></TITLE>
<LINK rel="stylesheet" type="text/css" href="style.css">
</HEAD>
<BODY <%=g_bodytag%>>
   <!-- #include file="start.asp" -->

   Welcome to Jo's Coffee!

   <!-- #include file="end.asp" -->
</BODY>
</HTML>
```

Creating the Template

We'll be using this basic structure as a template for all of the pages in our store. To make life easier for ourselves down the road we want to create an ASP page called `template.asp` that contains just these basic lines above.

Try It Out – Creating template.asp

1. Right-click on localhost/JoCoffee and select <u>A</u>dd | Acti<u>v</u>e Server Page. Call the page `template.asp`.

2. Copy and paste the entire contents of `default.asp` into this new file and save it.

What to Put on Your Home Page

We've already determined that our home page will contain three separate sections, mimicking our target business model:

❑   Machine retail

❑   Consumables retail

❑   Community

Try It Out – Creating the Home Page

1. Let's start by creating a table to structure the home page (`default.asp`), redoing the title that's already in-place using CSS and adding rows for each section of the home page:

```
<BODY <%=g_bodytag%>>
   <!-- #include file="start.asp" -->

   <!-- we have a TD to write into, so let's create our own table... -->
   <table cellspacing=0 cellpadding=0 width=100%>
```

115

```
    <!-- heading -->
    <tr><td class=bigheading>Welcome to Jo's Coffee!</td></tr>

    <!-- coffee machines... -->
    <tr><td><br></td></tr>
    <tr><td class=tableRed>Coffee Equipment</td></tr>

    <!-- coffee stuff... -->
    <tr><td><br></td></tr>
    <tr><td class=tableRed>Coffee Stuff</td></tr>

    <!-- coffee club... -->
    <tr><td><br></td></tr>
    <tr><td class=tableRed>Coffee Club</td></tr>

  <!-- end our table... -->
  </table>

  <!-- #include file="end.asp" -->
</BODY>
```

2. Now open `default.asp` in your browser and thanks to CSS, we already have something that looks half-decent:

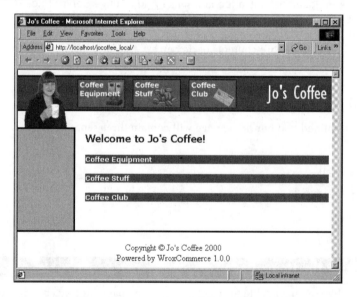

OK, but how is someone actually going to use that? Well, as I've said before, it's likely that people will bounce off this home page as soon as it's loaded, but it still has to do something.

The majority of e-commerce sites use the front page as a place to advertise special offers. Visit a site such as Computers4SURE.com and you'll be met with a plethora of products that they are particularly keen on selling you that day:

In Chapter 16, we'll learn how to assign certain products in our catalog as "Featured Items" and show how we can display them on the home page.

For example, joscoffee.com could have the following home page (we'll see how to do this in due course):

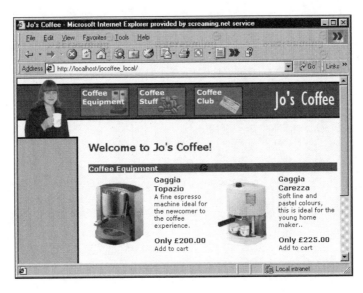

Displaying featured items from the product catalog works very well for coffee machines and coffee consumables, but what about the Coffee Club? Well, if we chose to feature "coffee news" on our site, we might display the last five news headlines here. Alternatively, if we had discussion groups, we might have a list of the last ten active discussions. Again, though, we must make sure that the user can quickly move from looking at this "Coffee Club Summary" section and into the main parts of the Coffee Club.

Summary

We began this chapter with a discussion on the basics of Web design, leading into a discussion on some of the overall design parameters we are going to use on Jo's site. We turned the basics of our prototype into ASP and HTML code.

We also saw how to structure the template of our site into a set of ASP include files and a Cascading Style Sheet. This means that whenever we need to change aspects of the site's navigation or the overall look and feel, we can just tweak these files and we're good to go.

In the next chapter, we'll look at some of the existing systems Jo has in place for managing her business, design the structure of the store's departments, and write some VB and ASP code to display them to the visitor.

Structuring the Online Store

In e-commerce, **catalog** refers to the online version of a traditional brochure, directory, or catalog that we might have used to sell our products offline. Simply, it's a list of all the goods and services we sell.

The catalog is divided into two parts:

❏ The database part represents how the catalog is arranged and stored in our site's database

❏ The presentation part represents the code that's used to present that database to the visitor as part of an engaging online shopping experience

This chapter will be probably the most involved of all the chapters in this book as it covers a number of different areas, including:

❏ Creating the database and presentation code

❏ Examining how we want to structure our catalog

❏ Getting data from existing line-of-business systems into our catalog

❏ Building the administration tools to manage our store

Designing the Store

Before we jump in and start writing code and building databases, we have to bring our minds back offline and start designing certain aspects of the store's layout and structure.

If we consider Jo's offline model, it is more than likely that she already divides her small retail store into a number of **departments** to help her customers find the stuff they need. She will usually arrange these departments in a way that makes use of the experience her customers have accumulated over years of shopping.

For example, high-ticket items like the espresso machines need to be presented nicely, not kept in their boxes on a low shelf in a dark corner of the store. Consumables like coffee, filters, etc. need to be arranged and kept together.

Let's take a customer looking for a particular blend of coffee. If he can't find it, he won't think of looking on a shelf in a completely different part of the store. Customers expect a grouping and arrangement common to all the other stores they have visited in their lives.

Organizing departments in an e-commerce store is largely an intuitive process. Unless you're crossing massive cultural boundaries, your own experience in finding your way around a store is most likely the same as your customers' ideas. Therefore, we can't give some magic trick or technique to help you get this right.

Navigation of departments in an e-commerce store is a very important part of a good shopping experience. You shouldn't have too many or too few departments in total, and you shouldn't have too many or too few items in each department. The depth of departments is important as well – visitors should be able to find the items they want in as few clicks as possible.

Department Structure

Here's the tree of departments on which we're going to base our site:

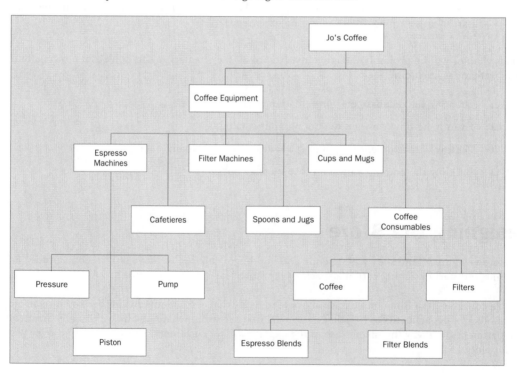

As you can see, we divide our store into two main departments, mimicking the decisions we've already made in our online business model:

❑ The top-level **Coffee Equipment** department has five, clearly defined sub-departments. The **Espresso Machines** sub-department has been further divided into three separate sections. This decision was made because the three different ways of making espresso (**Pressure**, **Pump**, and **Piston**) all have a very different market. Someone looking to spend $2,000 on a piston-based espresso machine probably won't be interested in a $40 Krups model. On the other hand, the filter machines that Jo sells are all targeted at a fairly similar market, so we don't subdivide that.

❑ **Coffee Consumables** is divided into two clear sections, as the types of products in each are wildly dissimilar. Additionally, the **Coffee** department is divided into two separate departments to target the two separate audiences.

Note that, although we've previously called CoffeeClub a department, it's not strictly part of the store and so isn't shown in this diagram.

Adding Departments

We created the `JoCoffee` database back in Chapter 2, but this is the first time we actually have a need to use it in earnest.

As we know by now, we intend to break our store up into a number of separate departments, and allow those departments to be arranged into a tree. After the departments are in place, we'll go ahead and build the `WroxCommerce` objects that can query this department structure, and then we will write the ASP code to present those departments to the visitor.

Obviously, our database is going to comprise a number of tables and rows inside tables. We want to make sure that across our entire database structure, we have consistency in terms of naming and design.

The most important design consideration for us at this stage is choosing a method for identifying each row. For proper database design, each row in each table must be uniquely identifiable through a key of some sort. The two main approaches to this are to use a unique ID field, which is usually an integer number of some sort, or to use a combination of fields (such as `FirstName`, `LastName`, `ZIPCode`).

Using a single integer field as a convention for identifying rows is the most efficient way of relating data in relational databases. We'll be using this method here, as we only have to match one column, which is usually quite short. The next decision we make is: "how big do we want the ID?"

My particular favorite method for identifying rows is to use a **Globally Unique Identifier**, or **GUID**. This is a 128-bit integer value and is capable at representing a number as high as 3.4×10^{38}. Its biggest strength, however, is that the code you use to create a GUID is written in such a way that no two identifiers are ever, ever, ever (without exception!) the same. This means that *you* can build a Jo's Coffee store with 500 products and those 500 products will never have the same ID as the 500 products in *my* store. That means we can, if we wanted, merge our two databases together and our unique IDs would never clash.

However, the usefulness of that functionality is possibly a little overkill for our operation here, so we're going use 32-bit integer values to represent our rows. As the biggest number we can represent using a 32-bit integer is nearly 4,300,000,000, it's big enough to ensure that we're unlikely to run out of space in our product catalog.

The naming convention we're going to use for ID fields is the singular name of the table with ID tacked on the end. For example, our Departments table will have an ID field called DepartmentID. We're also going to say that the ID column is always the first in the table, and will always be a 32-bit integer value. Finally, we're going to use SQL Server's Identity feature to automatically allocate IDs for each table.

Try It Out – Creating the Departments Table

1. Start SQL Server 7's Enterprise Manager, and open the JoCoffee database. Right-click on Tables and select New Table. The Table Designer will be opened, and you'll be prompted for a name. Enter Departments as the name and click OK:

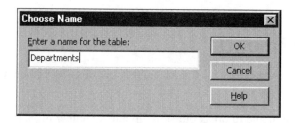

2. Now we will create the Departments table like this:

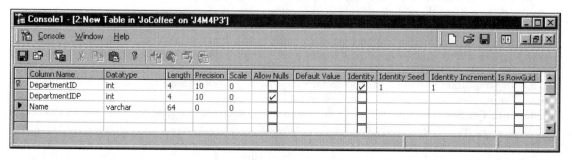

How It Works

As you can see from the table, we're going to give each department a name of up to 64 characters in length.

The other field, DepartmentIDP, will be used to structure the departments into a tree. This method for representing tree-like, or hierarchical, information in a database is pretty common. If you've never met it before, here's how it works.

Firstly, let's revisit our department structure diagram, but this time showing the possible IDs for each department. Note that we can't show the *actual* IDs in our diagram, as the IDENTITY field we're using in SQL Server won't guarantee you can recreate them exactly as seen here:

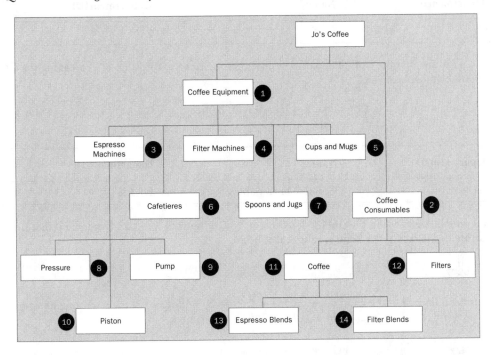

The first thing to note is that the **Jo's Coffee** department doesn't have an ID. This is because, in our store we're not actually going to create a department for that – the site itself can be considered to be the **Jo's Coffee** department.

Likewise with CoffeeClub, it's not part of the store and so doesn't have an ID.

Now that we have some example IDs, we can talk about how the DepartmentIDP field helps us represent the tree. Consider these two rows:

DepartmentID	Name	DepartmentIDP
13	Espresso Blends	11
14	Filter Blends	11

These two departments both have their DepartmentIDP field set to 11, meaning that they are parented by department whose ID is 11 – in this case **Coffee**.

Now look at the row for **Coffee**:

DepartmentID	Name	DepartmentIDP
11	Coffee	2

Now we can see that the **Coffee** department has a `DepartmentIDP` value of 2, meaning the **Coffee Consumables** department.

Lastly, look at the **Coffee Consumables** department. Notice that its `DepartmentIDP` value is null, meaning it's at the top of the department tree:

DepartmentID	Name	DepartmentIDP
2	Coffee Consumables	NULL

Based on this, we can find the sibling departments to **Coffee** with a `SELECT` statement that finds departments that share the same parent as **Coffee**:

```
SELECT * FROM Departments WHERE DepartmentIDP=2
```

We also can find all of the child departments of **Coffee** by finding all of the departments whose `DepartmentIDP` field is set to the ID of the **Coffee** department:

```
SELECT * FROM Departments WHERE DepartmentIDP=11
```

We'll be seeing more code that walks around the department tree later in the chapter and throughout the rest of the book.

Building Our Administration Tools

In order to both configure our site for testing and deployment, and manage the site once it's up and running, we need to have administration tools in place that let us add products, change departments around, view orders, etc.

In this section, we're going to start putting together the administration tools that will let us manage our site. These will also help us build the layout structure we've already defined.

Creating the Administration Page

Most Web applications, including e-commerce sites, have some mechanisms in place for managing the site over the Internet. In effect, administration tools like this are like a little intranet that can let you peer inside the site as it's running and make changes.

Our site is going to be administered through one page, which is "hidden" inside a folder called admin. I say "hidden" because there are a lot of sites out there that have an admin folder, or an admin.asp, so in a production environment it's smarter to choose a more unusual name – in much the same way as you might choose an unusual word for a password, rather than "password".

Try It Out – Creating an Administration Page

1. Open the InterDev project now and select the Project Explorer. Right-click on localhost/JoCoffee and select New Folder. Call this folder admin.

2. Now, right-click on the new admin folder and choose Add | Active Server Page. Call this page default.asp. The new default.asp will be created inside the admin folder in the Web project.

3. For the administration tool, we don't want to use the existing site template, but we do want to use some of the functions and services provided in site.asp. We also want to make sure that the code in end.asp that cleans up resources used by the page is also replicated.

Here's the code that needs to be added to admin/default.asp. You may recognize it as being very similar to the code that we added to the root default.asp earlier:

```
<% option explicit %>
<html>
<head>
    <!-- #include file="..\site.asp" -->
    <title><%=g_sitename%> Administration</title>
    <link rel="stylesheet" type="text/css" href="../style.css">
</head>
<body bgcolor=#ffffff>

    <!-- Start the page -->
    <font class=bigheading>Jo's Coffee Administration</font>
    <br><br><font class=small>

    <!-- Admin content will go here -->

    <!-- End the page -->
    </font>

<%

    ' Do we have a Visit object to close?
    If Not IsEmpty(m_visit) Then
        m_visit.ShutDown
        Set m_visit = Nothing
    End If

%>

</body>
</html>
```

How It Works

In this code example, we only use a single include file – `site.asp`. Because this file is in the folder below the `admin` folder, we need to use the `..\` to tell ASP where to find the file:

```
<!-- #include file="..\site.asp" -->
```

We also perform a similar trick with `style.css`:

```
<link rel="stylesheet" type="text/css" href="../style.css">
```

The only other really interesting point of note is the `ShutDown` method that we call when the page is ended. You may remember that code similar to this can be found in `end.asp` – its function is to properly stop the `Visit` object and free up any resources that may be in use, particularly the database connection:

```
If Not IsEmpty(m_visit) Then
    m_visit.ShutDown
    Set m_visit = Nothing
End If
```

Authentication

Of course, with any form of administrative tool, it's always smart to make sure you have a way of preventing unauthorized access to that tool.

In this example, we're going to build in very basic authentication. For brevity, our example will simply present a Password box to the user the first time they enter the page.

Try It Out – Authenticating the User

1. Add this code to `admin/default.asp`:

```
<font class=bigheading>Jo's Coffee Administration</font>
<br><br><font class=small>
```

```
<%
    'Are we logged on?
    If Session("AdminOK") = "" Then
        ' Start a form...
        Response.Write "<center><form action="""
        Response.Write Request("script_name")
        Response.Write """ method=post>"

        ' Render a password box and button...
        Response.Write "Password: "
        Response.Write "<input type=password name=password> "
        Response.Write
```

```
"<input type=submit value=""Login"">"

    ' End the form
    Response.Write "</form></center>"
Else %>
```

```
<!-- Admin content will go here -->
```

```
<!-- end the authentication check... -->
<% End If %>
```

```
<!-- end the page -->
</font>
```

2. Now place the following code at the top of `admin/default.asp`:

```
<% option explicit

' Are we trying to logon?
If Request("password") = "secret" Then
    Session("AdminOK") = True
End If
%>
```

```
<html>
<head>
```

How It Works

This works by checking the `Session` object for a variable called `AdminOK`. By default, this will be blank so the test for a blank string means that rather than rendering any administration code, the page will draw a form asking for a password:

```
If Session("AdminOK") = "" Then
    ' Start a form...
    Response.Write "<center><form action="""
    Response.Write Request("script_name")
    Response.Write """ method=post>"

    ' Render a password box and button...
    Response.Write "Password: "
    Response.Write "<input type=password name=password> "
    Response.Write "<input type=submit value=""Login"">"

    ' End the form
    Response.Write "</form></center>"
```

Here's what it looks like:

This form sends its results back to the same page, so we also need code that checks to see if the correct password was entered.

In a production environment, you might choose to implement a Users table that contains the details of any users that have administration rights. In our example, we just check for the static password secret:

```
If Request("password") = "secret" Then
    Session("AdminOK") = True
End If
```

If we enter the correct password the Session variable AdminOK will be equal to something other than a blank string, so the login form won't be displayed and the menu we're about to build for choosing administration options will be displayed.

The action Variable

We're going to use our administration page to perform all of the administration functions on our site. That means that our page has to perform different functions depending on which **mode** it's been placed in. For example, if we're in department-editing mode, we need to present a completely different user interface to that for the product-editing mode.

A really neat way of choosing which mode you're in is to use a query string variable and a VBScript Select Case statement.

This example (don't type this in) uses a query string variable called action to choose the mode:

```
<!-- what mode are we in? -->
<% Select Case LCase(Request.QueryString("action")) %>

    <!-- options... -->
    <% Case "Option1" %>
        <!-- Render the form for Option1 here -->

    <% Case "Option2" %>
        <!-- Render the form for Option2 here -->
```

```
<% Case "Option3" %>
    <!-- Render the form for Option3 here -->

<% Case "Option4" %>
    <!-- Render the form for Option4 here -->

<!-- menu? -->
<% Case Else %>
    <!-- render the menu here -->

<% End Select %>
```

If we don't understand the mode, we render the menu. We can understand the mode when ASP/VBScript is able to choose which case statement to execute. This technique allows us to present a different user interface depending on the mode. Effectively, this enables us to reuse pages for multiple activities, making the site easier to manage from a development perspective.

Building the Menu

At this point, we need to build the menu of administration options that we'll be expanding as we build functionality into our administration page.

To do this, we use a function called RenderOption that makes it a little easier to render the links and form the URLs that let the user navigate around the administration options.

Try It Out – Building a Menu Using Select Case

1. Here's the code to add to the admin/default.asp page:

```
' end the form
Response.Write "</form></center>"

Else %>

    <!-- Choose the Mode we're in  -->
    <% Select Case LCase(Request.QueryString("action")) %>

        <!-- menu? -->
        <% case else

            ' Function to draw menu options
            Sub RenderOption(name, action)

                ' Draw it out...
                Response.Write "<a href="""
                Response.Write Request("script_name")
                Response.Write "?action=" & action
                Response.Write """>"
                Response.Write name
                Response.Write "</a><br>"
```

```
            End Sub

            ' Render the menu options...
            RenderOption "Add Department", "adddepartment"

    End Select %>
```

```
<% End If %>
<!-- end the page -->
</font>
```

The `RenderOption` function simply lets us avoid having to repeat a lot of tedious `Response.Write` calls. Whenever we want a properly formatted option, `RenderOption` calls back into the `admin/default.asp` page via the following line:

```
Response.Write Request("script_name")
```

Tacking on an appropriate `action` variable in the query string for the request:

```
Response.Write "?action=" & action
```

If you recall, the query string is checked for a variable called `action` in the `Select Case` statement.

At the moment, we've only got one option, but as we work through the book, we'll be adding more `RenderOption` calls to add more options to the menu:

```
RenderOption "Add Department", "adddepartment"
```

Building the Add Department Form

Now that we have a way of presenting the various administration options to the user, we need to build the form that will let them add departments.

Try It Out – Building the Add Department Form

1. We've already decided that our `action` command for Add Department will be `adddepartment`, so here's the code that will present that form; add it to `admin/default.asp`:

```
<!-- Choose the Mode we're in  -->
<% Select Case LCase(Request.QueryString("action")) %>

    <% ' Do we want to add a department?
    case "adddepartment" %>

        <!-- Create a form -->
        <form action="<%=request("script_name")%>" method=post>
        <center><table cellspacing=0 cellpadding=3>
        <tr><td colspan=2 class=heading align=center>
```

```
                    Add Department
                    <br><br>
                    </td></tr>

                    <!-- Add the required fields... -->
                    <tr><td class=heading>Name: </td>
                    <td><input type=text name=name value="<%=request("name")%>"></tr>

                    <tr><td class=heading>Parent: </td>
                    <td><% RenderSelect Select_Departments, "departmentidp" %></tr>

                    <!-- Button... -->
                    <tr><td colspan=2 align=center>
                    <br><input type=submit value="Add Department">
                    </td></tr>

                    <!-- Hidden fields -->
                    <input type=hidden name=savenewdepartment value=1>

                    <!-- End the table -->
                    </table></center>
                    </form>

        <% case else

            ' Function to draw menu options
            Sub RenderOption(name, action)
```

2. Add this constant to the top of `site.asp`:

```
Const Select_Departments = 0
```

3. Now add this code to the bottom of `site.asp`:

```
Sub RenderSelect(TableID, TagName)

    ' Start the select statement...
    Response.Write "<select name=" & TagName & ">"

    ' Set a default (Select) option to prompt the user to select one...
    Response.Write "<option value="""">(Select)</option>"


    ' Select the items from the db...
    Dim query, IDColumn, NameColumn

    Select Case TableID

        ' Select out departments...
        Case Select_Departments
            Set query = Visit.Catalog.GetAllDepartments
```

```
            IDColumn = "DepartmentID"
            NameColumn = "Name"


    End Select


    ' Loop them all...
    Do While Not Query.EOF


        ' Draw it...  (check to see if it's selected too)
        Response.Write "<option value=""" & query(IDColumn) & """"
        If CStr(query(IDColumn)) = CStr(Request(TagName)) Then
            Response.Write " selected"
        End If
        Response.Write ">"
        Response.Write Query(NameColumn)
        Response.Write "</option>"


        ' Next...
        query.MoveNext


    Loop


    ' end the select statement...
    Response.Write "</select>"

End Sub
```

How It Works

The first thing we do is check the `action` variable in the query string to see what we're supposed to be doing. If it equals `adddepartment`, we display the Add Department form:

```
        case "adddepartment" %>
```

We begin the form by using the `request("script_name")` call to tell it to renter the page when the submit button is pressed.

```
        <form action="<%=request("script_name")%>" method=post>
```

Finally, we draw the appropriate fields for the form and an edit button:

```
            <!-- add the required fields... -->
            <tr><td class=heading>Name: </td>
            <td><input type=text name=name value="<%=request("name")%>"></tr>

            <tr><td class=heading>Parent: </td>
            <td><% RenderSelect Select_Departments, "departmentidp" %></tr>

            <!-- button... -->
```

```
<tr><td colspan=2 align=center>
<br><input type=submit value="Add Department">
</td></tr>
```

Before we close the form, we add a HIDDEN field called savenewdepartment. We'll use this later to detect when the submit button was pressed on that particular form and actually add the department required:

```
<!-- hidden fields -->
<input type=hidden name=savenewdepartment value=1>
```

Now on to RenderSelect! As we build our administration tools, we'll find it's quite useful to be able to present a list of all the rows in a table so that we can, for example, associate suppliers and manufacturers with products. (And we'll be doing that in Chapter 6.) Here, we're going to use RenderSelect to choose the parent department for a new department that we enter.

Firstly, we need to define a constant that tells RenderSelect from which table we want to display rows. At the moment, RenderSelect can only display the rows of the Departments table:

```
Const Select_Departments = 0
```

Notice how we pass the TableID and the TagName into RenderSelect as parameters:

```
Sub RenderSelect(TableID, TagName)
```

Therefore, as we want to see the rows of the Departments table, the TableID is Select_Departments, and the TagName is departmentid.

The first thing we do is create a SELECT tag, naming it after the TagName parameter (departmentid), and creating a blank option:

```
' Start the select statement...
Response.Write "<select name=" & TagName & ">"

' Set a default (Select) option to prompt the user to select one...
Response.Write "<option value="""">(Select)</option>"
```

Notice how we're using a Select Case statement to test the value of TableID. Later, we'll see how we can tweak the Select Case statement to test for other Select_ constants so that we can reuse RenderSelect in other forms:

```
Select Case TableID

    ' Select out departments...
    Case Select_Departments
```

Before we end the SELECT tag, we select out a complete list of the departments using the GetAllDepartments method. This method returns a recordset of the departments in alphabetical order:

```
Set query = Visit.Catalog.GetAllDepartments
```

After we've selected out the recordset, we also store the name of the column that represents the ID, and the column representing the name, and we use this information to render each row in the recordset as a row in the SELECT tag:

```
IDColumn = "DepartmentID"
NameColumn = "Name"
```

One possibly confusing line here is the one that tests query(IDColumn) against Request(TagName). If this page is represented for some reason (perhaps there was an error in filling the form), the last selected value will be shown on the new page:

```
If CStr(query(IDColumn)) = CStr(Request(TagName)) Then
    Response.Write " selected"
End If
```

The full usefulness of this function will become apparent as we build more tools.

Saving the Department

When the Add Department button is pressed, we can determine what to do by looking for the existence of the savenewdepartment hidden field that was included in the form.

However, first we need to build code into the Catalog object to save the department into the database.

Try It Out – Adding Code to Save a New Department to the Catalog Object

1. Open the WroxCommerce project, find the Catalog object and add this code:

```
' AddDepartment - creates a new department and returns the new DepartmentID...
Public Function AddDepartment(ByVal Name As String, _
                              Optional ByVal ParentID As Long) As Long

    Dim NewDepartment As New Recordset
    NewDepartment.Open "Departments", m_utility.DB.DB, adOpenKeyset, _
                    adLockOptimistic

    NewDepartment.AddNew

    NewDepartment("Name") = Name

    If ParentID <> 0 Then NewDepartment("DepartmentIDP") = ParentID
```

```
    NewDepartment.Update
    AddDepartment = NewDepartment("DepartmentID")

    ' Cleanup...
    NewDepartment.Close
    Set NewDepartment = Nothing

End Function
```

How It Works

We begin by creating a recordset that is capable of inserting the row:

```
Dim NewDepartment As New Recordset
NewDepartment.Open "Departments", m_utility.DB.DB, adOpenKeyset, _
                    adLockOptimistic
```

We then insert a new row and enter the details for the department:

```
NewDepartment.AddNew
NewDepartment("Name") = Name
```

Of particular note is that, if we don't supply a parent ID, we have to be careful not to set a value for the DepartmentIDP column.

```
If ParentID <> 0 Then NewDepartment("DepartmentIDP") = ParentID
```

If we don't explicitly set a value, it will default to null, which is exactly the action we want. Recall that in order to find the top-level departments in the tree, we ask for all those departments that have a null DepartmentIDP value.

Finally, we update the database and return the ID of the new department to the caller of this function:

```
NewDepartment.Update
AddDepartment = NewDepartment("DepartmentID")
```

Changing the Catalog Object

In Chapter 3, we built the foundations for our WroxCommerce object model. If you recall, we spoke about how one of the primary features of this object model was to abstract direct access to the database out of the reach of the presentation-tier developer so that the rules of the business could never be circumvented.

It's pretty obvious that to select out all of the top level departments in our database, we want to make a call like this:

```
<%
  Dim Departments
  Set Departments = Connection.Execute("SELECT * FROM departments " _
                                        WHERE departmentidp IS NULL")
%>
```

However, we don't want an ASP developer to be making a call like that, as it breaks the rules of 3-tier distributed design. Remember, we want the presentation-tier developer (and in this case, the presentation tier is ASP) to be abstracted from the database to stop her from breaking the tried and tested business rules that are built into the model. We'd rather she made this call, which ensures that she is using the correct business rules in the correct manner:

```
<%
    Dim Departments
    Set Departments = Visit.Catalog.GetDepartments
%>
```

Querying the Database

It's time now to revisit our Visual Basic project, so make sure you've got the WroxCommerce project open.

In the following *Try It Out* we're going to write a function (RunQuery) that can return queries from the database. The neat thing about this function is if you want a keyset query returned that you could scroll around and make changes to, you just set the AsKeyset parameter to True. Otherwise, its main function is to mitigate some of the hassle of building SQL strings. This function does it for you by examining the table name and the supplied Where and Order clause parameters.

Then we'll add a primitive function called QueryDepartments to the Catalog object, which makes calling that function to get rows from Departments even easier.

Try It Out – Querying the Database

1. Here's the function. Add it to the Database object:

```
' RunQuery - runs a query...
Public Function RunQuery(ByVal TableName As String, _
                    Optional ByVal ViewName As String, _
                    Optional ByVal Where As String, _
                    Optional ByVal Order As String, _
                    Optional ByVal AsKeyset As Boolean = False, _
                    Optional ByVal UseTable As Boolean = False) _
                    As Recordset

    Dim sql As String

    sql = "select * from "
    If ViewName = "" Or UseTable = True Then
        sql = sql & TableName
    Else
```

```
        sql = sql & ViewName
    End If

    If Where <> "" Then sql = sql & " where " & Where

    If Order <> "" Then sql = sql & " order by " & Order

    If AsKeyset = False Then
        Set RunQuery = DB.Execute(sql)
    Else
        Set RunQuery = New Recordset
        RunQuery.Open sql, DB, adOpenKeyset, adLockOptimistic
    End If

End Function
```

2. Add this method to the `Catalog` object:

```
' QueryDepartments - primitive to help us get at Departments...
Private Function QueryDepartments(Optional ByVal Where As String, _
                                  Optional ByVal Order As String = "Name", _
                                  Optional ByVal AsKeySet As Boolean = False) _
                                  As Recordset

    ' Call the DB object's RunQuery method...
    Set QueryDepartments = m_utility.DB.RunQuery("departments", , _
                                         Where, Order, AsKeySet)

End Function
```

3. Let's now add some methods that use our new `QueryDepartments` function. Add the following code to the `Catalog` object:

```
' GetDepartments - returns the top level store departments...
Public Function GetDepartments(Optional Byval AsKeyset As Boolean = False) _
                            As Recordset
    Set GetDepartments = QueryDepartments("DepartmentIDP is null", , AsKeyset)
End Function
```

4. For good measure, add this `GetAllDepartments` method to the `Catalog` object:

```
' GetAllDepartments - returns a list of all the store departments...
Public Function GetAllDepartments(Optional Byval AsKeyset As Boolean = False) _
                            As Recordset
    Set GetAllDepartments = QueryDepartments(, , AsKeyset)
End Function
```

5. Now we need to add a method to the `Catalog` object that can return information about a specific department:

```
' GetDepartment - returns a single department...
Public Function GetDepartment(ByVal DepartmentID As Long, _
                              Optional ByVal AsKeyset As Boolean = False) _
                    As Recordset
   Set GetDepartment = QueryDepartments("DepartmentID=" & DepartmentID, , _
                                   AsKeyset)
End Function
```

6. The last function we need to add to the `Catalog` object is one that can return the child departments of a department with a specific ID.

```
' GetChildDepartments - returns a list of departments from the ID of a parent
Public Function GetChildDepartments(ByVal DepartmentID As Long, _
                              Optional Byval AsKeyset As _
                              Boolean = False) As Recordset

   Set GetChildDepartments = _
       QueryDepartments("DepartmentIDP=" & DepartmentID, , AsKeyset)

End Function
```

How It Works

Let's begin with the first function we wrote in this *Try It Out* – `RunQuery`.

We begin by determining if we have a view or not. Later on, we will be building views to make access to data spread over a number of tables easier. When we do this, we'll be using this function by passing in both a table name (e.g. `Products`) and a view name (e.g. `vProducts`). By default, `RunQuery` will attempt to use the view, unless `UseTable` is set to `True`, in which case the base table will always be used:

```
If ViewName = "" Or UseTable = True Then
    sql = sql & TableName
Else
    sql = sql & ViewName
End If
```

When we reach this point in the code, the basic SQL statement will have been built, comprising just a `SELECT *`, and a table or view name.

The function then checks the `Where` and `Order` parameters to see if those clauses need to be tacked on to the end of the SQL string:

```
If Where <> "" Then sql = sql & " where " & Where

If Order <> "" Then sql = sql & " order by " & Order
```

After the SQL string has been formed, we need to decide how to execute it and then return the resulting recordset back out of the function. By default, the faster, forward-only version is called using the general `Execute` method on the DB object, which if you recall is a standard ADO `Connection` object. If we set `AsKeyset` to `True`, we can create a keyset query that will allow us to move around in the recordset, as well as letting us use the query to update information in the query.

```
If AsKeyset = False Then
    Set RunQuery = DB.Execute(sql)
Else
    Set RunQuery = New Recordset
    RunQuery.Open sql, DB, adOpenKeyset, adLockOptimistic
End If
```

You can see now why the `RunQuery` method is cool. Firstly, we just have to refer to the name of the table, and pass in the `Where` and `Order` clauses as optional parameters. In fact, notice how we set the default value for `Order` to `Name` in `QueryDepartments` – this means that whenever we omit the `Order` clause, by default we'll get a list of the departments in name order:

```
Private Function QueryDepartments(Optional ByVal Where As String, _
                                  Optional ByVal Order As String = "Name", _
                                  Optional ByVal AsKeySet As Boolean = False) _
                                  As Recordset
```

As we explained before, the `RunQuery` method itself is responsible for making up the SQL string and running the statement. This means that the `QueryDepartments` method will return a recordset back containing, in this case, all of the departments. Effectively, `RunQuery` will call this SQL statement:

```
SELECT * FROM Departments ORDER BY Name
```

We call this kind of function a **primitive** function. A primitive function is a function that's only visible to select group of methods and properties (usually all of the other methods and properties that are members of the object in which the primitive is defined). Its name is derived from the concept of using many of these little functions as building blocks to create larger, more complex functions.

We've discussed previously the `DepartmentIDP` field in terms of how it maintained a reference to its parent and that by doing this, it was possible to hold the departments as a tree. Well, the top level items in this tree have their `DepartmentIDP` values set to null, so the `Where` clause we pass back to our primitive is based on this assumption:

```
Public Function GetDepartments(Optional Byval AsKeyset As Boolean = False) _
                               As Recordset
    Set GetDepartments = QueryDepartments("DepartmentIDP is null", , AsKeyset)
End Function
```

This time, `RunQuery` will form this SQL:

```
SELECT * FROM Departments WHERE DepartmentIDP is null ORDER BY Name
```

See how we omit the `Where` clause from the call to `QueryDepartments` in the `GetAllDepartments` function previously, and so every department, regardless of position in the tree, will be returned back to the caller:

```
Set GetAllDepartments = QueryDepartments(, , AsKeyset)
```

Here's the SQL:

```
SELECT * FROM Departments ORDER BY Name
```

In the `GetDepartment` method, we just want to look up a department with a specific ID:

```
Set GetDepartment = QueryDepartments("DepartmentID=" & DepartmentID, , _
                                      AsKeyset)
```

`RunQuery` will create this SQL string:

```
SELECT * FROM Departments WHERE DepartmentID=27
```

The `GetChildDepartments` function has a similar nature to `GetDepartment`, but it's capable of returning a list of departments all of which share the same parent ID.

```
Set GetChildDepartments = _
    QueryDepartments("DepartmentIDP=" & DepartmentID, , AsKeyset)
```

Effectively, we give it a parent, and it gives us back the children:

```
SELECT * FROM Departments WHERE DepartmentIDP=1 ORDER BY Name
```

Try It Out – Testing the Form

1. Now, make sure you save and run the `WroxCommerce` project, and then add this code to `admin/default.asp`, immediately below our password check:

```
Session("AdminOK") = True
End If
```

```
' Are we trying to save a new department?
If Request("savenewdepartment") <> "" Then

    Dim NewDepartmentID
    if request("departmentidp") = "" then
        NewDepartmentID = Visit.Catalog.AddDepartment(Request("name"))
    else
        NewDepartmentID = Visit.Catalog.AddDepartment(Request("name"), _
                          Request("departmentidp"))
    end if

End If
```

2. Remember, because we're using IDENTITY fields, the IDs you get may be different to the diagram. However, it helps as you work through this book to have the same IDs. Try to add the departments in the same order as they are on the diagram and you should find that your IDs and my IDs match:

When you click **Add Department**, your new department will be added to the database, and will look something like this:

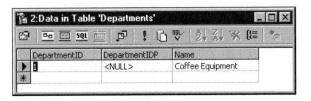

How It Works

The first thing we do is check to see if a savenewdepartment variable was passed through. If there was, we run the AddDepartment method of the Catalog object to create the new department. Remember that we can use the Select box that was added to the page by the RenderSelect clause to create a list of other departments. If we selected one of these, its ID will be placed in the departmentidp form variable, and this is passed through as a parameter to AddDepartment.

Try It Out – Adding the Remaining Departments

1. Now that our Add Department tool is working, we can go ahead and add the other departments from our earlier design:

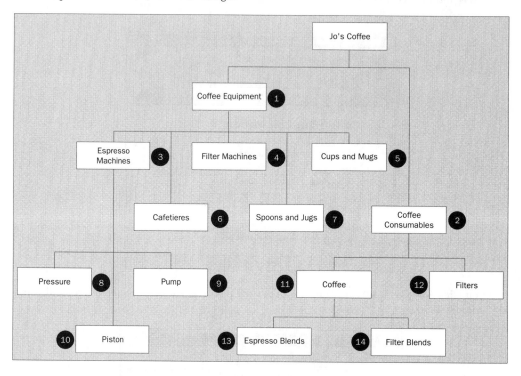

2. Remember, because we're using IDENTITY fields, the IDs you get may be different to the diagram. However, it helps as you work through this book to have the same IDs. Try to add the departments in the same order as they are on the diagram and you should find that your IDs and my IDs match.

Modifying the ASP Pages

Although we haven't got as far as storing actual products in our database, we can still develop pages capable of presenting the departments to the user. Later, we'll modify these pages to display product information.

1. Firstly, open our InterDev project and create a new ASP page called `dept.asp`.

2. When we built our first ASP pages in Chapter 4, we created a `template.asp` file that we could use as a foundation for any new pages we would create. Open this template file now and copy the contents into `dept.asp` so that both files look the same.

3. The next step is to tie the buttons at the top of the navigation bar into the `dept.asp` file. Open the `start.asp` include file, which if you recall contains the code that generates those buttons. All we have to do is link the images through to the `dept.asp` page, like this:

```
<!-- now we need to look at the first line in the layout.
This comprises Jo's head, the three site section buttons,
and the "Jo's Coffee" logo... -->
<tr>
   <td><a href="default.asp">
       <img src="i/johead.gif" border="0" </a></td> <!-- Jo's head -->
   <td><a href="dept.asp?id=1">
       <img src="i/machines.gif" border="0"> </a></td>  <!-- "Coffee Machines" button -->
   <td><a href="dept.asp?id=2"><img src="i/coffee.gif" WIDTH="106"
       HEIGHT="76" border="0"></a></td>    <!-- "Coffee" button -->
   <td><img src="i/club.gif" ></td>    <!-- "CoffeeClub" button -->
   <td><a href="default.asp">
       <img src="i/logo.gif" border="0" >   </a></td>  <!-- "Jo's Coffee" logo -->
</tr>
```

You'll need to check to make sure that the IDs in your database match the ID values passed to `dept.asp`, as the use of `IDENTITY` fields may have skewed the values you have.

4. Now add a new class to the `style.css` style sheet called `medheading`. Set the font to Tahoma, and give it a specific size of **12 pt** and an absolute weight of **Bold (700)**.

5. Save the changes you made to `start.asp` and make sure that you have `dept.asp` open. What we want to do first is display the name of the department at the top of the page by adding this code to `dept.asp`:

```
<!-- #include file="start.asp" -->
```

```
<%

    ' Use the GetDepartment method to get the department we were asked for...
    Dim Department
    Set Department = Visit.Catalog.GetDepartment(Request("id"))
```

```
    If Not Department.EOF Then

        ' Write the name of the department...
        Response.Write "<font class=medheading>"
        Response.Write Department("name")
        Response.Write "</font>"
        Response.Write "<br>"

    End If

    Department.Close
    Set Department = Nothing
%>
```

```
<!-- #include file="end.asp" -->
```

6. What we want to do next is display a list of the sub-departments in whatever department we're looking at. We can use the `GetChildDepartments` method to do this.

This code is slightly more bulky than it could be in order to accommodate the table we use to split the department list into two columns:

```
If Not Department.EOF Then

    ' Write the name of the department...
    Response.Write "<font class=medheading>"
    Response.Write Department("name")
    Response.Write "</font>"
    Response.Write "<br><br>"
```

```
    ' Get the child departments of the department we're looking at...
    Dim Children
    Set Children = Visit.Catalog.GetChildDepartments(Department("DepartmentID"))

    If Not Children.EOF Then

        ' Display the children...
        Dim num
        num = 0
        Response.Write "<table cellspacing=0 cellpadding=0 width=""100%"">"

        Do While Not Children.EOF

            ' We want two columns, so we use the 'num' variable to
            ' tell us when to start a new table row...
            if num mod 2 = 0 then
                if num <> 0 then Response.Write "</tr>"
                Response.Write "<tr>"
            end if

            ' Render the child department as a link, making that link call
            ' back into this page...
```

```
                    Response.Write "<td class=heading>"
                    Response.Write "<li><a href="""
                    Response.Write Request("script_name") & "?id=" & _
                              Children("DepartmentID")
                    Response.Write """>" & Children("Name") & "</a>"
                    Response.Write "</td>"

                    ' Next...
                    Children.MoveNext
                    num = num + 1

                Loop

                Response.Write "</tr></table>"
                Response.Write "<br><br>"

        End If

        Children.Close
        Set Children = Nothing

    End if
```

How It Works

Notice the calls to dept.asp have an ID value passed through to them. This refers to the department ID as stored in the Departments table:

```
<td><a href="dept.asp?id=1">
    <img src="i/machines.gif" WIDTH="103" HEIGHT="76" border=0>
    </a></td>   <!-- "Coffee Machines" button -->
<td><a href="dept.asp?id=2"><img src="i/coffee.gif" WIDTH="106"
    HEIGHT="76" border=0></a></td>   <!-- "Coffee" button -->
```

When we added the code to the buttons in start.asp, remember how we passed in the ID of the department through the query string for the page. Well, in the call to GetDepartment, we pass in that ID that we've discovered through use of the Request object:

```
Set Department = Visit.Catalog.GetDepartment(Request("id"))
```

Once we have a recordset containing just the department we want, we display its name.

```
If Not Department.EOF Then

    ' Write the name of the department...
    Response.Write "<font class=medheading>"
    Response.Write Department("name")
    Response.Write "</font>"
    Response.Write "<br>"

End If
```

Once we have the recordset containing the department we're interested in, we pass the ID of that department through to `GetChildDepartments` and this in turn will ask `RunQuery` to bring back a recordset of the departments where `DepartmentIDP` matches the department we're looking at:

```
Set Children = Visit.Catalog.GetChildDepartments(Department("DepartmentID"))
```

Once we've loaded the recordset of the children, we have to iterate through them all rendering them into a list. We actually want to build a list containing two columns, so we increment the value in `num` each time we render one, and check to see if this is an odd or even number using the `Mod` function:

```
if num mod 2 = 0 then
    if num <> 0 then Response.Write "</tr>"
    Response.Write "<tr>"
end if
```

This trick enables us to determine if a new row should be started before we render a new `<TD>` cell containing a link to the department itself. We only start a new table row each time `num` is an even number, and this gives us our two columns.

Here's what we end up with:

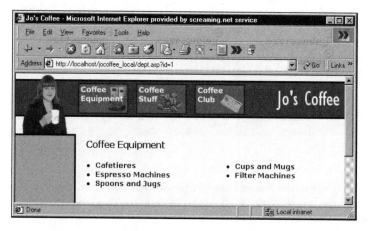

As you try clicking through the departments, you'll notice that the "recycling" method we use with `dept.asp` means that we only have to engineer this page once and it will work with any store department on the site. In the next chapter, we'll see how we can add products to our database and add some code to `dept.asp` that will display the products in any department on the system.

However, you may have noticed that when we "drill down" into the department tree, we have a usability issue. Drill down now through **Espresso Machines** and then **Piston**, and you'll notice that you arrive at a dead-end. There's no obvious way of navigating back up the tree.

1. To resolve this issue we change the heading of the department to allow for navigation back; add this to dept.asp:

```
' Write the name of the department...
Response.Write "<font class=medheading>"

' Loop up the parents, starting at our parent...
Dim buf, Parent, ParentID
ParentID = Department("DepartmentIDP")

Do While ParentID <> ""

    ' Get a list of all the previous departments, and add them to a string...
    Set Parent = Visit.Catalog.GetDepartment(ParentID)

    If Not Parent.EOF Then

        buf = "<a href=""" & Request("script_name") & "?id=" & _
            parentid & """>" & Parent("Name") & "</a>" & "\" & buf

        ' Get the next ID to look at...
        ParentID = Parent("DepartmentIDP")

    else

        ' Something's wrong... quit!
        ParentID = ""

    End If

    Parent.Close
    Set Parent = Nothing

Loop

' Render the parent list first...
Response.Write buf

Response.Write Department("name")
Response.Write "</font>"
Response.Write "<br><br>"
```

2. Before we explain the code, here's what we get:

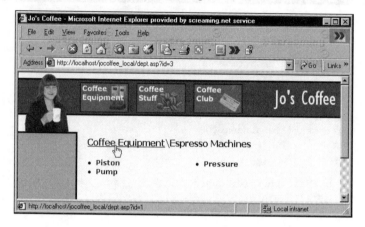

How It Works

The complexity of this code comes from the fact that it's more efficient to walk up a tree than it is to walk down it. What we do is use a Do...While loop to walk up the parent tree.

We start by knowing the ID of the department that is the parent of Espresso Machines and we set that value to a variable called ParentID:

```
ParentID = Department("DepartmentIDP")
```

Then we ask the Catalog object for the Departments row that represents that parent through GetDepartment:

```
Set Parent = Visit.Catalog.GetDepartment(ParentID)
```

We then insert the name of the department, along with a link that recycles the current ASP page with the parent's ID, at the beginning of buf:

```
buf = "<a href=""" & Request("script_name") & "?id=" & _
        parentid & """>" & Parent("Name") & "</a>" & "\" & buf
```

Then we reset the value of ParentID to be the value of the department we just got:

```
ParentID = Parent("DepartmentIDP")
```

When ParentID becomes " ", we know that we've reached the top of the tree and we can drop out of the loop. Finally, we use Response.Write to send the value of Buf back to the visitor's browser.

Try playing with that page and you'll discover that the department navigation is now a lot more usable.

Summary

In this chapter, we learned how to break up the departments in the store so that visitors to our site could use their knowledge and experience of offline shopping in our online environment.

Once we had decided on our department layout, and built our `Departments` table we set to work building the framework for the administration tools we'll use throughout the rest of this book to set up test cases and manage the site once it's live. We then used those tools to populate the `Departments` table with the departments we designed in the previous section.

With the departments stored in the database, we then built methods and properties into the `WroxCommerce` object model to let us query those departments and finally build ASP pages that used the model to render the department information to the user.

Building the Product Catalog

So far, we've managed to initialize a database, build the foundations of an object model, create an ASP template, structure the departments that make up our store, and write some pages that let us look around those departments. It may not sound like much, but we don't have that far to go from here to get a fully working site!

Next, we turn our attention to the products in the catalog itself. Somehow, we have to develop a database structure capable of holding the information on what we sell in such a way that our ASP code can pull out this information and display it to the visitor. Once we've done that, we're just one click away from having that visitor add products to their cart.

So within this chapter we're going to cover a lot of ground, we're going to be dealing with all three tiers of the development architecture, in that we'll:

- ❑ Design and create the database tables we need to store the product information
- ❑ Expand our object model so we can manipulate the new tables
- ❑ Enable our presentation tier to provide a front-end that will allow us to enter, retrieve and view the information that will make joscoffee.com an effective e-business

The Problems with Storing Product Information

One of the challenges we face when designing the schemas (a schema is a set of data that describes the structure of the database) that store our products is how we should store the rich set of data that exists for each type of product.

For example, if we're selling computer equipment, how do we store information specific to Windows CE devices in the same database that we use to store information specific to scanners? We can assume that there are some attributes common to both, like name, price, shipping information and so on, but there will be attributes unique to each type.

Consider the following table listing some of the data we may have to store:

	Windows CE Handheld	Scanner
Name	Cassiopeia E10	SnapScan 1212
Manufacturer	Casio	Agfa
Supplier	Computers-be-us	I like Scanners, Inc.
Price	$400	$100
Screen Resolution	200x400	
Scanning Resolution		600dpi x 600dpi
Carry case?	Yes	
Docking cradle?	Yes	
USB?		No

So you can see the total set of attributes we need to store gets larger the more types of products we have.

If we look at the types of products we sell, it's not hard to see we're going to have to store different sets of attributes for different types of products, as our offerings are quite diverse (after all, we sell both espresso machines and coffee filters!).

Curiously, the number of e-tailers that don't have this flexible attribute set problem is very small. Even a site that sells just CDs has to face the *dynamic attribute* challenge – classical music CDs, for example, hold details on the orchestra and conductor, whereas contemporary CDs don't.

When we look at our possible attribute sets we can immediately identify data that is common to all products (supplier, manufacturer, price, etc.) and we can hold all that information in a `Products` table.

We have two main options for storing the attribute information. We could store it in a text field so when we need to display it to the site visitor, we just render the field out to the browser. The alternative option is that we find some way of storing this information in a flexible structure that can grow as the number of different types of products we hold expands.

It's very easy to develop a structure that just holds the information as text, like this:

```
Cassiopeia E-10: "Screen Resolution:200x400, Carry Case: Yes, Docking Cradle: Yes"
Agfa SnapScan 1212: "Scanning Resolution:600dpi x 600dpi, USB: No"
```

But this text-based route steers us away from two important features. Firstly, we won't be able to present the user with rich searching tools like "*Show me all espresso machines using the pump system with greater than a 12 cup capacity*". Secondly, we won't be able to easily ask important decision support questions like "*How much more popular were Krups espresso machines with 8 cups capacity than Gaggia ones with 12 in the South West of the UK last quarter?*"

In this chapter, we'll be discussing how to build a system for holding dynamic attributes.

Building the Schemas

Relational database design lies outside the scope of this book, but to start with we're going to build a couple of tables that contain information common to each product (these tables aren't for handling dynamic attributes – those tables will be encountered later in the chapter). As we discussed above we're going to use a table to contain information about the products themselves; additionally we're going to build related tables to store information on the product manufacturers and the product suppliers. Once we've built the tables we'll then need to put some data in them to give us a basis to work from.

In setting up these tables we're not being exhaustive in the list of fields we include; as you work through the book and think about your own application scenarios I'm sure you will develop your own ideas about what further information you will need to store.

Let's kick off by building the `Products` table.

Try It Out – Building the Tables

1. Start SQL Server Enterprise Manager and drill down to the `JoCoffee` database, right-click on Tables, select New Ta<u>b</u>le…and enter Products as the table name.

2. Fill in the grid as shown in the accompanying screen shot. *Ensure the* `ProductID` *field is set to be a primary key. To do this, right-click on the field name and select* Set Primary Key.

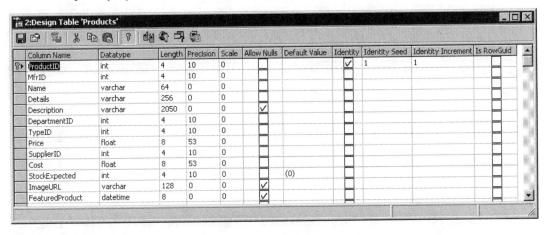

Here's what we we're going to store in each of the fields:

- ❏ `ProductID` – the unique 32-bit identifier for the product

- ❏ `MfrID` – the unique ID of the manufacturer (this is the foreign key linking to the `Mfrs` table we create below)

- ❏ `Name` – the name of the product

- ❏ `Details` – a one or two sentence description of the item

- ❏ `Description` – an in-depth description of what the product is and how it works

- ❑ DepartmentID –the unique ID of the department the product is in (the foreign key linking to the Departments table created in Chapter 5)
- ❑ TypeID – the type of product; this field will manage the dynamic attribute architecture we spoke about before
- ❑ Price – the current selling price of the product
- ❑ SupplierID – the unique ID of the supplier of the product (the foreign key linking to the Suppliers table we create below)
- ❑ Cost – the current cost of the product
- ❑ StockExpected – the number of days it will take your suppliers to get stock of an item (known as the supplier's *lead time*)
- ❑ ImageURL – the path to a GIF or JPG image on disk that holds an image of the product
- ❑ FeaturedProduct – indicates whether a product is a featured product on our Web site; if this is null, it's not a featured product, otherwise it holds the date when it became one

3. Save the table and close the grid to return to the main screen of Enterprise Manager.

4. Next, we want to create a table to contain details on the product manufacturers. Repeat the procedure for creating a new table in the JoCoffee database and enter Mfrs for the table name. Fill in the grid as shown below before saving the information. *Here note that the MfrID field should be set to be a primary key.*

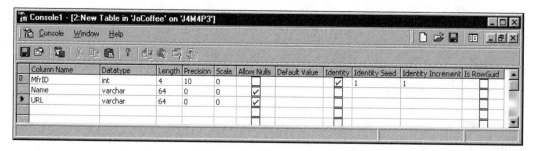

5. Follow the same process again to create a table called Suppliers (to be set up as shown below), which will hold information on our suppliers. *Here the primary key is the SupplierID field.*

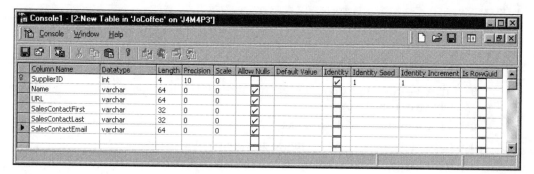

The only important thing to note on the Suppliers table is that we hold the first name, last name and e-mail address of our sales contact. In Chapter 8 we'll see how we can use this to e-mail our suppliers details of our orders.

6. Now we should start to populate the Mfrs and Suppliers tables. For the purposes of our project we're just going to add a single row of data to each table; in a real-life situation you may have to deal with the issues surrounding moving large chunks of data from your existing database to a new one.

In SQL Server Enterprise Manager right-click on the Mfrs table and select Open Table | Return all rows. Then enter the following into the table (the MfrID will be automatically added; you won't be able to edit this cell yourself):

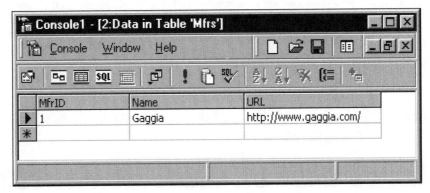

Remember, SQL Server will choose the MfrID value for us, so you may end up with a slightly different number to that shown here.

7. Close the Mfrs table, open the Suppliers table and add the following (again the SupplierID may be different in your table):

Views

A **view** can be thought of as a virtual table, in that it can mostly be used like a table, but it doesn't contain any data. A view is a pre-determined plan, stored in the database as a query, that allows us to control what parts of the database we allow the user of the view to see. This brings two obvious benefits. Firstly, using views allows us to impose some degree of security on database access as we can hold sensitive and non-sensitive information in the same table, because it's logically linked, but only allow users of the view to see the non-sensitive information. For example, a company may make use of a database with a table containing information on employees that includes their name, address and salary details. Here it may be appropriate to make the name and address details widely accessible via one view, but then build a view containing the salary details which is only available to certain members of the human resources department.

Secondly, the use of views allows us to customize the information displayed to the user – we can set up views that can combine and expose as much, or as little, of the information from the database as we need.

It's this second, ease of use, benefit that we're going to make most use of throughout the book. We're going to use views to allow us to easily combine and view data that, for relational database design reasons, is stored in different tables.

So, to start with we're going to set up a view (vProducts) that links the Products, Suppliers, Mfrs, and Departments tables together.

Try It Out – Creating the vProducts View

1. In the left-hand window of the Enterprise Manager, right click on the Views icon (a pair of eye glasses) under JoCoffee and select New View...

2. In the window that appears, right-click on the upper, gray pane and select Add Table... In the Add Table dialog, select the tables to be added (Products, Suppliers, Mfrs, and Departments tables) and click Add.

3. The four tables should now be in the gray pane; close the Add Table dialog. For convenience you may wish to drag them around the pane. You'll notice that some of the field names appear in bold text. This is because we defined them as primary key fields when we built the table earlier.

4. Click the appropriate check boxes and link the tables together as shown in the screen shot. To link the tables, highlight the column to be linked and drag it over to the column it should be linked with – a link will appear between the two columns if successfully done (unlinking can be achieved by right-clicking on the link and selecting Remove).

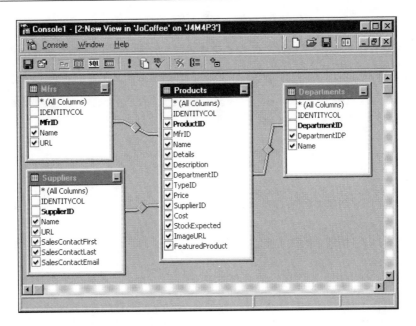

5. Click on the save icon on the top left hand corner on the window and this will prompt you with a **Save As** dialog box. Save the view as **vProducts**.

6. The next task is to resolve the name conflicts that currently exist within our view. As each individual table stands, identifiers like `Name` and `URL` are straightforward descriptions of data contained in those fields. However, when we link tables together in a view, each column needs to have a unique name and here we need to differentiate between the four occurrences of `Name` and two occurrences of `URL`.

To rename the columns firstly make sure that the Grid Pane is displayed by depressing the **Show/Hide Grid Pane** button on the toolbar.

7. Next to each of the columns shown, set unambiguous new names using the Alias edit column:

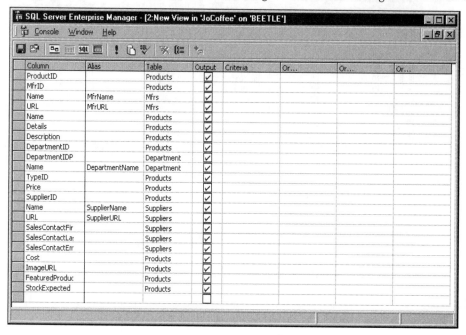

How It Works

The activities that we've just carried out above are translated into an SQL query that can be viewed in a pane in the View Designer (if you can't see the SQL, depress the Show/Hide SQL Pane button on the toolbar).

The SQL that will be used to retrieve the columns should look very similar to the following (although the order of the columns will depend on the order in which you worked through the exercise):

```
SELECT Products.ProductID, Products.MfrID,
   Mfrs.Name AS MfrName, Mfrs.URL AS MfrURL, Products.Name,
   Products.Details, Products.Description,
   Products.DepartmentID, Departments.DepartmentIDP,
   Departments.Name AS DepartmentName, Products.TypeID,
   Products.Price, Products.SupplierID,
   Suppliers.Name AS SupplierName, Suppliers.URL AS SupplierURL,
   Suppliers.SalesContactFirst, Suppliers.SalesContactLast,
   Suppliers.SalesContactEmail, Products.Cost, Products.ImageURL,
   Products.FeaturedProduct, Products.StockExpected
FROM Products INNER JOIN
   Suppliers ON
   Products.SupplierID = Suppliers.SupplierID INNER JOIN
   Mfrs ON Products.MfrID = Mfrs.MfrID INNER JOIN
   Departments ON
   Products.DepartmentID = Departments.DepartmentID
```

As we can see from the query, we are joining the Products table to three separate tables (Departments, Mfrs, and Suppliers) via an INNER JOIN statement linking related columns.

Storing Products

We've already discussed the need for some sort of database structure that can hold the dynamic attributes – this section will guide us through building such a scheme.

There are two main schools of thought about how to build a system like this. Both of them hold common elements in a `Products` table, which we've already built. They differ though in the following respects:

- ❑ Approach A – build another table structure that can hold dynamic data
- ❑ Approach B – dynamically build separate tables for each type of item that needs to be held

Although approach B offers performance and flexibility benefits, it is more complex to implement and is beyond the scope of this book. So, in this project we'll build another set of tables aimed at meeting our needs. To support the Web site we'll need tables to store information on:

- ❑ The different types of item stocked by Jo's Coffee
- ❑ The set of attributes each different type of item has
- ❑ The actual attributes themselves

Of course we'll need to build some type of view to be able to retrieve this information and also do some work to help our `WroxCommerce` engine to work with the data we'll hold in this structure.

Try It Out – Building Tables to Store Dynamic Attributes

1. We'll start off by creating a very simple `Types` table to define the different types of item that are stored in our catalog. Follow the normal procedure for creating a new table in the `JoCoffee` database, enter `Types` for the table name, and fill in the grid as shown (noting that the primary key is the `TypeID` field):

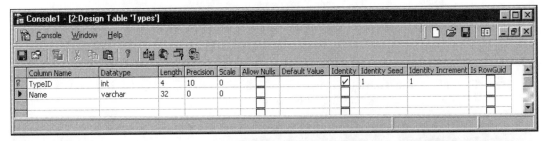

2. For the first part of this discussion, we only need a single type, so enter just the following into the created table (right-click on the table, select Open Table | Return all rows, enter Espresso Machines into the Name field and leave SQL Server to fill in the TypeID):

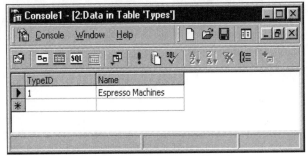

3. Next, we turn our attention to creating a table to keep track of the set of attributes that each different type has. Create an `AttributeStructure` table with the following structure (noting that `StructureID` is the primary key):

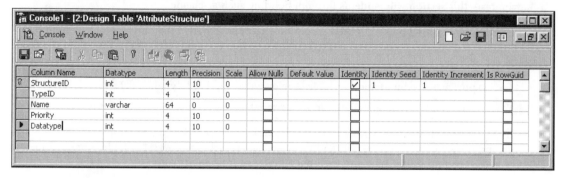

4. Now, we'll populate the `AttributeStructure` table and define the set of attributes for our **Espresso Machines** item type we added to the `Types` table in step 2:

    Remember, when you enter these, if SQL Server chose a `TypeID` other than 1 when you added the row to the `Types` table, you'll need to enter that value for that column.

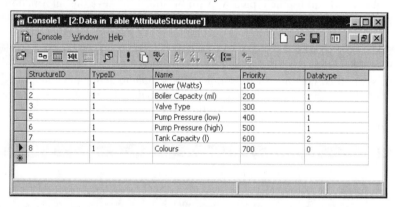

5. To hold the actual attribute data for each product, create an `Attributes` table as shown, with the `AttributeID` as the table's primary key:

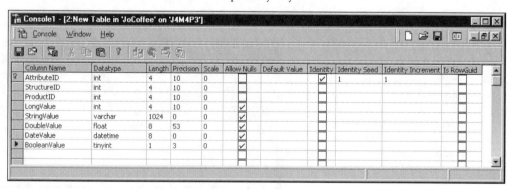

In this table the columns are used for the following purposes:

❑ AttributeID stores the unique ID of the attribute.

❑ StructureID refers to the attribute's definition in the AttributeStructure table.

❑ ProductID refers to the product's common attributes in the Products table.

❑ LongValue, StringValue, DoubleValue, DateValue, and BooleanValue provide storage for the five different sets of data type we accept for attributes. This lets us store our attribute data in the most efficient form possible, so if we want to store a long value, we don't have to convert it to a string and store it in Varchar field, we just store it in LongValue. We'll encounter this again below.

6. To make life easier for ourselves down the road, we need to set up a view that lets us quickly find attributes stored against a given product. Using the same steps as before create a new view that links the AttributeStructure and Attributes tables (as shown) and call it vAttributes:

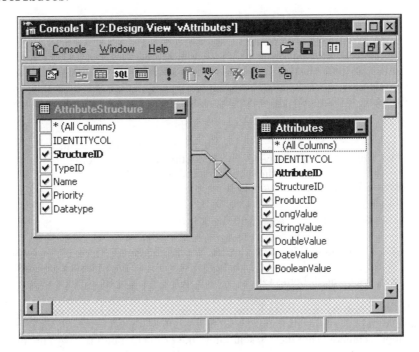

For this to work properly, you'll need to make sure that all rows from **AttributeStructure** are selected, even if there's no specific value set in **Attributes** for the product you're interested in. Right-click on the small diamond linking the two tables and select **Select All Rows from AttributeStructure**.

7. Our last step in this section is to put some mechanism in place, within the `WroxCommerce` engine, that will allow us to identify the five different types of data we are accepting for our attributes (as described in steps 3, 4 and 5). To do this return to the `WroxCommerce` project in Visual Basic and create a new **Standard Module**, call it **Globals** and enter the following:

```
Option Explicit

' AttributeTypes - holds the IDs for the different type of
' dynamic attribute data...
Public Enum AttributeTypes
   atInvalid = -1
   atString = 0
   atLong = 1
   atDouble = 2
   atDate = 3
   atBoolean = 4
End Enum
```

How It Works

Our `Types` table gives us a way of grouping the attributes together. As we saw before, certain types of item in the catalog have different sets of attributes. Our espresso machines may require a *Cup Capacity* attribute, whereas our coffee beans may require a *Strength* attribute. Using this table means when we add items to the catalog, we can assign them one of those types and then, just by looking at a single item, we understand not only the common attributes (through the `Products` table), but also which dynamic attributes apply.

Next, we set up the `AttributeStructure` table where each row represents a single attribute in the set identified by `TypeID`. We not only need to know the name of each one, but the order in which it appears in the list (`Priority`), and the type of data we want to hold (`Datatype`). The `Priority` column works by allowing us to use a query like

```
SELECT * FROM AttributeStructure ORDER BY Priority
```

to return the set of attributes in the correct order. We use the name `Priority` because `Order` is a *reserved word* in T-SQL (the dialect of SQL that SQL Server uses internally). You can find a list of reserved words, by looking in Books Online, which should have been installed along with SQL Server.

The last table we construct in this unit is the `Attributes` table – in our database structure we are using this one table to hold all of the attributes for all of the different products in the catalog. As mentioned before, our approach here is not the *best* solution to the problem, but it is *a* working one.

When we set up the `vAttributes` view the action of *selecting all rows* instructs SQL Server to perform an *outer* join, rather than an *inner* join like the ones we saw earlier. What this does is tell SQL Server that you're really interested in one set of data (in this case, we're really interested in the `AttributeStructure` table), but the data in the other table is optional. So, when SQL Server tries to join the `AttributeStructure` row called **Valve Type** to the row in the `Attributes` table that contains a specific value for that attribute, it will join the two rows even if there isn't a specific value set for **Valve Type** in the `Attributes` table. This brings us closer to the ideal of not having to specifically set attributes for items, which helps us keep the `Attributes` table smaller and response faster.

In this example, we have some sample data for a product with an ID of 1. The `ProductID` value for Valve Type is set to null, indicating that there is no specific value allocated for Valve Type in the attributes table.

As before, you can have a look at the SQL query generated in setting up the view – it should look something like this:

```
SELECT AttributeStructure.StructureID, AttributeStructure.TypeID,
    AttributeStructure.Name, AttributeStructure.Priority,
    AttributeStructure.Datatype, Attributes.ProductID,
    Attributes.LongValue, Attributes.StringValue,
    Attributes.DoubleValue, Attributes.DateValue,
    Attributes.BooleanValue
FROM AttributeStructure LEFT OUTER JOIN
    Attributes ON
    AttributeStructure.StructureID = Attributes.StructureID
```

Our last task was to create and build code in the `Globals` module that would allow us to identify the different types of data we can hold in our attributes. ADO (and OLE DB) defines a set of constants that can be used to identify the type of a column in an OLE DB provider. In order to query, accept and present our attribute data down the road, it helps to have a rich set of data types that we understand. We're using our own set of constants as ADO/OLE DB deals with a lot of different types and is overkill for our needs. You can see the implementation of our constants in the `AttributeStructure` table, where the different entries in the `Datatype` field correspond to the listing of the data types in the Visual Basic code we entered into the `Globals` module:

```
atString = 0
atLong = 1
atDouble = 2
atDate = 3
atBoolean = 4
```

Now that we've built the relevant parts of the data tier to allow us to store the product data we require, we now need to deal with the parts of the business and presentation tiers that will enable us to manipulate and view the data.

Adding and Viewing Basic Product Information

We're going to take two bites at dealing with the business and presentation tier coding, firstly we'll just look at how we can cope with the product information that is not dynamic and common to each product before we get to grips with the dynamic attributes.

Looking at the common product information gives us a good lead into this whole area; we're going to have to expand the WroxCommerce object model so that it understands the product storage tables in our database, adapt the presentation tier administration tool to allow us to add products to the database and then make sure customers can see the information we've carefully stored.

Try It Out – Expanding the Object Model

1. Return to the WroxCommerce VB project and find the Catalog object, then add the AddProduct method as below:

```
' AddProduct - creates a new product and returns the new ProductID...
Public Function AddProduct(ByVal MfrID As Long, ByVal Name As String, _
            ByVal Details As String, ByVal DepartmentID As Long, _
            ByVal TypeID As Long, ByVal Price As Double, _
            ByVal SupplierID As Long, ByVal Cost As Double, _
            Optional ByVal ImageURL As String, _
            Optional ByVal Description As String) As Long

    ' create a recordset capable of inserting the row...
    Dim NewProduct As New Recordset
    NewProduct.Open "Products", m_utility.DB.DB, adOpenKeyset, adLockOptimistic

    ' insert a new row...
    NewProduct.AddNew

    ' enter the details for the new product...
    NewProduct("MfrID") = MfrID
    NewProduct("Name") = Name
    NewProduct("Details") = Details
    NewProduct("DepartmentID") = DepartmentID
    NewProduct("TypeID") = TypeID
    NewProduct("Price") = Price
    NewProduct("SupplierID") = SupplierID
    NewProduct("Cost") = Cost

    ' enter the optional details...
    If ImageURL <> "" Then NewProduct("ImageURL") = ImageURL
    If Description <> "" Then NewProduct("Description") = Description

    ' update the database...
    NewProduct.Update

    ' return the ID of the new product to the caller...
    AddProduct = NewProduct("ProductID")

    ' cleanup...
    NewProduct.Close
    Set NewProduct = Nothing

End Function
```

The `AddProduct` method is a pretty straightforward way of inserting a new product into the `Products` table. Notice that as parameters to this method, we take all of the required common elements for a product and give the developer the opportunity to add an image URL and the description for the product.

2. In Chapter 5, we created the `GetDepartments` method on the `Catalog` object that was capable of returning all of the departments back to the developer. Now, we're going to duplicate that code to cover the other tables with which the `Products` table has relationships.

You may notice that these next code samples have considerable similarities – cutting and pasting will reduce the workload here!

3. Firstly, let's add the code which relates to the `Products` table to the `Catalog` object:

```
' QueryProducts - primitive to help us get at products...
Private Function QueryProducts(Optional ByVal Where As String, _
        Optional ByVal Order As String = "name", _
        Optional ByVal AsKeyset As Boolean = False) As Recordset
  Set QueryProducts = m_utility.DB.RunQuery("Products", "vProducts", _
                        Where, Order, AsKeyset)
End Function
```

```
' GetProducts - returns the top level store products
Public Function GetProducts(Optional ByVal AsKeyset As Boolean = False) _
                        As Recordset
  Set GetProducts = QueryProducts(, , AsKeyset)
End Function
```

```
' GetProductsInDepartment - returns all the products in the department...
Public Function GetProductsInDepartment(ByVal DepartmentID As Long, _
        Optional ByVal AsKeyset As Boolean = False) As Recordset
  Set GetProductsInDepartment = QueryProducts("DepartmentID=" & _
                        DepartmentID, , AsKeyset)
End Function
```

```
' GetProduct - returns all the products in the department...
Public Function GetProduct(ByVal ProductID As Long, _
        Optional ByVal AsKeyset As Boolean = False) As Recordset
    Set GetProduct = QueryProducts("ProductID=" & ProductID, , AsKeyset)
End Function
```

```
' GetFeaturedProducts - returns the featured products...
Public Function GetFeaturedProducts(ByVal DepartmentID As Long, _
        Optional ByVal AsKeyset As Boolean = False) As Recordset
  Set GetFeaturedProducts = QueryProducts("FeaturedProduct is not null", _
                        "FeaturedProduct", AsKeyset)
End Function
```

4. With the `Products` table handled, we need to write some code to get all of the manufacturers from the `Mfrs` table. Add this to the `Catalog` object as well:

```
' QueryMfrs - primitive to help us get at manufacturers...
Private Function QueryMfrs(Optional ByVal Where As String, _
        Optional ByVal Order As String = "name", _
        Optional ByVal AsKeyset As Boolean = False) As Recordset
```

```
    Set QueryMfrs = m_utility.DB.RunQuery("Mfrs", , Where, Order, AsKeyset)
End Function

' GetMfrs - returns all the manufacturers...
Public Function GetMfrs(Optional ByVal AsKeyset As Boolean = False) As Recordset
    Set GetMfrs = QueryMfrs(, , AsKeyset)
End Function

'GetMfr - returns a single manufacturer...
Public Function GetMfr(ByVal MfrID As Long, _
                Optional ByVal AsKeyset As Boolean = False) _
                As Recordset

    Set GetMfr = QueryMfrs("MfrID=" & MfrID, , _
                            As Keyset)

End Function
```

5. Similarly, we need to add the following code to the `Catalog` object to get all of the different product types from the `Types` table:

```
' QueryTypes - primitive to help us get at types...
Private Function QueryTypes(Optional ByVal Where As String, _
            Optional ByVal Order As String = "name", _
            Optional ByVal AsKeyset As Boolean = False) As Recordset
    Set QueryTypes = m_utility.DB.RunQuery("Types", , Where, Order, AsKeyset)
End Function

' GetTypes - returns all the types...
Public Function GetTypes(Optional ByVal AsKeyset As Boolean = False) As Recordset
    Set GetTypes = QueryTypes(, , AsKeyset)
End Function
```

6. Finally, add this code to retrieve the suppliers from the `Suppliers` table to the `Catalog` object as well:

```
' QuerySuppliers - primitive to help us get at Suppliers...
Private Function QuerySuppliers(Optional ByVal Where As String, _
            Optional ByVal Order As String = "name", _
            Optional ByVal AsKeyset As Boolean = False) As Recordset
    Set QuerySuppliers = m_utility.DB.RunQuery("Suppliers", , _
                            Where, Order, AsKeyset)
End Function

' GetSuppliers - returns all the suppliers...
Public Function GetSuppliers(Optional ByVal AsKeyset As Boolean = False) _
                            As Recordset
    Set GetSuppliers = QuerySuppliers(, , AsKeyset)
End Function
```

How It Works

The `AddProduct` method starts by creating a new ADO recordset that's pointed at the `Products` table on the current connection. The `AddNew` method (of the recordset) tells the recordset that a new row needs to be inserted into whatever table it's pointing at – in this case, the `Products` table:

```
' AddProduct - creates a new product and returns the new ProductID...
Public Function AddProduct(ByVal MfrID As Long, ByVal Name As String, _
            ByVal Details As String, ByVal DepartmentID As Long, _
            ByVal TypeID As Long, ByVal Price As Double, _
            ByVal SupplierID As Long, ByVal Cost As Double, _
            Optional ByVal ImageURL As String, _
            Optional ByVal Description As String) As Long

    ' create a recordset capable of inserting the row...
    Dim NewProduct As New Recordset
    NewProduct.Open "Products", m_utility.DB.DB, adOpenKeyset, adLockOptimistic

    ' insert a new row...
    NewProduct.AddNew
```

We describe the core details first, using the same notation to insert data into the recordset as we typically use to retrieve data from it. It's important to note that SQL Server won't physically write the row to the table until we call the `Update` method later in the function, so effectively these changes are cached until that time:

```
    ' enter the details for the new product...
    NewProduct("MfrID") = MfrID
    NewProduct("Name") = Name
    NewProduct("Details") = Details
    NewProduct("DepartmentID") = DepartmentID
    NewProduct("TypeID") = TypeID
    NewProduct("Price") = Price
    NewProduct("SupplierID") = SupplierID
    NewProduct("Cost") = Cost
```

After we've described the core details, we go ahead and describe the optional details. If we don't specifically assign values for a column in the new row, the default as defined in the table definition will be used. Failing that, null will be assigned. So in this case, if we don't have an `ImageURL`, then `ImageURL` will be set to null in the new row:

```
    ' enter the optional details...
    If ImageURL <> "" Then NewProduct("ImageURL") = ImageURL
    If Description <> "" Then NewProduct("Description") = Description
```

Finally, we tell the recordset to update itself, which performs the action of physically writing the row to the disk. SQL Server will automatically assign a value to any identity field and if that identity field is marked as a primary key (as it is here), we can retrieve that new ID back by querying the recordset at this time. This is exactly what we do immediately after the update, passing the new ID back out of the method:

```
    ' update the database...
    NewProduct.Update

    ' return the ID of the new product to the caller...
    AddProduct = NewProduct("ProductID")

    ' cleanup...
    NewProduct.Close
    Set NewProduct = Nothing

End Function
```

Moving on to the methods we set up for returning data from the tables, let's just concern ourselves with the `Product` table related code (as it contains code common to the other methods and a few extra bits).

Firstly, we create another primitive function to run queries on the `Products` table (just like we did when we built the `GetDepartments` method in the last chapter). Also, we pass in the name of our `vProducts` view to this function, so the `RunQuery` method of `DB` will attempt to use this view by default. This means when we try to use the recordset returned by the `GetProducts` method we'll be able to query the resulting recordset for things like `MfrName`, `SalesContactEmail` and so on.

```
' QueryProducts - primitive to help us get at products...
Private Function QueryProducts(Optional ByVal Where As String, _
            Optional ByVal Order As String = "name", _
            Optional ByVal AsKeyset As Boolean = False) As Recordset
  Set QueryProducts = m_utility.DB.RunQuery("Products", "vProducts", _
                        Where, Order, AsKeyset)
End Function

' GetProducts - returns the top level store products
Public Function GetProducts(Optional ByVal AsKeyset As Boolean = False) _
                        As Recordset
  Set GetProducts = QueryProducts(, , AsKeyset)
End Function
```

In this section, we have a `GetProductsInDepartment` method to help us access the products by department:

```
' GetProductsInDepartment - returns all the products in the department...
Public Function GetProductsInDepartment(ByVal DepartmentID As Long, _
            Optional ByVal AsKeyset As Boolean = False) As Recordset
  Set GetProductsInDepartment = QueryProducts("DepartmentID=" & _
                        DepartmentID, , AsKeyset)
End Function
```

This is a little bit different to what we've seen already in that we're actually passing in a snippet of a `WHERE` clause to `QueryProducts`. This action will prompt the `RunQuery` method (that `QueryProducts` refers to) to append a `WHERE` clause to the query, resulting in something like:

```
SELECT * FROM vProducts WHERE DepartmentID=27
```

The `GetFeaturedProducts` method is inserted for future use:

```
' GetFeaturedProducts - returns the featured products...
Public Function GetFeaturedProducts(ByVal DepartmentID As Long, _
            Optional ByVal AsKeyset As Boolean = False) As Recordset
  Set GetFeaturedProducts = QueryProducts("FeaturedProduct is not null", _
                        "FeaturedProduct", AsKeyset)
End Function
```

To start adding products to our database, we'll have to tweak our administration tools.

Adding Products Using the Administration Tool

In Chapter 5 we put together the framework for our administration tool and used it to add departments to our database. Now we have to revisit this tool to create a form that lets us add products.

Try It Out – Adding Products through the Presentation Tier

1. In our Visual InterDev Jo's Coffee project, open `admin/default.asp`. Add this code to the `Select Case` statement we built before to build the form to capture the new product's information:

```
<!-- End the table -->
</table></center>
</form>
```

```asp
<% ' do we want to add a product to the database...?
case "addproduct" %>

    <!-- create a form -->
    <form action="<%=request("script_name")%>" method=post>
    <center><table cellspacing=0 cellpadding=3>
    <tr><td colspan=2 class=heading align=center>Add Product<br><br></td></tr>

    <!-- add the required fields... -->
    <tr><td class=heading>Manufacturer: </td>
    <td>
    <% RenderSelect Select_Mfrs, "mfr" %>
    </td></tr>

    <tr><td class=heading>Name: </td>
    <td>
    <input type=text name=name value="<%=request("name")%>">
    </td></tr>

    <tr><td class=heading>Details: </td>
    <td>
    <textarea name=details rows=2 cols=40><%=request("details")%></textarea>
    </td></tr>

    <tr><td class=heading>Department: </td>
    <td>
    <% RenderSelect Select_Departments, "department" %>
    </td></tr>

    <tr><td class=heading>Type: </td>
    <td>
    <% RenderSelect Select_Types, "type" %>
    </td></tr>

    <tr><td class=heading>Price: </td>
    <td>
    <input type=text name=price value="<%=request("price")%>" size=10>
    </td></tr>

    <tr><td class=heading>Supplier: </td>
    <td>
```

171

```
        <% RenderSelect Select_Suppliers, "supplier" %>
        </td></tr>

        <tr><td class=heading>Cost: </td>
        <td>
        <input type=text name=cost value="<%=request("cost")%>" size=10>
        </td></tr>

        <!-- add the optional fields... -->
        <tr><td class=std>Image URL: </td>
        <td>
        <input type=text name=imageurl value="<%=request("imageurl")%>">
        </td></tr>

        <tr><td class=std>Description: </td>
        <td>
        <textarea name=desc rows=5 cols=40><%=request("description")%></textarea>
        </td></tr>

        <!-- button... -->
        <tr><td colspan=2 align=center>
        <br><input type=submit value="Add Product">
        </td></tr>

        <!-- hidden fields -->
        <input type=hidden name=savenewproduct value=1>

        <!-- end the table -->
        </table></center>
        </form>
```

```
<% case else
```

2. As we want to use the page to deal with another three tables, we need another three constants defined globally, so make the following additions to site.asp:

```
Const Select_Departments = 0
Const Select_Mfrs = 1
Const Select_Types = 2
Const Select_Suppliers = 3
```

3. Next we add some more code to the RenderSelect helper function in site.asp:

```
' select the items from the db...
Dim query, IDColumn, NameColumn
Select Case TableID

    ' select out departments...
    Case Select_Departments
        Set query = Visit.Catalog.GetAllDepartments
        IDColumn = "DepartmentID"
        NameColumn = "Name"

    ' select out manufacturers...
    Case Select_Mfrs
```

```
      Set query = Visit.Catalog.GetMfrs
      IDColumn = "MfrID"
      NameColumn = "Name"

   ' select out types...
   Case Select_Types
      Set query = Visit.Catalog.GetTypes
      IDColumn = "TypeID"
      NameColumn = "Name"

   ' select out suppliers...
   Case Select_Suppliers
      Set query = Visit.Catalog.GetSuppliers
      IDColumn = "SupplierID"
      NameColumn = "Name"
```

```
End Select
```

4. To open the form that lets us add products, we need to edit our `admin/default.asp` page. Add this menu option now:

```
' render the menu options...
RenderOption "Add Department", "adddepartment"
RenderOption "Add Product", "addproduct"
```

5. Next, add the product images to a folder called p.

6. Finally, we need to facilitate storing the product that we have entered into the page. Add the following code to the top of `admin/default.asp` after the `If...Then` statement that checks if we're trying to add a new department:

```
      NewDepartmentID = Visit.Catalog.AddDepartment(Request("name"), _
                      Request("departmentidp"))
   end if
```

```
End If
```

```
' are we trying to save a new product?
If Request("savenewproduct") <> "" Then

   ' we won't test this, we'll just try and add it...
   Dim NewProductID
   NewProductID = Visit.Catalog.AddProduct(Request("mfr"), Request("name"), _
        Request("details"), Request("department"), Request("type"), _
        Request("price"), Request("supplier"), Request("cost"), _
        Request("imageurl"), Request("desc"))

End If
```

```
%>
```

7. Next, we'll test our new form by trying to add a new product. *Before you open the administration page, make sure you get the* `WroxCommerce` *project running in Visual Basic.*

Enter the details for a Gaggia espresso machine into the administration page as shown here and select Add Product:

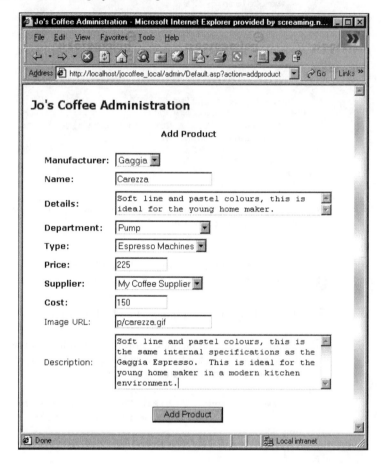

How It Works

That HTML form used to collect the new product information is pretty basic, so we won't go into too much detail here. Suffice to say we create a centered table and use each row to represent one field that we want to be able to edit, such as name, price, description, etc. We also use a HIDDEN field called `savenewproduct` to determine if we're supposed to be creating a new product when we run the page again. In the FORM tag we use the `Request("script_name")` server variable to create a page that calls itself when the submit button is pressed.

Again this form doesn't do anything with dynamic attributes – we're going to cover dynamic attribute editing after we've engineered our front-end ASP code to present the products to the visitor.

Within the page, we've again used the `RenderSelect` function that we originally used in the last chapter for the Add Department page. Originally, we only built the function to create a list of the departments in the database; here, we've modified it to do the same work with the manufacturers, types and suppliers tables.

So, when the user clicks **Add Product**, we look for the existence of the hidden savenewproduct field to determine if the form was filled in. To keep our example code simple, we don't check for the existence of the required field, or check to see if the Price and Cost fields were entered as valid values, we just attempt to call the AddProduct method of Catalog. The method inserts a new row into the Products table (if you access the vProducts view in SQL Server Enterprise Manager you'll be able to see how the new product is related to the supplier, manufacturer and type you selected).

Viewing the Products

Now we've entered the information, we need to make sure our visitors can read it.

To enable display we just need to make a few alterations to the dept.asp code; however, we do need to ensure prices are presented in the correct currency.

Try It Out – Viewing Products through the Presentation Tier

1. To ensure that the correct currency is displayed add this code to the bottom of site.asp:

```
Function FormatPrice(price)
    FormatPrice = "£" & FormatNumber(price, 2)
End Function
```

2. For displaying the items add this code to dept.asp, immediately after the part where we render the child departments:

```
End If

Children.Close
Set Children = Nothing

' now we need to show the products...
Dim Products
Set Products = Visit.Catalog.GetProductsInDepartment(Department("DepartmentID"))
If Not Products.EOF Then

    ' table header...
    Response.Write "<table width=100% cellspacing=0 cellpadding=0 border=0>"

    ' create somewhere to hold the details...
    Dim id, name, prodname, details, price, imageurl

    ' loop the items...
    num = 0
    Do While Not Products.EOF

        ' capture the details...
        id = Products("ProductID")
        name = Products("MfrName")
        prodname = Products("Name")
        details = Products("Details")
        price = Products("Price")
        imageurl = Products("ImageURL")
```

```
        ' add a separator line...
        Response.Write "<tr><td height=5></td></tr>"
        Response.Write "<tr><td height=1 colspan=4 bgcolor=#000000></td></tr>"
        Response.Write "<tr><td height=5></td></tr>"

        ' render the item's image...
        Response.Write "<tr><td valign=top>"
        If imageurl <> "" then
            Response.Write "<a href="""
            Response.Write "detail.asp?id=" & id
            Response.Write """>"
            Response.Write "<img src="""
            Response.Write imageurl
            Response.Write """ border=0>"
            Response.Write "</a>"
        End If
        Response.Write "</td>"

        ' render the item's name and short description...
        Response.Write "<td class=small valign=top>"
        Response.Write "<font class=heading>"
        Response.Write "<a href="""
        Response.Write "detail.asp?id=" & id
        Response.Write """>"
        Response.write name & " " & prodname
        Response.Write "</a>"
        Response.Write "</font><br>"
        Response.Write details
        Response.Write "</td>"

        ' render a space...
        Response.Write "<td>  </td>"

        ' render the item's price
        Response.Write "<td class=small align=right valign=top>"
        Response.Write "<font class=bigheading>"
        Response.Write FormatPrice(price)
        Response.Write "</font><br>"
        Response.Write "<a href="""
        Response.Write "basket.asp?id=" & id
        Response.Write """>"
        Response.Write "Buy it!"
        Response.Write "</a>"
        Response.Write "</td></tr>"

        ' next
        Products.MoveNext
        num = num + 1

    Loop

    ' table footer...
    Response.Write "</table>"

End If
Products.Close
Set Products = Nothing
```

```
        End if

        Department.Close
        Set Department = Nothing

        %>
```

How It Works

Our currency problem is that we want to show prices in the currency local to Jo's Coffee (Sterling) but the VBScript function `FormatCurrency` (which we would normally use) formats to the currency of whatever locale IIS is running in. Our site will be hosted on a server in the United States, so we need to make sure that we have a special function that always uses the £ symbol:

```
Function FormatPrice(price)
    FormatPrice = "£" & FormatNumber(price, 2)
End Function
```

This method is then used in the display code:

```
            ' render the item's price
            Response.Write "<td class=small align=right valign=top>"
            Response.Write "<font class=bigheading>"
            Response.Write FormatPrice(price)
            Response.Write "</font><br>"
            Response.Write "<a href="""
            Response.Write "basket.asp?id=" & id
            Response.Write """>"
            Response.Write "Buy it!"
            Response.Write "</a>"
            Response.Write "</td></tr>"
```

The main display code is fairly straightforward; we use `GetProductsInDepartment` to find all the products that are in the department we're looking at (and we determine the department ID by asking the `Response` object for its `ID` value), then we build a table and loop through each product displaying the name (made up of the manufacturer's name and the name of the product), the price, and the brief description that's stored in the `Details` column.

You can click on both the product name and the image to be taken to `detail.asp`, and you can also click on a link called **Buy it!** to be taken to `basket.asp`. We'll be building this `detail.asp` in the next section, and `basket.asp` in Chapter 7.

If we drill down into the site until we find the Pump department, we can see our new product:

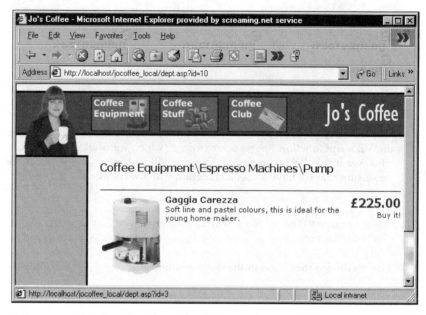

We made some important design decisions when building this page, so let's make them explicit now.

Design Decisions

We can split our design points up into two areas:

❑   Product Information

❑   Purchase Information

Product Information

It's important we display an image of the product. Society still has a history of shopping in environments where they can see and feel the products. While the latter isn't currently possible in an online shopping environment, we can show a picture (or even a video – although we're not going to tackle that in this book) of the product to the visitor. Traditionally, people are more comfortable exploring products when they can see an image of them on their screen.

This technique is complemented in the use of the `Details` column that's common to all products in the store. By creating a one or two sentence summary of what the product is, we can reinforce any impression they get from the picture with an extra level of detail.

In fact, the `dept.asp` will display a list of all the products in the department, whereas the `detail.asp` that we're yet to build will display all the extra attribute information and in-depth product commentary. So why do we need the image here, as well as on the detail page? Well, even when scanning a list of products, visitors still need to see the product in question, just like customers in an offline environment will look at entire shelf and *zoom-in* to products which interest them.
We've decided to make both the image and the product name click through to the detail page. This is simply convention – people expect that clicking on an image of a product will drill deeper down into the site to show a page dedicated to that product.

Purchase Information

The price we display in a large, clear manner; our aim is to impress upon the visitor that we're confident with the price (this technique is actually well used in offline retail environments). If we buried the price, or make it less obvious, the visitor may get the impression that we're not confident our price will make the grade.

While we're on the subject of price, it's critically important in an online environment that you don't use 'Price on Application', or 'Please Ask' pricing. In e-commerce sites, the *click-off* probability (where people abandon your site and click-off onto a competitor's site) is extremely high. You must share as much as you know about the product, especially the price and stock levels. If a visitor cannot find what they need to know without hassle, they'll simply abandon you and move on.

Another interesting thing on this page is the Buy It! button which we hope will be of use to returning visitors. Once we have dealt with the issues of displaying the dynamic attributes on the detail.asp page we'll be putting a Buy It! button there as well.

Our reasoning for putting this button in two places is that visitors who are investigating our offering are extremely unlikely to make a buy decision the moment they click on the appropriate department – even if they have decided on the exact product they want. Before committing, they will need to make sure your offer is as it seems by checking as much information as possible against information gathered from offline sources, other online sources (including competitors) and intuition. They will do this by clicking through to the detail page where they will expect to see a page dedicated to sharing everything that you as an e-tailer know about the product. If convinced, they can buy from that page; however, if they do go off and look elsewhere, putting a Buy It! button on the dept.asp page saves the returning visitor the effort of drilling down to the details page to place an order.

OK, now we come to the point where we confront the issue of dynamic attribute handling.

Adding and Viewing Product Detail

As discussed, when our visitor finds something that looks interesting, they'll attempt to drill down to find more information. This is the point at which we'll call upon our application to display the extra product attributes we have stored. To cope with this we'll find it convenient to expand our object model still further (indeed in this section we will add another object to the model) and make additions to our presentation layer.

The Product Object and Detail Presentation

Up to this point, we've used our WroxCommerce object model as little more than a device for running pre-programmed queries. In fact, it only has three individual objects.

When we use traditional object models, there's often a degree of *richness* whereby you can run methods or request properties that return other objects that you can then ask to do stuff. We've now reached a point where it makes sense to create a Product object that we can ask to do things like return a list of its attributes, add itself to the shopping cart and so on.

A single Product object will represent one row in the Products table or, to put it another way, one item in the site's catalog. We won't create this object using Server.CreateObject or something similar – rather we'll request properly configured objects, primarily through a method on the Catalog object. You may remember from Chapter 3 that this type of object can be termed a **Data** object within the context of our object model.

Try It Out – Creating the Product Object

1. Open the `WroxCommerce` project, create a new class module and call it **Product**, then enter this initial code:

```
Option Explicit

' use IUtility to call back into the Visit and Database objects...
Private m_utility As IUtility

' somewhere to hold information on the product we represent...
Private m_ID As Long
Private m_MfrID As Long
Private m_MfrName As String
Private m_MfrURL As String
Private m_Name As String
Private m_DepartmentID As Long
Private m_DepartmentName As String
Private m_Details As String
Private m_Description As String
Private m_DescriptionLoaded As Boolean
Private m_TypeID As Long
Private m_TypeName As String
Private m_Price As Double
Private m_SupplierID As Long
Private m_SupplierName As String
Private m_Cost As Double
Private m_StockExpected As Long
Private m_ImageURL As String
Private m_IsLoaded As Boolean

' Configure - set up IUtility...
Public Sub Configure(ByVal utility As IUtility, ByVal ID As Long)

    ' hold the utility object...
    Set m_utility = utility

    ' store the ID...
    m_ID = ID

End Sub
```

2. Next we need to make sure that we can create these objects; remember from our discussion of the object model in Chapter 3 that our design dictates that we'll do this through the `Catalog` **service** object. Open the `Catalog` object, and add the `GetProductObject` method as shown:

```
' GetProductObject - returns a configured Product object for the given id...
Public Function GetProductObject(ByVal id As Long) As Product

    ' create the new object...
    Set GetProductObject = New Product

    ' configure the new object. we pass through our own m_utility object...
    GetProductObject.Configure m_utility, id

End Function
```

3. Now let's return to the `Product` object and add the methods that will enable us to return common attributes. Firstly we set the `ID` property, so in `Product` add:

```
' ID property...
Public Property Get ID() As Long
   ID = m_ID
End Property
```

4. Next we need to put in place a method in `Product` that will allow us to load the information that isn't automatically held when the object is created:

```
' CheckLoad - makes sure the property values have been loaded...
Private Sub CheckLoad()

   ' have we already loaded?
   If m_IsLoaded = False Then


      ' get the record back from the Catalog object...
      Dim Query As Recordset
      Set Query = m_utility.Visit.Catalog.GetProduct(m_ID)
      If Not Query.EOF Then


         ' get the values back...
         m_MfrID = Query("MfrID")
         m_MfrName = Query("MfrName")
         m_MfrURL = Query("MfrURL")
         m_Name = Query("Name")
         m_Details = Query("Details")
         m_DepartmentID = Query("DepartmentID")
         m_DepartmentName = Query("DepartmentName")
         m_TypeID = Query("TypeID")
         m_Price = Query("Price")
         m_SupplierID = Query("SupplierID")
         m_SupplierName = Query("SupplierName")
         m_Cost = Query("Cost")
         m_StockExpected = Query("StockExpected")

         ' get back optional values...
         If Not IsNull(Query("ImageURL")) Then m_ImageURL = Query("ImageURL")

      End If
      Query.Close
      Set Query = Nothing

      ' flag...
      m_IsLoaded = True


   End If

End Sub
```

5. We can now create the other properties; again in `Product` add:

```
' Name property...
Public Property Get Name() As String

   ' see if the data has been loaded...
   CheckLoad

   ' return the name back...
   Name = m_Name

End Property
```

```
' MfrName property...
Public Property Get MfrName() As String

   ' see if the data has been loaded...
   CheckLoad

   ' return the name back...
   MfrName = m_MfrName

End Property
```

```
' Details property...
Public Property Get Details() As String
   CheckLoad
   Details = m_Details
End Property
```

```
' Price property...
Public Property Get Price() As Double
   CheckLoad
   Price = m_Price
End Property
```

```
' ImageURL property...
Public Property Get ImageURL() As String
   CheckLoad
   ImageURL = m_ImageURL
End Property
```

```
' StockExpected property...
Public Property Get StockExpected() As Long
   CheckLoad
   StockExpected = m_StockExpected
End Property
```

6. We'll handle the `Description` property differently – if there's no description specifically set against the object, we'll use the value against `Details` instead, so our last addition to `Product` in this section is:

```
' Description - returns the item description...
Public Property Get Description() As String

    ' have we loaded it?
    If m_DescriptionLoaded = False Then

        ' run a query...
        Dim Query As Recordset
        Set Query = m_utility.DB.DB.Execute("select Description from " & _
            "Products where ProductID=" & m_ID & " and Description is not null")
        If Not Query.EOF Then
            m_Description = Query("Description")
        Else
            m_Description = Details
        End If
        Query.Close
        Set Query = Nothing

        ' flag...
        m_DescriptionLoaded = True

    End If

    ' send it back...
    Description = m_Description

End Property
```

How It Works

The initial code may be mostly recognizable from the `Catalog` object. In fact, we can now say that it's convention that all of our objects have a `Configure` method that allows other objects in the model to pass through references to the `Visit` object, the database services and anything else we feel like making the `IUtility` interface do. However, in this example we also want to use the `Configure` method as a way of telling the new `Product` object which row in the `Products` table it actually represents, hence the `ID` parameter:

```
Option Explicit

' use IUtility to call back into the Visit and Database objects...
Private m_utility As IUtility

' Configure - set up IUtility...
Public Sub Configure(ByVal utility As IUtility, ByVal ID As Long)

    ' hold the utility object...
    Set m_utility = utility

    ' store the ID...
    m_ID = ID

End Sub
```

Additionally, we've added a bundle of private member variables to this class. We'll be using the Product object to represent a single instance of a product as we work with the object model. So, imagine we're working with a product object representing the Gaggia Coffee Classic and we want the price. The first time any of the attributes of the objects are requested, the product object will populate the member variables with the details from the database. However, it's important to note that we set the m_ID member variable to the same value as passed through as the ID parameter:

```
' somewhere to hold information on the product we represent...
Private m_ID As Long
Private m_MfrID As Long
Private m_MfrName As String
Private m_MfrURL As String
Private m_Name As String
Private m_DepartmentID As Long
Private m_DepartmentName As String
Private m_Details As String
Private m_Description As String
Private m_DescriptionLoaded As Boolean
Private m_TypeID As Long
Private m_TypeName As String
Private m_Price As Double
Private m_SupplierID As Long
Private m_SupplierName As String
Private m_Cost As Double
Private m_StockExpected As Long
Private m_ImageURL As String
Private m_IsLoaded As Boolean
```

This is because we want to let ASP developers create instances of these Product objects through methods like:

```
<%
    Dim Product
    Set Product = Visit.Catalog.GetProductObject(Request("ProductID"))
%>
```

We then moved on to code the GetProductObject method for the Catalog object. It works by firstly creating a new instance of a Product object. At this point, the object does not have a way of getting to the database or other objects in the model because its m_utility member is not set. So, once we've created the object, we call its Configure method passing in a reference to the Catalog object's own m_utility and the product ID that was requested through the ID parameter:

```
' GetProductObject - returns a configured Product object for the given id...
Public Function GetProductObject(ByVal id As Long) As Product

    ' create the new object...
    Set GetProductObject = New Product

    ' configure the new object. we pass through our own m_utility object...
    GetProductObject.Configure m_utility, id

End Function
```

In our discussion of good distributed application techniques, we mentioned that it's always best to create things the moment before you need them and get rid of them the moment you've finished. This is why in our `Configure` method for `Product`, we didn't open a query and capture any of the other information about the item we could determine from the `Products` table. Instead, we just hold the ID and we can use that to get the extra information when needed. Hence the ID property is quite straightforward; however, the other properties all make use of the `CheckLoad` method.

The `CheckLoad` method is responsible for this *just-in-time* loading effect that we want for most of the object properties. Basically, when the developer asks for the `Name` property, we first call `CheckLoad` (which sets the values for the `m_Name`, `m_MfrName`, etc. member variables) and then return the value from the relevant member variable. It's always best to do things on a just-in-time basis as it increases the scalability of the system. So, instead of always dragging everything back from the database whenever the object is created, we defer the query until such time as it's absolutely necessary. This prevents us from running queries when they are not needed (such as when the object is created, no attributes are requested and then it is deleted), and makes the total length of time that the data is taking up memory shorter (such as when several milliseconds pass between object creation and the first request for the attribute).

Let's have a look at the `CheckLoad` method to see how it works. Our first job is to see if it's already been called. If it has, we assume that everything's been loaded into memory; there's nothing to do, so we exit the function as fast as possible.

If it hasn't, we have some work to do; we use the `GetProduct` method on the `Catalog` object to return a recordset representing the item in which we're interested. Notice how we use the `m_ID` member variable, which we set when the `Configure` method was called:

```
' get the record back from the Catalog object...
Dim Query As Recordset
Set Query = m_utility.Visit.Catalog.GetProduct(m_ID)
If Not Query.EOF Then
```

Then we retrieve everything from the row and store it in the member variables. After we've closed the recordset, we set `m_IsLoaded` to `True`, so that next time `CheckLoad` is called, the method will exit without calling into the database:

```
' get the values back...
m_MfrID = Query("MfrID")
m_MfrName = Query("MfrName")
m_MfrURL = Query("MfrURL")
m_Name = Query("Name")
m_Details = Query("Details")
m_DepartmentID = Query("DepartmentID")
m_DepartmentName = Query("DepartmentName")
m_TypeID = Query("TypeID")
m_Price = Query("Price")
m_SupplierID = Query("SupplierID")
m_SupplierName = Query("SupplierName")
m_Cost = Query("Cost")
m_StockExpected = Query("StockExpected")
```

```
       ' get back optional values...
       If Not IsNull(Query("ImageURL")) Then m_ImageURL = Query("ImageURL")

    End If
    Query.Close
    Set Query = Nothing

    ' flag...
    m_IsLoaded = True
```

In CheckLoad, we don't get back the value for Description, as this could be very large. Instead, we run a separate query for this as described below. For the other properties that we've added in (to save on tedium we only created a few of the properties we could return) we make use of the CheckLoad method, for instance for the Name property we have:

```
' Name property...
Public Property Get Name() As String

   ' see if the data has been loaded...
   CheckLoad

   ' return the name back...
   Name = m_Name

End Property
```

As previously mentioned for the Description property, if there's no description specifically set against the object, we use the value against Details instead. What we're doing here is making a separate call to the database to get back the description when it's specifically requested. This is because the description may be extremely large, and we don't want it bloating memory if we only want the price, manufacturer, or whatever, of the object.

You'll notice that the function is very similar in nature to the one we saw previously – a flag (in this case, m_DescriptionLoaded) is checked to see if the function has been called before and, if it hasn't, a query is executed to retrieve the required value and, if it has, the function is exited as quickly as possible. In each case, the value stored in m_Description is returned to the caller.

```
   ' Description - returns the item description...
   Public Property Get Description() As String

   ' have we loaded it?
   If m_DescriptionLoaded = False Then

     ' run a query...
     Dim Query As Recordset
     Set Query = m_utility.DB.DB.Execute("select Description from " & _
       "Products where ProductID=" & m_ID & " and Description is not null")
     If Not Query.EOF Then
       m_Description = Query("Description")
     Else
       m_Description = Details
     End If
```

```
     Query.Close
     Set Query = Nothing

     ' flag...
     m_DescriptionLoaded = True

  End If

  ' send it back...
  Description = m_Description

End Property
```

With our new `Product` object in place, we can create our `detail.asp` page.

Try It Out – Creating detail.asp

1. Open the JoCoffee Visual InterDev project and create a new ASP page called `detail.asp`. Copy the code out of `template.asp` so the two files look the same.

2. As for `dept.asp`, when the visitor requests this page, they'll also pass through the ID of the product they're interested in, so enter this code into `detail.asp`:

```
<!-- #include file="start.asp" -->
```

```
<%
   ' load the product...
   Dim Product
   Set Product = Visit.Catalog.GetProductObject(Request("id"))
%>
```

```
<%
   ' close the product...
   Set Product = Nothing
%>
```

```
<!-- #include file="end.asp" -->
```

That's all the code we need to create an instance of the `Product` object we're interested in, and then clean it up again when we're not. Notice how we use ASP's `Request` object to pass in the ID we're interested in through any of the five request collections. Typically, the `QueryString` collection would contain the value we're interested in.

3. As it stands this page doesn't do too much, so add the following:

```
<%
   ' load the product...
   Dim Product
   Set Product = Visit.Catalog.GetProductObject(Request("id"))
%>
```

```
<table width=100% cellspacing=0 cellpadding=0 border=0>

   <!-- add the heading -->
   <tr><td colspan=5 class=bigheading>
   <%
      Dim mfrname, prodname
```

```
    mfrname =Product.MfrName
    prodname = Product.Name
    Response.Write mfrname & " " & prodname
%>
</td></tr>

<!-- add a spacer -->
<tr><td><br></td></tr>

<!-- add the product image... -->
<tr><td valign=top><%
    If Product.ImageURL <> "" Then
        Response.Write "<img src="""
        Response.Write Product.ImageURL
        Response.Write """>"
    End If
%></td>

<!-- product description, and other stuff... -->
<td>   </td>
<td valign=top class=heading>
<%

    ' render the description
    Response.Write Product.Description
    Response.Write "<br><br>"

%>
</td>

<!-- product price and cart button... -->
<td>   </td>
<td align=right valign=top class=heading>
<font class=bigheading><%=FormatPrice(Product.Price)%></font>
<br>
<a href="basket.asp?id=<%=Product.ID%>">Buy it!</a>
</td></tr>

</table>

<%
    ' close the product...
    Set Product = Nothing
%>
```

We start our code example by using the GetProductObject method to retrieve a Product object referencing the product with the ID specified in the id query string variable. We then create a simple HTML table and use the MfrName and Name properties of the product object to write the full product name to the browser. As MfrName is called first, it's at this point that CheckLoad is called and all of the product information, minus the description, is loaded from the database into the object. This means that when Name is called, the name is already loaded into the member variable and can simply be returned. We also have some code in there to see if an image has been specified, and we also write out the description, price and a Buy It! button.

4. Let's test our handiwork; make sure you're running the WroxCommerce VB project, then attempt to view the details for the **Gaggia Carezza**. Here's what you should see:

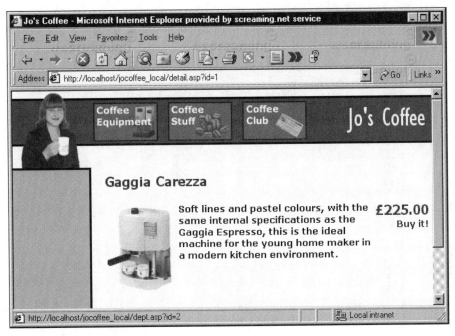

So far this isn't much different to what dept.asp does. But now, we can start working towards getting the dynamic attributes working.

Supporting Dynamic Attributes

We're now turning into the home straight; we have to expand the functionality of the Product object to enable it to retrieve all attributes and facilitate retrieval and setting of individual attributes, then enable our presentation layer to display this information.

Try It Out – Enabling the Product Object

1. Let's return to the WroxCommerce VB project and add the Attributes property to the Product object:

```
' Attributes - returns a list of the attributes...
Public Property Get Attributes() As Recordset

    ' run a query to get all of the attributes for this object back,
    ' even if there are no attributes specifically set...
    Set Attributes = m_utility.DB.DB.Execute("select * from vAttributes " & _
            "where typeid=" & m_TypeID & " and (ProductID=" & ID & _
            " or ProductID is null) order by Priority")

End Property
```

2. Now we can retrieve a list of all the attributes, let's get to grips with getting and setting attribute data. Firstly, add this method to the `Product` object which returns the value of the appropriate `Datatype` column:

```
' GetAttributeType - returns the data type of the attribute...
Public Function GetAttributeType(ByVal StructureID As Long) As Long

    ' query it...
    Dim Query As Recordset
    Set Query = m_utility.DB.DB.Execute("select Datatype from " & _
            "AttributeStructure where StructureID=" & _
            StructureID)

    ' is it valid?
    If Not Query.EOF Then
        GetAttributeType = Query("Datatype")
    Else
        GetAttributeType = atInvalid
    End If

    ' cleanup...
    Query.Close
    Set Query = Nothing

End Function
```

3. Now that we have a way of determining which row we want to save our data into, we can write an `Attrib` property that will allow us to get and set attribute data. First of all, the `Get` part:

```
' Attrib - gets the value for an attribute...
Public Property Get Attrib(ByVal StructureID As Long) As Variant

    ' we need to select out the appropriate value...
    Dim Query As Recordset
    Set Query = m_utility.DB.DB.Execute("select * from vAttributes " & _
            "where ProductID=" & ID & " and StructureID=" & StructureID)
    If Not Query.EOF Then

        ' which column do we want?
        Select Case Query("Datatype")

            Case atString
                If Not IsNull(Query("StringValue")) Then
                    Attrib = Query("StringValue")
                End If

            Case atLong
                If Not IsNull(Query("LongValue")) Then
                    Attrib = Query("LongValue")
                End If

            Case atDouble
                If Not IsNull(Query("DoubleValue")) Then
                    Attrib = Query("DoubleValue")
                End If
```

```
        Case atDate
          If Not IsNull(Query("DateValue")) Then
            Attrib = Query("DateValue")
          End If

        Case atBoolean
          If Not IsNull(Query("BooleanValue")) Then
            Attrib = Query("BooleanValue")
          End If

      End Select

    End If
    Query.Close
    Set Query = Nothing

End Property
```

4. Then, the `Let` part:

```
' Attrib - sets a value for an attribute...
Public Property Let Attrib(ByVal StructureID As Long, ByVal newval As Variant)

    ' if we're trying to set an empty value, we may as well delete the row...
    If IsEmpty(newval) Then

        ' delete it...
        m_utility.DB.DB.Execute "delete from Attributes where ProductID=" & _
                        ID & " and StructureID=" & StructureID


    Else

        ' try to select the attribute we want...
        Dim SetAttrib As New Recordset
        SetAttrib.Open "select * from Attributes where ProductID=" & _
            ID & " and StructureID=" & StructureID, m_utility.DB.DB, _
            adOpenKeyset, adLockOptimistic
        If SetAttrib.EOF Then

            ' there's not one there already, so create one!
            SetAttrib.AddNew
            SetAttrib("ProductID") = ID
            SetAttrib("StructureID") = StructureID

        End If


        ' set the value...
        Select Case GetAttributeType(StructureID)

          Case atString
            SetAttrib("StringValue") = newval
          Case atLong
            SetAttrib("LongValue") = newval
          Case atDouble
            SetAttrib("DoubleValue") = newval
```

```
      Case atDate
        SetAttrib("DateValue") = newval
      Case atBoolean
        SetAttrib("BooleanValue") = newval

    End Select

    ' update the row...
    SetAttrib.Update

    ' close
    SetAttrib.Close
    Set SetAttrib = Nothing

  End If

End Property
```

How It Works

The Attributes property we initially add simply runs a database query to select rows from the vAttributes view we built earlier where we know the product type, and we also know the product ID. The vAttributes view was deliberately structured (using an outer join) so that it will always return a complete set of attributes for the product, even if not all attributes have been set for the product.

Before we turned our attention to building the Attrib property for getting and setting attribute data (incidentally we couldn't use the word *Attribute* for the property because this is a VB reserved word) we added the GetAttributeType method. This method queries the AttributeStructure table to find out what data type is accepted by the attribute we're trying to set. This method will also tell us if we're trying to set an invalid attribute by virtue of the fact we'll receive atInvalid if we pass this an unknown attribute.

This code works by first querying the AttributeStructure table for the row with a given StructureID:

```
Dim Query As Recordset
Set Query = m_utility.DB.DB.Execute("select Datatype from " _
        "AttributeStructure where StructureID=" & _
        StructureID)
```

In fact, we only ask SQL Server to return the Datatype column, as this is the only one we're interested in right away. If we get back an empty recordset, we know that the StructureID was invalid, otherwise we return the value in the Datatype column:

```
' is it valid?
If Not Query.EOF Then
  GetAttributeType = Query("Datatype")
Else
  GetAttributeType = atInvalid
End If
```

Once we know which row we want to save our data into, we return to the Attrib property. When we try to access this property, we'll always have the StructureID value that uniquely identifies the attribute we want to set.

In the Get part of the property we start off by pulling the row from the vAttributes view that matches the given StructureID and the given ProductID. If we get nothing back, we know that there's no specific value set for that particular attribute on that particular product and do nothing.

```
' Attrib - gets the value for an attribute...
Public Property Get Attrib(ByVal StructureID As Long) As Variant

    ' we need to select out the appropriate value...
    Dim Query As Recordset
    Set Query = m_utility.DB.DB.Execute("select * from vAttributes " & _
            "where ProductID=" & ID & " and StructureID=" & StructureID)
    If Not Query.EOF Then
```

Once we have the attribute value, we have to look at the Datatype column to determine which column actually contains the data we're looking for. So, if we know we're looking at a "long" field, we pull data from the LongValue column, and so on:

```
        ' which column do we want?
        Select Case Query("Datatype")

            Case atString
                If Not IsNull(Query("StringValue")) Then
                    Attrib = Query("StringValue")
                End If

            Case atLong
                If Not IsNull(Query("LongValue")) Then
                    Attrib = Query("LongValue")
                End If

            Case atDouble
                If Not IsNull(Query("DoubleValue")) Then
                    Attrib = Query("DoubleValue")
                End If

            Case atDate
                If Not IsNull(Query("DateValue")) Then
                    Attrib = Query("DateValue")
                End If

            Case atBoolean
                If Not IsNull(Query("BooleanValue")) Then
                    Attrib = Query("BooleanValue")
                End If

        End Select

    End If
    Query.Close
    Set Query = Nothing

End Property
```

Then we come to the `Let` part. By convention, we decide that if we don't want to set a value for an attribute, we don't want it taking up space in the database. So, if `newval` comes through as `Empty`, we delete the row. If there was no row there (no attribute was set), this statement won't throw an error, so we don't need to do any error checking.

```
' Attrib - sets a value for an attribute...
Public Property Let Attrib(ByVal StructureID As Long, ByVal newval As Variant)

    ' if we're trying to set an empty value, we may as well delete the row...
    If IsEmpty(newval) Then

        ' delete it...
        m_utility.DB.DB.Execute "delete from Attributes where ProductID=" & _
                    ID & " and StructureID=" & StructureID
```

If we do choose to set a value for an attribute, the first thing we have to do is SELECT the existing one. If there is one there, we just want to change the value. If there isn't, we want to create a new one. If we do have to create a new row, we have to set the `ProductID` and the `StructureID`:

```
    Else

        ' try to select the attribute we want...
        Dim SetAttrib As New Recordset
        SetAttrib.Open "select * from Attributes where ProductID=" & _
                ID & " and StructureID=" & StructureID, m_utility.DB.DB, _
            adOpenKeyset, adLockOptimistic
        If SetAttrib.EOF Then

            ' there's not one there already, so create one!
            SetAttrib.AddNew
            SetAttrib("ProductID") = ID
            SetAttrib("StructureID") = StructureID

        End If
```

Whether the row already exists, or whether it's new, we need to do the same thing. We use the `GetAttributeType` method that we built earlier to determine which column we want to save the values in and then use a `Select Case` statement to make that happen. Finally, we update and close the row, and this action saves the changes to disk:

```
        ' set the value...
        Select Case GetAttributeType(StructureID)

          Case atString
            SetAttrib("StringValue") = newval
          Case atLong
            SetAttrib("LongValue") = newval
          Case atDouble
            SetAttrib("DoubleValue") = newval
          Case atDate
            SetAttrib("DateValue") = newval
          Case atBoolean
            SetAttrib("BooleanValue") = newval

        End Select
```

```
    ' update the row...
    SetAttrib.Update

    ' close
    SetAttrib.Close
    Set SetAttrib = Nothing

  End If

End Property
```

Now we have a property capable of returning a complete set of dynamic attributes for our product, we can turn our attention to displaying those attributes on the detail page.

Try It Out – Adding Dynamic Attributes to detail.asp

1. Although we've defined the different types of data type an attribute can be in our VB code, we need to make that information available to our ASP code. The first thing to do is to replicate the VB enumeration we created earlier in the **Globals** module of the VB project, by adding these lines to the top of `site.asp`:

```
' globally define certain site metrics, such as its name and domain...
const g_sitename = "Jo's Coffee"
const g_domainname = "joscoffee.com"

' globally define attribute datatypes...
Const atInvalid = -1
Const atString = 0
Const atLong = 1
Const atDouble = 2
Const atDate = 3
Const atBoolean = 4
```

2. Next we need to add the code to create a table to display the attributes to `detail.asp`:

```
<!-- product description, and other stuff... -->
<td>   </td>
<td valign=top class=heading>
<%

  ' render the description
  Response.Write Product.Description
  Response.Write "<br><br>"

  ' get the attributes...
  Dim Attributes
  Set Attributes = Product.Attributes
  If Not Attributes.EOF Then
```

```
        ' start a table...
        Response.Write "<table cellspacing=0 cellpadding=0>"

        ' loop the attributes
        Do While Not Attributes.EOF

            ' render the name
            Response.Write "<tr><td class=std>"
            Response.Write Attributes("name") & ": "
            Response.Write "</td><td class=std>"

            ' do we have a value set for this attribute and product?
            If Not IsNull(Attributes("ProductID")) Then

                ' what data type do we have?
                Select Case Attributes("Datatype")

                    case atString
                        Response.Write Attributes("StringValue")
                    case atLong
                        Response.Write Attributes("LongValue")
                    case atDouble
                        Response.Write _
                            FormatNumber(Attributes("DoubleValue"), 2)
                    case atDate
                        Response.Write Attributes("DateValue")
                    case atBoolean
                        If Attributes("BooleanValue") = "True" Then
                            Response.Write "True"
                        Else
                            Response.Write "False"
                        End If

                End Select

            Else
                Response.Write "<font color=#c0c0c0>?</font>"
            End If

            ' finish the row...
            Response.write "</td></tr>"

            ' next...
            Attributes.MoveNext

        Loop


        ' end the table...
        Response.Write "</table>"

    End If
    Attributes.Close
    Set Attributes = Nothing
%>
</td>
```

How It Works

Our first job is to load the attributes definition from the Product by requesting the Attributes property. If you recall, this queries the vAttributes view to get a set of all the valid attributes from the product, whether specific values have been assigned or not:

```
' get the attributes...
Dim Attributes
Set Attributes = Product.Attributes
If Not Attributes.EOF Then
```

We then walk the attributes list. Irrespective of the data type, we render the name of the attribute by asking for the Name column of the Attributes recordset. We then query the Datatype column and use this in combination with a Select Case to decide how to render the values. We use the IsNull function to determine if an attribute has been set for the specific item:

```
' loop the attributes
Do While Not Attributes.EOF

    ' render the name
    Response.Write "<tr><td class=std>"
    Response.Write Attributes("name") & ": "
    Response.Write "</td><td class=std>"

    ' do we have a value set for this attribute and product?
    If Not IsNull(Attributes("ProductID")) Then

        ' what data type do we have?
        Select Case Attributes("Datatype")

            case atString
                Response.Write Attributes("StringValue")
            case atLong
                Response.Write Attributes("LongValue")
            case atDouble
                Response.Write _
                    FormatNumber(Attributes("DoubleValue"), 2)
            case atDate
                Response.Write Attributes("DateValue")
            case atBoolean
                If Attributes("BooleanValue") = "True" Then
                    Response.Write "True"
                Else
                    Response.Write "False"
                End If

        End Select
```

As you can see, we use the Attributes property to select out the set of attributes defined for the specific item type we're looking at. The way we do this query means that we'll get rows out of the vAttributes view even if there's no specific value set for that attribute and for that product.

We can detect if there is no value set for that attribute/product pair, because ProductID will be null in this case. We test for this and, if there isn't one set, we render a small, gray question mark. If there is one set, we test the Datatype column from the query to determine how we should draw it:

```
            Response.Write "<font color=#c0c0c0>?</font>"
        End If

        ' finish the row...
        Response.write "</td></tr>"

        ' next...
        Attributes.MoveNext

    Loop


    ' end the table...
    Response.Write "</table>"

End If
Attributes.Close
Set Attributes = Nothing
```

Although we can now render any attribute information we like into the visitor's browser, we still don't have a way of entering that information into the database.

Setting Attribute Values

The form we set up here would be ideal for allowing us to alter the common attributes against the products, but for space we're going to keep it simple here and only enable dynamic attributes to be changed – we'll go into more detail on setting common attributes later on in the book.

Try It Out – Adding Attributes to the Database

1. To create a form that lets us edit attribute information, we need to edit our admin/default.asp page. Open this page now, and add this menu option:

```
' render the menu options...
RenderOption "Add Department", "adddepartment"
RenderOption "Add Product", "addproduct"
RenderOption "Edit Products", "editproducts"
```

2. So that we can choose which product we want to edit, the editproducts option will just display a list of the products as links. Clicking on one of those links will open up a form that we can use to change the attribute information. Enter this code as one of the options in the Select Case statement in the body of admin/default.asp:

```
<% ' do we want to edit products?
case "editproducts"

    ' display a list of the products for editing...
    Dim Products
    Set Products = Visit.Catalog.GetProducts
    Do While Not Products.EOF
    ' draw the link...
        Response.Write "<a href="""
        Response.Write Request("script_name")
```

```
         Response.Write "?action=editproduct&id=" & Products("ProductID")
         Response.Write """>"
         Response.Write Products("MfrName") & " " & Products("Name")
         Response.Write "</a>"

         ' next
         Products.MoveNext

      Loop
      Products.Close
      Set Products = Nothing
%>
```

3. Next, we need to add this code to the Select Case in the body of admin/default.asp to display the attribute editing form:

```
<% ' do we want to edit a single product?
case "editproduct"%>

   <!-- start the form -->
   <form action="<%=request("script_name")%>" method=post id=form1 name=form1>
   <center><table cellspacing=0 cellpadding=3>
   <tr><td colspan=2 class=heading align=center>Edit Product<br><br></td></tr>

   <%
   ' get the product object...
   Dim Product
   Set Product = Visit.Catalog.GetProductObject(Request("id"))

   ' write the name of the product out...
   Response.Write "<tr><td class=heading>"
   Response.Write "Name: "
   Response.Write "</td><td class=std>"
   Response.Write Product.MfrName & " " & product.Name
   Response.write "</td></tr>"

   ' get the attributes...
   Dim Attributes, Value
   Set Attributes = Product.Attributes

   ' loop the attributes rendering an edit field for each...
   Do While Not Attributes.Eof

      ' render the name
      Response.Write "<tr><td class=heading>"
      Response.Write Attributes("Name") & ": "
      Response.Write "</td><td>"

      ' get the current value for the attribute...
      value = Product.Attrib(Attributes("StructureID"))

      ' what kind of edit field do we want?
      Select Case Attributes("Datatype")
         case atString
            Response.Write "<input type=text name=values value="""
            Response.write value
            Response.Write """>"

         case atLong
            Response.Write "<input type=text name=values value="""
```

```
            Response.write value
            Response.Write """ size=5>"

      case atDate
            Response.Write "<input type=text name=values value="""
            Response.write value
            Response.Write """ size=10>"

      case atDouble
            Response.Write "<input type=text name=values value="""
            Response.write value
            Response.Write """ size=8>"

      case atBoolean
            Response.Write "<select name=values>"
            Response.Write "<option value=0"
            if value = 0 then Response.Write " selected"
            Response.Write ">No</option>"
            Response.Write "<option value=0"
            if value = 1 then Response.Write " selected"
            Response.Write ">Yes</option>"
            Response.Write "</select>"

   End Select

   ' we need to make an array holding the structure ID too...
   Response.Write "<input type=hidden name=structureids value="""
   Response.Write Attributes("StructureID")
   Response.Write """>"

   ' finish the row...
   Response.write "</td></tr>"

   ' next
   Attributes.MoveNext

Loop
Attributes.Close
Set Attributes = Nothing

' finish...
Set Product = Nothing
%>

<!-- button... -->
<tr><td colspan=2 align=center>
<br><input type=submit value="Save Changes">
</td></tr>

<!-- hidden fields -->
<input type=hidden name=saveproduct value=<%=Request("id")%>>

<!-- finish the form -->
</table></center>
</form>
```

This works in a very similar fashion to the attribute display code we saw on detail.asp, as
we use the Attributes property of the Product object to return the set of attributes
definitions and values for the type of product it represents. This time, however, we use the
Datatype column to determine the appearance of the editing field presented to the user.

Now we need to save that attribute information back into the database. Building and handling dynamic forms in ASP is a common challenge. Most of the time when using forms in ASP, you're capturing a fixed set of data. In this case, that isn't true as we may at some point change the `TypeID` on our Gaggia Carezza and end up with a completely different set of attributes – hence our form will have a completely different set of fields. Our challenge is to make the code which checks and accepts data from the form adapt to the structure of the dynamic attribute set stored in the database.

What we have done is make each of the fields on our dynamic form have the same name. This means that we can ask ASP to return the field values as an array. Once we have an array, we can loop through setting attributes as we go.

4. Finally, add this code to `admin/default.asp` at the top of the page, just beneath the `If…Then` statement that checks if we're trying to save a new product :

```
' are we trying to save a product?
If Request("saveproduct") <> "" then

    ' get the product back...
    Set Product = Visit.Catalog.GetProductObject(Request("saveproduct"))

    ' start looping the array of StructureIDs stored in the hidden fields...
    Dim n
    For n = 1 to Request("structureids").Count

        ' do we have a value, or is it null?
        If Trim(Request("values")(n)) <> "" then

            ' store the value...
            Product.Attrib(Request("structureids")(n)) = _
                            Request("values")(n)

        Else

            ' set the value to null...
            Product.Attrib(Request("structureids")(n)) = Empty

        End If

    Next

    ' cleanup...
    Set Product = Nothing

End If
```

In our form, we store the `StructureID` in a hidden field called `structureids`. When we have more than one field on the form, this will become an array (we can treat it as an array even if there's only one field). When we come to save the form we loop through this set of IDs. Whenever we find one, we can jump to the matching field data that's stored in the `values` array. Again, we create an array by making everything have the same name. (In fact, this is why we implemented the Boolean field as a `SELECT` box, rather than a checkbox. Checkboxes behave rather strangely in arrays – if they're not selected, they don't occupy a space in the array. `SELECT` boxes and `INPUT` fields that aren't checkboxes always have an entry irrespective of the value chosen.)

Try It Out – Testing the Form

At last we're in a position to see the results of our handiwork.

1. Firstly start the
WroxCommerce VB project,
then the Visual InterDev
project, and select Edit
Products and Gaggia
Carezza. Then enter the data
into the fields as shown:

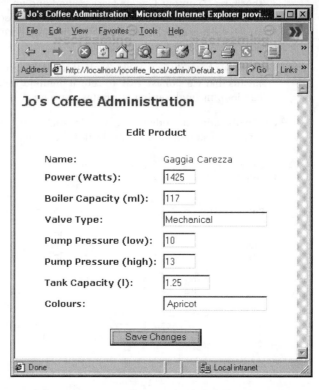

When you hit **Save Changes**, the attributes will be saved into the database leading to
something of the form:

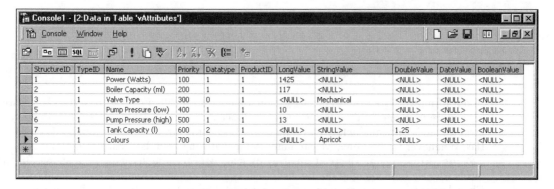

StructureID	TypeID	Name	Priority	Datatype	ProductID	LongValue	StringValue	DoubleValue	DateValue	BooleanValue
1	1	Power (Watts)	100	1	1	1425	<NULL>	<NULL>	<NULL>	<NULL>
2	1	Boiler Capacity (ml)	200	1	1	117	<NULL>	<NULL>	<NULL>	<NULL>
3	1	Valve Type	300	0	1	<NULL>	Mechanical	<NULL>	<NULL>	<NULL>
5	1	Pump Pressure (low)	400	1	1	10	<NULL>	<NULL>	<NULL>	<NULL>
6	1	Pump Pressure (high)	500	1	1	13	<NULL>	<NULL>	<NULL>	<NULL>
7	1	Tank Capacity (l)	600	2	1	<NULL>	<NULL>	1.25	<NULL>	<NULL>
8	1	Colours	700	0	1	<NULL>	Apricot	<NULL>	<NULL>	<NULL>

2. Now if we refresh our `details.asp` page we should see the data:

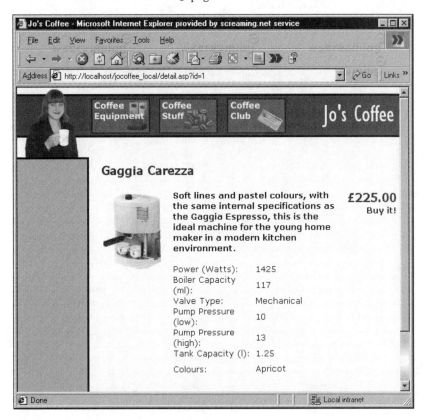

Summary

We started out this chapter with a quick discussion on how product attributes work, before we leapt into building the first of our tables for handling products, manufacturers, suppliers and product types. We then discussed a method for holding dynamic attributes so different kinds of products in our catalog could have different attributes. This could be used for allowing coffee beans to have information about the region and roast, while coffee machines could have information about power, boiler capacity, etc.

In addition to constructing tables, we also built some views to aid our interaction with the database.

We then moved on to support this development by expanding our object model by adding functionality to our existing objects and creating a new data object – the `Product` object. The coding approaches used in Visual Basic (for the business tier development) and ASP (for the presentation tier development) built on what we learned in the last chapter, and added a greater degree of richness to the object model.

Finally, we used the new methods and properties to allow administrators to add new products and set attributes for existing products and tweaked the ASP pages to enable detailed product information to be presented to the site visitors.

The Shopping Basket

Traditionally, to let people make purchases from your e-commerce site you give them the ability to build a list of the products or services they want and then confirm that choice once they've committed to make a purchase from you. This list is usually known as a **shopping cart** in the US and **shopping basket** in the UK. The process of committing the purchase and submitting credit card and address information is called **checking out**. On most good e-commerce sites, your order will not be processed until you see the **receipt** or **summary page**. This page will typically break down the order into quantities, addresses, and payment methods. You will be invited to confirm the order by clicking on some form of "Yes, I am sure" button or link. Only at this point have you actually committed to the order.

In this chapter, we'll be building the shopping basket for our site, and we'll be referring to it as basket because Jo's Coffee is a British company. To enable us to add basket functionality to our site we will:

- ❑ Create two tables – one to keep track of all the baskets and one to keep track of all the items in the baskets
- ❑ Extend our `WroxCommerce` object model by building a new `Basket` object
- ❑ Create a new ASP page, which we will use to display our basket
- ❑ Make the contents of the basket visible anywhere in joscoffee.com by adding a summary of it to the left-hand navigation bar

Holding State

One of the challenges with Web development that's always been around is that of keeping track of who's using your site at any particular moment.

The Web is described as being inherently **stateless**, that's to say when a browser requests a page, that page is served, but no persistent connection exists between the Web server and the visitor to the site. That same visitor can immediately request another page, but the Web server cannot be confident that it is, in fact, the same visitor. From an architectural standpoint this is great because when building a system with a persistent connection you have to maintain information about that user in memory. If keeping track of one user requires 1K of memory and you have 10,000 users, you've lost 10MB of server memory just in that instance. If each user has a database connection that takes 7K, you've lost an additional 70MB! By building Web servers in such a way that the user is immediately disconnected after the page is served, all the resources are freed.

What happens then is that the number of users using a particular site at any given time is actually quite small, especially if your pages are served quickly. Anyway, the idea with a Web application is that the number of users connected at any given moment in time should be as small as possible, so Web servers are built in a connectionless manner, leading to **statelessness**.

The ASP `Session` object was created to overcome the problems of statelessness. ASP employs the `Session` object to create a construct whereby visitors to a Web server can be identified even though no persistent connection exists. Through that identification process the Web server develops an understanding of which visitor is requesting which pages and can therefore associate certain metrics with that user. In this chapter, we'll be using the `Session` object to associate an instance of a basket in our database.

Creating the Tables for a Shopping Basket

When a visitor adds an item to his or her basket, we need to add that item to a list so that later on we can retrieve that list and present it to them before they checkout, and we can also iterate through that list when constructing their final order.

We will have to add two tables to the `JoCoffee` database: `Baskets` and `BasketItems`. The `Baskets` table holds a list of the baskets that are currently open on the system. The `BasketItems` table holds the actual list of products that the visitor wants to buy. We use the `Baskets` table to group the rows in the `BasketItems` table together so that we can determine the contents of a visitor's basket whenever we need to, separating one person's basket items out from all the items in all the baskets.

Try It Out – Building the Baskets Table

1. Start up SQL Server and create the `Baskets` table now:

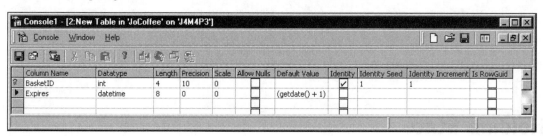

How It Works

One of the interesting things about that table is the use of the `Expires` column. Notice how the default value of that column is 24 hours in the future from the time the row was created. We do this so that we can safely delete rows that are older than this at any time. Although ASP informs us when a session has ended through the `OnSessionEnd` event, on an e-commerce site it is better to let people get at their basket a few days in the future. Ours is set for 24 hours, but we could set it for a week or a month. Then all we need to do is hold a reference to the `BasketID` in a **cookie** on the visitor's computer and we can retrieve the basket and its contents whenever he or she comes back.

A cookie is a commonly used site-engineering device that enables a server to place a piece of information on a visitor's computer. The server and browser work together to check for the existence and contents of this cookie, and in our case, we're going to use it to store a reference to the basket in our database.

Try It Out – Building the BasketItems Table

1. Now create the `BasketItems` table:

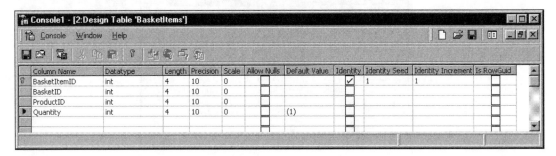

How It Works

As you can see, this is another pretty simple table. We have a `BasketItemID` that uniquely identifies the row, we have a link to the `Baskets` table through `BasketID`, a link to the product we want to buy through the `ProductID` and finally we hold the quantity of items we want to buy. We default the quantity of items we want to 1.

The vBasketItems View

When we're displaying the list of items to the user when they checkout, and when we're doing our order processing, it's useful to have a view around that can calculate totals, and bring information back about the product we want.

Try It Out – Building the vBasketItems View

1. Now create the `vBasketItems` view, which is linked to the `vProducts` view which we created earlier:

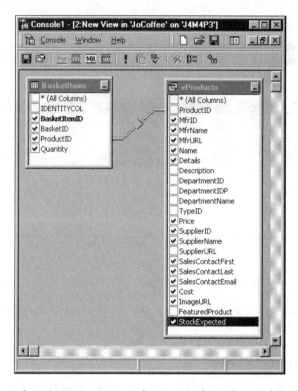

At the moment, this view just returns information about the product that's added to the basket. What would be smart would be to make the view return the total price and total cost of the row, based on whatever value was stored in the `Quantity` column.

We can do this by adding the `LinePrice` and `LineCost` columns to the view's SQL statement that makes up this view.

2. Change the SQL statement as shown below:

```
SELECT BasketItems.BasketItemID, BasketItems.BasketID,
    BasketItems.ProductID, vProducts.MfrID, vProducts.MfrName,
    vProducts.MfrURL, vProducts.Name, vProducts.Details,
    vProducts.Price, vProducts.SupplierID,
    vProducts.SupplierName, vProducts.SalesContactFirst,
    vProducts.SalesContactLast, vProducts.SalesContactEmail,
    vProducts.Cost, vProducts.ImageURL,
    vProducts.StockExpected, BasketItems.Quantity,
    BasketItems.Quantity * vProducts.Price AS LinePrice,
    BasketItems.Quantity * vProducts.Cost AS LineCost
FROM BasketItems INNER JOIN
    vProducts ON BasketItems.ProductID = vProducts.ProductID
```

Modifying the Object Model

As we saw before with the product catalog, once our basket tables are in place, we need to start adapting the `WroxCommerce` object model to work with the new tables.

Modifying the Visit Object

It's at this stage that we need to backtrack a little and modify our VB project so it understands the ASP intrinsic objects, and then modify our `Visit` object so we can pass the `Session` object through from ASP. It's through this `Session` object that we'll be able to access the ID of the visitor's basket from within the `WroxCommerce` components.

Try It Out – Modifying the Visit Object

1. First of all, we need to link our project into the ASP object model in a similar manner to the way we linked in the ADO object model in Chapter 3.

Open the `WroxCommerce` project. Select Project | References from the menu and check Microsoft Active Server Pages Object Library. Click OK:

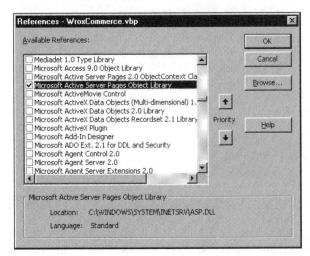

2. Now we want to hold a reference to the ASP `Session` object around for as long as the `Visit` object is around (for the life of the page), so add this member variable at the top of the `Visit` code alongside the other member variable definitions. We'll also add a member variable that will hold the ID of the basket:

```
' these variables hold the objects that are in the next hierarchical
' level in our object model...
Private m_catalog As Catalog

    ' this variable holds a reference to Session level stuff...
    Private m_Session As Session
    Private m_BasketID as Long
```

3. We're going to pass a reference to the Session object through the Configure method, store it in our m_session member variable and then query it for session-level information (specifically here, the ID of the basket), so change the definition of this method in Visit to look like this:

```
' Configure - tells the Visit object a little about the site...
Public Sub Configure(ByVal sitename As String, ByVal maildomain As String, _
                     ByVal strDBString As String, ByVal Session As Session)

    ' Copy the site name, etc...
    m_sitename = sitename
    m_maildomain = maildomain

    ' Copy the database details...
    m_strDBString = strDBString

    ' Hold the Session information...
    Set m_Session = Session

    If Not m_Session Is Nothing Then

        ' Capture the BasketID...
        m_BasketID = CLng(m_Session("BasketID"))

    End If

End Sub
```

4. Because other objects in the model might want access to the Session object, we should add a property to the IUtility interface to allow this. Add this code to IUtility:

```
' Session - returns the ASP session...
Public Property Get Session() As Session
End Property
```

5. Now we need to implement this new property in the Visit object. Remember, you can use the drop-down lists at the top of the code editor to create the framework for the property. In fact, if you use this technique, it will add the verbose ASPTypeLibrary.ISessionObject identifier, rather than the shorthand Session we used in the interface definition:

```
Private Property Get IUtility_Session() As ASPTypeLibrary.ISessionObject
    Set IUtility_Session = m_Session
End Property
```

6. Finally, make sure we get rid of the `m_Session` reference by adding this code to `Visit`'s `Shutdown` method:

```
' Shutdown - releases any resources we may have open...
Public Sub Shutdown()

    ' Do we have a database?
    If Not m_db Is Nothing Then

        ' Shutdown the database...
        m_db.Shutdown
        Set m_db = Nothing

    End If

    ' Clean up any other objects...
    Set m_catalog = Nothing
    Set m_Session = Nothing

End Sub
```

7. Of course, because we've changed the definition of our object model, we need to alter our ASP code. Pass the `Session` object to the `Configure` method by altering the `Visit` function found inside `site.asp` to this:

```
' Site - this function returns an instance of the site back to the caller.
' If one doesn't exist, it will create one...
Function Visit

    ' Do we have one?
    If IsEmpty(m_visit) Then

        ' Create an instance of a visit  object...
        Set m_visit = Server.CreateObject("WroxCommerce.Visit")

        m_visit.Configure g_sitename, g_domainname, "driver=SQL Server;" & _
                        "DATABASE=JoCoffee; UID=JoCoffeeWeb;PWD=eermlate;" & _
                        "SERVER=localhost", Session

    End If

    ' Return the visit object back...
    Set Visit = m_visit

End Function
```

The upshot of all this, is that as soon as our `Visit` object is created, we can ask the ASP `Session` object to return to us the ID of the basket that the user is currently using. (We'll see how we can create baskets a little later on and then set the ID of the newly created baskets against the session variable.)

Creating the Basket Object

Just as we created a `Product` object to represent a single instance of a product in the catalog, we're going to create a `Basket` object to represent a single instance of a basket in the system. More specifically, we're going to use `Basket` objects to represent the basket the user is currently filling.

Try It Out – Building the Basket Object

1. Create a new class module in the VB project and call it `Basket`. Add this code:

```
Option Explicit

' Use IUtility to call back into the Visit and Database objects...
Private m_utility As IUtility

' Somewhere to hold information on the basket we represent...
Private m_ID As Long

' Configure - set up IUtility...
Public Sub Configure(ByVal utility As IUtility, ByVal ID As Long)

    ' Hold the utility object...
    Set m_utility = utility

    ' Store the ID...
    m_ID = ID

End Sub
```

2. Let's create a property to return the ID of the basket back. Add this code to the `Basket` object:

```
' ID - returns the ID of the basket...
Public Property Get ID() As Long
    ID = m_ID
End Property
```

3. Finally, add the `Basket` property to the `Visit` object:

```
' Basket - returns the Basket that we're using...
Public Property Get Basket() As Basket

    ' Do we have a BasketID?
    If m_BasketID = 0 Then

        ' Create a new basket row...
        Dim NewBasket As New Recordset
        NewBasket.Open "Baskets", IUtility_DB.DB, adOpenKeyset, adLockOptimistic
        NewBasket.AddNew
```

```
        ' Update the row and get issued an ID...
        NewBasket.Update

        ' Get the ID back and store it locally, and in the Session...
        m_BasketID = NewBasket("BasketID")
        m_Session("BasketID") = m_BasketID

        ' Cleanup...
        NewBasket.Close
        Set NewBasket = Nothing

    End If

        ' Create and return an instance of a Basket object...
        Set Basket = New Basket
        Basket.Configure Me, m_BasketID

End Property
```

How It Works

You'll notice that that code is extremely similar to that which we saw when building our Product object. Well, that's because we've decided that, by convention, all objects in the model share the same initialization scheme – in our case, this is using a Configure method to pass in IUtility and the ID of the row that the object represents:

```
Public Sub Configure(ByVal utility As IUtility, ByVal ID As Long)

    ' Hold the utility object...
    Set m_utility = utility

    ' Store the ID...
    m_ID = ID

End Sub
```

When we want to gain access to the basket through ASP, we'll ask the Visit object for its Basket property. This property will check to see if we already have a basket and, if we don't, it will create the appropriate row in the Baskets table to store the new BasketID in the ASP Session:

```
' ID - returns the ID of the basket...
Public Property Get ID() As Long
    ID = m_ID
End Property
```

The first time the user requests the Basket property, the ID of the basket will be 0. In the Configure method, we query the Session for the variable BasketID and store it in m_BasketID. Therefore, if BasketID is empty, m_BasketID will be 0.

When we test the ID in the `Basket` property and it turns out to be 0, we create a new row in the `Baskets` table and then store this ID both in the member variable m_BasketID and in the `Session` variable `BasketID`:

```
' Create a new basket row...
Dim NewBasket As New Recordset
NewBasket.Open "Baskets", IUtility_DB.DB, adOpenKeyset, adLockOptimistic
NewBasket.AddNew

' Update the row and get issued an ID...
NewBasket.Update

' Get the ID back and store it locally, and in the Session...
m_BasketID = NewBasket("BasketID")
m_Session("BasketID") = m_BasketID
```

Next time the `Visit` object is created (the next time a page is requested), the `Session` object will indicate that it already has a `BasketID` and so a new one won't be created. Either way, a new `Basket` object will be created and configured with the ID – whether that's a new ID, or an old one:

```
Set Basket = New Basket
Basket.Configure Me, m_BasketID
```

The Basket Object's Methods

Before we go on to wiring the basket functionality into the ASP pages, we need to add a number of methods to the `Basket` object that will let us add to, delete from and change quantity of items in the basket. These are all simple methods so we won't discuss them in too much detail.

Try It Out – Adding Methods to the Basket Object

1. Add the following code to the `Basket` object:

```
' Contains - checks to see if an item exists...
Public Function Contains(ByVal ProductID As Long) As Long

    ' Run the query...
    Dim Query As Recordset
    Set Query = m_utility.DB.DB.Execute("select Quantity from BasketItems " & _
            "where BasketID=" & ID & " and ProductID=" & ProductID)

    ' Is it in the basket?
    If Not Query.EOF Then
        ' Return the quantity...
        Contains = Query("Quantity")
    Else
        ' Return zero...
        Contains = 0
    End If
```

```
    ' Cleanup
    Query.Close
    Set Query = Nothing

End Function
```

2. Now add the code for the `Add` method:

```
' Add - adds an item to the basket...
Public Sub Add(ByVal ProductID As Long)

    ' Is it already there?
    If Contains(ProductID) <> 0 Then

        ' Add one to the quantity...
        Increment ProductID

    Else

        ' Add a new row...
        Dim NewItem As New Recordset
        NewItem.Open "BasketItems", m_utility.DB.DB, adOpenKeyset, _
                    adLockOptimistic
        NewItem.AddNew

        ' Configure...
        NewItem("BasketID") = ID
        NewItem("ProductID") = ProductID
        NewItem("Quantity") = 1

        ' Update and close...
        NewItem.Update
        NewItem.Close
        Set NewItem = Nothing

    End If

End Sub
```

3. The next method of the `Basket` object is the opposite of the previous one. Now create a `Remove` method:

```
' Remove - removes an item from the basket...
Public Sub Remove(ByVal ProductID As Long)
    m_utility.DB.DB.Execute "delete from BasketItems where " & _
                        "BasketID=" & ID & " and ProductID=" & ProductID
End Sub
```

4. Next, add the `ChangeQuantity` method:

```
' ChangeQuantity - sets the quantity in the basket...
Public Sub ChangeQuantity(ByVal ProductID As Long, ByVal Quantity As Long)

    ' Is it already there?  if not, add it...
    If Contains(ProductID) = 0 Then Add ProductID

    ' Now set the quantity...
    m_utility.DB.DB.Execute "update BasketItems set Quantity=" & _
                            Quantity & " where BasketID=" & ID & _
                            " and ProductID=" & ProductID

End Sub
```

5. Now add the `Increment` method to the `Basket` object:

```
' Increment - adds one to the quantity in the basket...
Public Sub Increment(ByVal ProductID As Long)

    ' If it's not there already, add it...
    If Contains(ProductID) = 0 Then
       Add ProductID
    Else
        ' increment the quantity...
       m_utility.DB.DB.Execute "update BasketItems set Quantity=Quantity+1 " & _
                    "where BasketID=" & ID & " and ProductID=" & ProductID
    End If

End Sub
```

6. Now add the reverse of the `Increment` method – the `Decrement` method, which removes an item from the basket if the quantity drops to zero:

```
' Decrement - removes one from the quantity...
Public Sub Decrement(ByVal ProductID As Long)

    ' If it's "1", remove it...
    If Contains(ProductID) = 1 Then
       Remove ProductID
    Else
        ' Decrement the quantity...
       m_utility.DB.DB.Execute "update BasketItems set Quantity=Quantity-1 " & _
                    "where BasketID=" & ID & " and ProductID=" & ProductID
    End If

End Sub
```

7. Lastly, the `RemoveAll` method:

```
' RemoveAll - removes everything from the basket...
Public Sub RemoveAll()
   m_utility.DB.DB.Execute "delete from BasketItems where BasketID=" & ID
End Sub
```

8. Before we finish with the `Basket` object for the time being, we need a property that can return a recordset of items in the basket back to the ASP code using the `vBasketItems` view:

```
' Items - returns all the items in the basket...
Public Property Get Items(Optional ByVal AsKeyset As Boolean = False) _
                    As Recordset
   Set Items = m_utility.DB.RunQuery("BasketItems", "vBasketItems", _
                              "BasketID=" & ID, "Name", AsKeyset)

End Property
```

How It Works

The `Contains` method checks to see if an item is in the basket. If the basket contains any items at all, the quantity of items in the basket is returned, otherwise 0 is returned:

```
' Is it in the basket?
If Not Query.EOF Then
   ' Return the quantity...
   Contains = Query("Quantity")
Else
   ' Return zero...
   Contains = 0
End If
```

The `Add` method works by querying the `Basket` to see if the item is already in the basket by using the `Contains` method:

```
If Contains(ProductID) <> 0 Then
```

If it is, we call the `Increment` method, which increments the number of that particular item by one:

```
' Increment - adds one to the quantity in the basket...
Public Sub Increment(ByVal ProductID As Long)

   ' If it's not there already, add it...
   If Contains(ProductID) = 0 Then
      Add ProductID
   Else
      ' increment the quantity...
      m_utility.DB.DB.Execute "update BasketItems set Quantity=Quantity+1 " _
                  "where BasketID=" & ID & " and ProductID=" & ProductID
   End If

End Sub
```

If the item is not in the basket, we create a new `Recordset` object and use that to insert a new row into the `BasketItems` table. Notice how we add the basket ID to that row, along with the product ID we originally asked for through the `ProductID` parameter and a default quantity of 1:

```
Dim NewItem As New Recordset
NewItem.Open "BasketItems", m_utility.DB.DB, adOpenKeyset, _
              adLockOptimistic
NewItem.AddNew

' Configure...
NewItem("BasketID") = ID
NewItem("ProductID") = ProductID
NewItem("Quantity") = 1
```

The `Remove` method will remove the row or rows from the `BasketItems` table, based on the ID of the basket that we store as a member variable of the object and whatever product ID we were given. Usually, there will be either no rows, or a single row, as the `Decrement` method will reduce the quantity if there is more than one of the object. In addition, since SQL Server will not throw an error if a row does not exist, there's no need for any error checking here:

```
' Remove - removes an item from the basket...
Public Sub Remove(ByVal ProductID As Long)
    m_utility.DB.DB.Execute "delete from BasketItems where " & _
                        "BasketID=" & ID & " and ProductID=" & ProductID
End Sub
```

Before the `ChangeQuantity` method resets the quantity in the basket, it checks to see if the item is already present. If the item is not there, it is first added, using the `Add` method:

```
' ChangeQuantity - sets the quantity in the basket...
Public Sub ChangeQuantity(ByVal ProductID As Long, ByVal Quantity As Long)

    ' Is it already there?  if not, add it...
    If Contains(ProductID) = 0 Then Add ProductID

    ' Now set the quantity...
    m_utility.DB.DB.Execute "update BasketItems set Quantity=" & _
                        Quantity & " where BasketID=" & ID & _
                        " and ProductID=" & ProductID

End Sub
```

Adding the Basket to Our ASP Code

In the previous code examples in Chapter 6, we've seen Buy It! buttons that have been wired into `basket.asp`. Let's now add the functionality provided by the `Basket` object to our `basket.asp`.

1. Create a new ASP page called `basket.asp` in Visual InterDev and copy the contents from `template.asp` into it so that both files are identical.

2. When we request `basket.asp` after clicking on a Buy It! button we pass the ID of the item we're interested in through the `Request` variable's `id`; this is similar to both `dept.asp` and `detail.asp`.

Add this code to the top of `basket.asp` to add the item to the basket:

```
<% option explicit

   ' Do we want to add an item to the basket?
   If Request("id") <> "" Then
      Visit.Basket.Add Request("id")
   End If
%>
<HTML>
<HEAD>
```

3. Run both the Visual Basic project and the Visual InterDev project, then find the Gaggia Carezza. Click on its Buy It! button; the new `Baskets` row will be created, the ID of that new row stored in a `Session` variable and a row for the item will be added to `BasketItems`.

4. Ask Enterprise Manager to show you the contents of the `Baskets` table by finding it in the Tables list, right-clicking on it, and selecting Open Table | Return all rows. If the data in the table appears to be missing, you may have to refresh it, which you can do by right-clicking on the Tables object and choosing Refresh.

Here's what the `Baskets` table now looks like:

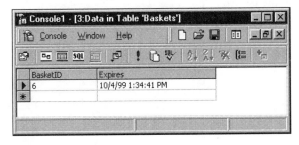

Notice how the `Expires` column has been automatically set to a date 24 hours in the future.

5. Now let's look at the `BasketItems` table:

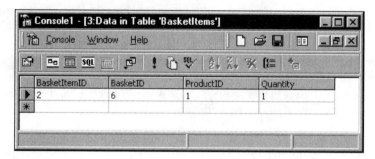

6. Now if you refresh the browser page, the `Add` method will be called again and the quantity will be incremented.

Ideally, we want to stop that happening, so that the customer doesn't order products by mistake. Therefore, we redirect the customer back into the `basket.asp` page again from `basket.asp`, but this time we don't pass through an ID so `Add` won't be called the second time around.

Here's the code that you should add in at the top of `basket.asp`:

```
' Do we want to add an item to the basket?
If Request("id") <> "" Then

    ' Add the item...
    Visit.Basket.Add Request("id")

    ' Bounce to stop the Refresh problem...
    Response.Buffer = true
    Response.Clear
    Response.Redirect Request("script_name")

End If
```

Now if the visitor refreshes the page, the ID variable won't be set in the query string and so another item will not be added to the basket.

Presenting the Basket

Of course, the basket is of little use unless we can present it to the visitor properly, and that's what we're going to do in the following Try It Out.

1. Add this code to `basket.asp`:

```
<!-- #include file="start.asp" -->
```

```
<!-- start a table... -->
<font class=bigheading>Your Basket</font>
<br><br>
<table width=100% cellspacing=0 cellpadding=2>
<%

    ' Get the items from the basket...
    Dim Items
    Set Items = Visit.Basket.Items

    If Not Items.EOF Then

        ' Put a heading on the row...
        Response.Write "<tr bgcolor=#c0c0c0>"
        Response.Write "<td class=heading>"
        Response.Write "Item"
        Response.Write "</td><td class=heading colspan=2>"
        Response.Write "Quantity"
        Response.Write "</td><td class=heading>"
        Response.Write "Each"
        Response.Write "</td><td class=heading>"
        Response.Write "Total"
        Response.Write "</td></tr>"

        ' Loop the items...
        Dim num, Total
        num = 0
        Total = 0

        Do While Not Items.EOF

            ' Start the row - use num to color each row...
            Response.Write "<tr bgcolor="
            if num mod 2 = 0 then
                Response.Write "#f0f0f0"
            else
                Response.Write "#ffffe0"
            end if
```

```
      Response.Write ">"

      ' Draw the name of the item...
      Response.Write "<td class=heading>"
      Response.Write Items("MfrName") & " " & Items("Name")
      Response.Write "</td>"

      ' Draw the quantity...
      Response.Write "<td class=std>"
      Response.Write Items("Quantity")
      Response.Write "</td>"

      ' Draw some buttons...
      Response.Write "<td class=small>"
      Response.Write "<a href="""
      Response.Write Request("script_name")
      Response.Write "?less=" & Items("ProductID")
      Response.Write """>Less</a>"
      Response.Write " | <a href="""
      Response.Write Request("script_name")
      Response.Write "?more=" & Items("ProductID")
      Response.Write """>More</a>"
      Response.Write " | <a href="""
      Response.Write Request("script_name")
      Response.Write "?del=" & Items("ProductID")
      Response.Write """>Delete</a>"
      Response.Write "</td>"

      ' Draw the price per item...
      Response.Write "<td class=std align=right>"
      Response.Write FormatPrice(Items("Price"))
      Response.Write "</td>"

      ' Draw the line total...
      Response.Write "<td class=heading align=right>"
      Response.Write FormatPrice(Items("LinePrice"))
      Total = Total + Items("LinePrice")
      Response.Write "</td></tr>"

      ' Next...
      Items.MoveNext
      num = num + 1

Loop

' Add the total...
Response.Write "<tr><td><br></td></tr>"
Response.Write "<tr bgcolor=#c0c0c0>"
Response.Write "<td colspan=4 align=right class=heading>"
Response.write "Total:"
Response.Write "</td><td align=right class=heading>"
Response.Write FormatPrice(total)
Response.Write "</td></tr>"
```

```
    Else

        ' Render a message...
        Response.write "<tr><td class=heading align=center>"
        Response.Write "Your basket is empty!"
        Response.Write "</td></tr>"

    End if
    Items.Close
    Set Items = Nothing

%>

<!-- end the table... -->
</table>

<!-- #include file="end.asp" -->
```

How It Works

This code is quite simple, albeit lengthy. We start by requesting a list of the items that are in the basket from the Basket object:

```
Dim Items
Set Items = Visit.Basket.Items
```

This list is selected from the vBasketItems view, so we have access to the common attributes stored in the Products table.

We can use the LinePrice column to automatically return the price multiplied by the quantity. We also maintain a variable called Total, which contains the total value of the basket when we've finished:

```
Response.Write "<td class=heading align=right>"
Response.Write FormatPrice(Items("LinePrice"))
Total = Total + Items("LinePrice")
```

Here's what the basket looks like so far:

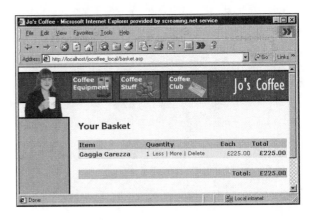

Changing Quantities

Next to the quantity in our basket, we've already added links for **Less**, **More** and **Delete**. These links call back into our `basket.asp` page with an instruction to decrement, increment or delete the given product from the basket. Let's add the code that uses these links.

Try It Out – Adding the Ability to Change Quantities to basket.asp

1. Here's how we can change the code in `basket.asp` to deal with the three quantity options:

```
<% option explicit
```

```
' Do we want to change the items in the basket?
If Request("id") <> "" or Request("less") <> "" or _
              Request("more") <> "" or Request("del") <> "" Then

   ' Add an item?
   If Request("id") <> "" then
      Visit.Basket.Add Request("id")
   End If

   ' Have less?
   If Request("less") <> "" then
      Visit.Basket.Decrement Request("less")
   End If

   ' Have more?
   If Request("more") <> "" then
      Visit.Basket.Increment Request("more")
   End If

   ' Remove an item?
   If Request("del") <> "" then
      Visit.Basket.Remove Request("del")
   End If
```

```
   ' Bounce to stop the Refresh problem...
   Response.Buffer = true
   Response.Clear
   Response.Redirect Request("script_name")

End if

%>
<HTML>
```

How It Works

The first line in the code snippet checks to see if we're trying to manipulate the basket in some way by examining the query string variables:

```
If Request("id") <> "" or Request("less") <> "" or _
                Request("more") <> "" or Request("del") <> "" Then
```

If we are trying to change something, we use a few If...Then statements to decide which one of the various methods on the Basket object we wish to run:

```
' Add an item?
If Request("id") <> "" then
   Visit.Basket.Add Request("id")
End If

' Have less?
If Request("less") <> "" then
   Visit.Basket.Decrement Request("less")
End If

' Have more?
If Request("more") <> "" then
   Visit.Basket.Increment Request("more")
End If

' Remove an item?
If Request("del") <> "" then
   Visit.Basket.Remove Request("del")
End If
```

Remember, whenever we ask the Visit object for the Basket object, some intelligence is used to drag the current basket ID from the session variables. This action means that whenever we do ask for the Basket object, we're always referring to the unique basket that is owned specifically by the visitor who has requested the page.

Making the Basket Accessible

If you click on the picture of Jo to go back to the site's home page, you'll notice that you no longer have an easy route to the basket. What we need is a link that will let us find our way back to the basket when we're ready to checkout.

A neat way of doing this is to always show the visitor the number of items in the basket and the total value of that basket. Once we have the capability to do this, we can render the basket summary into the left-hand navigation bar and offer the visitor the opportunity to navigate back to the basket page through a link.

To do this, we need to add a few methods to the Basket object, and we also need to add some code to the methods that alter the basket contents.

Try It Out – Displaying Details of the Basket in the Navigation Bar

1. First of all, let's create some member variables at the top of the definition for `Basket`:

```
' Somewhere to hold information on the basket we represent...
Private m_ID As Long
```

```
' These variables hold the cart totals...
Private m_Total As Double
Private m_NumItems As Long
Private m_TotalsLoaded As Boolean
```

2. Here's an internal helper function of the `Basket` object called `CheckTotals` (similar to `CheckLoad` method that we added to the `Products` object) that can load the totals if needed:

```
' CheckTotals - see if we need to load the totals...
Private Sub CheckTotals()

    ' Have we loaded the totals?
    If m_TotalsLoaded = False Then

        ' Reset...
        m_NumItems = 0
        m_Total = 0

        ' Run a query to get the totals back...
        Dim Query As Recordset
        Set Query = m_utility.DB.DB.Execute("select Sum(Quantity), " & _
                    "Sum(LinePrice) from vBasketItems where BasketID=" & ID)

        If Not Query.EOF Then

            ' Get the values back...
            If Not IsNull(Query(0)) Then
                m_NumItems = Query(0)
                m_Total = Query(1)
            End If

        End If

        Query.Close
        Set Query = Nothing

        ' Flag...
        m_TotalsLoaded = True

    End If

End Sub
```

3. Then, it's a simple matter of creating a `NumItems` property in the `Basket` object to return the number of items in the basket:

```
' NumItems - returns the number of items in the basket...
Public Property Get NumItems() As Long
   CheckTotals
   NumItems = m_NumItems
End Property
```

4. And a `Total` property to return the total value:

```
' Total - returns the number of items in the basket...
Public Property Get Total() As Double
   CheckTotals
   Total = m_Total
End Property
```

5. Before we can use that, we need to change the following methods of the `Basket` object, which alter the basket so they invalidate the totals that are in place. Therefore, we need to add the following line:

```
m_totalsloaded = false
```

To the top of these methods:

- ❑ Add
- ❑ Remove
- ❑ ChangeQuantity
- ❑ Increment
- ❑ Decrement
- ❑ RemoveAll

So that you get:

```
' Add - adds an item to the basket...
Public Sub Add(ByVal ProductID As Long)

   m_TotalsLoaded = False

   ' Is it already there?
   If Contains(ProductID) <> 0 Then

      ' Add one to the quantity...
      Increment ProductID

   Else
```

```
' Remove - removes an item from the basket...
Public Sub Remove(ByVal ProductID As Long)
    m_TotalsLoaded = False
    m_utility.DB.DB.Execute "delete from BasketItems where " & _
                "BasketID = " & ID & " And ProductID = " & ProductID
End Sub


' ChangeQuantity - sets the quantity in the basket...
Public Sub ChangeQuantity(ByVal ProductID As Long, ByVal Quantity As Long)
    m_TotalsLoaded = False
    ' Is it already there?  if not, add it...
    If Contains(ProductID) = 0 Then Add ProductID

    ' Now set the quantity...
    m_utility.DB.DB.Execute "update BasketItems set Quantity=" & _
                            Quantity & " where BasketID=" & ID & _
                            " and ProductID=" & ProductID

End Sub


' Increment - adds one to the quantity in the basket...
Public Sub Increment(ByVal ProductID As Long)
    m_TotalsLoaded = False
    ' If it's not there already, add it...
    If Contains(ProductID) = 0 Then
        Add ProductID
    Else
        ' increment the quantity...
        m_utility.DB.DB.Execute "update BasketItems set Quantity=Quantity+1 " & _
                    "where BasketID=" & ID & " and ProductID=" & ProductID
    End If

End Sub


' Decrement - removes one from the quantity...
Public Sub Decrement(ByVal ProductID As Long)
    m_TotalsLoaded = False
    ' If it's "1", remove it...
    If Contains(ProductID) = 1 Then
        Remove ProductID
    Else
        ' Decrement the quantity...
        m_utility.DB.DB.Execute "update BasketItems set Quantity=Quantity-1 " & _
                    "where BasketID=" & ID & " and ProductID=" & ProductID
    End If

End Sub

' RemoveAll - removes everything from the basket...
Public Sub RemoveAll()
    m_TotalsLoaded = False
    m_utility.DB.DB.Execute "delete from BasketItems where BasketID=" & ID
End Sub
```

6. Add this code to `start.asp`:

```
<td bgcolor="#ffcc99" background="i/lbg.gif" width="112" valign=top>
   <!-- in here is where we'll be adding the left navigation bar -->
   <br><table width=100% cellspacing=0 cellpadding=0>
   <tr><td class=heading align=center>Your Basket</td></tr>
   <tr><td class=small align=center>

<%
   If Visit.Basket.NumItems = 0 Then
      Response.Write "...is empty"
   Else
      ' Draw the number of items...
      Response.Write "Contains "
      Response.write Visit.Basket.NumItems & " item"

      If Visit.Basket.NumItems <> 1 Then Response.Write "s"

      ' Draw the value...
      Response.Write "<br>"
      Response.Write FormatPrice(Visit.Basket.Total)

      ' Draw a link...
      Response.Write "<br>"
      Response.Write "<a href="""
      Response.Write "basket.asp"
      Response.Write """><b>View Basket</b></a>"
   End If
%>
   </td></tr>
   </table>
</td>
```

How It Works

Now if we look at one of the other pages in the site, we can see our basket summary and our visitor has an easily accessible link back to the basket when he or she wants to checkout:

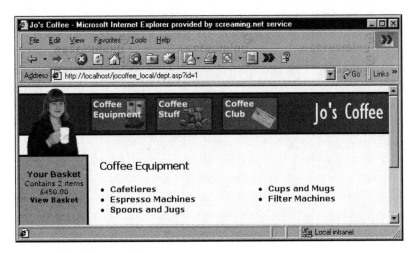

Let's look at the code!

Because querying the database to determine the total number of items and total value of the basket might be quite slow, we only want to do it whenever it's necessary. We use m_TotalsLoaded to determine if the totals have been loaded:

```
Private m_TotalsLoaded As Boolean
```

We want each page in the site to display the summary, so we place the code that displays the new basket summary in the left-hand navigation bar in start.asp. This page is part of the standard template we use throughout the site.

The code we're using in start.asp is very simple. Firstly, we ask the Visit object for the Basket, which returns a Basket object representing the unique basket of that particular visitor. We then call NumItems to find out it if it has any items (which calls the internal CheckTotals function the first time it's called to make sure the object has fresh values for this and the basket total). If the basket contains items we render a little summary of how many items it contains and the total value of goods:

```
' Draw the number of items...
Response.Write "Contains "
Response.write Visit.Basket.NumItems & " item"

If Visit.Basket.NumItems <> 1 Then Response.Write "s"

' Draw the value...
Response.Write "<br>"
Response.Write FormatPrice(Visit.Basket.Total)
```

Finally, we render a link to basket.asp so the visitor can view the details and, if they want, purchase the goods:

```
' Draw a link...
Response.Write "<br>"
Response.Write "<a href="""
Response.Write "basket.asp"
Response.Write """><b>View Basket</b></a>"
```

Summary

In this chapter, we saw how to build the tables and objects necessary to store the users' shopping baskets. We began by building two tables (`Baskets` and `BasketItems`) and a view (`vBasketItems`). We then modified the `Visit` object so that it can handle `Session` objects. This enables us to access the ID of the visitor's basket from within our `WroxCommerce` objects. We then constructed a `Basket` object. A `Basket` object is used to represent each instance of a basket in the site.

We also saw how we could present the basket to the visitor, through a `basket.asp` page and allowed customers to vary the quantity of each item.

Finally, we showed a summary of the basket's contents so that the customer could quickly navigate back to the basket when he or she wanted to checkout.

In the next chapter, we'll see how we can turn that basket into an order when the Checkout button is pressed.

The Checkout

Once the visitor has made a commitment to purchase a selection of goods and services from you, he or she has to go through the **checkout**. The checkout process is a continuation of the basket or cart metaphor that we met in the previous chapter. Once a visitor has passed through the checkout, we call them a customer.

In fact, an online checkout process is little more than a glorified data capture operation. It's at this stage that we ask the customer for their billing and shipping addresses, and their credit card information. Once we have that information, we can proceed with validating that the customer has the means to pay, and that we have the ability to send the goods to them.

Therefore, in this chapter we're going to discuss:

❑   Drop shipping

❑   How to store the customer's details and what to store

❑   How to keep track of the current customer

❑   Splitting up the order into groups (or **parts**) depending on the supplier

❑   Dealing with tax

❑   Building a checkout page

Before we get into the code of this chapter, we'll begin with a quick introduction to the world of drop shipping.

Drop Shipping

Drop shipping is the term given to the process of asking your suppliers to ship goods to your customers on your behalf. In this model, the retailer doesn't keep stock (or keeps very little stock) and relies on the stock management and distribution skills of its suppliers to satisfy orders the customer places.

In joscoffee.com, we'll be assuming that Jo's suppliers have agreed to drop ship, so that Jo can concentrate on maintaining the site and creating a sense of community with her customers. However, there's a lot of code that needs to be implemented so that we can acquire the customers' details and their orders, and then pass them on to the relevant supplier, which is what we will be discussing in this and the following chapter.

Persuading Your Supplier to Drop Ship

As a small coffee retailer, we do not have the cash to buy a lot of stock. This means that, in the offline world, we could only hold stock of a select number of machines – in other words, we couldn't sell every machine by every manufacturer, nor could we hold enough stock to satisfy all of the orders we were able to get. Or, if we did, our operating capital was affected, making our business less resistant to change.

However, suppliers can hold stock of an entire product range or ranges, and they can hold enough to meet demand. As long as we pay the suppliers for their shipping costs, it makes no odds to them if they ship directly to our customers or to us exclusively:

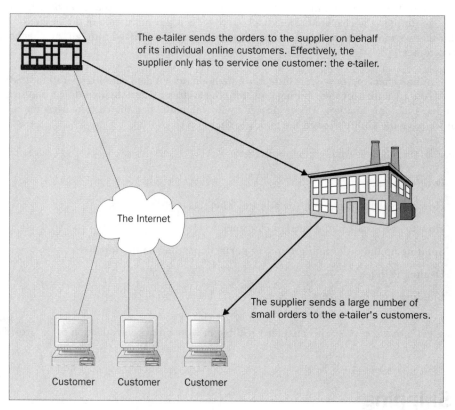

The e-tailer sends the orders to the supplier on behalf of its individual online customers. Effectively, the supplier only has to service one customer: the e-tailer.

The Internet

The supplier sends a large number of small orders to the e-tailer's customers.

Customer   Customer   Customer

Purchasing products on the Internet is often cheaper than doing so from a store, because the overheads to run an online store are less than those to run an offline store. Jo has to rent her offline store and buy stock to sell in the store (some of which is slow selling and will sit on the shelves for several months). If her suppliers drop ship to her customers, she only has to worry about maintaining the Web site, as stock will not be bought until it is needed. The only increase in costs occurs in shipping costs (as the supplier has to make lots of small shipments instead of a few large ones); however, the customers themselves usually pay for the cost of shipment as an additional charge.

Another reason why products are often cheaper on the Internet is because e-commerce sites usually significantly reduce their profit margins on each product, in the hope of gaining market share.

Our customers never directly raise customer service queries with the supplier – the retailer remains their first line of support. In addition, our supplier doesn't have to deal with the risk of selling to our customers – we still pay the supplier even if the customer turns out to be making a fraudulent order.

However, we are still sending a large number of orders through its system. At this point, we're still making phone calls or sending faxes – we're not actively reducing administration costs in the supplier's organization, which is the subject of the next section...

The Holy Grail of Drop Shipping

In the world of e-business, the ability to directly tap into your supplier's computer systems and directly create orders without having to involve labor at the supplier is something of a holy grail. There are two reasons why only a very small number of e-commerce ventures manage to totally circumvent the human administrative processes inside their suppliers:

❑ **Negotiation**. To be allowed to start messing about in your supplier's computer sandbox is going to take some fancy talking. No one likes to allow outside parties into the systems that, effectively, are the foundation of their organization.

❑ **Cost**. Integrating two computer systems together so that they operate as one smooth whole is extremely expensive. Chances are that if you're a small retailer, you can't afford to do it.

To connect into your supplier's system through an **EDI** (**electronic data interchange**) system you have to paint an extremely lucrative picture. You have to show it that going through the cost and hassle of connecting your business systems to its business systems is worthwhile. The truth is that, today, the only companies that can justify this are large e-tailers like Amazon.com and Buy.com.

Nevertheless, we're still left with the challenge of reducing the administrative costs to the supplier's business. An easy way for us to do this is to send the orders in through e-mail. If we sit down with the supplier and describe a format for the e-mail that suits it best, we can streamline communication between it and us, therefore reducing costs. We can also try to describe goods using the product codes and description that the supplier uses. If we convince it to make available an up-to-date stock level and pricing schedule each night, either through a download or an e-mail mechanism, we can eliminate the problem of placing orders for products it doesn't have. Finally, the last neat thing we can do is let it into sections of our site's administration (which is our extranet) so that it can see order details.

In short, without directly tying the two systems together (which is prohibitively expensive for most of you reading this), the only thing we can do is try to supply the data that the supplier needs to process the order in as close a format as possible to its existing business systems.

Happily, this situation will change as the industry matures as people innovate new ways of letting companies cooperate. One company working on solutions is Microsoft through its BizTalk initiative (http://www.biztalk.org/).

Drop Shipping from Multiple Suppliers

In an offline business model, companies don't usually deal with a single supplier. Jo probably dealt with one or more coffee suppliers, and several more that supplied machines. Once we move online, we may find that some suppliers don't carry all of the goods we want to sell, and so we have to deal with a number of alternative suppliers.

As we start to design our software and systems for getting goods from our suppliers to our customers, we have to be careful to accommodate multiple supplier relationships. In the offline business world, when we receive an order from a customer that contains a number of items, we regard it as a single whole order, irrespective of how many suppliers were actually used. However, in the online world, we can reevaluate that thinking and use a better solution.

What we do is split the order into different parts – one part for each supplier. We then authorize payment for, and instruct each supplier to ship, each part separately:

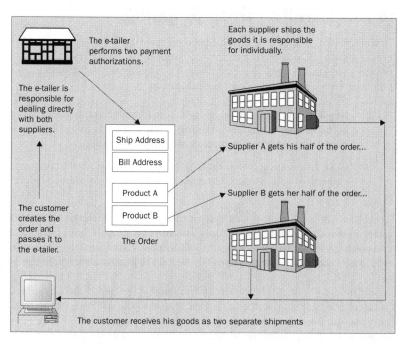

This method can be confusing to the customer as, typically, they expect an order to be satisfied in a single shipment, unless they have received separate notification that some lines in the order cannot be satisfied due to stock deficiencies. In this section, we'll see a technique for showing the customer how their order is separated into parts – each part representing an individual supplier.

In the remainder of this chapter, we'll be seeing how we can build database schemas and objects for handling drop shipping from multiple suppliers.

Storing Customer Details

However you structure the checkout portion of your site, you have to capture the customer's name, e-mail address, and physical address information. If we store that information so the customer can be identified on return visits to the store, we create a **membership and personalization** environment. From this point, we can leverage our identification of the customer to market the site to them further, and involve them in other community activities.

The best way to hold customer data is to create one table for holding their names, e-mail addresses, and passwords, and another table that can be used to hold an address book. By creating a separate address book, a customer who routinely purchases coffee for his mother can easily select her address from his book, rather than having to retype it. It's this kind of feature that helps make an e-commerce site compelling to revisit.

Try It Out – Creating Our Customers' Addresses and Address Books

1. Start up SQL Server and create the Customers table like this:

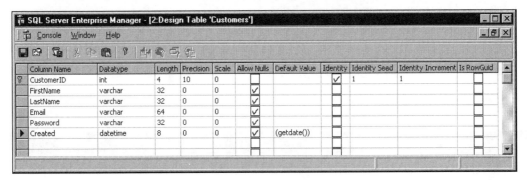

2. The table for holding addresses is just as straightforward:

Notice how we use the `CustomerID` field in the `Addresses` table to associate addresses with a particular customer in the `Customers` table.

Storing Credit Cards

A number of e-tailers hold their customers' credit card information in their databases so when those customers come back to the site they don't have to re-type that information.

Whether you choose to hold your customers' credit card details in your database is a serious decision. You have to be sure that your security is never going to be circumvented to a degree that someone could steal that list. For example, Amazon.com from the very beginning have been storing their customers' credit card details. (In fact, they have four of my cards on record).

However, imagine what would happen to Amazon's share price if one day someone (not necessarily a hacker; it could be a disgruntled employee) had stolen this database and made it publicly available. In fact, shortly before this book went to press, a hacker who gained access to the database of an e-commerce site selling CDs, published the numbers and expiration dates of 25,000 credit cards on his Web site. This could be the situation you find yourself in as owner of an e-commerce site, and illustrates the importance of deciding whether or not to store credit card numbers based upon all of your resources (security setup, exclusivity of who can access the data, etc.).

Most medium to large organizations shouldn't have too much trouble making sure that this database remains impervious to inside and outside attack. However, if the risk is too great, there's no shame in asking your customers to re-key the details whenever they make a purchase. In fact, UK super-site Jungle.com does not hold credit card information. If in doubt, err on the side of caution.

For Jo's Coffee, we're going to hold our customers' credit card information in the database.

Try It Out – Creating the Cards Table

1. Create the following `Cards` table to hold the details of our customers' credit cards:

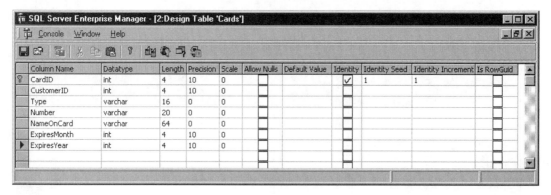

Again, notice how we use the `CustomerID` column to associate the card with an entry in the `Customers` table.

Keeping Track of the Current Customer

In the previous chapter, we kept track of the visitor's basket by using the ASP Session object and creating a new Basket object. Well, now we need to do the same thing to keep track of the current customer.

1. Keeping track of the customer's ID is the easy part. Add this global variable to the Visit object:

```
' This variable holds a reference to the Session level stuff...
Private m_Session As Session
Private m_BasketID As Long
Private m_CustomerID As Long
```

2. Then, in the Configure method of the Visit object place the following code:

```
' Hold the Session...
Set m_Session = Session
If Not m_Session Is Nothing Then

    ' capture the BasketID...
    m_BasketID = CLng(m_Session("BasketID"))
    m_CustomerID = CLng(m_Session("CustomerID"))

End If
```

This is the same place from which we retrieved the possible BasketID from the Session object.

3. We now need to create a new class module in Visual Basic called Customers and add this code to it:

```
Option Explicit

' Use IUtility to call back into the Visit and Database objects...
Private m_utility As IUtility

' Configure - set up IUtility...
Public Sub Configure(ByVal utility As IUtility)

    ' Hold the utility object...
    Set m_utility = utility

End Sub
```

4. Next, add this code to `Customers` to retrieve customer information:

```
' QueryCustomers - primitive to help us get at customers...
Private Function QueryCustomers(Optional ByVal Where As String, _
                        Optional ByVal Order As String = "lastname", _
                        Optional ByVal AsKeyset As Boolean = False) _
                        As Recordset

    Set QueryCustomers = m_utility.DB.RunQuery("Customers", , Where, _
                                            Order, AsKeyset)
End Function
```

```
' GetCustomer - returns a single customer...
Public Function GetCustomer(ByVal CustomerID As Long, _
                        Optional ByVal AsKeyset As Boolean = False) _
                        As Recordset

    Set GetCustomer = QueryCustomers("CustomerID=" & CustomerID, , AsKeyset)

End Function
```

5. Now, we need to alter the `Visit` object so that we can get hold of the `Customers` object when we need it. Firstly, add this global variable to the `Visit` object:

```
' These variables hold the objects that are in the next hierarchical
' level in our object model...
Private m_catalog As Catalog
Private m_customers As Customers
```

6. Add this property to the `Visit` object, to return a properly configured `Customers` object back to the caller:

```
' Customers - returns an instance of a Customers object...
Public Property Get Customers() As Customers

    ' Do we have one already?
    If m_customers Is Nothing Then
        ' Create and configure
        Set m_customers = New Customers
        m_customers.Configure Me
    End If

    ' Return the Customers...
    Set Customers = m_customers

End Property
```

7. Finally, add this code to `Visit` object's `Shutdown` method:

```
' Shutdown - releases any resources we may have open...
Public Sub ShutDown()
```

```
    ' Do we have a database?
    If Not m_DB Is Nothing Then

        ' Shutdown the database...
        m_DB.ShutDown
        Set m_DB = Nothing

    End If

    ' Clean up any other objects...
    Set m_catalog = Nothing
    Set m_Session = Nothing
    Set m_customers = Nothing

End Sub
```

How It Works

By adding the following line, each time the `Configure` object is called, we examine the session variables to exact the ID of the current customer:

```
    m_CustomerID = CLng(m_Session("CustomerID"))
```

Just as the `Catalog` object lets us perform tasks in the object model related to the product catalog, we need to create the `Customers` object that lets us handle the customers in our database. We require the `Customers` object to hold a pointer back to the `IUtility` interface exposed by the `Visit` object (this is identical to the way we started the `Catalog` object):

```
    Private m_utility As IUtility

    Public Sub Configure(ByVal utility As IUtility)

        Set m_utility = utility

    End Sub
```

The `QueryCustomers` method is similar in nature to the `QueryProducts` method we built earlier. It asks `RunQuery` to select rows from the `Customers` table based on the parameters passed through:

```
    Private Function QueryCustomers(Optional ByVal Where As String, _
                                    Optional ByVal Order As String = "lastname", _
                                    Optional ByVal AsKeyset As Boolean = False) _
                                    As Recordset

        Set QueryCustomers = m_utility.DB.RunQuery("Customers", , Where, _
                                                   Order, AsKeyset)
    End Function
```

241

In `GetCustomer`, we leverage that method by asking it to return the customer row with the given ID:

```
Public Function GetCustomer(ByVal CustomerID As Long, _
                            Optional ByVal AsKeyset As Boolean = False) _
                            As Recordset

    Set GetCustomer = QueryCustomers("CustomerID=" & CustomerID, , AsKeyset)

End Function
```

We've seen code similar to that in the `Customers Property Get` before too. When we built the `Catalog` object, we wanted the `Visit` object to be responsible for creating instances of it. Here we're doing the same thing – we create an instance of the object the very first time the property is requested and cache it. Then, each subsequent time the property is requested, we return the cached version. This reduces the total number of objects required per page and aids scalability.

```
Public Property Get Customers() As Customers

    ' Do we have one already?
    If m_customers Is Nothing Then
      ' Create and configure
      Set m_customers = New Customers
      m_customers.Configure Me
    End If

    ' Return the Customers...
    Set Customers = m_customers

End Property
```

Shipping Methods

E-commerce sites commonly give their customers a number of different shipping options so that they can get a speed/cost trade off with which they are happy. If a customer needs an item urgently (perhaps as a present), he or she will often be happy to pay a high price for express delivery. If there is no hurry customers will often prefer the slower, but cheaper option.

There are various options for charging your customers. You might want to consider charging by weight (especially if you stock a lot of heavy items) or by distance (especially if you are expecting a significant overseas market). Some companies provide discounts on shipping for customers who are bulk buying.

To keep things simple, we're going to allow customers of joscoffee.com to select from next-day delivery and 3-day delivery, and store these options in a table called `Shipping`.

Try It Out – Creating the Shipping Table

1. Here's the Shipping table:

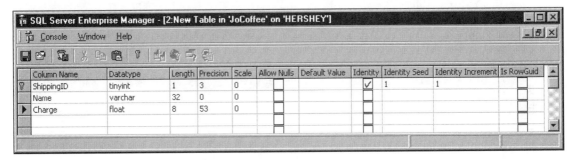

2. For the purposes of this example, quickly tap these shipping options into the Shipping table for use later on:

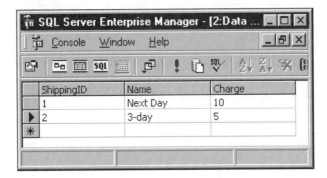

Don't forget – ShippingID is configured as an IDENTITY field, so your IDs may not be the same as the ones we're using here.

Splitting Up the Order

With the database schema in place to hold the customers' details, we need to create the schema that's capable of holding the orders that have been placed, or are in the process of being placed, on the system.

Earlier in the chapter, we spoke about how we can split the order up into several parts and then send each part over to the individual suppliers. In this section, we'll learn how we can take the contents of the basket and create an individual order, and then use one or more order parts to satisfy the request. To begin with, we'll create three new tables.

Try It Out – Creating the Tables for Orders

1. To start with, let's create a table that's capable of keeping track of the orders that exist, the `Orders` table:

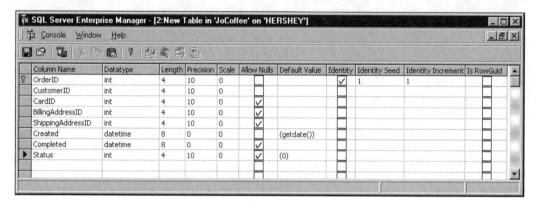

2. Now add the `OrderParts` table as shown in the following screenshot:

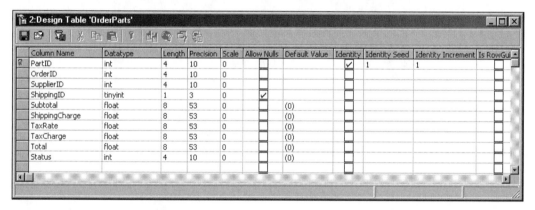

3. Finally, create another table called `OrderLines`:

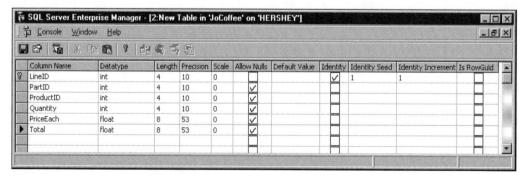

How It Works

As a business rule, we say that each part of an order must share the same customer, credit card, shipping address, and billing address, so the `Orders` table lets us associate those particulars with an order. We'll see more of the `Status` column later, but it is responsible for telling us what state the order is in, e.g. Processing, Completed, or Cancelled. Although an order requires a credit card, and billing and shipping addresses, we allow these to be null inside the table because we'll be populating these fields as the customer moves through the process of supplying this information; in other words, we don't specify all of this data in one go.

In `OrderParts`, we want to keep a reference back to the row in the `Orders` table that it relates to, and hold a reference to the supplier that is going to handle that part of the order. Additionally, we want to keep track of who is responsible for shipping the order. We begin with the `ShippingID` column blank, because we'll be populating this as the customer goes through the process of committing the order.

We also need to hold values for the shipping charge, subtotal, tax rate, and total for the order part. This is for two reasons. Firstly, we are going to be storing historical values in this table, so we want to store a snapshot of the shipping charge and tax rate values that were valid when the order was placed. If these values change over time, our historical accounting data in these tables won't be skewed. Secondly, we want to relieve some of the processing burden on both the database and the application components by storing the results of calculated values such as `TaxCharge` and `Total`.

The `OrderLines` table holds the detail of each item. We use it to store the historical value of the price of the product (`PriceEach`), and the calculated total value of the line of the order (`Total`).

Creating the Views

As we walk through the process of capturing the order, and as we try to process the order once it's been committed, we'll need some views to make life a little easier.

The vOrderParts View

The first view we'll create, `vOrderParts`, is designed to join the `OrderParts` and `Shipping` tables together. However, because we will only be setting the reference to the `Shipping` table at the very end of the order capture process, we want to use a **left outer join** so that we include all the information from the `OrderParts` table, but not necessarily all the information from the `Shipping` table.

Try It Out – Creating the vOrderParts View

1. Create a new view called `vOrderParts`, and add the `OrderParts` table and the `Shipping` table (in that order).

2. Select the columns as shown in this screenshot:

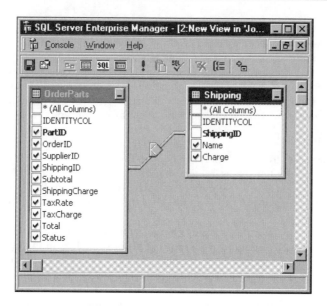

3. Right-click on the line joining the two tables and select Properties. Then select All rows from OrderParts from the Include rows frame:

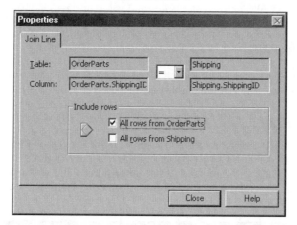

4. To make the naming more obvious on the columns from the Shipping table, we will rename the Name column to ShippingName and the Charge column to CurrentShippingCharge. To do this, open the Grid pane of the Design View window, and specify ShippingName as the Alias of the Name column and CurrentShippingCharge as the Alias of the Charge column.

5. Here's the SQL for the view, which should appear in the SQL pane of the Design View window:

```
SELECT Shipping.Name AS ShippingName,
    Shipping.Charge AS CurrentShippingCharge,
    OrderParts.PartID, OrderParts.OrderID,
```

```
        OrderParts.SupplierID, OrderParts.ShippingID,
        OrderParts.Subtotal, OrderParts.ShippingCharge,
        OrderParts.TaxRate, OrderParts.TaxCharge,
        OrderParts.Total, OrderParts.Status
FROM OrderParts LEFT OUTER JOIN
        Shipping ON
        OrderParts.ShippingID = Shipping.ShippingID
```

The vOrderLines View

Our second view is called vOrderLines and its purpose is to join OrderLines and vProducts together. This will give us instant access to all of the product specific information for each line in the order. However, we won't see all of the dynamic attribute information that we store against each product.

Try It Out – Creating the vOrderLines View

1. Create a new view called vOrderLines, which looks like this:

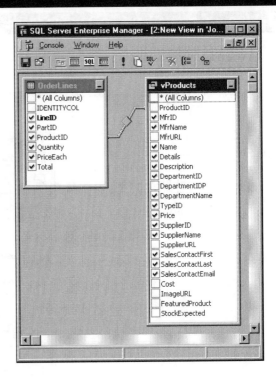

2. As in the previous Try It Out, alias the Price column of the vProducts view to CurrentPrice. The SQL for this view should look like this:

```
SELECT OrderLines.LineID, OrderLines.PartID,
        OrderLines.ProductID, OrderLines.Quantity,
        OrderLines.PriceEach, OrderLines.Total, vProducts.MfrID,
        vProducts.MfrName, vProducts.Name, vProducts.Details,
        vProducts.Description, vProducts.DepartmentID,
```

247

```
        vProducts.DepartmentName, vProducts.TypeID,
        vProducts.Price AS CurrentPrice,
        vProducts.SupplierID,
        vProducts.SupplierName, vProducts.SalesContactFirst,
        vProducts.SalesContactLast,
        vProducts.SalesContactEmail
   FROM OrderLines INNER JOIN
        vProducts ON OrderLines.ProductID = vProducts.ProductID
```

The vOrderSplit View

One of the steps involved in populating the tables that we built earlier in this chapter is determining how many parts each order has, based on the products in the basket. In the time-honored tradition of getting the database to do most of the work, we're going to create a view called vOrderSplit that can take a basket and tell us which individual suppliers the basket uses. We can then query the vOrderSplit view, walk through the results, and create the rows that are needed in the OrderParts table.

Try It Out – Creating the vOrderSplit View

1. Create a new view called vOrderSplit, which comprises the BasketItems tables and the Products table.

2. Select only the BasketID column from the BasketItems table and the SupplierID column from the Products table.

3. Then right-click anywhere on the gray background of the Design View window and select <u>G</u>roup By. You should get this:

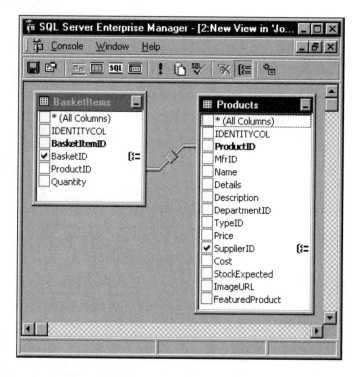

4. The SQL for the `vOrderSplit` view should look like this:

```
SELECT Products.SupplierID, BasketItems.BasketID
FROM BasketItems INNER JOIN
    Products ON
    BasketItems.ProductID = Products.ProductID
GROUP BY Products.SupplierID, BasketItems.BasketID
```

How It Works

It's the `GROUP BY` clause that does the magic in this case. What we have done here is created a view that we can query by passing in a basket ID and get back a list of the unique suppliers. To get the supplier IDs, however, we first had to join the `BasketItems` and `Products` tables together. Once that was done, we used the `GROUP BY` clause to aggregate the results.

Creating the Objects

Let's just recap where we are. In the checkout page of joscoffee.com, we allow the visitors to place orders. However, Jo's suppliers are drop shipping the customers' orders, so we need to make sure that each supplier only gets orders for items that it can provide. Therefore, we're going to split each order into parts (one for each supplier), which are in turn split into lines (each of which holds a single item), and hold the information in the `Orders`, `OrderParts`, and `OrderLines` tables respectively.

We now need to add the objects, methods, and properties into the `WroxCommerce` object model that will deal with creating the rows in the tables we just built.

Try It Out – Creating the Orders Object

1. To start off, create a new object called `Orders` in the `WroxCommerce` project and add this code:

```
Option Explicit

' Use IUtility to call back into the Visit and Database objects...
Private m_utility As IUtility

' Configure - set up IUtility...
Public Sub Configure(ByVal utility As IUtility)

    ' Hold the utility object...
    Set m_utility = utility

End Sub
```

2. Now add this global variable to the `Visit` object:

```
' These variables hold the objects that are in the next hierarchical
' level in our object model...
Private m_catalog As Catalog
```

```
Private m_customers As Customers
Private m_orders As Orders
```

3. Next, add this property to the `Visit` object:

```
' Orders - returns an instance of a Orders object...
Public Property Get Orders() As Orders

    ' Do we have one already?
    If m_orders Is Nothing Then
        ' Create and configure
        Set m_orders = New Orders
        m_orders.Configure Me
    End If

    ' Return the Orders...
    Set Orders = m_orders

End Property
```

The `Orders` property is much like the one we built earlier in the chapter for returning instances of the `Customers` object. As a reminder, it creates a single instance of the `Orders` object the first time it's called and holds a cached copy throughout the life of the `Visit` object.

4. Finally, add this code to `Visit` object's `Shutdown` method:

```
' Shutdown - releases any resources we may have open...
Public Sub ShutDown()

    ' Do we have a database?
    If Not m_DB Is Nothing Then

        ' Shutdown the database...
        m_DB.ShutDown
        Set m_DB = Nothing

    End If

    ' Clean up any other objects...
    Set m_catalog = Nothing
    Set m_customers = Nothing
    Set m_Session = Nothing
    Set m_orders = Nothing

End Sub
```

5. Add this routine to the `Basket` object. This `Split` function makes a call to the `SplitBasket` method of the `Orders` object, which we will create in the next step:

```
' Split - splits the basket up into lots of order rows...
Public Function Split() As Long
    Split = m_utility.Visit.Orders.SplitBasket(ID)
End Function
```

6. With everything in place, we can go ahead and write the `SplitBasket` method, which is responsible for populating the tables. Add this method to the `Orders` object:

```
' SplitBasket - splits a basket into Orders, OrderParts and OrderLines...
Public Function SplitBasket(ByVal BasketID As Long) As Long

    ' Get started by creating a new order...
    ' Assign this order to the customer by asking the Visit object
    ' for its CustomerID.
    Dim Order As New Recordset
    Order.Open "orders", m_utility.DB.DB, adOpenKeyset, adLockOptimistic
    Order.AddNew
    Order("customerid") = m_utility.Visit.CustomerID
    Order.Update

    ' Pass the new order ID back...
    SplitBasket = Order("orderid")

    ' We'll be using these variables as we go...
    Dim Query As Recordset
    Dim OrderPart As Recordset
    Dim OrderLine As Recordset
    Dim SubTotal As Double

    ' Use the vOrderSplit view to determine the separate suppliers...
    Dim SupplierList As Recordset
    Set SupplierList = m_utility.DB.DB.Execute( _
                       "select * from vOrderSplit where BasketID=" & BasketID)

    ' Loop the suppliers...
    Do While Not SupplierList.EOF

        ' Create a new part...
        Set OrderPart = New Recordset
        OrderPart.Open "orderparts", m_utility.DB.DB, adOpenKeyset, _
                        adLockOptimistic
        OrderPart.AddNew

        ' Set the supplier and order id...
        OrderPart("orderid") = Order("orderid")
        OrderPart("supplierid") = SupplierList("SupplierID")

        ' Update the part straightaway to get an ID back that
        ' we can then add to the new order lines...
```

```
OrderPart.Update

' We'll use this to keep track of the subtotal...
SubTotal = 0

' Use vBasketItems to find the products in the basket
' that use that supplier. Then, walk this list and update.
Set Query = m_utility.DB.DB.Execute( _
              "select * from vBasketItems where BasketID=" & BasketID & _
              " and SupplierID=" & SupplierList("supplierid"))
Do While Not Query.EOF

    ' Add an order line...
    Set OrderLine = New Recordset
    OrderLine.Open "orderlines", m_utility.DB.DB, adOpenKeyset, _
                adLockOptimistic
    OrderLine.AddNew

    ' Associate the line with an order part...
    OrderLine("partid") = OrderPart("partid")

    ' Copy the details from the basket...
    OrderLine("productid") = Query("productid")
    OrderLine("quantity") = Query("quantity")
    OrderLine("priceeach") = Query("price")
    OrderLine("total") = Query("lineprice")

    ' Update and close the new order line...
    OrderLine.Update
    OrderLine.Close
    Set OrderLine = Nothing

    ' Add the line total to subtotal...
    SubTotal = SubTotal + Query("lineprice")

    ' Next
    Query.MoveNext

Loop
Query.Close
Set Query = Nothing

' Set the subtotal in the order part...
OrderPart("subtotal") = SubTotal

' Update and close the order part...
OrderPart.Update

' With the part finished, ask another method to
' update the calculated totals...
CalculatePartTotals OrderPart("partid")
```

```
    ' Cleanup the orderpart
    OrderPart.Close
    Set OrderPart = Nothing

    ' Next...
    SupplierList.MoveNext

Loop

  ' Close the suppliers...
  SupplierList.Close
  Set SupplierList = Nothing

  ' Close the order...
  Order.Close
  Set Order = Nothing

End Function
```

7. Enter this code for the `CalculatePartTotals` method to the `Orders` object:

```
' CalculatePartTotals - updates the totals when subtotal, shipping or
' tax values change...
Public Function CalculatePartTotals(ByVal PartID As Long)

    ' Get the part from the database...
    Dim Part As New Recordset
    Part.Open "select * from OrderParts where PartID=" & PartID, _
            m_utility.DB.DB, adOpenKeyset, adLockOptimistic

    ' Do the calculations...
    Part("taxcharge") = Part("subtotal") * Part("taxrate")
    Part("total") = Part("subtotal") + Part("shippingcharge") _
                  + Part("taxcharge")

    ' Update and close...
    Part.Update
    Part.Close
    Set Part = Nothing

End Function
```

8. Back at the beginning part of this section, we spoke about shipping methods and charges. These three methods will let us extract them from the database and use them in the order capture process. Add them to the `Orders` object now:

```
' QueryShipping - query the shipping table...
Private Function QueryShipping(Optional ByVal Where As String, _
                               Optional ByVal Order As String = "charge", _
                               Optional ByVal AsKeyset As Boolean = False) _
                               As Recordset
```

```
        Set QueryShipping = m_utility.DB.RunQuery("Shipping", , _
                            Where, Order, AsKeyset)
    End Function


    ' GetShipping - returns all the shipping methods...
    Public Function GetShipping(Optional ByVal AsKeyset As Boolean = False) _
                        As Recordset
        Set GetShipping = QueryShipping(, , AsKeyset)
    End Function


    ' GetShippingMethod - returns all the shipping methods...
    Public Function GetShippingMethod(ByVal ShippingID As Long, _
                            Optional ByVal AsKeyset As Boolean = False) _
                        As Recordset
        Set GetShippingMethod = QueryShipping("shippingid=" & ShippingID, _
                            , AsKeyset)

    End Function
```

9. Finally, we need to create some methods that can query the orders in the database; add these to Orders as well:

```
    ' QueryOrders - query the Orders table...
    Private Function QueryOrders(Optional ByVal Where As String, _
                        Optional ByVal Order As String = "orderid", _
                        Optional ByVal AsKeyset As Boolean = False) _
                        As Recordset
        Set QueryOrders = m_utility.DB.RunQuery("Orders", , Where, _
                                Order, AsKeyset)
    End Function


    ' GetOrders - returns all the orders...
    Public Function GetOrders(Optional ByVal AsKeyset As Boolean = False) _
                        As Recordset
        Set GetOrders = QueryOrders(, , AsKeyset)
    End Function


    ' GetOrder - returns a single order...
    Public Function GetOrder(ByVal OrderID As Long, _
                        Optional ByVal AsKeyset As Boolean = False) As Recordset
        Set GetOrder = QueryOrders("orderid=" & OrderID, , AsKeyset)
    End Function
```

How It Works

We've seen code very much like that above when we created the Customers object, so we'll just focus on the SplitBasket and CalculatePartTotals methods here.

The first thing we do in the SplitBasket method is create a new row in the Orders table. We add the ID of the customer (we'll build the CustomerID property of the Visit object later in the chapter, so don't worry), update the row, and grab the new ID for the order. This ID is returned out of the method:

```
Order.AddNew
Order("customerid") = m_utility.Visit.CustomerID
Order.Update

' Pass the new order ID back...
SplitBasket = Order("orderid")
```

Next, we use our `vOrderSplit` view to return a list of the suppliers unique to the particular set of objects held in the basket:

```
Set SupplierList = m_utility.DB.DB.Execute(_
                "select * from vOrderSplit where BasketID=" & BasketID)
```

We then loop through these suppliers. As we come across each supplier in the `SupplierList` recordset, we create a new row in the `OrderParts` table, and configure it with the order ID and the supplier ID:

```
Do While Not SupplierList.EOF

    ' Create a new part...
    Set OrderPart = New Recordset
    OrderPart.Open "orderparts", m_utility.DB.DB, adOpenKeyset, _
                adLockOptimistic
    OrderPart.AddNew

    ' Set the supplier and order id...
    OrderPart("orderid") = Order("orderid")
    OrderPart("supplierid") = SupplierList("SupplierID")

    ' Update the part straightaway to get an ID back that
    ' we can then add to the new order lines...
    OrderPart.Update
```

Next, we get a list of the products from the `vBasketItems` view that pertains to the supplier at which we're current looking. Effectively, we're going to copy the relevant data from the `vBasketItems` view into the `OrderLines` table. Note that we store a snapshot of the price in the `OrderLines` table. This prevents our data from being corrupted whenever we alter prices in the future. We also keep track of the subtotal of the current order part:

```
Set Query = m_utility.DB.DB.Execute(_
                "select * from vBasketItems where BasketID=" & BasketID & _
                " and SupplierID=" & SupplierList("supplierid"))
Do While Not Query.EOF

    ' Add an order line...
    Set OrderLine = New Recordset
    OrderLine.Open "orderlines", m_utility.DB.DB, adOpenKeyset, _
                adLockOptimistic
    OrderLine.AddNew
```

```
' Associate the line with an order part...
OrderLine("partid") = OrderPart("partid")

' Copy the details from the basket...
OrderLine("productid") = Query("productid")
OrderLine("quantity") = Query("quantity")
OrderLine("priceeach") = Query("price")
OrderLine("total") = Query("lineprice")

' Update and close the new order line...
OrderLine.Update
OrderLine.Close
Set OrderLine = Nothing

' Add the line total to subtotal...
SubTotal = SubTotal + Query("lineprice")
```

After we've added all the appropriate rows to OrderLines, all that remains is to store the subtotal in the OrderParts row, update that row, and then call CalculatePartTotals:

```
' Set the subtotal in the order part...
OrderPart("subtotal") = SubTotal

' Update and close the order part...
OrderPart.Update

' With the part finished, ask another method to
' update the calculated totals...
CalculatePartTotals OrderPart("partid")
```

The CalculatePartsTotals method is responsible for updating the calculation columns in the OrderParts table. Every time the items in the table change, or we change the shipping method or tax rate, we call this function:

```
Public Function CalculatePartTotals(ByVal PartID As Long)

    ' Get the part from the database...
    Dim Part As New Recordset
    Part.Open "select * from OrderParts where PartID=" & PartID, _
            m_utility.DB.DB, adOpenKeyset, adLockOptimistic

    ' Do the calculations...
    Part("taxcharge") = Part("subtotal") * Part("taxrate")
    Part("total") = Part("subtotal") + Part("shippingcharge") _
                    + Part("taxcharge")

    ' Update and close...
    Part.Update
    Part.Close
    Set Part = Nothing

End Function
```

The trick with this method is to select the appropriate `OrderParts` row from the database, and update the `TaxCharge` and `Total` columns based on the information stored in the `TaxRate` and `ShippingCharge` columns. We haven't seen a way of altering `TaxRate` or setting `ShippingCharge` yet – this is something we'll do later.

Try It Out – Creating the Order Object

1. Create a new class module called `Order` and add these variable declarations:

```
Option Explicit

' Use IUtility to call back into the Visit and Database objects...
Private m_utility As IUtility

' Somewhere to hold information on the order we represent...
Private m_ID As Long
Private m_CustomerID As Long
Private m_CardID As Long
Private m_BillingAddressID As Long
Private m_ShippingAddressID As Long
Private m_Created As Date
Private m_Completed As Date
Private m_Status As Long
Private m_IsLoaded As Boolean
```

2. Now add a `Configure` method; as before this method is called to give the object a reference back to the `IUtility` interface. We also pass in the ID of the row in the `Orders` table that we're interested in:

```
' Configure - set up IUtility...
Public Sub Configure(ByVal utility As IUtility, ByVal ID As Long)

    ' Hold the utility object...
    Set m_utility = utility

    ' Store the ID...
    m_ID = ID

End Sub
```

3. `CheckLoad` is called by any of the properties that return information about the order. It simply selects out the row and stores the values contained therein in member variables on the object:

```
' CheckLoad - makes sure the property values have been loaded...
Private Sub CheckLoad()

    ' Have we already loaded?
    If m_IsLoaded = False Then
```

```
        ' Get the record back from the Catalog object...
        Dim Query As Recordset
        Set Query = m_utility.Visit.Orders.GetOrder(m_ID)

        If Not Query.EOF Then
            ' Get the values back...
            m_CustomerID = Query("customerid")
            If Not IsNull(Query("cardid")) Then m_CardID = Query("cardid")
            If Not IsNull(Query("billingaddressid")) Then _
                        m_BillingAddressID = Query("billingaddressid")
            If Not IsNull(Query("shippingaddressid")) Then _
                        m_ShippingAddressID = Query("shippingaddressid")
            If Not IsNull(Query("created")) Then m_Created = Query("created")
            If Not IsNull(Query("completed")) Then _
                        m_Completed = Query("completed")
            m_Status = Query("status")
        End If

        Query.Close
        Set Query = Nothing

        ' Flag...
        m_IsLoaded = True

    End If

End Sub
```

4. Finally, we write a bundle of properties to return information about the order. Notice that we call `CheckLoad` at the start of most of these properties:

```
Public Property Get ID() As Long
    ID = m_ID
End Property
```

```
Public Property Get CustomerID() As Long
    CheckLoad
    CustomerID = m_CustomerID
End Property
```

```
Public Property Get BillingAddressID() As Long
    CheckLoad
    BillingAddressID = m_BillingAddressID
End Property
```

```
Public Property Get ShippingAddressID() As Long
    CheckLoad
    ShippingAddressID = m_ShippingAddressID
End Property
```

```
Public Property Get CardID() As Long
    CheckLoad
    CardID = m_CardID
End Property

Public Property Get Status() As Long
    CheckLoad
    Status = m_Status
End Property

Public Property Get Created() As Date
    CheckLoad
    Created = m_Created
End Property

Public Property Get Completed() As Date
    CheckLoad
    Completed = m_Completed
End Property
```

Dealing with Tax

The way sales tax is handled varies between different countries, and regions within some countries. For example, in the United States, you only pay sales tax on mail order or e-commerce orders if the company has offices in the state that you're resident in, usually between 6 to 8%. In the UK, you pay VAT (Value Added Tax) of 17.5% on most goods (although a few categories, including books, are zero rate) no matter where you live in the country.

The most important thing when dealing with tax is getting the customer to tell you what tax rate they should be charged at. You cannot, for example, ask them, "Do you want to pay tax? Yes or No."

Dealing with Variable Tax Rates

If you live in the US (or any another country that has variable sales tax rates depending on where you live compared to where the company you're buying from is based), the easiest way to work out the tax rate is to present the users with a drop-down list of the available states and ask them to choose the one in which they live. Giving the user a finite set of 50 options is a lot easier than trying to interpret the multitude of values available in everyday English. For example, if a customer chooses Arizona from a drop-down list, you know instantly that he or she lives in Arizona, whereas if you provide a free-entry field you could get things like AZ, Arizona, Arzna, or Ariz. Once you know the state, you simply assign the tax rate of the order appropriately.

> **You should seek professional advice before deciding how to handle sales tax in your e-commerce solution.**

The same concept applies for countries that have a flat tax rate throughout. A UK-based company can simply present the customers with a drop-down list of countries. If they choose UK, the tax rate is set to 17.5%, if they don't, it's set to 0%.

In our example, we're going to charge sales tax on all orders at 17.5%, so that we can keep this example as simple as possible.

Just as a side note regarding duty: Most e-commerce sites that ship internationally do not concern themselves with the tax or duty rates in the importing country. When goods are shipped overseas, it's assumed that the government of the country that the goods are going to will levy the appropriate taxes.

Setting the Tax Rate on the Order

Once we know what the rate is going to be, all we need to do is assign a tax rate to each order part through a property on the `Order` object that we're going to write now.

We know that all the goods that Jo is selling should be taxed at the same rate. However, if your site sells items that do not need to have a sales tax applied, you should make sure that you assign a tax rate to each order item, not to each order part.

Try It Out – Building the TaxRate Property

1. Add the following code to the `Order` object:

```
' TaxRate - sets the tax rate for the order...
Public Property Let TaxRate(ByVal newval As Double)

    ' Get the parts in the order...
    Dim parts As Recordset
    Set parts = m_utility.Visit.Orders.GetOrderParts(m_ID, True)

    Do While Not parts.EOF
        ' Set the rate for the part...
        m_utility.DB.DB.Execute "update orderparts set taxrate=" & _
                            newval & " where partid=" & parts("partid")

        ' Now, recalculate the tax totals, etc. for the part...
        m_utility.Visit.Orders.CalculatePartTotals parts("partid")

        ' Next
        parts.MoveNext
    Loop

    parts.Close
    Set parts = Nothing

End Property
```

How It Works

The only function that the `TaxRate` property performs is to grab hold of all the parts in the order and then loop through them one by one updating the `TaxRate` column in the `OrderParts` table. Each time the `TaxRate` property is set, `CalculatePartTotals` is called to update the calculated values that are stored in this table.

Note, the GetOrderParts method is implemented on page 305, so don't compile WroxCommerce.dll just yet

Calling the SplitBasket Method

At this point we've built the `Orders` and `Order` objects, which help to populate the `Orders`, `OrderParts`, and `OrderLines` tables. The method that is actually responsible for these tables being populated is `SplitBasket`. However, we have not yet created any code that calls the `SplitBasket` method, and that is the purpose of the following exercise. We will call this method from the `Visit` object.

To do this, we're going to add an `OrderID` property to the `Visit` object that will return the ID of the order on which we're working. The first time this property is called, `SplitBasket` will be called and the appropriate rows will be created, based on the ID of the basket that's also stored inside `Visit`. By doing it this way we we, we have the 'just in time' approach that is vital in environments that need to scale, such as this. The idea is that we don't waste resources by running long, complex routines that do a number of writes to the database before we really need them.

Using this approach has an interesting side effect. If people go through some of the checkout process, but don't commit to it (they click out before confirming), we'll end up with rows in the database that don't point to real orders that have been received. Fortunately, we can identify which orders aren't committed to by looking at the `Status` column in the `Orders` table – a column we'll be seeing more of in the next chapter.

Periodically, we'll have to run a batch process that clears out this dead data. However, this data is still quite useful to keep, as it tells us whereabouts in the checkout process our potential customers are clicking out of the page. We can use that information to improve our site.

Try It Out – Calling SplitBasket from the Visit Object

1. To implement the `OrderID` property,, we need to add a member variable to the `Visit` object that can hold the ID:

```
' this variable holds a reference to Session level stuff...
Private m_Session As Session
Private m_BasketID As Long
Private m_CustomerID As Long
Private m_OrderID As Long
```

2. Implementing the `OrderID` property is pretty easy. We simply check to see if we have an order ID of 0, and if we do, we call `SplitBasket`. Add this code to the `Visit` object as well:

```
' OrderID - returns an order ID for the basket...
Public Property Get OrderID() As Long

    ' Do we have one? If not, split the order up...
    If m_OrderID = 0 Then
        m_OrderID = Orders.SplitBasket(m_BasketID)
        m_Session("OrderID") = m_OrderID
    End If
```

```
        ' Return it...
        OrderID = m_OrderID

End Property
```

In a similar manner to how we're storing the basket and customer IDs, we're holding our current order ID in a `Session` variable. So, whenever we create an instance of the `Visit` object, we need to retrieve it.

3. Add this code to the `Configure` method of `Visit`:

```
' Hold the session information...
Set m_Session = Session

If Not m_Session Is Nothing Then

    ' Capture the BasketID...
    m_BasketID = CLng(m_Session("BasketID"))
    m_CustomerID = CLng(m_Session("CustomerID"))
    m_OrderID = CLng(m_Session("OrderID"))
End If
```

4. Now we add a small property to return a configured `Order` object back. By calling the existing `OrderID` property from this new property, we can automatically split the order if that is required. Add the following code to the `Visit` object:

```
' Order - returns a configured Order object...
Public Property Get Order() As Order
    Set Order = New Order
    Order.Configure Me, OrderID
End Property
```

5. One other useful thing to know is if we already have an order configured. Add this `IsOrder` method to the `Visit` object:

```
' IsOrder - do we have an order?
Public Function IsOrder() As Boolean

    ' test for an order...
    If m_OrderID = 0 Then
        IsOrder = False
    Else
        IsOrder = True
    End If

End Function
```

We won't actually be looking at how to process the order until the next chapter, although now we're in an excellent position to try and obtain the money out of our customers' pockets, and get our suppliers to send them the goods they order. To recap we've:

- ❏ Created tables to store the orders, order parts, and order lines (`Orders`, `OrderParts`, and `OrderLines`)

- ❏ Created views to make our coding simpler (`vOrderParts`, `vOrderLines`, and `vOrderSplit`)

- ❏ Created objects to populate our tables (`Orders` and `Order`)

- ❏ Called the `SplitBasket` method of the `Orders` object from the `Visit` object

The remainder of this chapter talks about how we can build a page for capturing the order information (credit cards, addresses, etc.) and increasing our customers' confidence by securing our server.

Building the Checkout

In the rest of this chapter, we're going to build our checkout page, called `checkout.asp`. The `checkout.asp` page is, actually, one of the most challenging ones to build – mainly because it has to deal with customers flitting about entering details of addresses and credit cards. However, with a good architecture, you can create a good, stable solution.

First, though, we need to make the checkout process accessible from the customer's basket...

Try It Out – Linking the Checkout to the Basket

1. The first step is to create a new `checkout.asp` page that will be used to capture the details of the checkout process. Open the `JoCoffee` Visual InterDev project and create a new ASP page called `checkout.asp` page. As we've done before, copy the contents of `template.asp` into this new page so they both look the same.

2. Now add this code to `basket.asp`:

```
' Add the total...
Response.Write "<tr><td><br></td></tr>"
Response.Write "<tr bgcolor=#c0c0c0>"
Response.Write "<td colspan=4 align=right class=heading>"
Response.write "Total:"
Response.Write "</td><td align=right class=heading>"
Response.Write FormatPrice(total)
Response.Write "</td></tr>"

' Go to the checkout...
Response.Write "<tr><td><br></td></tr>"
Response.Write "<td colspan=5 align=center class=heading>"
Response.Write "<a href="""
Response.Write "checkout.asp"
Response.Write """>Proceed to checkout</a>"
Response.Write "</td></tr>"
```

Now if you refresh the page you'll see a link enabling you to get to the checkout:

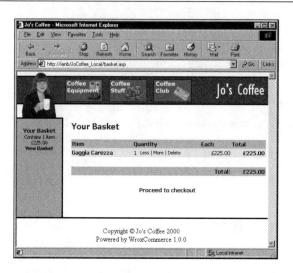

The Checkout Process Flowchart

In our administration code, we used the `select case request("action")` trick to make the page behave differently depending on how we approached it. We'll be using the same method in `checkout.asp` to mimic this flowchart:

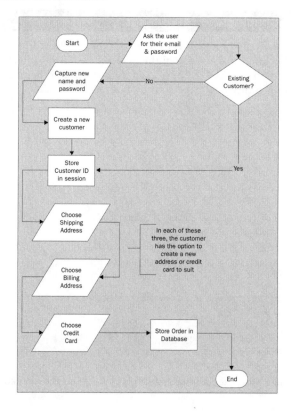

Step 1 – Capture the E-mail Address and Password

According to the flowchart, the first thing we have to do is capture the e-mail address and password of the customer. In an e-commerce environment, we need the customer's e-mail address to properly communicate with him or her during the order fulfillment process. The password is only needed if the customer is a returning one who's already been through the checkout process once before.

Try It Out – Creating a Form to Obtain the E-mail Address and Password

1. First of all, add this code to the top of `checkout.asp`:

```
<% Option Explicit

    ' Somewhere to store problems...
    Dim problem

%>
```

2. Let's create the form for obtaining the e-mail and password by adding this code to `checkout.asp`:

```
<!-- #include file="start.asp" -->

<!-- heading -->
<font class=bigheading>Checkout</font>
<br><br>

<% ' What do we want to do?
select case lcase(request("action")) %>

    <% ' log on the user...
    case else %>

        <!-- table and form... -->
        <form action="<%=request("script_name")%>" method=post>
        <center><table width=400 cellspacing=0 cellpadding=3
                    bgcolor=#e0e0e0 border=1>
        <tr><td><table cellspacing=0 cellpadding=2 width=100%>

        <!-- if we have a problem, render it... -->
        <% if problem <> "" then %>
            <tr><td bgcolor=#ff0000 class=heading colspan=2>
            <font color=#ffffff><%=problem%></font></td></tr>
            <tr><td><br></td></tr>
        <% end if %>

        <!-- draw the e-mail field... -->
        <tr><td class=heading>
        Your e-mail address:
        </td><td>
        <input type=text name=email value="<%=request("email")%>">
        </td></tr>

        <!-- now, ask if they're coming back... -->
```

```
<tr><td class=small colspan=2>
<input type=radio name=return value=0>
I have never shopped at Jo's Coffee before
</td></tr>

<tr><td class=small colspan=2>
<input type=radio name=return value=1 checked>
I am a returning customer.  My password is:
<input type=password name=password size=10
                      value="<%=request("password")%>">
</td></tr>

<!-- add the button -->
<tr><td><br></td></tr>
<tr><td colspan=2 align=center>
<input type=submit value="Continue">
</td></tr>

<! -- end it -->
</table></td></tr>
</td></tr></table></center>
<input type=hidden name=logoncustomer value=1>
</form>

<% end select %>

<!-- #include file="end.asp" -->
```

How It Works

When we add some items and try to checkout our basket this is the screen we'll see (don't try it yet though, we've got some more coding to do first):

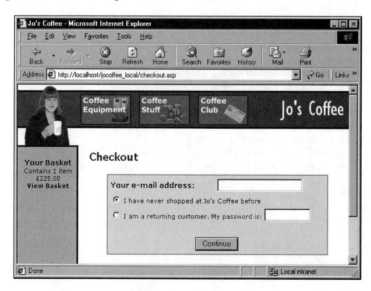

Note that just before we closed the form, we added a HIDDEN field to the form called
logoncustomer:

```
<input type=hidden name=logoncustomer value=1>
```

What this does is tell us what we expect the page to do when it's re-entered – we'll be reusing this page for a number of tasks as we build it, so we need to make sure we have mechanisms in place to let the form know what it's supposed to do.

What we also need is a method for returning problems back to the visitor if anything goes wrong. We can do this through a variable called problem, which we can populate to describe the problems that occurred to the visitor. We added this variable at the start of the Try It Out, so now we need to make it do something.

Try It Out – Dealing with a Problem

1. Add this code to the top of checkout.asp:

```
<% option explicit

    ' Somewhere to store problems...
    dim problem

    Sub AddToProblem(buf)
        if problem <> "" then problem = problem & "<br>"
        problem = problem & buf
    end sub

%>
```

How It Works

The code in AddToProblem makes it a little easier for us to present problems. Basically, there are a number of points of failure when we may want to tell the user something was missing from the form or incorrect – this function helps us present the problems in a clearer fashion by appending a BR tag to the end of each issue. For example, if the user specifies neither a City nor a Region, we can say:

```
You must enter a city.<br>
You must enter a region.
```

We'll see this function in use throughout this code.

The Visual Basic Code for Logging the User In

For now, we must turn our attention to creating the Visual Basic code for logging the user into the checkout process, and ensuring that the password for the specified e-mail address is correct. If the e-mail address is new, we create a new customer.

Try It Out – Adding the Visual Basic Code to Login the User

1. We begin by adding properties for getting and setting the customer ID to the `Visit` object:

```
' CustomerID - get the current customer id...
Public Property Get CustomerID() As Long
    CustomerID = m_CustomerID
End Property
```

```
' CustomerID - set the current customer id both in the object
' and in the Session...
Public Property Let CustomerID(ByVal newval As Long)
    m_CustomerID = newval
    m_Session("CustomerID") = m_CustomerID
End Property
```

2. Now we need to ask the `Customers` object to validate the customer and return any problems back to the caller. If successful, the `Customers` object will also store the current user ID in the ASP session. Way back in this chapter, we changed the `Visit` object's `Configure` method so that it would pull this customer ID from the session each time it was called. The upshot of this is that when we log a user into the site, they remain logged on until they close the browser, time out the session, or explicitly log off.

Add this code to the `Customers` object in the VB project:

```
' CheckLogon - attempts to logon a user based on an e-mail and password
Public Function CheckLogon(ByVal EMail As String, ByVal Password As String, _
                    ByRef Problem As Variant) As Boolean

    ' Make sure the problem is blank...
    Problem = ""

    ' Try to find a customer with a matching e-mail address. We use the Replace
    ' function to make sure that if the e-mail address was entered with
    ' apostrophes, we gracefully handle any problems.
    Dim query As Recordset
    Set query = m_utility.DB.DB.Execute("select * from customers " & _
                "where email='" & Replace(EMail, "'", "''") & "'")

    ' Is there such a customer?
    If Not query.EOF Then
        ' Do the passwords match?
        If LCase(Password) = LCase(query("password")) Then
            ' We're fine. Log on the customer using the CustomerID
            ' property of the Visit object...
            m_utility.Visit.CustomerID = query("customerid")

            ' Flag it as successful...
            CheckLogon = True
```

```
    Else
        ' Add it to the problem...
        Problem = "The password you entered is invalid."
    End If
    Else
' Add it to the problem...
    Problem = "There is no customer with the e-mail address you specified."
    End If

    ' Close...
    query.Close
    Set query = Nothing

End Function
```

3. Now add this function to the Customers object, which we can use to create new customers:

```
' CreateCustomer - create a new customer from the e-mail address...
Public Function CreateCustomer(ByVal EMail As String) As Long

    ' First of all, check to see if there's a customer with this e-mail...
    Dim query As Recordset
    Set query = m_utility.DB.DB.Execute("select * from customers " & _
                            "where email='" & Replace(EMail, "'", "''") & "'")

    ' Only create the record there are no results in "query"...
    If query.EOF Then
        ' Create a new record...
        Dim NewCustomer As New Recordset
        NewCustomer.Open "select * from customers", m_utility.DB.DB, _
                    adOpenKeyset, adLockOptimistic
        NewCustomer.AddNew

        ' Set the value...
        NewCustomer("email") = EMail

        ' Update the record...
        NewCustomer.Update

        ' Pass the ID back to the caller...
        CreateCustomer = NewCustomer("customerid")

        ' Close the record...
        NewCustomer.Close
        Set NewCustomer = Nothing

    End If

    ' Close query...
    query.Close
    Set query = Nothing

End Function
```

How It Works

Let's start with the `CheckLogon` function!

The first thing we do is select from the `Customers` table by e-mail address. We assume each customer has a unique e-mail address. The `Replace` function used to form the query prevents the code from crashing if the user enters an apostrophe into the e-mail address:

```
Set query = m_utility.DB.DB.Execute("select * from customers " & _
            "where email='" & Replace(EMail, "'", "''") & "'")
```

If there is no row, then we assume that the e-mail address was invalid and prompt the user to try again by returning the error message back through the `Problem` parameter and into the `problem` variable we added earlier:

```
Problem = "There is no customer with the e-mail address you specified."
```

If we have a row, then we do have a customer with that e-mail address. All we have to do is check the password. We use the `LCase` function on both sides of the test to make a case insensitive comparison. If the password matches, we use the `CustomerID` property on the `Visit` object to set the current customer. If you recall, this action not only updates the `m_CustomerID` member variable of the `Visit` object, but also updates the session variables:

```
If LCase(Password) = LCase(query("password")) Then
   ' We're fine. Log on the customer using the CustomerID
   ' property of the Visit object...
   m_utility.Visit.CustomerID = query("customerid")

   ' Flag it as successful...
   CheckLogon = True
Else
   ' Add it to the problem...
   Problem = "The password you entered is invalid."
End If
```

In the `CreateCustomer` function, we only want to create a new customer if we don't already have one with the same e-mail address (remember, e-mail addresses are the method through which we uniquely identify customers). We use the same test here as we did in `CheckLogon`. If the e-mail address is unique, we create a new row in the `Customers` table:

```
Set query = m_utility.DB.DB.Execute("select * from customers " & _
                        where email='" & Replace(EMail, "'", "''") & "'")

' Only create the record there are no results in "query"...
If query.EOF Then
   ' Create a new record...
   Dim NewCustomer As New Recordset
   NewCustomer.Open "select * from customers", m_utility.DB.DB, _
                   adOpenKeyset, adLockOptimistic
   NewCustomer.AddNew
```

```
    ' Set the value...
    NewCustomer("email") = EMail

    ' Update the record...
    NewCustomer.Update
```

At this time, all we know about the customer is his or her e-mail address. `CreateCustomer` does not set the `CustomerID` property of the `Visit` object – we do this in the ASP code.

The ASP Code for Logging the User In

Now that our `WroxCommerce` object model is capable of logging on users, we need to turn our attention back to the ASP code.

There are two key features to the ASP code we are going to create in the next Try It Out:

❑   Firstly, we're going to check if the required information has been filled out.

❑   Secondly, we're going to do some interesting logic with regards to the radio buttons. If the user doesn't select I am a returning customer but enters a password anyway, we'll attempt to log them in as an existing user anyway.

Try It Out – Creating the ASP Code to Login the User

1. Here's the ASP code, which should be added at the top of the `checkout.asp` page after the `AddToProblem` method:

```
Sub AddToProblem(buf)
    if problem <> "" then problem = problem & "<br>"
    problem = problem & buf
end sub
```

```
' Are we trying to logon? We added this hidden field in our form design.
If Request("logoncustomer") <> "" Then
    ' Do we have an e-mail?
    If Request("email") = "" Then
        addtoproblem "You must enter your e-mail address."
    End If
    If Request("return") = "1" and Request("password") = "" Then
        addtoproblem "You must enter your password."
    End If

    ' Did we do it?
    If problem = "" Then

        ' Are we creating a new customer?
        Dim customerid
        Dim newcustomer

        If Request("return") = "0" and Request("password") = "" Then
```

```
            ' Create a new customer?
            customerid = Visit.Customers.CreateCustomer(Request("email"))

            If customerid = 0 Then
                ' We already have a customer with that e-mail
                addtoproblem "There is already a customer listed " & _
                            "with that e-mail address.  You should log " & _
                            "into your existing account by entering " & _
                            "your password."
            else
                ' Tell WroxCommerce what customer we are, and then
                ' flag us as a new customer
                Visit.CustomerID = customerid
                newcustomer = True
            End If

        else

            ' we need to check the password...
            Visit.Customers.CheckLogon Request("email"), Request("password"), _
                                    problem
            newcustomer = False

        End If

        ' Bounce if all OK. This prevents confusion with page refreshes.
        If problem = "" Then

            ' Set up for a redirect...
            Response.Buffer = True
            Response.Clear

            ' If we're a new customer, we need to bounce to a
            ' page where we can get the rest of the info, otherwise
            ' try to capture a billing address...
            If newcustomer = True Then
                Response.Redirect Request("script_name") & "?action=getname"
            Else
                Response.Redirect Request("script_name") & _
                                "?action=addresses&type=billing"
            End If

        End If

    End If

End If
%>
<HTML>
<HEAD>
    <!-- #include file="site.asp" -->
```

How It Works

We begin by checking the form variables to see if we were passed an e-mail address and password. If either of those is missing, we use the AddToProblem routine, which presents the problem to the user; otherwise, we proceed to either try and create a new account, or log the user in:

```
If Request("email") = "" Then
    addtoproblem "You must enter your e-mail address."
End If
If Request("return") = "1" and Request("password") = "" Then
        addtoproblem "You must enter your password."
End If
```

This If statement determines if the user checked on the I have never shopped at Jo's Coffee before option button, as the default action in this case is that we want to create a new customer. However, we are also working on the assumption that the customer may not have remembered to check on the I am a returning customer option, and may have gone ahead and entered his or her password. The second part of the If statement checks for this and assumes that if the user has entered a password they meant to check on I am a returning customer:

```
If Request("return") = "0" and Request("password") = "" Then
```

Depending on what happened after this check, we either try to create a new customer with CreateCustomer, or we try to log in an existing customer with CheckLogon. Either one of these functions can throw errors – CreateCustomer will throw an error if the e-mail address has already been used. If all goes well though, we set the customer ID manually:

```
customerid = Visit.Customers.CreateCustomer(Request("email"))

If customerid = 0 Then
    ' We already have a customer with that e-mail
    addtoproblem "There is already a customer listed " & _
                "with that e-mail address.  You should log " & _
                "into your existing account by entering " & _
                "your password."
else
    ' Tell WroxCommerce what customer we are, and then
    ' flag us as a new customer
    Visit.CustomerID = customerid
    newcustomer = True
End If
```

CheckLogon will throw an error if the e-mail address has not been used, or if the password is invalid. If all goes well, CheckLogon will set the customer ID itself:

```
Visit.Customers.CheckLogon Request("email"), Request("password"), _
                            problem
newcustomer = False
```

Finally, if the user does manage to log on, we need to bounce to a different page using a
`Response.Redirect`. If the customer is new (the `newcustomer` flag has been set to `True`), we need
to get their name and chosen password by setting the `action` to `getname`; otherwise, we have to get a
billing address:

```
If newcustomer = True Then
    Response.Redirect Request("script_name") & "?action=getname"
Else
    Response.Redirect Request("script_name") & _
                      "?action=addresses&type=billing"
End If
```

The Customer Object

The design of our `Customers` table dictates that we only need to know a few things about our
customers. We require their names, e-mail addresses, and passwords. Credit card and address
information is held in separate tables.

Try It Out – Creating a Customer Object

1. Create a new object called `Customer` in the `WroxCommerce` project and add this code:

```
Option Explicit

' Use IUtility to call back into the Visit and Database objects...
Private m_utility As IUtility

' Somewhere to hold information on the product we represent...
Private m_ID As Long
Private m_FirstName As String
Private m_LastName As String
Private m_EMail As String
Private m_Password As String
Private m_Created As Date
Private m_IsLoaded As Boolean


' Configure - set up IUtility...
Public Sub Configure(ByVal utility As IUtility, ByVal ID As Long)

    ' hold the utility object...
    Set m_utility = utility

    ' store the ID...
    m_ID = ID

End Sub

' CheckLoad - makes sure the property values have been loaded...
Private Sub CheckLoad()

    ' Have we already loaded?
```

```
    If m_IsLoaded = False Then


        ' Get the record back from the Catalog object...
        Dim query As Recordset
        Set query = m_utility.Visit.Customers.GetCustomer(m_ID)
        If Not query.EOF Then
            ' Get the values back...
            If Not IsNull(query("firstname")) Then m_FirstName = query("firstname")
            If Not IsNull(query("lastname")) Then m_LastName = query("lastname")
            If Not IsNull(query("email")) Then m_EMail = query("email")
            If Not IsNull(query("password")) Then m_Password = query("password")
            If Not IsNull(query("created")) Then m_Created = query("created")
        End If

        query.Close
        Set query = Nothing

        ' Flag...
        m_IsLoaded = True

    End If

End Sub


Public Property Get FirstName() As String
    CheckLoad
    FirstName = m_FirstName
End Property


Public Property Get LastName() As String
    CheckLoad
    LastName = m_LastName
End Property


Public Property Get EMail() As String
    CheckLoad
    EMail = m_EMail
End Property


Public Property Get Password() As String
    CheckLoad
    Password = m_Password
End Property


Public Property Get Created() As String
    CheckLoad
    Created = m_Created
End Property


Public Property Get Name() As String
    Name = FirstName & " " & LastName
End Property
```

As you can see, this code is notionally similar to the code we saw before to implement the Order object, so we won't go into detail on it here.

2. To round this off, we'll create this property in the Visit object to return a Customer object back when requested. This is similar in nature to the Order property. Place this code at the bottom:

```
' Customer - returns a customer object...
Public Property Get Customer() As Customer
    Set Customer = New Customer
    Customer.Configure Me, CustomerID
End Property
```

Step 2 – Capture the New Customer's Name and Password

Next, we need to capture the extra information that we need to know about our new customer. For starters, this will just be his or her name and password. In the previous step, we used the newcustomer flag to determine if the user was new, and if so route him or her through to the "getname" case on our select lcase(request("action")) line, which determines how the checkout.asp page should look and what functionality it should provide. In the following exercise, we're going to add the code to get a new customer's name and password to checkout.asp.

Try It Out – Adding the getname Case

1. Here's the code that will create the form we need to ask the user for his or her name and password. It should be added to checkout.asp, immediately above the Case Else statement we built in the previous step. This is similar in nature to the form we created earlier in the chapter, so we'll keep duplications in our discussions to a minimum!

```
<% ' What do we want to do?
select case lcase(request("action")) %>

    <%' Capture the name of the visitor...
    case "getname" %>

        <!-- table and form... -->
        <form action="<%=Request("script_name")%>" method=post>
        <center>
        <table width=400 cellspacing=0 cellpadding=3 bgcolor=#e0e0e0 border=1>
        <tr><td><table cellspacing=0 cellpadding=2 width=100%>

        <!-- heading -->
        <tr><td class=heading colspan=2>
        Please tell us a little about yourself...
        </td></tr>
        <tr><td><br></td></tr>

        <!-- If we have a problem, draw it... -->
        <% If problem <> "" Then %>
```

```
            <tr><td bgcolor=#ff0000 class=heading colspan=2>
            <font color=#ffffff><%=problem%></font></td></tr>
            <tr><td><br></td></tr>
        <% End If %>

        <!-- draw the fields... -->
        <tr><td class=heading>
        Your first name:
        </td><td>
        <input type=text name=firstname value="<%=Request("firstname")%>">
        </td></tr>
        <tr><td class=heading>
        Your last name:
        </td><td>
        <input type=text name=lastname value="<%=Request("lastname")%>">
        </td></tr>
        <tr><td class=heading>
        Your password:
        </td><td>
        <input type=password name=password value="<%=Request("password")%>">
        </td></tr>
        <tr><td class=heading>
        Confirm password:
        </td><td>
        <input type=password name=confirm value="<%=Request("confirm")%>">
        </td></tr>

        <!-- add the button -->
        <tr><td><br></td></tr>
        <tr><td colspan=2 align=center>
        <input type=submit value="Continue">
        </td></tr>

        <! -- End it -->
        </table></td></tr>
        </td></tr></table></center>
        <input type=hidden name=updatecustomer value=1>
        <input type=hidden name=action value="<%=Request("action")%>">
        </form>

    <% ' log on the user...
    case else %>

        <!-- table and form... -->
        <form action="<%=request("script_name")%>" method=post>
```

2. At present the WroxCommerce objects don't know how to update customer information, so we need to add this method to our Customer object:

```
' Update - updates information for the customer...
Public Function Update(Optional ByVal FirstName As String, _
                       Optional ByVal LastName As String, _
```

```
                        Optional ByVal EMail As String, _
                        Optional ByVal Password As String)

    ' Get the customer record for updating...
    Dim UpdateQuery As New Recordset
    UpdateQuery.Open "select * from customers where customerid=" & m_ID, _
                     m_utility.DB.DB, adOpenKeyset, adLockOptimistic

    ' Set the values that need setting...
    If FirstName <> "" Then UpdateQuery("firstname") = FirstName
    If LastName <> "" Then UpdateQuery("lastname") = LastName
    If EMail <> "" Then UpdateQuery("email") = EMail
    If Password <> "" Then UpdateQuery("password") = Password

    ' Update the database and close the query...
    UpdateQuery.Update
    UpdateQuery.Close
    Set UpdateQuery = Nothing

End Function
```

3. To clear this bit up, we just have to write a little ASP code in `checkout.asp` to validate the form and call the `Update` method:

```
    ' If we're a new customer, we need to bounce to a
    ' page where we can get the rest of the info, otherwise
    ' try to capture a billing address...
    If newcustomer = True Then
        Response.Redirect Request("script_name") & "?action=getname"
    Else
        Response.Redirect Request("script_name") & _
                          "?action=addresses&type=billing"
    End If

        End If

    End If

End If
```

```
' Do we want to update the customer info?
If Request("updatecustomer") <> "" Then

    ' Do we have the bits we need?
    If Request("firstname") = "" Then
        addtoproblem "You must enter your first name."
    End If
    If Request("lastname") = "" Then
        addtoproblem "You must enter your last name."
    End If
    If Request("password") = "" Then
```

```
            addtoproblem "You must enter your password."
    Else
        If LCase(Request("password")) <> LCase(Request("confirm")) Then
            addtoproblem "Both passwords you enter must match exactly."
        End If
    End If


    ' Did we do it?
    If problem = "" Then


        ' Update the customer.  We don't need to update the e-mail...
        visit.Customer.Update Request("firstname"), _
                            Request("lastname"), , Request("password")


        ' Bounce over to capture the billing address...
        Response.Buffer = True
        Response.Clear
        Response.Redirect Request("script_name") & _
                        "?action=addresses&type=billing"


    End If

End If
```

```
    %>
    <HTML>
    <HEAD>
```

How It Works

The code in this step produces the following form:

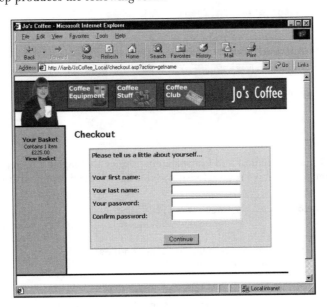

As in the first instance where we use a HIDDEN field called logoncustomer, we use one in the getname case called updatecustomer to indicate to ASP that it needs to update the customer when the form is submitted. We do a similar trick by including the HIDDEN field that will send the action value back into the form. That way, when we submit the form, the page stays in getname mode and won't redisplay the first page:

```
<input type=hidden name=updatecustomer value=1>
<input type=hidden name=action value="<%=Request("action")%>">
```

In the Update method, we use optional parameters so we can pick and choose the fields we want to update – we're not forced to update all of the fields against a customer each time we use the method:

```
Public Function Update(Optional ByVal FirstName As String, _
                       Optional ByVal LastName As String, _
                       Optional ByVal EMail As String, _
                       Optional ByVal Password As String)
```

Whatever specific values we want to set, we still work on the principle of selecting a recordset containing just the customer row we're interested in:

```
UpdateQuery.Open "select * from customers where customerid=" & ID, _
                  m_utility.DB.DB, adOpenKeyset, adLockOptimistic
```

Before we update the customer information, we check for the existence of all the appropriate form fields and look to see if the two passwords we passed in match:

```
If Request("firstname") = "" Then
    addtoproblem "You must enter your first name."
End If
If Request("lastname") = "" Then
    addtoproblem "You must enter your last name."
End If
If Request("password") = "" Then
    addtoproblem "You must enter your password."
Else
    If LCase(Request("password")) <> LCase(Request("confirm")) Then
        addtoproblem "Both passwords you enter must match exactly."
    End If
End If
```

Finally, we use the Update method and immediately bounce the page off to get the billing address. This is the same page to which we redirect visitors who have logged on to existing accounts:

```
visit.Customer.Update Request("firstname"), _
                      Request("lastname"), , Request("password")

' Bounce over to capture the billing address...
Response.Buffer = True
Response.Clear
Response.Redirect Request("script_name") & _
                  "?action=addresses&type=billing"
```

Step 3 – Adding Addresses

The next two steps are choosing a billing address and a shipping address. However, because the customer might be new, or he or she might want to use different addresses to the ones we have in the database (if he or she moves, wants to send a gift, etc.), we also need to develop a page for capturing addresses.

Try It Out – Creating the Visual Basic Code to Add Addresses

1. First of all, we need to add some methods to the `Customers` object that can return addresses back to the caller:

```
' QueryAddresses - primitive to help us get at addresses...
Private Function QueryAddresses(Optional ByVal Where As String, _
                                Optional ByVal Order As String = "address1", _
                                Optional ByVal AsKeyset As Boolean = False) _
                                As Recordset
    Set QueryAddresses = m_utility.DB.RunQuery("Addresses", _
                                               , Where, Order, AsKeyset)

End Function
```

```
' GetAddress - returns a single address...
Public Function GetAddress(ByVal AddressID As Long, _
                           Optional ByVal AsKeyset As Boolean = False) _
                           As Recordset
    Set GetAddress = QueryAddresses("AddressID=" & AddressID, , AsKeyset)
End Function
```

```
' GetCustomersAddresses - returns all the addresses a customer has...
Public Function GetCustomersAddresses(ByVal CustomerID As Long, _
                Optional ByVal AsKeyset As Boolean = False) As Recordset
    Set GetCustomersAddresses = QueryAddresses("CustomerID=" & _
                                               CustomerID, , AsKeyset)

End Function
```

2. Then, add some code to the `Customers` object that can create the addresses:

```
' CreateAddress - creates a new address record...
Public Function CreateAddress(ByVal CustomerID As Long, _
              ByVal Name As String, ByVal Company As String, _
              ByVal Address1 As String, ByVal Address2 As String, _
              ByVal City As String, ByVal Region As String, _
              ByVal PostalCode As String, ByVal Country As String, _
              ByVal Phone As String) As Long

    ' Create a new address record...
    Dim NewAddress As Recordset
    Set NewAddress = New Recordset
    NewAddress.Open "addresses", m_utility.DB.DB, adOpenKeyset, adLockOptimistic
    NewAddress.AddNew
```

```
' Populate it...
NewAddress("customerid") = CustomerID
NewAddress("name") = Name
If Company <> "" Then NewAddress("company") = Company
NewAddress("address1") = Address1
If Address2 <> "" Then NewAddress("address2") = Address2
NewAddress("city") = City
NewAddress("region") = Region
NewAddress("postalcode") = PostalCode
NewAddress("country") = Country
If Phone <> "" Then NewAddress("phone") = Phone

' Close it, but send the ID back to the caller...
NewAddress.Update
CreateAddress = NewAddress("addressid")
NewAddress.Close
Set NewAddress = Nothing

End Function
```

3. Next, instead of adding more code to the Customers object, we need to add a couple of methods to the Customer object:

```
' Addresses - returns all of the addresses the customer has...
Public Property Get Addresses(Optional ByVal AsKeyset As Boolean) As Recordset
    Set Addresses = _
        m_utility.Visit.Customers.GetCustomersAddresses(m_ID, AsKeyset)
End Property
```

```
' HasAddresses - returns True if the customer has addresses...
Public Function HasAddresses() As Boolean

    ' Test to see if the address recordset we get is empty...
    Dim query As Recordset
    Set query = Addresses
    If query.EOF Then
        HasAddresses = False
    Else
        HasAddresses = True
    End If
    query.Close
    Set query = Nothing

End Function
```

How It Works

Notionally similar again to the code used to create customers, the CreateAddress method adds a new row to the database and uses the parameters to populate the columns. For optional columns (Company, Address2, and Phone), we leave the database values as null if they are not explicitly stated:

```
NewAddress.Open "addresses", m_utility.DB.DB, adOpenKeyset, adLockOptimistic
NewAddress.AddNew

' Populate it...
NewAddress("customerid") = CustomerID
NewAddress("name") = Company
If Company <> "" Then NewAddress("company") = Company
NewAddress("address1") = Address1
If Address2 <> "" Then NewAddress("address2") = Address2
NewAddress("city") = City
NewAddress("region") = Region
NewAddress("postalcode") = PostalCode
NewAddress("country") = Country
If Phone <> "" Then NewAddress("phone") = Phone
```

Try It Out – Creating the ASP Code to Add Addresses

1. Add this code to the top of `checkout.asp`:

```
<% option explicit

' Somewhere to store problems...
dim problem

Sub AddToProblem(buf)
    if problem <> "" then problem = problem & "<br>"
    problem = problem & buf
end sub
```

```
If Request("action") = "addresses" Then

    ' Check to see if there are any addresses
    If Visit.Customer.HasAddresses = False Then

        ' Bounce...
        Response.buffer = True
        Response.clear
        Response.Redirect Request("script_name") & _
                        "?action=getaddress&type=" & request("type")

    End If

End If
```

```
' Are we trying to logon?  we added this hidden field in our form design...
If Request("logoncustomer") <> "" Then
```

2. The next stage is to present the form capable of capturing the address information. This code is fairly similar to what we've seen before, but we also pass a HIDDEN field through with the type. This lets us know whereabouts in the order capture process we are. Add this to `checkout.asp`, too:

```
<input type=hidden name=updatecustomer value=1>
<input type=hidden name=action value="<%=Request("action")%>">
</form>
```

```
<% ' Capture the new address...
case "getaddress" %>

    <!-- table and form... -->
    <form action="<%=Request("script_name")%>" method=post>
    <center><table width=400 cellspacing=0 cellpadding=3
                    bgcolor=#e0e0e0 border=1>
    <tr><td><table cellspacing=0 cellpadding=2 width=100%>

    <!-- heading -->
    <tr><td class=heading colspan=2>
    Please enter an address...
    </td></tr>
    <tr><td><br></td></tr>

    <!-- If we have a problem, draw it... -->
    <% If problem <> "" Then %>
        <tr><td bgcolor=#ff0000 class=heading colspan=2>
        <font color=#ffffff><%=problem%></font></td></tr>
        <tr><td><br></td></tr>
    <% End If %>

    <!-- draw the fields... -->
    <tr><td class=heading>
    Name:
    </td><td>
    <input type=text name=name value="<%=Request("name")%>">
    </td></tr>
    <tr><td class=std>
    Company name:
    </td><td>
    <input type=text name=company value="<%=Request("company")%>">
    </td></tr>
    <tr><td class=heading>
    Address 1:
    </td><td>
    <input type=text name=address1 value="<%=Request("address1")%>">
    </td></tr>
    <tr><td class=std>
    Address 2:
    </td><td>
    <input type=text name=address2 value="<%=Request("address2")%>">
    </td></tr>
    <tr><td class=heading>
    Town/City:
    </td><td>
    <input type=text name=city value="<%=Request("city")%>">
    </td></tr>
```

```
<tr><td class=heading>
Region/State:
</td><td>
<input type=text name=region value="<%=Request("region")%>">
</td></tr>
<tr><td class=heading>
Postal code/ZIP:
</td><td>
<input type=text name=postalcode value="<%=Request("postalcode")%>">
</td></tr>
<tr><td class=heading>
Country:
</td><td>
<input type=text name=country value="<%=Request("country")%>">
</td></tr>
<tr><td class=std>
Phone:
</td><td>
<input type=text name=phone value="<%=Request("phone")%>">
</td></tr>

<!-- add the button -->
<tr><td><br></td></tr>
<tr><td colspan=2 align=center>
<input type=submit value="Continue">
</td></tr>

<! -- End it -->
</table></td></tr>
</td></tr></table></center>
<input type=hidden name=createaddress value=1>
<input type=hidden name=type value="<%=Request("type")%>">
<input type=hidden name=action value="<%=Request("action")%>">
</form>
```

```
<% ' log on the user...
case else %>
```

3. Finally, add some code to checkout.asp to check to see if the form was filled in properly and make the call to CreateAddress:

```
' Bounce over to capture the billing address...
Response.Buffer = True
Response.Clear
Response.Redirect Request("script_name") & _
                "?action=addresses&type=billing"

    End If

End If
```

```
' Do we want to create a new address?
If Request("createaddress") <> "" Then

    ' Do we have the bits we need?
    If Request("name") = "" Then
        addtoproblem "You must enter a name."
    End If
    If Request("address1") = "" Then
        addtoproblem "You must enter the first address line."
    End If
    If Request("city") = "" Then
        addtoproblem "You must enter the city."
    End If
    If Request("region") = "" Then
        addtoproblem "You must enter the region (or state)."
    End If
    If Request("postalcode") = "" Then
        addtoproblem "You must enter the postal code (or ZIP)."
    End If
    If Request("country") = "" Then
        addtoproblem "You must enter the country."
    End If

    ' Did we do it?
    If problem = "" Then

        ' Update the customer...
        Visit.Customers.CreateAddress Visit.CustomerID, _
                Request("name"), Request("company"), Request("address1"), _
                Request("address2"), Request("city"), Request("region"), _
                Request("postalcode"), Request("country"), Request("phone")

        ' Bounce over to choose the address we want.  We pass
        ' through the type we were working with on the form...
        Response.Buffer = True
        Response.Clear
        Response.Redirect Request("script_name") & _
                        "?action=addresses&type=" & Request("type")

    End If

End If

%>
<HTML>
<HEAD>
```

How It Works

Here's the form that is created in this step:

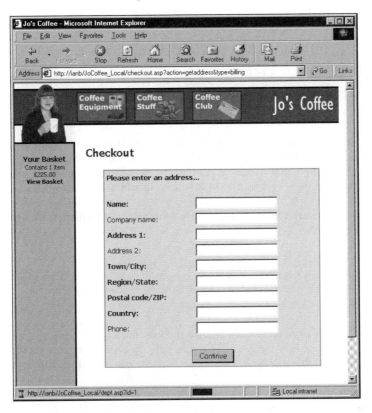

To deal with new customers that will have no addresses registered, we need to present a form capable of capturing their addresses. We'll then be reusing that form later for customers who want to register new addresses.

The desired action is that if a customer has come back to the site, or already has an address registered, we present a list of the addresses and let the customer choose the one he or she wants. Don't forget that after they've entered a billing address, they'll have an address registered and we can prompt them to use that one for their shipping address. After the user either logs on to an existing account, or creates one by supplying a new name and password, we redirect to the `action` statement called `addresses`, which will present a list of addresses.

As we want to add a new customer's address to our database, we need to create a form into which he or she can enter an address. To implement this in `checkout.asp` we need to use an action statement called `getaddress`. Let's look at the code we use to achieve this.

At the top of checkout.asp, just before we implement the logoncustomer functionality, we check to see if the customer has any addresses and, if not, redirect the page once more:

```
If Visit.Customer.HasAddresses = False Then

    ' Bounce...
    Response.buffer = True
    Response.clear
    Response.Redirect Request("script_name") & _
                   "?action=getaddress&type=" & request("type")
End If
```

When we redirect the page, we pass through the type query string value that indicates what type of address we want to capture. Internally, we make no distinction between billing and shipping addresses. We treat them both equally – that way we don't have to hassle the customers to enter the same address twice on occasions where they want to ship to their billing address.

After validating the form variables to make sure we have all the information we need, we call the CreateAddress method:

```
Visit.Customers.CreateAddress Visit.CustomerID, _
        Request("name"), Request("company"), Request("address1"), _
        Request("address2"), Request("city"), Request("region"), _
        Request("postalcode"), Request("country"), Request("phone")
```

After the new address has been added, we bounce the user back to the Choose Address form, which we'll build in Step 4. Notice how we've continued to pass the type of form along through each aspect of this operation in the form variable type. This type variable can contain either the value billing or shipping:

```
Response.Redirect Request("script_name") & _
                 "?action=addresses&type=" & Request("type")
```

Step 4 – Choosing Addresses

Now that the customer can enter addresses, we need to write the code that will let them choose existing addresses for either billing or shipping, or create new addresses entirely.

To do this, we just need to use the Addresses property of the Customer object and let the customer use radio buttons to pick the one he or she wants.

Try It Out – Allowing the User to Select an Address

1. Add this code to checkout.asp immediately above case "getaddress":

```
<input type=hidden name=updatecustomer value=1>
<input type=hidden name=action value="<%=Request("action")%>">
</form>
```

```
<% ' choose the address...
case "addresses" %>

    <!-- table and form... -->
    <form action="<%=Request("script_name")%>" method=post>
    <center><table width=400 cellspacing=0 cellpadding=3
                 bgcolor=#e0e0e0 border=1>
    <tr><td><table cellspacing=0 cellpadding=2 width=100% border=0>

    <!-- heading -->
    <tr><td class=heading colspan=2>
    Please choose a <%=Request("type")%> address...
    </td></tr>
    <tr><td><br></td></tr>

    <!-- get the addresses... -->

    <%
      Dim addresses
      set addresses = Visit.Customer.Addresses
      Do While not addresses.EOF
         ' Draw the radio button...
         Response.write "<tr><td align=right>"
         Response.write "<input type=radio name=address " & _
                        "value=" & addresses("addressid") & ">"

         ' Draw the address...
         Response.write "</td><td class=small>"
         RenderAddress addresses
         Response.write "</td></tr>"

         ' Next...
         addresses.MoveNext

      Loop
      addresses.Close
      set addresses = Nothing
    %>

    <!-- add an extra button to let the visitor create a new address -->
    <tr><td align=right>
    <input type=radio name=address value=-1>
    </td><td class=small>
    Create a new address...
    </td></tr>

    <!-- add the button -->
    <tr><td><br></td></tr>
    <tr><td colspan=2 align=center>
    <input type=submit value="Continue">
    </td></tr>
```

```
        <! -- End it -->
        </table></td></tr>
        </td></tr></table></center>
        <input type=hidden name=createaddress value=1>
        <input type=hidden name=type value="<%=Request("type")%>">
        <input type=hidden name=action value="<%=Request("action")%>">
        </form>
```

```
    <% ' Capture the new address...
    case "getaddress" %>
```

2. Add this helper function to the bottom of the `checkout.asp` page:

```
<% end select %>
```

```
<%  ' RenderAddress - draws an address...
Sub RenderAddress(address)

    Response.write address("name") & "<br>"
    If not isnull(address("company")) Then _
        Response.write address("company") & "<br>"
    If not isnull(address("address1")) Then _
        Response.write address("address1") & "<br>"
    If not isnull(address("address2")) Then _
        Response.write address("address2") & "<br>"
    If not isnull(address("city")) Then _
        Response.write address("city") & "<br>"
    If not isnull(address("postalcode")) Then _
        Response.write address("postalcode") & "<br>"
    If not isnull(address("country")) Then _
        Response.write address("country") & "<br>"

End Sub   %>
```

```
    <!-- #include file="end.asp" -->
</BODY>
</HTML>
```

3. Back in Step 3, we checked for the `action` value of `addresses` and used that to see if the customer actually had addresses registered against them. We now need to revisit that logic and use it to set the address that the customer chose – or if she selected **Create a new address**, we need to bounce her off to the form that can capture a new address.

Here's the code we need to add to `checkout.asp`:

```
If Request("action") = "addresses" Then

    ' Check to see if there are any addresses
    If Visit.Customer.HasAddresses = False Then

        ' Bounce...
```

```
                Response.buffer = True
                Response.clear
                Response.redirect Request("script_name") & _
                               "?action=getaddress&type=" & Request("type")


        Else

            ' Have we been given an address?
            If Request("address") <> "" Then

                ' Did we get a real address, or were we asked to create a new one?
                If Request("address") <> "-1" Then

                    ' Set the address against the order...
                    If lcase(Request("type")) = "billing" Then

                        ' Set the billing address...
                        Visit.Order.BillingAddressID = Request("address")

                        ' Then bounce to get the shipping address...
                        Response.buffer = True
                        Response.clear
                        Response.redirect Request("script_name") & _
                                       "?action=addresses&type=shipping"

                    Else

                        ' Set the shipping address...
                        Visit.Order.ShippingAddressID = Request("address")

                        ' Now that we have a shipping address, update the tax rate for
                        ' the order. (In this example, we're just adding a flat rate of
                        ' 17.5% throughout)
                        Visit.Order.TaxRate = 0.175

                        ' Then bounce to get the payment info...
                        Response.buffer = True
                        Response.clear
                        Response.redirect Request("script_name") & "?action=cards"
                    End If

                Else

                    ' Create a new address...
                    Response.buffer = True
                    Response.clear
                    Response.redirect Request("script_name") & _
                                   "?action=getaddress&type=" & Request("type")

                End If

        End If
```

```
        End If

    End If
```

4. An important point to note is that this is the first time we've seen the `Basket.Order` property in action, and therefore the first time we've actually gone ahead and created a single `Orders` row, and an appropriate number of `OrderParts` and `OrderLines` rows in the database. We're using it to set the billing and shipping addresses for the order by updating the appropriate columns in the `Orders` row.

Here are the properties that need to be added to the `Order` object to do this:

```
' BillingAddressID - set the billing address...
Public Property Let BillingAddressID(ByVal newval As Long)

    ' Open the record and update the values...
    Dim query As New Recordset
    query.Open "select * from orders where orderid=" & m_ID, _
               m_utility.DB.DB, adOpenKeyset, adLockOptimistic
    query("billingaddressid") = newval
    query.Update
    query.Close
    Set query = Nothing

End Property
```

```
' ShippingAddressID - set the shipping address...
Public Property Let ShippingAddressID(ByVal newval As Long)

    ' Open the record...
    Dim query As New Recordset
    query.Open "select * from orders where orderid=" & m_ID, _
               m_utility.DB.DB, adOpenKeyset, adLockOptimistic
    query("shippingaddressid") = newval
    query.Update
    query.Close
    Set query = Nothing

End Property
```

How It Works

This is what the code in this step of our 8-step checkout process produces:

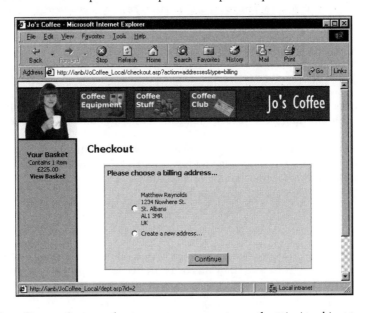

To get the address list, we first use the `Customer` property on the `Visit` object to return a new `Customer` object based on whatever customer ID is held in the session. (Remember that when we created or logged on the user, we stored that ID in the session variables and we changed the `Visit.Configure` method to bring back that ID each time.) We then request the `Addresses` property of that `Customer` object, which in turn returns a recordset of the customer's addresses:

```
Dim addresses
set addresses = Visit.Customer.Addresses
```

We then loop through this list, rendering each one together with a radio button. Each radio button's value is set to the `addressid` column value:

```
Do While not addresses.EOF
   ' Draw the radio button...
   Response.write "<tr><td align=right>"
   Response.write "<input type=radio name=address " & _
                   "value=" & addresses("addressid") & ">"

   ' Draw the address...
   Response.write "</td><td class=small>"
   RenderAddress addresses
   Response.write "</td></tr>"

   ' Next...
   addresses.MoveNext

Loop
```

The button with `value -1` prompts for a new address:

```
<!-- add an extra button to let the visitor create a new address -->
<tr><td align=right>
<input type=radio name=address value=-1>
</td><td class=small>
Create a new address...
</td></tr>
```

Note how we're using a helper function called `RenderAddress` to show the user the address. We'll also be using this later on when we're presenting the order back to the customer for confirmation.

Our first check determines if we were trying to create a new address. If `Request("address")` is not `"-1"`, we know we're referring to an existing address; otherwise we want to bounce the user to the `action` statement that allows for the creation of new addresses:

```
Response.redirect Request("script_name") & _
                  "?action=getaddress&type=" & Request("type")
```

If we want to use an existing one, we test to see if we want a billing or shipping address and use either the `Order` object's `BillingAddressID` or `ShippingAddressID` property as appropriate:

```
If lcase(Request("type")) = "billing" Then

    ' Set the billing address...
    Visit.Order.BillingAddressID = Request("address")

    ' Then bounce to get the shipping address...
    Response.buffer = True
    Response.clear
    Response.redirect Request("script_name") & _
                      "?action=addresses&type=shipping"

Else

    ' Set the shipping address...
    Visit.Order.ShippingAddressID = Request("address")

    ' Now that we have a shipping address, update the tax rate for
    ' the order. (In this example, we're just adding a flat rate of
    ' 17.5% throughout)
    Visit.Order.TaxRate = 0.175

    ' Then bounce to get the payment info...
    Response.buffer = True
    Response.clear
    Response.redirect Request("script_name") & "?action=cards"
End If
```

Now, we haven't built either of those properties at this time, and this is precisely what we will do in a moment. Additionally, if we have a billing address, we bounce to the action statement capable of getting a shipping address, otherwise we bounce to the one we haven't built yet that will allow the user to select or add credit cards.

Step 5 – Capturing Credit Card Information

Now we can move on to the task of adding or selecting the credit card that the customer wishes to use to pay for the order.

In fact, this process is almost identical to the process for adding and selecting addresses – we present forms to choose a credit card that is registered against the customer or capture details of a new one. The only big difference is that we have to let the customer choose which type of credit card they wish to use. For Jo's Coffee, we're going to say that the payment options are fixed in that she only accepts Visa or MasterCard.

A large proportion of the Internet population still has considerable reservations concerning sending their credit cards down a secure link directly into a computerized order processing system and prefer instead to phone or fax in payment details. Paradoxically, it has been proven that the risk of theft of credit card details by employees taking them over the phone or fax is something like 1,000 times higher than for credit card details being deposited directly into a computer system through a secure server. If you would like to allow the customers the option of giving their credit card details via phone, you should place your phone number on the Web page, so that the customer may call you at their convenience.

Our first step is to add methods to the Customers and Customer objects to determine if the customer has any credit card registered, and provide a way to query for them if they do.

Try It Out – Adding the Visual Basic Code that Captures Credit Card Details

1. Firstly, add some methods to the Customers object:

```
' QueryCards - primitive to help us get at cards...
Private Function QueryCards(Optional ByVal Where As String, _
                      Optional ByVal Order As String = "number", _
                      Optional ByVal AsKeyset As Boolean = False) _
                      As Recordset
   Set QueryCards = m_utility.DB.RunQuery("Cards", , Where, Order, AsKeyset)
End Function
```

```
' GetCard - returns a single Card...
Public Function GetCard(ByVal CardID As Long, _
                      Optional ByVal AsKeyset As Boolean = False) As Recordset
   Set GetCard = QueryCards("CardID=" & CardID, , AsKeyset)
End Function
```

```
' GetCustomersCards - returns all the Cards a customer has...
Public Function GetCustomersCards(ByVal CustomerID As Long, _
             Optional ByVal AsKeyset As Boolean = False) As Recordset
   Set GetCustomersCards = QueryCards("CustomerID=" & CustomerID, , AsKeyset)
End Function
```

2. Secondly, add this `Cards` property to the `Customer` object that can return the customer's cards to us, and also a `HasCards` function to tell is if he or she has cards registered:

```
' Cards - returns all of the cards the customer has...
Public Property Get Cards(Optional ByVal AsKeyset As Boolean) As Recordset
    Set Cards = m_utility.Visit.Customers.GetCustomersCards(m_ID, AsKeyset)
End Property
```

```
' HasCards - returns True if the customer has cards...
Public Function HasCards() As Boolean

    ' Test to see if the address recordset we get is empty...
    Dim query As Recordset
    Set query = Cards
    If query.EOF Then
        HasCards = False
    Else
        HasCards = True
    End If
    query.Close
    Set query = Nothing

End Function
```

3. Finally, add this method to the `Customers` object, which we can use to create new cards:

```
' CreateCard - creates a new card record...
Public Function CreateCard(ByVal CustomerID As Long, ByVal CardType As String, _
                        ByVal Number As String, ByVal NameOnCard As String, _
                        ByVal ExpiresMonth As Integer, _
                        ByVal ExpiresYear As Integer) As Long

    ' Create a new card record...
    Dim NewCard As New Recordset
    NewCard.Open "cards", m_utility.DB.DB, adOpenKeyset, adLockOptimistic
    NewCard.AddNew

    ' Populate it...
    NewCard ("customerid") = CustomerID
    NewCard ("type") = CardType
    NewCard ("number") = Number
    NewCard ("nameoncard") = NameOnCard
    NewCard ("expiresmonth") = ExpiresMonth
    NewCard ("expiresyear") = ExpiresYear

    ' Close it, but send the ID back to the caller...
    NewCard.Update
    CreateCard = NewCard ("cardid")
    NewCard.Close
    Set NewCard = Nothing

End Function
```

Try It Out – Adding the ASP Code that Captures Credit Card Details

1. The first thing we did back when we were asking the customer for the address he or she wanted to use, was check to see if any were registered and, if not, redirect them over to a form to capture a new address. Now we need to do the same thing for credit cards.

Here's the code we need to use, which should be placed at the top of checkout.asp:

```
' Do we have any card details?
If Request("action") = "cards" Then

    ' Check to see If there are any...
    If Visit.Customer.HasCards = False Then
      ' Bounce...
      Response.buffer = True
      Response.clear
      Response.redirect Request("script_name") & "?action=getcard"
    End If

End If

' Do we want to create a new address?
If Request("createaddress") <> "" Then
```

2. If no cards exist, the customer will be redirected through to the action statement called getcard. Here's what that looks like; place this code directly above case "addresses":

```
        <input type=hidden name=updatecustomer value=1>
        <input type=hidden name=action value="<%=Request("action")%>">
        </form>
```

```
        <% ' capture a new credit card...
        case "getcard" %>

           <!-- table and form... -->
           <form action="<%=Request("script_name")%>" method=post>
           <center><table width=400 cellspacing=0 cellpadding=3
                          bgcolor=#e0e0e0 border=1>
           <tr><td><table cellspacing=0 cellpadding=2 width=100%>

           <!-- heading -->
           <tr><td class=heading colspan=2>
           Please enter the credit card information...
           </td></tr>
           <tr><td><br></td></tr>

           <!-- If we have a problem, draw it... -->
           <% If problem <> "" Then %>
              <tr><td bgcolor=#ff0000 class=heading colspan=2>
              <font color=#ffffff><%=problem%></font></td></tr>
```

```
        <tr><td><br></td></tr>
      <% End If %>

      <!-- draw the fields... -->
      <tr><td class=heading>
      Type of card:
      </td><td>
      <select name=type>
      <option value="">(Select)</option>
      <option value="visa">Visa</option>
      <option value="mastercard">MasterCard</option>
      </select>
      </td></tr>
      <tr><td class=heading>
      Name on card:
      </td><td>
      <input type=text name=name value="<%=Request("name")%>">
      </td></tr>
      <tr><td class=heading>
      Card number:
      </td><td>
      <input type=text name=number value="<%=Request("number")%>">
      </td></tr>
      <tr><td class=heading>
      Expires (mm/yyyy):
      </td><td>
      <input type=text name=expiresmonth
                  value="<%=Request("expiresmonth")%>" size=2>
      <input type=text name=expiresyear
                  value="<%=Request("expiresyear")%>" size=4>
      </td></tr>

      <!-- add the button -->
      <tr><td><br></td></tr>
      <tr><td colspan=2 align=center>
      <input type=submit value="Continue">
      </td></tr>

      <! -- End it -->
      </table></td></tr>
      </td></tr></table></center>
      <input type=hidden name=createcard value=1>
      <input type=hidden name=action value="<%=Request("action")%>">
      </form>

  <% ' choose the address...
  case "addresses" %>
```

3. Now that we can present the form, we need to quickly validate the details and then create a row in the `Cards` table. Add this code to the top of `checkout.asp`:

```
' Do we want to create a new card?
If Request("createcard") <> "" Then

    ' Do we have the bits we need?
    If Request("type") = "" Then _
        addtoproblem "You must select the type of card."
    If Request("name") = "" Then _
        addtoproblem "You must enter the name on the card."
    If Request("number") = "" Then _
        addtoproblem "You must enter the number on the card."
    If Request("expiresmonth") = "" Then _
        addtoproblem "You must enter an expiry month."
    If Request("expiresyear") = "" Then _
        addtoproblem "You must enter an expiry year."

    ' Did we do it?
    If problem = "" Then

        ' Update the customer...
        Visit.Customers.CreateCard Visit.CustomerID, Request("type"), _
            Request("number"), Request("name"), _
            Request("expiresmonth"), Request("expiresyear")
        ' Bounce over to choose the card we want to use...
        Response.Buffer = True
        Response.Clear
        Response.Redirect Request("script_name") & "?action=cards"

    End If

End If

' Do we have any card details?
If Request("action") = "cards" Then
```

In our validation code, we don't check to make sure the expiration date on the card is valid to keep the example brief. A neat way of doing this in the real world is to provide a drop-down box to let the user choose the month and another that can be used to choose the year.

Here's the form that's produced by this step (although you won't be able to see this yet, because we need to add the code from Step 7):

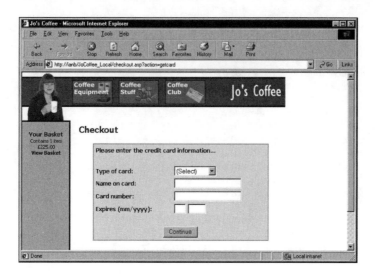

Step 6 – Choosing Credit Cards

Now that we have a way of letting the users store card details, we need let the customer choose the card he or she wants to use for the order. One thing we must be careful of here is that we should never send the full card number back down to the browser. This is an extra security step that shows our customers that we take every step to ensure credit card security.

Therefore, rather than displaying the whole number, we'll display the first four digits and a check digit. Typically for Visa and MasterCard, the first four digits are a code assigned to a card issuer and the last digit is a check digit, so using these numbers ensures that the numbers we send back are pretty useless except to the card holder who's unlikely to have two cards from the same issuer with the same check digit. As we'll most likely render card details quite often, we'll create a function in the Visit object called GetSafeCCNumber that will return this abbreviated string.

Try It Out – Allowing the User to Select a Credit Card

1. Add this code to the Visit object:

```
' GetSafeCCNumber - takes a full credit card number and strips
'                   out the important numbers...
Public Function GetSafeCCNumber(ByVal Number As String) As String

    ' Do we have a string at all?
    If Number <> "" Then

        ' Is the string long enough?
        If Len(Number) > 5 Then

            ' Add the first four digits...
            Dim buf As String
            buf = Left(Number, 4)
```

```
        ' Replace the middle however many digits with dots...
        buf = buf & String(Len(Number) - 5, ".")

        ' Add the last digit...
        buf = buf & Right(Number, 1)

        ' Return the value...
        GetSafeCCNumber = buf

    Else

        ' Just write back the first digit...
        GetSafeCCNumber = Left(Number, 1) & String(Len(Number) - 1, ".")

    End If

  End If

End Function
```

Our code sample starts by checking that we got a card number, and that the number is longer than five digits. If it isn't, we send back just the first digit and use the String function to add a list of dots to the end. Otherwise, we write the first four digits, use the String function to add however many dots we need (the length of the string minus five – four for the first, one for the end), and then the last digit on the card.

We can then use this function when we get the customer's registered credit cards and present them in a similar manner to how we presented the addresses:

2. Go back to the Visual InterDev project and add this code to checkout.asp, immediately above Case "getcard":

```
<input type=hidden name=updatecustomer value=1>
<input type=hidden name=action value="<%=Request("action")%>">
</form>
```

```
<% ' Ask the customer to choose a credit card...
case "cards" %>

    <!-- table and form... -->
    <form action="<%=Request("script_name")%>" method=post>
    <center>
    <table width=400 cellspacing=0 cellpadding=3 bgcolor=#e0e0e0 border=1>
    <tr><td><table cellspacing=0 cellpadding=2 width=100% border=0>

    <!-- heading -->
    <tr><td class=heading colspan=2>
    Please choose a card...
    </td></tr>
    <tr><td><br></td></tr>
```

```
<!-- get the cards... -->
<%
    Dim cards
    set cards = Visit.Customer.Cards

    Do While not cards.EOF

        ' Draw the radio button...
        Response.write "<tr><td align=right>"
        Response.write "<input type=radio name=card value=" & _
                       cards("cardid") & ">"

        ' Draw the address...
        Response.write "</td><td class=small>"
        Response.write cards("nameoncard") & "<br>"
        Response.write cards("type") & " "
        Response.write Visit.GetSafeCCNumber(cards("number"))
        Response.Write "<br>"
        Response.write "Expires: " & _
                       cards("expiresmonth") & "/" & cards("expiresyear")
        Response.write "</td></tr>"

        ' Next...
        cards.MoveNext

    Loop

    cards.Close
    set cards = Nothing
%>

<!-- add an extra button to let the visitor create a new address -->
<tr><td align=right>
<input type=radio name=card value=-1>
</td><td class=small>
Create a new card...
</td></tr>

<!-- add the button -->
<tr><td><br></td></tr>
<tr><td colspan=2 align=center>
<input type=submit value="Continue">
</td></tr>

<! -- End it -->
</table></td></tr>
</td></tr></table></center>
<input type=hidden name=action value="<%=Request("action")%>">
</form>

<% ' capture a new credit card...
case "getcard" %>
```

As we've suggested before, the code to handle the credit cards is very similar to the code to handle addresses, so we won't go into great detail. The same thing applies – we create a recordset of all the customer's cards, render a list of them, and render an option for the customer to create a new card if he or she wants.

3. The middle step for getting this credit card stuff working is to add a property to the `Order` object that will let us set the credit card we want to use for the order.

Add this property to the `Order` object in `WroxCommerce`:

```
' CardID - set the shipping address...
Public Property Let CardID(ByVal newval As Long)

    ' Open the record...
    Dim Query As New Recordset
    Query.Open "select * from orders where orderid=" & m_ID, _
            m_utility.DB.DB, adOpenKeyset, adLockOptimistic
    Query("cardid") = newval
    Query.Update
    Query.Close
    Set Query = Nothing

End Property
```

4. Finally, we need to tweak the code we added to `checkout.asp`, which checks for the existence of a credit card, so that it will set the credit card for the order:

```
' Do we have any card details?
If Request("action") = "cards" Then

    ' Check to see If there are any...
    If Visit.Customer.HasCards = False Then

        ' Bounce...
        Response.buffer = True
        Response.clear
        Response.redirect Request("script_name") & "?action=getcard"
```
```
    Else

        ' Have we been given an address?
        If Request("card") <> "" Then

            ' Did we get a real address, or were we asked to create a new one?
            If Request("card") <> "-1" Then

                ' Set the card...
                Visit.Order.CardID = Request("card")

                ' Then bounce over to confirm the order...
                Response.buffer = True
                Response.clear
```

```
                    Response.redirect Request("script_name") & "?action=confirm"

        Else

            ' Bounce over to get a new card...
            Response.buffer = True
            Response.clear
            Response.redirect Request("script_name") & "?action=getcard"

        End If

    End If

    End If

End If
```

Here's what the code in this step will produce (as before, you'll need the code from Step 7 before you can run this and see it for yourself):

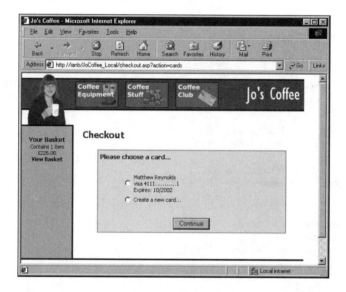

Step 7 – Showing the Order and Presenting Shipping Options

E-commerce conventions dictate that before an order can be processed, it has to go through a process where it is presented to the customer so that the customer can be confident there are no hidden costs. One such hidden cost is usually shipping costs.

When we built our Orders and OrderParts tables, we put the ShippingID and ShippingCharge columns into the OrderParts table, not the Orders table. In a situation where the customer has an order that must be satisfied by separate suppliers, the customer will be asked to choose different shipping options. This lets the customer opt for a slower delivery in situations where one part of the order is not as critical as another, and reduce or increase shipping costs as required.

However, now that we have captured the address and credit card information, and we've taken the cart (basket) and processed it into a bundle of rows in OrderLines and OrderParts, we can present a summary of the order to the user. We'll present this as one order, but in cases where the order has more than one part, we'll present different subtotals, shipping options, and totals, and explain why the order has been split up.

To present the order to the user, and to process the order later on, we need a couple of properties that can help us get information about the parts of the order, and the items in each part.

Try It Out – Presenting the Order to the User

1. Here are some methods to add to the Orders object that do just that:

```
' QueryOrderParts - primitive to help us get at OrderParts...
Private Function QueryOrderParts(Optional ByVal Where As String, _
                Optional ByVal Order As String, _
                Optional ByVal AsKeyset As Boolean = False) As Recordset
    Set QueryOrderParts = m_utility.DB.RunQuery("OrderParts", _
                "vOrderParts", Where, Order, AsKeyset)
End Function
```

```
' GetOrderParts - returns the parts for a given order...
Public Function GetOrderParts(ByVal OrderID As Long, _
                Optional ByVal AsKeyset As Boolean = False) As Recordset
    Set GetOrderParts = QueryOrderParts("orderid=" & OrderID, , AsKeyset)
End Function
```

```
' GetOrderPart - returns a single OrderPart...
Public Function GetOrderPart(ByVal OrderPartID As Long, _
                Optional ByVal AsKeyset As Boolean = False) As Recordset
    Set GetOrderPart = QueryOrderParts("OrderPartID=" & OrderPartID, , AsKeyset)
End Function
```

```
' QueryOrderLines - primitive to help us get at OrderLines...
Private Function QueryOrderLines(Optional ByVal Where As String, _
                Optional ByVal Order As String, _
                Optional ByVal AsKeyset As Boolean = False) As Recordset
    Set QueryOrderLines = m_utility.DB.RunQuery("OrderLines", _
                "vOrderLines", Where, Order, AsKeyset)
End Function
```

```
' GetOrderLines - returns the lines for a given part...
Public Function GetOrderLines(ByVal PartID As Long, _
                Optional ByVal AsKeyset As Boolean = False) As Recordset
    Set GetOrderLines = QueryOrderLines("partid=" & PartID, , AsKeyset)
End Function
```

2. Here are some properties to add to the `Order` object that call into the methods we just added to the `Orders` object:

```
' Parts - return the parts of the order...
Public Property Get Parts(Optional ByVal AsKeyset As Boolean) As Recordset
    Set Parts = m_utility.Visit.Orders.GetOrderParts(m_ID, AsKeyset)
End Property
```

```
' Lines - returns the lines for a part of the order...
Public Property Get Lines(ByVal PartID As Long, _
                          Optional ByVal AsKeyset As Boolean) As Recordset
    Set Lines = m_utility.Visit.Orders.GetOrderLines(PartID, AsKeyset)
End Property
```

3. Now that `WroxCommerce` can tell us all about the order, we need to use those methods and properties to present the order to the customer for confirmation. However, in the first instance, we need to ask the customer to choose the shipping method he or she wants to use for each part. Add this code to `checkout.asp`, immediately above `Case "cards"`:

```
<input type=hidden name=updatecustomer value=1>
<input type=hidden name=action value="<%=Request("action")%>">
</form>
```

```
<% ' Present the order to the user for confirmation...
case "confirm" %>

    <!-- table and form... -->
    <form action="<%=Request("script_name")%>" method=post>
    <table cellspacing=0 cellpadding=2 width=100% border=0>

    <!-- present the shipping and billing addresses -->
    <%
        ' Draw the billing address...
        Dim address
        set address = Visit.Customers.GetAddress(Visit.Order.BillingAddressID)
        Response.write "<tr><td class=small width=50% colspan=2>"
        Response.write "<b>Billing address:</b><br>"
        RenderAddress address
        address.close
        set address = Nothing

        ' Now draw the shipping address...
        set address = Visit.Customers.GetAddress(Visit.Order.ShippingAddressID)
        Response.write "</td><td class=small width=50% colspan=2>"
        Response.write "<b>Shipping address:</b><br>"
        RenderAddress address
        Response.write "</td></tr>"
        address.close
        set address = Nothing
    %>
    <tr><td><br></td></tr>
```

```
<!-- present the credit card -->
<%
    ' Draw the credit card...
    Dim card
    set card = Visit.Customers.GetCard(Visit.Order.CardID)
    Response.write "<tr><td colspan=4 class=small>"
    Response.write "<b>Payment details:</b><br>"
    Response.write card("nameoncard") & "<br>"
    Response.write card("type") & " " & _
                    Visit.GetSafeCCNumber(card("number")) & "<br>"
    Response.write "Expires: " & card("expiresmonth") & "/" & _
                    card("expiresyear")
    Response.write "</td></tr>"
%>
<tr><td><br></td></tr>

<!-- present each part of the order with totals, etc... -->
<%
    Dim parts, partnum, lines, shipping

    ' We'll be using this to determine how many parts
    ' need a shipping option set against them...
    Dim NumNeedingShippingID
    NumNeedingShippingID = 0

    ' Get the parts back and Then loop them...
    set parts = Visit.Order.Parts
    partnum = 1

    Do While Not parts.EOF

        ' Draw the part...
        Response.write "<tr><td class=heading bgcolor=#000080 colspan=4>"
        Response.write "<font color=#ffffff>Order Part " & partnum & "</font>"
        Response.write "</td></tr>"

        ' Get the lines in the part...
        set lines = Visit.Order.Lines(parts("partid"))

        Do While Not lines.EOF

            ' Draw the line...
            Response.write "<tr><td class=small>"
            Response.write lines("mfrname") & " " & lines("name")
            Response.write "</td><td class=small>"
            Response.write lines("quantity")
            Response.write "</td><td class=small>"
            Response.write FormatPrice(lines("priceeach"))
            Response.write "</td><td class=small>"
            Response.write FormatPrice(lines("total"))
            Response.write "</td></tr>"
```

```
        ' Next
        lines.MoveNext

Loop
lines.Close
set Lines = Nothing

' Add the subtotal...
Response.write "<tr bgcolor=#e0e0e0>"
Response.write "<td colspan=3 align=right class=small>"
Response.write "Subtotal: "
Response.write "</td><td class=small>"
Response.write FormatPrice(parts("subtotal"))
Response.write "</td></tr>"

' Draw in the tax...
Response.write "<tr bgcolor=#e0e0e0>"
Response.write "<td colspan=3 align=right class=small>"
Response.write "Tax ("
Response.write FormatNumber(parts("taxrate") * 100, 1)
Response.write "%): "
Response.write "</td><td class=small>"
Response.write FormatPrice(parts("taxcharge"))
Response.write "</td></tr>"

' Start the row to deal with the shipping...
Response.write "<tr bgcolor=#e0e0e0>"
Response.write "<td colspan=3 align=right class=small>"

' First of all, do we know how we're shipping this?
If not isnull(parts("shippingid")) Then

    ' We know the method and cost - just write it out...
    Response.write parts("shippingname")
    Response.write "</td><td class=small>"
    Response.write FormatPrice(parts("shippingcharge"))
    Response.write "</td></tr>"

Else

    ' Get the possible shipping methods back...
    Response.write "Shipping method:"
    Response.write "</td><td>"
    Response.write "<select name=shipping>"
    set shipping = Visit.Orders.GetShipping

    do while not shipping.eof

        Response.write "<option value=" & shipping("shippingid") & ">"
        Response.write shipping("name")
        Response.write " (" & formatprice(shipping("charge")) & ")"
        Response.write "</option>"
```

```
                    ' Next
                 shipping.MoveNext

            loop
            shipping.Close
            set shipping = Nothing

            ' Add a hidden field - this will help us match
            ' choices to parts later...
            Response.write "<input type=hidden "
            Response.Write "name=shippingpart value=" & parts("partid") & ">"

            ' Keep track of how many parts need a shipping id...
            NumNeedingShippingID = NumNeedingShippingID + 1

        End If

        ' End the shipping row...
        Response.write "</td></tr>"

        ' If we know the shipping we have the grand total...
        If not isnull(parts("shippingid")) Then
            Response.write "<tr bgcolor=#c0c0c0>"
            Response.write "<td colspan=3 align=right class=small>"
            Response.write "<b>TOTAL:</b>"
            Response.write "</td><td class=small>"
            Response.write FormatPrice(parts("total"))
            Response.write "</td></tr>"
        End If

        ' Next...
        parts.MoveNext
        partnum = partnum + 1
        Response.write "<tr><td><br></td></tr>"

    Loop
    parts.Close
    Set parts = Nothing
%>

<!-- add the button -->
<tr><td><br></td></tr>
<tr><td colspan=4 align=center>
<%
    ' Do we want to submit the order? If we've specified shipping IDs for
    ' each part, Then yes we do, otherwise we want to re-run the form

    If NumNeedingShippingID <> 0 Then
        Response.write "<input type=submit value=""Continue"">"
        Response.write "<input type=hidden name=action value=""" & _
                    Request("action") & """>"
    Else
        Response.write "<input type=submit value=""Place Order"">"
```

```
        Response.write "<input type=hidden name=action value=""placeorder"">"
      End If
%>
</td></tr>

<! -- End it -->
</table></td></tr>
</form>
```

```
<% ' ask the customer to choose a credit card...
case "cards" %>
```

4. Admittedly, that's a pretty lengthy code sample! However, what it does is quite simple. Here's what you could expect to see:

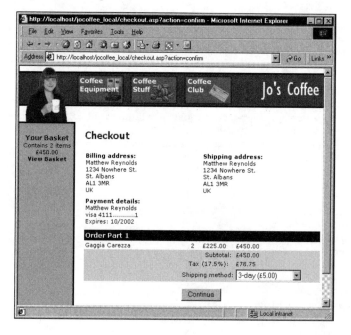

How It Works

We start by returning the billing and shipping addresses that the user gave us when the order was placed:

```
' Draw the billing address...
Dim address
set address = Visit.Customers.GetAddress(Visit.Order.BillingAddressID)
Response.write "<tr><td class=small width=50% colspan=2>"
Response.write "<b>Billing address:</b><br>"
RenderAddress address
address.close
set address = Nothing
```

```
' Now draw the shipping address...
set address = Visit.Customers.GetAddress(Visit.Order.ShippingAddressID)
Response.write "</td><td class=small width=50% colspan=2>"
Response.write "<b>Shipping address:</b><br>"
RenderAddress address
Response.write "</td></tr>"
address.close
set address = Nothing
```

We then render out the details of the credit card he or she wishes to use:

```
Dim card
set card = Visit.Customers.GetCard(Visit.Order.CardID)
Response.write "<tr><td colspan=4 class=small>"
Response.write "<b>Payment details:</b><br>"
Response.write card("nameoncard") & "<br>"
Response.write card("type") & " " & _
               Visit.GetSafeCCNumber(card("number")) & "<br>"
Response.write "Expires: " & card("expiresmonth") & "/" & _
               card("expiresyear")
Response.write "</td></tr>"
```

Next, we grab the parts that make up the order and loop through each of them. We create a heading that splits off each order part from the other parts on the page:

```
set parts = Visit.Order.Parts
partnum = 1

Do While Not parts.EOF

    ' Draw the part...
    Response.write "<tr><td class=heading bgcolor=#000080 colspan=4>"
    Response.write "<font color=#ffffff>Order Part " & partnum & "</font>"
    Response.write "</td></tr>"
```

Having grabbed the parts, we can get the lines that make up each part. We then render each item together with the quantity ordered and the total for the line:

```
set lines = Visit.Order.Lines(parts("partid"))

Do While Not lines.EOF

    ' Draw the line...
    Response.write "<tr><td class=small>"
    Response.write lines("mfrname") & " " & lines("name")
    Response.write "</td><td class=small>"
    Response.write lines("quantity")
    Response.write "</td><td class=small>"
    Response.write FormatPrice(lines("priceeach"))
    Response.write "</td><td class=small>"
```

```
Response.write FormatPrice(lines("total"))
Response.write "</td></tr>"

' Next
lines.MoveNext

Loop
```

We then calculate the subtotal for the part, which simply comprises the sum of all the lines, and how much tax the customer should expect to pay, both as a percentage and as an amount:

```
' Add the subtotal...
Response.write "<tr bgcolor=#e0e0e0>"
Response.write "<td colspan=3 align=right class=small>"
Response.write "Subtotal: "
Response.write "</td><td class=small>"
Response.write FormatPrice(parts("subtotal"))
Response.write "</td></tr>"

' Draw in the tax...
Response.write "<tr bgcolor=#e0e0e0>"
Response.write "<td colspan=3 align=right class=small>"
Response.write "Tax ("
Response.write FormatNumber(parts("taxrate") * 100, 1)
Response.write "%): "
Response.write "</td><td class=small>"
Response.write FormatPrice(parts("taxcharge"))
Response.write "</td></tr>"
```

Next, we allow the customer to make a decision regarding the shipping method for the part. If a shipping method hasn't been chosen (and we don't choose one by default, so the first time this page is displayed, none of the parts will have a shipping method set against them), we grab a list of the possible methods from the database and present them to the user as a drop-down list. Note that it's essential here that we give the user an indication of how much each shipping option will cost:

```
Response.write "Shipping method:"
Response.write "</td><td>"
Response.write "<select name=shipping>"
set shipping = Visit.Orders.GetShipping

do while not shipping.eof

    Response.write "<option value=" & shipping("shippingid") & ">"
    Response.write shipping("name")
    Response.write " (" & formatprice(shipping("charge")) & ")"
    Response.write "</option>"

    ' Next
    shipping.MoveNext
```

```
loop
shipping.Close
set shipping = Nothing

' Add a hidden field - this will help us match
' choices to parts later...
Response.write "<input type=hidden "
Response.Write "name=shippingpart value=" & parts("partid") & ">"

' Keep track of how many parts need a shipping id...
NumNeedingShippingID = NumNeedingShippingID + 1
```

Note also that when we walk through the parts, we keep track of how many parts don't have shipping methods set against them in the `NumNeedingShippingID` local variable – so each time we draw one of the drop-down lists with the shipping methods in it, we add one to this variable. Once we've iterated through the complete list of parts, we examine this variable:

```
If NumNeedingShippingID <> 0 Then
    Response.write "<input type=submit value=""Continue"">"
    Response.write "<input type=hidden name=action value=""" & _
                   Request("action") & """>"
Else
    Response.write "<input type=submit value=""Place Order"">"
    Response.write "<input type=hidden name=action value=""placeorder"">"
End If
```

If it's not zero, we know that we're still not at a point where the order can be confirmed, as the final shipping details and charges are still being fleshed out. In this case, we need to examine the choice that the user made in the drop-down list and set the shipping method for the part appropriately.

In the case where `NumNeedingShippingID` is zero, the shipping methods for each part have been properly determined and so we can go ahead and approve the order.

If a shipping method has been chosen, we simply draw the name of the method together with how much we charge:

```
Response.write parts("shippingname")
Response.write "</td><td class=small>"
Response.write FormatPrice(parts("shippingcharge"))
Response.write "</td></tr>"
```

Additionally, if a shipping method has been chosen, we display the grand total for the part:

```
If not isnull(parts("shippingid")) Then
    Response.write "<tr bgcolor=#c0c0c0>"
    Response.write "<td colspan=3 align=right class=small>"
    Response.write "<b>TOTAL:</b>"
    Response.write "</td><td class=small>"
    Response.write FormatPrice(parts("total"))
    Response.write "</td></tr>"
End If
```

Before we can let the customer approve the order, we need to write some code that will set the shipping method for each part. The code will also retrieve the current shipping charge as it appears in the Shipping table and copy this value into the appropriate OrderParts row.

Try It Out – Setting the Shipping Methods

1. Add this method to the Orders object:

```
' SetShippingMethod - sets the shipping method for a part...
Public Function SetShippingID(ByVal PartID As Long, ByVal ShippingID As Long)

    ' We need to get the whole shipping method back because we'll
    ' be adding the current charge into the row...
    Dim Shipping As Recordset
    Set Shipping = GetShippingMethod(ShippingID)

    If Not Shipping.EOF Then

        ' Set the shipping ID and the charge...
        m_utility.DB.DB.Execute "update OrderParts set " & "ShippingID=" & _
                        ShippingID & ", ShippingCharge=" & _
                        Shipping("charge") & " where PartID=" & PartID

        ' recalculate the part...
        CalculatePartTotals PartID

    End If
    Shipping.Close
    Set Shipping = Nothing

End Function
```

2. We need to add a similar object to the Order object itself. In fact, we'll implement it as a property:

```
Public Property Let ShippingID(ByVal PartID As Long, ByVal ShippingID As Long)
    m_utility.Visit.Orders.SetShippingID PartID, ShippingID
End Property
```

3. Now we need to write the ASP code in checkout.asp that will call the ShippingMethod property on the order. We primed this functionality earlier by adding a HIDDEN field called shippingpart to the confirmation form that contains a list of the OrderParts that require a shipping method to be set. All we have to do is examine and walk through this to set the IDs, like this:

```
' Are we trying to set shipping information?
If Request("action") = "confirm" Then

    ' Loop the shipping parts...
    Dim ShippingPart, num
```

```
    num = 1

For Each ShippingPart in Request("shippingpart")

    ' Set the ID we chose from the drop down...
    Visit.Order.ShippingID(ShippingPart) = Request("shipping")(num)

    ' Next
    num = num + 1

Next

End If
```

```
'Do we have any card details?
If Request("action") = "cards" Then
```

How It Works

This allows us to set the shipping method to either **Next Day** or **3-day** and the **TOTAL** will be changed as required:

The trick behind this is to put multiple values into the shippingpart HIDDEN field – and remember this field contains the actual IDs taken from the OrderParts table. If we had more than one part to the order that required shipping methods, shippingpart might look something like "100,101,150". All we have to do is use the For Each ... Next construct to walk through each ID in the array and extract the appropriate value from the shipping <SELECT> tag – each value in this array references an ID in the Shipping table:

```
For Each ShippingPart in Request("shippingpart")

    ' Set the ID we chose from the drop down...
    Visit.Order.ShippingID(ShippingPart) = Request("shipping")(num)

    ' Next
    num = num + 1

Next
```

We use the num local variable to keep track of where we are in the shipping array. As we walk through, we simply use the ShippingID property of the Order object to set the appropriate ID on the part.

Finally, note the use of `CalculatePartTotals` in the `SetShippingID` method:

```
CalculatePartTotals PartID
```

We use that to update the calculated values on `OrderParts`, so whenever we change the shipping method, it's probable that the costs of shipping have changed, and so the tax charge and total need to be calculated.

Step 8 – Approving the Order

Thanks to the code we've already done, when the customer clicks the Continue button after making his or her shipping method selections, we'll automatically present the complete total for each part and offer up a Place Order button, which is capable of passing the order through to the order processing components of the site. In this chapter, we'll just be setting a flag in the database and telling the customer that the order has been sent for processing. Chapter 9 is concerned with processing the order, so this will be a fairly perfunctory explanation.

To confirm an order, we have to adjust the `Status` field (which acts as a flag) in the `Orders` table to indicate that processing now has to proceed. As a housekeeping measure, we also have to empty the basket and reset some of the `Session` variables we're using.

Try It Out – Approving the Order

1. Here's the method to add to the `Orders` object:

```
' PlaceOrder - confirms the order...
Public Function PlaceOrder(ByVal OrderID As Long)

    ' Update the flag...
    m_utility.DB.DB.Execute "update Orders set Status=1 where " & _
                        "OrderID=" & OrderID

    ' Is this the current order?
    If OrderID = m_utility.Visit.OrderID Then
        ' Reset the sessions...
        m_utility.Visit.ResetOrder
    End If

End Function
```

2. The `PlaceOrder` method uses the `ResetOrder` method of the `Visit` object, which we haven't seen yet. Add this to the `Visit` object:

```
' ResetOrder - clears out the cart and resets internals...
Public Function ResetOrder()

    ' Clean out the basket...
    If m_BasketID <> 0 Then
        Basket. EmptyBasket
```

```
        m_BasketID = 0
        m_Session("BasketID") = Empty
    End If

    ' Clean out the order...
    m_Session("OrderID") = Empty

End Function
```

3. The `ResetOrder` method uses the `EmptyBasket` method of the `Basket` object, which we haven't seen either! Place this code into the `Basket` object:

```
' EmptyBasket - removes the basket from the database...
Public Function EmptyBasket()

    ' Delete the lines, then delete us...
    m_utility.DB.DB.Execute "delete from BasketItems where BasketID=" & ID
    m_utility.DB.DB.Execute "delete from Baskets where BasketID=" & ID

End Function
```

4. Create this property of the `Order` object that can call `PlaceOrder`:

```
' PlaceOrder - places the order...
Public Function PlaceOrder()
    m_utility.Visit.Orders.PlaceOrder m_ID
End Function
```

5. Now all that remains is to implement the ASP code designed to call `PlaceOrder`. We pass the `action` statement `placeorder` when the **Place Order** button is pressed. Add this code to `checkout.asp`:

```
<% ' place the order...
case "placeorder" %>

    <% ' only place the order if we have one...
        If Visit.IsOrder = True then Visit.Order.PlaceOrder %>

    <table cellspacing=0 cellpadding=0>
    <tr><td class=heading>Thank you!</td></tr>
    <tr><td class=small>Your order has been placed.</td></tr>
    </table>

<% ' present the order to the user for confirmation...
case "confirm" %>
```

How It Works

When the visitors click on **Place Order** to confirm their order they will see the following page:

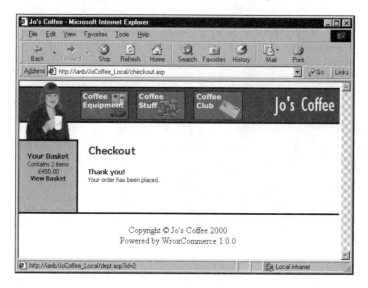

One important thing to get right here is to test to see if we have an order before we try and place one:

```
<% ' only place the order if we have one...
   If Visit.IsOrder = True then Visit.Order.PlaceOrder %>
```

What would happen without this line is, if the user refreshed the page, the Order property of the Visit object would go ahead and create a new blank order and, worse still, mark it as ready for processing.

Ideally, PlaceOrder should check to see if the order as it appears in the database is valid as part of the business rules for the application.

By testing to see if we have an order, if the user refreshes the page, the PlaceOrder method won't be called and spurious orders won't be created.

That's it! We can now capture everything we need to know when an order is placed.

Summary

In this chapter, we went through the process of getting the customer's name, address, and credit card number so that we can authorize payment and send the order up to our supplier. We also examined how, when doing business online, it makes sense to get our suppliers to handle all of the order fulfillment aspects of the transaction, rather than sticking to a model where we have to keep stock of the items that we want to sell.

We looked at the Checkout Process Flowchart and the eight major steps that our checkout.asp has to perform to follow that flowchart. The eight steps are:

- ❏ Capturing the e-mail address and password
- ❏ Capturing the new customer's name and password
- ❏ Adding addresses
- ❏ Choosing addresses
- ❏ Capturing credit card information
- ❏ Choosing credit cards
- ❏ Showing the order and presenting shipping options
- ❏ Approving the order

The next chapter covers what we have to do to create an order-processing pipeline. We can take the information we captured during the process described here and use the pipeline to authorize credit cards and raise orders to the supplier. In addition, our checkout.asp page is currently not secure, so our customer's credit card numbers could be intercepted as they travel over the Internet to us. We'll discuss secure communications in more detail in Chapter 10.

Order Processing

There are many operations, in all spheres of life, which can only be achieved by moving through a number of steps in a logical ordered manner. For example when building a house we can't put the windows in before the foundations and the walls have been constructed. The same is true for us when we think about moving an order through our application; for example we need to know what the order is for before we attempt to bill the customer.

To approach this whole area of order processing we'll be showing how we can use the commonly accepted concept of a **pipeline** to help keep all of the different aspects of the order synchronized. Here we'll have to incorporate into our pipeline solution the functionality we need to interact with the different systems involved, which include inventory control, credit card authorization, and audit trails.

This is going to be a pretty involved chapter that will give the Jo's Coffee site the ability to resolve commercial transactions. We'll be seeing how we can build an order-processing pipeline to handle the orders as they come into the site and we'll build a pipeline architecture that will be flexible enough to allow us to cope with new requirements and opportunities.

So our route through this chapter (if you like, our pipeline for addressing order processing!) has the following outline:

- ❑ Designing the pipeline
- ❑ Starting the `WroxProcessor` component that will support transactional operations
- ❑ Adding functionality to the component to allow construction of an audit trail
- ❑ Adding functionality to facilitate notification of those associated with the pipeline
- ❑ Enabling the `WroxCommerce` and `WroxProcessor` components to move orders through the pipeline
- ❑ Creating an extranet to allow order viewing and supplier interaction
- ❑ Dealing with credit cards

> **There's a lot of code in this chapter – remember the files for Jo's Coffee project can be downloaded from www.wrox.com.**

Let's start with a look at what sort of pipeline we need to build for Jo.

The Jo's Coffee Order Processing Pipeline

You may not have realized it, but at this point, we've already built one part of our order-processing pipeline. When the customer clicks the **Place Order** button at the checkout, our new order has been placed into a state where it's ready to move through the rest of the pipeline.

Here's what the order pipeline we're going to build for Jo's Coffee looks like:

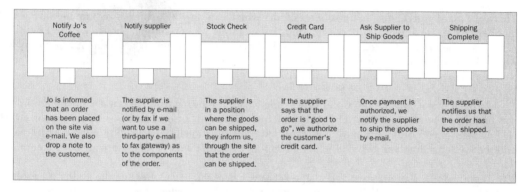

The illustration of the process as a pipeline is particularly useful in that, apart from showing the logical steps needed to process an order (which we associate with individual parts of the pipeline, which we term **connectors**), it also shows that, at any point in the process, the order can drop out from the pipe if something goes wrong. At different points in the pipeline, each connector can return a YES or NO response indicating success or failure. A YES response will cause the order to advance to the next connector in the pipeline. A NO will cause a different action. For example, if the Credit Card Authorization connector fails, we might invite the customer to call us so that we can obtain a new card. At that point, we can hold the order at that point in the pipeline and, if we get updated details we ask our order processor to re-execute that connector, or if nothing is forthcoming we cancel the order.

Each connector is able to handle a specific set of tasks, each of which is responsible for contributing to the final YES or NO response of the connector as a whole. For example the Notify Jo's Coffee connector will:

❑   Send an e-mail to jo@joscoffee.com to say there is a new order

❑   Create an **audit trail** (log of information relating to the transaction) entry containing the text of Jo's message

❑   Send an e-mail to the customer indicating that the order has been received

❑   Create an audit trail entry containing the text of the customer's message

That connector will only return a YES value if all four of those tasks completed successfully. If any or all of them fail, the order will not advance to the next connector in the pipeline.

Those of you who have used **Microsoft Transaction Server** (**MTS**), or in fact, any form of transaction manager, will be familiar with this concept, and we'll be using Microsoft Transaction Server in our pipeline to make sure everything is managed properly. We'll be going into MTS in detail later in the chapter to explain how it is crucial to our transaction processing.

The order does not naturally move through the pipeline; at each point in the pipeline some external event that is deemed successful has to push it further on. At certain points, we may have to involve another party to indicate a value of success or failure of a connector. Our Stock Check connector, for example, will require the supplier to indicate that they have the goods and are in a position to ship them so that we can proceed to the Credit Card Authorization connector. In our system the supplier can indicate this fact either by logging in directly to a special part of the Jo's Coffee site, or by faxing or phoning Jo to say that the order is good to go.

> *As with many parts of this book our treatment follows only one of a range of options. For example, if our supplier had the appropriate system, we could set the Stock Check connector to respond to automatic inventory status updates provided by the supplier when we request a particular item.*

We will, however, be careful to build our pipeline so that it can be adapted to fit the needs of (and the opportunities presented to) the business as it changes over time. Thus if our suppliers (or even just one supplier) moved to a system that supported e-mail based inventory updates we can merely replace the Stock Check connector to respond to this change.

Breaking Down the Pipeline

Now we've introduced the pipeline we need to elaborate on the tasks each connector will handle.

> *Remember that in Chapter 8 we split our order into individual order parts to improve communication with our suppliers. In this section, we'll be pushing each order* part *down the pipeline separately, not the order as a whole.*

For example, let's say order 27 contains two parts (with IDs of 100 and 101) that come from different suppliers. Each part will be given its own pipeline and treated separately. However, orders containing multiple quantities from the same supplier would not be subdivided into order parts. So, if I ordered a single notebook PC from Supplier A as an order, or if I ordered one hundred of them, in each case only one order part would exist.

For reference, here's what each connector in our pipeline does; we'll be building objects to handle each of these as we work through the chapter:

Connector	Task
Notify Jo's Coffee	Send e-mail to `jo@joscoffee.com` to say there is a new order.
	Send e-mail to the customer indicating that the order has been received.
Notify Supplier	Send e-mail to the supplier informing them of the new order.
Stock Check	Wait for the supplier to indicate that the order can be shipped.
	Update the database to indicate the new status of the order.
Credit Card Authorization	Send the payment information to the credit card processing gateway.
	Update the database to indicate the new status of the order.
Ask Supplier to Ship Goods	Send e-mail to the supplier asking them to ship the goods.
Shipping Complete	Wait for the supplier to indicate that the order has been shipped.
	Update the database to indicate the new status of the order.

In our breakdown, we haven't included information about when actions are recorded in the audit trail. As a rule of thumb, anything that happens inside the pipeline should be recorded in an audit trail in as much detail as possible. So, when we send an e-mail, we store the text of the e-mail, including the recipients, in the audit trail. We'll discuss the audit trail in more detail presently and we'll learn how to build such a trail later in this section.

Building the Pipeline

In this section, we'll cover a lot of ground as we learn how to build the order-processing pipeline for Jo's Coffee and here we'll be:

- Discussing Microsoft Transaction Server (MTS)
- Creating the component that will work inside MTS
- Building an interface that can talk to each pipeline connector
- Adding functionality to the component to allow construction of an audit trail
- Adding functionality to facilitate notification of those associated with the pipeline, like the proprietor Jo, the customer, and the supplier
- Creating the first connectors in the pipeline that will carry out notification of Jo, the customer, and the supplier
- Putting in place the code to enable the appropriate part of the pipeline to be executed

First we need to understand how we are going to make use of MTS.

MTS

We won't go into Microsoft Transaction Server (MTS) in great detail, but basically MTS is a component-based run-time environment that is closely integrated with ASP and IIS and enables Visual Basic developers to build scalable, distributed applications. It manages the registering and the instantiating of COM components from within Web pages and can support large numbers of concurrent users by efficiently managing system resources. Additionally, it provides support for **transactions**.

In the context of our order pipeline, let's make quite sure that we fully understand what the word **transaction** means and what its implications are.

Transactions

Take an example from database manipulation; let's say we want to carry out the following operations:

- ❑ **Query 1** – Write a row to `TableA`
- ❑ **Query 2** – Update a row in `TableB`
- ❑ **Query 3** – Delete a set of rows from `TableC`

In a **transactional environment**, we define those three operations to be part of a single transaction. We want that transaction to be **atomic**, this means if one part of it fails, the transaction shouldn't happen. In the real world, if Query 2 fails, we would already have executed Query 1 and added the row to `TableA`, so we effectively have to remove the row from `TableA` by **rolling back** the operation.

Rolling back is the name given to the process of the database equivalent of an undo. So, if a column was changed from Alex to Ollie, a rollback will change it back to Alex. If we didn't do this rollback, we'd say that the system had lost **consistency** because part of a transaction would have been performed without the rest of it happening.

Our point about consistency is important – imagine a bank transfer to move funds between two of your accounts. Simplistically we can say that the transaction has two parts:

- ❑ **Part A** – Deduct money from first account
- ❑ **Part B** – Add money to second account

If the second part in the transaction failed, you would have lost money as the balances became inconsistent – effectively the money from the first account would have disappeared into the ether. It's imperative that in any form of transactional system a single transaction either all happens perfectly or doesn't happen at all. Of course, in our example of Jo's Coffee, we're going to use transactions to catch exceptions so when something goes critically wrong we want to be shielded from the effects as much as possible.

In addition to the **atomic** and **consistent** aspects of programming in transactional environments, there are two more aspects:

- ❑ Transactions must be **isolated** (that is one can't interfere with another, so continuing our bank analogy, if we transfer money between two of Edward's accounts, we don't want Niamh knowing anything about it).
- ❑ Transactions must also be **durable**, meaning that once they are completed they are known to be properly stored in the underlying data store.

These four properties of transactional environments are summarized in the acronym **ACID** – Atomic, Consistent, Isolated and Durable.

MTS and Transactions

The principle with MTS is that, once it's installed on a computer, it is then possible to create components that take part in the transactional environments it can create and so have the ACID benefits of such an environment. This is great news as developing your own environment to handle transactions would involve a lot of pain.

To use MTS you mark the Visual Basic objects as wishing to partake in transactions (we'll do this for real in a little while) and then the COM-subsystem and MTS work together to let instances of the object enjoy the benefits of running in the environment. So, in our database example MTS will ensure the row from `TableA` is automatically removed if Query 2 fails, and if Query 3 fails the row from `TableA` is removed and the changes made to `TableB` are undone. At the end, you're guaranteed that all of the systems involved in the transaction are at the state they were before you started working with them.

MTS also requires us to group our components together into **packages**. Those components can be off-the-shelf components, or ones written by you in Visual Basic, Visual C++ or another tool. In our case, we're interested in the `WroxProcessor` component that's going to be written in Visual Basic. We're building an e-commerce site, so we are going to put together a package that represents the application of processing orders on that site. If it were an airline reservation system, we'd most likely create a package for that application and use it to group together communications objects, database management objects, ticket printing objects and so on.

In order for this environment to work, other parts of the system that are involved have to understand their role. So, SQL Server has to understand when it's part of a transaction in order to handle the commit and rollback functions that the components might be reliant on.

As we detailed in Chapter 2, MTS should have been already installed from the Windows NT Option Pack.

Right, now we've got the theory under our belts let's move on to the practical.

Creating the WroxProcessor Component

As we mentioned, MTS uses the concept of grouping components related to single application together into packages. To kick off our pipeline construction we're going to build a Jo's Coffee package, create a new Visual Basic project with objects specifically designed to handle order processing, and then configure this new `WroxProcessor` component to work inside MTS.

> **There is a bug that can prevent Visual Basic and MTS from communicating properly. If when you run the VB project, you see a message indicating the "MTS is not installed or is the wrong version",** *re-install* **Service Pack 4.**

One of the libraries we reference during this next section – Microsoft CDO for NTS 1.2 Library (Collaboration Data Objects for NT Server) is, as its name implies, only available in Windows NT Server so you may have to modify this code depending on the platform you're using.

Try It Out – Creating a Component to Work Under MTS

1. For starters, create a new Visual Basic ActiveX DLL project and save it as `WroxProcessor`. Ideally, you should try to keep related projects together, so if you've saved your `WroxCommerce` components in a folder called `c:\Projects\WroxCommerce`, save the new project as `c:\Projects\WroxProcessor`.

2. Our new project requires a number of references to other libraries, such as ADO and MTS itself. Select Project | References...from the menu and check on:

❑ Microsoft CDO for NTS 1.2 Library – used for sending e-mails (we'll detail this later).

❑ Microsoft Transaction Server Type Library – used for communicating with MTS.

❑ Microsoft ActiveX Data Objects 2.1 Library – used for communicating with ADO and, through ADO, SQL Server.

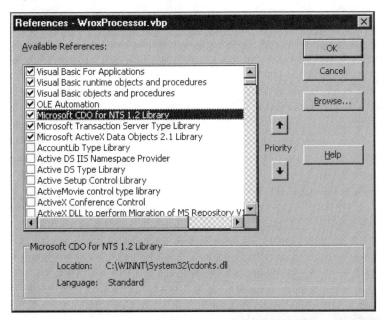

3. To do the actual pipeline work, we're going to create a new Visual Basic class module called `OrderProcessor`. This object will be the one that we create whenever we want to do anything with the order, and it will also be the component that we install in the MTS package.

Create a new class module via Project | Add Class Module, rename it OrderProcessor, and then, using the Properties window, change the MTSTransactionMode property to 4 – RequiresNewTransaction:

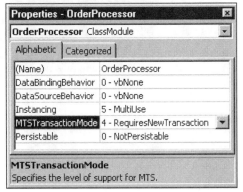

4. Next, to implement the object we need to add the following code to `OrderProcessor`:

```
Option Explicit

' this variable holds mail domain.
Private m_strMailDomain As String

' this variable holds the connection string needed to connect to the database...
Private m_strDBString As String

' transaction information...
Private m_PartID As Long
Private m_ObjectContext As ObjectContext

' implement...
Implements ObjectControl

' Configure - set up the object based on values from WroxCommerce
Public Sub Configure(ByVal strDBString As String, ByVal strMailDomain As String, _
    ByVal Commerce As Object)

    ' store mail domain
    m_strMailDomain = strMailDomain

    ' copy the database details...
    m_strDBString = strDBString

End Sub


' Activate - we have been activated inside the context of a transaction...
Private Sub ObjectControl_Activate()

    ' capture our object context from MTS...
    Set m_ObjectContext = GetObjectContext

End Sub

' CanBePooled - can this object be pooled?
Private Function ObjectControl_CanBePooled() As Boolean
    ObjectControl_CanBePooled = False
End Function

' Deactivate - we are no long running inside a transaction...
Private Sub ObjectControl_Deactivate()

    ' release our object context...
    Set m_ObjectContext = Nothing

End Sub

' ObjectContext - pass the object context on...
Public Property Get ObjectContext() As ObjectContext
 Set ObjectContext = m_ObjectContext
End Property
```

How It Works

The first thing we need to discuss here is the setting of the MTS transaction modes; as you probably saw when you set that property there are actually five different modes which can be described as follows:

❑ **0 – NotAnMTSObject** – This is the default state for an object. It simply means that the object doesn't support MTS and that MTS should ignore it and not attempt to manage it.

❑ **1 – NoTransactions** – This indicates that the object explicitly does not want to run in a transactional environment. If a transaction is running, this object will not be included in the transaction.

❑ **2 – RequiresTransactions** – This indicates that the object absolutely requires transactions. If a transaction is already running (we'll learn more about how transactions are created and destroyed later), it will be enrolled in that transaction. If a transaction is not running, a new one will be created.

❑ **3 – UsesTransactions** – This indicates that the object is happy to run in a transactional environment, but it doesn't have to.

❑ **4 – RequiresNewTransaction** – This indicates that the object needs a brand new transaction in which to operate.

The last of these modes is the one we have chosen to create our new `OrderProcessor` object in, and later we'll see how setting `MTSTransactionMode` to this property will create the transaction we require.

Once it's time to start moving the order through the pipeline we'll be creating an instance of `WroxProcessor.OrderProcessor` and calling its `Configure` method from the `WroxCommerce` objects. Thus we have added to the object a `Configure` method (which is similar to its counterpart in the `WroxCommerce.Visit` object). This call will pass over certain pieces of environmental information; specifically, where to find the database connection, the name of the e-mail domain, and a reference to the `WroxCommerce` object that created it. By passing over the `Visit` object, we can derive more information about the environment, and have complete access to the `WroxCommerce` object model should we need it later during our transactional processing:

```
Option Explicit

' this variable holds mail domain.
Private m_strMailDomain As String

' this variable holds the connection string needed to connect to the database...
Private m_strDBString As String

' transaction information...
Private m_PartID As Long
Private m_ObjectContext As ObjectContext

' implement...
Implements ObjectControl

' Configure - set up the object based on values from WroxCommerce
Public Sub Configure(ByVal strDBString As String, ByVal strMailDomain As String, _
    ByVal Commerce As Object)
```

```
     ' store mail domain
     m_strMailDomain = strMailDomain

     ' copy the database details...
     m_strDBString = strDBString

 End Sub
```

The code `Implements ObjectControl` indicates that we want MTS to call back into us to tell us when we become involved in the transaction. When we include this line, we then have to implement the three functions that are part of the `IObjectControl` interface. The `Implements` keyword is a contract with VB that states we're committed to providing the various methods and properties of whatever interface we're talking about (we encountered this before with the `IUtility` interface that we built back in Chapter 6).

The `Activate` method is called when MTS decides to make our object active. Inside it, we call a global function defined inside the MTS library, called `GetObjectContext`, to grab hold of an object that will later use to call back into MTS to commit and abort transactions, as well as learning more about the transactional environment:

```
 ' Activate - we have been activated inside the context of a transaction...
 Private Sub ObjectControl_Activate()

    ' capture our object context from MTS...
    Set m_ObjectContext = GetObjectContext

 End Sub
```

The `Deactivate` method is called when MTS decides there's no longer a need for our method, and so we cleanup our `m_ObjectContext` variable at that time:

```
 ' Deactivate - we are no long running inside a transaction...
 Private Sub ObjectControl_Deactivate()

    ' release our object context...
    Set m_ObjectContext = Nothing

 End Sub
```

We also implement the `CanBePooled` method; but the results are currently ignored by MTS. This feature is supported on Windows 2000, providing your objects are built with support for free threading. VB6 doesn't support that, but Visual C++ does. Either way, creating objects in this manner is beyond the scope of this book.

```
 ' CanBePooled - can this object be pooled?
 Private Function ObjectControl_CanBePooled() As Boolean
  ObjectControl_CanBePooled = False
 End Function
```

Our last piece of code passes on our transaction environment to other objects in the pipeline that may need them:

```
' ObjectContext - pass the object context on...
Public Property Get ObjectContext() As ObjectContext
  Set ObjectContext = m_ObjectContext
End Property
```

After creating a suitable project, let's put the component into an MTS package.

Try It Out – Creating the MTS Package

1. To create our MTS package, we have to have a compiled version of the project available to import into it. From the menu, select File | Make WroxProcessor.dll...and save the new DLL.

2. MTS will only talk nicely with a VB component if the project has been compiled in **binary compatibility** mode. This is a way of telling VB that the identifiers that it uses to identify each of the ActiveX objects in the project, and any unique interfaces that those objects may support should not change between compilation or editing. To set binary compatibility on, select Project | WroxProcessor Properties from the menu, change to the Component tab and check on Binary Compatibility:

3. Installing our new components inside MTS and creating the package is a simple process of walking through one Wizard to create the package, then another to put the component in the package.

331

Open Transaction Server Explorer (via Start | Programs | Windows NT 4.0 Option Pack | Microsoft Transaction Server). Drill down inside the management tree until you find My Computer. Right-click on Packages Installed and select New | Package:

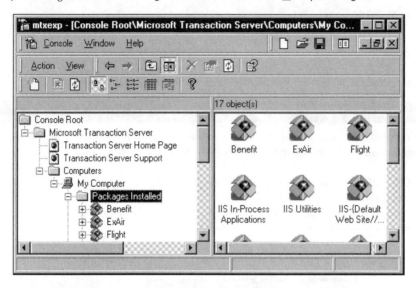

4. In the first Wizard window that appears, click Create an empty package (we're not going to show all of the pages for the Wizard in this discussion, as it's pretty simple to follow) and enter the name for the new package as JoCoffee. Click Next.

5. When asked for the user account, leave Interactive user checked on and click Finish. What this does is tell MTS to impersonate the user that made the call into the object and use all of the security settings for that user. In our case, this means that the anonymous IIS user will be the one that MTS will impersonate, so the objects that MTS creates will have the same rights as the anonymous IIS user.

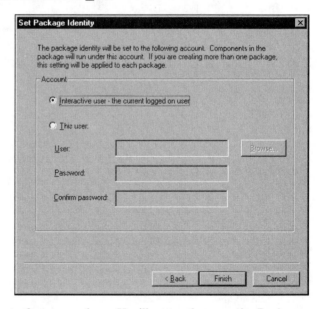

That's all that we have to do to create the new package. You'll notice that now the Packages Installed object contains a JoCoffee package.

6. To install our `WroxProcessor` component into the package we'll be working though another Wizard. Expand out the JoCoffee node, right-click on Components, choose New | Component and click the Install new components button.

7. Click the Add files...button and browse to the `WroxProcessor` DLL we created a moment ago. Selecting Open will cause the path of the DLL and all of the components that the DLL contains that can be executed in the MTS environment to be displayed in the dialog. Click Finish to save the component:

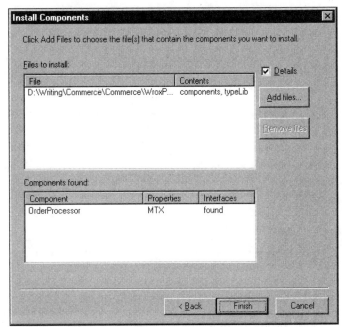

8. After the components have been imported, the MTS Explorer will display the only object in the DLL we just imported. If you're interested, you can drill down inside the component looking at the methods and properties that it supports:

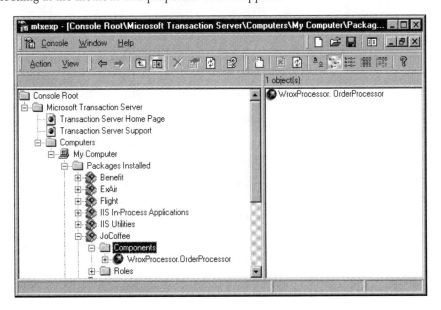

So far, we've managed to configure our VB project so that it will run properly inside Microsoft Transaction Server. We haven't actually done anything to build up the pipeline at all yet; that's all about to change starting with the next section.

The IConnector Interface

The first thing we're going to do is build a common interface that we can use to talk to each pipeline connector. Back in Chapter 3, we built the `IUtility` interface as an way of letting objects in our object model communicate, without having to expose the methods and properties on `IUtility` to the ASP presentation layer.

Remember, in order to adhere for our rules for 3-tier client/server design, we don't want the ASP developer being able to circumvent the business rules that we define in the business objects – direct access to IUtility would allow the developer to circumvent the rules.

Now, we're going to use the same approach to creating connectors in our pipeline by building the `IConnector` interface. Each connector in the pipeline is going to be implemented as a separate object and in some ways our pipeline design can be taken as a type of object model:

Connector Object	Task
PipelineNotifyOwner	Send e-mail to jo@joscoffee.com to say there is a new order.
	Send e-mail to the customer indicating that the order has been received.
PipelineSignalSuppliers	Send e-mail to the supplier informing them of the new order.
PipelineSupplierOK	Wait for the supplier to indicate that the order can be shipped.
	Update the database to indicate the new status of the order.
PipelinePaymentAuth	Send the payment information to the credit card processing gateway.
	Update the database to indicate the new status of the order.
PipelineSupplierToShip	Send e-mail to the supplier asking them to ship the goods.
PipelineSupplierOK	Wait for the supplier to indicate that the order has been shipped.
	Update the database to indicate the new status of the order.

As we said before, we need to make the structure of the pipeline as flexible as possible, to make the process of inserting a new connector into the pipe, or replacing an existing connector with a new one, a smooth an operation as possible. To do this, we'll define a common set of properties and methods that each connector object must implement, so that anything that needs to talk to the pipeline, including the `OrderProcessor` object and the other objects in the pipeline, are able to use this common language (this is the fundamental principle behind Microsoft's Component Object Model (COM) architecture, by the way).

Try It Out – Creating the IConnector Interface

1. To create the IConnector interface, create a new class module in the WroxProcessor Visual Basic project and call it IConnector. Add the following code:

```
Option Explicit

' IConnector - common interface for pipeline connectors

' ID - return the ID of the connector...
Public Property Get ID() As String
End Property

' Name - return the name of the connector...
Public Property Get Name() As String
End Property

' Process - tell the connector to go ahead and start working...
Public Function Process(ByVal Processor As OrderProcessor, _
        ByRef RunNextConnector As Boolean) As Boolean
End Function
```

How It Works

We've tried to keep the common interface for connectors as simple as possible in this example. All we need to do is ask them for their ID and their name, and tell them when it's time to go away and try to do their part of the processing job.

This brings us to a very important point about how we can identify the objects that we create.

Connector IDs

One of the neatest things about COM is the really useful **Globally Unique Identifier**, or **GUID**. A GUID is basically a really, really, really large number (128 bits in length), and is created in such a way that it's not possible for the same number to be created on two separate machines (or, in fact, on the same machine).

> *What this means overall, is that if you use these numbers to identify objects that you create, no one else in the world will end up using the same IDs to identify their objects.*

When you run your project in Visual Basic, or you compile the project, VB creates GUIDs for each of the objects in your project. (In fact, it also creates them for a whole host of other things related to COM, but the important thing here is that it creates one for each object.) If we also use GUIDs to identify each object that makes up a connector in our pipeline, not only are we guaranteed never to have problems identifying them ourselves, but we can also share our pipeline components with other people using WroxCommerce.

VB spends most of its time hiding the inner workings of COM from developers like you and I, so discovering the GUID that represents each object in the pipeline isn't as easy as if we were writing in Visual C++, for example. Later in the chapter, we'll see how we can retrieve the GUIDs for our connector objects, as this will prove invaluable in moving through the pipeline.

The ID property of our IConnector interface will return the ID of the connector back to the caller in the form of a string, and we'll see how this works later on when we start using our IConnector interface.

Pipeline Support Code

In the breakdown of each connector, you'll notice that there are a few tasks that are common to several connectors, for example:

❑ Adding things to the audit trail

❑ Sending notifications by e-mail to Jo, the customer, and the supplier

Before we move on to implementing the pipeline connectors themselves we'll deal with these common tasks as part of the supporting infrastructure for the pipeline. There are several points during this chapter where we'll have to step back from implementing specific connectors and build such support code.

To begin with, we look at the part of the project dealing with the audit trail; let's kick off by examining in more detail what we mean by an audit trail.

Audit Trail

An audit trail is absolutely essential in any system that performs transactions, as it provides a level of accountability to anything you do. Would you, for example, trust a bank that didn't accurately record information on transactions performed on your account?

In this chapter, we'll be building an auditing system that we can use down the road to examine the path an order took from original inception to final resolution. The system will allow us to ask, among other questions, "What was the authorization code of that credit card transaction?" and "When did we e-mail the customer to tell him that his order has been delayed?"

How much information you keep in your audit trail is up to you. Too little information and the system is not as useful as it might be; too much and you'll find you spend most of your time managing the audit trail tables. In this chapter, we're going to err on the side of verbose, so feel free to change the level of auditing to suit your particular tastes.

We do, however, have a paradox to deal with. Basically, if some part of the transaction fails, no parts of the transaction will be allowed to happen. This includes the auditing information, meaning that if we do cancel the MTS transaction, the audit trail will not be written, so we won't be able to tell what went wrong. This is great if all we want to report in the audit trail is successful events, but bad if we want to report errors or exceptions to the pipelining process. For Jo's Coffee, to keep things simple, we're not going to let this worry us.

Building a system capable of handling audit trails is actually very simple. The one we build here will have a single table (`Audit`), and a single method for inserting entries into that table which will form a part of our support code.

Try It Out – The Audit Trail I: Building the Audit Table

1. Open the SQL Server Enterprise Manager, drill down to the JoCoffee database, right-click on Tables, select New Table...and enter Audit as the name.

2. Fill in the grid as shown and save the table (note the `AuditID` column is the primary key):

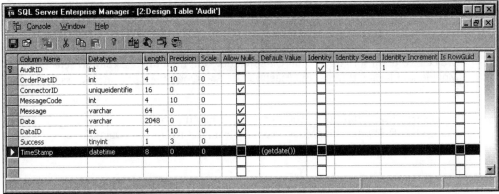

How It Works

Some of the columns in that table are talking about stuff we haven't fully introduced yet, but in summary we have:

❑ `AuditID` – the identifier for the audit entry.

❑ `OrderPartID` – all of the audit trail entries will be related to exactly one `OrderPartID`, meaning we can easily grab hold of a processing history for each part of the order.

❑ `ConnectorID` – this will store the GUID representing the `ConnectorID` (the SQL Server `uniqueidentifier` data type is specifically used for holding GUIDs). The `ConnectorID` column can be null as the core object that manages the pipeline may throw its own messages.

❑ `MessageCode` – each connector will be able to issue its own unique integers, that are stored in `MessageCode`, and there will be exactly one code for each activity the connector may wish to note in the audit trail.

❑ `Message` – a field that allows extra information about the audit entry to be stored if required (for example this field could contain information relating to any e-mail that is sent).

❑ `Data` – a field that allows extra information about the audit entry to be stored if required.

❑ `DataID` – a field that allows extra information about the audit entry to be stored if required.

❑ `Success` – this is used to indicate whether the entry is notifying us of something that went right, or something that went wrong.

❑ `TimeStamp` – this holds both the date and time of the audit log entry. The default value of this column has been set to `getdate()`, which is a SQL Server scalar function that returns the current server date and time.

Now we have the database structure in place – all one table of it – we now need to build the code in the Visual Basic project that will allow us to connect to and write to the table.

Try It Out – The Audit Trail II: Connecting to the Database

1. We're going to connect to the database in `WroxProcessor` in the same manner as we did in `WroxCommerce`.

To do this, we'll simply include the `Database.cls` object file in the `WroxProcessor` project. To do this, right-click on **Class Modules** in the Project Explorer, select **Add | Class Module** and locate, through the **Existing** tab, and **Open** the `Database` class that belongs to `WroxCommerce`.

However, because this object was not using transactions inside `WroxCommerce`, you need to change its MTSTransactionMode property from 0 – NotAnMTSObject to 3 – UsesTransactions.

> By doing this, the next time you return to the **WroxCommerce** project and try to run it, VB will throw a message indicating that the project has to be in binary compatibility mode. You should alter the project properties, via **Project | WroxCommerce Properties** and set this project to be binary compatible.

2. After including the `Database` class module, we need to make some standard changes to the `OrderProcessor` object in `WroxProcessor`. Create a member variable for holding a database connection:

```
'variable holds new database
Private m_DB As Database
```

3. Next, we need to create a property to return the database back. This should be added to the bottom of the `OrderProcessor` object:

```
' DB - return the database object...
Public Property Get DB() As Database

    ' do we have one?
    If m_DB Is Nothing Then

        ' create it...
        Set m_DB = New Database
        m_DB.Configure m_strDBString

    End If

    ' return it...
    Set DB = m_DB

End Property
```

4. We also need to add a `ShutDown` method to the end of `OrderProcessor`:

```
' ShutDown - close the database...
Public Function ShutDown()

    ' do we have a connection?
    If Not m_DB Is Nothing Then
        m_DB.ShutDown
        Set m_DB = Nothing
    End If

End Function
```

5. And finally, to make sure `ShutDown` gets called, add this destructor to `OrderProcessor`:

```
' Called when the object is destroyed
Private Sub Class_Terminate()
    ShutDown
End Sub
```

Try It Out – The Audit Trail III: Adding Entries

1. To support our audit trail we need to add a couple of methods to `WroxProcessor`; the `AddAudit` function will enable us to add entries to the audit trail and the `RecordError` method will notify the site owner that something went badly wrong in the case of VB errors occurring in the pipeline.

Add the following code to the `OrderProcessor` object:

```
' AddAudit - add an entry to the audit trail...
Public Function AddAudit(ByVal Connector As IConnector, _
    ByVal MessageCode As Long, ByVal Success As Boolean, _
    Optional ByVal Message As String, _
    Optional ByVal Data As String, _
    Optional ByVal DataID As Long) As Long

    ' create a new item...
    Dim NewAudit As New Recordset
    NewAudit.Open "Audit", DB.DB, adOpenKeyset, adLockOptimistic
    NewAudit.AddNew

    ' set it...
    NewAudit("OrderPartID") = m_PartID
    If Not Connector Is Nothing Then _
            NewAudit("ConnectorID") = Connector.ID
    NewAudit("MessageCode") = MessageCode
    If Message <> "" Then NewAudit("Message") = Message
    If Data <> "" Then NewAudit("Data") = Data
    NewAudit("DataID") = DataID
    If Success = True Then
        NewAudit("Success") = 1
    Else
        NewAudit("success") = 0
    End If
```

```
' finish...
NewAudit.Update
AddAudit = NewAudit("AuditID")
NewAudit.Close
Set NewAudit = Nothing

End Function

' Record the fact an error occurred...
Public Function RecordError(ByVal Area As String, _
            Optional ByVal Connector As IConnector)

    ' get the text for the message...
    Dim MessageText As String
    MessageText = "OrderPartID: " & m_PartID & Chr(13)
    MessageText = MessageText & "Number: " & Err.Number & Chr(13)
    MessageText = MessageText & "Description: " & _
                Err.Description & Chr(13)
    MessageText = MessageText & "Source: " & Err.Source & Chr(13)

    ' get the name for the audit log...
    Dim AreaText As String
    If Connector Is Nothing Then
    AreaText = "Pipeline:" & Area
    Else
    AreaText = Connector.Name & ":" & Area
    End If

    ' send the message over via e-mail...
    Dim NewMail As New CDONTS.NewMail
    NewMail.Send "server@" & m_strMailDomain, "admin@" & m_strMailDomain, _
                AreaText, MessageText

    ' tell MTS not to do  roll everything back and make it look like nothing
happened...
    ObjectContext.SetAbort

End Function
```

2. Each of the activities that each connector performs will have its own message code that has to be written into the audit trail. We need to store these codes globally in the `WroxProcessor` project. Add a new global-style module (not a class module), to the project and call it `MessageCodes`. Then, add this code:

```
Option Explicit

' PipelineCodes - things that can happen to the pipeline itself...
Public Enum PipelineCodes
 PipelineError_VBError = 10001
 PipelineError_NotInTransaction = 10002
End Enum
```

Those are two of the message codes that the pipeline itself can write into the audit trail. We'll be seeing how this works later on.

How It Works

The AddAudit method is quite straightforward (apart from asking for a PartID property that we haven't yet implemented) in that it simply creates and populates a row in the Audit table.

The next part of the code, addressing the handling of any Visual Basic error that occurs in our pipeline, deserves more attention. We use VB's standard exception handling routines to discover the point at which the error occured, and the RecordError method to notify the owner something went badly wrong.

The method uses the built-in Visual Basic error reporting object Err to discover what error actually occurred and this object is then used to build the MessageText string, which forms the body of the text added to the audit trail:

```
' Record the fact an error occurred...
Public Function RecordError(ByVal Area As String, _
            Optional ByVal Connector As IConnector)

' get the text for the message...
Dim MessageText As String
MessageText = "OrderPartID: " & m_PartID & Chr(13)
MessageText = MessageText & "Number: " & Err.Number & Chr(13)
MessageText = MessageText & "Description: " & _
            Err.Description & Chr(13)
MessageText = MessageText & "Source: " & Err.Source & Chr(13)
```

Additionally, the connector is used in combination with the Area parameter to indicate in the audit trail exactly where the error occurred. We then send the message via e-mail and abort the transaction with the SetAbort method. If the transaction is aborted, none of the audit trail information will be included in the transaction, meaning that we have to signal the administration team in another manner.

```
' get the name for the audit log...
Dim AreaText As String
If Connector Is Nothing Then
AreaText = "Pipeline:" & Area
Else
AreaText = Connector.Name & ":" & Area
End If

' send the message over via e-mail...
Dim NewMail As New CDONTS.NewMail
NewMail.Send "server@" & m_strMailDomain, "admin@" & m_strMailDomain, _
            AreaText, MessageText

' tell MTS not to do  roll everything back and make it look like nothing
happened...
ObjectContext.SetAbort

End Function
```

This is the only instance in the pipeline where if we ask MTS to abort the transaction it can have repercussions on the system, as it's very much a last gasp approach. Wherever possible in your VB code, attempt to pre-empt and handle VB errors so that you can gracefully roll back stuff that MTS cannot roll back itself.

For instance, MTS cannot roll back credit card authorizations from the payment gateway we discuss later in the chapter, so if you have to get out of the transaction for any reason, you have to be able to manually undo that operation. If an error happens somewhere in the pipeline that's not properly handled, there's a possibility here that payment could be authorized, yet you'd never know about it, which is a potentially embarrassing problem.

In short, it's good practice to code defensively and try to make sure that your code is capable of testing for (and subsequently handling) the majority of errors that can occur.

That concludes the audit trail end of things for the moment, let's now move on to the second part of the support code we discussed – that concerning e-mail notifications.

Notification Systems

The other common piece of functionality required by the connectors is the ability to send e-mail. In this chapter, we're going to be using Collaboration Data Objects for NT Server (CDONTS) to do the actual sending of the e-mail (we created a reference, in the `WroxProcessor` component, to this library when we created the project). If you're not running on Windows NT Server, or you don't want to use CDONTS, you can easily modify this code to handle any of the off-the-shelf ASP e-mail components, like Server Object's ASPMail (`http://www.serverobjects.com/`) or Dimac's JMail (`http://www.dimac.net/`).

One word of warning though – you will need to make sure that the **Microsoft SMTP Service** is running, and configured properly, otherwise no e-mails will be sent. Although there are a number of ways to send e-mail these days (MAPI, Lotus Notes, etc.), we're going to work from the premise of using standard Internet mail driven by SMTP. We're not going to concern ourselves with the intricacies of getting the e-mails actually sent – this is another area where you will have to negotiate with your ISP.

Try It Out – Implementing Notification

1. Here's the `SendEmail` method that should be added to the `OrderProcessor` object:

```
' SendEmail - send e-mail from a connector...
Public Function SendEMail(ByVal Connector As IConnector, _
    ByVal MessageID As Long, ByVal Subject As String, _
    ByVal ToName As String, ByVal ToEMail As String, _
    ByVal Message As String, Optional ByVal FromName As String, _
    Optional ByVal FromEMail As String) As Boolean

    ' set up an error handler...
    On Error GoTo Problem

    ' prepare cdo...
    Dim NewMail As New CDONTS.NewMail

    ' who is the mail from?
    ' CDONTS likes to see recipients in the format...
    ' "John Doe<john@wrox.com>" or "john@wrox.com"
    If FromName = "" Then
```

```
' if nothing specified, send it from the "server"...
NewMail.From = "Fred<server@" & m_strMailDomain & ">"

Else

' send it from the one we specified...
NewMail.From = FromName & "<" & FromEMail & ">"

End If

' who is it to?
NewMail.To = ToName & "<" & ToEMail & ">"

' the message...
NewMail.Subject = Subject
NewMail.Body = Message

' send it...
NewMail.Send

' indicate that we were ok...
SendEMail = True
GoTo Finish

Problem:

' an error occured, log it and return false...
SendEMail = False

Finish:

' we need to record the result in the audit trail...
Dim AuditText As String
AuditText = "To: " & ToName & "<" & ToEMail & ">" & Chr(13)
AuditText = AuditText & _
    "From: " & FromName & "<" & FromEMail & ">" & Chr(13)
AuditText = AuditText & "Subject: " & Subject & Chr(13)
AuditText = AuditText & Chr(13)
AuditText = AuditText & Message

' send it out...
AddAudit Connector, MessageID, SendEMail, _
        "E-mail sent to " & ToEMail, AuditText

End Function
```

How It Works

This is the first method where we encounter the kind of exception handling we're going to be using in each method implemented by the connectors and supporting code (remember our `AddAudit` method doesn't follow this exception-handling paradigm because of the paradox that we report errors using the audit trail, so if we can't update the trail, we can't report the errors!).

The SendEMail function takes a whole bundle of parameters indicating where the mail should go, what connector ordered it, and what order part the connector was processing. The first thing it does is set up the standard VB error handling, where if any errors are encountered the Problem label is jumped to. After the method has created the CDONTS NewMail object, we set the address that the mail is from.

We can assume that if no From address is specified then the mail is from the server, so we make a name up based on the mail domain that we already know and an arbitrary name – in this case Fred. Once we've set the From address, we define a To address, put the subject and the message body in place and send it off. If everything goes right, we set the return result to True and jump to the end of the function in order to update the audit trail.

After putting some of the supporting code in place, let's move on to build our first connector object.

Starting the Pipeline

You may not realize it at this point, but we have already implemented one tiny part of the order pipeline. The PlaceOrder method we added to the Orders object in the last chapter is the very first stage in the PipelineNotifyOwner connector. After we've created this new object, we'll need to rewrite the PlaceOrder method to create an instance of the WroxProcessor.OrderProcessor object and do the work.

In fact, although we're creating the object now, it'll be several more pages before we are in a position to actually do something. After we've created the object, we'll look at how transactions are handled in our application, how we can select which connector to execute; we'll add a little more support type code and then we'll build the code that enables the connector to fulfill its responsibilities.

Anyway let's make a start and create this new connector object.

Try It Out – Creating PipelineNotifyOwner

1. Create a new class module in WroxProcessor and call it PipelineNotifyOwner and set its MTSTransactionMode property to 2 – RequiresTransaction. As we saw previously this tells MTS that the object will participate in an existing transaction, but if a transaction doesn't exist, it should create a new one.

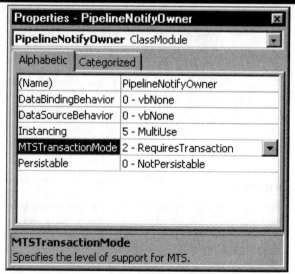

344

2. We start the coding by adding the following:

```
Option Explicit

' Indicate that this is a connector object...
Implements IConnector
```

The `Implements` keyword tells Visual Basic that this object will be implementing all of the properties and methods supported on the `IConnector` interface we built a moment ago. You can see these methods that you need to implement by dropping down the list in the top-left hand corner of the editing window and selecting `IConnector`.

3. For the moment, implement these methods and properties as stub functions:

```
' ID - return the ID of the connector...
Public Property Get IConnector_ID() As String
End Property

' Name - return the name of the connector...
Public Property Get IConnector_Name() As String
End Property

' Process - tell the connector to go ahead and start working...
Public Function IConnector_Process(ByVal Processor As OrderProcessor, _
        ByRef RunNextConnector As Boolean) As Boolean
End Function
```

4. To see the new component inside MTS, the *easiest* thing to do is delete the entire JoCoffee MTS package and recreate it, re-importing the *newly compiled* VB project as you go (follow through the steps we outlined at the head of the chapter).

If you do this you should see both the new `PipelineNotifyOwner` and `IConnector` objects. You can also see how MTS intends to handle transactions for each object by selecting View | Property View from the menu:

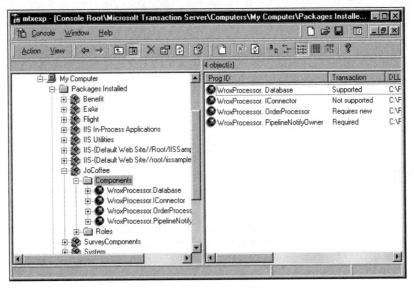

5. Next, we need to see how to find the GUID of our connector. As we mentioned before, we're going to use GUIDs to uniquely identify each connector that may exist throughout the world. Because Visual Basic does a lot of abstraction from the GUID that physically identifies the COM object that implements `PipelineNotifyOwner`, we can't assume that GUID is correct or will stay static. For this reason we can't say that a connector's GUID as we perceive it from the context of a WroxCommerce-driven site is the *same* as the GUID that implements that class.

The GUID you're about to find on your computer will, by its very nature, be different to the one you'll see in this book, and later we'll be showing you a technique to make it easier to handle these GUIDs.

To determine the GUID we're going to use for the connector, open up MTS Explorer, find the `PipelineNotifyOrder` object, right-click on it and choose **Properties**. The long string in the middle of the dialog called **CLSID** is the GUID that we're after. Select it, and copy it to the clipboard.

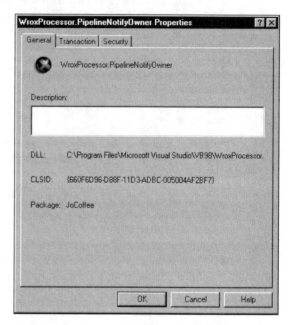

6. Now, create a new module in the `WroxProcessor` VB project and call it **GUIDs**. (This is a normal, global-style module, not a class module.) Add this code:

```
' Pipeline Connector GUIDs
Global Const GUID_PipelineNotifyOwner = _
        "{Add your computer-specific GUID here}"
```

For example, as an illustration, the GUID shown above gives:

```
' Pipeline Connector GUIDs
Global Const GUID_PipelineNotifyOwner = _
        "{660F6D6D96-D88F-11D3-ADBC-005004AF2BF7}"
```

Progressing Orders

We're now at a point where we can actually try to move the order through the pipeline.

We may well end up in a position where we have to call the pipeline object from outside of an ASP page, although the first call we make will be in response to the user pressing the **Place Order** button on the checkout page. That's one of the reasons why we rolled the pipeline objects out into their own VB project.

Before we start coding we should outline how MTS deals with our application.

Running Transactions

One of the hardest things to understand when using MTS is who actually creates and destroys the transactions! In most development activities, the developer is responsible for explicitly changing the environment to suit his or her needs, for example opening a connection to a database, or destroying a window. In MTS, there is no concept of explicitly creating or destroying a transaction. All that you do is indicate how an object participates in a transaction and MTS does the rest. A transaction is closed either when all the objects have indicated their result, or all the objects involved within a transaction have terminated.

In our example here, our `OrderProcessor` object has been set to 4 – RequiresNewTransaction meaning that whenever a call into a method on that object is made, a new transaction must be created. Our `PipelineNotifyOwner` component is set to 2 – RequiresTransaction meaning that if a transaction doesn't exist, one should be created, otherwise the component should run inside the context of an existing transaction. In our particular case, `PipelineNotifyOwner` will be created by `OrderProcessor`, which specifies that it has to run inside a transaction, so the use of 2 – RequiresTransaction here really just indicates that we want to keep running inside the context of that transaction. Conversely, all of our `WroxCommerce` objects in the other project are each set to 0 – NotAnMTSObject meaning that they do not support transactions in any way.

Here's a flow diagram indicating what happens as the order is placed:

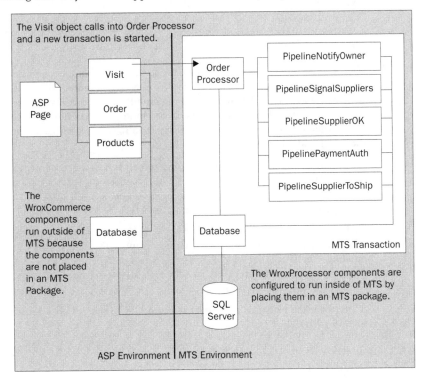

Throughout the lifetime of the objects involved in the transaction, each of the objects has the opportunity to vote on whether or not they were successful. This is not a majority rules decision, as the *atomic* requirement of transactional environments indicates that either everything succeeds, or everything fails. If we detect that one single thing has gone wrong during execution, not one part of the work done by the objects in the transaction will be allowed to succeed. We'll see later in this chapter how we can inform MTS of the success or failure of each part.

Let's move on to the coding, which will involve jumping between our `WroxCommerce` and our `WroxProcessor` projects.

Try It Out – Moving an Order through the Pipeline

1. The first call we need to add to `WroxCommerce` is the one that instantiates and configures an instance of the `OrderProcessor` object. Add this code to the `Visit` object:

```
' StartOrderProcessor - create a new order processing object...
Public Function StartOrderProcessor() As Object

  ' create and initialize...
  Set StartOrderProcessor = CreateObject("WroxProcessor.OrderProcessor")
  StartOrderProcessor.Configure m_strDBString, m_strMailDomain, Me

End Function
```

Notice how in that function we pass the database connection and mail server domain over to the new processor through the `Configure` method.

2. Next we need to change the `PlaceOrder` method that exists inside the `Orders` object. When a call into `WroxProcessor.OrderProcessor` is made, MTS will be given the opportunity to start a transaction. Because we've specified that `OrderProcessor` requires a new transaction through the **MTSTransactionMode** property being set to **RequiresNewTransaction**, MTS will create a new transaction the instant the `Configure` method is called on the `OrderProcessor` object.

However, at this point, nothing is going to call the `StartOrderProcessor` method that we added to the `WroxCommerce.Visit` object; therefore the `Configure` method on the `OrderProcessor` object will not get called and so no transaction will be created. Moreover, the pipeline won't be asked to do anything!

To fix this, we need to alter the call to `PlaceOrder` that exists inside the `Orders` object. The adjustment we're going to make involves looping through the possible parts for the order, creating a new instance of the `OrderProcess` object each time, hence creating a new transaction for each order part. We'll then call the `Go` method in `OrderProcessor` (which we build in the next section).

So, replace the previous `PlaceOrder` method in the `WroxCommerce.Orders` object with the following:

```
' PlaceOrder - confirms the order...
Public Function PlaceOrder(ByVal OrderID As Long)

  ' processor...
  Dim Processor As Object
```

```
' get the parts...
Dim Parts As Recordset
Set Parts = GetOrderParts(OrderID)
Do While Not Parts.EOF

    ' start a processor and, implicitly, a transaction...
    Set Processor = m_utility.Visit.StartOrderProcessor

    ' process the part...
    Processor.Go Parts("PartID")

    ' close the processor...
    Set Processor = Nothing

    ' next...
    parts.MoveNext

Loop
Parts.Close
Set Parts = Nothing

' is this the current order?
If OrderID = m_utility.Visit.OrderID Then

    ' reset the sessions...
    m_utility.Visit.ResetOrder

End If

End Function
```

3. Now we move back to `WroxProcessor` to look at running a connector. When we press the **Place Order** button on the site, the `PlaceOrder` method in the `Order` object will create an instance of the `OrderProcessor` object for each part of the transaction and call the `Go` method.

The `Go` method will determine the current status of the order and, from there, determine the action to be taken. Therefore, if it sees that nothing has been done with the order thus far, it knows to find and call the first connector.

So, to `OrderProcessor` add:

```
' Go - run the next stage of the pipeline!
Public Function Go(ByVal PartID As Long) As Boolean

    ' establish an error handler...
    On Error GoTo problem

    ' store the part that we're working with...
    m_PartID = PartID
```

```
' make sure we're running as a safe, secure, reliable transaction...
' if we're not, quit...
If ObjectContext.IsInTransaction = True Then
Else

    ' indicate that we can't run in this environment...
    AddAudit Nothing, PipelineError_NotInTransaction, False

End If

    ' tell MTS the transaction was successful...
    ObjectContext.SetComplete

    ' jump over the error handler...
    GoTo finish

problem:

    ' log the fact some error occurred...
    RecordError "Go"

finish:

End Function
```

How It Works

The Go method is worthy of closer examination; the first thing that the method does is query MTS to determine whether or not a transaction was successfully created. If this object is not running within the context of a transaction, we choose to do nothing, because we don't want to proceed with the work if we cannot guarantee a safe environment for it to execute in:

```
' make sure we're running as a safe, secure, reliable transaction...
' if we're not, quit...
If ObjectContext.IsInTransaction = True Then
Else

    ' indicate that we can't run in this environment...
    AddAudit Nothing, PipelineError_NotInTransaction, False

End If
```

To capture any errors that occur we use the On Error GoTo Problem and RecordError lines:

```
' establish an error handler...
On Error GoTo problem

' log the fact some error occurred...
RecordError "Go"
```

We use the `SetComplete` method to tell MTS that the transaction was successful:

```
' tell MTS the transaction was successful...
ObjectContext.SetComplete
```

Remember, we make a distinction between unexpected occurrences – like a database connection being down, or a code error – and an exception we understand happening. For good defensive coding we want to define a fixed set of paths that the execution of the code can take. These can include both successful paths and unsuccessful paths.

As we discussed during the adding of entries to the audit trail, we want to catch as many errors as we can. For instance, if we expect a customer to have a last name defined, but it was actually null in the database, we'd want to be able to detect and handle that, rather than letting the standard VB error handling catch it and take us out of the processing in an unexpected manner.

The way we have that set up here is that VB will take us over to `RecordError` and cancel the transaction. As we are taking steps to handle all possible exceptions in our software we use `SetAbort` to handle really unexpected stuff, and `SetComplete` the rest of the time.

Code Testing

To see this in action, put a breakpoint on the line:

```
If ObjectContext.IsInTransaction = True
```

Next, run *both* VB projects (`WroxCommerce` and `WroxProcessor`), and the Visual InterDev project. Then work through the site and place an order on the site. The moment the **Place Order** button is pressed, the VB project will break and you can examine the transactional environment.

Open the **Immediate** window in the VB environment and enter this code:

```
?ObjectContext.IsInTransaction
```

This code asks MTS to tell us if we are running in a transaction. This should return `True`. You can double-check this by using the MTS Explorer to examine the currently executing transactions. The **Transaction Statistics** object in the management tree provides a snapshot of the currently executing transactions:

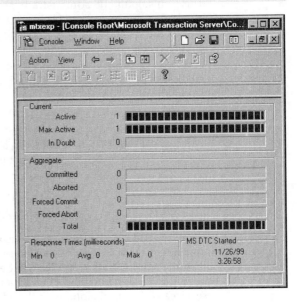

At this point, you may find your code doesn't work for whatever reason and you have to make a change to the `WroxProcessor` component. This is not as straightforward as we might like, but it is important, as throughout this chapter we'll be constantly re-compiling and testing our code.

If you try to compile the DLL to the same file as before, the file will most likely be in a situation where it is locked as it's still being held open by the Web server you're using. If this happens, you'll see a message box indicating **Permission Denied**.

The server will tend to hold objects open like this so that the next person who requests the object won't have to wait for it to be loaded. However, for developers who need to update the objects repeatedly to get things working, this can be a real pain.

> To release the server's grip on the components so they can be recreated you could reboot the computer! Alternatively if you're using Personal Web Server on Windows 95 or Windows 98 and you have Visual Studio/Visual C++, your best bet is to kill the **INETINFO** process that will be running on your machine. Use the Process Viewer utility that comes with Visual C++ to locate and kill **INETINFO.EXE**. Users of Windows NT 4 Workstation and Server can use the batch file approach detailed below.

So, for those of you using NT, let's step through a batch file approach to stopping the service. NT based Web servers work by defining a general *administration* service that all of the other Internet services plug into. This means that if you stop the Web server service (technically called the **World Wide Web Publishing Service**), the objects will *still* be loaded into memory, as it's the administrative service that does this on behalf of the Web server service.

❑ Make this line the first line of a Notepad file:

```
NET STOP IISADMIN
```

❑ This will stop the IIS administrative service, and its dependent services. On Windows NT Server, this means the **Microsoft SMTP Service** and the **FTP Publishing Service** as well as the **World Wide Web Publishing Service**. Windows NT Workstation users only get the Web publishing service.

❑ After you've stopped the services, you need to restart the dependent services. When the first dependent service is started, the administrative service will be started automatically. Add this line:

```
NET START W3SVC
```

❑ Windows NT Workstation users can stop here, as you don't have any other dependent services. Windows NT Server users need to add this:

```
NET START MSFTPSVC
NET START SMTPSVC
```

❑ Save the batch file somewhere easily accessible on your computer as `RESTART.BAT`.

❑ If you try and run the file, you'll be asked if you really do want to stop all of the dependent services. Enter `Y` and press return. The dependent services will be stopped, then the administration service will be stopped (after that's done it will release the lock on your DLL and you'll be able to compile it again), and finally of the dependent services will restart, along with the administration service.

Now try compiling the DLL again. If the **Permission Denied** error appears, run RESTART.BAT and try again. If the system, still doesn't want to play the game, shut down Visual Basic (after ensuring you've saved the project) then re-open VB and try re-compiling the DLL.

> *You may find, even if you haven't used Visual InterDev, that you have to close and re-open (after ensuring you've saved the work) Visual Basic before it lets you re-compile the DLL.*

Now that we've proven that our new `OrderProcessor` object gets called inside MTS, and that a new transaction gets created, we can decide which connector in the pipeline needs to be executed.

Choosing the Connector

As you may have gathered, the Go method will be called each time some action on the order part needs to be performed. So far, we've seen this only at the point when **Place Order** is pressed, but Go may be called when a supplier logs into our extranet to record that an order has been shipped (more later), or when Jo asks the system to resubmit a credit card for authorization.

We need to have a way of choosing which connector needs to be called depending on what we know about the status of the order. In fact, we already have a way of getting the status of the order through the Status column on the OrderParts table, so we'll be using this to decide the action to be taken.

Early on in this chapter we discussed how we'd make the pipeline as flexible as possible by letting people add, remove or swap out connectors. It's through this Status value that we will provide this functionality. For example, let's say a Status value of 10 means that an order should be sent to the warehouse and we need to swap out that connector for one that can send the order directly to a supplier. In that case we can alter the Go method and make it do something different when a Status value of 10 is found.

Try It Out – Implementing Connector Selection

1. Modify the Go method by adding to it the following portions of code:

```
' Go - run the next stage of the pipeline!
Public Function Go(ByVal PartID As Long) As Boolean

    ' store the part that we're working with...
    m_PartID = PartID

    ' store some flags...
    Dim Result As Boolean
    Dim RunNextConnector As Boolean

    ' make sure we're running as a safe, secure, reliable transaction...
    ' if we're not, quit...
    If ObjectContext.IsInTransaction = True Then

        ' put the connector somewhere...
        Dim Connector As IConnector

        ' get the order part back...
        Dim OrderPart As Recordset
        Set OrderPart = DB.RunQuery("OrderParts", "", "PartID=" & PartID)
        If Not OrderPart.EOF Then
```

```
' what stage is the part at?
Select Case OrderPart("Status")

' start of the order...
Case 0
 Set Connector = New PipelineNotifyOwner

End Select

Else

' indicate that the order part was missing...
AddAudit Nothing, PipelineError_PartNotFound, False

End If
OrderPart.Close
Set OrderPart = Nothing

' did we get one?
If Not Connector Is Nothing Then

' note down what we're doing...
AddAudit Connector, PipelineInfo_StartingConnector, True

' attempt to run the connector...
RunNextConnector = False
Result = Connector.Process(Me, RunNextConnector)

' flag the result...
If Result = True Then
AddAudit Connector, PipelineInfo_ConnectorOK, True
Else
AddAudit Connector, PipelineInfo_ConnectorFailed, False
End If

Else

' log the fact we can't do anything...
AddAudit Nothing, PipelineError_NothingToDo, False

End If

Else

' indicate that we can't run in this environment...
AddAudit Nothing, PipelineError_NotInTransaction, False

End If

' tell MTS the transaction was successful...
ObjectContext.SetComplete

' do we want to automatically run the next connector?
If RunNextConnector = True And Result = True Then

' call back into us to go again!
Go = Go(PartID)
```

```
    Else

    ' store the result against this call...
    Go = Result

    End If

    ' jump over the error handler...
    GoTo Finish

Problem:

    ' log the fact some error occurred...
    RecordError "Go"

Finish:

End Function
```

2. We'll also have to make these changes to the `PipelineCodes` enumeration in the `MessageCodes` module:

```
' PipelineCodes - things that can happen to the pipeline itself...
Public Enum PipelineCodes

    ' error codes...
    PipelineError_VBError = 10001
    PipelineError_NotInTransaction = 10002
    PipelineError_PartNotFound = 10003
    PipelineError_NothingToDo = 10004

    ' information codes...
    PipelineInfo_StartingConnector = 20001
    PipelineInfo_ConnectorOK = 20002
    PipelineInfo_ConnectorFailed = 20003
    PipelineInfo_MasterOrderUpdated = 20004

End Enum
```

3. The final step here is to add code so that the connector's `ID` and `Name` properties work as required. Replace the `Get` stub function we currently have in `PipelineNotifyOwner` with:

```
Private Property Get IConnector_ID() As String
    IConnector_ID = GUID_PipelineNotifyOwner
End Property

Private Property Get IConnector_Name() As String
    IConnector_Name = "PipelineNotifyOwner"
End Property
```

4. Try running the application code (again firstly by running both VB projects, then running the Visual InterDev project) and work right the way through the purchase process – after it's finished it should cause two lines to be added to the audit trail. To see them go to SQL Server Enterprise Manager and open the `Audit` table:

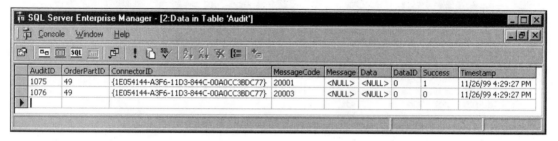

The first line in the trail indicates that we started the `PipelineNotifyOwner` connector, and the second line indicates that the connector failed. In fact, it only failed because we didn't ask it to do anything...

How It Works

The main purpose of the code added to the `Go` method is to determine which connector needs to be executed. Notice how when we create the `PipelineNotifyOwner` connector we use the data type of the `Connector` local variable to indicate that, rather than the specific `PipelineNotifyOwner` interface, we want the general `IConnector` interface. This means that in the rest of the pipeline management code we can treat every pipeline connector object that we create in the same way.

```
' put the connector somewhere...
Dim Connector As IConnector

' get the order part back...
Dim OrderPart As Recordset
Set OrderPart = DB.RunQuery("OrderParts", "", "PartID=" & PartID)
If Not OrderPart.EOF Then

' what stage is the part at?
Select Case OrderPart("Status")

' start of the order...
Case 0
  Set Connector = New PipelineNotifyOwner

End Select
```

Particularly here this means calling the `Process` method defined in the `IConnector` interface:

```
' attempt to run the connector...
RunNextConnector = False
Result = Connector.Process(Me, RunNextConnector)
```

In addition to this, the AddAudit method will ask the IConnector-supporting object to return its ID and name (more later).

One of the interesting things to note here is that connectors are able to tell the processor that it's OK to automatically move on to the next connector in the pipe. They can do this by setting the RunNextConnector variable to True, but this is only valid if the Process method has returned a True result. When this happens, the Go method is called again:

```
' do we want to automatically run the next connector?
If RunNextConnector = True And Result = True Then

    ' call back into us to go again!
    Go = Go(PartID)

Else

    ' store the result against this call...
    Go = Result

End If
```

We need to do this with our first connector, as there's no way of signaling into the processor that the second connector, which involves sending e-mail to suppliers, should proceed. We'll see this in action in a little while. It's important that the Status column is properly updated when automatically moving to the next connection, otherwise you risk creating an endless loop.

When you're running inside a transaction, SQL Server will only allow you to create and use one query at a time, meaning you cannot open one query and then open another before closing the first. This means you have to be very careful to write your code so that only one database connection is required at a time. Also, do not call AddAudit when you already have a query open, as AddAudit will fail. This is the main reason why we're not allowing access to the WroxCommerce object model from inside the order processor – the WroxCommerce object model we've built so far does not follow this strict rule.

Now that we've built the framework methods capable of notifying the owner that an order has been placed, we need to finish that off, and then move on to building supporting code to complete the other stages of the order-processing pipeline.

More OrderProcessor Support Code

It's likely that the connectors in our pipeline will require a bevy of information as they try to do their work. However, as we stated earlier, it's not possible to let the connectors have access to the rich WroxCommerce object model because of the restriction that we can only hold one query open at any one time when running inside a transaction. To solve this problem, we have to build a number of functions on the OrderProcessor object that can help us learn more about the order we're trying to process.

We'll break the code we're adding to OrderProcessor down into bite-sized chunks to make it clear what's happening.

Try It Out – Adding Further Supporting Code to OrderProcessor

1. Firstly let's complete the properties for the `OrderProcessor` object:

```
' MailDomain - return the mail domain...
Public Property Get MailDomain() As String
 MailDomain = m_strMailDomain
End Property
```

```
' PartID - return the order part ID...
Public Property Get PartID() As String
 PartID = m_PartID
End Property
```

2. Next we start on the information for the connectors, here's a method to return the ID of the order that owns the part:

```
' GetOrderID - returns the OrderID...
Public Function GetOrderID() As Long

 ' run the query...
 Dim Query As Recordset
 Set Query = DB.RunQuery("OrderParts", , "PartID=" & m_PartID)
 If Not Query.EOF Then
 GetOrderID = Query("OrderID")
 End If
 Query.Close
 Set Query = Nothing

End Function
```

3. Then a method to return the ID of the customer who owns the order part:

```
' GetCustomerID - returns the customer ID...
Public Function GetCustomerID() As Long

 ' run the query...
 Dim Query As Recordset
 Set Query = DB.RunQuery("Orders", , "OrderID=" & GetOrderID)
 If Not Query.EOF Then
 GetCustomerID = Query("CustomerID")
 End If
 Query.Close
 Set Query = Nothing

End Function
```

4. We make the customer's e-mail contact details available through:

```
' GetCustomerContact - get the customer's e-mail and name...
Public Function GetCustomerContact(ByRef CustomerName As String, _
          ByRef CustomerEMail As String)

 ' get the id...
 Dim CustomerID As Long
```

```
CustomerID = GetCustomerID
If CustomerID <> 0 Then

    ' run the query...
    Dim Query As Recordset
    Set Query = DB.Runquery ("Customers", , "CustomerID=" & CustomerID)
    If Not Query.EOF Then

    ' get the values...
    CustomerName = Query("firstname") & " " & Query("lastname")
    CustomerEMail = Query("email")

    End If
    Query.Close
    Set Query = Nothing

End If

End Function
```

5. Next, we need some code to update the status of both the order part and the master order:

```
' SetPartStatus - update the status of the OrderPart to reflect the next
' point in the pipeline...
Public Function SetPartStatus(ByVal Status As Long)

    ' update the query...
    DB.DB.Execute "update OrderParts set Status=" & Status & _
                  " where PartID=" & PartID

End Function
```

```
' SetOrderStatus - update the status of the whole order...
Public Function SetOrderStatus(ByVal Status As Long, _
        Optional ByVal Connector As IConnector)

    ' what order do we have?
    Dim OrderID As Long
    OrderID = GetOrderID
    If OrderID <> 0 Then

        ' update the query...
        DB.DB.Execute "update Orders set Status=" & Status & _
                      " where OrderID=" & OrderID

        ' add something to the audit...
        AddAudit Connector, PipelineInfo_MasterOrderUpdated, True, Status

    End If

End Function
```

At last we have enough of the supporting code in place to move on and get the connectors doing something.

Doing the Work

Now it's time to make the connector try and fulfill its task to notify Jo and the customer that the order has been placed.

Try It Out – Notification of Order Placement

1. Here's the code to add to the `PipelineNotifyOwner` object to provide the implementation of the `Process` method:

```
' Process - do this connector's work...
Private Function IConnector_Process(ByVal Processor As OrderProcessor, _
        ByRef RunNextConnector As Boolean) As Boolean

    On Error GoTo Problem

    ' first thing we have to do is notify Jo that there is a new order...
    Processor.SendEMail Me, PNO_NotifyOwner, _
        "Order Received - Part ID " & Processor.PartID, _
        "Owner", "owner@" & Processor.MailDomain, _
        "An order was received."

    ' second thing we have to do is notify the customer...
    Dim CustomerName As String
    Dim CustomerEMail As String
    Processor.GetCustomerContact CustomerName, CustomerEMail
    If CustomerName <> "" And CustomerEMail <> "" Then

        ' get the email address...
        Processor.SendEMail Me, PNO_NotifyCustomer, _
            "Your order has been received!", _
            CustomerName, CustomerEMail, _
            "Your order, reference " & Processor.PartID & " was received!"

        ' tell the processor to update the status of the part...
        Processor.SetPartStatus 1

        ' now update the status of the master order...
        Processor.SetOrderStatus 1

        ' tell the processor that we want to move onto stage 2...
        RunNextConnector = True

        ' indicate success...
        IConnector_Process = True

    Else
        Processor.AddAudit Me, PNO_NoCustomer, False
    End If

    ' jump over the error handler...
    GoTo Finish

Problem:
```

```
    ' flag the error...
    Processor.RecordError "Process", Me

Finish:

End Function
```

This method is made quite simple by using a lot of the helper functions that we spent time building earlier. For example, e-mail is sent using the `SendEMail` method, which also helpfully adds information about the mail that was sent to the audit trail. Otherwise, this function doesn't do too much except adjust the `Status` column in the `OrderParts` table to 1 through use of the `SetPartStatus` helper, and update the `Status` in the master `Orders` table to indicate that the order is proceeding. This means that next time `Go` is called, it will try and find the next connector in the pipeline.

In our example, the messages we've sent are not very informative. In a real world situation, it would make sense to e-mail the customer a copy of the order summary so she or he can spot any problems.

2. Each connector will be responsible for maintaining its own set of message codes. Here's the set for the `PipelineOrderNotify` connector that need to be added to the `MessageCodes` module below the previous `End Enum` statement:

```
' PipelineNotifyOwner codes...
Public Enum PNOCodes

    ' information codes...
    PNO_NotifyOwner = 30001
    PNO_NotifyCustomer = 30002

    ' error codes...
    PNO_NoCustomer = 30101

End Enum
```

If you try running the application through to the checkout again, and then look inside the audit log, you'll notice that the last entry has a code of **10004** which maps onto the error code of `NothingToDo`.

In the rest of this chapter, we'll work through the construction of the other connectors in the pipeline; next up in the pipeline is the connector relating to supplier notification.

Signaling Suppliers

The next connector in the pipeline (`PipelineSignalSuppliers`), telling our suppliers about the order, is technically very similar to the `PipelineNotifyOwner` object we just finished implementing. However, as we said before, it's a good idea to abstract the pipeline components to such a degree that alternative ones can be slotted in as easily as possible. In one case, our business model may dictate that we check stock levels in a warehouse, rather than sending an e-mail to our suppliers, but in each separate business model, we'll most likely want to send e-mail to the customer, hence the need for two separate connectors.

Try It Out – Creating PipelineSignalSuppliers

1. As this connector is so similar to the first one, we'll go through the code relatively quickly. Our first job is to create a new class module called `PipelineSignalSuppliers` in `WroxProcessor` and make it support the `IConnector` interface. Don't forget to change the `MTSTransactionMode` property on this object to **2 – RequiresTransaction**:

```
Option Explicit

' Indicate that this is a connector object...
Implements IConnector

Private Property Get IConnector_ID() As String
 IConnector_ID = GUID_PipelineSignalSuppliers
End Property

Private Property Get IConnector_Name() As String
 IConnector_Name = "PipelineSignalSuppliers"
End Property

' Process - do this connector's work...
Private Function IConnector_Process(ByVal Processor As OrderProcessor, _
      ByRef RunNextConnector As Boolean) As Boolean

 On Error GoTo Problem

 ' jump over the error handler...
 GoTo Finish

Problem:

 ' flag the error...
 Processor.RecordError "Process", Me

Finish:

End Function
```

2. To get that object working inside MTS, you'll need to go through the hoops we outlined previously. This may seem like a bit of a pain, but it's the only way to *guarantee* that your changes will be visible inside the MTS environment! Firstly, save the project.

3. Next, compile the project; as before, if you get the **Permission Denied** message box it's time to run through the Web server restart procedure we outlined previously.

If a message appears concerning breaking compatibility, say **OK**. We're going to re-import the MTS package.

4. Delete the JoCoffee package from MTS Explorer, recreate the JoCoffee package and import the new DLL into the new JoCoffee package.

5. Once the `PipelineSignalSuppliers` object is there, you'll need to find the GUID of the object. Right-click on the object (take care to get the correct one), select **Properties**, and copy the GUID into the `GUIDs` module. Here's what mine looks like:

```
' Pipeline Connector GUIDs
Global Const GUID_PipelineNotifyOwner = _
        "{1E054144-A3F6-11D3-844C-00A0CC3BDC77}"
Global Const GUID_PipelineSignalSuppliers = _
        "{FC0E5E0E-A441-11D3-844E-00A0CC3BDC77}"
```

6. Next, we need to look at how to integrate the object into the pipeline. Once the object has been imported into MTS, we're ready to alter the `Go` method so that it can call the new object. You can do this by altering the `Select Case` statement in the middle of the `OrderProcessor` object:

```
' what stage is the part at?
Select Case OrderPart("Status")

  ' start of the order...
  Case 0
  Set Connector = New PipelineNotifyOwner
  Case 1
  Set Connector = New PipelineSignalSuppliers

End Select
```

Now, whenever the processor comes across an order part that has a status set to 1, it knows that it's supposed to use the `PipelineSignalSuppliers` connector. At the moment, the only time this can happen is when `Go` is first called and `PipelineNotifyOwner` suggests that the processor should automatically move on to the next connector.

7. Now is a good time to test the code – put a breakpoint on the `Select Case` statement, run the VB project and the Visual InterDev project, and place an order through the site. VB should break twice: once to notify the owner, and once to signal suppliers.

8. In our example, we're going to assume that our supplier is capable of receiving notifications via e-mail. We're also going to assume that our supplier will be communicating with us via a special section of our administration tools (that we'll be covering in the next section).

For this reason, the notification message we will send will not contain any detail about the order itself. If we wanted, we could easily append an order summary to the message. Just as easily, rather than sending the message to the supplier via e-mail directly, we could enlist an e-mail-to-fax gateway that could fax the order through to the supplier. In this instance, the supplier would have to contact Jo by phone to tell her whether or not the order can be completed.

> **You can find companies providing e-mail-to-fax gateways in most of the popular search engines.**

The first thing we need to do is add some additional support code to the `OrderProcessor` object that can return the ID of the supplier, and some more to return the e-mail contact information:

```
' GetSupplierID - returns the supplier ID...
Public Function GetSupplierID() As Long

    ' run the query...
    Dim Query As Recordset
    Set Query = DB.RunQuery("OrderParts", , "PartID=" & m_PartID)
    If Not Query.EOF Then
    GetSupplierID = Query("SupplierID")
    End If
    Query.Close
    Set Query = Nothing

End Function

' GetSupplierContact - returns the contact information for the supplier...
Public Function GetSupplierContact(ByRef SupplierName As String, _
            ByRef SupplierEMail As String)

    ' get the id...
    Dim SupplierID As Long
    SupplierID = GetSupplierID
    If SupplierID <> 0 Then

        ' run the query...
        Dim Query As Recordset
        Set Query = DB.RunQuery("Suppliers", , "SupplierID=" & SupplierID)
        If Not Query.EOF Then

        ' get the values...
        SupplierName = Query("SalesContactFirst") & " " & _
                    Query("SalesContactLast")
        SupplierEMail = Query("SalesContactEmail")

        End If
        Query.Close
        Set Query = Nothing

    End If

End Function
```

9. With this code in place, we can now implement the `Process` method for the `PipelineSignalSuppliers` object:

```
' Process - do this connector's work...
Private Function IConnector_Process(ByVal Processor As OrderProcessor, _
                            ByRef RunNextConnector As Boolean) As Boolean

On Error GoTo Problem

    ' get hold of the supplier...
    Dim SupplierName As String
    Dim SupplierEMail As String
```

```
            Processor.GetSupplierContact SupplierName, SupplierEMail
            If SupplierName <> "" And SupplierEMail <> "" Then

                ' get the email address...
                Processor.SendEMail Me, PSS_SignalSupplier, _
                    "An order has been received!", _
                    SupplierName, SupplierEMail, _
                    "The order, #" & Processor.PartID & " has been received."

                ' tell the processor to update the status of the part...
                Processor.SetPartStatus 2

                ' tell the processor *not* to move on...
                RunNextConnector = False

                ' indicate success...
                IConnector_Process = True

            Else
                Processor.AddAudit Me, PSS_NoSupplier, False
            End If

            ' jump over the error handler...
            GoTo Finish

        Problem:

            ' flag the error...
            Processor.RecordError "Process", Me

        Finish:

End Function
```

10. Of course we need to add message codes for the `PipelineSignalSupplier` connector that need to be added to the `MessageCodes` module:

```
'PipelineSignalSuppliers codes
Public Enum PSSCodes

        'information codes...
        PSS_SignalSupplier = 31001
        'error codes...
        PSS_NoSupplier = 31101

End Enum
```

The code we go through there is pretty much the same as in the first connector we built. The two important things to note are that we advance the order status to 2, and we do not ask the processor to move onto the next connection. At this point, the pipeline will stall.

We've deliberately stopped the pipeline at this point because we can't progress the order further until the supplier tells us that we can go ahead. There may be a good reason why the supplier will tell us we can never go ahead, such as one of the items in the order will never be produced again, but it's likely that they'll eventually tell us they are in a position to ship our order. In the next section, we'll see how we can enhance our administration tools to let the suppliers see into our order database and progress the order.

Creating an Extranet

So far, we haven't created any tools that let us see the orders that exist within the system. When we create those tools, we can either choose to let them be accessible only to Jo and others within the organization (an **intranet**), or we can let the tools be used by partners to the organization. We call an intranet that lets people outside of the organization have access to it an **extranet**. One point though, just because others can access the extranet does not mean that it's publicly available. Extranets have a controlled access so that, for example, one supplier cannot see another supplier's orders.

Within the next section we're going to address three main topics:

❑ Enabling Jo to look at orders in the system

❑ Enabling suppliers to appropriately view orders

❑ Building the third section of the pipeline – the `PipelineSupplierOK` connector

The first two of these will involve returning to the `WroxCommerce` component and building tools that will allow database interrogation and display through our soon-to-be-enhanced presentation layer. The third topic sees us back in the `WroxProcessing` project.

Viewing Orders

Our initial move is going to be adding some methods to `WroxCommerce` to return the orders that have been placed. In the last chapter, we built quite a few of these, so all that remains is to add a method that can return the unprocessed orders back.

Try It Out – Examining Orders in the Database

1. Firstly, we need to create an enumeration that holds the possible order status codes. Open the `WroxCommerce` project and add this to the `Globals` module:

```
' OrderStatus - what's happened to the order...
Public Enum OrderStatus
 statusUncommited = 0
 statusProcessing = 1
 statusCommited = 2
 statusCancelled = 3
End Enum
```

2. In the `PipelineNotifyOwner` connector, you may have noticed that we set the order status to 1, indicating that the order status was now one of *processing*. We can use this status code to return the orders that have not been completed, with this method that should be added to the `Orders` object:

```
' GetNewOrders - returns unprocessed orders...
Public Function GetNewOrders(Optional ByVal AsKeyset As Boolean) _
            As Recordset
 Set GetNewOrders = QueryOrders("status=1", "created desc", AsKeyset)
End Function
```

3. In these administrative tools, we're going to be dealing most of the time with a single order. Add this method to the `Orders` object to return a properly configured `Order` object:

```
' GetOrderObject - return an object for an order...
Public Function GetOrderObject(ByVal OrderID As Long) As Order

    ' create and configure...
    Set GetOrderObject = New Order
    GetOrderObject.Configure m_utility, OrderID

End Function
```

4. The last function to add to the `Orders` object at this stage is one that can return some human-readable words about the order status:

```
' GetStatusText - returns a string representing the status of the order...
Public Function GetStatusText(ByVal Status As Integer) As String

    ' select the text...
    Select Case Status

    Case statusUncommited
    GetStatusText = "Not commited"
    Case statusProcessing
    GetStatusText = "In process"
    Case statusCommited
    GetStatusText = "Sent to supplier"
    Case statusCancelled
    GetStatusText = "Cancelled"

    Case Else
    GetStatusText = "Unknown (" & Status & ")"

    End Select

End Function
```

5. Finally for this session of coding in `WroxCommerce`, add this method, that returns a supplier, to the `Catalog` object:

```
' GetSupplier - returns a single supplier...
Public Function GetSupplier(ByVal SupplierID As Long, _
    Optional ByVal AsKeyset As Boolean = False) As Recordset
    Set GetSupplier = QuerySuppliers("SupplierID=" & SupplierID, , _
                AsKeyset)
End Function
```

6. Now we return to our Jo's Coffee Visual InterDev project. Initially we need to edit the `default.asp` page within the `admin` folder. Locate the `Case Else` statement at the bottom, and add this code:

```
' render the menu options...
RenderOption "Add Department", "adddepartment"
RenderOption "Add Product", "addproduct"
RenderOption "Edit Products", "editproducts"
Response.Write "<tr><td><br></td></tr>"
RenderOption "View New Orders", "viewneworders"
```

7. Let's now use the methods we've just built in the `admin/default.asp` page. To get a list of the new orders we naturally need the `GetNewOrders` method. Add the following to the `case` statement at the top of the page where we previously created statements to handle `adddepartment` and `editproduct`:

```
<% ' do we want to view the orders?
case "viewneworders" %>

  <%
  ' get a list of the orders...
  Dim orders
  Set orders = Visit.Orders.GetNewOrders
  If Not orders.EOF Then

    ' start the table...
    Response.Write "<center>"
    Response.Write "<table cellspacing=0 cellpadding=0 width=400>"

    ' draw the orders...
    Do While Not orders.EOF

      ' use a helper to present the orders...
      RenderOrder orders, True

      ' next
      orders.MoveNext
      response.write "<tr><td><br></td></tr>"

    Loop

    ' end the table...
    Response.Write "</table></center>"

  End If
  orders.Close
  Set orders = Nothing
  %>
```

8. In our administration tools, we want to create the functions that will assist in the general presentation of information, and to present order data we'll use the RenderOrder method. However, when we're looking at orders, we have two different possible views:

❑ If Jo or someone in her employ is looking at an order, we can assume that they are able to see all privileged information, including credit card details, supplier information, and costs.

❑ If someone outside Jo's Coffee – either a customer looking at his or her order details online (this is covered in Chapter 14), or a supplier looking at an order (which we'll deal with in a moment), we don't want to provide some of those details.

To indicate whether we want to present this privileged information or not we'll use a parameter called IsAdmin. The RenderOrder method that needs to be added to site.asp is detailed below. For readability we have, firstly, broken the code up into smaller chunks broken by explanation, and secondly, used multiple Response.Write statements so the interesting bits don't get submerged in formatting tags.

First of all, we run a routine to detect the kind of value we've been passed and turn it into an Order object. So, if we get passed a recordset, we assume that we're interested in the current record in that recordset and create a new Order object based on that row, or if we get passed an integer, we assume it refers to an order ID and create an Order object based on the raw ID:

```
' RenderOrder - method to present an order to the user...
function RenderOrder(ByVal order, IsAdmin)

    ' convert whatever we got into something useful...
    Select Case typename(order)

      case "Recordset", "Fields"
        Set order = Visit.Orders.GetOrderObject(order("OrderID"))

      case "Integer", "Long"
        Set order = Visit.Orders.GetOrderObject(order)

    End Select
```

Next, we render some information about the order. Specifically, we write out the order ID, the date it was created and, if it's been committed or cancelled, we render the date that that happened on. Finally, we render the status, using the GetStatusText helper of the Orders object in combination with the status code:

```
' header...
    Response.Write "<tr><td class=heading colspan=3 bgcolor=#ff0000>"
    Response.Write "<font color=#ffffff>"
    Response.Write "Order Number " & order.ID
    Response.Write "</font>"
    Response.Write "</td></tr>"

    ' add the dates...
    Response.Write "<tr><td class=std>"
    Response.Write "Date entered: "
    Response.Write "</td><td class=std colspan=2>"
    Response.Write order.Created
    Response.Write "</td></tr>"
```

```
if order.Status = 2 or order.Status = 3 then
  Response.Write "<tr><td class=std>"
  Response.Write "Date completed: "
  Response.Write "</td><td class=std colspan=2>"
  Response.Write order.Completed
  Response.Write "</td></tr>"
end if

' add the status
Response.Write "<tr><td class=std>"
Response.Write "Status: "
Response.Write "</td><td class=std colspan=2>"
Response.Write Visit.Orders.GetStatusText(order.Status)
Response.Write "</td></tr>"

' spacer...
Response.Write "<tr><td><br></td></tr>"
```

Next, we run a routine to get a recordset representing the current customer by pulling the customer ID from the `Order` object and passing it to the `Customers` object. We then see the name being rendered, before we check to see if we're an administrator through the `IsAdmin` parameter and, if so, render out the e-mail address. We consider the e-mail address of the customer to be privileged information, hence the reason why it's available only to administrators (remember, we're calling anyone who works for Jo an administrator):

```
' customer information...
Dim customer
Set customer = Visit.Customers.GetCustomer(order.CustomerID)
If Not customer.EOF Then

  Response.Write "<tr><td class=heading>"
  Response.Write "Customer: "
  Response.Write "</td><td class=std colspan=2>"
  Response.Write customer("FirstName") & " " & _
              customer("LastName")
  Response.Write "</td></tr>"

  ' if we're admin, display e-mail...
  If IsAdmin Then
    Response.Write "<tr><td class=heading>"
    Response.Write "E-mail: "
    Response.Write "</td><td class=std colspan=2>"
    Response.Write "<a href=""mailto:"
    Response.Write customer("EMail")
    Response.Write """>"
    Response.Write customer("EMail")
    Response.Write "</a>"
    Response.Write "</td></tr>"
  End If

  ' spacer...
  Response.Write "<tr><td><br></td></tr>"
```

After we've rendered out the customer name, we pull out the billing address, shipping address, and credit card information and render this. Again, we check to see if we're an administrator before we display the credit card information, as this too is privileged information:

```
' if we're admin, display billing information...
Dim address
If IsAdmin Then
  Set address = _
   visit.Customers.GetAddress(order.BillingAddressID)
  If Not address.EOF Then

    ' draw it...
    Response.Write "<tr><td class=heading>"
    Response.Write "Billing address:"
    Response.Write "</td><td colspan=2 class=std>"
    Response.Write address("Name") & "<br>"
    if not isnull(address("Company")) Then _
      Response.Write address("Company") & "<br>"
    Response.Write address("Address1")
    if not isnull(address("Address2")) Then _
      Response.Write ", " & address("Address2")
    Response.Write "<br>"
    Response.Write address("City") & ", "
    Response.Write address("Region") & ", "
    Response.Write address("PostalCode") & ", "
    Response.Write address("Country")
    if not isnull(address("Phone")) Then _
      Response.Write "<br>" & address("Phone")
    Response.Write "</td></tr>"

    ' spacer...
    Response.Write "<tr><td><br></td></tr>"

  End If
  address.Close
  Set address = Nothing
End If

' display the shipping information...
Set address = _
   visit.Customers.GetAddress(order.ShippingAddressID)
If Not address.EOF Then

  ' draw it...
  Response.Write "<tr><td class=heading>"
  Response.Write "Shipping address:"
  Response.Write "</td><td colspan=2 class=std>"
  Response.Write address("Name") & "<br>"
  if not isnull(address("Company")) Then _
     Response.Write address("Company") & "<br>"
  Response.Write address("Address1")
  if not isnull(address("Address2")) Then _
     Response.Write ", " & address("Address2")
  Response.Write "<br>"
  Response.Write address("City") & ", "
  Response.Write address("Region") & ", "
  Response.Write address("PostalCode") & ", "
  Response.Write address("Country")
```

```
      if not isnull(address("Phone")) Then _
          Response.Write "<br>" & address("Phone")
      Response.Write "</td></tr>"

  End If
  address.Close
  Set address = Nothing

  ' if we're admin, display card information...
  If IsAdmin Then

    ' get the card...
    Dim card
    Set card = Visit.Customers.GetCard(order.CardID)
    If Not card.EOF Then

      ' spacer...
      Response.Write "<tr><td><br></td></tr>"

      ' card info...
      Response.Write "<tr><td class=heading>"
      Response.Write "Card details: "
      Response.Write "</td><td class=std colspan=2>"
      Response.Write card("type")
      Response.Write " "
      Response.Write card("number")
      Response.Write " ("
      Response.Write card("expiresmonth")
      Response.Write "/"
      Response.Write card("expiresyear")
      Response.Write ")"
      Response.Write "</td></tr>"

    End If
    card.Close
    Set card = Nothing

  End If

End If
customer.Close
Set customer = Nothing

' spacer...
Response.Write "<tr><td><br></td></tr>"
```

After we've done that, we use the `Parts` property of the `Order` object to get a recordset of the order parts that we can then loop and render:

```
' render the parts...
Dim parts, lines
Set parts = Order.Parts
Do While Not parts.EOF

  ' draw the part...
  Response.Write "<tr bgcolor=#f0f0f0>"
  Response.Write "<td class=heading colspan=2>"
  Response.Write "Part Number " & parts("PartID")
```

```
Response.Write "</td></tr>"
Response.Write "<tr bgcolor=#f0f0f0>"
Response.Write "<td class=std colspan=3 align=right>"
Response.Write "Status: <b>"
Select Case parts("Status")
  Case 0
   Response.Write "Notify owner"
  Case 1
   Response.Write "Notify supplier"
  Case 2
   Response.Write "Waiting for supplier approval"
  Case 3
   Response.Write "Credit Card Authorization"
  Case 4
   Response.Write "Notify supplier"
  Case 5
   Response.Write "Waiting for supplier to ship"
  Case 6
   Response.Write "Completed"
  Case Else
   Response.Write "Unknown (" & parts("Status") & ")"
End Select
Response.Write "</b></td></tr>"

' display the supplier info if we're admin...
If IsAdmin Then

  Dim supplier
  Set supplier = _
     Visit.Catalog.GetSupplier(parts("SupplierID"))
  If Not supplier.EOF Then

   ' draw the supplier
   Response.Write "<tr><td class=heading>"
   Response.Write "Supplier:"
   Response.Write "</td><td class=std colspan=2>"
   Response.Write supplier("Name")
   Response.Write "<br>"
   Response.Write supplier("SalesContactFirst") & " " & _
         supplier("SalesContactLast")
   Response.Write "<br>"
   Response.Write "<a href=""mailto:"
   Response.Write supplier("SalesContactEMail")
   Response.Write """>"
   Response.Write supplier("SalesContactEMail")
   Response.Write "</a>"
   Response.Write "</td></tr>"

   ' spacer...
   Response.Write "<tr><td><br></td></tr>"

  End If
  supplier.Close
  Set supplier = Nothing

End If
```

At this point, we've rendered out the number of the part, and the status. As you've seen, the status of the order part maps directly onto the position in the order-processing pipeline that we're currently at. So, if the order part status is set to 2, we're waiting for supplier approval and we use a `Select Case` statement to give the user this information.

An interesting part about this code is the fact that for the order status, we use a method on the `Orders` object to return a string indicating a human-readable message, but for the order part status, we use code directly in the `OrderParts` object. This is because the pipeline status is actually dependent on the structure of the `OrderProcessor` object. We don't want to create an `OrderProcessor` object at this point, as we don't want the overhead of creating transactions, so we use a `Select Case` statement and enter the presentation messages directly into the code. If we change the structure of the pipeline, we also have to change this code.

After rendering the statement, we see if we're an administrative user through `IsAdmin` to decide if we need to know the contact information at the supplier.

```
' get the lines...
   Set lines = Order.Lines(parts("PartID"))
   Do While Not lines.EOF

      Response.Write "<tr><td class=std>"
      Response.Write lines("Quantity")
      Response.Write "x "
      Response.Write lines("MfrName") & " " & lines("Name")
      Response.Write "</td><td class=std align=right>"
      Response.Write "@ "
      Response.Write FormatPrice(lines("PriceEach"))
      Response.Write " = "
      Response.Write "</td><td class=std align=right>"
      Response.Write FormatPrice(lines("Total"))
      Response.Write "</td></tr>"

      ' next
      lines.MoveNext

   Loop
   lines.Close
   Set lines = Nothing

   ' totals...
   Response.Write "<tr><td colspan=2 align=right class=std>"
   Response.Write "Shipping ("
   Response.Write parts("ShippingName")
   Response.Write "):"
   Response.Write "</td><td align=right class=std>"
   Response.Write FormatPrice(parts("ShippingCharge"))
   Response.Write "</td></tr>"

   Response.Write "<tr><td colspan=2 align=right class=std>"
   Response.Write "VAT @ "
   Response.Write parts("TaxRate") * 100 & "%"
   Response.Write ":"
   Response.Write "</td><td align=right class=std>"
   Response.Write FormatPrice(parts("TaxCharge"))
   Response.Write "</td></tr>"
```

```
Response.Write "<tr><td colspan=2 align=right class=heading>"
    Response.Write "Total:"
    Response.Write "</td><td align=right class=heading>"
    Response.Write FormatPrice(parts("Total"))
    Response.Write "</td></tr>"

    ' next
    parts.MoveNext
    Response.Write "<tr><td><br></td></tr>"

Loop
parts.Close
Set parts = Nothing

End Function
```

Finally, as we come to each part in the order, we grab a recordset containing the lines of that part using the `Lines` property. We then walk through this recordset rendering each line until we've finished, at which point we render the shipping information, tax and totals.

Remember, the password to access the administrative pages is `secret`.

So, after all that code has been added to the project we should obtain the following:

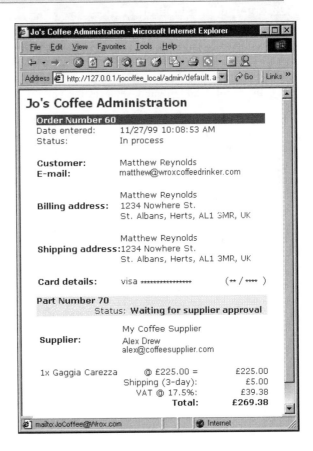

Now that we have the tools to see what orders are in the system, we need to provide a way for the supplier to look at the order to see what needs to be done.

Supplier Access

As we outlined before, although we want the supplier to have access to our system we need to limit it – we don't want them to see sensitive information about our customers or other suppliers.

To authenticate supplier access to our system, we're going to tweak the code we wrote on the admin pages to accept the word **secret** so that our supplier can enter his or her e-mail address to gain access. This is, obviously, not the level of security you want to implement on a real-world version of this system, so make sure you implement an authentication scheme that fits in with your company's policies.

> This whole area of security is very important – we touch on it in later chapters but our advice is that you take professional advice before going live with systems that could potentially allow highly sensitive information into the public domain.

Try It Out – Enabling Suppliers Access

1. Again in this section we'll be expanding the functionality of our original object model and working with the WroxCommerce project. In Chapter 8, we implemented a method on the Customers object called CheckLogon. We're now going to add a similar method to the Catalog object called CheckSupplierLogon. This method will take the e-mail address of the supplier and, if valid, set a session variable to indicate the ID of the logged in supplier.

Quite obviously this method isn't appropriate for a real-world environment, as anyone may know the supplier's e-mail address, but is sufficient here to demonstrate the general principles we want to get across.

Add this method to the Catalog object:

```
' CheckSupplierLogon - attempts to log on a supplier based on the e-mail...
Public Function CheckSupplierLogon(ByVal SalesContactEMail As String, _
                              ByRef Problem As Variant) As Boolean

   ' make sure the problem is blank...
   Problem = ""

   ' try to find a supplier with a matching e-mail address...
   ' we use the Replace function to make sure that if the
   ' e-mail address was entered with apostrohes, we gracefully
   ' handle any problems...
   Dim Query As Recordset
   Set Query = m_utility.DB.DB.Execute("select * from Suppliers where
SalesContactEMail='" & Replace(SalesContactEMail, "'", "''") & "'")

   ' is there such a supplier?
```

```
If Not Query.EOF Then

    ' we're fine. log on the supplier...
    m_utility.Visit.SupplierID = Query("SupplierID")

    ' flag it as OK...
    CheckSupplierLogon = True

Else

    ' add it to the problem...
    Problem = "There is no supplier with the e-mail address you specified."

End If

' close...
Query.Close
Set Query = Nothing

End Function
```

2. Like the `CustomerID` property we added to the `Visit` object in Chapter 8, we now have to add a `SupplierID` property. Add this member variable to the `Visit` object:

```
' this variable holds a reference to the ASP Session object...
Private m_Session As Session
Private m_BasketID As Long
Private m_CustomerID As Long
Private m_OrderID As Long
Private m_SupplierID As Long
```

3. Continuing with the `Visit` object, we need to change the `Configure` method to retrieve the supplier ID from the `Session` object whenever the `Visit` object is created:

```
' hold the session...
Set m_Session = Session
If Not m_Session Is Nothing Then

    ' capture the BasketID...
    m_BasketID = CLng(m_Session("BasketID"))
    m_CustomerID = CLng(m_Session("CustomerID"))
    m_OrderID = CLng(m_Session("OrderID"))
    m_SupplierID = CLng(m_Session("SupplierID"))

End If
```

4. Then, to the same object, we add a couple of property calls and a method to check to see if a supplier is logged on:

```
' SupplierID - get the current supplier ID...
Public Property Get SupplierID() As Long
  SupplierID = m_SupplierID
End Property


' SupplierID - set the current supplier ID both in the object and in the
' session...
Public Property Let SupplierID(ByVal newval As Long)
  m_SupplierID = newval
  m_Session("supplierID") = m_SupplierID
End Property


' IsSupplierLoggedOn - detect if a supplier is connected...
Public Function IsSupplierLoggedOn() As Boolean
  If SupplierID = 0 Then
  IsSupplierLoggedOn = False
  Else
  IsSupplierLoggedOn = True
  End If
End Function
```

5. Now we've modified the object model, we have to return to the presentation layer. Firstly, we tweak the code that examines the results of the login form to see if it's a valid supplier. Make these changes to the code in `admin/default.asp`:

```
' are we trying to logon?
If Request("password") <> "" Then

  ' are we logging on as admin?
  If Request("password") = "secret" Then
   Session("AdminOK") = True
  Else

    ' check to see if we're a supplier...
    Dim problem
    if Visit.Catalog.CheckSupplierLogon(Request("password"), _
        problem) = True Then Session("AdminOK") = True

  End If

End If
```

Now, when we fill in the password field, we can either supply **secret** to log in as us, or we can enter the e-mail address of a supplier.

Early on in Chapter 6 we populated the Suppliers table with a sample supplier, which had the e-mail, address alex@coffeesupplier.com, so we can use that for testing.

6. We need to present a different set of options to the suppliers that use our site, than we have for our own use. To do this, we can use the `IsSupplierLoggedOn` method of the `Visit` object.

We need to add an `If...Then...Else` statement around the entire code `Select Case` statement that apportions most of the work in the administration pages. Firstly, add this code before the `Select Case` statement in `default.asp`:

```
<% ' what do we want to do?
    If Visit.IsSupplierLoggedOn = False Then
      Select Case LCase(Request("action")) %>
```

Then, add this code after it:

```
<%    End Select

  Else

      ' supplier-only options
      Select Case LCase(Request("action"))

      Case Else
        ' render the options...
        RenderOption "View Pending Orders", "vieworders"

      End Select

  End If

End If ' admin OK...
```

The upshot of what you're trying to do is run the first `Select Case` statement if the logged on user is *not* a supplier, and run the second `Select Case` statement if the user is.

The first select statement option will manage the existing options we have already built on the `admin/default.asp` page, whereas the second will manage the new options just for suppliers. Breaking the options into two `Select Case` statements controlled through the `IsSupplierLoggedOn` property stops the supplier from hacking the query string for the page in an attempt to access the privileged options. We can represent this as:

```
' is anyone logged on?
If Session("AdminOK") = False Then
  present the form to ask for the password...
Else

  ' are we a supplier?
  If Visit.IsSupplierLoggedOn = False Then

    run the original Select Case statement...
```

```
Else

    run the new Select Case statement, which is only
    to be used by suppliers...

End If

End If
```

As with all pieces of code, if you have any problems remember that you can always refer to the full project download available from www.wrox.com.

7. Next, we want to get a list of the order that the supplier is responsible for, but only on orders that have not been **committed** or cancelled. A committed order is one that's gone all the way through the order pipeline and the goods are now either on their way to, or have been received by, the customer.

We can obtain this list by selecting out all of the order parts that the supplier is responsible for, but combining that query with orders that have a status code of statusProcessing, which is defined in the WroxCommerce Globals module as 1. The SQL that addresses this query is:

```
SELECT *
FROM Orders
WHERE OrderID IN
 (SELECT OrderID
 FROM OrderParts
 WHERE SupplierID = 1) AND Status = 1
```

When this SQL statement is adapted, taking account of the variables we are using, we need to add the following method to the Orders object:

```
' GetPendingOrdersForSupplier - returns the uncompleted orders that a
' supplier is responsible for...
Public Function GetPendingOrdersForSupplier(ByVal SupplierID As Long, _
        Optional ByVal AsKeyset As Boolean) As Recordset

    ' where...
    Dim Where As String
    Where = "OrderID in (select OrderID from OrderParts where " & _
        "SupplierID=" & SupplierID & ") and Status=" & statusProcessing

    ' run the query...
    Set GetPendingOrdersForSupplier = _
            QueryOrders(Where, "created", AsKeyset)

End Function
```

8. When we present the orders, we only want to show the supplier the order parts that he or she is responsible for, so we'll have to tweak the RenderOrder function, but firstly, we need to add some code to admin/default.asp to present the pending orders. Add this code to the second, supplier-specific Select Case statement:

```
Else

    ' supplier-only options
    Select Case LCase(Request("action"))

            ' present the pending orders...
        Case "vieworders"

            ' get a list of the orders..
            Set orders = _
            Visit.Orders.GetPendingOrdersForSupplier(Visit.SupplierID)
            If Not orders.EOF Then

                ' start the table...
                Response.Write "<center>"
                Response.Write "<table cellspacing=0 cellpadding=0 border=0>"

                ' loop
                Do While Not orders.EOF

                    ' draw the order...
                    Response.Write "<tr><td class=heading>"
                    Response.Write "<a href="""
                    Response.Write request("script_name") & _
                        "?action=vieworder&id=" & orders("orderid")
                    Response.Write """>"
                    Response.Write "Order Number " & orders("orderid")
                    Response.Write "</a> </td><td class=small>"
                    Response.Write orders("created")
                    Response.Write "</td></tr>"

                    ' next
                    orders.MoveNext

                Loop

                ' end the table...
                Response.Write "</table>"
                Response.Write "</center>"

            Else
                Response.Write "There are no pending orders."
            End If
            orders.Close
            Set orders = Nothing
```

Once the appropriate orders have been selected from the database and sent to the browser, the supplier can click on the order number to be brought to another page that presents the order.

9. The step is to add a method to the `Orders` object which will allow the appropriate information to be retrieved:

```
' GetOrderPartsForSupplier - returns the parts for a given order that are
' handled by a given supplier...
Public Function GetOrderPartsForSupplier(ByVal OrderID As Long, _
    ByVal SupplierID As Long, _
    Optional ByVal AsKeyset As Boolean = False) As Recordset
  Set GetOrderPartsForSupplier = QueryOrderParts("OrderID=" & _
    OrderID & " and SupplierID=" & SupplierID, , AsKeyset)
End Function
```

10. Then a method to the `Order` object (not the different object):

```
' PartsForSupplier - return the parts for the order handled by a
' specific supplier...
Public Property Get PartsForSupplier(ByVal SupplierID As Long, _
        Optional ByVal AsKeyset As Boolean) As Recordset
  Set PartsForSupplier = _
    m_utility.Visit.Orders.GetOrderPartsForSupplier(m_ID, _
            SupplierID, AsKeyset)
End Property
```

11. We can now go ahead and tweak the `RenderOrder` helper function that resides in `site.asp`:

```
' render the parts...
Dim parts, lines
If Visit.IsSupplierLoggedOn = False Then
   Set parts = Order.Parts
Else
   Set parts = Order.PartsForSupplier(Visit.SupplierID)
End If
Do While Not parts.EOF
```

12. The whole point of this exercise is to get the supplier to say whether the order should advance down the pipeline. We will, therefore, need a little button they can press to say whether they're prepared to ship the order. When that happens, we'll authorize the customer's credit card (dealt with in the next section) and then we'll re-signal the supplier to say that it's time to ship.

Add this code to `admin/default.asp`:

```
Else

    ' supplier-only options
    Select Case LCase(Request("action"))

        ' view a single order...
        Case "vieworder"

            ' get hold of the order...
            Dim order
            Set order = Visit.Orders.GetOrderObject(request("id"))
```

```
' start a table
Response.Write "<center>"
Response.Write "<table cellspacing=0 cellpadding=0 border=0>"

' present the order...
RenderOrder order, False

' get the order part back...
Dim part
Set part = order.PartsForSupplier(Visit.SupplierID)
If Not part.EOF Then

    ' we only want to ask the supplier to advance the order if the
' pipeline is at stage 2 or 4...
    If part("Status") = 2 or part("Status") = 5 then

        ' add a button...
        Response.Write "<tr><td><br></td></tr>"
        Response.Write "<tr><td class=heading colspan=3 " & _
                "align=center>"
        Response.Write "Supplier: Is this OK? "
        Response.Write "<a href="""
        Response.Write Request("script_name") & _
                "?action=advance&id=" & request("id")
        Response.Write """>Yes</a>"
        Response.Write "</td></tr>"

    End If

End If

' end the table
Response.Write "</table>"
Response.Write "</center>"

' present the pending orders...
Case "vieworders"
```

As we mentioned, we use the `RenderOrder` helper to present the order to the user. We set the `IsAdmin` parameter to `False` so that the supplier can't see anything other than those details we intend them to see; specifically this prevents them from seeing the customer's e-mail address and credit card number.

After we've presented the order, we then grab the appropriate `OrderPart` row back from the database, so we can decide if we want to offer the supplier the option of advancing the order down the pipeline. The supplier will be notified once more in addition to this to indicate that the order has been shipped.

We use the `Status` column in the `OrderParts` table to decide what stage in the pipeline the order is in and whether or not the supplier is allowed to move it. The supplier is only allowed to move the order when the status is either 2 (can the order be fulfilled?) or 5 (has the order been shipped?). For example, a `Status` code of 3 indicates that the processor should attempt to process the credit card. If the supplier sees that code at this point, the supplier should not be able to advance the order down the pipeline, as this is Jo's responsibility.

13. However, to advance the order we need to add some more code to `admin/default.asp`:

```
Else

    ' supplier-only options
    Select Case LCase(Request("action"))

        ' advance the order...
        Case "advance"

            ' create an order processor...
            Dim processor
            Set processor = Visit.StartOrderProcessor
            processor.Go request("id")
            Set processor = Nothing

            Response.Write "<tr><td class=heading>"
            Response.Write "Your instructions have been recorded."
            Response.Write "</td></tr>"

        ' view a single order...
        Case "vieworder"
```

The point of this code is to create an instance of the `OrderProcessor` object and then tell it to advance the order down the pipeline using the `Go` method. This works in exactly the same way as when we called the `Go` method from the `PlaceOrder` method on the `WroxCommerce.Orders` object.

What we've been trying to do with these order-processing components is design them in such a way that we abstract the other parts of the application away from the machinations of what they actually do. So, when we first call `Go` from the `PlaceOrder` method, neither the `WroxCommerce` components, nor the `PlaceOrder` method should care what happens next. In our case, we have the pipeline sending out e-mails, but we could authorize credit cards, ring a little bell attached to the server, or whatever. By using this generic approach to progressing the order each time we need anything to happen, we can abstract the workings of the pipeline away from any of the components involved, and away from any ASP code, as is shown in this example.

Of course, nothing will happen unless we tell the processor what to do…

Enabling Supplier Confirmation

The next connector object we build for the pipeline will have two functions. We'll be using it both here, as the third connector in our pipeline, to indicate that the supplier is in a position to ship the order, and later as the final connector for the supplier to tell us that the order has been shipped successfully.

Try It Out – Creating PipelineSupplierOK

1. Before we begin, add this code to the `OrderProcessor` object. The pipeline support code we build later on will use this method to determine the status of the order part that it has been asked to process.

```
' GetPartStatus - returns our current status...
Public Function GetPartStatus() As Long

    ' run the query...
    Dim Query As Recordset
    Set Query = DB.RunQuery("OrderParts", , "PartID=" & PartID)
    If Not Query.EOF Then
    GetPartStatus = Query("Status")
    End If
    Query.Close
    Set Query = Nothing

End Function
```

Now we need to build a new connector object. As this is now the third time we've done this, we'll move through the coding pretty quickly.

2. Create a new class module called `PipelineSupplierOK`. Set the MTSTransactionMode property to 2 – RequiresTransaction and then add this code:

```
Option Explicit

' Indicate that this is a connector object...
Implements IConnector

Private Property Get IConnector_ID() As String
End Property

Private Property Get IConnector_Name() As String
 IConnector_Name = "PipelineSupplierOK"
End Property

' Process - do this connector's work...
Private Function IConnector_Process(ByVal Processor As OrderProcessor, _
        ByRef RunNextConnector As Boolean) As Boolean

On Error GoTo Problem

  ' tell the processor to update the status of the part...
  Processor.SetPartStatus Processor.GetPartStatus + 1

  ' tell the processor to move on to the next step...
  RunNextConnector = True
```

```
' indicate success...
IConnector_Process = True

' jump over the error handler...
GoTo Finish

Problem:

' flag the error...
Processor.RecordError "Process", Me

Finish:

End Function
```

One thing to note about that `Process` method is that, in this state, it already does everything we intend it to. All it has to do is advance the `Status` flag by one (which it does by using the `GetPartStatus` method on the processor) and return `True`. When we've written the credit card authorization connector, this action will automatically get the credit card authorized. Once that's been done successfully, we'll automatically ask the supplier to ship.

Again this is somewhat simplistic; out there in the real world you could find yourself in the situation that a credit card clearance takes so much time that the supplier sells out of the requested items! This is yet another situation where you need to fully understand your own business situation when building your own e-commerce solution.

3. Compile the VB project. If you get messages about compatibility, select **Break Compatibility**. Again if the **Permission Denied** error appears, you'll need to carry out the Web server restarting process (appropriate to your machine) that we covered a few pages back in the discussion on the `PipelineSignalSuppliers` connector.

4. Once that's done, delete and recreate the **JoCoffee** package in the MTS Explorer and import the new DLL. Use MTS Explorer to find the properties for the `PipelineSupplierOK` component and copy the GUID into the **GUIDs** module, like this:

```
' Pipeline Connector GUIDs
Global Const GUID_PipelineNotifyOwner = _
    "{1E054144-A3F6-11D3-844C-00A0CC3BDC77}"
Global Const GUID_PipelineSignalSuppliers = _
    "{FC0E5E0E-A441-11D3-844E-00A0CC3BDC77}"
Global Const GUID_PipelineSupplierOK = _
    "{BDEADE43-C265-11D0-BCED-00A0C90AB50F}"
```

5. Then, alter the `IConnector_ID` method of the `PipeLineSupplierOK` object to look like this:

```
Private Property Get IConnector_ID() As String
  IConnector_ID = GUID_PipelineSupplierOK
End Property
```

6. Finally, to integrate the new connector into our pipeline we need to add another `Case` statement to the `Go` method of the `OrderProcessor` object:

```
' what stage is the part at?
Select Case OrderPart("Status")

    ' start of the order...
    Case 0
    Set Connector = New PipelineNotifyOwner
    Case 1
    Set Connector = New PipelineSignalSuppliers
    Case 2
    Set Connector = New PipelineSupplierOK

End Select
```

7. To test this out, put a breakpoint at the start of the `Go` method on the processor and log on as a supplier using `alex@coffeesupplier.com`. Find an order that's waiting for your action and click the `Yes` link to advance the order. Step through the `Go` method and you'll see how the `Status` flag is advanced and then `Go` is called one more time. This time, however, the processor doesn't know what to do with a `Status` value of 3, so the processing will stop. However, if you go back to the order view, you'll notice that it says that the order is waiting for credit card authorization:

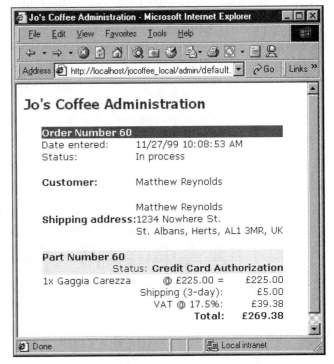

When we've finished the pipeline, what will actually happen is that as soon as the supplier confirms they can ship the order our pipeline will go away and try to authorize the payment. If the authorization is successful, the order details page can be refreshed to show a message that says, "Ship the order, please!" If the authorization is not successful, they'll see a status message indicating that the order is waiting for authorization.

Credit Card Authorization

Credit card authorization is possibly the most nebulous aspect of e-commerce. Finding real-world, specific information about how to get to a position where you can accept credit cards online is hard. Searching for "credit card merchant services" and "how do I take credit cards online" in the major search engines yields links pointing not to impartial advice, but rather to companies providing services to online merchants. This leads to a great deal of plowing through **brochureware** (the term given to a Web site that merely reproduces the marketing information a company releases on paper), but not too many hard facts. Brochureware sites have traditionally represented the first step a company takes on the road to becoming an e-business, but most companies find such a site cannot enhance customer communications to the extent that a more complete e-business site can.

In this section we'll go some way to explaining exactly what's going on, so you can better understand what's involved in getting cash out of your customers wallets and into your account. We'll be covering how to do this both in the United States and in the United Kingdom as the procedures are broadly the same.

Within this particular section we'll be looking at the following areas:

❑   Interacting with banking networks

❑   Remote credit card transactions

❑   Building the pipeline connector that facilitates credit card transactions (`PipelinePaymentAuth`)

❑   Viewing the audit trail

❑   Handling failure

> **Again, this is a complicated area; to fully implement credit card handling you'll have to talk to your bank, and will probably want to take advice from a consultant working in e-commerce in your tax region. This chapter should help you well on the way though!**

Two Separate Networks

The problem of obtaining payment from your customer starts when you consider the way that the banks organize their computer systems. Naturally, everything a bank does is computerized, so you would expect that electronically signaling them in some way and asking them to send you some money would be quite easy.

In general this isn't the case, because banks are mainly connected using a network that doesn't work over TCP/IP like the Internet does. Effectively, each bank has its own extranet, which rather than running on TCP/IP, usually runs on **X.25** (X.25 is another network protocol like TCP/IP). We don't need to worry about protocol differences, other than to note that this means the bank's servers and the Web servers that run your business run on separate networks.

Into this picture we need to add the credit card companies that Jo's customers use. They sit outside the X.25 network of the banks but still need to communicate securely with the bank. The solution we've illustrated is the case where the communication is carried out via a dedicated leased line (a fixed, defined connection between two points – here the bank and the credit card company):

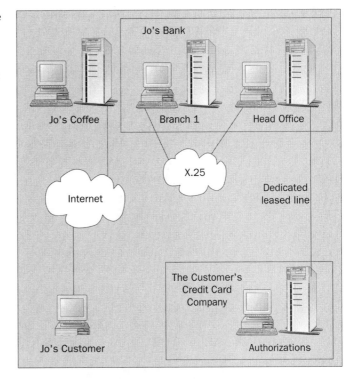

So we have the problem that the Jo's Coffee Web site and Jo's customers are both communicating over the Internet, and the credit card companies used by Jo's customers, and Jo's bank, are communicating over a different system. Our mission (which we've chosen to accept) is to get the payment request that the server needs to make over to our bank, and then have that bank get the money from the relevant customer.

Talking to the Bank

There is no way that a bank will place their core processing systems on a publicly accessible network like the Internet where it becomes overly susceptible to attack. Rather, they will use their legacy X.25 network as a firewall to prevent security attacks from being made on them. In recent years, most of the banks have rolled out Web access for customers to carry out simple operations but these are simply a Web presentation of their underlying systems and they go to great lengths to ensure they are properly protected.

In order for someone to communicate with a financial institution over its X.25 network, there has to be a degree of negotiation in order for the bank to feel confident about the organization that wants access. The bank needs to know the inquiring company is not only legitimate and credible but has appropriate security procedures. For example, to directly connect to certain banks, a company has to place the server not only in a secure location, but also store the servers and routers in a separate, lockable cage. Daily backup tapes from this system are ejected down a chute, through a slot in the cage and stored offsite. The tapes themselves are secured with at least three separate keys, also held offsite, each key being held by a different individual. All three keys have to be brought together in order to decrypt the tapes.

389

This is a route that small operators like Jo are unlikely to want to go down, so they usually employ a company to act as a **payment gateway** between the public IP-driven Internet and private, X.25-driven bank network:

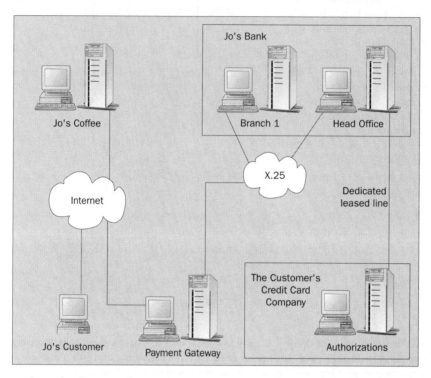

As you can see from the diagram, the payment gateway sits in the middle of the whole mess and can connect to both the Internet and the bank's X.25 network. Jo's server can make a request to the bank via the payment gateway by signaling the request over the Internet to that gateway and having the gateway *translate* the request to the bank. The bank then uses its credit card authorization technology to signal down to the customer's credit card company to perform the transaction. If all works well, the money gets transferred into Jo's account, minus the bank's authorization fees, and minus that small cut which the payment gateway takes.

An Overview of Credit Card Transactions

When credit card companies first started doing business, all the transactions that went through their system required the customer to present the card to a cashier, who would ask the customer to sign a slip that was then sent away for processing. That sort of transaction is then associated with a **merchant ID** so that the payment processing services know where to transfer the money. A merchant gets a merchant ID through negotiation with their bank, (which will usually involve the bank ensuring the merchant is legitimate and trustworthy).

These transactions have a commission charge associated with them which is supposed to cover the bank's risk insofar as if the merchant actually touches the physical card, the bank still coughs up the cash if the payment is fraudulent.

Card Not Present

Card Not Present (CNP) is a concept that's been around for a long time and is usually referred to when handling mail order purchases that come in by phone. A merchant that wants to accept *card not present* orders has to go through another round of negotiations with the bank to obtain a separate ID. The main reason for assigning this separate ID is that the bank is not responsible for the risk involved in this transaction and they will most likely decide to charge a higher rate of commission.

This seems paradoxical; as the bank has no risk, how can they justify higher commissions? The answer is that even without handling the risk, they still have greater administrative costs with handling fraudulent transactions, and in many cases they fund investigations into companies and individuals that are involved. Having two separate IDs helps their accounting; if a CNP transaction turns out to be fraudulent, it is the merchant that is responsible for the risk and has to absorb these costs.

> **This is an important point: you are financially responsible for all fraudulent transactions put through your site; if someone makes a purchase with a stolen card and you ship it, you pay for it. This is why you often find retailers who are only willing to ship to the same address the card is registered at.**

Today we find that the majority of companies have electronic credit card terminals for capturing card information, rather than the old paper-based systems of yesteryear. If the merchant can get hold of the customer's card, it is swiped through the machine; in CNP transactions, the number is manually punched into the keypad on the top of the box.

E-Commerce and Credit Cards

Now that the banks have started to recognize the Internet as a legitimate economic phenomenon, it's necessary for online traders to go back to their bank and negotiate yet another ID in addition to the card-present and card-not-present ones they already have. This ID is often called an **e-commerce merchant ID**. An important point is that it is technically not necessary to obtain this separate e-commerce merchant ID. If you have a card-not-present ID, you could use that in combination with your existing electronic payment terminal. However, if the bank gets wind of the fact that you're doing it, they will ask you to stop and get an e-commerce merchant ID. It's a bit of a mystery why the banks have decided that merchants must seek another ID for online purchases, but it's most likely related to some hidden, risk-reduction agenda.

As a side note, if you design your payment processing pipeline so that it sends e-mails to you with the customer's card details, make sure that e-mail is securely encrypted using something like PGP (which we discuss in Chapter 10) or SMIME. Do not let them send the credit card information as clear-text.

It's at this point that writing this book gets difficult for me, and getting an ID gets difficult for you. If you choose to get an e-commerce specific merchant ID you're on your own. Each bank in the US and the UK has its own rules and procedures for this, so pick up the phone and talk to them. This is a developing area, and currently not all bank personnel (especially in the UK) will be up to speed in this area, so a degree of patience and a great deal of explanation may be in order. Persevere though, because it can be done. For additional help, the payment gateway companies often have expertise and advice that they can share to help you get through this process with your sanity intact.

Once you have an ID, you can enlist the services of any of the payment gateways to send authorization requests to your bank on your behalf. In a little while we'll show you how you can send transactions over to one of these gateways.

391

Bureau Services

If you're a brand new company, or your bank is not so switched on, you may find it extremely difficult to get an e-commerce ID.

If you can't get an e-commerce merchant ID (or you just don't want one), you can use a **bureau service**. A bureau service is an intermediary that has their own relationship with a bank and puts your transactions through their account on your behalf. They will charge a higher percentage than you could get through your bank, but some bureau services will absorb the risk of the transaction, so you could consider the extra percentage as being an insurance policy.

There are, as you might expect, a number of companies providing this service, including iBill.com in the US and NetBanx.com in the UK.

Charging the Customer

In this section, we'll be building a connector in the pipeline that can communicate with a gateway service to process our credit cards.

Gateway Services

There are a whole host of companies offering payment gateway services, and a few of them are listed below. This is a rapidly expanding area and it appears that banks themselves are entering the area (but it's still likely the model we developed before will be appropriate – the bank will operate a gateway; you won't communicate with their main systems directly). Remember, a payment gateway service is simply a service organization that has a connection to both the Internet and your bank's computer system.

You open an account with the gateway service, supplying them with your e-commerce merchant ID. When they pass over the processing request to the bank, the bank uses the e-commerce merchant ID to track who you are in order to route the money back.

It is critically important that you shop around when looking for this service, as picking one that's too expensive, or one that does not deal with transactions properly, will have a profound effect on your business. To find them, use Yahoo or Netscape's Open Directory (http://directory.netscape.com/) to find their competitors. Each one will charge different setup and administration fees and varying levels of commission.

United States		United Kingdom	
CyberCash	http://www.cybercash.com/	BT BuyNet	http://www.btbuynet.com/
First Data	http://www.firstdata.com/	Cable & Wireless Web Commerce	http://www.web-commerce.co.uk
CardService International	http://www.cardservice.com/	WorldPay	http://www.worldpay.com/
IC Verify	http://www.icverify.com/	DataCash	http://www.datacash.com/

A Payment Gateway for Jo'sCoffee

In our example, we're going to use DataCash as our payment gateway. In this example, we'll be able to use DataCash's test merchant ID and card numbers so we can get going without having to negotiate with a bank.

If you're using a bureau service, or an existing offline payment terminal, you'll have to tweak the connector we build here (`PipelinePaymentAuth`) to make it similar to the `PipelineSupplerOK` connector we created to ask the supplier to tell us if the order can be shipped.

The connector we build in this section will automatically advance the order down the pipeline once the card has been authorized, or signal us if the card has been rejected.

DataCash

Like all payment gateways, DataCash establishes a **point-of-presence** on the Internet that we can communicate with in order to perform credit card transactions. DataCash passes the transaction requests we send to it over to the bank, and passes any replies from our bank back to us. To do this DataCash is attached to and accessible through the Internet via a connection mediated by an Internet Service Provider (ISP). Additionally it goes through the requisite hurdles and obtains a separate leased X.25 line to each bank it deals with.

Thus we send your requests to DataCash over the Internet and it then deals with moving the specific request over to your bank's X.25 network. Irrespective of which bank your customer deals with, DataCash will only talk to your bank. It relies on your bank having a connection to the credit card processing system of your customer's bank.

> **DataCash can only directly support UK banks and American Express both in the UK and the US. So, if you're using Bank One, Wells Fargo or any of the other US banks, you will need to use a different payment gateway. The principles you see here will be largely similar to the procedures your chosen company will expect; simply tweak the code that talks to DataCash to talk to your chosen gateway company's components.**

To start working with DataCash, all you have to do is open an account with it. This is a simple process and the main purpose of it is to let DataCash know who your bank is and what your e-commerce merchant ID is. Once that's done, DataCash will return you back a user name and password that you need to use with its service.

For the purposes of this example, we're going to use a sample account that is free to use for testing.

To facilitate communication between Internet based e-commerce sites and themselves, DataCash supplies an ASP component that can be used within the site to talk to its service. We'll need this component to make sure our `PipelinePaymentAuth` connector can fulfill its assigned tasks.

Try It Out – Installing the DataCash components

1. Firstly, visit the DataCash site at http://www.datacash.com/. Click on the Software link and look for the Microsoft logo. Alongside that there will be (correct at the time of writing) a link that says FTP server accompanied by text saying A variety of ZIP files (..). Click on this to be taken to an FTP site where you can download the latest version of the components.

2. The README file indicates which of the available download options does what. You most likely will only need the DataCash_ASP_NR.ZIP file – this is the version without the Visual Basic support libraries. However, when moving the components to your production machine, you may need the version with the support libraries: DataCash_ASP.ZIP. Download whichever file suits your needs and save it somewhere on your computer.

3. Extract the ZIP file to an appropriate folder and run Setup.exe.

4. The setup program will install the components into the chosen folder and will properly register the components for use.

Try It Out – Creating PipelinePaymentAuth

1. We've built a few connectors now, so the process is probably starting to look pretty familiar. Firstly, create a new class module called PipelinePaymentAuth. Set the MTSTransactionMode property to 2 – RequiresTransaction and then add this code:

```
Option Explicit

' Indicate that this is a connector object...
Implements IConnector

Private Property Get IConnector_ID() As String
End Property

Private Property Get IConnector_Name() As String
  IConnector_Name = "PipelinePaymentAuth"
End Property

' Process - do this connector's work...
Private Function IConnector_Process(ByVal Processor As OrderProcessor, _
        ByRef RunNextConnector As Boolean) As Boolean

  On Error GoTo Problem

  ' jump over the error handler...
  GoTo Finish

Problem:

  ' flag the error...
  Processor.RecordError "Process", Me

Finish:

End Function
```

2. Compile the VB project. If you get messages about compatibility, select **Break Compatibility**. As before if the **Permission Denied** error appears, you'll need to carry out the Web server restarting process (appropriate to your machine) that we covered back in the PipelineSignalSuppliers connector discussion.

3. Once that's done, delete and recreate the **JoCoffee** package in the MTS Explorer and import the new DLL. Use MTS Explorer to find the properties for the `PipelinePaymentAuth` component and copy the GUID into the `GUIDs` module, like this:

```
' Pipeline Connector GUIDs
Global Const GUID_PipelineNotifyOwner = _
      "{1E054144-A3F6-11D3-844C-00A0CC3BDC77}"
Global Const GUID_PipelineSignalSuppliers = _
      "{FC0E5E0E-A441-11D3-844E-00A0CC3BDC77}"
Global Const GUID_PipelineSupplierOK = _
      "{BDEADE43-C265-11D0-BCED-00A0C90AB50F}"
Global Const GUID_PipelinePaymentAuth = _
      "{6285D4A4-A4B1-11D3-844F-00A0CC3BDC77}"
```

4. Then, alter the `IConnector_ID` method of the `PipelinePaymentAuth` object to look like this:

```
Private Property Get IConnector_ID() As String
    IConnector_ID = GUID_PipelinePaymentAuth
End Property
```

5. Once again, to integrate the connector into the pipeline, alter the `Go` method of the `OrderProcessor` object so that it looks like this:

```
' what stage is the part at?
Select Case OrderPart("Status")

  ' start of the order...
  Case 0
    Set Connector = New PipelineNotifyOwner
  Case 1
    Set Connector = New PipelineSignalSuppliers
  Case 2
    Set Connector = New PipelineSupplierOK
  Case 3
    Set Connector = New PipelinePaymentAuth

End Select
```

Remember, when we built the `PipelineSupplierOK` connector we asked it to automatically move onto the next connector in the pipeline. This means that when the supplier clicks the **Order OK** link, credit card authorization will automatically occur.

Now we have the connector built, we need to add some code to various parts of the `WroxProcessor` project to leverage the DataCash components.

Try It Out – Communicating with DataCash

1. To use the DataCash components from the WroxProcessor project, we need to include a reference to its libraries. Select Project | References...from the menu and check on DataCash Payment Authorisation for Windows NT:

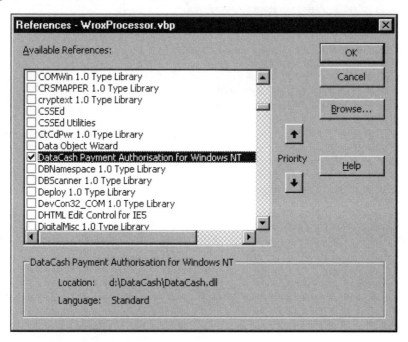

2. As you might have suspected, we're going to need a few basic functions. Add these to the OrderProcessor object (the GetReferenceNumber method may look odd right now, but we'll explain it in a little while):

```
' GetReferenceNumber - number suitable for credit card transactions...
Public Function GetReferenceNumber() As Long
    GetReferenceNumber = 2000000 + PartID
End Function

' GetCardID - returns the Card ID...
Public Function GetCardID() As Long

    ' run the query...
    Dim Query As Recordset
    Set Query = New Recordset
    Set Query = DB.RunQuery("Orders", , "OrderID=" & PartID)
    If Not Query.EOF Then
        GetCardID = Query("CardID")
    End If
    Query.Close
    Set Query = Nothing
```

```
End Function

' GetPaymentDetails - return the details of the payment...
Public Function GetPaymentDetails(ByRef CardNumber As String, _
    ByRef ExpiresMonth As Integer, ByRef ExpiresYear As Integer)

    ' get the card...
    Dim CardID As Long
    CardID = GetCardID
    If CardID <> 0 Then

            ' run the query...
            Dim Query As Recordset
            Set Query = DB.RunQuery("Cards", , "CardID=" & CardID)
            If Not Query.EOF Then

                ' get the values...
                CardNumber = Query("Number")
                ExpiresMonth = Query("ExpiresMonth")
                ExpiresYear = Query("ExpiresYear")

            End If
        Query.Close
        Set Query = Nothing

    End If

End Function
```

3. Still in the `OrderProcessor` object, add the following `GetAmount` method which we use to determine the total value of an order part:

```
' GetAmount - returns the amount of the order part...
Public Function GetAmount() As Double

    ' run the query...
    Dim Query As Recordset
    Set Query = New Recordset
    Set Query = DB.RunQuery("OrderParts", , "PartID=" & PartID)
    If Not Query.EOF Then
        GetAmount = Query("Total")
    End If
    Query.Close
    Set Query = Nothing

End Function
```

4. Of course we need to implement the `Process` method for the `PipelinePaymentAuth` connector to get the connector to authorize the payment. Here's the code we need:

```
' Process - do this connector's work...
Private Function IConnector_Process(ByVal Processor As OrderProcessor, _
                                    ByRef RunNextConnector As Boolean) As Boolean

    On Error GoTo Problem

    ' get the card id...
    Dim CardID As Long
    CardID = Processor.GetCardID
    If CardID <> 0 Then

        ' get the card and payment details...
        Dim CardNumber As String
        Dim ExpiresMonth As Integer
        Dim ExpiresYear As Integer
        Processor.GetPaymentDetails CardNumber, ExpiresMonth, ExpiresYear
        If CardNumber <> "" And ExpiresMonth <> 0 And _
            ExpiresYear <> 0 Then

            ' get the amount of the otder...
            Dim Amount As Double
            Amount = Processor.GetAmount
            If Amount <> 0 Then

                ' get a reference number for the transaction...
                Dim Reference As Long
                Reference = Processor.GetReferenceNumber
                If Reference <> 0 Then

                    ' log the fact we're going to try...
                    Processor.AddAudit Me, PPA_AttemptingAuth, True

                    ' create an instance of the datacash component...
                    Dim Result As Integer
                    Dim DataCash As New DataCash
                    Result = DataCash.Authorise("new-auth.datacash.com", _
                             9070, "0123456789ABCDEF", "auth", _
                             CardNumber, ExpiresMonth, ExpiresYear, "", _
                             Reference, "21859999", "fred", Amount, 0, _
                             "c:\temp\datacash.log", 60, "GBP", "")

                    ' a result of one means the transaction was ok!
                    If Result = 1 Then

                        ' form a message for the audit trail...
                        Dim Data As String
                        Data = "Card issuer: " & DataCash.Issuer & Chr(13)
                        Data = Data & "Card country: " & _
                                DataCash.Country & Chr(13)
                        Data = Data & "Timestamp: " & _
                                DataCash.TimeStamp & Chr(13)
                        Data = Data & "Unique ref: " & _
                                DataCash.UniqueRef & Chr(13)
```

```
                        ' add it to the audit log...
                        Processor.AddAudit Me, PPA_AuthSuccessful, _
                        True, "Auth code: " & DataCash.AuthCode, Data

                        ' proceed...
                        RunNextConnector = True
                        Processor.SetPartStatus 4

                        ' return ok!
                        IConnector_Process = True

                    Else

                        ' e-mail the owner that the authfailed...
                        Processor.SendEMail Me, PPA_NotifyOwnerFailed, _
                                "Authorization Failed - Part ID " & _
                                Processor.PartID, "Owner", "owner@" & _
                                Processor.MailDomain, _
                                "Authorization of order part " & _
                                Processor.PartID & " failed."

                        ' add the result to the audit trail...
                        Processor.AddAudit Me, PPA_AuthFailed, False, _
                        "Result #" & Result & ", " & DataCash.AuthCode

                    End If

                Else
                    Processor.AddAudit Me, PPA_NoReferenceNumber, False
                End If

            Else
                Processor.AddAudit Me, PPA_NoAmount, False
            End If

        Else
            Processor.AddAudit Me, PPA_NoPaymentDetails, False
        End If

    Else
        Processor.AddAudit Me, PPA_NoCard, False
    End If

    ' jump over the error handler...
    GoTo Finish

Problem:

    ' flag the error...
    Processor.RecordError "Process", Me

Finish:

End Function
```

5. During the function we make use of a number of audit trail codes and these need to be added to MessageCodes; the code for that is as follows:

```
' PipelinePaymentAuth codes...
Public Enum PPACodes

    ' information codes...
    PPA_AttemptingAuth = 33001
    PPA_AuthSuccessful = 33002
    PPA_AuthFailed = 33003
    PPA_NotifyOwnerFailed = 33004

    ' error codes...
    PPA_NoCard = 33101
    PPA_NoPaymentDetails = 33102
    PPA_NoReferenceNumber = 33103
    PPA_NoAmount = 33104

End Enum
```

6. You can test the results that come back from DataCash by putting a breakpoint at the beginning of the method and stepping through and looking at the return codes. Feel free to put your own credit card number in. Nothing will happen on the test account; the DataCash servers will return a random result. A return code of 1 from the Authorise method means that the transaction was successful, anything else means that it was not.

How It Works

We started the coding with the OrderProcessor object; the GetPaymentDetails method is used to get hold of the card number, expiry month and expiry year of the card that's been associated with the order. We use the GetCardID method to determine the card ID that was used and run a simple query to return a recordset that represents that card:

```
' GetCardID - returns the Card ID...
Public Function GetCardID() As Long

    ' run the query...
    Dim Query As Recordset
    Set Query = DB.RunQuery("Orders", , "OrderID=" & GetOrderID)
    If Not Query.EOF Then
        GetCardID = Query("CardID")
    End If
    Query.Close
    Set Query = Nothing

End Function
```

```
' get the card...
   Dim CardID As Long
   CardID = GetCardID
   If CardID <> 0 Then

         ' run the query...
         Dim Query As Recordset
         Set Query = DB.RunQuery("Cards", , "CardID=" & CardID)
         If Not Query.EOF Then
```

If we can find the card, we return the details back out of the function through the ByRef-style parameters. The GetAmount method is used to determine the total value of an order part. If you recall, at various times during the checkout when tax rates and shipping methods are chosen, we hold the results of the calculations in the OrderParts table for each access. Here, we extract the total from the Total column:

```
' run the query...
   Dim Query As Recordset
   Set Query = DB.RunQuery("OrderParts", , "PartID=" & GetOrderID)
   If Not Query.EOF Then
      GetAmount = Query("Total")
```

There is quite an amount that can be said about the Process method we just coded. The first few things we do are concerned with checking to make sure we know everything we need to know about the order. This includes:

❑ The ID of the credit card – which is used to get the details of the card

❑ The amount for authorization

❑ The reference number of the order

All of these use the various methods we put together a little earlier:

```
CardID = Processor.GetCardID

Amount = Processor.GetAmount

Reference = Processor.GetReferenceNumber
```

The DataCash.Authorise method is the one that does all the work of authorizing the transaction. Its first job is to connect to the DataCash payment gateway server that's somewhere on the Internet (in our example here, we're using the server at **new-auth.datacash.com**), establishing the security and encryption protocols for safely passing the card data over the Internet, and then passing over the data. Once that's done, the payment gateway looks at the account details to figure out who you are, determines which bank to pass the request to, and then translates the request to the protocol specified by the bank, sends it down the X.25 line, and listens for the results.

401

We go into the `Authorise` method in more detail in Appendix A, but in the code you can see here the card details, the amount, and the reference number we grabbed a little earlier. Together with this is the client number and password for the test account – "21859999" and "fred":

```
Result = DataCash.Authorise("new-auth.datacash.com", _
                    9070, "0123456789ABCDEF", "auth", _
                    CardNumber, ExpiresMonth, ExpiresYear, "", _
                    Reference, "21859999", "fred", Amount, 0, _
                    "c:\temp\datacash.log", 60, "GBP", "")
```

In the real world, you'd provide your own client number and password here.

> **If you get problems with your pipeline timing out try, for sample purposes, setting `Result=1` and commenting out the DataCash code**

DataCash expects to see reference numbers of more than six digits, which is why we add 2,000,000 (in the `GetReferenceNumber` method) to our Part ID to form this unique reference number. Once all that is in place, we go ahead and create the `DataCash` object and make our call.

Appendix A contains details about the DataCash API, particularly the so-called **magic numbers** and return codes. Magic numbers are used for testing purposes and return either a random result, or a well-known result. For example, the card number 5473000000000114 will always result in the **Retain Card** message, whereas 4111111111111111 results in a random result, which could include a successful authorization. In our connector example, we only proceed whenever a card is authorized, so you might like to use 5473000000000015 as this card number will always guarantee a successful transaction.

If the authorization worked (the card was valid, the money was in the account, etc.), the `Authorise` method will return 1. In this case, we use the `DataCash` object to return information about the transaction, including a unique reference number, time stamp, country, card issuer and, most importantly, an authorization code. The credit card companies use this to authenticate transactions, so if you ever have any recourse with the banks as to the validity of the transaction, they will ask you to supply this number.

```
' a result of one means the transaction was ok!
        If Result = 1 Then

                ' form a message for the audit trail...
                Dim Data As String
                Data = "Card issuer: " & DataCash.Issuer & Chr(13)
                Data = Data & "Card country: " & _
                    DataCash.Country & Chr(13)
                Data = Data & "Timestamp: " & _
                    DataCash.TimeStamp & Chr(13)
                Data = Data & "Unique ref: " & _
                    DataCash.UniqueRef & Chr(13)
```

In addition to writing an entry into the audit log, we also set the `RunNextConnector` parameter to `True` and set the status of the part to 4, which is the connector that indicates to the supplier that it's time to ship the order:

```
                ' add it to the audit log...
                Processor.AddAudit Me, PPA_AuthSuccessful, _
                True, "Auth code: " & DataCash.AuthCode, Data

                ' proceed...
                RunNextConnector = True
                Processor.SetPartStatus 4
```

If the transaction was not successful, we send e-mail to the site owner indicating that the transaction failed. In the audit log, we note down this fact, along with the reason why the transaction was rejected. Whenever a transaction is invalid, the `DataCash` object allows access to a textual error through the `AuthCode` method:

```
' e-mail the owner that the authfailed...
Processor.SendEMail Me, PPA_NotifyOwnerFailed, _
        "Authorization Failed - Part ID " & _
        Processor.PartID, "Owner", "owner@" & _
        Processor.MailDomain, _
        "Authorization of order part " & _
        Processor.PartID & " failed."

' add the result to the audit trail...
Processor.AddAudit Me, PPA_AuthFailed, False, _
"Result #" & Result & ", " & DataCash.AuthCode
```

An important thing to watch with the structure of this method is the error trapping. Notice we check each of the values we want to work with in a set of nested `If` statements. Any one of those statements can drop the execution out of the function and back to the order processor. By default, if this happens the return function for the method will be `False`, indicating to the `OrderProcessor.Go` method that something went wrong and something needs to be done. By convention, we say that anything *good* is handled in the top part of the `If` statement, whereas anything *bad* is handled at the bottom. That's why we see this pattern of `AddAudit` calls adding potential problems into the audit trail towards the end of the function:

```
        Else
            Processor.AddAudit Me, PPA_NoReferenceNumber, False
        End If

    Else
        Processor.AddAudit Me, PPA_NoAmount, False
    End If

    Else
        Processor.AddAudit Me, PPA_NoPaymentDetails, False
    End If

Else
    Processor.AddAudit Me, PPA_NoCard, False
End If

' jump over the error handler...
GoTo Finish

Problem:

' flag the error...
Processor.RecordError "Process", Me
```

When we carry out a test, we use the `AuthCode` method of the `DataCash` object to get back a string representing what went wrong if the transaction was declined, or an authorization code if it went OK (you can find more information on the error codes in Appendix A). We write the results in the audit trail and, if the authorization was successful, we signal the processor that the method executed properly and ask it to proceed to the next connector:

```
' add it to the audit log...
            Processor.AddAudit Me, PPA_AuthSuccessful, _
            True, "Auth code: " & DataCash.AuthCode, Data
```

Incidentally, when you work with your own site, the area of credit card validation can represent another small minefield. For instance, there is potential that the credit card bureau will charge for the authorization attempt even if it is unsuccessful with a bogus (or mistyped) card number being entered. We won't go into any detail here but there are a number of digit checking methods (for instance, all American Express card numbers are 15 digits in length and should start with either the digits 34 or 37) and checksum calculations that we can use for local validation of the card number.

On the other hand, it may become more commonplace for payment gateways to offer sophisticated tools for online authorization of cards, including verifying credit limits and holding lists of fraudulent cards, which would take some of the pressure off site builders.

Let's move on to consider the audit trail we've carefully built up in more detail.

Viewing the Audit Trail

Throughout the pipeline process we've been collecting a bundle of information in the audit trail, but so far we don't have any way to view the information. To do this, we will be tweaking the `RenderOrder` code, but first we need a method on the `Orders` object that can return the audit trail for an order part.

Try It Out – Exposing the Audit Trail

1. Firstly, return to the `WroxCommerce` project. Add the following method to the `Orders` object:

```
' GetAuditTrail - returns the audit trail for an order part...
Public Function GetAuditTrail(ByVal PartID As Long, _
    Optional ByVal AsKeyset As Boolean) As Recordset
Set GetAuditTrail = m_utility.DB.RunQuery("Audit", , _
    "OrderPartID=" & PartID, "AuditID", AsKeyset)
End Function
```

We've seen functions like that hundreds of times at this point, but what's interesting about this one is that we specify the order clause as `AuditID`. As this column is a SQL Server identity field, the numbers will always go up, and sorting on a 4-byte integer column is quicker than sorting on an 8-byte date column.

2. Next, back in Visual InterDev, we can add some presentation code to the `RenderOrder` function found in `site.asp`. It should be placed immediately below the `If...End If` statement that renders the supplier information:

```
' also, if we're admin, draw the audit log...
If IsAdmin Then

   ' get the log...
   Dim audit
   Set audit = Visit.Orders.GetAuditTrail(parts("PartID"))
   If Not audit.EOF Then

     ' start a table...
     Response.Write "<tr><td colspan=3>"
     Response.Write "<table cellspacing=0 cellpadding=0>"

     ' loop
     Do While Not audit.EOF

        Response.Write "<tr><td class=small>"
        Response.Write audit("Timestamp")
        Response.Write " </td><td class=small>"
        Select Case audit("MessageCode")

' sample explanations for the message codes ...
     case 10001
        response.write "VB Error"
     case 10002
        response.write "Not in transactional environment"
     case 10003
        response.write "Path specified was not found"
     case 10004
        response.write "Nothing to do"
     case 20001
        response.write "Connector started"
     case 20002
        response.write "Connector successful"
     case 20003
        response.write "Connector failed"
     case 20004
        response.write "Master order updated"

        Case Else
          Response.Write "Unknown (" & _
               audit("MessageCode") & ")"

        End Select
        Response.Write " </td><td class=small>"
        Response.Write audit("Message")
        Response.Write " </td></tr>"

        ' next
        audit.MoveNext

     Loop

     ' end a table...
     Response.Write "</table>"
     Response.Write "</td></tr>"
     Response.Write "<tr><td><br></td></tr>"

   End If
   audit.Close
   Set audit = Nothing

End If
```

In our code snippet we've added some example cases to the `Select Case` statement to render out an explanation for some of the messages that can be in the audit trail – the list is incomplete but you get the idea. Once you've finished this off, you'll find that the `RenderOrder` helper function now provides a great deal of information about the history of the order.

Once appropriate error messages have been added in, the audit trail might look like this after the second attempt to authorize a card succeeded, (we'll see how to re-submit a card for authorization in the next section):

Part Number 66

Status: **Waiting for supplier to ship**

Supplier: My Coffee Supplier
Alex Drew
alex@coffeesupplier.com

```
11/28/99 7:30:46 PM Connector started
11/28/99 7:30:47 PM Owner notified            E-mail sent to owner@joscoffee.com
11/28/99 7:30:47 PM Customer notified         E-mail sent to matthew@wroxcoffeedrinker.com
11/28/99 7:30:47 PM Master order updated       1
11/28/99 7:30:47 PM Connector successful
11/28/99 7:30:47 PM Connector started
11/28/99 7:30:47 PM Supplier signalled         E-mail sent to alex@coffeesupplier.com
11/28/99 7:30:47 PM Connector successful
11/28/99 7:33:20 PM Connector started
11/28/99 7:33:20 PM Connector successful
11/28/99 7:33:20 PM Connector started
11/28/99 7:33:20 PM Attempting authorization
11/28/99 7:34:21 PM Notified owner of failure  E-mail sent to owner@joscoffee.com
11/28/99 7:34:21 PM Authorization failed       Result #-4, Local Timeout
11/28/99 7:34:21 PM Connector failed
11/28/99 7:39:44 PM Connector started
11/28/99 7:39:44 PM Attempting authorization
11/28/99 7:39:46 PM Authorization successful   Auth code: 874814
11/28/99 7:39:46 PM Connector successful
11/28/99 7:39:46 PM Nothing to do
```

Handling Failure

If the authorization fails, Jo will receive an e-mail indicating that the payment could not be authorized. We then need to supply a way for her to reattempt the authorization. If this authorization does fail, it could either be a network or gateway fault (in which case the same card details will most likely work on a reattempt), or a problem with the card. Although we aren't going to tackle the re-authorization issue, there are of course a number of options at this point – we could add an editing tool that allowed Jo to change the credit card details, as they exist in the database, or we could get in touch with the customer and request that they re-enter their details.

If Jo wants to advance the order down the pipeline for any reason (say a supplier has phoned her to say that the item can be shipped, rather than logging in over the site), she needs a link on the site that can advance the order down the pipeline. This is similar in nature to the link we added to the supplier's view of the extranet to signal that the order could be fulfilled. We can do this by adding two bits of code to the site.

Try It Out – Failure Handling

1. Firstly, alter the code that draws out the pending orders to **admin/default.asp**, like this:

```
<% ' do we want to view the orders?
case "viewneworders" %>

    <%
    ' get a list of the orders...
    Dim orders
    Set orders = Visit.Orders.GetNewOrders
    If Not orders.EOF Then

        ' start the table...
        Response.Write "<center><table cellspacing=0 cellpadding=0>"

        ' draw the orders...
        Dim parts
        Do While Not orders.EOF

            ' use a helper to present the orders...
            RenderOrder orders, true

            ' get the parts...
            Set parts = Visit.Orders.GetOrderParts(orders("OrderID"))
            Do While Not parts.EOF

                ' add an advance option...
                Response.Write "<tr><td colspan=3 align=center class=heading>"
                Response.Write "<a href="""
                Response.Write request("script_name") & _
                        "?action=advance&id=" & parts("PartID")
                Response.Write """>"
                Response.Write "Advance part " & parts("PartID")
                Response.Write "</a></td></tr>"

                ' next
                parts.MoveNext

            Loop
            parts.close
            set Parts = nothing

            ' next
            orders.MoveNext
            Response.Write "<tr><td><br></td></tr>"

        Loop
```

2. Then, add this code, which is similar in nature to the code used by the supplier to advance the order:

```
<% ' advance the order on a stage...
Case "advance"

  Set processor = Visit.StartOrderProcessor
  processor.Go request("id")
  Set processor = nothing

  Response.Write "<tr><td class=small>"
  Response.Write "The order has been advanced."
  Response.Write "</td></tr>"
  %>
```

```
<% ' do we want to view the orders?
case "viewneworders" %>
```

Now when Jo clicks the **Advance Order** nnn link, the order processor will be started and asked to process the supplied order number.

Finalizing the Order

The last two stages of the pipeline are nothing special compared to what we've already done; we're going to set up the fifth connector in our pipeline (`PipelineSupplierToShip`) to address order shipping and enhance the `PipelineSupplierOK` object to finish it all off.

Try It Out – Creating PipelineSupplierToShip

1. This can be achieved easily by copying the `PipelineSignalSuppliers` object and renaming it `PipelineSupplierToShip`. Change the text of the e-mail message that gets sent from this object and redo all of the work you did to get the VB project compiled and re-imported into the MTS environment. Don't forget to get the new GUID for the object and update the GUIDs module.

2. Some of the code does need to be adapted; namely the code that adjusts the position in the pipeline (`SetPartStatus`), and the message codes added to the audit trail:

```
' Process - do this connector's work...
Private Function IConnector_Process(ByVal Processor As OrderProcessor, _
                                    ByRef RunNextConnector As Boolean) As Boolean

  On Error GoTo Problem

  ' get hold of the supplier...
  Dim SupplierName As String
  Dim SupplierEMail As String
  Processor.GetSupplierContact SupplierName, SupplierEMail
```

```
If SupplierName <> "" And SupplierEMail <> "" Then

    ' get the email address...
    Processor.SendEMail Me, PSTS_SignalSupplier, _
        "An order is ready to ship!", SupplierName, _
        SupplierEMail, "The order, #" & Processor.PartID & _
        " can now be shipped."

    ' tell the processor to update the status of the part...
    Processor.SetPartStatus 5

    ' tell the processor *not* to move on...
    RunNextConnector = False

    ' indicate success...
    IConnector_Process = True

Else
    Processor.AddAudit Me, PSTS_NoSupplier, False
End If
```

```
' jump over the error handler...
GoTo Finish

Problem:

' flag the error...
Processor.RecordError "Process", Me

Finish:

End Function
```

3. You'll also need to add these message codes to the `MessageCodes` module:

```
' PipelineSupplierToShip codes...
Public Enum PSTSCodes

    ' information codes...
    PSTS_SignalSupplier = 34001

    ' error codes...
    PSTS_NoSupplier = 34101

End Enum
```

4. Then, to integrate the connector into the pipeline, change this code on the Go method of OrderProcessor:

```
' what stage is the part at?
Select Case OrderPart("Status")

    ' start of the order...
    Case 0
    Set Connector = New PipelineNotifyOwner
    Case 1
    Set Connector = New PipelineSignalSuppliers
    Case 2
    Set Connector = New PipelineSupplierOK
    Case 3
    Set Connector = New PipelinePaymentAuth
    Case 4
    Set Connector = New PipelineSupplierToShip
    Case 5
    Set Connector = New PipelineSupplierOK
End Select
```

We use the PipelineSupplierOK object once more to leverage the code we've already written to give the opportunity to indicate when the order has been shipped. All the suppliers have to do is click on the **Yes** link and the order pipeline status will be automatically advanced to 6 – and that's the top of the next section.

Try It Out – Finishing the Order

1. After the supplier has indicated that the order has been completed, the order processor needs to examine all of the parts to the order to determine if it's been completed. If it has, the Status on the master Orders table needs to be set to statusCommited (2). This tells us that nothing else needs to be done with the order.

    When the supplier indicates that the order has been shipped, the Status on the order part will be set to 6 and the Go method will be called again. Add this code to the Go method of OrderProcessor:

```
' do we want to automatically run the next connector?
If RunNextConnector = True And Result = True Then

    ' what's our status? if our status is 6 we've finished...
    If GetPartStatus = 6 Then

    ' check all the parts on the order, make sure they're all six...
    Dim OK As Boolean
    OK = True
    Dim Query As Recordset
    Set Query = DB.RunQuery("OrderParts", , "OrderID=" & GetOrderID)
    Do While Not Query.EOF
```

```
' check the value...
If Query("Status") <> 6 Then
   OK = False
   Exit Do
End If

' next
Query.MoveNext

Loop
Query.Close
Set Query = Nothing

' is everything finished?
If OK = True Then

   ' set the master status...
   SetOrderStatus 2

   ' flag the result...
   Go = True

End If

Else

' call back into us to go again!
Go = Go(PartID)

End If

Else

' store the result against this call...
Go = Result

End If
```

When this connector is finished, the processor will check the part status to determine if it's OK, that is, the connector has finished, and the order has been shipped. The processor then grabs all of the order parts for the order and checks each Status in turn looking for ones that are not finished – ones with a Status column that is not 6. If all of the parts have finished properly, the Status on the master order in the Orders table is set to 2, indicating that the order as a whole has finished.

Canceling an Order

In this chapter, we've worked on the assumption that it is possible to complete the order. In some cases, it might not be possible; for example, a supplier may not be able to get stock for several weeks, in which case the customer will most likely go elsewhere. Alternatively, the customer may not be willing to provide a valid credit card for reauthorization. In these cases, it will be necessarily to cancel the order.

We won't be showing you how to cancel an order in this section, but there are only two things of which you have to be careful. Firstly, if you've authorized the customer's credit card, you have to refund the money. Secondly, if you have taken the choice to integrate the pipeline with your own warehouse, you have to remember to reallocate the stock back into the warehouse.

Finally, in order to set an order as cancelled all that's required is to set the `Status` column in `Orders` table to `statusCancelled`, or 3.

Summary

In this pretty involved chapter we started off by introducing the concept of an order pipeline. An order pipeline is a construct that defines how an order moves through the different parts of the system, from initial creation to final fulfillment. We built a new VB project to encapsulate the components involved in processing the pipeline and imported these components into a new Microsoft Transaction Server package.

We then went through the process of creating connectors for the pipeline capable of signaling Jo when a new order had come in, and asking our supplier whether it was possible to ship the order (thanks to the architecture of the pipeline, it's possible to switch out the connector that signals the supplier for one that connects to a system in a warehouse to check stock levels). We tweaked our administration tools not only to present the orders to us, but also present the relevant parts of the order to our supplier who can, from that point, signal us to indicate whether or not an order can be shipped.

We then discussed how credit card processing works in an online environment, most importantly pointing out the need for a payment gateway, which is responsible for sitting between our bank's computer system and our server, which is generating payment requests. We also talked about how it's necessary to approach our bank for another merchant ID specifically for online retail.

After integrating the pipeline with the DataCash payment gateway, we built connectors that signaled the supplier once more to ask them to ship the goods to our customer and provided a mechanism by which they could indicate to us that the order has been shipped and that we could go ahead and flag the order as completed.

Secure Communications

In e-commerce transactions, you ask your customers to hand over personal, confidential information. Because of this, those customers expect you to take steps to ensure that that information remains confidential, both as it moves over the Internet on its way to you, and when you've actually received the data. This chapter talks about how you can employ the secure communications protocol **Secure Sockets Layer (SSL)** to encrypt the communications between the customer's browser and your e-commerce site.

We are *not* going to be dealing with the thorny problem of securing your server and ensuring that the data you receive (and the content of your web site) is protected from malicious attack. To secure your Web application, careful thought has to be applied to the configuration of the operating system, the Web server software, and the database. Not only do you have to ensure the system is set up correctly to start with but you also need to install upgrades to the software you use as soon as any security holes are found and fixing patches released. Obviously, this is a complex area and when starting your e-commerce site it's best to take professional advice (maybe from your chosen ISP) on how to approach server security. More details can be found in *Professional ASP Techniques for Webmasters, ISBN 1861001797* also by *Wrox Press.*

> The topics and examples discussed in the book should be considered as recommendations and guidelines and should only be implemented as part of a properly investigated security policy. It's beyond the scope of this book to detail such a policy, although the techniques here have a role to play in a properly designed system. Having a properly secured infrastructure is paramount to the professional behavior and appearance of any e-business, so make sure you understand all of the issues involved and consider seeking professional advice.

After all that, what is the scope of this chapter? Well we hope to give you a bit of background on the technology which enables data to be transferred securely over the Internet specifically we're going to discuss:

- ❑ **Cryptography** and **encryption**
- ❑ The use of **certificates**
- ❑ How to obtain a certificate
- ❑ Adapting `checkout.asp` to make it secure

To run through some of the practical work contained in the chapter you're going to need access to a computer running Windows NT Server with IIS installed. Don't worry if you haven't; this chapter will give you a good overview of this technology area anyway and if you're deploying a solution up to an ISP you'll want to know about certificates when you discuss the type of hosting support they offer (ISP hosting is covered in Chapter 12).

Cryptography

Cryptography is the process of encoding any kind of information in such a way that persons it was not intended for cannot easily understand it.

Imagine I want to send the word *hello* to a friend via a postcard and snail-mail. I might choose to write *hello* by encrypting it as *ifmmp*. Under this scheme I shift each letter forward by one, so *h* becomes *i*, *e* becomes *f*, and so on. At this point, only the people who know the encryption scheme I'm using (or guess it) can decrypt my message because they know that they are supposed to rotate each letter back by one. Therefore, even though my message has been transmitted through a fundamentally insecure medium, anyone who handles the information as it passes down to its final destination won't necessarily be able to understand it.

The use of a postcard in this example is deliberate. In most scenarios, the Internet is about as secure as a postcard. Each packet that is sent from your computer to the server you're connected to, and vice versa, can be considered to be a postcard that can be read by anyone in-between. Each postcard is chock full of information. This information could be a sensitive e-mail to a competing company asking for a job, your complete DNA fingerprint, sensitive medical information, or credit card details. On its way from your computer to the server, that postcard is likely to move through any number of points (typically around eight or 10 individual points) including routers, firewalls, etc. in your own company, and hardware at your ISP and in the Internet's main communications providers.

Realistically, in order for your confidentiality to be compromised as it passes around the Internet someone has to be deliberately looking for it – there's simply too much for someone to watch every single packet! Your employer might not trust you not to use company resources for browsing job sites, and someone at your ISP may be deliberately examining each packet on their network looking for credit card information using a so-called sniffer program. Unluckily for you, low-cost technology exists today that can present your credit card number, or potential employment locations to these people as plain as the text on this page.

So the trick then is to encrypt the data as it passes around, so instead of seeing a Visa number of *4111 1111 1111 1111* they see *4587 3457 1474 4293*. In fact, most encryption software will go further than that by scrambling every character, including spacers; it will use the entire ASCII character set and typically the string will contain more characters. Quality encryption systems are likely to produce something more like *jkh(*&#\$OSLHY&*(*&9][3844GV*%(*.

Breaking Encryption

Encryption methodology has been used for hundreds of years, so it's not something that's just come along.

The challenge that we face today is that, as computers get more powerful, breaking encryption becomes easier. Take our simple encryption example above – if you have an idea that all that's happened is the letters in the alphabet have been jumbled about somehow, all you have to do is try every single possible permutation until you get something you understand, known as the **brute-force method**. If you had to do that by hand, it might take a while, but doing it with an average PC would take less than a second. Therefore, we need to think about using a scheme sufficiently complex that breaking it using a brute-force method like that will take several years to do.

It is possible, today, to encrypt our sensitive data to a level where it cannot easily be broken, and therefore understood, as it moves around the Internet. The technology used to secure Web servers uses an encryption technique called **Public Key Cryptography**, or **PKC**.

How Public Key Cryptography Works

Without getting deep into the scientific mechanics of how PKC does its stuff, broadly you take two huge prime numbers (and by huge we mean numbers of the magnitude 1,000,000,000,000,000) and multiply them together to get an absolutely enormous number. You then take that enormous number and perform some mathematical operation on the message to get an encrypted message. To decrypt the message, simply perform the mathematical reverse of the encryption operation on the encrypted message. If you're wondering why math applies to text-based messages, don't forget that computers consider letters of the alphabet, and any special character such as punctuation, as numbers. So, the letter A is considered by a computer to be the number 65, and so on.

The general premise behind this is that, if the number used for the actual operation is sufficiently large (30 or so digits), it would take an astonishingly long time to brute-force every possible permutation to decrypt the message.

Now we're faced with the issue that someone in the world is the intended audience for our message. However, how do we tell our friend Ollie what the decryption **key** for the message is, without letting anyone else intercept the key as it moves over to him? Also, what happens if someone can get hold of that key and use it to encrypt messages that will then appear to come from us? We could be framed for anything!

The solution is in the fact that we take two numbers and generate the big number from it. We say that one of those numbers is private, and never leaves my computer – that's the **private key**. We then make the other one generally available so anyone can get hold of it, and we call this one the **public key**. Together, both keys are referred to as a **private/public key pair**, or simply **key pair**.

> You can find my public key by searching for **matthew@bitsonthewire.com** at **ldap://certserver.pgp.com/**.

At this point, I need to reiterate that I won't be going into the mathematical stuff that drives all of this. If I did, this book would be twice as long just from that discussion! What I hope to do is tell you enough about it that you get a grip of what's going on.

Let's get back to how I would send Ollie a message. Basically, in order to do that, I need to get hold of his public key and use it in combination with my private key to encrypt the message. Once that's done, I transmit it to him by saving it on a floppy disk and driving round to his house. If I get car-jacked on the way, the thieves won't be able to read the message because they need Ollie's private key to decrypt it. If my car and myself successfully get to his house, he uses his private key and my public key to decrypt the message.

Here's a diagram that clarifies what's going on:

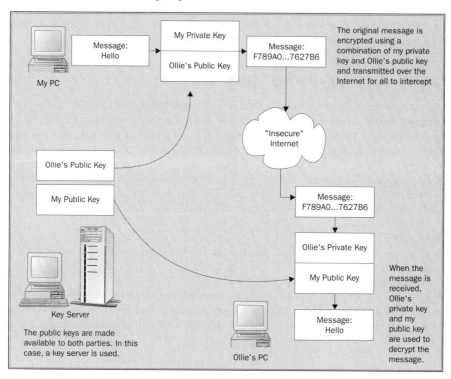

Let's just tidy up some terminology at this point – our original encryption example (shifting the letters around) can be termed **symmetric encryption** as both the sender and the receiver know the key to encrypting and decrypting the information. In contrast the public/private key method is termed **asymmetric encryption** since the same key cannot be used for encryption and decryption.

What's all this got to do with E-commerce?

Now that we have an understanding of how Public Key Cryptography works, we need to talk about why it's an appropriate technology to use for securing Web servers.

In a secure Web server scenario, we simply replace one of the PCs with a Web server. The Web server (or rather the company that maintains the Web server) has a private key for itself and shares a public key with the world. Although it's not apparent, when you're communicating with a secure Web server, you are using a key pair during the interaction (although it's a little more complex than the situation we outlined above).

Connections established with a secure Web server can be identified by the https in the URL string, as opposed to just http. (The s stands for secure.) In Internet Information Server, https connections are established through a standard called **Secure Sockets Layer 3.0** (or **SSL 3.0**). When you use such connections a little yellow padlock icon will appear on the browser status bar.

Without going into too much detail about the SSL workings, when you connect to a secure Web server, the server will send a **certificate** to you (more about this soon). A public key can be extracted from this certificate and this public key can be used as part of the encryption process which allows you to communicate sensitive information (like your credit card number) to the server.

The Need for Certificates

In environments where a degree of trust exists between the two parties, this approach works quite well. For example, if I want Ollie to have confidence that the message was from me, all I have to do is phone him up and tell him that, yes, that public key is mine and he can be sure that anything that can be decrypted by him using that public key was indeed from me.

However, there's an added degree of complexity when dealing with people you don't know. For example, when I click the buy button on Amazon.com, how do I know that the server I'm going to is really controlled by Amazon.com and not someone electronically impersonating them? Alternatively, if it's a company I'm not familiar with, how do I know that there's a real company behind it?

The way this problem is solved is by using **server certificates**. A certificate is a bit of data that your Web browser can use to determine the identity of the server that is handling your secure HTTP request. However, just having a certificate that says, 'yes, I'm an Amazon.com server' doesn't do much for your confidence, unless you're sure you can trust the information presented by the certificate.

Certificate Authorities

Note that although anyone can create and issue certificates, there are a few trusted third parties (termed **Certificate Authorities – CAs**) who are generally recognized within the Internet community to provide a reliable confirmation that a public key is being issued by the person whose name is on the certificate. Examples of Certificate Authorities are:

- ❑ VeriSign (www.verisign.com) – or in their UK partner in this area, BT Trustwise (www.trustwise.com)
- ❑ Belsign (www.belsign.be)
- ❑ Xcert Software (www.xcert.com)

As part of the yearly fee that these companies charge to issue a certificate, they perform a check to ensure the business that the certificate is for is a legitimate one (what type of procedures they go through to achieve this will probably be described in the **Certification Practices Statement – CPS** – which may be found on the Web site of the CA).

So, if you visit the secure checkout section of Amazon.com and look up their certificate, you'll notice that their certificate was issued by a company named VeriSign and by implication, you know that VeriSign has done a check on your behalf to ensure that the Amazon.com server is owned by a legitimate business.

Although we've mentioned three CAs here, there are an ever-growing number of these organizations and thus choosing a CA to **enroll** with takes some careful consideration.

In summary a certificate from a recognized Certificate Authority:

❑ Lets the visitor to the site ensure that the information capture pages secured by the certificate do indeed belong to the site to which he/she thinks it belongs.

❑ Provides an encryption key that is used by the server and browser together to create an extremely secure conduit through which encrypted versions of the HTTP traffic move.

Additionally, although we aren't going to mention it further, the SSL protocol addresses a third important area of security – it detects if the data being transmitted has been messed with during its journey over the Internet.

We'll cover the mechanics of how to obtain a certificate in the next section.

Obtaining a Certificate

In this chapter, to show you more about certificates, we'll be taking you through the process of obtaining a certificate and installing it on the server so that we can practice using secure servers.

> **This form of server security is *not* available on Personal Web Server, so if you're using this to develop on you'll have to hunt down a computer running Windows NT Server with IIS installed and perform these exercises there.**

Remember to respect the critical nature of most servers and, if you're not responsible for the servers in your organization or department, remember to check with the person who is! If you haven't got access to a server don't worry – we've made the discussion easy to follow.

Incidentally, if you are looking to deploy your solution up to an ISP, it's worth checking with them how they handle certificates before you go out and get one yourself.

In this book, we'll be looking at obtaining a certificate from VeriSign.

This book is focused towards developing an actual e-commerce solution, and as such on occasion we need to use a specific vendor as an example of how to make something happen. In this section, we're using VeriSign to obtain a secure server certificate. This is not an endorsement of their products or services and Wrox Press has not received payment of any kind for featuring them. You should shop around and investigate the offerings of all the different vendors before committing to a specific Certificate Authority.

Test Certificates

VeriSign actually offers a way of obtaining a test certificate so that you can familiarize yourself with how this whole aspect of server security works without having to spend a bean. However, you can't use that certificate in a production environment.

Before we can obtain the test certificate we need to create a test key.

> Note: if when working through this example you choose to get your own key to test, don't use `joscoffee.com` as the site you submit through to VeriSign. Use your own site, or just invent one for the purposes of the exercise!

Try It Out – Creating a Test Key

1. To create a test key, the first step is to ask IIS to generate a **Key Request** for you. You then pass this over to the Certificate Authority who uses it to generate your actual certificate. To do this, open the IIS Management Console and click on the **Key Manager** button on the toolbar:

2. When the **Key Manager** has loaded, select the **WWW** node, then **Key | Create New Key** from the menu. The first thing you'll be asked for is a filename in which to store the request:

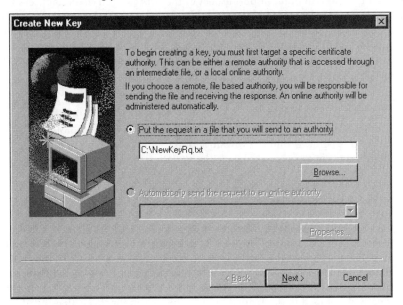

3. Later on, when we connect to VeriSign, we'll copy and paste the contents of that file onto a form on VeriSign's site. For now, click **Next** to save the file in the default location.

421

4. The next step is to supply the name, password, and key length for the keys. The name is just an arbitrary name that you choose to assign. The password is important, as you'll need to use it later on when you install the key.

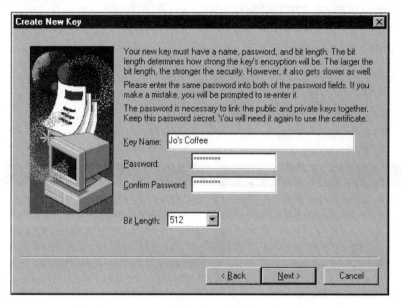

The Bit **L**ength is another import aspect of the process. International users will have only one option here: 512. Domestic US users will have the option of using 1024-bit length encryption. The larger this number, the slower, but more secure, encryption and decryption will be. The reason for the difference between the US and the rest of the world is that, at the time of press, the US government sometimes controls the possible security levels available for encryption systems.

Indeed, due to the internal workings of the SSL the actual level of encryption you can use for the SSL *communication* between a site visitor and your server will be, at best, 128-bit encryption if you're in the US or Canada, or 40-bit if you're in another part of the world. Just to clarify this point; within the workings of SSL different levels of encryption are used at different points in the process, hence the variation in numbers between the communication set-up encryption (selected above) and the actual communication itself. This variation in encryption levels is the reason why some US banking institutions, like Bank One (http://www.bankone.com/), cannot be accessed from outside of the United States.

Again this is the situation at the time of press and is likely to change, since there is a lot of movement in the US towards lifting export controls of strong encryption products. A lot of this has been driven by the fact that there are a number of ways around these laws. The most commonly available public key cryptography program, **Pretty Good Privacy** (**PGP**), is available worldwide (although it's not used for Web server security), even though it was originally developed in the United States. The reason for this is that the algorithms used in the program were published in a book, sent overseas and other developers built a complementary product, which was totally compatible with the formats defined in the US product. This means that, for PGP at least, all international users are able to enjoy strong encryption security.

You can download PGP International at http://www.pgpi.com/.

After filling out the name, password and bit length, click <u>N</u>ext.

5. The next thing we have to do is tell the Wizard the name of the site we're trying to secure:

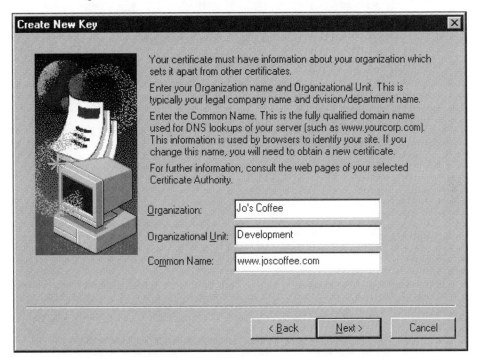

It's obviously important that you get this right, but if you typically access the site through http://joscoffee.com and enter the common name as joscoffee.com and then try to browse to the secure site at https://www.joscoffee.com/, the browser will throw an error claiming the certificate does not match the site. So, if you rig the checkout.asp page to https://www.joscoffee.com/, make sure you enter the common name as www.joscoffee.com (later in this chapter, we'll be altering checkout.asp to make it connect to the secure server).

6. Click <u>N</u>ext when you've specified the common name for the site.

7. The next thing to do is specify where the business that owns the certificate is located. This is a fairly simple form, but note that everything appears to be in the wrong order:

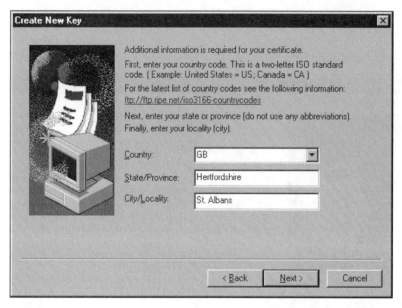

Click <u>N</u>ext once you've completed the dialog.

8. The penultimate part of the process is to put your own personal details into the certificate. People will attempt to contact this person if they have questions about the certificate, or site security, so make sure it's accurate:

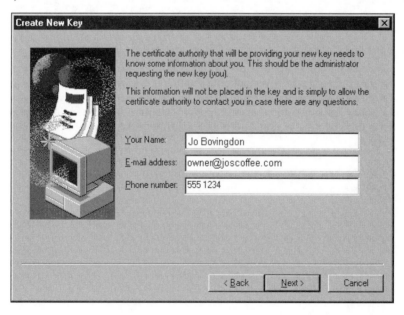

9. Click <u>N</u>ext and you'll see a final page explaining what the next steps are. As we're covering the next steps here, just click Finish. Another confirmation window will appear – click OK to dismiss it.

10. When you've finished, this is what the Key Manager will look like this:

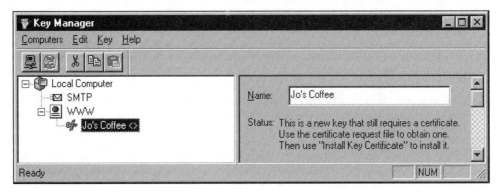

The strike through the key icon next to Jo's Coffee indicates that the key has not been certificated yet and so cannot be used.

Obtaining a Test Certificate

Now that our Key Request file has been created, we can visit VeriSign and ask them to create a new key for us. We won't be showing you the Web pages from the VeriSign site throughout this process as, despite being somewhat long, they're quite straightforward to complete. The test certificate procedure is liable to change with time, but the steps we outline below over the next couple of sections will provide effective guidelines.

Try It Out – Obtaining a Test Certificate from VeriSign

1. VeriSign occasionally moves the signup page for trial certificates, so the best place to find it is to visit the site as http://www.verisign.com/ and find a link saying something along the lines of Trial, Free Trial Web Server ID or Create a Test ID. It'll ask you for some basic marketing information before you move on to getting the actual key.

> Although the process we're about to go through is for a test ID, when you come to obtain a full ID you can use in production environments, the process is extremely similar.

2. After a quick check that you have installed the necessary Web server software, are able to make a secure connection outside any firewall, and that you have read the license agreement, you are requested to submit a **CSR** (**Certificate Signing Request**). A CSR is another name for that which we created earlier from the Key Manager; the terms CSR, key request, and certificate request are all interchangeable.

3. What VeriSign wants us to do at this point is to send it the CSR that we created earlier. To do this, you just have to find the file we previously specified (by default, this is `c:\NewKeyRq.txt`), open it, and paste the contents into the form. Then click on Continue to proceed.

If in your request you asked for a 512-bit length key, the VeriSign Web site at this point will warn you that it's not such a good idea. This is true if you're in the US, where you should ask for a 1024-bit length key, but if you are outside the US, press Continue to ignore the message.

4. VeriSign will then ask you to identify yourself and your company. Fill out the form as usual and click Accept.

5. What you do next, is wait for VeriSign to e-mail your new certificate to you. This e-mail contains instructions on how to install both the test server ID and the test CA root (which we discuss below).

The certificate you are issued with is a legitimate, usable server certificate. The question is what prevents you from using that test certificate in a production environment? Well, for one thing, the certificate is only valid for 14 days, but you could just remember to renew every two weeks. The other reason is the existence of **Certificate Authority Roots**.

Certificate Authority Roots

Not only is it necessary to prove to visitors to a site that the site is what it says it is, but it's also necessary to prove the authenticity of the organization that produced that certificate (in fact, the specifications for the certificates are readily available, so there's no reason why people can't even make their own). To handle this eventuality, there is the concept of **Certificate Authority Roots** or **CAR**.

Each certificate that is created for general consumption has to be linked to another certificate called a CAR. People who care can then view the root authority of the certificate they are examining to make sure that it's legitimate. In fact many browsers come with CA root certificates from some of the more widely used CAs already installed.

You can see the certificates that are installed on your computer by selecting Tools | Internet Options...from the menu of Internet Explorer, switching to the Content tab and clicking Certificates. Change to the Trusted Root Certification Authorities to see the roots. By default, Microsoft installs some VeriSign certificates along with a few others from other companies together with the cryptographic components of Windows and Internet Explorer. The reason why different authorities appear to have a number of different roots is that they create a number of roots for different tasks. For example VeriSign might create a root for secure server certificates, another for software publishers using AuthentiCode (a technology for signing software to identify the producer of the software), and so on.

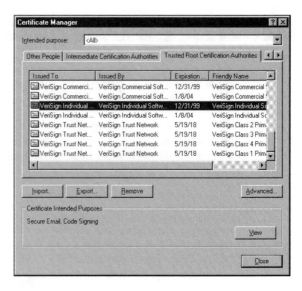

To get around the problem of test certificates being used in production environments, VeriSign effectively limits the number of machines that the test certificates can be installed on, and then indicates that they are just to be used in development environments. Additionally, Web users would not normally have CA Test certificate roots installed on their browser as being trusted.

Now we'll install the test root certificate on our server.

Try It Out – Installing the Test Certificate Authority Root

1. Follow the link, provided in the VeriSign e-mail and work through the instructions – you will quickly reach a dialog similar to that shown:

2. To install the certificate, click the Install Certificate…button. This will display a short Wizard which you can just click through using the default options.

3. After that is done, revisit the Certificate Manager dialog in Internet Explorer through the Tools | Internet Options menu option, and you'll see the root certificate now appears in the Trusted Root Certification Authorities tab. When our Web server pushes our server certificate down to the browser (after we've installed it, obviously), it will attempt to match this certificate up with the test root we just installed. If the test root is not there, the certificate will not work – thereby proving that VeriSign's method for limiting use of the certificates to development environments works, as only development boxes will have this root installed!

Try It Out – Installing the New Certificate

1. The test certificate appears as a block of data appended to the bottom of the e-mail and looks something like this:

```
-----BEGIN CERTIFICATE-----
EIDCWjACRdDCECBeEKHnAEN9C1zUtCBHeA4LDEYXKoDIRvENWQEEBQAwGaIxFjJU
OgEVYAoTDVZDcAlRaRdELNBJbmCxLzAFRgKVEAsTPnO3LyL2IXEpc2CnOiRjN2Ev
SmVwb3NdT9EeV9EZXNWQYBNIK1OYO9PcC4gQnRgImCmKiBMaWFELBBSVTQEMRYw
RAYDVQQLEz1Gb3IgVmVyaVNpZ24gYXV0aG9yaXplZCZ0ZXN0aW5nIG9ubHkuIE5v
IGFzc3VyYW5jZXMgKEMpVlMxOTk3MB4XDTk5MTAxOTAwMDAwMFoXDTk5MTEwMjIz
NTk1OVowgYIxCzAJBgNVBAYTAkdCMRYwFAYDVQQIEw1IZXJ0Zm9yZHNoaXJlMRMw
EQYDVQQHFApTdC4gQWxiYW5zMRQwEgYDVQQKFAtKbydzIENvZmZlZTEUMBIGA1UE
CxQLRGV2ZWxvcG1lbnQxGjAYBgNVBAMUEXd3dy5qb3Njb2ZmZWUuY29tMFwwDQYJ
KoZIhvcNAQEBBQADSwAwSAJBALpiXjZaGhxF0ykiFZuGek5U8vhz/Kg5aTT5BdUp
fy20ObyZSXPjmLpGo2FhoNMfRZSPxQ4xtmxIxBBQYcRnXUECAwEAATANBgkqhkiG
9w0BAQQFAANBABgYHh3dhduwW39X9OUp1RH4GAtMyzHtadZ4B9GbdqmavWU/N8k0
96omKVeU2XBGu3C+01KuVNjaSAslf4ebfW0=
-----END CERTIFICATE-----
```

2. In order to install the key, you need to create a new text file (using Notepad, or some similar tool) and copy that block of text into it.

3. Then, using the Key Manager, highlight the Jo's Coffee key and select Key | Install Key Certificate...from the menu. Navigate to the file that you created a moment ago and open it. When prompted, enter the password you originally entered when you created the key request.

4. Key Manager will then prompt to ask you the addresses and ports on the server to which you want to bind the certificate. You should make sure the certificate is bound to whatever IP address your Web server actually uses (if you're working locally, remember `localhost` has the address 127.0.0.1). By default, SSL will use port 443. This screenshot illustrates what the binding dialog might look like:

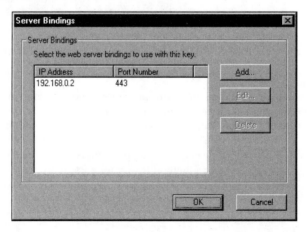

5. Once you press OK, you need to select Computers | Commit Changes Now from the menu to tell IIS about the new certificate and bindings.

Using the New Certificate

Luckily for us, IIS actually makes it remarkably easy to create a Web site that is secure to communicate with. In fact, we already achieved that by virtue of the fact that we've installed the certificate! Remember, a certificate like the one we're using here is intended to make the site visitor confident that the site does belong to the organization that he or she thinks it does.

The certificate performs no authentication of the user to ensure they should be using the site. If you need this kind of authentication, you'll have to either use the built-in NT security, or implement your own scheme.

To clarify, if your **Default Web Site** entry in the IIS metabase uses `c:\InetPub\wwwroot` as its root folder for the non-secure version, if you then connect to the same server through SSL, IIS will still continue to use `c:\InetPub\wwwroot` as its source of files, but this time it will encrypt each file as its sent down to the client. What this means is that when our **Proceed to Checkout** button is clicked, we just have to enter the `ACTION` element of the `FORM` tag as `https://www.joscoffee.com/` and we've finished. We don't have to build another folder on the site or configure another site to point at it to have a secure connection. So, if you request http://www.joscoffee.com/checkout.asp or https://www.joscoffee.com/checkout.asp, ASP will try to execute the same script at `c:\InetPub\wwwroot\checkout.asp` and you'll get the same results – only the latter will be encrypted on its way down to the browser.

You can test to see if the new certificate works by trying to make it throw an error.

Try It Out – Testing out the New Certificate

1. When we created the certificate request, we told the Key Manager that the **Friendly Name** for our site was www.joscoffee.com. We then bound that address to the IP 192.168.0.2. However, if we try to navigate directly to the IP address, IE will detect that the name in the **Address** bar of the browser doesn't match the certificate the server issues and will throw an error, like this one:

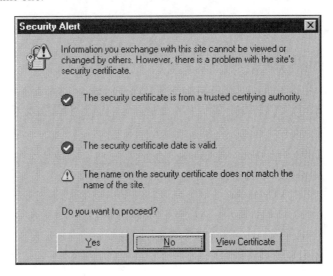

429

2. If you click the <u>V</u>iew Certificate button, you can zoom into the certificate to see exactly what's going on. Once there, you can confirm that the certificate is indeed for the site you requested. Make sure you click through to the Certification Path tab and examine the fact that our certificate is within the VeriSign test key that we installed earlier.

3. Close the certificate and click <u>Y</u>es to view the page. Notice how the little padlock icon appears on the status bar indicating that you're viewing the page over a secure connection.

As a general note, IE will assume that, when you're viewing pages over a secure connection, everything that's used on that page should come from the *same* secure source. Usually, the only thing affected by this caveat is images that come from other servers, such as banner ads. It's a good idea to use some ASP code to remove banner ads, or other external resources, if the page is being called over a secure link. A neat way of doing this is to use the `Request.ServerVariables` collection in ASP, like this:

```
If Request.ServerVariables("https") = "on" Then
   Response.Write "This is a secure connection!"
Else
   Response.Write "This is *not* a secure connection."
   Response.Write "<img src=""http://banners.company.com/banner.gif"">"
End If
```

There are a few server variables you can use pertaining to secure servers. Here they are:

`HTTPS`	Determine if it is a secure connection. Returns on if it is, off if it isn't.
`HTTPS_KEYSIZE`	Number of bits in the Secure Socket Layer connection key size. For example, 40.
`HTTPS_SECRETKEYSIZE`	Number of bits in the server certificate. For example, 512.
`HTTPS_SERVER_ISSUER`	A string representing the organization that issued the certificate.
`HTTPS_SERVER_SUBJECT`	A string representing the subject field in the certificate.

Obtaining a Full ID

Thanks to the way VeriSign has structured its trial ID program, you've already learned enough to install a full, production use, ID on your server. To do this, you'll need to give VeriSign a few hundred bucks and prove your identity and your company's legal status to it. Full details can be found on its site.

> Remember, you don't *have* to use VeriSign for your secure ID's. Shop around to make sure you're getting the best deal.

Making checkout.asp Secure

In fact, the only really tricky thing about secure connections is that fact that http://www.joscoffee.com and https://www.joscoffee.com are not considered by IIS/ASP to be the same site. What this means is that any session variables you create on the non-secure site will be lost as you move over to the secure one. The easiest way to get around the problem is to pass the relevant session variables through in the query string or the form variables when you make the request for the secure page. However, this extra work can be a bit of a nightmare if you have structured your session variables in a particularly tricky manner. Luckily for us, we haven't.

In fact, the only thing we have to do to move the customer's context over to the secure server is to pass the ID of the basket. Usually, when passing IDs like this around, they are passed through form variables, as that way they don't appear in the browser's address bar and are therefore a little trickier to forge. This is why you typically see Proceed to checkout buttons, rather than links.

Try It Out – Adding a Proceed to Checkout Button to basket.asp

1. Here's the code to change in `basket.asp` that adds a button to visit the secure `checkout.asp`:

```
' add the total...
Response.Write "<tr><td><br></td></tr>"
Response.Write "<tr bgcolor=#c0c0c0>"
Response.Write "<td colspan=4 align=right class=heading>"
Response.Write "Total:"
Response.Write "</td><td align=right class=heading>"
Response.Write FormatPrice(total)
Response.Write "</td></tr>"
```

```
' go to the checkout...
Response.Write "<tr><td><br></td></tr>"

' add a form first...
Response.Write "<form action= 'https://localhost/jocoffee_local/checkout.asp'
method=post>"
Response.write "<tr><td colspan=5 align=center>"
Response.write "<input type=submit value=""Proceed to Checkout"">"
Response.write "</td></tr>"
Response.write "<tr><td><br></td></tr>"

' add the basket id to a HIDDEN field on the form...
Response.write "<input type=hidden name=basketid value="
Response.Write Visit.Basket.ID
Response.Write ">"

' End the form
Response.write "</form>"

' If the customer can't use the secure link doesn't work,
' provide an insecure method...
Response.Write "<tr><td colspan=5 align=center class=heading>"
Response.Write "<a href=""checkout.asp"">"
Response.Write "If you are having problems with the secure server...</a>"
Response.Write "</td></tr>"
```

How It Works

Note that on the ACTION attribute of the FORM, we specify the URL to go to in full. This is because if we used the server variables to detect the name of our server, we might come back with joscoffee.com, which would not match the name on the certificate. To ensure the name always matches, we must specify the name in full.

> **Don't forget that the certificate you obtained for testing will not be for www.joscoffee.com – remember to replace the ACTION attribute with whatever server suits you.**

The original development of this project did not take place on a box called www.joscoffee.com so the FORM's ACTION attribute was changed to the path on localhost that pointed to checkout.asp. In the development version, when Proceed to Checkout was clicked an error was obtained saying the server did not match the certificate name, and the developer then simply confirmed that it was OK. You'll have to play around with the code on the form to make it work for you. Basically, though, whatever machine you're running the site on should have the certificate installed and the ACTION for the FORM should point to the exact same checkout.asp file you built in Chapter 8, only this time the URL should start https://.

Something you may also want to think about is offering a way of getting to any checkout page without *having* to use the secure connection. Some companies, or even ISPs, configure their proxy servers so that secure connections cannot be made. Therefore, if you set up your servers so only secure connections are allowed, you could potentially stop customers from getting to your store.

Using the Basket over the Secure Connection

Here's a screenshot of the authors checkout.asp page as viewed over the secure link. Here IE was told to ignore the warning that the name on the certificate (www.joscoffee.com) did not match localhost:

> **There is a rather frustrating bug in IE that when the warning is displayed, the FORM variables are lost when you OK the warning. For this reason, you need to click the Back button and then click the Proceed to Checkout button again. IE won't prompt you with the warning second time around and, more importantly, the FORM variables are passed through so checkout.asp will work as desired.**

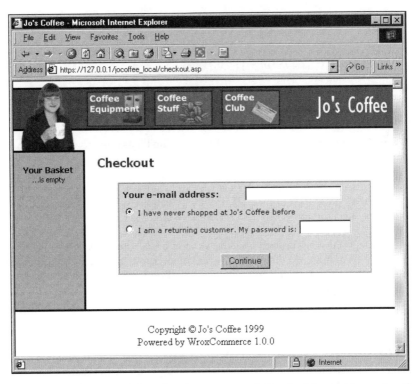

Notice on the screenshot that the address for the page is an https:// address. Also notice the little padlock on the status bar indicating the connection is a secure one. However, the most important thing to notice here is that we did literally *nothing* to the code to start transmitting pages securely! IIS makes this very easy.

However, you'll also notice that the basket is empty. This is because of the problem we stated earlier – https://localhost/ and http://localhost/ are considered by IE to be two different sites. ASP's Session mechanism maintains **state** (values and variables) through cookies, and a cookie can only be associated with a single site. For this reason, when the cookies for https://localhost/ are examined to determine the internal session ID that ASP is looking for, ASP discovers there is no ID and creates a separate session.

Try It Out – Setting the BasketID when Moving to a Secure Server

1. First off, we have to return to the WroxCommerce project and create a method on the Visit object that can set the basket ID. We'll look up the basket ID from the FORM variables that were passed through to the page:

```
' SetBasket - sets the basket ID when moved to a secure server...
Public Function SetBasket(ByVal BasketID As Long)

    ' set the ID, and then set the session...
    m_BasketID = BasketID
    m_Session("BasketID") = m_BasketID

End Function
```

2. Now, at the top of `checkout.asp`, add this code:

```
    ' did we get given a basketid?
   If Request.Form("BasketID") <> "" Then
      Visit.SetBasket Request("BasketID")
 End If
```

How It Works

Now when you click the **Proceed to Checkout** button, you'll continue to use the same basket you did in the not-secure connection.

As a side note to this, the navigation and **View Cart** links now take you to secure versions of the pages. On secure pages, it's a good idea to turn off all the navigation and marketing links, and don't forget that you can do this by checking for the `HTTPS` server variable.

Incidentally, although moving through a secure version of the site works just fine, it's a good idea to try to dissuade people from doing it; the actual process of encrypting the pages and the extra negotiation required to establish a secure connection puts extra load on the server and creates an experience for the user that's much less responsive than its not-secure counterpart.

Summary

In this chapter, we've given you a bit of a taster for the topic of secure Web connections. This quick overview of cryptography, encryption in the computing world using keys, the Secure Sockets Layer protocol, Certificates, and Certificate Authorities will hopefully have given you some feeling for the issues that need to be addressed to ensure customer confidence in communicating with your site.

We haven't explored the topic of controlling access to your Web site, or of securing the data contained within your site, and strongly advise you take professional advice on how to implement operating system, Web server, Web page and database security to maintain a fully secure site.

Building on the theoretical discussion of secure communications, we looked at obtaining and installing a test certificate from VeriSign. Subsequently, we used this in developing a secure checkout option. This involved:

❑   Adding code to our `basket.asp` page to direct us to the secure checkout

❑   Altering the `WroxCommerce.Visit` object and `checkout.asp` page to allow basket information to be transferred to the secure connection

Searching

Letting visitors easily find products in your store is paramount to providing a smooth and enjoyable shopping experience. As we mentioned in previous chapters, visitors will come to your site with a clear idea of what they want. It's a common misconception that they come to browse, which is why the e-mall paradigm has never really taken off, and this is why it's extremely important to make it as easy as possible for customers to determine if you can sell them what they want as smoothly as possible.

In this chapter, we'll see how we can add simple search functionality to the site to complement the existing navigation for moving around the store's departments. Specifically, we'll look at:

❑ Choosing which fields to search on

❑ Removing unnecessary words, such as "the", "and", and "a"

❑ Using quotes and Boolean operators (specifically OR and AND) to define the search

❑ Using SQL Server's Full-Text Searching tool

❑ Implementing a Search tool in joscoffee.com

Building the Search Object to Create a Search

We're going to add a Search object to the WroxCommerce object model that we can use to provide the customer with search functionality. The Search object is really very simple; along with the usual Configure method, there is just one function of this object, also called Search.

Try It Out – Creating a Search Object

1. We can start moving on this fairly quickly by creating a new class module in Visual Basic and calling it `Search`. Add this code to the new `Search` module:

```
Option Explicit

' use IUtility to call back into the Visit and Database objects...
Private m_utility As IUtility


' Configure - set up IUtility...
Public Sub Configure(ByVal utility As IUtility)

    ' Hold the utility object...
    Set m_utility = utility

End Sub
```

2. As we did before with, among others, the `Customers` and `Orders` objects, we need to provide a way to access this object through the `Visit` object. First of all, add this member variable to the `Visit` object:

```
' these variables hold the objects that are in the next hierarchical
' level in our object model...
Private m_catalog As Catalog
Private m_customers As Customers
Private m_orders As Orders
Private m_search As Search
```

3. Secondly, add the `Search` property to the `Visit` object:

```
' Search - returns an instance of a Search object...
Public Property Get Search() As Search

    ' Do we have one already?
    If m_search Is Nothing Then

        ' Create and configure
        Set m_search = New Search
        m_search.Configure Me

    End If

    ' Return the Search object...
    Set Search = m_search

End Property
```

4. Finally, add this line to the `Shutdown` method of the `Visit` object:

```
Set m_catalog = Nothing
Set m_Session = Nothing
Set m_customers = Nothing
Set m_orders = Nothing
Set m_search = Nothing
```

Choosing the Fields to Search

Now that we've built the Search object, we need to add methods and properties to it so that the caller can make it find things in the database as the users request. The next step is to decide what parts of the database we want to search.

It's quite common for a site to offer both a **quick search** and an **advanced search**. In my opinion, this split is indicative of the kinds of relics we see as the Web matures. Typically, the quick search is presented as a simple text box as part of the navigation of each page. Visitors naturally gravitate towards this for their searching and if the quick search does not cover an adequate number of database fields, they may simply click out and go elsewhere. A good example of this one is bookstore sites that do not include the ISBN number as part of the quick search. Visitors cannot be relied upon to hunt around looking for an advanced search.

The best way around this for modern sites is to scrap the advanced search option and do one, decent quick search. That's what we'll be doing here, so we need to decide the best spread of database columns to search.

However, there are two major issues with this approach:

❏   Firstly, the more fields you search, the more horsepower the database will require to find the results you're looking for, and so if you have a *considerable* number of products in your database, you may want to make the search quite restrictive in terms of the fields that are searched.

❏   Secondly, the less refined the search, the more results you'll find. Therefore, if you're looking for a book called "The Behan Effect" by using the keyword "Behan" on a typical book site, you'll also find anything written by anyone called "Behan".

Luckily for us, both those issues are only really felt in large e-commerce sites. Jo's Coffee is quite a small site, so we should be able to get away with providing a single search box.

Intuitively, we can guess that we'll definitely need to search these fields from the vProducts view:

❏   Product name – Name

❏   Short product details – Details

❏   Longer product description – Description

Optionally, we could also search on the department name, meaning that searching for the word "Pump" will find anything in the "Espresso Machines: Pump" department. However, this is likely to create a lot of results if someone looks for "Coffee", so we'll give this one a miss.

We are, however, storing a ton of extra data about products in the dynamic attribute structure we built back in Chapter 6 and we should really provide a way of searching this too, as it's likely this will contain some useful information. Searching for the word "solenoid" across the dynamic attributes will yield all products that feature the word "solenoid" – in our case, this is most likely to be espresso machines featuring solenoid valves.

Putting Keywords into an Array

When the visitor enters a search query, he or she is likely to specify a number of words, rather than just specifying a single word to match. In addition, it's quite likely that the search query will contain superfluous information, like extra spaces, illegal characters, etc.

Another thing to consider when running searches is the possibility of **noise words**. Noise words are simply words that don't usually do much to narrow down search results, like "the", "and", "a", "with", "this", etc. When we do our search, we want to filter out all of the noise words to try to get a better match.

The final decision to make is whether you default to an OR query, or to an AND query. To clarify, if someone on your site searches for Gaggia Carezza, do you look for products that match Gaggia *or* Carezza, or Gaggia *and* Carezza? Most Web site search engines, like Yahoo or Excite, will do an OR match and only perform an AND match when quotes are used. Therefore, if you type "Gaggia Carezza", they'll go away and find everything containing Gaggia *and* Carezza. In our search "engine", we can't rely on the visitor entering the quotes so, by default we're going to treat multiple words as if they are AND-ed together.

The trick, then, is to build a method in the `Search` object that can take the search string that the visitor gives us, and strip out all of the white space and non-alphanumeric characters. The method should then make up an array containing all of the words we want to look for, and remove the noise words until we finally end up with an array containing the words for which we want to look.

Try It Out – Adding the Search Function to the Search Object

5. Add the following code for the `Search` function to the `Search` object:

```
' Search - find the search string in the database...
Public Function Search(ByVal RawWords As String, _
                       Optional ByVal UseOr As Boolean, _
                       Optional ByVal AsKeyset As Boolean) As Recordset

    ' To optimize things a little, make the test string all lower case...
    RawWords = LCase(RawWords)

    ' Then, make up a new string that contains just alphanumerics...
    Dim Buf As String
    Dim Char As String
    Dim n As Integer
    Dim ok As Boolean

    For n = 1 To Len(RawWords)

        ' Check the character we're looking at...
        ok = False
        Char = Mid(RawWords, n, 1)
        If Char >= "a" And Char <= "z" Then ok = True
        If Char >= "0" And Char <= "9" Then ok = True
        If Char = " " Then ok = True

        ' Should it be added?
```

```
        If ok = True Then
            Buf = Buf & Char
        End If

    Next


    ' Next, use the Split function to make an array of words...
    Dim Words As Variant
    Dim Word As Variant
    Words = Split(Buf, " ")

    ' Make up an array for the keywords...
    ReDim keywords(UBound(Words)) As Variant

    ' Next, remove the noise words...
    Dim num As Integer
    For Each Word In Words

        ' Remove any white space...
        Word = Trim(Word)

        ' If it's less than three chars, it's noise...
        If Len(Word) >= 3 Then

            ' Check it...
            If Word <> "the" And Word <> "and" And Word <> "this" _
                        And Word <> "that" Then
                ' add it to the final match list...
                keywords(num) = Word
                num = num + 1
            End If

        End If

    Next

End Function
```

How It Works

We add an extra parameter to the `Search` method called `UseOr` that will allow us to adjust our default functionality from doing a "Gaggia *and* Carezza" search to a "Gaggia *or* Carezza" search:

```
Public Function Search(ByVal RawWords As String, _
                    Optional ByVal UseOr As Boolean, _
                    Optional ByVal AsKeyset As Boolean) As Recordset
```

Our first job with this method is to change the search string we are given through the `RawWords` parameter into all lower case letters. As we don't care about case-sensitivity when we're searching, we drop all the letters to a known case here to optimize the operation slightly:

```
    RawWords = LCase(RawWords)
```

The next section takes out everything that's not a letter or a number or a space, so things like quotes and apostrophes are removed, leaving the spaces in to delimit the text:

```
For n = 1 To Len(RawWords)

    ' check the character we're looking at...
    ok = False
    Char = Mid(RawWords, n, 1)
    If Char >= "a" And Char <= "z" Then ok = True
    If Char >= "0" And Char <= "9" Then ok = True
    If Char = " " Then ok = True

    ' should it be added?
    If ok = True Then
        Buf = Buf & Char
    End If

Next
```

Next, we use the built-in Split function to create an array of the discrete words in the query:

```
Dim Words As Variant
Dim Word As Variant
Words = Split(Buf, " ")

' Make up an array for the keywords...
ReDim keywords(UBound(Words)) As Variant
```

Finally, we iterate through this list to remove anything that's less than three characters and anything that looks like a noise word:

```
Dim num As Integer
For Each Word In Words

    ' Remove any white space...
    Word = Trim(Word)

    ' If it's less than three chars, it's noise...
    If Len(Word) >= 3 Then

        ' Check it...
        If Word <> "the" And Word <> "and" And Word <> "this" _
                    And Word <> "that" Then
            ' add it to the final match list...
            keywords(num) = Word
            num = num + 1
        End If

    End If

Next
```

For this example, our noise list is extremely limited – feel free to make your own list more extensive!

Efficient Text Searches in SQL Server

Those of you who have spent any time at all trying to optimize SQL queries will understand that one of the most expensive operations (in terms of memory consumption) you can ask a database server to perform is a general text search, like the ones we're trying to do here. Hence, indexes are used to make access to the data stored in a relational database easier.

An **index** is a software device used by relational databases (like SQL Server) to speed access to rows in database tables. It takes its name from an index you might find in a book like this. Indexes are structured so that they're easy to scan and usually contain small amounts of data with references to the full bulk of the data. For example, if you were to use this book's index to find information about indexes, you'd flip to the index, find "I", look down until you found "Indexes" and then examine each bulk of data referenced by each page number until (we hope) you found the information you were looking for.

Indexes are typically used to arrange columnar information into alphanumeric order. SQL Server mimics the way that you yourself might look for information, along with other algorithms worked out by the people who have been putting these things together over the past few decades.

For example, if we want to select out customers that have a last name beginning with "C" from our `Customers` table, we create an index on the last name column to make this query faster. In short, we ask SQL Server to make a list of all the possible last names and arrange them in alphabetical order. Then, whenever we want to find all the customers with a last name beginning with "C", SQL Server flicks open the index at "C", walks down the index and forms a query containing all the references to all of the last names until it reaches "D".

However, the moment you start asking questions like, "Which last names *end* in 'C'?" or, "Which product descriptions *contain* the word 'espresso'?" the standard SQL Server indexes cannot help, as they were not designed to enable this kind of functionality. We'll discuss how to cope with these types of queries later in the chapter.

Microsoft SQL Server comes with a tool called Query Analyzer that can help you understand what SQL Server does behind the scenes when you ask it to run a query. Let's run some simple SQL queries in the Query Analyzer.

Try It Out – Querying the JoCoffee Database Using the Query Analyzer

1. Using the SQL Server Enterprise Manager, find the `JoCoffee` database and select Tools | SQL Server Query Analyzer from the toolbar. This will launch the Query Analyzer and a new query pane will be opened for you.

2. By default, the selected database will be the `master` database, so use the drop-down list in the top right-hand corner of the window to change this to `JoCoffee`.

443

3. Enter this SQL statement into the query window and select Query | Execute from the menu:

```
SELECT * FROM Products WHERE name='carezza'
```

This is one of the simplest SQL statements there is. It is asking SQL to select all rows (by using *) from the `Products` table where the name is carezza.

If you've done any database work at all, you're probably more than familiar with this kind of tool. Query Analyzer will go away, run the query, and display any results to you in a table at the bottom of the window. However, this doesn't help us to understand what SQL Server is doing.

4. Now, with the SQL query still in the query pane, select Query | Display Estimated Execution Plan from the menu. This time, Query Analyzer will run the query, but instead of the query results, it will display a graphical view of what SQL Server *might* have done if it were to run this query. (I use the word *might* here because this is a best guess – SQL Server may handle this differently in practice.) Here's what it looks like:

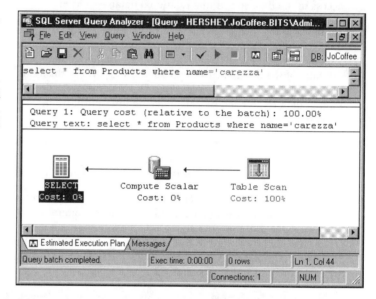

> **Database optimization (the process of using the various tools supplied by a Database Management System to make access to the data that an application requires as responsive as possible) is a bit of an art, and it's something we're not going to go into too deeply here. Rather, we'll discuss some of the major problems databases face and how we can overcome some of them. There is, however, one overriding rule: "table scans are bad!"**

If you look at the view Query Analyzer returns, notice how the Table Scan icon is displayed in red. What basically happens in a table scan is, if SQL Server can't think of a really quick, neat way of getting the data it will examine *each and every row* in the table and test each one. This is almost OK for small tables, but it's a definite no-no with large tables. In short, the bigger the table gets, the slower your query will run.

5. Luckily, table scans are fairly easy to defeat for queries like the one we've just run. All we have to do is create an index on the `Name` column and the next time we run the query, SQL Server will use the index, rather than examining each row in the table.

Although the Enterprise Manager comes with handy tools for creating and managing indexes, we can create them from SQL. Execute this SQL statement to create an index on the Name column:

```
CREATE INDEX ProductName ON Products(Name)
```

6. Now if you select <u>Q</u>uery | <u>D</u>isplay Estimated Execution Plan, SQL Server will display this:

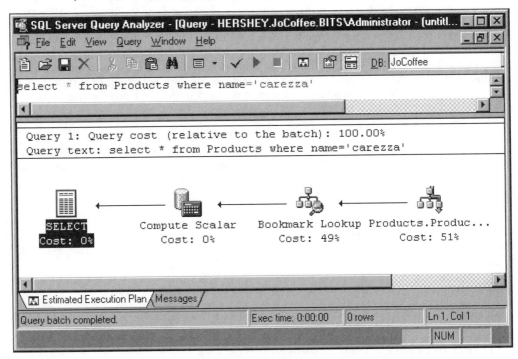

The rightmost icon indicates that an Index Seek was performed to find the data, which is substantially more efficient and scalable. The Bookmark Lookup icon that also appears is a partner of the Index Scan – you'll notice it's not shown in the screenshot showing the table scan.

Full-Text Searching

No matter how many indexes we create, however, we won't be any closer to making our text searching more efficient. That's because rather than searching for this:

```
SELECT * FROM Products WHERE Name='carezza'
```

We actually want to search for products where Name *contains* Carezza with a statement like this:

```
SELECT * FROM Products WHERE Name LIKE '%carezza%'
```

The bad news is that SQL Server indexes can't help us out with the second type of query, so we're back to table scans. Try it by entering the second SQL statement shown above and viewing its execution plan.

The first statement looks for an exact match, so only if the Name field exactly matches carezza with nothing tacked onto the end or the beginning will SQL consider it a match and include it in the results.

Actually, the vast majority of the time SQL Server works in a case-insensitive mode, so CareZZa, cAREZZA and any combination in between will match.

The LIKE predicate we've used in the second statement will match any strings where the word carezza appears in any part of the string, so mycarezza, yourcarezzatoo and carezzaforme will all match.

There is a very big "but" to this. Normal SQL Server indexes are structured in such a way that they cannot be used to speed searches where the search term exists anywhere in the string. They are great for matching the beginning of a string (like the "last name begins with C idea" we saw before, which can be executed with LastName LIKE 'C%'), but not for matching middle sections of strings. To get an understanding of why, imagine flipping the index in the back of the book and looking for any page where the index term contains the letters "th" anywhere in it. That form of index falls apart, as it relies on you knowing the beginning of the search string.

Coming back to our discussion on optimization, it's easy to see why we now have a problem. With the LIKE '%whatever%' query, SQL Server has no option but to perform the search using a table scan. As we know, table scans are very, very bad. Fortunately for us, SQL Server comes with a service called **Full-Text Indexing**, and this can help us speed up queries of this type.

Full-Text Indexing is a separate service derived from the technology found in **Microsoft Index Server**. What happens is that the indexing service pulls all of the text out of your database, arranges it into a special index called a **catalog**, and stores that index outside SQL Server. You can then ask SQL Server to use that catalog in queries where you want to perform full-text searching.

Full Text Indexing is a kludge, so here are some points to remember:

❑ Full-text catalogs exist outside SQL Server and are maintained by a separate service called **Microsoft Search Service**.

❑ Full-Text Indexing is only available on Windows NT Server.

❑ Changes to the data are not automatically reflected in the catalog, as they are with regular indexes. You will have to schedule SQL Server to rebuild the catalog periodically to make sure it's up to date. The catalogs will not be backed up along with the database, so if you have to restore for any reason, you'll also have to take some time to rebuild the indexes.

❑ You can only have one full-text index per table, but this index can span as many columns as you like. In fact, in order to work, the indexing engine requires a column that it knows will be unique (usually the primary key column, as you will see in our example here), and this column is matched with one or more columns containing the data to be searched.

Installing Full-Text Indexing

Full Text Indexing is not installed with SQL Server by default, so you may have to run the setup from the original SQL Server disk in order to install this component. You can tell if it is by pulling down the Tools menu from the Enterprise Manager. If Full-Text Indexing is grayed out, you may need to install it.

Thanks to a small bug in SQL Server, the option may be grayed out even if it is installed, as the service may not have started properly. To check, expand the Support Services object in the Enterprise Manager tree and look for an object called Full-Text Search. If this is there, it's installed OK but hasn't started properly – right-click on it and select Start. Otherwise, you'll have to install it.

Try It Out – Create an Index on the Products Table

1. To create an index on the Products table, make sure the JoCoffee database is selected and choose Tools | Full-Text Indexing from the toolbar. This will open the Full-Text Indexing Wizard; you can click right through the first page, as it's just blurb about what the Wizard does.

2. The first question you'll be asked is which table you want to index. Select the Products table and click Next:

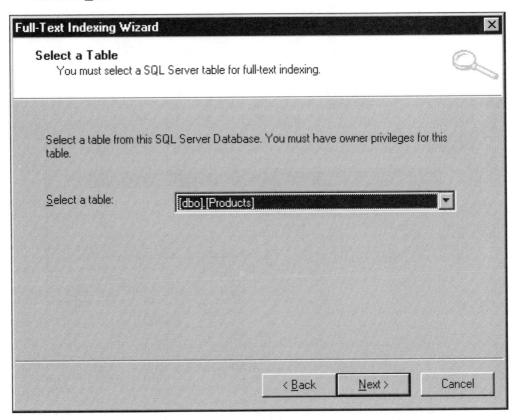

3. The next step is to choose the unique index for the table. We only have one – the primary key index we placed on the ProductID column. Click Next.

4. The next step in the Wizard asks us to choose on which columns we want to index. Any text-based columns can be included in a full-text search, but in our case, we're only interested in the `Name`, `Details`, and `Description` columns. Select these and click **Next**:

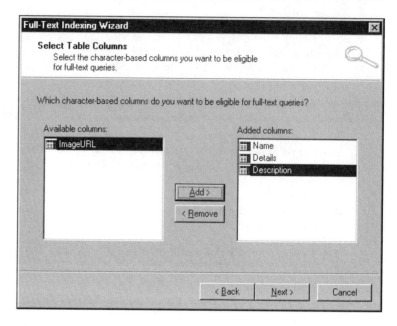

5. After this, we're asked to select the catalog we wish to use to store the full-text indexing data in. You can store many full-text indexes in a single catalog, but it's a good idea to try and separate them depending on how large each index is and for what reasons an index is used. We don't have an index, so enter the name as My Catalog and click **Next**:

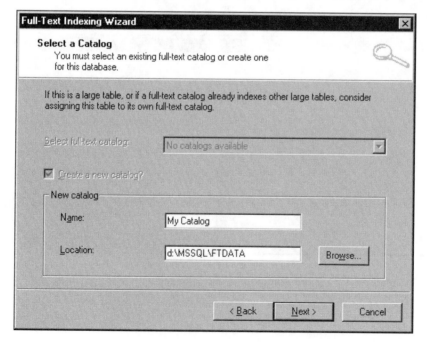

6. The final step in the Wizard is to define a schedule for the index population. As I mentioned before, full-text indexes do not automatically change themselves as the data they relate to changes, therefore they must be updated in a batch mode. If you want to define a schedule now, do so, but this should obviously fit in with whatever schedule you have arranged for server maintenance. Click Next when you've finished.

7. The final page of the Wizard asks you to confirm the actions you've specified, so click Finish.

8. Before we've finished with the index creation process, we need to perform an initial population of the catalog so that we can use it. Use the Enterprise Manager to locate the Full-Text Catalogs object inside the JoCoffee database object. When you select this, the current catalogs on the database will be shown in the right-hand pane, including the new catalog we just created:

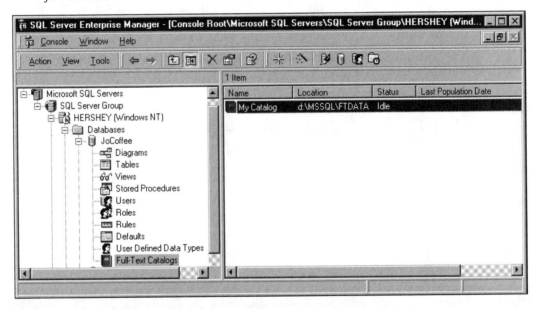

9. Right-click on My Catalog and select Start Population | Full Population. It will take SQL Server a moment to perform the population.

Try It Out – Using Full-Text Indexes

1. With our full-text index in place, you'll notice that we're still performing a table scan if we run:

```
SELECT * FROM Products WHERE Name LIKE '%carezza%'
```

2. That's because in order to use full-text indexes, we have to explicitly tell SQL Server to do so. Try this statement instead:

```
SELECT * FROM Products WHERE CONTAINS(name, 'carezza')
```

3. Here's what our execution plan looks like:

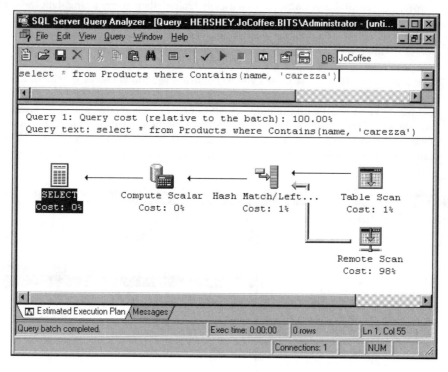

How It Works

You'll notice that this statement does not include the SQL % wildcard operator. This execution plan shows that 98% of the query's work was performed in a **Remote Scan** – a scan that took place outside of SQL Server's control, in this case the Microsoft Search Service.

Try It Out – Full-Text Indexing on the Attributes Table

Recall how we are interested in searching inside both the Products table and the dynamic attributes table? Well, we'll need to create a similar index on the Attributes table, so go through these steps:

1. Right-click on the **Attributes** table in the Enterprise Manager. Select <u>F</u>ull-Text Index Table | <u>D</u>efine Full-Text Indexing on a Table.

2. Click <u>N</u>ext to dismiss the blurb.

3. Select the existing PK_Attributes primary key index.

4. Add the StringValue column to the **Added columns** list.

5. Select the My Catalog catalog.

6. Click <u>N</u>ext to ignore the scheduling options.

7. Click Finish.

Once the index has been created, locate My Catalog in the Full-Text Catalogs management object, right-click on it, and select <u>S</u>tart Population | <u>F</u>ull Population.

Building the Query

Once we have the list of words that make up the search, and SQL Server is configured to handle full-text indexing, we need to make the SQL query up that will do the actual searching.

Remember how we want to search across a number of the columns in the vProducts view? To make the search work, we'll need to query each of the columns separately for the existence of the keywords and glue the results for each column together using OR operators in the SQL string. When we look for keywords, we're going to use the SQL keyword LIKE so that we can look for keywords that occur as a part of a longer string.

Try It Out – Adding the Ability to Search to the Search Method

1. Add this code to the end of the Search method of the Search class module:

```
'Add it to the final match list...
keywords(num) = Word
num = num + 1
End If

End If


Next
```

```
' Do we have any keywords?
If num > 0 Then

    ' After removing the noise, make up a string...
    Dim Where As String
    Dim ColumnName As String
    Dim First As Boolean

    For n = 1 To 3

        ' What column are we looking for?
        Select Case n

            Case 1
                ColumnName = "Name"
            Case 2
                ColumnName = "Details"
            Case 3
                ColumnName = "Description"

        End Select
```

```
                     ' If we're not the first one, tack on an OR...
                     If n <> 1 Then
                         Where = Where & " or "
                     End If

                     ' Loop the words...
                     Where = Where & "Contains(" & ColumnName & ", '"
                     First = True

                     For Each Word In keywords

                         ' Is it the first word?
                         If First = True Then
                             First = False
                         Else

                             ' If it's not the first, we need an AND or an OR...
                             If UseOr = True Then
                                 Where = Where & " OR "
                             Else
                                 Where = Where & " AND "
                             End If

                         End If

                         ' Tack on the word...
                         Where = Where & Word

                     Next
                     Where = Where & "')"

                 Next

                 ' Adjust the clause to deal with the view anomaly...
                 Where = "ProductID in (SELECT ProductID FROM Products WHERE " & _
                         Where & ")"

                 ' Now that we have the clause, run the query...
                 Set Search = m_utility.DB.RunQuery("Products", "vProducts", _
                         Where, "name", AsKeyset)

             End If

     End Function
```

How It Works

First of all, we don't do anything if there's no need, and in this case we can check to see if there's any need by examining the number of keywords we found. In the case of failed searches, we simple return Nothing out of the function:

```
If num > 0 Then
    ...
End If
```

Otherwise, if we find some keywords we need to set up a loop that will repeat the examination operation on the specific columns we're interested in – and earlier on in the chapter we decided that three columns would be adequate: product name, product details, and product description:

```
Select Case n

    Case 1
        ColumnName = "Name"
    Case 2
        ColumnName = "Details"
    Case 3
        ColumnName = "Description"

End Select
```

For each of these columns, we iterate through the keywords in our array, tacking each one onto the end of the Where clause as we go. Before each of the second, third, and fourth columns, we add on either an OR or an AND operator depending on what value we specified for the UseOr parameter:

```
For Each Word In keywords

    ' Is it the first word?
    If First = True Then
        First = False
    Else

        ' If it's not the first, we need an AND or an OR...
        If UseOr = True Then
            Where = Where & " OR "
        Else
            Where = Where & " AND "
        End If

    End If

    ' tack on the word...
    Where = Where & Word

Next
```

Say we look for Carezza, if the Details column of a particular Products row contains this keyword, or the Description field does, then that row will pass the test and be returned.

There is one little gotcha with the SQL free-text searching. If you query a view for a column that exists inside a free-text index, SQL Server will throw an error claiming that the column in the "table" (and remember, full-text index is mistaking our view for a table) is not full-text indexed. To get around this, we have to run the query on the Products table directly, and then pass the rows that matched into a separate query, which does the work on the vProducts view that contains all of the data in which we're interested. We do this using a SELECT...IN clause, and we'll see that complete clause in a moment.

If we run the `Search` method with the search string Carezza, here's the `WHERE` clause that will get passed back to the caller through the `Where` parameter of the `RunQuery` method:

```
ProductID IN
    (SELECT ProductID FROM Products WHERE
        CONTAINS(Name, 'carezza')
        OR CONTAINS(Details, 'carezza')
        OR CONTAINS(Description, 'carezza'))
```

The `RunQuery` method itself will use this `WHERE` clause to form a SQL statement that looks like this:

```
SELECT * FROM vProducts WHERE
    ProductID IN
        (SELECT ProductID FROM Products WHERE
            CONTAINS(Name, 'carezza')
            OR CONTAINS(Details, 'carezza')
            OR CONTAINS(Description, 'carezza'))
```

Including the Dynamic Attributes

We've successfully written some code that will search the columns in the `vProducts` view, but what about the dynamic attributes?

As you know, the data for dynamic attributes is stored in the `Attributes` table. Frustratingly, this data for the attributes is stored under a different mechanism to the products; in the `Products` table we have one row per product that is sold, but in the `Attributes` table, we have zero or more rows for each product. We can get around this by selecting out the IDs of the matching rows in the `Attributes` table and then joining this with the results found from the `vProducts` view.

Try It Out – Completing the Search Method

1. Add this code to the `Search` method of the `Search` class module:

```
' Adjust the clause to deal with the view anomaly...
Where = "ProductID in (SELECT ProductID FROM Products WHERE " & _
        Where & ")"
```

```
' Before we run the query, we need to select out the
' dynamic attribute columns...
Dim AttribWhere As String

For Each Word In keywords

    ' Do we need to add an AND or OR?
    If AttribWhere <> "" Then
        If UseOr = True Then
            AttribWhere = AttribWhere & " OR "
        Else
            AttribWhere = AttribWhere & " AND "
        End If
    End If
```

```
            ' Add the word...
            AttribWhere = AttribWhere & "Contains(StringValue, '" & Word & "')"

    Next

    ' Combine the two where clauses together...
    Where = Where & " OR ProductID IN " & _
        "(SELECT ProductID FROM Attributes WHERE " & AttribWhere & ")"

    ' Now that we have the clause, run the query...
    Set Search = m_utility.DB.RunQuery("Products", "vProducts", _
                    Where, "name", AsKeyset)
```

How It Works

The additional code we've added performs a similar job on the keywords we worked with before, but this time selects matches out of the `Attributes` table. In fact, because only one column in this table contains string data (`StringValue`), we only perform the match on the `StringValue` column:

```
    AttribWhere = AttribWhere & "Contains(StringValue, '" & Word & "')"
```

We then combine the results of this sub-query with the main query, so now we search all three of the `vProducts` columns, and the dynamic string attributes:

```
    Where = Where & " OR ProductID IN " & _
            (SELECT ProductID FROM Attributes WHERE " & AttribWhere & ")"
```

Now the WHERE clause we pass through to `RunQuery` looks like this:

```
ProductID IN
    (SELECT ProductID FROM Products WHERE
        CONTAINS(Name, 'carezza')
        OR CONTAINS(Details, 'carezza')
        OR CONTAINS(Description, 'carezza'))
OR ProductID IN
    (SELECT ProductID FROM Attributes WHERE
        CONTAINS(StringValue, 'carezza'))
```

… which `RunQuery` converts to create the actual SQL statement:

```
SELECT * FROM vProducts WHERE
    ProductID IN
        (SELECT ProductID FROM Products WHERE
            CONTAINS(Name, 'carezza')
            OR CONTAINS(Details, 'carezza')
            OR CONTAINS(Description, 'carezza'))
    OR ProductID IN
        (SELECT ProductID FROM Attributes WHERE
            CONTAINS(StringValue, 'carezza'))
```

Building a Search Tool

As we've said before, the search tools we put on Jo's Coffee will be one of the features most often used by visitors to the site. Visitors will naturally gravitate towards a search box if they have a manufacturer or product name in mind, so it's essential that we make it easily accessible from all pages on the site.

In our case, a good place for it is the left-hand navigation bar, just below where we added the basket summary.

Try It Out – Adding a Search Box

1. Open `start.asp` and add this code beneath the code that rendered the basket:

```
<tr><td class=heading align=center>Your Basket</td></tr>
<tr><td class=small align=center>
<%
   If Visit.Basket.NumItems = 0 Then
      Response.Write "...is empty"
   Else

      ' Draw the number of items...
      Response.Write "Contains "
      Response.write Visit.Basket.NumItems & " item"

      If Visit.Basket.NumItems <> 1 Then Response.Write "s"

      ' Draw the value...
      Response.Write "<br>"
      Response.Write FormatPrice(Visit.Basket.Total)

      ' Draw a link...
      Response.Write "<br>"
      Response.Write "<a href="""
      Response.Write "basket.asp"
      Response.Write """><b>View Basket</b></a>"

   End If
%>
</td></tr>
```

```
<!-- search -->
<tr><td><br></td></tr>
<form action="search.asp" method=post>
<tr><td class=heading align=center>Search</td></tr>
<tr><td class=small align=center>
<input type=text name=search value="<%=request("search")%>" size=6>
<input type=submit value="Go">
</td></tr>
</form>
```

Here's the search box in place:

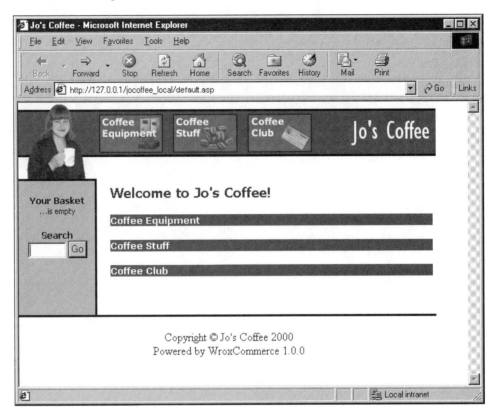

Presenting the Results

You'll notice that the form we created in that code calls an ASP page called `search.asp` that we need to create now.

Try It Out - Building search.asp

1. Create a new ASP page called `search.asp` and copy the contents from `template.asp` into it so both files look identical.

2. Then, add this code:

```
<!-- #include file="start.asp" -->
```

```
<!-- start a table -->
<font class=bigheading>Search</font>
<br><br>
<table width=100% cellspacing=0 cellpadding=2 border=0>
```

```
<%
    If Request("search") <> "" Then

        ' Run the search...
        Dim results
        Set results = Visit.Search.Search(Request("search"), , True)

        ' Did we get anything at all?
        If Not results Is Nothing Then

            ' Did we find anything?
            If Not results.eof Then

                ' Draw the results here...

            Else
                response.write "<tr><td class=small>"
                response.write "No results were found."
                response.write "</td></tr>"
            End If
            results.Close

        Else

            ' The search terms were invalid!
            response.write "<tr><td class=small>"
            response.write "There was a problem with your search terms."
            response.write " Please try again."
            response.write "</td></tr>"

        End If
        Set results = Nothing

    End If
%>

<!-- end the table... -->
</table>

<!-- #include file="end.asp" -->
```

How It Works

As you can see from the code example, all we have to do to search our product catalog is to call the
Search method of the Search object with the string that we want to find. In this case, the string has
been passed in through the Request variables:

```
If Request("search") <> "" Then

    ' Run the search...
    Dim results
    Set results = Visit.Search.Search(Request("search"), , True)
```

If the `Search` method does not return a recordset (in which case it returns `Nothing`), we know that the search terms were invalid and the method could not do any work. We can then return a message back to the visitor explaining this:

```
If Not results Is Nothing Then

    …

Else

    ' The search terms were invalid!
    response.write "<tr><td class=small>"
    response.write "There was a problem with your search terms."
    response.write " Please try again."
    response.write "</td></tr>"

End If
```

If the search terms were valid and we do get a recordset back, we need to display the search results back to the visitor. Typically, when search terms are displayed to the user, they're displayed in a number of pages, usually with 10 or 25 results on a page. However, in order to keep our example here brief, we're going to miss out the ability to show search results in multiple pages, meaning that even the longest searches will come back as a single page. However, our product catalog is quite small and we take steps to cut out lengthy results by removing noise words, so this should not create too much of a problem.

It's up to you how you display the results, but at the very least you should display enough text about the item to let the visitor decide if it's worth clicking through to take a closer look. Sometimes, you'll even find an image of the product listed alongside the text to further prompt the visitor to click through. We're going to implement that in `search.asp` now.

Let's move on and write our code to tell the user all about the products he or she has found in our product catalog.

Try It Out – Adding the Code to Draw the Search Results

1. Add this code to `search.asp`:

```
If Not results.EOF Then

    ' draw the number of results...
    Response.Write "<tr><td class=heading colspan=4>"
    Response.Write results.RecordCount & " item"
    if results.RecordCount <> 1 then Response.Write "s"
    Response.Write " found.</td></tr>"

    ' draw the results here...
    Dim Num

    Do While Not results.EOF
```

```
                 ' draw a line...
                 Response.Write "<tr><td>"
                 Response.Write "<img src=""i/td.gif"" width=1 height=5>"
                 Response.Write "</td></tr><tr><td colspan=7 bgcolor=#000000>"
                 Response.Write "<img src=""i/td.gif"" width=1 height=1>"
                 Response.Write "</td></tr><tr><td>"
                 Response.Write "<img src=""i/td.gif"" width=1 height=5>"
                 Response.Write "</td></tr>"

                 ' draw the item number...
                 Response.Write "<tr><td class=small valign=top>"
                 Response.Write Num + 1 & ". "

                 ' draw the item picture...
                 Response.Write "</td><td> "
                 Response.Write "</td><td valign=top>"
                 If Not IsNull(results("ImageURL")) Then
                    Response.Write "<a href="""
                    Response.Write "detail.asp?id=" & results("productid")
                    Response.Write """>"
                    Response.Write "<img src="""
                    Response.Write results("ImageURL")
                    Response.Write """ border=0>"
                    Response.Write "</a>"
                 End If

                 ' draw the item name and description
                 Response.Write "</td><td> "
                 Response.Write "</td><td valign=top class=small>"
                 Response.Write "<font class=heading>"
                 Response.Write "<a href="""
                 Response.Write "detail.asp?id=" & results("productid")
                 Response.Write """>"
                 Response.Write results("mfrname") & " " & results("name")
                 Response.Write "</a></font><br>"
                 Response.Write results("details")

                 ' draw the item price...
                 Response.Write "</td><td> "
                 Response.Write "</td><td valign=top class=small align=right>"
                 Response.Write "<font class=bigheading color=#800000>"
                 Response.Write formatprice(results("price"))
                 Response.Write "</font><br>"
                 Response.Write "<a href="""
                 Response.Write "basket.asp?id=" & results("productid")
                 Response.Write """>Buy it!</a>"
                 Response.Write "</td></tr>"

                 ' Next...
                 results.MoveNext
                 Num = Num + 1

            Loop

        Else
```

How It Works

This code sample takes off from the point where the `Search` method has returned us a recordset. We start a loop to walk through all of the items that were found, and render each one into a table. We add the product image (if there is one), and then draw the name of the product and the short description. We make both the name and the image links that drill down into the further information page:

```
' draw the item picture...
Response.Write "</td><td> "
Response.Write "</td><td valign=top>"
If Not IsNull(results("ImageURL")) Then
   Response.Write "<a href="""
   Response.Write "detail.asp?id=" & results("productid")
   Response.Write """>"
   Response.Write "<img src="""
   Response.Write results("ImageURL")
   Response.Write """ border=0>"
   Response.Write "</a>"
End If

' draw the item name and description
Response.Write "</td><td> "
Response.Write "</td><td valign=top class=small>"
Response.Write "<font class=heading>"
Response.Write "<a href="""
Response.Write "detail.asp?id=" & results("productid")
Response.Write """>"
Response.Write results("mfrname") & " " & results("name")
Response.Write "</a></font><br>"
Response.Write results("details")
```

To continue the theme we met when we were rendering the items as we navigated through the departments back in Chapter 6, we show the visitor the price of the item, and we give him or her a quick way of adding it to the cart:

```
' draw the item price...
Response.Write "</td><td> "
Response.Write "</td><td valign=top class=small align=right>"
Response.Write "<font class=bigheading color=#800000>"
Response.Write formatprice(results("price"))
Response.Write "</font><br>"
Response.Write "<a href="""
Response.Write "basket.asp?id=" & results("productid")
Response.Write """>Buy it!</a>"
Response.Write "</td></tr>"
```

Here's how it looks after we search for Carezza:

Summary

In this chapter, we looked at how we could go about building objects to handle searching the product catalog to help the visitor find relevant items. We talked about how it was important to split up the keywords that make up the original query and how certain noise words should be removed to prevent the visitor from becoming swamped with half-relevant results.

We then saw how we could configure SQL Server to handle full-text searches, where we are searching for results that *contain* a specified word and don't merely start with it. To do this we used SQL Server's Full-Text Indexing tool.

We then built the Search function of the Search object, which built queries to perform these searches. We then called the Search method from a search box, which we attached to the left-hand navigation bar. Finally, we displayed the results of the search in a results page called search.asp. This page listed the number of results found and some details about each product, including price, picture, and a short description.

Hosting and Deployment

Once you've put your e-commerce site together, you need to make it available on the Internet. In this chapter, we're going to assume that you're not going to host your site in-house, so our discussion is geared towards outsourcing your hosting to an **Internet Service Provider** (**ISP**) that can manage the servers and the connection to the Internet. If you are planning on hosting in-house, we're assuming that you either have (or will gain) the skills to do this, or are going to seek professional advice. In that case we hope that you will find some interesting background information here.

The information in this chapter is accurate at the time of going to press, but the rapidity of development of the Internet will, inevitably, mean some of the more specific detail becomes quickly outdated. The underlying approach to the topic should, however, give you a good perspective on the main issues and a feel for the marketplace. E-commerce is evolving quickly and ISPs are continually adapting their services to address this movement.

Finding an Internet Service Provider to host your site is a tricky proposition. The ISP that you choose will have a profound and lasting impact on your online business. Choose one that's too cheap and you run the risk of not being able to present a quality storefront to your visitors, and hence not getting many customers; choose one that's too expensive and you risk having all of your profit absorbed into hosting costs.

This chapter is going to cover two main areas:

❑ An examination of the issues surrounding finding a suitable host for your site – what general points you need to consider regarding hosting architectures, hosting locations, and the type of service you may expect.

❑ A discussion of how we go about deploying our e-commerce site – we'll discuss creating the production database, installing the VB components we've built and copying the ASP pages that provide the presentation layer of our application.

> **We're not going to cover security issues again in this chapter – undoubtedly discussion of such matters, including the installation of appropriate software, will form part of your negotiations with the ISP you choose to host your e-commerce site.**

To start with, let's get an appreciation of the area we're getting into by looking at what it would involve to host a site.

What does Hosting Involve?

Hosting a site is not a trivial exercise; remember, to have a quality presence on the Web you're going to want your site to be available 24 hours a day, 7 days a week (a timescale often represented as 24/7). For interest, let's break down the costs self-hosting might incur:

Hardware Costs

It's usually wise to purchase server units from a big name, such as Compaq, IBM, or Dell. These servers should have a lot of memory and hard disk space, and the hard disk space should be configured in a RAID array (more later). You also need to have redundant units to hand in case you need to quickly replace a machine. If you're doing high availability hosting (again more later), you're going to need to invest in **load balancing** hardware. Apart from the cost of the servers, money will have to be invested in the networking hardware required to link the servers together, and link the servers to the company network. Linking to the company network means you require **firewalls** to defend against attacks from the company network, as well as another set of firewalls to defend against attack from the Internet. Finally, you'll require uninterruptible power supplies (several of the larger ISPs have backup generators on site, so even if the power fails to the building, the servers keep running).

Software Costs

Broadly, this falls into three categories:

❑ Licenses for the actual server software, such as Microsoft Windows NT Server and Microsoft SQL Server 7

❑ Licenses (in some cases like SQL Server 7) for connecting the software to the Internet

❑ Network management software to monitor your servers

Bandwidth Costs

You need to provide access to the Internet, and this is usually where the economies of scale of being a large ISP come into play. First of all, you need to source Internet connectivity from at least two different providers, in order to provide redundancy should there be a problem upstream (we talk about this more later). Secondly, you have to buy enough bandwidth to cover your busiest times. An ISP hosting a number of businesses may well find that, although there will be commonalities in usage patterns, they can take advantage of all their bandwidth at all points during the day. Chances are that you'll be paying for bandwidth you're unlikely to use.

Service Costs

If you're buying servers from a big name brand, you're going to want to pay for onsite service. Depending on how good your redundancy is, you most likely don't need a top line *immediate service* contract, but you'll need some cover. If you're building servers in-house from components, you'll need someone on hand to build new machines, upgrade aging machines and repair machines.

Environmental Costs

This roughly falls into two areas:

❑ The servers must be physically secure (from damage, theft etc.)

❑ The servers will require cool, dry air 24/7 – basically they'll want a round-the clock air conditioned environment

Management Costs

You'll also require staff to look after the servers. A large ISP is likely to have a team of extremely qualified personnel with experience at detecting problems before they happen, resolving difficulties quickly and optimizing the server environment for maximum efficiency. They also need to be available 24/7, ideally onsite. At the time of writing, this is very much a sellers market; so expect to pay a lot for staff with the necessary skills.

For a small company like Jo's Coffee, the cost of the resources outlined above, not to mention the requirement for an employee to spend time maintaining and optimizing the use of the resources is just not a cost effective or practical option.

Jo's Coffee Site

During the forthcoming sections we'll look at a number of different aspects concerned with hosting but we know, from our design and coding, what software requirements we need to meet to run Jo's Coffee:

- ❑ Microsoft Windows NT Server 4.0 SP4
- ❑ Internet Information Server 4
- ❑ Active Server Pages
- ❑ Microsoft ActiveX Data Objects 2.1
- ❑ Microsoft SQL Server 7

If you're looking to run a site based on the same software and your chosen ISP doesn't supply that software as part of their dedicated server solution, you'll need to go out and purchase copies of NT Server and SQL Server, together with the appropriate client access licenses for management and administrative activities. In addition to that, you'll also need to purchase the **SQL Server 7 Internet Connector**. This Internet Connector is required whenever SQL Server 7 exposes data to the Internet and comes at extra cost. Currently, NT Server 4 does *not* require one of these Internet Connectors. However, the version of IIS that will ship with Windows 2000 will require Internet Connectors for **Active Directory Services**. Active Directory Services has a similar licensing model to SQL Server 7, and is used internally by Windows 2000, hence the need for an Internet Connector.

> **Microsoft licensing rules and regulations are fraught with complications and difficulties, especially for server-side solutions. If you are in a position where you will be purchasing Microsoft server products, seek professional advice from a Microsoft Certified Solution Provider.**

So, what can we expect from an ISP?

Finding a Host

Most ISPs offer a host of similar services, which is great for you as someone wanting to host a site, because there is a lot of competition. Prices will vary, basically, on competence and feature sets. The better an ISP is, typically the more they will charge for their services. If your ISP is incapable of maintaining a decent quality connection to the Internet, your site will be unresponsive or worse – just plain unavailable.

In Chapter 9, we discussed the differences in credit card authorization procedures and gateways between the United States and the United Kingdom. If we continue that theme here, we can say that generally speaking, hosting is cheaper in the US than in the UK and so there's an incentive to host in the US to save money. We'll be talking about hosting locations later in this chapter.

Unfortunately, at the time of writing, there are no really good UK-centric online resources for finding hosting companies capable of hosting sites like Jo's, so if you do want to host in the UK, you'll have to pick up a magazine from the newsstand. If you want to host in the US, one resource for finding hosts is offered by CNet (webhostlist.internetlist.com).

Simple Hosting

When you're shopping around for hosts, the way we've built the site in this book means that we have to be careful and study which services the ISP provides, as many will fall short of our requirements. The main reason for this is that we've created our own Visual Basic components. Traditionally, ISPs don't like to put homegrown components on **shared servers**, as they may misbehave and impact other sites. A shared server is one where many sites are hosted on a single server and is commonly the cheapest way of hosting ASP Web sites. The ISPs main concern is that, with a component, they can't actually see what's going on, but with ASP they can.

> Some ISPs will now allow customers to install homegrown components on shared servers, providing the ISP can see the source code and compile up the DLLs themselves.

In situations like this, most ISPs prefer their customers to get either dedicated or co-located servers:

❑ **Dedicated servers** basically mean that when you take out the service, they buy and configure a specific box for just you to use and plug it into their network

❑ **Co-located** means that you supply the box and they put it on their network

Either way, no other customer's site will be able to run on the box – it is yours and yours alone. Dedicated is often a better bet than co-located, as they will manage the server for you. This means they will monitor the activity on the server to determine where and when problems may occur, upgrade software and swap out hardware when it fails (or looks like it's going to fail). Some companies also include the cost of licenses for Windows NT Server and SQL Server in your monthly fee, whereas others insist that you buy them separately.

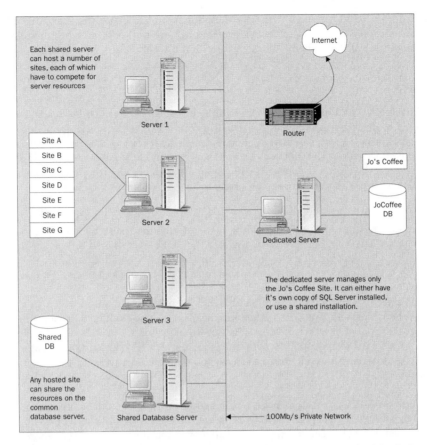

All ISPs will handle setting up your site's domain for you. In fact, if you don't already have the domain, most will be more than happy to register it for you, although there are literally hundreds of domain registration bureaus out there, such as AllDomains.com, uk2.net and Register.com. Your ISP will most likely be able to handle your e-mail requirements, too.

While that simple solution will work for relatively low use sites, if you're trying to build a Web site that will experience a *lot* of traffic, you're going to have to step up to a high-end hosting solution. This latter type of solution may not necessarily be immediately applicable to someone like Jo, but as word gets around who knows...

High Availability Hosting

Provisioning service for a high-end Web site is substantially trickier than just renting some space at an ISP and putting a box in it. If you have a site that's experiencing a lot of traffic, you'll need to step up to high availability hosting. Typically, this means building a **server farm**. A server farm is based on the same technology that your dedicated server uses, but you basically have a number of servers doing the work. So, rather than having one machine serving 100,000 pages a day, you could have four machines serving 25,000 each.

Unfortunately for us, building a high-end server farm for running a major site is actually a bit of an art and if you have serious money to spend, seek professional advice. We'll move through this discussion rapidly as it's not central to the theme of the chapter, but it's stuff you might need to know about in the future.

Load Balancing

The first rule of high availability hosting is that you need lots of servers. This spreads the site traffic out among a **cluster** of machines and provides a scenario where, rather than buying one incredibly expensive high-end server, you can buy a collection of cheaper servers that do the same job. So, rather than buying a Quad Pentium III Xeon server, you can buy, say, four 2-way Pentium II servers. Each of these four servers in the cluster is configured into a **load-balancing** environment, whereby requests to the cluster as a whole are shared between all of the available servers in the cluster.

When running in a load-balancing environment such as this, visitors to the site are directed to one of the four servers in the application cluster, spreading the load such that no servers in the cluster experience considerable load when the others are virtually idle. When the overall load on the site grows (because the site becomes more popular), the cluster can be upsized simply by adding more servers. The other great reason for using a cluster is that if one machine goes down, you still have a Web site.

There are a number of ways of building a load-balancing environment, all of which, as you've probably guessed, have their pros and cons. The easiest (or cheapest) way to do it is to use a **round robin Domain Name Services** (**DNS**) configuration. In this scenario, when visitor A's Web browser requests the Internet Protocol (IP) address for www.joscoffee.com, she is issued with IP xxx.xxx.xxx.1, visitor B gets IP xxx.xxx.xxx.2, and so on. Although cheap and easy to configure, if machine 1 goes down, visitor A can no longer see the site.

Microsoft Windows NT Server 4 Enterprise Edition comes with a load balancing service, called Windows NT Load Balancing Service. This service can be used with anywhere between two and 32 servers in the cluster, and the general principle is that each machine in the cluster shares the same IP address. So, when a request comes through to the server, one of the machines in the cluster will pick it up and start servicing it. Not only can Load Balancing Service be used for providing high availability for Web services, but it can be used for a number of TCP/IP based services, such as proxies, Virtual Private Networking and streaming media. Each machine running the service emits a heartbeat every few seconds to the other nodes. If a machine stops emitting this heartbeat, the other nodes assume it is unavailable and take over its workload.

One way to balance a cluster is to use a hardware-based load balancing solution (such as Cisco Local Director). This product can determine the load experienced by a machine and direct new visitors to less busy machines in the cluster automatically. It can also automatically swap out machines that have failed, and swap in new machines.

Database Servers

Finally, we come on to the database server. The `WroxCommerce` components will need to constantly query the database to enable the ASP layer to present the site to the user, so this is obviously a critical part of the solution. We could get away with a single high-end database server, but if this dies for any reason, the entire Web site will have a catastrophic problem. In this situation, we say there would be a "single point of failure" and, short of the ISP simply vanishing off of the planet, there should *never* be one of these single points of failure in your solution. To eliminate the single failure point for these database requests, create two identical machines to be the database server and connect them together using the Microsoft Cluster Service, again included with Windows NT 4 Enterprise Edition.

An important thing to note here is that previously we were balancing Web requests across a collection of servers; now we're talking about balancing database requests from the cluster of Web servers across two, *additional*, database servers. Microsoft Cluster Service only supports two machines, and these machines have to be identical. This is in marked contrast to the Load Balancing Service that can support up to 32 machines of varying configurations.

Once we have all of the servers, we have to provide connectivity between the parts. In these situations, a private network is usually constructed to connect all of the parts of the server farm together. Sectioning off the traffic to manage the network is done to prevent other network traffic from bogging down communication between the servers in the farm. Private communication is typically done over a 100Mb/s network, but as the price of gigabit Ethernet continues to fall, we'll see more server farms enjoying gigabit connectivity for private communication.

Once we put it all together, here's what our high availability hosting solution looks like:

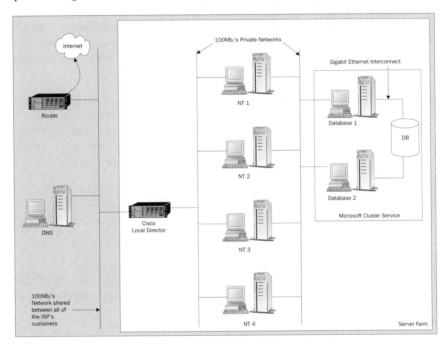

Pricing

Finding pricing information for hosts providing the basic dedicated rack in a server solution is relatively straightforward, although as we discussed before, you'll have to investigate each ISP carefully to determine their ability to provide the service you need. Basically, you pay for what you get, so the more money you spend, the closer to a **backbone** (see following discussion) your provider will be and the more money they spend on systems administration and support. The rest of this chapter details a lot of points you should look out for. Remember to factor in the cost of software licenses for companies that do not provide you with software, as this can be a considerable cost in its own right.

Pricing for clustered solutions is a little harder to come by, because no two solutions are the same (apart from local clustering, some companies offer geographically dispersed solutions). A good way to find other ISPs is to trace the connection to major Web properties, such as eBay, Yahoo and CNet and see which service providers they use.

Hosting Location

The location of your ISP will go a long way to determining both the cost of the service, and the speed your visitors will perceive. By location, we're talking not just about the physical, real world location of your ISP, but rather the location in the not so real Internet world.

When you connect to the Internet from your computer at home through a normal modem, you dial into your ISP's network (possibly through something as low bandwidth as a telephone) and become part of their network. Unless you're using a really big ISP provider, they'll also have an account with another ISP that provides a slightly larger line to them that gets shared between you and the other dial up customers that your ISP has. This continues up the chain until, eventually, all of the ISPs' networks are connected together. The largest lines connecting the bigger networks together are termed **backbones**, and these are typically owned by telecommunications companies such as MCI, AT&T and Sprint.

Obviously, when provisioning service for your site, you have to pay attention to where your ISP is in the general scheme of things. For example, if your ISP is buying bandwidth from an ISP, who's buying bandwidth from another ISP, who's then buying bandwidth from another, customers are going to have to be routed through three networks in order to get to your site. This is undesirable because it will take more time to download and navigate through your site.

The size of the ISP will generally decide its buying power. Remember, all of the bandwidth they buy has to be shared between their entire set of dial-up customers (if they have any) and all of their hosting customers. Therefore, if they only have a single T1 line (more later) to their ISP, everyone's going to be sharing that small pipe. When choosing an ISP, pay attention to their commitment to ensuring the bandwidth they buy is sufficient for their customers' needs, and the frequency with which they upgrade their networks capability in response to an expanding customer base.

Wherever possible, buy your service from an ISP that's directly connected to an Internet backbone. This reduces the number of hops that your customer has to go through to get to your site, which should help in making your site more responsive.

Technical Information

An ISP will have to buy a connection to the Internet through either a single dedicated line, or a set of dedicated lines. Each type of line available has a standard designation so you know its capacity. Here's a quick breakdown of the capacity of those lines:

Line Designation	Capacity	Comments
T0	56Kb/s	The speed of a standard new home computer modem
T1	1.54Mb/s	
E1	2Mb/s	European (including UK) equivalent of a T1
T3	45Mb/s	
OC-1	51Mb/s	

Line Designation	Capacity	Comments
OC-3	155Mb/s	
OC-12	622Mb/s	Average speed of an Internet backbone connection
OC-48	2.4Gb/s	
OC-192	9.6Gb/s	

Remember, MB means megabytes, whereas Mb means megabits. OC is used to describe the speeds of the next generation of high-speed connections. They always run over fiber and one OC means approximately one T3.

In the diagram shown, Jo has chosen to host her site with a second tier provider, meaning that her ISP buys bandwidth from a large ISP. Whenever traffic needs to get in or out of her server, it has to be squeezed down a T3. This is fine for a single customer using a dial-up connection, but if she had around a thousand concurrent connections, this would create a bottleneck. If she hosted at the large ISP directly, she wouldn't experience a bottleneck unless she had around 11,000 concurrent connections.

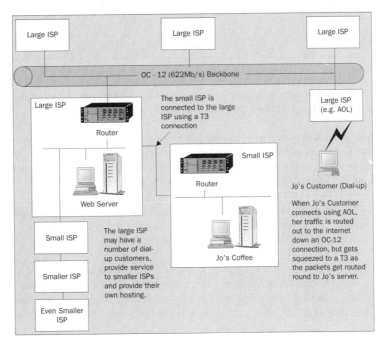

Another consideration when going for an ISP is how many pipes they have. They may well have a 45Mb/s connection to the Internet, but what happens when the provider of that connection experiences a problem and can no longer route traffic in or out? If the ISP buys bandwidth from a number of different providers, there is a level of redundancy, much like the redundancy we saw when building our server clusters, and therefore the good news is that there will be a reduced possibility that you'll discover your site has no connectivity.

Implications of Foreign Hosting

NeoTrace by NeoWorx (http://www.neoworx.com/) provides an excellent tool for finding out where in the world a server is. They maintain a database of router whereabouts, meaning that they can draw a map of where the packets actually go. Here's what happens when we connect to a server in Texas from London:

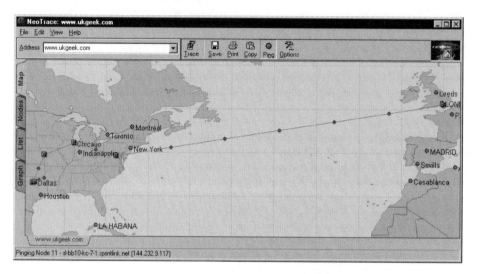

In this case, the packets are routed through from a dial-up connection, over to a UK-based ISP and then shot over the Atlantic to a Sprint backbone connection. The packets are then routed through to one of Sprint's connections in Dallas and then down to the ISP.

The US is the cheapest country in which to host, so there is an incentive for foreign companies like Jo's to host here. What you need to determine is where your customers are in relation to the servers, so that you can estimate the likely paths that visits to the sites may take, and therefore how they will perceive the performance of the site in terms of downloading and moving through the site.

The quality of the UK backbone infrastructure and the quality of the transatlantic pipes connecting the UK's backbone to the US's is such that, providing you source a good ISP in the US, there's no reason why your customers in the UK cannot experience excellent performance.

LastMinute.com, for example, uses a US-based ISP that has a presence in London, so their site is actually hosted in the UK. Excite.co.uk shares the same servers as Excite.com over in Silicon Valley, whereas Yahoo.co.uk is hosted in Stockholm! EU.Microsoft.com shares the same servers as Microsoft.com in Seattle and QXL uses a set of servers in London.

Support Services

Downtime has now become such an important consideration in the Internet world that large companies are publicly ridiculed for their problems in this area; Amazon.com's downtimes of as little of half-an-hour are now routinely recorded on Internet news sites.

When discussing downtime, companies usually use a percentage figure, such as 99% or 95% service availability. However, while obviously insane service figures such as 50% are easily spotted, it's worthwhile doing the math on the higher figures: Given that there are 525,600 minutes in a year, 95% availability actually means you lose 26,280 minutes in a year, or 18 complete days. So, your 24/7 online retail operation is going to lose nearly three weeks simply because your ISP can't do more than 95%. 99% does slightly better, losing you 3.6 days over the course of a complete year.

Maintenance

Usually ISPs will quote downtime as *planned maintenance time*. This time is usually given over to activities that improve the quality of service that you and your visitors will receive and you should always factor this in, mainly to ignore any ISP that claims 0% downtime. Any ISP that doesn't bother to maintain, upgrade or otherwise enhance their internal operations will most likely experience a catastrophic failure that will firmly put that 0% figure into the realms of fiction. You will experience some downtime during the operation of your company – the trick is to minimize its effect on your business by trying to schedule downtime during quiet periods. Foreign companies hosting in the US beware; a number of ISPs will perform maintenance on Thanksgiving when the US is quiet, but being the last Thursday in November, your UK business may well not be.

The bottom line is this: the support that your ISP provides to you will dictate how you handle downtime. A good ISP will e-mail you, perhaps a month in advance, indicating the exact 30-minute slot when you will lose your servers. This gives you time to plan, but it's probably not worth warning your customers in advance, as the chances of them caring enough to remember are slim.

Unplanned Faults

The other issue that you have to deal with is if your ISP experiences an unplanned fault. There are two things to think about here:

❑ Firstly, you have to know as quickly as possible that your server has gone down – there are a number of services that will constantly watch your site and let you know when it's down, such as Red Alert (http://www.redalert.com/).

❑ Secondly, you have to find out when the server will be up again – depending on the kind of failure, your ISP may be able to e-mail you and tell you about the problems, or post a message on their Web site (unless they've gone down completely!). Otherwise, you'll have to phone into the ISP to find out what's going on and when it will be remedied.

Your ISP will also issue a Service Level Agreement where the level of service you can expect is outlined; if they don't live up to their end of the bargain, you may well be entitled to compensation.

Most ISPs will also allow you to manage your dedicated server or servers through a remote control package (examples being Compaq's Carbon Copy or Symantec's PC Anywhere). All of the server flavors of Windows 2000 will also feature the terminal services featured in the current Windows NT Server 4.0 Terminal Server Edition, so expect to see easier management of remote systems in the future.

Disaster Recovery and Fault Tolerance

Assuming the ISP you choose is sufficiently capable of providing a service, the only other things you have to worry about are the servers themselves. As everyone knows, computers are notoriously tricky things and will almost always crash when you're least expecting it. That's one of the reasons why it's a good idea to invest in redundant technology, both on a macro level (such as having machines to take over when one goes wrong) and on a micro level.

The most common micro-level redundancy technology to watch for is **RAID**. RAID (or Redundant Array of Inexpensive, or Independent, Devices) is a hard disk management technology where a number of drives (an array) are treated as a single disk. RAID makes disks more tolerant to faults, and can automatically restore data should one of the drives in the array fail. RAID comes in many configurations, and in software and hardware implementations. For your database server, use the highest level possible – hardware controlled, hot-swappable, so-called RAID 5. This level provides the ability for system administrators to remove the offending drive, slot in a new one, and have the data on the failed drive be recovered all without bringing down the machine. Your ISP will be able to advise you on your options.

The best method for keeping a server alive goes under the maxim that prevention is better than cure. Your ISP should be able to constantly monitor the health of the servers that host your site and spot problems when they occur. Modern server hardware is able to analyze itself constantly and report back possible problems to the systems administrators through network management products (such as Hewlett-Packard's OpenView or Intel's LANDesk). A good ISP should be able to e-mail you when an alert comes in to indicate that one of the servers may be experiencing a problem and that it may have to be taken offline or restarted to fix the potential fault.

Backups

Backups are also a critically important element of your hosting scenario, although not in the way you might imagine. The VB components and ASP pages posted on the server will simply be copies of the versions on your development machines, and so you'll always have a backed up copy of this development work available. Therefore, it's not important to backup the code that runs the site. What is important to back up, however, is the SQL Server database. There are a number of ways you can do this:

- ❏ Configure the database to backup to a tape drive. Your ISP will have to handle swapping the tapes, as you are unlikely to have daily access to the server.

- ❏ Use Data Transformation Services, or Publications, to export the database to another SQL Server database on your network on a regular basis. As Jo's Coffee is storing sensitive customer information in its database, it wouldn't be wise to use the Internet to transfer this data as it could be intercepted on its way over to the other server. However, it's neat to have a copy of the database off site, so consider using a dial-up connection to pull a Subscription off the server.

- ❏ Use SQL Server backup to backup the database to a file, and then use a Backup Service Provider. These companies provide tape-based and online backup services by taking files sent to them over the Internet, encrypting them and holding them until you need to restore a backup.

External Factors

There are also external factors that can affect your ISP's ability to deliver quality service. For example, what happens to your ISP if the power to its building is turned off? What happens if it's in an area of the country with an unusually high thirst for bandwidth (as happens in some areas of Silicon Valley)? What security measures are in place to stop someone breaking in and stealing all of the servers? It's always wise to learn as much about your ISP as possible – another case where asking around and taking advice can help out. At least, armed with the information we've just given you, you'll be in a position to ask the right questions and understand some of the answers.

OK, after we've found an appropriate ISP and they've set a server up for us, we now have to deploy our application.

Deploying the Site

Deployment of a site like Jo's Coffee is a three-part operation involving:

- ❏   Creating and populating the SQL Server database at the ISP
- ❏   Copying over and installing the components
- ❏   Copying over the ASP pages

Throughout this section, we'll be referring to the **production server**. A production server is a server that's located at our host ISP and will be the one from which we actually run our online business (in contrast to the **development servers** which we've been using thus far to build our site).

Creating and Populating the Database

Thanks to the fact that SQL Server can be configured remotely using the management console, creating and copying the database is possibly the simplest part of the entire operation. The only thing you have to watch out for is the settings for the client connection. By default, this is set to be a Named Pipes connection, and this only operates over the NetBIOS protocol. To configure remote servers over the Internet, the client access protocol must be set to TCP/IP.

Try It Out – Creating the JoCoffee Database at the ISP

1. You can set the default client access protocol using the Client Network Utility in the Microsoft SQL Server 7.0 program group after installation (Start | Programs | Microsoft SQL Server 7.0 | Client Network Utility). Set the default to TCP/IP, like this:

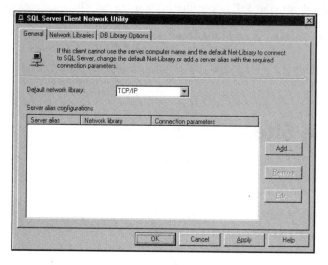

2. To export the data, open the Enterprise Manager and find the JoCoffee database. Right-click and select All Tasks | Export Data. This will start the DTS Export Wizard.

3. The first thing this Wizard asks is the source of the data. This will be your development server.

4. After pressing Next, you'll be asked where you want to copy the data to. This should be the remote database, and you'll have to provide the relevant SQL Server logon information to connect to this remote database.

5. After clicking Next you'll be asked what you want to transfer. To perform this operation, select Transfer objects and data between SQL Server 7.0 databases:

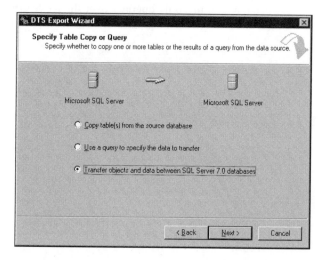

6. After clicking Next, you'll be asked to choose the objects you want to copy. Leave the options as selected and choose Next:

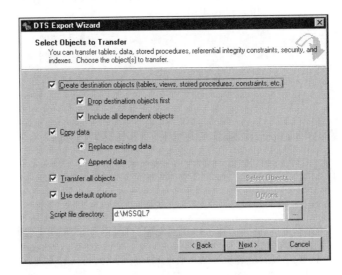

7. The final question you'll be asked regards scheduling the operation, or saving the DTS package. When replicating the database (which is a topic we won't be covering here), creating a DTS package defines what information is included in the DTS operation. Therefore, if you were to save what you'd done so far as a package, you could run the package at a later date and the operation would be repeated.

You have the option of scheduling the package to be run either on a specific date and time in the future, or at a recurring date and time. The recurring option is useful for pushing a copy of the production server onto the development server on a daily basis by way of a backup.

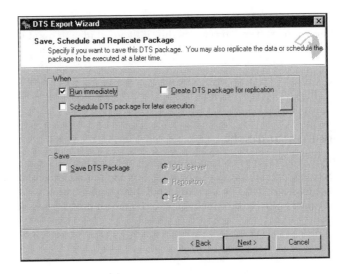

8. After you've saved and scheduled the package (or, alternatively, chosen the default option of not saving and running immediately), you'll be given the chance to confirm the settings and perform the transformation operation. A window will then be displayed showing the current status of the operation until it's finished:

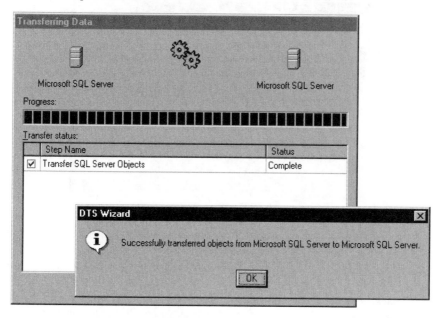

Installing the Components

Installing the components typically means connecting to the server using the remote management tool that your ISP suggests (as we mentioned before, this will most likely be a product such as Compaq's Carbon Copy or Symantec's PC Anywhere).

The first time you push the components onto the server, chances are that the runtime files that Visual Basic requires won't be on the server. To remedy this, it's a good idea to do at least the first installation using a package created by the VB Package and Deployment Wizard add-in.

The resulting package that is created is quite large, which is why it's a good idea to do this the first time to install the relevant runtime files and then just copy the new DLL over and register it each time thereafter.

Payment Gateway Components

Visual Basic may not be able to properly deploy the relevant files for the payment gateway used as part of your payment-processing pipeline, such as DataCash, on the remote machine. Wherever possible, copy the original setup package, that you used to install the payment gateway on your development boxes, and execute the package to ensure that you experience no problems in that department.

Copying Updated Component Versions Over Already Installed Versions

When you do need to copy over a new version, you'll most likely find that IIS, Active Scripting and the COM subsystem maintains a permanent reference to the old DLL, meaning that you will not be able to replace the DLL. To fix this problem, you need to stop the IIS Admin Service. We first came across this issue in Chapter 9 where, if you recall, we built RESTART.BAT to restart IIS for us and release the lock on the DLL.

Because we're in a production environment again, chances are that the moment we restart the IIS service, IIS will reload our component and we're back where we started. The technique then is to manually stop IIS, install the new components, and call RESTART.BAT to start all of our dependent services again. We use RESTART.BAT to make life a little easier – we could restart each service manually. Remember, your production server may well not have RESTART.BAT installed, so you will most likely have to create a new one.

> Note, if you're hosting on a shared server you'll have to talk to your ISP about them compiling up and installing the components.

Try It Out – Stopping the IIS Admin Service

1. You can either stop the service using <u>C</u>ontrol Panel | Services, or you stop the service using the NET command from the command line, like this:

```
NET STOP IISADMIN
```

2. Here's what happens:

3. At this stage, install the new components.

4. Once the components are in place, you should recreate the Microsoft Transaction Server (MTS) package. We first did this back in Chapter 9. You can do this by exporting the package from the development server and importing it into the local server. MTS's management console only allows you to manage servers accessible through NetBIOS, so you'll have to perform this task through your remote control package.

5. Now, run RESTART.BAT to start the IIS services.

Visual InterDev Remote Application Deployment

One of the options you get when installing the Windows NT Option Pack is to install the Visual InterDev Remote Application Deployment (RAD) feature. This feature allows you to post components into remote MTS packages. However, there are inherent security problems with the way RAD has been designed, so it's not a good choice to use in production environments. However, it can help in development environments if you're testing on multiple servers.

Copying the Code

Once the database and the components have been installed at your ISP, it's time to copy over the code. There are three ways in which you can do this:

❑ Use the administrative remote control program to transfer the files over – most remote control programs come with file transfer utilities

❑ Use FTP to manually transfer the files that have changed

❑ Use Visual InterDev to copy the Web application to another server

FTP is the quick and dirty option for this, but it does work. However, you have to be careful to make sure you copy all of the correct files, otherwise you'll end up with a hybrid Web application that's half one version, half another. Visual InterDev does a good job of copying Web sites around, and is likely the better choice if you've been building the pages in Visual InterDev as recommended throughout this book.

To copy a site from within Visual InterDev, you first of all have to have put the application together using Visual InterDev. If you followed the instructions we set out in Chapter 2, you should be ready to go. If you haven't you'll most likely find it easier to use FTP.

Try It Out – Copying a Site using Visual Interdev

1. To copy the Web application, select Project | Web Project | Copy Web Application…from the menu.

2. Then, simply plug in the names of the remote server, click on OK, and the project will be copied:

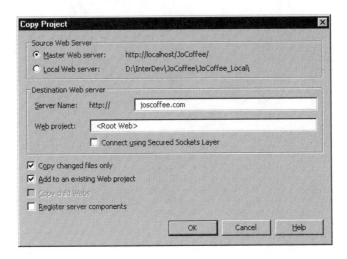

3. We want to configure the Web site to be the only, and therefore the *root* Web site, on the server. This is shown with the <Root Web> in the screenshot. If we were sharing this server, rather than it being a dedicated solution, our ISP would give us a different We̲b project to enter into the dialog.

4. For this to work, the FrontPage Server Extensions must have been installed on the remote server. It's likely that your ISP would have done this for you. However, if you need to do it manually, you can find it as part of the Windows NT Option Pack. You can configure the FrontPage Extensions using the supplied management console.

Summary

At the start of this chapter, we began with a Web site on a development box and, we hope, ended up with a fully functioning production site that can attract visitors!

During the course of the chapter, we learned a little bit about what is involved in hosting web sites and what an ISP does for its customers. We highlighted some of the areas you may like to consider when choosing an ISP, such as the location of the company relative to Internet backbones and the attitude of the ISP towards downtime, disaster recovery, and fault tolerance.

As a result of our considerations, we suggested that for a site built like Jo's Coffee (which involves a set of homegrown Visual Basic components), the best solution would be to go for a dedicated hosting solution. Depending on the traffic we expect, we could run everything on a single machine at our ISP; otherwise we could invest in a clustered solution to handle large quantities of traffic better.

Finally, we saw how we can deploy our application – the database, the components and the ASP pages – over to the new server.

The material covered in this chapter will have given you a good grounding in the basic matters you need to consider when thinking about where to host your e-commerce solution. We don't pretend we've given you all the answers (in fact in a book like this we can't attempt to), again we emphasize you'll need to take professional advice about issues like security.

483

Privacy

One of the hottest topics currently exercising the minds of those concerned with the development of the Internet is that of privacy. As Web technology matures, more and more information is being collected about individual Internet users and new technology is being developed that can help understand and take advantage of patterns this potentially sensitive information. Not only is information being gathered on broad social groups, but also on individuals like you or me.

This chapter discusses in broad terms the kinds of issues faced by both the people who run Web sites and the people who use them, and then focuses down on showing you how to create a privacy statement. More specifically, in this chapter we'll discuss:

❑ What a privacy statement is

❑ The business practices of companies, which are causing privacy to become an issue

❑ What our privacy policy is going to be

❑ Companies that monitor privacy statements

❑ Creating a privacy statement

❑ Organizations that are helping to maintain the privacy of Internet users

Privacy Statements

Today, the only way to share your company's views on privacy with the general public is to create a **privacy statement**. This statement is a broad outline detailing what information you collect about your visitors, and what you intend to do with it once you have it.

Once you place this statement in a prominent location on your site, visitors and customers will be able to quickly discover exactly what privacy risks they might expose themselves to simply by being there. (As a word of caution, although the majority of people are mildly careful about privacy, you will find that some visitors are positively fanatical about protecting their privacy.)

In this section, we're going to create our own privacy statement for Jo's Coffee and post it on the site.

Researching Privacy Statements

Before creating our own privacy statement, it's a good idea to research some others that have been put together by leading Web sites.

Typically, you'll find links to privacy statements at the bottom of each page. Here are some example privacy statements that are worth taking a look at:

- ❑ Microsoft – http://www.microsoft.com/info/privacy.htm
- ❑ Yahoo – http://docs.yahoo.com/info/privacy/
- ❑ Buy.com – http://www.buy.com/corp/faq.asp#privacy
- ❑ Wired – http://www.hotwired.com/home/digital/privacy/
- ❑ Amazon.com – http://www.amazon.com/exec/obidos/subst/misc/policy/privacy.html
- ❑ American Express – http://home3.americanexpress.com/corp/consumerinfo/privacy/privacystatement.asp
- ❑ Nortel Networks – http://www.nortelnetworks.com/help/legal/#privacy
- ❑ Productopia – http://www.productopia.com/privacy/0,1945,1-0-0,00.html
- ❑ Readers Digest – http://www.readersdigest.com/privacy/privacy.html

The spread of sites there is deliberately broad to illustrate that a wide variety of sites have privacy policies, irrespective of the aims of the organization.

Once you know where to find existing privacy statements that you can research, it's just a matter of balancing your business requirements with the ethics of your client, organization, and yourself.

Threats to Privacy

A very real fear for the Internet community is that, without sufficient self-governing and policing, privacy will be abused to the extent that government will have no choice but to start bringing in legislation where there is none, or strengthening it where there is. This would most likely stifle innovation. It's important, then, that as an owner of an e-commerce property you get on the bandwagon and keep privacy control firmly in the hands of yourself and your peers. Additionally, if you don't have a privacy policy that is acceptable to your customers it is inevitable that you will lose them.

Banner Ads

DoubleClick (http://www.doubleclick.net/) became famous (and astonishingly wealthy) for serving up the ubiquitous banner ads that you see emblazoned across the tops of most information-centric Web sites. They already have the technology to determine which country you're in so that they can serve different banners to different localities. This means when viewing pages on AltaVista from the UK, I might see an advertisement for a new British Investment Trust, but when viewing the site from the US, I might see an advertisement for a car that's just been launched in the US. DoubleClick also has technology to associate you with activities on other DoubleClick-enabled sites. Therefore, if you search for "Volkswagens" on AltaVista, you may well find adverts for Volkswagens, or even their competitors, popping up on other DoubleClick sites.

Although we're talking about DoubleClick in this section, there are a number of companies offering this banner aggregation service that also have similar technology. DoubleClick happens to be the largest.

DoubleClick and Abacus Direct

One of the most recent events, which worried privacy advocates, was the merger between DoubleClick and the US's leading researcher of catalog buying behavior: Abacus Direct (abacus-direct.com). Broadly speaking, what this lets the two organizations do is create a scenario where it's now possible to establish a physical name and address for the person to whom they're serving the banner ads. Presently, banner ads are completely anonymous, so even though they can guess where you live and what you do, they don't *know* exactly. To quote Tony White, Abacus' CEO at the time of the merger announcement: "We will be relating everything to a name and address. We'll hang additional data on that."

Luckily, the only way they can tell to whom a specific browser belongs, is to collect your name and address when you make an online purchase and match it against the existing Abacus database. This process is called **tagging**. Once the browser has been tagged, as you move around the Internet and hit DoubleClick banners, the two companies are able to build up a profile of what sites you like to look at. Worse still, there's a possibility that if you were visiting a site for a car manufacturer, DoubleClick could *immediately* send your phone number over to a local car dealer who might phone you up and try to sell you the car!

The only caveat to this is that DoubleClick has to have the cooperation of the online merchant to tag the browser. However, as one of these online merchants, do you want to sell your customer's privacy for the chance of having DoubleClick market your services at them more efficiently in the future? Only one online merchant has to provide the tagging service. To stop this from happening, you'd need the cooperation of every online retailer from Jo's Coffee up to Amazon.

Although some of this sounds horrible, don't forget that the amount of information that these particular companies (and companies like them) collect is so vast that your own personal information is probably protected by a lot of noise. Statistically speaking, today you would have to be fairly unlucky to get targeted as a result of this technology. However, this technology is being developed every day and some people perceive tactics like this as an affront to their civil liberties. I hope that you're starting to see why you, as part of the greater Internet community, should be concerned about privacy issues.

> **You can find out more about what companies are doing to either protect or damage your privacy by visiting any technical news site and searching for Privacy. Additionally, there is a listing of pressure groups at the end of the chapter.**

Privacy Guidelines

In the next section, we're going to use a tool to help us put together our privacy statement. However, we first need to broadly decide what our privacy policy is going to be. Here are some general questions which we need answers to, and the responses we are basing the rest of the chapter on.

❑ Will we share our customers' information with other companies?

No. We want to make sure that our customers feel comfortable handing over addresses and other demographics.

❑ Will we track customers as they move around the site?

Yes. What visitors do once they get to the site provides valuable information about what user interface stimuli work and whether the flow (how typical users are expected to work through the site to accomplish tasks, such as find goods, buy, find company information, etc.) works.

❑ Will we capture information not related to the purchase, such as social security numbers?

No. There's no need to collect this information and the customer will lose confidence if we do.

❑ Will we capture survey information?

Yes. In the next chapter, we will see how we can outsource customer service surveys to a third-party called BizRate. However, what it actually asks for on that survey is out of our control, as are its privacy practices.

❑ Will we provide ways for customers to discover, and change, information we have about them?

Yes. We'll provide an e-mail address they can use to find out the information we hold and change or delete information as applicable.

TRUSTe.org

Back in Chapter 10 we spoke about how server certificates only worked if you could be certain that the certificate had been issued by a reputable source. The same issue applies here – how do you know that the privacy policy you read on a site is accurate and truthful?

TRUSTe.org was founded as an independent organization whose mandate is to examine the privacy statements of sites on the network and make sure that they are being adhered to. It operates as a watchdog, so it is able to investigate an organization that it has certified if Internet users take issue with that company. Although its powers are limited, it can perform third party audits and will refer the organization in question to relevant law enforcement agencies in the case of, in its own words, "egregious or malicious breaches".

TRUSTe is a good way to let your visitors know that your privacy policy is legitimate. Note that TRUSTe is not the only company that monitors privacy statements; the Better Business Bureau Online (http://www.bbbonline.com/) also offers a similar service to TRUSTe.

TRUSTe is, obviously, deeply interested in the whole privacy movement and keeps helpful resources on its site that detail legislation, surveys, and other information at http://www.truste.org/webpublishers/pub_privacy.html. You can also find interesting privacy resources at other sites, including:

- ❑ http://www.cookiecentral.com/
- ❑ http://www.privacy.org/
- ❑ http://www.epic.org/
- ❑ http://hotwired.lycos.com/Lib/Privacy/
- ❑ http://www.eff.org/

The Process

TRUSTe's services are not free, but it is a non-profit organization. The fees you pay in order to join the scheme go into investigations, marketing of the brand and service, and working towards ensuring online privacy practice doesn't fall into the hands of the legislators.

At the time of going to press (February 2000), you could expect to pay these fees to become a TRUSTe licensee:

Annual Revenue	Annual Licensee Fee
Less than $1m	$299
$1m to $5m	$399
$5m to $10m	$499
$10m to $25m	$1,499
$25m to $50m	$2,499
$50m to $75m	$3,499
More than $75m	$4,999

To become a licensee, you must perform these steps:

- ❑ Create a privacy statement – we'll be doing this later in the chapter
- ❑ Read and sign the license agreement – send two signed copies to TRUSTe along with a copy of the privacy statement and the fee
- ❑ Complete the self-assessment
- ❑ Wait until TRUSTe contacts you with the results of your application

489

Self-Assessment

The self-assessment is a detailed questionnaire where you're asked to provide information on exactly how your company deals with data you collect from your customers. You can find a copy of it at http://www.truste.org/webpublishers/pub_selfassessment.html.

The TRUSTe Trustmark

In order to build the reputation of its service, TRUSTe has created the TRUSTe **Trustmark**, a small graphic to be placed somewhere on your site that indicates that you've been checked out by TRUSTe.

Here's the Trustmark on Yahoo's site:

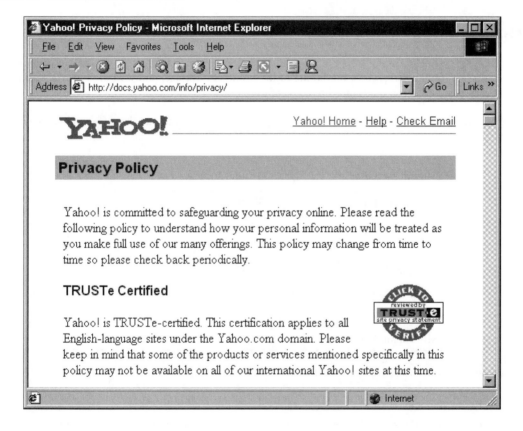

By clicking on the Trustmark, you're taken to a secure page that shows you that the Trustmark is legitimate:

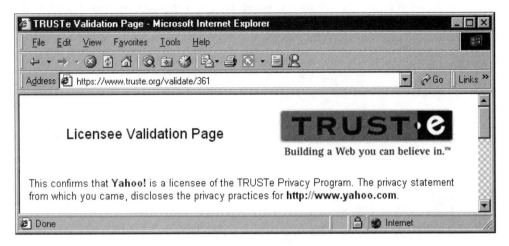

> **If you choose to use TRUSTe, do not post the Trustmark until your application has been approved. Also, if you have no intention of using TRUSTe, do not use their Trustmark, name or other logos, as you could find yourself liable for legal action.**

The Privacy Wizard

To help you put your privacy statement together, TRUSTe provides a Privacy Wizard that you can work through. You can use this Privacy Wizard irrespective of whether you choose to become a TRUSTe licensee – in fact, I recommend you do whichever route you decide to take.

You can find the Wizard at http://www.truste.org/wizard, but as all Web sites are free to move their content about, you may have to hunt around for it.

We'll now work through the Wizard to create a Privacy Statement for Jo's Coffee. However, because the pages are quite large, we won't reproduce them as they appear on the site; rather we'll just walk through the questions they ask and discuss our responses – you might want to walk through the Wizard as you read. All of the questions they ask are optional, so you can miss out anything that's not appropriate or relevant.

Try It Out – Using the Privacy Wizard

1. The first set of responses they want to collect concern contact information regarding the site and the person responsible for its privacy practices, including:

- ❑ Company name

    Jo's Coffee

- ❑ Web site name

    joscoffee.com

- ❑ Name, physical address, phone number, and e-mail address of the person to contact regarding privacy

2. Secondly, we're asked about the kinds of information that we collect and what areas of the site we collect it in, including:

- ❑ Contact information, such as name, addresses, and e-mail

    Jo's Coffee collects all of this information to process the orders, and collects name and e-mail addresses for the community features.

- ❑ Financial information, such as credit card numbers and salary

    Jo's Coffee collects credit card numbers to process the orders.

- ❑ Unique identifiers, such as Social Security (or National Insurance) numbers

    Jo's Coffee doesn't collect anything like that.

- ❑ Demographic information

    Jo's Coffee doesn't collect that, either.

3. In the next section, the Wizard asks for some more information that we can collect:

- ❑ Does the Web server log any information such as browser type or IP address?

    Yes.

- ❑ Does the Web site use cookies?

    Yes, ASP uses cookies to keep track of `Session` *variables.*

- ❑ Does the site use an advertising aggregator, such as DoubleClick or MatchLogic?

    No.

> **MatchLogic (www.matchlogic.com) is a targeted marketing company, like DoubleClick.**

- ❑ Does the site have links to other sites?

    Yes, we could publish links to manufacturers' sites, and people in our community features may also publish links.

❏   Does the organization/company have **special relationships** such as "Powered By" partners?

No.

> **Special Relationships is a term used for companies that have a negotiated a close relationship and are capable of sharing potentially privileged information thanks to this relationship.**

4.   Next, they ask some more questions regarding the types of features we have on the site:

❏   Does the site offer chat rooms, forums, and/or message boards?

Yes, our community features have those.

❏   Does the company have measures in place to prevent the loss, misuse, or alteration of information?

Yes.

❏   Is the information you collect supplemented by third parties?

No (this would apply to the DoubleClick/Abacus Direct merger we talked about earlier).

❏   Is the Web site, or portions of it, directed at children under the age of 13?

No.

> **There are special implications for sites targeting children, as they are typically less aware of potential privacy breaches than adults are.**

❏   Does the site collect the date of birth of its visitors?

No.

5.   The third major area to answer questions on concerns the intentions you have towards using the information you collect:

❏   Web servers will, usually, automatically log IP addresses and domain names. How is this data used?

Jo's Coffee uses it for system administration.

❏   How are cookies used?

Jo's Coffee uses cookies to track session-level information.

❏   How is the contact information on the order form used?

It's just used to send the goods to the customer.

❏   How does the site use the financial information that's collected?

It's used to bill the customer.

6. The next section governs something called the **Fair Information Practices** defined by the US government, you can find out more about this at http://www.junkbusters.com/ht/en/fip.html.

If you're not in the US, you will need to examine the laws that apply in your own country. For example, those in the UK should refer to http://www.hmso.gov.uk/acts/acts1998/19980029.htm, which covers the Data Protection Act of 1998.

The Fair Information Practices dictate that you should provide users with the opportunity to decide whether third parties should have access to their information. In addition, you need to provide ways for the visitors to have their data removed from your database through one of these methods:

- ❑ E-mail
- ❑ Visiting a URL
- ❑ Sending postal mail
- ❑ By phone

We want visitors to e-mail Jo at jo@joscoffee.com, as we want to show our visitors that we take a personal, hands-on approach to rectifying privacy problems.

Additionally, the Fair Information Practices dictate that the user should be able to view and correct inaccuracies in the data that is held, through one or more of the methods illustrated above.

7. That's all there is to complete the Wizard! Here's the privacy statement that is generated:

```
Privacy Statement for joscoffee.com

 Jo's Coffee has created this privacy statement in order to demonstrate our firm
commitment to privacy. The following discloses our information gathering and
dissemination practices for this website: joscoffee.com.

We use your IP address to help diagnose problems with our server, and to
administer our Web site.

Our site uses cookies to keep track of your shopping cart.

This site contains links to other sites. joscoffee.com is not responsible for the
privacy practices or the content of such Web sites.

Our site uses an order form for customers to request information, products, and
services. We collect visitor's contact information (like their email address) and
financial information (like their account or credit card numbers). Contact
information from the order form is used to send orders to our customers. Users may
opt-out of receiving future mailings; see the choice/opt-out section below.
Financial information that is collected is used to bill the user for products and
services.
```

```
Public Forums
This site makes chat rooms, forums, message boards, and/or news groups available
to its users. Please remember that any information that is disclosed in these
areas becomes public information and you should exercise caution when deciding to
disclose your personal information.

Security
This site has security measures in place to protect the loss, misuse and
alteration of the information under our control. (*Please elaborate on the
security measures that you have in place.)

Choice/Opt-Out
This site gives users the following options for removing their information from
our database to not receive future communications or to no longer receive our
service.

You can send email to jo@joscoffee.com

Correct/Update
This site gives users the following options for changing and modifying information
previously provided.

email jo@joscoffee.com

Contacting the Web Site
If you have any questions about this privacy statement, the practices of this
site, or your dealings with this Web site, you can contact

Jo Bovingdon
Jo's Coffee
jo@joscoffee.com
```

TRUSTe strongly recommends that you edit the privacy statement that its Wizard generates to make it 100% applicable to your site. In fact, some of the information in the Wizard needs expanding – in our example, we're asked to elaborate on the security measures that we have in place to keep personal information secure:

```
Security
This site has security measures in place to protect the loss, misuse and
alteration of the information under our control. (*Please elaborate on the
security measures that you have in place.)
```

Once we're happy with the privacy statement, we just have to create a page on the site called privacy.asp and create a link to this page called **Privacy Policy** that appears at the bottom of each page. Adding the link to end.asp will automatically integrate it into the standard template and therefore it will appear on each page in the site.

Protecting Your Privacy

In this chapter, we've learned a lot about companies that are trying to take users' rights to privacy away; but for balance let's have a quick look at some individuals and organizations that are trying to keep privacy intact. We'll break this down into two areas:

❑   **Pressure Groups**

❑   **Infomediaries**

Pressure Groups

As you know, the Web is very good at tying people together to achieve common goals. For this reason, there are a number of organizations around that are trying to make sure that your privacy remains intact, and the following listing of organizations is just the tip of the iceberg.

Junkbusters (junkbusters.com)

Junkbusters is a pressure group that is dedicated to eliminating not only online junk mail, but also offline stuff.

Headed by Jason Catlett, Junkbusters runs an information site (translated into many different languages), which gives you scripts on how to deal with telemarketers, how to get yourself off junk e-mail lists, and how to get your name off commercial mailing lists.

It offers a Web-based service called Junkbusters Declare, that can help you build a declaration of exactly the kinds of junk mail you do and don't want, and find companies that have your details. Additionally it has a free software product called the Internet Junkbuster Proxy. This is a simple proxy server that can filter out banner ads and cookies. Note that even though the word server is used, it's actually a very simple application that will happily run on a laptop or a home PC.

Electronic Privacy Information Center (epic.org)

EPIC is a public interest research center in Washington, DC. It was established in 1984 to focus public attention on emerging civil liberties and to protect privacy, the First Amendment, and constitutional values.

It offers a news service where it can share news articles concerning privacy with the general public (including an e-mail newsletter) and supply resources and other documents concerning privacy.

Privacy International (privacyinternational.org)

Privacy International is a human rights group founded in 1990 as a watchdog on surveillance by governments and corporations. It is based in London and has offices in Washington, DC. Privacy International offers similar services to EPIC, including news and privacy resources. In fact, the two groups often work together.

Infomediaries

Like with most Internet-related topics, there are a number of innovators out there trying to help the privacy cause, while at the same time making a bit of cash for themselves.

The big movers in this area are companies that define themselves as **infomediaries**. An infomediary offers itself up as a way of securely protecting your sensitive information at a secure location, in terms of a collective online community. In this context, all Amazon.com shoppers could be considered to be a single online community. The infomediary then controls which information is distributed to the online retailer, effectively protecting the community from any tricks that the retailer might play to extract more information than the community has chosen to give.

There are companies developing hardware and software products that can help you remain anonymous and private as you perform any Internet-related tasks. Some are already available. Here are a few:

- ❑ Novell's DigitalMe (http://www.digitalme.com/)
- ❑ PrivaSeek (http://www.privaseek.com/)
- ❑ Lumeria (http://www.lumeria.com/)
- ❑ Enonymous (http://www.enonymous.com/)
- ❑ ZeroKnowledge (http://www.zeroknowledge.com/)

Summary

In this chapter, we looked at what privacy issues exist today and the kinds of things companies can do to learn more about you and abuse your privacy. In particular we discussed how marketing organizations can place banner ads which can be targeted towards your interests and purchasing history.

We then moved on to discuss how to let visitors know about your organization's privacy policy by posting your policy on your Web site. We introduced TRUSTe, an independent organization acting as a watchdog and investigator of privacy practices. We discussed how to go about gaining a TRUSTe Trustmark by making a commitment to take care of your customers' privacy; specifically, we looked at the steps involved in creating a privacy statement with the help of the Privacy Wizard on TRUSTe's Web site. Finally, we introduced some privacy advocates and touched on the concepts of infomediaries and pressure groups.

Customer Service

As the number of **e-tailers** in the United States increases, the number of industry experts mocking the level of customer service also increases. Customer service is, today, one of the most important aspects of moving your business online, and a lot of what you've learned in the offline world maps right onto the online one. Luckily for you, most online retailers don't do a good job of customer service, leaving you in a prime position to create a competitive advantage. But, as you know, things in this industry move quickly, so don't rest on your laurels.

The critically poor customer service levels in the e-commerce industry stem from the fact that, originally, the only people who bought online were skilled computer users who thought in a similar way to the programmers who designed and built the sites. Now that an increasing number of non-technical people are using e-commerce, the need for customer service has grown – a major need has been to provide what are, effectively, technical support services to the sites themselves. Additionally, the impersonal nature of the Web and online shopping effectively increases the distance between you and your customer, meaning more tender, loving care is needed to keep your customers happy.

In this section, we'll be talking about the tools and services you can provide to help bridge the gap between you and your customers. Naturally, the ideas in this section just scrape the surface of possible customer service tools that you could implement on your site. An important source of more ideas is the staff of your company and your friends. Ask them to report to you whenever they have a problem with someone's site as they do their own personal shopping at home – you'll quickly find all kinds of good ideas (and things to avoid).

In this chapter the customer service strategies that we're going to cover are:

- ❑ Toll-free numbers to provide customer support
- ❑ E-mail interaction between vendor and customer for addressing queries
- ❑ Gaining feedback from your customers
- ❑ Providing order tracking
- ❑ Automatic e-mailing to customers for order support

While some of the discussion in this chapter is somewhat general, we're going to carry out further work on Jo's Coffee by adding a customer service page and implementing order tracking and automatic e-mailing.

Let's start by stepping back from Internet based interactions and look at why, and how, we can use telephone support to enhance our e-commerce organization.

Toll-Free Numbers

Even though you're operating an online service, it's very important you have a quality telephone infrastructure that your customers and potential customers can use to contact someone in your organization if they have a pre-sales or a post-sales question.

The philosophy that, because you're an online company, everyone will want to contact you through e-mail is simply not correct. In some very specific market segments, it may be the case that the vast majority will contact you through e-mail (typically, we find this tendency in computer-related retail sites). Niche markets, like the one Jo's in, are likely to experience a larger amount of customers who are less confident of carrying out online transactions, and are therefore likely to create a greater load on operators.

One of the most important reasons to offer an effective telesales operation is to capture the address and credit card portion of the order. A surprisingly high number of people are not comfortable with sending a credit card number over the Internet and prefer to telephone in their orders. Naturally, an easy way of dealing with an offline transaction such as this is to have a telephone operator tap the order into the tools the customer would use if they weren't so wary of the consequences. If that customer receives a busy signal, or spends too long on hold, it's likely he or she will abandon the call and move on to another merchant.

Unfortunately it's not uncommon to come across telephone operators who have never used the Internet and can easily say some pretty impolitic things to technically literate customers. Since you want to ensure *all* contact with your organization is as pleasant as possible it might be a good idea to put together an FAQ, that's updated daily, for the staff who answer the phones.

Customer Service E-mails

When dealing with customers online, you'll find that there are two distinct types of people; those who'll prefer to interact with you over the phone (and as we've seen, this type of person may even phone you to place orders), and those who'll prefer to contact you by e-mail.

To provide an organized way of allowing people to contact your company you may want to offer a variety of e-mail addresses; for example an e-commerce company might offer the following:

❑   sales@joscoffee.com – e-mails pertaining to actual sales of the product

❑   support@joscoffee.com – e-mails pertaining to issues with getting the product working properly

❑   service@joscoffee.com – e-mails pertaining to general customer service issues

- ❑ webmaster@joscoffee.com – e-mails pertaining to Web-related issues with the site
- ❑ advertising@joscoffee.com – if you offer advertising on your site, e-mails pertaining to advertising opportunities
- ❑ partnering@joscoffee.com – e-mails pertaining to enquiries into entering into a business relationship with the company

Providing e-mail addresses for different parts of your organization (even if, in a small company only one person actually answers the e-mail) is a very simple proposition; but this must be managed effectively in order for it to be a constructive customer service tool.

What this basically means is, if you have a service@joscoffee.com e-mail address, make sure that the person dealing with that in box can turn the enquiries round quickly. There is nothing more frustrating than having a customer service e-mail fall completely on deaf ears, or take a very long time to receive an answer. E-mail might be an asynchronous medium, yet the person sending the message is still keen to have a response. What seems like an hour or so to you may well seem like a day to the customer. Most customers expect a turnaround in a 24-hour period, but turning around queries faster than this may well give you a competitive advantage.

Additionally you should make sure that you regularly check that each of these e-mail addresses works. A good way to do this is to periodically test the e-mail addresses you use by running code similar to this:

```
' SendMail - routine to send a test e-mail
Sub SendMail(email)

    ' Create an instance of the collaboration object...
    Dim CDO
    Set CDO = WScript.CreateObject("CDONTS.NewMail")

    ' Send the mail...
    CDO.Send "testmailer@joscoffee.com", email, _
     "Test Mail to " & email, _
     "This is a test of the Jo's Coffee e-mail address."

    ' Cleanup...
    Set CDO = Nothing

End Sub

' Send the test mails...
SendMail "sales@joscoffee.com"
SendMail "support@joscoffee.com"
SendMail "service@joscoffee.com"
SendMail "webmaster@joscoffee.com"
SendMail "advertising@joscoffee.com"
SendMail "partnering@joscoffee.com"
```

Later in this chapter, where we consider automatic e-mails, we'll see how we can use the Windows NT Scheduler and Windows Script Host to run batch processes.

Contact Forms

A lot of sites use contact forms that invite people to communicate with the company through a Web-based form, such as the one shown below. Although these forms are not as flexible as having a list of e-mail addresses, they can be used for a number of reasons including focussing customer input, or avoiding abuse of e-mail facilities by people attaching massive or malicious files.

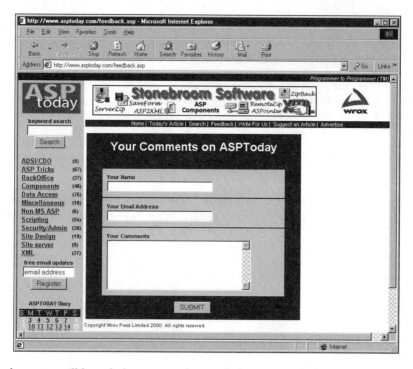

All modern browsers will launch the customer's e-mail client upon clicking on a link that is specified as an e-mail address through the mailto: protocol. However, there are certain circumstances where the user will not have access to a mail client such as if they're using a browser on a handheld computer or mobile phone, or if they're using the site from a public Web kiosk.

Some reasons for *not* using forms like this on your site are:

❑ The customer has no record of sending the e-mail. Because the process does not involve the customer's e-mail client in any way, the customer cannot look back to see when e-mails were sent. This could be particularly important in defusing problematic customer service issues.

❑ Bounced messages may not get routed back properly.

❑ Replies may not get back to the customer if they misspell their e-mail address.

❑ Lack of appropriate tools. Some customers may not be comfortable sending e-mails without running them through spell checkers. Customers who are visually challenged may not wish to cram their message into a hard to read box on a form. By inviting the user to use their regular e-mail client, you ensure that they will have minimum difficulty in getting in touch.

Pagers and Cell Phones

If you are an e-tailer who is often away from an Internet connection, it's a neat idea to have your pager signaled whenever a customer service issue comes on. Most mobile communications companies offer gateways that can send messages through your phone by providing an e-mail address such as `6025551234@mobile.att.net`. Therefore, it's usually straightforward to get your server to page you. If your phone does not have an e-mail address, there are companies out there that will route your messages through to the phone network on your behalf.

Frustratingly, this is easiest to achieve when using a customer service form, as you simply instruct the ASP code behind the form to send e-mail to another To: address. However, Microsoft Outlook's Rules Wizard and Outlook Express' Inbox Assistant can automatically respond to certain triggers, like the account name the message was intended for, and forward a message to your cellular phone's or pager's e-mail address. These rely on the e-mail client being open, and there must be a connection to the Internet available. If you're using Microsoft Exchange Server, you can get around this problem using Event Triggers, as these can route messages irrespective of the state of the client (you'll still need an Internet connection, however).

In fact, as wireless Internet services become commonplace, you may well find that you can manage your entire e-tail operation while relaxing on a fishing boat in the middle of nowhere!

Now let's add a customer service page to `joscoffee.com` so that customers can contact the staff at Jo's Coffee.

Try It Out – Creating a Customer Service Page

1. To create our customer service page for joscoffee.com, we first have to add a link to the left navigation bar. Enter this code into `start.asp`, directly beneath the code that renders the search box:

```
<!-- search -->
<tr><td><br></td></tr>
<form action="search.asp" method=post>
<tr><td class=heading align=center>Search</td></tr>
<tr><td class=small align=center>
<input type=text name=search value="<%=request("search")%>" size=6>
<input type=submit value="Go">
</td></tr>
</form>

<!-- Render a customer service link -->
<tr><td class=small align=center>
<a href="service.asp">Customer<br>Service</a>
</td></tr>
<tr><td><br></td><br>
```

2. Now, create a new file called `service.asp` and copy the contents of `template.asp` into it so both are identical.

3. In this incarnation, `service.asp` doesn't contain any dynamic code, so simply make your page look like this:

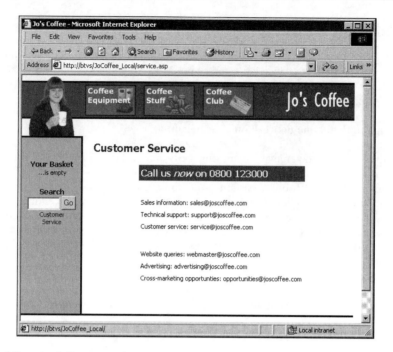

By adding the following code:

```
<!-- #include file="start.asp" -->
```

```
<table cellspacing="0" cellpadding="0" width="100%" border=0>

    <!-- heading -->
    <tr><td class="bigheading">Customer Service</td></tr>
    <tr><td><br></td></tr>

    <tr><td align=center><table cellspacing=0 cellpadding=4>

    <tr><td class=medheading bgcolor=#ff0000>
    <font color=#ffffff>Call us <i>now</i> on 0800 123000</font>
    </td></tr>
    <tr><td><br></td></tr>

    <tr>
    <td class=small>Sales information: <a href="">sales@joscoffee.com</a>
    </td></tr>
    <tr>
    <td class=small>Technical support: <a href="">support@joscoffee.com</a>
    </td></tr>
    <tr>
    <td class=small>Customer service: <a href="">service@joscoffee.com</a>
    </td></tr>
    <tr><td><br></td></tr>
    <tr>
    <td class=small>Website queries: <a href="">webmaster@joscoffee.com</a>
    </td></tr>
```

```
<tr>
<td class=small>Advertising: <a href="">advertising@joscoffee.com</a>
</td></tr>
<tr>
<td class=small>Cross-marketing opportunties: <a
    href="">opportunities@joscoffee.com</a>
</td></tr>

</table></td></tr>

</table>

<!-- #include file="end.asp" -->
```

4. After you've created the page, you have a simple but effective way of sharing your contact information with your customers and visitors alike. However, visitors to the site may well choose to look for a link called Contact Us, rather than Customer Service specifically, so it's a good idea to add a simple link at the bottom of the template that also points to service.asp.

Order Status E-mails

As you know, from the time the customer clicks Place Order to the time when the delivery truck turns up at the door, her order goes through many different stages.

A really easy way to keep the customer in the loop is to send off e-mails as the order progresses through each stage. Amazon.com is notably good at doing this, although most e-tailers fire off e-mails when goods are shipped, orders are received, and so on. Although we didn't go into this when we produced our own e-mails of this type in Chapter 9, it's a good idea to include helpful information so the customer doesn't have to hunt around trying to find contact numbers, returns policies, links to the Web site and so forth

One of the easiest things to do from ASP-driven Web sites is fire off e-mails. Windows NT Server comes with a built-in feature called **Collaboration Data Objects for NT Server** (or **CDONTS**) and, as its name implies, it's only available in Windows NT Server. We'll be using CDONTS later on when we consider automatic e-mails. If you're not running your site from Windows NT Server, or simply don't want to use CDONTS, there are plenty of components that can be used, including the free JMail from Dimac (http://www.dimac.net/).

Here are some places where it makes sense to automatically send e-mails:

❑   On order receipt – when a customer clicks Place Order, send out a summary of the order and reiterate the details of the addresses and payment method used, along with the items he/she should expect and when to expect them.

❑   On shipment from the supplier – when the supplier lets you know that the order has been shipped, pass on the message to the customer.

❑   When the order has been placed on back order – when the supplier lets you know that the order cannot be fulfilled, pass this information on to the customer (we'll see more about this later).

❑ When payment has been declined – if there is an issue with the payment method the customer has used, invite them to supply another card by calling the customer service line. We'd prefer they didn't e-mail the card details to us as they probably wouldn't do this in a secure (as in encrypted) fashion.

❑ A few days after the order has been shipped – as a follow up to say thank-you and to see if the order was to their satisfaction (another topic we consider later).

Obtaining Customer Feedback

One method of getting feedback from your customer after an order is to use a rating service like BizRate.com. Again this shouldn't be taken as an endorsement, but, we want to show practical information. Its service is free, and we'll discuss how they can afford to provide the service later. What happens is, on the receipt page of your site (after the customer clicks **Place Order** and is thanked for their custom) a box is added offering the customer the opportunity to comment on your service by filling out a survey. Both the image in the box, the survey, and all the backend processing is managed by BizRate.com.

Here's how it might look on joscoffee.com:

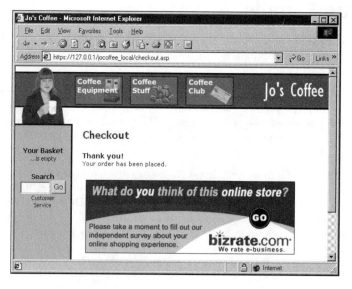

When and if the customer clicks the Go button, a new browser pops up offering the customer the opportunity to fill out a fairly complex survey form.

A demo survey can be found at http://www.bizrate.com/merchant_info/, where the kinds of questions your customer is asked are:

❑ Merchant ratings – a series of five questions, scored out of ten. The questions are "Ease of ordering", "Product selection", "Product information", "Product prices" and "Web site navigation and looks".

❑ Shopping on the Web – a series of questions about the size of order you placed and some questions about which media prompted you to visit that merchant, including TV, radio, print, etc.

❑ Site features – a series of questions asking which *tool* on the site was used to buy the product, including conventional search tools, gift registries, express orders and featured products.

❑ Repetition of business – a series of questions probing when you last shopped at the site, and when you're likely to shop there again.

❑ Categories – a list of categories that you can use to select the type of product that was purchased.

❑ Expectations – a score out of ten regarding the "Expectations of this online purchase", as in how well the site performed in relation to your expectations.

❑ Shopping components – a general set of "out of ten" questions probing what you generally look for when shopping online: "Ease of ordering", "Product selection", "Product information", "Product prices", "Web Site Navigation and Looks", "On-time Delivery", "Product Representation", "Level and Quality of Customer Support", "Posted Privacy Policies", "Product Shipping and Handling".

❑ Demographics – a series of questions intended to find out who you are, whether you're married and how much you earn.

Another thing you can expect from BizRate is the follow-up survey. A short time after you fill out the survey, you'll be sent an e-mail inviting you to do another survey to investigate what happened in the days following your **Place Order** click. In this survey, you're asked:

❑ Has the order been delivered – and if so, was it correct, did you return anything, etc.

❑ Satisfaction – a series of five questions scored out of ten: "On-time Delivery", "Product Representation", "Level and Quality of Customer Support", "Posted Privacy Policies", "Product Shipping and Handling".

❑ If you contacted the vendor's customer service by phone, you're asked questions about why you called it, and what level of service was received.

❑ General perception – how do you generally rate customer service levels in the industry, what kinds of customer service should online merchants provide, etc.

❑ Overall experience – a question, scored out of ten, regarding your overall dealings with the merchant.

❑ "Are you likely to shop again?" – yes or no!

When you sign up as a BizRate merchant, it will periodically send you reports based on this survey so you can see how you're doing. You also receive an overall rating, marked out of five, which you can use on your site to proclaim that you are a quality e-tailer – if, of course, you score highly enough to want to advertise their findings!

What's neat about their service is that it's completely independent, and your customers will perceive this as proof that you're making an effort to get in touch with how they perceive your business and, fundamentally, that their responses will shape the way that members of the Internet public perceive you. In our example above for illustration we've simply shown the BizRate banner. If we were going to actively use the service it would be wise for us to write some text introducing BizRate and indicating why we've chosen to partner with them.

What's in it for BizRate?

BizRate's motivation for providing this service is two-fold. By putting a BizRate button on each receipt page they are getting free advertising space from you that they are using to build a brand for virtually no cost. They can then use this brand to drive your existing and new customers to a **shopping portal** (a Web site that offers links to a wide range of e-tailers) at BizRate.com where they can search for merchants on a category-by-category basis. Your BizRate rating also appears by your name. The issue is here that not only are you listed, but your competitors are too, and if one of your competitor's has a higher rating than you... But, then you're faced with the age-old adage of "can you afford not to be there?"

Primarily, BizRate is attempting to use you to get eyeballs to its shopping portal. As a side effect of providing this service, BizRate also collects a huge quantity of information, again at very little cost, about shopping attitudes of the industry as a whole.

It should be noted BizRate is very keen to promote its own privacy policies. The surveys it asks your customers to fill out are general in nature and don't ask for specifics, like name and address. They do ask for your e-mail, but it's an optional question and it uses this to send you a follow-up query a few days after the purchase to further track the performance of the merchant. It then takes this general, demographic data, collates it and sells it. This does have an impact on any privacy policy you have, so it's worth mentioning the details of the arrangement with BizRate in the policy.

However, if that's shocked you a little, remember that most of the way people make money out of the Internet, when they're not physically selling goods or services like an e-tailer, is by collecting eyeballs. BizRate does provide a neat service, at no charge, and you do end up having your site listed in a large shopping portal. Perhaps the most compelling reason for working with it is that it is building perception of customer service as an important differentiator. It is letting you compete with e-tailers that sell by simply being the cheapest by making it more relevant that you are customer service focused, and providing a tool that your customers can use to get a realistic indication of the levels of customer service you provide.

Merchant Listings

As mentioned earlier, part of the shopping portal it provides is a service whereby you can find merchants by a particular category. Once you find a merchant, you can view a Report Card that tells you quite a lot about the merchant in general:

❏ Description of services

❏ Ordering methods supported (online, by phone, by fax)

❏ Delivery methods available (including international)

❏ Payment methods available

❏ Special features

❏ Return policy

❏ Physical address and contact details for the customer service manager

Another neat thing it offers is a breakdown of the survey scores the merchant has received, along with the overall BizRate rating.

Adding the Service

Naturally, BizRate makes it as easy as possible to get signed up with its service. After filling out a short application form, you'll be contacted by e-mail indicating whether your application has been approved or declined. After this, you simply visit a Web page where you'll find eight lines of HTML that should be added to your `checkout.asp`. After that, simply wait for the reports to come in.

Order Tracking

The **WISMO call** has long been a serious drain on the resources of traditional offline mail order companies. WISMO stands for "Where is my order?" and describes a phone call into your organization that performs no other function than to provide the caller with an idea of whereabouts on the planet his or her order is.

For an e-tailer, there's no need whatsoever to pay for calls into your toll-free number for your customers to find out the status of their orders. In this section we'll see how they can visit joscoffee.com, log into their account and view the status of any orders they have placed.

Implementing this strategy offers scope for improving our previous work – it would be a good idea to include a link to the ASP page we're about to build, in the e-mails that get sent out by the order-processing pipeline that we built in Chapter 9.

Identifying the Customer

The first job in implementing a system like this is to add a link to the navigation bar that lets the customers get to the WISMO tool, which for the customer, we'll refer to as "Order Tracking". WISMO might not mean too much to our customers!

Try It Out – Implementing Order Tracking in JosCoffee.com

1. Add this code to `start.asp`, above the code that renders the Customer Service link:

```
<!-- Order Tracking -->
<tr><td><br></td></tr>
<tr><td class=small align=center>
<a href="tracking.asp">Order<br>Tracking</a>
</td></tr>
<tr><td><br></td></tr>

<!-- Render a customer service link -->
<tr><td class=small align=center>
<a href="service.asp">Customer<br>Service</a>
</td></tr>
```

2. Now, create a new ASP file called `tracking.asp` and copy the contents of `template.asp` into this so both files look identical.

3. Our first job is to provide the customer with a way of logging into his or her account, and we'll do this by testing to see if he/she is logged on. If the customer is not logged on, we display a form to capture his or her e-mail address and password. We can then reuse the code we used in checkout.asp to validate and log on the user.

First of all, we need to add a method to the Visit object that determines if the user is already logged on:

```
' IsLoggedOn - Is the customer logged on?
Public Function IsLoggedOn() As Boolean

   ' Test for a customer...
   If m_CustomerID = 0 Then
    IsLoggedOn = False
   Else
    IsLoggedOn = True
   End If

End Function
```

This simple code looks at the m_CustomerID value. If it is 0, we assume the customer is not logged on. You may recall that when we took the user through the checkout (Chapter 8), we logged them onto their customer account with Customers.CheckLogon, or created a new one with Customers.CreateCustomer (this ID was also stored in the Session variables). Either way, when the user identified themselves, we placed that ID in the m_CustomerID member variable.

4. Now we can write the ASP code in tracking.asp that uses the IsLoggedOn method and presents the form:

```
<!-- #include file="start.asp" -->
```

```
<% ' Are we logged on?
If Visit.IsLoggedOn = False Then %>

  <!-- Heading -->
  <font class=bigheading>Logon to your account</font>

  <!-- Start the form -->
  <form action="<%=request("script_name")%>" method=post>
  <center><table cellspacing=0 cellpadding=5>

  <% ' Did we have a problem?
   if problem <> "" then
     response.write "<tr>"
     response.write "<td class=heading bgcolor=#ff0000 "
     response.write "colspan=2>"
     response.write "<font color=#ffffff>"
     response.write problem
     response.write "</font></td></tr>"
   end if %>
```

```
   <!-- Render the fields -->
   <tr><td class=heading>
   E-mail address:
   </td><td>
   <input type=text name=email value="<%=request("email")%>">
   </td></tr>
   <tr><td class=heading>
   Password:
   </td><td>
   <input type=password name=password value="<%=request("password")%>">
   </td></tr>

   <!-- Render the button -->
   <tr><td colspan=2 align=center>
   <input type=submit value="Continue">
   </td></tr>

   <!-- End the form -->
   </table></center>
   </form>

<% else %>

   <!-- View the orders... -->
   <table cellspacing=0 cellpadding=0 width=100%>
   <%
   %>
   </table>

<% end if %>
```

```
<!-- #include file="end.asp" -->
```

The code here firstly looks at if we haven't logged on; if we haven't we need to render a heading and start the form.

Next we check a variable called `problem` (we'll be giving this a value when we call the `CheckLogon` method in this next step, to see if the e-mail address and password supplied are valid) and, if there's something in it, write out the problem to the visitor.

Finally, we render the e-mail and password fields. If the `IsLoggedOn` method tells us that the user was logged on, we set up a table in which we'll be rendering the orders.

5. Thanks to the work we did in `checkout.asp`, logging onto the account is straightforward. Add this code to the top of `tracking.asp`:

```
<% option explicit
```

```
' Log on the customer...
dim problem
```

```
If Request("email") <> "" Then
  Visit.Customers.CheckLogon request("email"), _
          request("password"), problem
End If

%>
```

`<HEAD>`

The `CheckLogon` method deals with validating the customer's e-mail address and password and reports any problems through the reference to the `problem` local variable. If everything is OK, the internal `m_CustomerID` and `Session` variables are updated to reflect the customer's ID – functionality we met back in Chapter 8.

6. In order to get hold of the orders a customer has placed, we need to add a method to the `Orders` object, which simply queries the list of orders in the database with the given customer ID. We also check to make sure the `status` is not 0, – so we know something has happened with the order such as it has been put in for processing, it has been processed, cancelled etc. Here's the code:

```
' GetCustomerOrders - returns the orders for a given customer...
Public Function GetCustomerOrders(ByVal CustomerID As Long, _
        Optional ByVal AsKeyset As Boolean) As Recordset

  Set GetCustomerOrders = QueryOrders("customerid=" & CustomerID & _
                  " and status <> 0", , AsKeyset)

End Function
```

7. To add some depth to our object model, it's also a good idea to add a property to the `Customer` object that calls into the `GetCustomerOrders` method:

```
' Orders - returns a list of the orders...
Public Property Get Orders(Optional ByVal AsKeyset As Boolean) _
          As Recordset
  Set Orders = m_utility.Visit.Orders.GetCustomerOrders(m_ID, AsKeyset)
End Property
```

8. Now we're ideally placed to generate a list of the orders. What we're going to do is reuse this page so that it not only displays a list of all the orders the customer has ever placed, but also display details on an order when they click through. To do this, we're going to use a query string field called `id`. Add this code to `tracking.asp`:

```
<!-- View the orders... -->
<table cellspacing=0 cellpadding=0 width=100%>
<%
  ' Are we looking at a specific order?
  If Request("id") = "" Then
```

```
    ' Draw a heading...
    Response.write "<tr><td class=bigheading>"
    Response.write "Your Orders"
    Response.write "</td></tr>"
    Response.write "<tr><td><br></td></tr>"

    ' Get a list of all of the orders...
    Dim orders
    set orders = Visit.Customer.Orders

    If not orders.EOF Then

      ' Loop the orders...
      do while not orders.EOF
        ' Render a link to view the order details...
        Response.write "<tr><td class=heading>"
        Response.write "<a href="""
        Response.write Request("script_name") & "?id="
        Response.write orders("orderid")
        Response.write """>"
        Response.write "Order Number " & orders("orderid")
        Response.write "</a>"

        ' Display the time the order was placed
        Response.write "</td><td class=std>"
        Response.write orders("created")

        ' Display the status of the order
        Response.write "</td><td class=std>"
        Response.write Visit.Orders.GetStatusText(orders("status"))
        Response.write "</td></tr>"

        ' Next
        orders.MoveNext

      loop

    else
      Response.write "<tr><td class=heading>"
      Response.write "You have not placed any orders."
      Response.write "</td></tr>"
    End If

  Else

    ' Here's where we'll view a specific order...

  End If
End If
%>
</table>
```

How It Works

If you run all that code now, you'll see something like this:

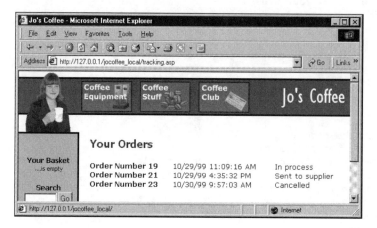

Simply, all the code does is use the `Orders` property of the `Customer` object to go away and get a list of the orders that have something happening to them – that they're being processed, the supplier's been asked to ship, or they've been cancelled. We then iterate through that list of orders rendering a link to call back into the `tracking.asp` page, the date of the order, and the status. We pull the text for the status code back from the `GetStatusText` method that we created in Chapter 9.

When the customer clicks on one of the links, we need to render the details of that particular order. Let's add some code to do that.

Try It Out – Rendering the Details of a Specific Order

1. We can reuse the `RenderOrder` helper function that we created in Chapter 9 to present the order. Here's the code that we need to add to `tracking.asp`:

```
Else

    ' Here's where we'll view a specific order...
    Dim order
    Set order = Visit.Orders.GetOrder(Request("id"))

    If not order.EOF Then

        ' Draw the heading...
        Response.write "<tr><td class=bigheading>"
        Response.write "Order Number " & order("orderid")
        Response.write "</td></tr>"
        Response.write "<tr><td><br></td></tr>"

        ' Use the RenderOrder helper function...
        RenderOrder order, False
```

```
    End If

    order.Close
    set order = Nothing

  End If
  %>
  </table>
```

At this point, we've presented a perfectly functional feature that lets your customers know the exact status of their current orders, and also provides historical information for orders they have placed in their overall dealings with your company.

This whole area presents more opportunities for you to build on the simple option we have presented – depending on the nature of your business you could think about implementing a system that allows for partial shipments, where some items in the order have been shipped and others are on order.

Integrated Shipment Tracking

One of the easiest WISMO problems to solve is the situation of a drop shipment where your supplier has sent off the package, it's en-route to the customer, and your customer wants to know where it is.

Whichever shipper you use to get your products to your customers' doors, chances are they have a way of uniquely identifying each package in their system – usually called a **tracking number**. If you're lucky, they also offer tools on their Web site that your customer can use to find out where a given package is in their system. UPS and FedEx both offer this service.

The beauty of the system is that, providing your customer can get the tracking number of the package, they can see exactly where it is. So, if you live in Tempe, Arizona and the Tempe, Arizona depot received your package at 2 a.m., you know there's a fairly good chance of getting your package that day. If it's still in Connecticut, you know it'll be a while.

Again this opens up another area for building on the Jo's Coffee application as it currently stands – depending on the shipper you may be able to obtain the tracking number of the shipment you ask them to send. You could then expand the application to enabling storing of this number in the database and subsequent presentation of it back to the customer. Even more impressively, you could alter the presentation layer to provide a link to the appropriate page on your shipper's site showing the status of the order.

Back Orders and Cancellations

As you may know, there is a degree of immediacy when buying stuff over the Internet. This stems from the fact that when a customer wants to buy something, they're mostly used to retail environments where they can get hold of their purchases immediately. For this reason, it's easy for customers to become frustrated when they're trying to get hold of the products they want and the online vendor they've chosen (you!) does not appear to be able to come up with the goods.

In any retail scenario, there's a good chance that the customer will want something that you can't give to them simply because there is short supply. In an offline retail environment, if a store doesn't have what you want, you can simply go find another store that can supply the item. This is also applicable for online retail, but there's often a delay between the time when you place the order and the time you learn that the merchant can't come up with the goods (yet another area for consideration in your e-commerce solution is to show product availability).

The single greatest source of frustration with e-commerce is placing an order online expecting it to arrive the next day, and on that next day checking the merchant's order tracking feature to discover the goods have been placed on back order. The frustration is not with the mechanics of our demand and supply economy, but rather the fact that the time it's going to take the customer to get the goods has now been lengthened.

When you learn a customer's order has been placed on back order, make sure that you tell them about it as soon as possible. The most obvious way to do this is through e-mail, but you may even find it beneficial to contact them by phone. Relying on the customer to log back into the site and check order status is the least preferable method of first alert. If there are a number of vendors selling the item that you offer they will, most likely, cancel the order and go to another merchant. This can be frustrating, but the last thing you want to do *ever* is create a customer service engagement so nightmarish that the customer avoids you forever, so don't be frightened to share the bad news with the customer. If you are selling into a niche market there is a fair likelihood that the customer will stick with you anyway – but they'll still want to know how long they can expect to wait.

Contact Details

Chances are that if your customer is using this feature, they have some customer service issues they're trying to resolve and this is their first port of call. Usually, WISMOs are simply the result of your shipping company taking a little longer than the customer expected to route goods through to them. Here the shipping tracking functionality we spoke about a little while ago could be especially useful in showing when the delay is with the shipping company, not the supplier.

However, if the customer is not satisfied by the information they find out in Order Tracking, it's good practice to route them to an escalation process as soon as possible. After a cursory look through the information they can find online, they will want to contact you – either through e-mail, or by phone. It makes sense, then, on this page to proactively offer up the customer service e-mail and toll-free phone number, like this:

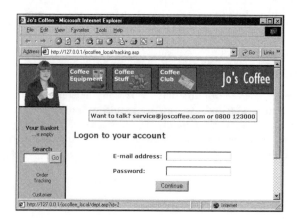

For maximum effect, it's important you put this on each of the order tracking pages – not least the one before the user has logged in, as is shown here. A customer that cannot log into their account is already frustrated enough, without having to hunt around for contact details. Of course, a customer that comes into the site specifically looking for contact information will most likely search out the Customer Service or Contact links that we talked about earlier.

Automatic 'Fire-and-Forget' E-mails

Most of the customer service methods we've seen here have been reactive rather than proactive. However, customers often appreciate it when a retailer makes an effort to ensure that transactions have been conducted to the service level the retailer desires.

An easy way of providing a level of proactive service is to use what we term here **fire-and-forget** e-mails. In this scenario, you create an e-mail when a trigger occurs, but don't actually send it until sometime in the future. The most obvious application for this is to send e-mails like:

```
Dear Tim,

We shipped an order to you on the 13th comprising the following:

1x Gaggia Coffee Classic Espresso Machine

You should have received this item by now. If you haven't please reply to this
message to talk to me, or alternatively phone 0800 123000.

If you have any other comments to make about your dealings with Jo's Coffee,
please let us know.

Regards,

Jo
```

When your supplier lets you know that this order has been shipped, create this e-mail, but don't send it out until five days have passed. An easy way to do this is to store the e-mails in a database table and write a simple process that checks to see if any need sending and, if they do, sends them. Although, for simplicity we've not done it here, one could envisage a number of methods of automating the message text generation.

To implement this strategy we're going to need to:

❑ Create a database table

❑ Create an appropriate view allowing us to access the information we require

❑ Build the `FireAndForget` service object that implements the e-mail sending operation

❑ Create a script that schedules the sending of the e-mails

Again, this is going to involve using the CDONTS library that we came across in Chapter 9. Don't forget that the NTS in CDONTS stands for NT Server. As this implies, CDONTS is available only to servers running Windows NT 4.0 – again we won't be concerning ourselves with the server configuration issues required to enable mail sending.

Try It Out – Creating the Database Table

1. Here's the structure for a database table called `FireAndForget` that can be used to hold the e-mails:

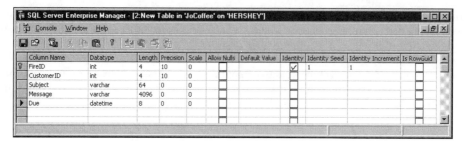

2. We'll also need this `vFireAndForget` view that joins the `FireAndForget` and `Customers` tables:

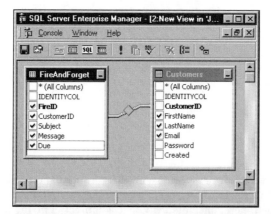

Try It Out – Creating the FireAndForget Object

1. To facilitate this fire-and-forget e-mail system, create a new class module in the `WroxCommerce` VB project called `FireAndForget`. Add this code:

```
Option Explicit

' Use IUtility to call back into the Visit and Database objects...
Private m_utility As IUtility
```

```
' Configure - set up IUtility...
Public Sub Configure(ByVal utility As IUtility)

    ' Hold the utility object...
    Set m_utility = utility

End Sub
```

2. Then, add this property to the `Visit` object. Unlike the `Customers` and `Orders` objects we've met up to this point, we're not going to hold onto the `FireAndForget` objects after they've been used, as this object will be used rarely in the course of the systems operation. Here's the `FireAndForget` property:

```
' FireAndForget - create an instance of the FireAndForget object...
Public Function FireAndForget() As FireAndForget
    Set FireAndForget = New FireAndForget
    FireAndForget.Configure Me
End Function
```

Try It Out – Queuing the E-mails

1. To queue the e-mails, we need to create a method that will let us add e-mails to the `FireAndForget` table. Add this method to the `FireAndForget` object:

```
' AddEMail - adds an e-mail to the queue...
Public Function AddEMail(ByVal CustomerID As Long, _
            ByVal Subject As String, ByVal Message As String, _
            ByVal DaysDelay As Integer, _
            Optional ByVal StartDate As Date) As Long

    ' Get the date the e-mail is supposed to go on...
    Dim SendDate As Date

    If Year(StartDate) <> 1899 Then
        SendDate = Now
    Else
        SendDate = StartDate
    End If

    SendDate = DateAdd("d", DaysDelay, SendDate)

    ' Create a new row...
    Dim EMail As New Recordset
    EMail.Open "FireAndForget", m_utility.DB.DB, adOpenKeyset, adLockOptimistic
    EMail.AddNew

    ' Set the values...
    EMail("customerid") = CustomerID
    EMail("subject") = Subject
    EMail("message") = Message
    EMail("due") = SendDate
```

```
    ' Update...
    EMail.Update
    AddEMail = EMail("fireid")

    EMail.Close
    Set EMail = Nothing

End Function
```

How It Works

This is a fairly simple function. Firstly, the date the e-mail is sent on is examined. Unlike most data types, when you create one it does not correctly report the fact that it's 'empty' using the IsEmpty function. However, if you query an 'empty' Date variable for it's year, you receive the value 1899. So, we'll be using the Year function and looking for a value of 1899 to test to see if we have an 'empty' date. Usually, this is specified as the number of days from the current date to send the mail on:

```
    If Year(StartDate) <> 1899 Then
        SendDate = Now
    Else
        SendDate = StartDate
    End If

    SendDate = DateAdd("d", DaysDelay, SendDate)
```

An alternate start date can be specified to send e-mails on a specific day in the future (such as on your customer's birthday, etc.).

Secondly, a new row is created in the FireAndForget table and is configured with the text of the message, the customer ID, the subject, and the date:

```
    Dim EMail As New Recordset
    EMail.Open "FireAndForget", m_utility.DB.DB, adOpenKeyset, adLockOptimistic
    EMail.AddNew

    ' Set the values...
    EMail("customerid") = CustomerID
    EMail("subject") = Subject
    EMail("message") = Message
    EMail("due") = SendDate
```

Finally, the row is updated and the new ID of the row in FireAndForget is returned:

```
    EMail.Update
    AddEMail = EMail("fireid")
```

To ask this method to send e-mail to the customer today informing them that the order has been shipped, and another to tell them in five days that they should have received it, you can use something like this:

```
' Tell them what happened today...
Visit.FireAndForget.AddEMail Visit.CustomerID, "Order Shipped", _
            "Your order has been shipped.", 0

' ask them again in five days time...
Visit.FireAndForget.AddEMail Visit.CustomerID, "Follow-up", _
            "Did you get your order?", 5
```

This is example code and doesn't have to be added to the project at this time. We'll see in the next section an appropriate point for calling this code.

Try It Out – Sending the E-mails

Of course, having e-mails sitting in a database doesn't help your customers get an idea of what's going on! What we have to do now is create a mechanism that can extract and send those e-mails.

1. To start with, select Project | References...from the menu and check Microsoft CDO for NTS 1.2 Library.

2. Then, add this method to the FireAndForget object:

```
' Process - sends out the pending e-mails...
Public Function Process()

    ' Send the mails through this...
    Dim cdo As CDONTS.NewMail

    ' Get a list of the e-mails that need to go...
    Dim query As Recordset
    Set query = m_utility.DB.RunQuery("FireAndForget", "vFireAndForget", _
                "GetDate() > Due", , True)

    Do While Not query.EOF

        ' Create the e-mail object...
        Set cdo = New CDONTS.NewMail

        ' Send the mail...
        cdo.Send "service@joscoffee.com", query("email"), query("subject"), _
            query("message")

        ' Cleanup
        Set cdo = Nothing

        ' Next
        query.MoveNext

    Loop

    query.Close
    Set query = Nothing

End Function
```

How It Works

The trick with the `Process` method is to ask the database to return only those e-mails that are due to go out by using the SQL Server scalar function `GetDate()` in combination with the `Due` column:

```
Dim query As Recordset
Set query = m_utility.DB.RunQuery("FireAndForget", "vFireAndForget", _
                "GetDate() > Due", , True)
```

Then, the list of results is looped and CDONTS is used to send the e-mail out. Note that we set the return address for the mail to `service@joscoffee.com`. This ensures that if the customer has any issue with the message, they can click Reply and get straight back in touch:

```
Do While Not query.EOF

    ' Create the e-mail object...
    Set cdo = New CDONTS.NewMail

    ' Send the mail...
    cdo.Send "service@joscoffee.com", query("email"), query("subject"), _
        query("message")

    ' Cleanup
    Set cdo = Nothing

    ' Next
    query.MoveNext

Loop
```

Scheduling the E-mails

We still haven't seen a way of making that `FireAndForget.Process` method run on a regular basis. One of the easiest ways to do this is to use **Windows Script Host** and **Windows NT Scheduler** – the former a technology we touched on earlier in the chapter regarding regularly testing our customer server e-mail addresses.

Windows Script Host

In Chapter 3, when we introduced the concept of ActiveX, we spoke about a technology called Active Scripting that was used by ASP to actually run the code embedded in your pages. We also alluded to the fact that other applications are also able to leverage Active Scripting functionality. One such application is **Windows Script Host**.

Windows Script Host works in a similar way to batch files that have been around for a number of years. Simply, it allows you to build a file containing commands written in any of the languages that the installation of Active Scripting on your machine supports (Active Scripting ships with VBScript and JScript support, but third-party developers have written language plug-ins for PERL and others). Because it is powered by Active Scripting, it acts as an ActiveX component container and can therefore make calls into any ActiveX component.

In the next section we'll see how we can build a small file containing VBScript code capable of establishing a connection to the WroxCommerce Visit object. Then we'll see how this same file can create an instance of the FireAndForget object and call the Process method to get it to process the e-mails stored in the database.

Try It Out – Running Processes Regularly by using the Windows Script Host

1. Here's the code to create and configure the Visit object and then call the Process method. Open Notepad, enter the code below and save to a file called ProcessMails.vbs:

```
' Create and configure the visit object...
Dim visit
Set visit = WScript.CreateObject("WroxCommerce.Visit")
visit.Configure "Jo's Coffee", "joscoffee.com", "driver=SQL " & _
"Server;DATABASE=JoCoffee;UID=JoCoffeeWeb;PWD=eermlate;SERVER=localhost"

' Call the FireAndForget process...
visit.FireAndForget.Process
' Cleanup
visit.ShutDown
Set visit = Nothing
```

When we want to run code in Windows Script Host, we use WScript.CreateObject, rather than Server.CreateObject. Otherwise, the code should be very familiar. Now all we have to do is configure NT's Task Scheduler to run this for us.

2. First of all, we have to make sure that the Task Scheduler service is running. Open **Control Panel** and locate **Services**. Then scroll down the pane until you find the service (note that prior to IE5, this service was called **Scheduler**, as opposed to **Task Scheduler**, so you may need to hunt around for it). Whatever the name on your system, make sure it's started and also make sure it's configured to start on system startup.

3. Open a command prompt now – you can see what jobs are scheduled by simply entering:

```
AT
```

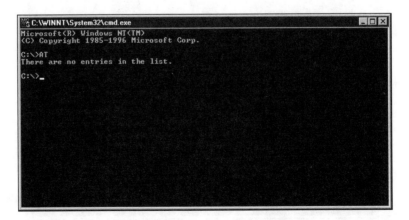

4. Naturally, in a scenario like ours, we want to run the process at least once a day, and we can use this to specify each day:

```
AT 1am /EVERY:Sunday,Monday,Tuesday,Wednesday,Thursday,Friday,Saturday
c:\Scripts\ProcessMails.vbs
```

Unfortunately, you do have to enter the name of each day in full – abbreviations are not allowed. Of course, it could be the case that we want to run the script even more regularly than that, and to do this you have to create a different job for each time slot.

5. Run the AT command again to examine the results:

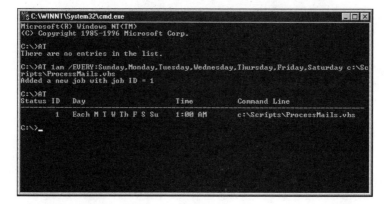

6. If you want to delete an event (unfortunately, you can't change an event – you have to delete and recreate it), you can use the /delete command. You need to know the ID of the event ahead of time, so run the AT command to get a list of the events that are registered.

7. Select the event you want and note its ID. Run this command:

```
AT idNumber /delete
```

8. Run the AT command again to examine the results:

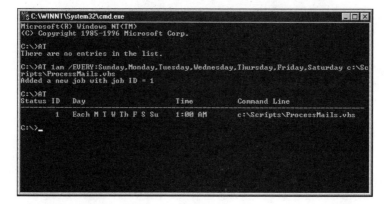

Summary

In this chapter, we learned about the importance of providing quality customer service in an online environment. We learned about some tools to help bridge the gap between the customer and the vendor such as:

- ❑ Toll-free phone numbers – just like offline retail operations require toll-free numbers we saw that online ones do as well.

- ❑ Customer service e-mails – we saw the importance of presenting contact addresses to the user, learned about how small e-tailers can respond quickly to queries through pager technology and a little about contact forms.

- ❑ BizRate.com – we saw how this online pioneer is helping us learn more about our customers, at the same time as creating a neat shopping portal.

- ❑ Order tracking – we saw how we can reduce the number of "Where is my order?" (WISMO) calls into the company by showing the customer where their order is through the site.

- ❑ Fire-and-Forget e-mails – we saw how we can queue e-mails for future sending to proactively enhance the shopping experience and make sure a transaction went smoothly.

During our examination of these topics we enhanced the Jo's Coffee application by:

- ❑ Adding a customer service page

- ❑ Adding functionality to our existing object model by enabling order tracking

- ❑ Expanding our object model by adding the `FireAndForget` service object and a supporting database table to facilitate e-mailing

- ❑ Scheduled the e-mails for sending at defined times

During the chapter we highlighted a number of areas where you might want to build upon the attributes we've described within the Jo's Coffee project.

Creating an Online Community

All the way back in Chapter 1, we spoke at length about online communities and how they can be a powerful tool to make a Web site successful. The premise is simple: give potential customers a compelling reason to come to the store even if they have no intention to buy. Belonging to a community creates loyalty and so customers are more likely to buy from you, as opposed to your competitor.

In the next stage of e-commerce/e-business evolution, we'll see more companies simply acting as an agency to let people with similar interests communicate. Although the message will be primarily one of sharing and communication, these sites will build in an underlying message promoting the fact that the site can also supply the various goods and services that make whatever market sector or interest group they're involved with more exciting.

In this section, we'll be seeing how Jo can create a community of people who want to talk about coffee-related subjects. Jo can then become an active part of this community herself by chatting with the visitors to the site, and sharing her knowledge and experience. This community environment is only one click away from a selling environment from which Jo can profit. It's almost as if she's sponsoring the meetings of a club of coffee enthusiasts.

In this chapter, we're going to look at building an online community by:

- ❑ Implementing a newsletter of Jo's Coffee announcements
- ❑ Implementing a discussion group called All About Coffee

Newsletters

One of the most common ways of keeping in contact with your customers and regular visitors to the site is to have an online **newsletter**. This feature is also known as a **mailing list** and is often run by a computer called a **list server**.

Most of us are familiar with these, as our inbox fills up with them every day. Despite their bad press, some people do find them an excellent way for keeping up to date with what's going on at a particular company in terms of special deals or other information. As we discussed in our chapter on privacy, it's very important that you don't abuse the trust afforded to you by subscribers by behaving irresponsibly. Usually, this means not adding people to your mailing list until they specifically ask to be added (**opt-in**), and not selling, renting or giving their names to other companies without their express permission.

Implementing a Newsletter

There are, as with everything, a few ways you can implement a newsletter; the options we'll quickly discuss are:

❑ Constructing our own

❑ Buying a mailing list package

❑ Using an online service

To build your own online newsletter, simply collect a list of names and e-mail addresses in your database and periodically run a script that fires off your e-mail to each of them. This can be done using Windows Script Host and SQL Server, but the main issue with this is that as the list grows in size, your server could start to experience severe load. Coverage of the Windows Script Host is beyond the scope of this book, but if you would like to learn more about it, please refer to the *Windows Script Host Programmer's Reference* by Dino Esposito (Wrox Press, ISBN 1-861002-65-3).

Buying a mailing list package will allow you to supply it with a list of e-mail addresses and, in a similar manner to a homegrown solution, it will fire off your newsletter to each person on that list. The advantage with using an off-the-shelf package is that it is cheaper and faster than developing your own.

The third option here is to use an online service that deals with the whole problem for you. **ListBot,** which is part of Microsoft's bCentral service (http://www.bcentral.com), lets you set up your own mailing list, and provides methods for letting people subscribe and unsubscribe either through a Web site or through e-mail. In this chapter, we'll be implementing a mailing list using ListBot. However, one thing you should be aware of with this service is that the e-mail will come from the @listbot.com domain, which will not help build your online brand.

> **As we've said before, there are lots of competing services out there, so make sure you shop around to make sure you're getting the one that best suits your needs.**

ListBot

The ListBot Web site can be found at http://www.listbot.com. If you choose to use ListBot as your mailing list tool, you have two options available to you: ListBot Free (which is free) and ListBot Gold (which costs $99 a year). One of the biggest benefits to ListBot Gold is that you won't have third-party advertisements in your mails.

Here are some key features of ListBot:

❑ Multiple lists on one account – so you can create a single **list owner** account with them and build as many mailing lists as you like.

❑ Assorted newsletter types – **announcement** (traditional newsletters), **discussion** (everyone gets a copy as the list goes on) or **moderated lists** (the owner has to approve messages before they get distributed).

❑ Reports – ListBot can send out daily or weekly **reports** to the list owner detailing the subscribers to the list.

❑ Demographics – ListBot Gold can collect **demographic information**, such as salary, number of children, etc. However, collecting this kind of data isn't very fashionable right now as privacy issues are very much in the news, so you most likely do not want to collect demographics for a mailing list.

As this is a technical book, we're not going to go through the details of how to actually create a list in ListBot – if you can handle constructing an order processing pipeline from scratch then you can handle filling in a few forms!

The account you create at ListBot has an e-mail address of accountname@listbot.com, so Jo's one is called joscoffee@listbot.com. Depending on the type of list you create, something different will happen each time a message is sent over to that account. Jo's one is configured as an announcement list that only she can post to; hence each time she sends e-mail over to joscoffee@listbot.com, everyone on the list receives a copy. So, every two weeks, or whatever period she chooses, she simply sends out the newsletter to that address and ListBot handles the distribution to those people that have registered.

After we've created our ListBot list, we want to add it in as an option on the home page. ListBot automatically provides the appropriate HTML that needs embedding into the page to present the list and we'll see this code at the end of the following exercise. When we created our list, we didn't ask for any demographic information to be collected, so the only field we have is our e-mail address.

Try It Out – Implementing ListBot

1. ListBot provides HTML code that should be added to the page so that visitors to the site can subscribe to the newsletter. Here's the mess of code we have to add to default.asp. The code also includes a link over to the list archive, which is hosted by ListBot as part of the service:

```
<!-- coffeeclub... -->
<tr><td><br></td></tr>
<tr><td class="tableRed">Coffee Club</td></tr>
```

```
<tr><td>
<!-- Begin ListBot Code -->
<form method="post" action="http://www.listbot.com/cgi-bin/subscriber">
<table border=0><tr><td colspan=2 class=small>
Join our mailing list!<br>
Enter your email address below,<br>
then click the 'Join List' button:<br>
</td></tr><tr><td>
<input type=text name="e_mail">
<input type=hidden name="list_id" value="joscoffee">
<input type=hidden name="Act" value="subscribe_list">
</td><td>
<input type=image src="http://www.listbot.com/subscribe_button.gif"
            border=0 width=88 height=31
            alt="Click here to join our mailing list!">
</td></tr><tr><td colspan=2>
```

```
<font size=1 face="arial">
<a href="http://www.listbot.com/" target="_top">Powered by ListBot</a></font> |
<font size=1 face="arial">
<a href="http://www.listbot.com/archive/joscoffee" target="_top">
View List Archive</a></font><br>
</td></tr></table>
</form>
<!-- End ListBot Code -->
</td></tr>

<!-- end our table... -->
```

How It Works

Our home page now looks like this:

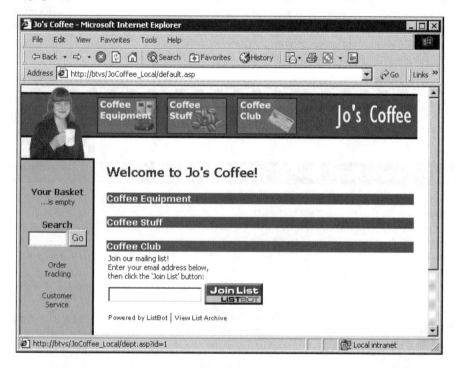

What to Put in the Newsletter

You'll have to experiment with what you choose to put in the newsletter, but whatever you do put in there should be compelling and interesting to its recipients. Most importantly, it has to promote the online brand that you are trying to create (so, in our example, we're promoting the Jo's Coffee brand), and it has to push visitors back to the site. A common way of pulling visitors back to the site is to run special sales promotions or site surveys, and these are certainly something you can advertise in the newsletter.

Speaking of advertising, there's no reason why you can't sell advertising space in your newsletter. We'll discuss marketing in greater detail in Chapter 18, but to jump ahead a little, one of the most promising ways to advertise right now is to do so in targeted mailing lists. If you could find someone who wanted to specifically target your customers (not your competitors, obviously!), you might well be able to sell them sponsorship of the newsletter. It is important, however, that you make sure that any sponsorship deals do not violate your privacy policy.

Original content is also a good way to make a newsletter interesting. Naturally, if the recipient of your newsletter has enjoyed one because there was some interesting stuff in it, she'll be more likely to read, and less likely to unsubscribe from, the newsletter. In Jo's case, good original content would be a review of a local coffee bar, or a recipe for a particular espresso-based coffee drink. One final point; you may want to consider including graphics in the mail, as Amazon have begun to do recently.

Discussion Groups

One of the neatest ways to involve Web site visitors in a compelling community experience is to implement **discussion groups**, which are also known as **bulletin boards** or **message boards**. A discussion group, as the name implies, allows a discussion to be held on the Web site itself. Whereas Jo's newsletter is just a method for her to announce new products, sales, or new features on the site, a discussion group is a facility that allows Jo and her customers to discuss coffee related matters. While the newsletters are a one-way communication, discussion groups can involve hundreds of people in conversation.

Here's a screenshot of the ASP Forum on the Wrox Press Web site:

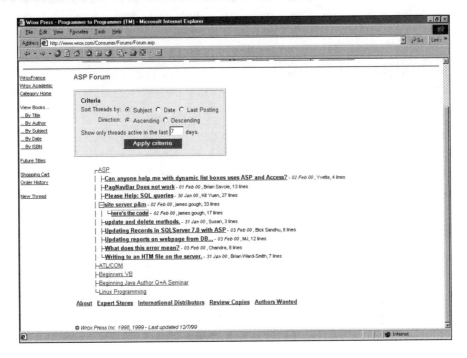

Although building a discussion group from scratch is not that hard to do (easier than what we've done thus far, certainly!), we're going to be using an off-the-shelf package for our discussion group's needs. We're doing this to illustrate how it's possible to build a quality Web experience through a combination of homegrown software and bought-in software. Most good Web sites are a hybrid mix of these. For example, Buy.com uses its own cart and catalog components, its own application integration software and an off-the-shelf package for customer management called Business Evolution (http://www.businessevolution.com/). Buying in software improves your innovation cycle by giving you the power to concentrate on your company's core competencies, while still giving customers the tools they expect or need in response to new opportunities and competition.

Doug Dean's EZsite Forum 3

Throughout this chapter, we're going to be working with Doug Dean's EZsite Forum 3. These components are used on a number of sites around the world and provide a comprehensive set of tools for creating engaging discussion groups. You can find more information on the capabilities of these components at the EZsite Forum 3 site at http://www.dougdean.com/.

> **Again, to make the book as practical as possible we're working with a specific product; as stated previously, this coverage should not be taken as a recommendation.**

Try It Out – Setting Up the Forum

1. Firstly, we have to obtain EZsite Forum 3 from http://www.dougdean.com/. At the time of going to press, these components cost $349 per processor. An evaluation version is available for download.

2. After downloading the components, you have to unzip them into a folder (on my machine I unzipped to a folder called `D:\EZForum`) on your computer. You should now have:

- ❑ Four folders (`Forums`, `Documentation`, `Database`, and `Components`)
- ❑ Two ASP pages (`OnLineDocumentation.asp` and `ForumManager.asp`)
- ❑ A license agreement (`License.txt`)
- ❑ An HTML page (`GettingStarted.htm`)

3. You will usually get two DLLs, one for Visual Basic 5 (`EzsiteForum3.dll`) and one for Visual Basic 6 (`EzsiteForum3VB6.dll`). You need to rename the appropriate DLL to `EZsiteForum3.dll`. If you've downloaded the trial version, the names will have a `T` at the end (`EzsiteForum3T.dll` and `EzsiteForum3VB6T.dll`), which you should keep so that the DLL is called `EzsiteForum3T.dll`.

4. Now we need to manually register `EZsiteForum3.dll` in the `Components` folder. If you're not familiar with how to register a component, you need to go to the Start menu and select Run, then type regsvr32 "d:\EZForum\Components\EZsiteForum3.dll" into the box and click OK:

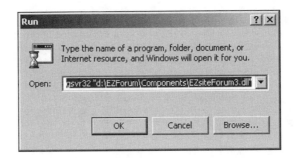

5. Our next task is to create the forum; by default, the components are designed to run in a Microsoft Access environment, but they can be configured to operate in a SQL Server environment, which is what we're using for Jo's site. To do this, there is a SQL script supplied with the components that, when executed, will create all of the tables needed to handle the discussion forums. As these SQL scripts create tables, you should check through them to make sure they don't clash with any of the tables or views that are already a part of your database. In our case, none of the tables clash with ones we've built so far, so we're OK to run the script on the `JoCoffee` database.

The best way to run a lengthy SQL script in SQL Server 7 is to use the Query Analyzer. Open SQL Server's Enterprise Manager, select the `JoCoffee` database, and select **Tools | SQL Server Query Analyzer** from the menu. When the Query Analyzer loads, it will default to the `master` database, so you should use the drop-down list in the top-right corner of the query window to select `JoCoffee`.

6. When that's done, select **File | Open** from the menu and open the `EZsiteForumSchema.sql` file (this is located in the `EZForum\Database` folder). When that's done, select **Query | Execute** from the menu.

7. When the components render the forum information, graphics will be embedded into the results. To make these graphics available, copy the `graphics` folder and all of its contents (located under the `Forums` folder) into the `JoCoffee_Local` folder that provides the content for our site.

Try It Out – Managing the Forum

1. ASP-driven tools are supplied to help us manage the forum when it's installed. In the `EZForum` folder, there is an ASP page called `ForumManager.asp`. Copy this file into the same `admin` directory in which the main site's administrative tools are.

2. We need to tweak `ForumManager.asp` a little to get it working with the site. Load `ForumManager.asp` into the editor and make these changes:

```
<% Response.Buffer = True %>
<% Response.Expires = 0 %>

<HTML><HEAD><TITLE>EZsite Forum Manager</TITLE></HEAD>

<%
```

```
'########## INTIALIZE THE FORUM OBJECT ##########
Set ObjForum = Server.CreateObject("EZsiteForum.ForumManager")
ObjForum.DSN = "Provider=SQLOLEDB.1;Persist Security Info=False;" & _
    "User ID=JoCoffeeWeb;Password=eermlate;Initial Catalog=JoCoffee;" &_
    "Data Source=localhost"

'~~~~~ If you want the Forum Id's to show on the
'   managers forum list page, set ShowForumID to true
ObjForum.ShowForumID = true

'The Forum Site Account ID can be displayed
'next to each Forum Site Name. A forum site's
'Account ID can be used as an argument in the
'ListForums() method in order to list only those
'forums within this Forum Site group.
ObjForum.ShowAccountID = true


'====== NEW FEATURES 4/15/1999 =====================
' Advanced developers properties.
' See AfterNewForumURL.asp file for documentation.
'ObjForum.AfterNewForumURL = "AfterNewForumURL.asp"
'ObjForum.AfterNewForumOn = true
'ObjForum.AfterNewForumValuesOn = true
'===================================================

ObjForum.ImagePath = "../graphics/"

ObjForum.Manager
%>

</HTML>
```

How It Works

We include the following line at the top of the page, as the components require it to be buffered:

```
<% Response.Buffer = True %>
```

When a page is buffered, ASP runs the page completely through and generates the entire HTML before sending it down to the client. The default operation is to send the content as the page is generated.

The first line we altered tells the components to use our SQL Server database, rather than an Access database:

```
ObjForum.DSN = "Provider=SQLOLEDB.1;Persist Security Info=False;" & _
    "User ID=JoCoffeeWeb;Password=eermlate;Initial Catalog=JoCoffee;" &_
    "Data Source=localhost"
```

By default, the components will attempt to use a DSN called DSNForum; this line gives it an alternate connection string.

The second line we change tells the components where to find the graphics files used in presentation:

```
ObjForum.ImagePath = "../graphics/"
```

In this case, it's in the `graphics` folder, so we have to use the "`..`" directive to tell the components to come back out of the `admin` folder to find the files.

The final line of code, which we did not alter, does the actual job of rendering the forum manager, as we'll now examine:

```
ObjForum.Manager
```

Try It Out – Using the Forum Manager

1. Open the Forum Manager now by browsing to `admin/ForumManager.asp`. You'll be asked to enter a user name and password. The user name is Forum Site, the password is password:

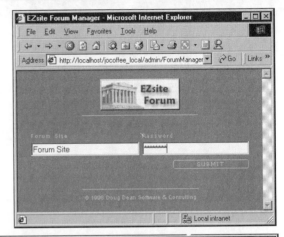

2. The only thing we have to do in the Forum Manager for now is change the title and description for the forum. Once you've logged in, you'll be presented with a list of the forums available in the site. Click on the little pencil icon to the left of [change this text to your forum title]. Change the AUTHOR of the forum to Jo Bovingdon, the TITLE to All About Coffee and finally change the TEXT to A discussion forum about coffee. Totally free and relaxed... Say what you think!

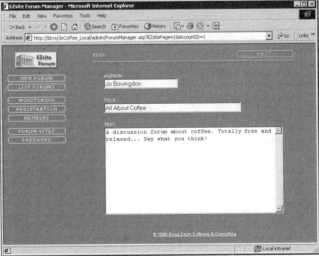

3. Click Next (in the top right-hand corner) and you'll be asked to confirm the changes. Click Save.

4. One thing we need to note down for when we're actually presenting the forum to the visitor is the ID number of the forum. In our case, this is the small 1 to the left of the forum name:

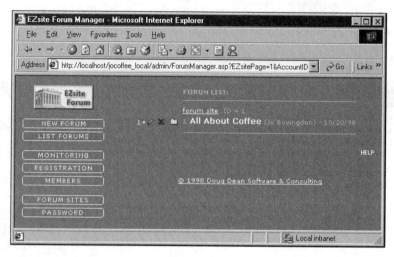

Presenting the Forum

We now need a way of presenting the forum to the visitors of the site. To do this, we need to build a separate page for presenting the forum.

Looking back at the code we had before for the Forum Manager, the last line in our ASP block was:

```
ObjForum.Manager
```

The `Manager` method on the `EZsiteForum.ForumManager` object has been built to render all of the management tools to the site's administrator. In a way, the component has implemented both its business and presentation layers in compiled components, rather than having the presentation layer in ASP. This makes it substantially easier to deploy the components on remote systems, as there's no plumbing work. However, this does limit the amount of customization that can be done to the presentation layer.

We're about to use the `EZsiteForum.Forum` object to perform the same trick. We'll set up the component and then call a method that will render the forum. However, because of the way we've built our site, there are some conflicts with the way EZsite presents its part. Mainly, these have to do with forms stretching out our layout and corrupting it.

To remedy this, we're going to put the forum into a separate frame set, and we'll see how to do that in a little while.

Try It Out – Plumbing in the Forum

1. To plumb in the forum, we need to create links on the navigation bar, and on the home page, to a page called `forum.asp` that we're going to build in the next section. To add a link to the forum to the **Coffee Club** button on the top navigation bar, open `start.asp` and change this code:

```
<!-- now we need to look at the first line in the layout.
This comprises Jo's head, the three site section buttons,
and the "Jo's Coffee" logo -->

  <tr>
    <td><a href="default.asp">
    <img src="i/johead.gif" border="0" WIDTH="112" HEIGHT="76">
    </a></td> <!-- Jo's head -->
    <td><a href="dept.asp?id=1">
    <img src="i/machines.gif" WIDTH="103" HEIGHT="76" border=0>
    </a></td> <!-- "Coffee Machines" button -->
    <td><a href="dept.asp?id=2">
    <img src="i/coffee.gif" WIDTH="106" HEIGHT="76" border=0>
    </a></td>  <!-- "Coffee" button -->
    <td><a href="forum.asp">
    <img src="i/club.gif" WIDTH="105" HEIGHT="76" border=0>
    </a></td>  <!-- "Coffee Club" button -->
    <td><a href="default.asp">
    <img src="i/logo.gif" border="0" WIDTH="174" HEIGHT="76">
    </a></td>  <!-- "Jo's Coffee" logo -->
  </tr>
```

2. Secondly, we need to add a link to the home page, to the right of the form that we use to ask visitors to sign up for the newsletter. To do this, we need to wrap a table around the ListBot form and put our link into the right-most of two table cells. Here's the code we need to change in `default.asp`:

```
<tr><td>
<table cellspacing=0 cellpadding=0 width=100%>
<tr><td>
    <!-- Begin ListBot Code -->
    <form method="post"
    action="http://www.listbot.com/cgi-bin/subscriber">
    <table border=0><tr><td colspan=2 class=small>
    Join our mailing list!<br>
    Enter your email address below,<br>
    then click the 'Join List' button:<br>
    </td></tr><tr><td>
    <input type=text name="e_mail">
    <input type=hidden name="list_id" value="joscoffee">
    <input type=hidden name="Act" value="subscribe_list">
    </td><td>
    <input type=image src="http://www.listbot.com/subscribe_button.gif"
    border=0 width=88 height=31 alt="Click here to join our mailing
    list!"></td></tr><tr><td colspan=2
```

```
<font size=1 face="arial"><a href="http://www.listbot.com/"
target="_top">Powered by ListBot</a></font> |
<font size=1 face="arial"><a
href="http://www.listbot.com/archive/joscoffee"
target="_top">View List Archive</a></font><br>
</td></tr></table>
</form>
<!-- End ListBot Code -->
</td><td align=right valign=top class=heading>
<a href="forum.asp">Talk about coffee at our Coffee Club</a>
</td></tr></table>
</td></tr>
```

Try It Out – Building forum.asp

1. We should now move on to create the new forum.asp page; add a new ASP page to the project and add the following code:

```
<HTML>
   <HEAD>

   <!-- #include file="site.asp" -->
   <TITLE><%=g_sitename%></TITLE>

   <!-- do the frames... -->
   <frameset rows="30, *">
      <frame src="forumtop.asp" name=forumtop noresize scrolling=no>
      <frame src="forumdata.asp" name=forumdata>
   </frameset>

   </HEAD>
   <BODY>
   </BODY>
</HTML>
```

The only reason why we require the site.asp page for our new forum.asp page is to provide the g_sitename constant for the caption at the top.

2. As you've probably guessed, we need to build two pages to present the forum – one for the top of the frameset, one for the bottom. The top section simply provides a link back to the main site, so set up a new page called forumtop.asp and add the following:

```
<% option explicit %>
<HTML>
<HEAD>
   <!-- #include file="site.asp" -->
   <TITLE><%=g_sitename%></TITLE>
   <LINK rel="stylesheet" type="text/css" href="style.css">
</HEAD>
<BODY leftmargin=0 topmargin=0>
   <table width=100% height=100%>
      <tr><td class=heading align=center>
```

```
      <a href="default.asp" target=_top>
      Return to <%=g_sitename%>
      </a></td></tr>
   </table>
</BODY>
</HTML>
```

Again, `site.asp` is included to provide the name of the site.

3. The last page in the set you need to create is `forumdata.asp`, which will present the forum and all of the associated visitor-side tools to the visitor. Here's the code for the new page:

```
<% response.buffer = true %>
<HTML>
<HEAD>
   <!-- #include file="site.asp" -->
   <TITLE><%=g_sitename%></TITLE>
   <LINK rel="stylesheet" type="text/css" href="style.css">
</HEAD>
<BODY>
<%
   ' create the forum components...
   Dim ObjForum
   Set ObjForum = Server.CreateObject("EZsiteForum.Forum")

   ' configure the forum...
   ObjForum.DSN = "Provider=SQLOLEDB.1;Persist Security Info=False;" & _
      "User ID=JoCoffeeWeb;Password=eermlate;Initial Catalog=JoCoffee;" &_
      "Data Source=localhost"
   ObjForum.ImagePath = "graphics/"

   ' present the forum...
   ObjForum.ShowForum(1)
%>
</BODY>
</HTML>
```

How It Works

In `forumdata.asp` the only code we really need to comment on is this:

```
   ' configure the forum...
   ObjForum.DSN = "Provider=SQLOLEDB.1;Persist Security Info=False;" & _
      "User ID=JoCoffeeWeb;Password=eermlate;Initial Catalog=JoCoffee;" &_
      "Data Source=localhost"
   ObjForum.ImagePath = "graphics/"

   ' present the forum...
   ObjForum.ShowForum(1)
```

The user of the `DSN` and `ImagePath` properties have previously been discussed when we modified the `ForumManager.asp` page, and here we're using them for the same reasons. Otherwise, the only other line of note concerns the presentation of the forum, where the ID of the forum (which we noted down when using the Forum Manager) is passed into `ShowForum`.

Here's what the forum looks like before we enter any comments:

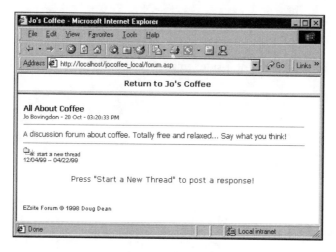

Notice how the bar at the top of the frameset contains a convenient way to jump back to the site proper. If we wanted, we could make this bar look more like the actual top navigation bar on the site. When discussion threads are added to the forum, here's what happens:

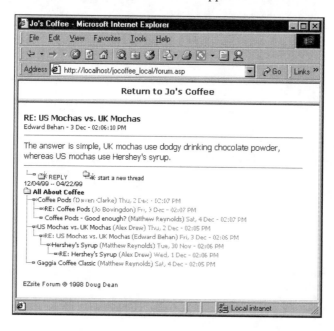

As you can imagine, with a lot of conversations going on, that list can get quite large and requires some degree of management.

Try It Out – Managing Threads

1. You can use the `CollapseThreads` property to create an Explorer-like navigation view through the discussion tree. Add this code to `forumdata.asp`:

```
' configure...
    ObjForum.DSN = "Provider=SQLOLEDB.1;Persist Security Info=False;" & _
        "User ID=JoCoffeeWeb;Password=eermlate;Initial Catalog=JoCoffee;" &_
        "Data Source=localhost"
ObjForum.ImagePath = "graphics/"
ObjForum.CollapseThreads = True
```

2. Now if we look at our forum, we see this:

More Forum Options

EZsite Forum comes with a bundle of options for manipulating the way that your forums look, including:

- ❑ **Moderated** – You can put together your discussion forums in such a way that a moderator has to approve all posts before they are made public. Jo could use this to ensure that inflammatory comments were *not* posted on her site.

- ❑ **Frame-based** – You can split the view we've created so far into two frames. This makes navigation a little easier by providing easier access to the message tree when displaying lengthy posts.

- ❑ **Membership** – You can require people to register and log on to the message forums before they are allowed to make posts.

- ❑ **Multiple forums** – The components can handle a virtually unlimited number of discussion forums.

Remember, you can find more information on the capabilities of these components at the EZsite Forum 3 site at http://www.dougdean.com/.

Summary

In this chapter, we implemented some of the community features that we started talking about in Chapter 1 when we discussed Jo's business migration strategy. The purpose of these features is to make sure that customers keep coming back to our site even if they do not want to buy anything.

We discussed the importance of a newsletter, to make announcements regarding new products and services, and then saw how to put together a simple newsletter using MSN's ListBot service. This allows Jo to communicate with her customers and potential customers on a regular basis, drawing them back into the store.

We then looked at discussion groups, which allow conversations between Jo's customers, and between Jo and her customers. We took a detailed look at the role of commercial software in discussion groups – particularly Doug Dean's EZsite Forum 3. With this it is simple to quickly build a discussion board for people who wanted to share ideas and knowledge about coffee-related subjects.

Up-sell, Cross-sell, and Recommendations

As a retailer, you probably know what people like to buy, or should buy, when they visit your store. Maybe you have a batch of coffee that's nearing its sell-by date and want to move it quickly, or maybe your customer may also like a set of batteries to go with his portable espresso machine.

In this chapter, we're going to examine how we can actively pitch a product or products to customers of the store. Specifically, we'll be showing you:

- ❑ How to **up-sell** better products to your customers

- ❑ How to **cross-sell** complementary products to your customers (e.g. cross-sell coffee to someone buying a coffee machine)

- ❑ How to put featured items on the home page

We'll round the chapter off by briefly looking at Amazon.com's system for making sales recommendations.

Making Suggestions

As we mentioned in the introduction, the ability to suggest to customers that they should make additional purchases is a powerful e-commerce sales tool. Generally speaking, there are three sorts of recommendations you can make:

- ❑ **Up-sell** – try to sell the customer a product that's "better" than the one she is looking at. For example, if she's looking at a Toyota, try to sell her a Lexus (naturally, depending on your retail strategy, better here may simply mean higher margin).

- ❑ **Cross-sell** – try to sell the customer a complementary product. For example, selling batteries with toys.

- ❑ **Dynamic recommendation** – try to sell the customer additional goods that you think he or she may like, based on what other customers and the customer have already purchased.

We're going to begin by talking about up-selling and cross-selling. We'll then move on to discuss dynamic recommendations at the end of the chapter.

The Suggestion Matrix

In order to make effective suggestions, you first have to build a **suggestion matrix**. This is a table that defines what you're trying to sell, and how you're trying to sell it.

Here's a very simple suggestion matrix for a Gaggia Espresso coffee machine and beans. We assume that the customer is about to make a purchase from the column on the left. For each purchase, we check to see what kind of sale is appropriate.

Purchase: Suggestions:	Gaggia Carezza Machine	Rich, Espresso Blend	Expensive, Italian Blend
Gaggia Carezza Machine		Cross-sell	Cross-sell
Rich, Espresso Blend			Up-sell
Expensive, Italian Blend			

If there's no entry in the cell, no form of up-selling or cross-selling is appropriate. For example, if someone wanted to buy the Rich, Espresso Blend, we don't want to try selling them the Rich, Espresso Blend or a new espresso machine. Depending on the number of products we have available, they may well feel swamped by our suggestions.

An interesting thing to come out of this is that cross-selling and up-selling have a direction. It doesn't make much sense for us to try to suggest they buy a cheaper product if they've already gone for the high-end Italian one. Therefore, however we structure the tools for entering these recommendations into the product catalog, we'll have to make sure they operate in one direction only.

The Suggestions Table

What we'll do now is create a database table that is capable of holding the data in that matrix, and any other cross-sell or up-sell suggestions we wish to make. We'll call this new table `Suggestions`. Once the table is populated with data, whenever we display information about a certain product, we can use it to find our suggestions.

So, if we view information for the Gaggia Carezza, we look up the ID for that product in the `Suggestions` table and pull out the details of the products that are linked to it.

Try It Out – Creating the Database Table

1. Our first step in developing our suggestion system is to build a database table to represent our selling matrix. Create this table called `Suggestions`:

Column Name	Datatype	Length	Precision	Scale	Allow Nulls	Default Value	Identity	Identity Seed	Identity Increment	Is RowGuid
SuggestionID	int	4	10	0			✓	1	1	
ProductID	int	4	10	0						
RelatedProductID	int	4	10	0						
SellType	smallint	2	5	0						

How It Works

This is a pretty simple table. Its main function is to associate a product ID with another product ID. `ProductID` can be taken to represent the left-most column in matrix we built before. Finally, we store a `SellType` column, which represents the type of relation for which we're looking.

In fact, we'll probably not talk about the kind of suggestion we're making to the visitor, as we'll just be presenting a simple list of associated products. We will be using this, however, for internal administration.

With somewhere to store the matrix, we just need to create an administrative interface for inserting rows into the `Suggestions` table. This involves adding methods to the `WroxCommerce` objects, and building some ASP code.

Try It Out – Editing the Matrix

1. Firstly, let's add some code to `WroxCommerce` project. Open the `Globals` standard module and add this enumeration to the end:

```
' SuggestionType - the type of suggestion we're making...
Public Enum SuggestionType
    suggestUp = 0
    suggestCross = 1
End Enum
```

2. Next, add this method to the `Product` object:

```
' AddSuggestion - add a suggested product...
Public Function AddSuggestion(ByVal RelatedProductID As Long, _
                        ByVal SuggestionType As Integer) As Long

    ' Create a new suggestion...
    Dim NewSuggestion As New Recordset
    NewSuggestion.Open "Suggestions", m_utility.DB.DB, _
                adOpenKeyset, adLockOptimistic
    NewSuggestion.AddNew
```

547

```
' Add the suggestion...
NewSuggestion("ProductID") = ID          ' ID of the current product
NewSuggestion("RelatedProductID") = RelatedProductID
NewSuggestion("SellType") = SuggestionType

' Close and return the ID of the new row in the Suggestions table
NewSuggestion.Update
AddSuggestion = NewSuggestion("SuggestionID")
NewSuggestion.Close
Set NewSuggestion = Nothing

End Function
```

3. The final part of our matrix-building exercise is to create the ASP code to present the administrative interface. If you recall, our administrative code is in a separate file: admin/default.asp. Open this file now and look for the case statement that's used to present the editing form to the administrator. This will look like:

```
<% ' do we want to edit a single product?
case "editproduct"%>
```

4. At the end of this case statement, before the **Save Changes** button is added, add this code:

```
' finish...
Set Product = Nothing
%>
```

```
<!-- add a field to enter a up/cross sell -->
<tr><td class=heading>Suggested sale:</td>
<td>
<select name=SuggestionID>
<option value="">(Select)</option>
<%
    Set Products = Visit.Catalog.GetProducts
    Do While Not Products.EOF

        ' make sure we're not the product in question...
        If Products("ProductID") <> CLng(Request("ID")) Then

            ' render the product...
            response.write "<option value="""
            response.write Products("ProductID")
            response.write """>"
            response.write Products("MfrName") & " " & Products("Name")
            response.write "</option>"

        End If

        ' next
        Products.MoveNext
```

```
      Loop
      Products.Close
      Set Products = Nothing
%>
</select>
 
<select name=SuggestionType>
    <option value=0>Up-sell</option>
    <option value=1>Cross-sell</option>
</select></td></tr>
```

```
<!-- button... -->
<tr><td colspan=2 align=center><br>
<input type=submit value="Save Changes"></td></tr>
```

5. When the user clicks **Save Changes**, we need to add that recommendation. Add this code to the top of the admin/default.asp page:

```
' are we trying to save a product?
If Request("saveproduct") <> "" then

    ' Get the product back...
    Set Product = Visit.Catalog.GetProductObject(Request("saveproduct"))
```

```
    ' Do we have a suggestion?
    If request("SuggestionID") <> "" Then
        Product.AddSuggestion Request("SuggestionID"), _
                              Request("SuggestionType")
    End If
```

```
    ' Start looping the array of StructureIDs store in the hidden fields...
    Dim n
    For n = 1 to Request("structureids").Count

        ' Do we have a value, or is it null?
```

How It Works

We've seen methods like AddSuggestion a thousand times by this point so, briefly, all it does is insert a row into the Suggestions table based on the product the object itself represents (the ID of which is held in ID), and the parameters supplied in the call:

```
    ' Add the suggestion...
    NewSuggestion("ProductID") = ID        ' ID of the current product
    NewSuggestion("RelatedProductID") = RelatedProductID
    NewSuggestion("SellType") = SuggestionType
```

We then alter the functionality of the **Edit Product** page to include a `<SELECT>` box containing the complete list of available products. We get this list as a recordset provided by the `GetProducts` method of the `Catalog` object:

```
Set Products = Visit.Catalog.GetProducts
```

After we've drawn all of the products, we draw a short list to describe the type of suggestion we're making. The ID of each of the options (0 or 1) will be written directly into the `Suggestions` table:

```
<select name=SuggestionType>
   <option value=0>Up-sell</option>
   <option value=1>Cross-sell</option>
</select></td></tr>
```

In our example here, we've added a drop-down box to allow the user to select the product that's to be added to the suggestion. With a large product catalog, this is not a very sound plan, as bringing back that list could take considerable server time and bandwidth. In addition, lengthy drop-down boxes are very difficult for the visitor to use adequately. In most cases, it's better to leave this as a text box and invite the user to enter the ID of the product they require directly. Remember, you can find the ID of a product by navigating to it on the Web site and looking at the URL of the page. The ID of the product will be preceded by `id`, like this:

```
http://localhost/jocoffee_local/detail.asp?id=1
```

If you choose to do this, leave the name of the text box as `SuggestionID` and you won't have to change any other code.

Finally, the code for the Save Changes button is changed so that it listens to see if we selected a product in the `SuggestionID SELECT` list (if you recall, this is the one containing the product list) and, if we do, uses the `AddSuggestion` method we wrote earlier to add the suggestion to the database:

```
If request("SuggestionID") <> "" Then
   Product.AddSuggestion Request("SuggestionID"), _
                         Request("SuggestionType")
End If
```

Testing the Code

At this point, we can't test our code because we don't have enough test data in the database to do it. We need to add a new product type and a new manufacturer. As we haven't built administrative tools to add product types or manufacturers, we need to do this manually using SQL Server's Enterprise Manager.

Try It Out – Adding Data to the Database

1. Add this to the Types table:

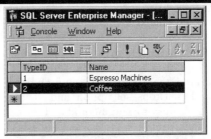

2. Add this to the Mfrs table:

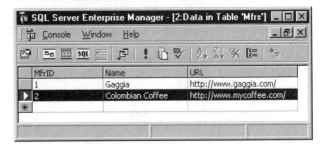

3. We're now ready to add two new products to the database. Run the WroxCommerce Visual Basic project and go to the admin/default.asp page. As a reminder, the password for the administrative page is secret.

4. Once you have the administration menu, select **Add Product**. Make the product look like this:

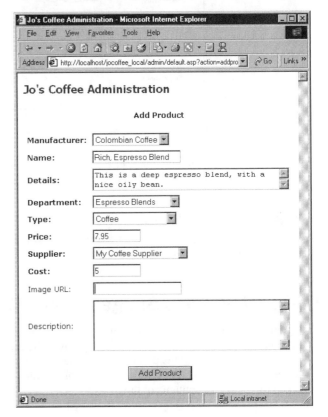

5. After that product has been added to the database, click on Add Product again, but this time call the product **Expensive, Italian Blend.** Set the **Price** to 15.00 and the **Cost** to 12.50. Keep everything else the same.

6. Back at the administration menu (the first page that appears after you log on), select **Edit Products** and then select **Gaggia Carezza.** It's now time to enter the cross-sell for this product. From the **Suggested sale** drop-down list, select **Colombian Coffee Rich, Espresso Blend,** and the **Cross-sell** option, and click **Save Changes.** As we discussed before, this will call our `AddSuggestion` method and store that cross-sell in the matrix:

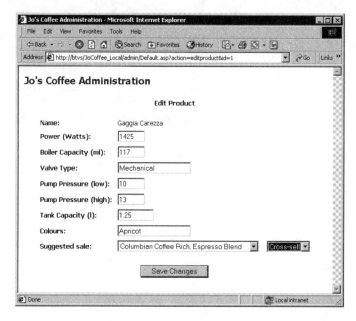

7. As we want to give the user two cross-sell suggestions, edit the product once more and select **Colombian Coffee Expensive, Italian Blend,** select **Cross-sell,** and then click **Save Changes** again.

8. To complete our selling suggestions, we want to up-sell visitors from the **Rich, Espresso Blend** to **Expensive, Italian Blend.** Click Edit Products, click **Rich, Espresso Blend,** and then add this up-sell to the matrix using the form.

Presenting Sales Suggestions – Before the Checkout

The first place to present our sales suggestion is going to be when the visitor is actively looking at the product. However, this is most likely not going to be the most "suggestive" place to make such a recommendation as, at this point, the potential customer is not necessarily committed to making an order. In the next section, we'll be reusing some code to show how the same sales suggestion can be made on the entire contents of the basket.

Try It Out – Presenting Suggestions on Product Pages

1. Our first step, as always, is to tweak the `WroxCommerce` objects to return the recommendations back. All we have to do is join the `Suggestions` and `Products` tables together. Add this method to the `Catalog` object:

```
' GetSuggestions - return a list of cross/up sells...
Public Function GetSuggestions(ByVal ProductID As Long, _
                               Optional ByVal AsKeyset As Boolean) _
                   As Recordset

    ' Run the query...
    Set GetSuggestions = QueryProducts("ProductID in (select " & _
        "RelatedProductID from Suggestions where ProductID=" & _
        ProductID & ")", , AsKeyset)

End Function
```

2. Now add this property, which calls the `GetSuggestions` method, to the `Product` object:

```
' Suggestions - return the suggested products...
Public Property Get Suggestions(Optional ByVal AsKeyset As Boolean) _
                    As Recordset
    Set Suggestions = m_utility.Visit.Catalog.GetSuggestions(ID, AsKeyset)
End Property
```

3. Now we just have to add some code to `detail.asp` to present the suggestions. This code uses a helper function called `RenderSuggestions`, which we'll meet in a moment. This code should go towards the bottom of the page, after the code that renders the **Buy it!** button:

```
<!-- product price and basket button... -->
<td>   </td>
<td align=right valign=top class=heading>
<font class=bigheading><%=FormatPrice(Product.Price)%></font>
<br>
<a href="basket.asp?id=<%=Product.ID%>">Buy it!</a>
</td></tr>
```

```
<!-- suggestions... -->
<%
Dim suggestions
Set Suggestions = Product.Suggestions

If Not Suggestions.EOF Then

    ' Start a table...
    response.write "<tr><td><br></td></tr>"
    response.write "<tr><td colspan=2></td><td colspan=3>"
    response.write "<table cellspacing=0 cellpadding=0 border=0>"
    response.write "<tr><td class=heading>We suggest...</td></tr>"
```

```
    ' Draw the suggestions...
    RenderSuggestions suggestions

    ' End the table...
    response.write "</table>"
    response.write "</td></tr>"

End If

Suggestions.Close
Set Suggestions = Nothing
%>
```

4. As we mentioned, the code above won't do anything until we build the
    RenderSuggestions helper function. Like all our helper functions, this should be added to
    our site.asp:

```
' RenderSuggestions - helper to present suggestions...
Sub RenderSuggestions(suggestions)

    ' Loop...
    Do While Not suggestions.EOF

        Response.Write "<tr><td class=small>"
        Response.Write "<a href="""
        Response.Write "detail.asp?id=" & suggestions("productid")
        Response.Write """>"
        Response.Write suggestions("mfrname") & " " & _
                        suggestions("name")
        Response.Write "</a> "
        Response.Write "</td><td class=small align=right>"
        Response.Write FormatPrice(suggestions("price"))
        Response.Write "</td></tr>"

        ' Next
        suggestions.MoveNext

    Loop

End Sub
```

5. Here's what our Gaggia Carezza page looks like now, with the suggestion in place:

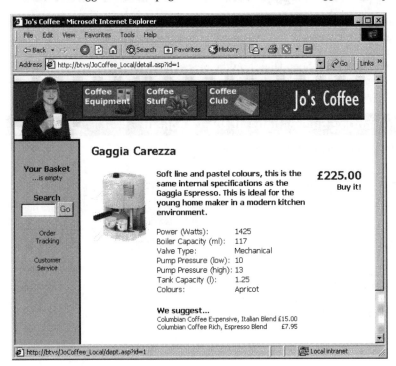

Don't forget to take a look at the Rich, Espresso Blend to see an up-sell to the Italian blend!

How It Works

When we call the GetSuggestions method, it will select rows from the vProducts view based on the ProductID column of the Suggestions table:

```
Set GetSuggestions = QueryProducts("ProductID in (select " & _
    "RelatedProductID from Suggestions where ProductID=" & _
    ProductID & ")", , AsKeyset)
```

If you recall back to our introduction to the suggestions system, the Suggestions table contains a ProductID column and a RelatedProductID column. In our situation here, when we pass in a ProductID representing the Gaggia Carezza, we will receive back two rows – one referencing the Rich, Espresso Blend, and one referencing the Expensive, Italian Blend.

Our RenderSuggestions helper function doesn't really do much other than loop through a recordset of suggestions made by the system administrator, and draw the results. However, we will need the same effect in the next section, so it makes sense to reuse the code by adding it to site.asp instead of placing it with the code that calls it in detail.asp.

Presenting Sales Suggestions – At the Checkout

As we mentioned briefly before, trying to make sales suggestions before the checkout isn't an effective tactic. You can see this aspect of human nature in your local supermarket. Customers are far more susceptible to suggestion-based, impulse buying once their shopping mission has been accomplished. How many people seek out Soap Digest on the newsstand, compared to people who buy it while waiting in line at the checkout?

Try It Out – Presenting Suggestions at the Checkout

1. Add this code to the `Catalog` object:

```
' GetBasketSuggestions - get suggestions based on a basket...
Public Function GetBasketSuggestions(ByVal BasketID As Long, _
                                    Optional ByVal AsKeyset As Boolean) _
                                    As Recordset

    ' Run the query...
    Set GetBasketSuggestions = QueryProducts("ProductID in (select " & _
        "RelatedProductID from Suggestions where ProductID in " & _
        "(select ProductID from BasketItems where BasketID=" & _
        BasketID & ")) and ProductID not in (Select ProductID " & _
        "from BasketItems where BasketID=" & BasketID & ")", , AsKeyset)

End Function
```

2. And, again, add this property to the `Basket` object:

```
' Suggestions - returns a list of suggestions...
Public Property Get Suggestions(Optional ByVal AsKeyset As Boolean) _
                                As Recordset
    Set Suggestions = _
        m_utility.Visit.Catalog.GetBasketSuggestions(ID, AsKeyset)
End Property
```

3. All that remains is to add this code to `basket.asp`. This is pretty much the same code we saw before, but the message is a tad more polite, we put the table in a different place and, of course, we ask the basket to return its recommendations, not an individual product:

```
' add the total...
Response.Write "<tr><td><br></td></tr>"
Response.Write "<tr bgcolor=#c0c0c0>"
Response.Write "<td colspan=4 align=right class=heading>"
Response.Write "Total:"
Response.Write "</td><td align=right class=heading>"
Response.Write FormatPrice(total)
Response.Write "</td></tr>"
```

```
' Suggestions...
Dim suggestions
Set suggestions = Visit.Basket.Suggestions

If Not suggestions.EOF Then

    ' Start a table...
    Response.Write "<tr><td><br></td></tr>"
    Response.Write "<tr><td colspan=5 align=center>"
    Response.Write "<table cellspacing=0 cellpadding=0 border=0>"
    Response.Write "<tr><td class=heading>"
    Response.Write "May we also suggest..."
    Response.Write "</td></tr>"

    ' Draw the suggestions...
    RenderSuggestions suggestions

    ' End the table...
    Response.Write "</table>"
    Response.Write "</td></tr>"

End If

suggestions.Close
Set suggestions = Nothing
```

How It Works

We can test this out by adding the Gaggia Carezza and the cheaper brand coffee to the basket. If we do this, the site will ask us if we'd like to buy the better coffee...

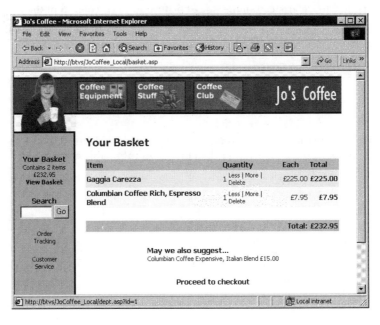

The point where we present the potential customer with the basket is the optimum place to make a suggestion. To do this, we have to write a query (in GetBasketSuggestions) that looks at the items in the basket, taking care not to suggest items that are already there. The SQL to do that is quite tricky, so here it is for clarity, assuming a BasketID of 66:

```
SELECT *
FROM vProducts
WHERE ProductID IN
        (SELECT RelatedProductID
         FROM Suggestions
         WHERE ProductID IN
           (SELECT ProductID
            FROM BasketItems
            WHERE BasketID = 66)) AND
      ProductID NOT IN
        (SELECT ProductID
         FROM BasketItems
         WHERE BasketID = 66)
```

As you can see, this query is actually four SELECT statements in one. Let's see how it's built up.

1. Firstly, we know the basket ID, so we select out all of the items in the basket:

```
SELECT ProductID
FROM BasketItems
WHERE BasketID = 66
```

2. We then take the results from that and mimic the action of the GetSuggestions method we built earlier in the chapter. If you recall, the GetSuggestions method creates a list of products that are referenced in the RelatedProductID column of the Suggestions table:

```
SELECT RelatedProductID
FROM Suggestions
WHERE ProductID IN
    (SELECT ProductID
     FROM BasketItems
     WHERE BasketID = 66)
```

3. Once we've gone that far, we pass all of the suggested products to the vProducts view. We prefer to work with the view rather than the Products table as it provides us with more detailed information:

```
SELECT *
FROM vProducts
WHERE ProductID IN
        (SELECT RelatedProductID
         FROM Suggestions
         WHERE ProductID IN
           (SELECT ProductID
            FROM BasketItems
            WHERE BasketID = 66))
```

4. Finally, we don't want to include items that are already in the basket, so in case we've already taken up a suggestion (or the customer has been lucky and chosen to buy goods we would otherwise offer):

```
SELECT *
FROM vProducts
WHERE ProductID IN
        (SELECT RelatedProductID
         FROM Suggestions
         WHERE ProductID IN
            (SELECT ProductID
             FROM BasketItems
             WHERE BasketID = 66)) AND
      ProductID NOT IN
        (SELECT ProductID
         FROM BasketItems
         WHERE BasketID = 66)
```

Remember that the join is in two parts because, although we want a set of products to suggest, we don't want to suggest items that have already been added. The NOT IN clause at the end stops this from happening.

Featured Items

Now that we've learnt how to up-sell and cross-sell products to our customers, let's turn our attention to the sort of promotions that e-commerce sites have on their home pages – **featured items**.

One of the most useful places on the site to make sales suggestions is the home page, and up until this point, we haven't paid it much attention at all. Luckily, back in Chapter 6 we added a column called FeaturedProduct to the Products table that we can now use to add featured items to the home page.

When you have any content at all on the home page of the site, it's essential that it gets changed and rotated as often as possible to give regular visitors the impression that it's always changing and improving. The design of the Products table helps us do this by defining FeaturedProduct as a datetime data type, meaning we can use it to store the exact moment in time that an item became a featured item. That means that whenever we want to know how long a product has been on the front page, we just examine this column. It also means that when we add items to the featured items list, by selecting out and ordering on FeaturedProduct, we can make sure the newly featured items appear at the top of the list.

To set featured items, all we have to do is provide a method for setting the FeaturedProduct column in the Product object, and then alter our administration pages.

Try It Out – Setting Featured Items

1. When we built our `Product` object originally, we didn't add the code to get and set the `FeaturedProduct` column, so our first move is to add a member variable for holding the value:

```
Private m_ImageURL As String
Private m_FeaturedProduct As Date
Private m_IsLoaded As Boolean
```

2. When we load the product data from the database, we need to also load the `FeaturedProduct` column. Add this code to the `CheckLoad` method of the `Product` object:

```
If Not IsNull(Query("ImageURL")) Then m_ImageURL = Query("ImageURL")
If Not IsNull(Query("FeaturedProduct")) Then _
    m_FeaturedProduct = Query("FeaturedProduct")
m_StockExpected = Query("StockExpected")
```

3. Next, we need a property to get the `FeaturedProduct` value:

```
' FeaturedProduct property...
Public Property Get FeaturedProduct() As Date
    CheckLoad
    FeaturedProduct = m_FeaturedProduct
End Property
```

4. Add this `IsFeaturedProduct` function:

```
' IsFeaturedProduct - tells us if this is a featured product...
Public Function IsFeaturedProduct() As Boolean

    ' We can detect if a date is Empty (i.e., it was null in the database)
    ' by looking at the year...
    If Year(FeaturedProduct) <> 1899 Then
        IsFeaturedProduct = True
    Else
        IsFeaturedProduct = False
    End If

End Function
```

5. We have enough methods and properties now to make the `Product` object capable of telling us if it is featured, but we need to add a property to set the `FeaturedProduct` column in accordance with whatever the administrator tells us to do:

```
' SetFeaturedProduct - set this item to be a featured product...
Public Sub SetFeaturedProduct(ByVal IsFeatured As Boolean)

    ' Firstly, check that we're setting it to something different...
    If IsFeaturedProduct <> IsFeatured Then

        ' Get the record from the db...
        Dim update As New Recordset
        update.Open "select * from Products where ProductID=" & ID, _
                    m_utility.DB.DB, adOpenKeyset, adLockOptimistic

        ' Set it..
        If IsFeatured = True Then
            update("featuredproduct") = Now
        Else
            update("featuredproduct") = Empty
        End If

        ' Update it...
        update.update
        update.Close
        Set update = Nothing

    End If

End Sub
```

How It Works

Visual Basic has some problems identifying a date value as being `Empty`. Unlike most data types, when you create one it does not correctly report the fact that it is `Empty` using the `IsEmpty` function. However, if you query an empty date variable for its year, you receive the value 1899. Therefore, we'll be using the `Year` function and looking for a value of 1899 in the `IsFeaturedProduct` function:

```
If Year(FeaturedProduct) <> 1899 Then
    IsFeaturedProduct = True
Else
    IsFeaturedProduct = False
End If
```

The `FeaturedProduct` property returns the value in the `FeaturedProduct` column from the `Products` table. If we get 1899, we assume that the `FeaturedProduct` column in the database was null, hence it is not a featured product; otherwise, we assume it is.

In the `SetFeaturedProduct` method, we don't want to do anything unless the status of the item has changed:

```
If IsFeaturedProduct <> IsFeatured Then
```

This is mainly to stop the featured new item from popping back up to the top of the list if we happen to call `SetFeaturedItem` again with `IsFeatured` set to `True`.

Once we've determined that it's changed, we select the row from the database and set the `FeaturedProduct` column either to the current date and time, or to `Empty`:

```
If IsFeatured = True Then
    update("featuredproduct") = Now
Else
    update("featuredproduct") = Empty
End If
```

Note that setting a column to `Empty` in ADO results in the column being set to null.

Try It Out – Altering the Administrative Tools

1. Now it's just a simple matter of tweaking the `admin/default.asp` page that we were editing earlier on in this chapter. Add this code to the page, above the code we added to display the cross-sell/up-sell drop-down:

```
Loop
Attributes.Close
Set Attributes = Nothing
```

```
%>

<!-- add a field to set a featured product -->
<tr><td class=heading>Featured product:</td>
<td>
<select name=FeaturedProduct>
<%
    ' Render the options
    Response.Write "<option value=1"
    If product.IsFeaturedProduct Then Response.Write " selected"
    Response.Write ">Yes</option>"
    Response.Write "<option value=0"
    If Not product.IsFeaturedProduct Then Response.Write " selected"
    Response.Write ">No</option>"
%>
</select>
</td></tr>

<!-- finish... -->
<% Set Product = Nothing %>

<!-- add a field to enter a up/cross sell -->
<tr><td class=heading>Suggested sale:</td>
<td>
```

Notice how, in `admin/default.asp`, we use the `IsFeaturedProduct` function to adjust the default item of the `<SELECT>` box so that the user knows the status of the item.

2. Let's now add the code to the page to save the featured item back. We can add this code directly above the code we used to insert any new suggestion into the database:

```
' Do we have a featured item?
If request("FeaturedProduct") = "0" Then
    Product.SetFeaturedProduct False
Else
    Product.SetFeaturedProduct True
End If

' Do we have a suggestion?
If request("SuggestionID") <> "" Then
    Product.AddSuggestion Request("SuggestionID"), Request("SuggestionType")
End If
```

How It Works

To test that lot, run the Visual Basic WroxCommerce project and navigate to the administrative tools. Once there, find the Gaggia Carezza and set the **Featured product** field to **Yes** and click **Save Changes**. Check the FeaturedProduct column in the database to see for yourself how the database is altered to reflect this activity.

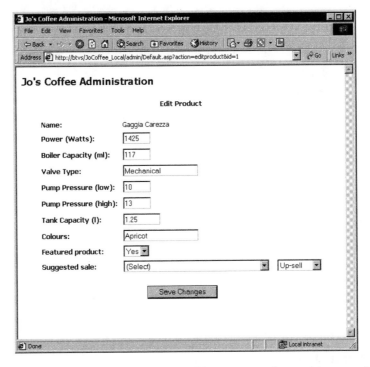

We're now just a couple of steps away from being able to present featured items to the visitor. This involves adding a method to the Catalog object, and changing the site's default.asp.

Try It Out – Displaying the Featured Products

1. Firstly, add this method to the `Catalog` object:

```
' GetAllFeaturedProducts - return a list of everything that's featured...
Public Function GetAllFeaturedProducts(Optional ByVal AsKeyset As Boolean) _
                                       As Recordset
   Set GetAllFeaturedProducts = QueryProducts( _
       "FeaturedProduct is not null", "FeaturedProduct Desc", AsKeyset)
End Function
```

2. We can now use the `GetAllFeaturedProducts` method to return a list of the featured items by editing `default.asp`. Add this code to `default.asp`, above the code we added in the previous chapter to present a few of the community features:

```
<!-- heading -->
<tr><td class="bigheading">Welcome to Jo's Coffee!</td></tr>

   <!-- coffee machines... -->
   <tr><td><br></td></tr>
   <tr><td class=tableRed>Coffee Equipment</td></tr>
```

```
<tr><td><br></td></tr>

<!-- featured products -->
<tr><td><table cellspacing=0 cellpadding=2 width=100% border=0>
<%
' select them...
Dim featured, num, price, product
Set featured = Visit.Catalog.GetAllFeaturedProducts

' loop...
num = 0
Do While Not featured.EOF

   ' Get the product...
   Set product = Visit.Catalog.GetProductObject(featured("productid"))

   ' Start a row?
   If num mod 2 = 0 Then
      If num <> 0 then Response.Write "</tr>"
      Response.Write "<tr>"
   Else
      Response.Write "<td> </td>"
   End If

   ' Draw the item's picture...
   Response.Write "<td valign=top>"
   If product.ImageURL <> "" Then
      Response.Write "<img src="""
      Response.Write product.ImageURL
      Response.Write """>"
   End If
```

```
' Draw the item details...
Response.Write "</td>"
Response.Write "<td> </td>"
Response.Write "<td class=small valign=top>"
Response.Write "<font class=heading>"
Response.Write "<a href="""
Response.Write "detail.asp?id=" & featured("productid")
Response.Write """>"
Response.Write product.MfrName & " " & product.Name
Response.Write "</a>"
Response.Write "</font>"
Response.Write "<br>"
Response.Write product.Details

' Draw the item price...
Response.Write "<br><div style=""text-align:right"">"
Response.Write "<font class=bigheading>"
Response.Write FormatPrice(product.Price)
Response.Write "</font>"
Response.Write "</div>"
Response.Write "</td>"

' Next
featured.MoveNext
num = num + 1

Loop

' Close...
featured.Close
Set featured = Nothing
%>
</table></td></tr>

    <!-- coffee stuff... -->
    <tr><td><br></td></tr>
    <tr><td class=tableRed>Coffee Stuff</td></tr>

    <!-- coffee club... -->
    <tr><td><br></td></tr>
    <tr><td class=tableRed>Coffee Club</td></tr>
```

How It Works

Again, this is a fairly typical piece of presentation code that you're probably used to seeing by now. We start by using `GetAllFeaturedProducts` to return a list of the products, which we then loop through:

```
Dim featured, num, price, product
Set featured = Visit.Catalog.GetAllFeaturedProducts

' loop...
num = 0
Do While Not featured.EOF
```

We want to present the featured items in a grid with two columns in each row, so we check the value of num on each iteration to see if it is an even number. If it is, we have to start a new row, otherwise we add a spacer column:

```
If num mod 2 = 0 Then
    If num <> 0 then Response.Write "</tr>"
    Response.Write "<tr>"
Else
    Response.Write "<td> </td>"
End If
```

Then, we create three columns for each item: one for the image, one for a spacer, one for the product information. We add a link to the product and show the short description and the price. We use a DIV tag for the price to keep the code sample simpler by not having to add an extra table:

```
' Draw the item's picture...
Response.Write "<td valign=top>"
If product.ImageURL <> "" Then
    Response.Write "<img src="""
    Response.Write product.ImageURL
    Response.Write """>"
End If

' Draw the item details...
Response.Write "</td>"
Response.Write "<td> </td>"
Response.Write "<td class=small valign=top>"
Response.Write "<font class=heading>"
Response.Write "<a href="""
Response.Write "detail.asp?id=" & featured("productid")
Response.Write """>"
Response.Write product.MfrName & " " & product.Name
Response.Write "</a>"
Response.Write "</font>"
Response.Write "<br>"
Response.Write product.Details

' Draw the item price...
Response.Write "<br><div style=""text-align:right"">"
Response.Write "<font class=bigheading>"
Response.Write FormatPrice(product.Price)
Response.Write "</font>"
Response.Write "</div>"
Response.Write "</td>"
```

Here's what it looks like if we add another product to the database and set that as a featured item too. Notice how, because we created the Topazia second, it appears before the Carezza in the presentation:

Recommendation-Based Selling

The holy grail of suggestion-based shopping is the ability to make qualified cross-sell and up-sell suggestions based on data you've obtained about your customers from their shopping habits.

Amazon.com is the most visible user of this kind of technology, offering sales recommendations when the visitor is examining a book, CD, or movie, as well as offering the visitor a way of saying, "What do you recommend to me?"

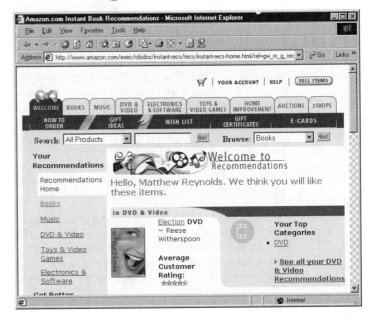

A detailed breakdown of this recommendation technology is beyond the scope of this book, but we can take a 30,000-foot view of some of the technology Amazon uses to drive it.

Examining Customer Habits

Amazon's recommendation technology is based on examining the real-world buying habits of its customers. For most sites wishing to implement this kind of technology, there's a hurdle there already. Amazon has a lot of customers and has processed a *lot* of orders in its relatively short life, giving it an enviable base of data on which to run its queries.

Amazon's recommendation system is, effectively, cross-selling you products in a similar manner to the way we've rigged Jo's Coffee to do this in this chapter. What's different is that whereas in Jo's Coffee we have to manually define the cross-sell matrix, Amazon has software to do this automatically.

The first stage in the recommendation process is to take a snapshot of the orders currently in the system and passing them over to a **recommendation processor**:

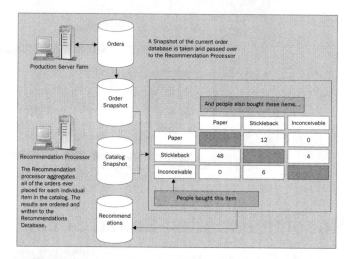

This processor also has a snapshot of the current catalog. The recommendation process starts in row one of the catalog looking for orders containing that item:

❏ Whenever an order is found, all the other orders that customer has made with a date earlier than the one being examined are selected. (As this works on a snapshot basis, the recommendation processor will only examine each order once.)

❏ A row is added to (or found in) the recommendations matrix for each item in the first order.

❏ The products in all of the previous orders are examined. A column is added to the recommendation matrix for each unique product. The value in the intersection of the row representing the product in the master order, and the column in the previous order is incremented. This is called the **tally**.

❏ Once all of the orders are processed, each row in the recommendation matrix is processed. The columns are selected out, highest tally value first. The first selected item will, therefore, be the most common other product that's bought by customers that buy the product in the first column. The second will be the next most popular, and so on. The top "x" number of products (say five or ten) can then be inserted into a cross-sell table, similar in nature to our Suggestions table.

In our diagram, we can see that customers who bought the book Paper, also placed a total of 12 orders for the book, Stickleback, but placed no orders for another book called Inconceivable. We can therefore suggest to other people interested in Paper that Stickleback might be worth taking a look at. Although we haven't covered the algorithms for this next bit, there is an argument that suggests if four people who bought Stickleback also bought Inconceivable, then Inconceivable might not be a bad recommendation for Paper. To add that recommendation to the Suggestions table, the recommendation process would have to look one, two, or several more levels deep into the matrix to try to weed out other likely cross-sell opportunities.

At the end of this extremely involved process, Amazon will have dynamically created a Suggestions table containing data based on the real-world ordering habits of its customers. Therefore, whenever it displays a CD, book, movie, etc., it just has to select out other products based on its Suggestions table, much like we did earlier on.

Personal Recommendations

That explains how Amazon can suggest other products when a customer is actively examining one, but how does it do the "View your Personal Recommendations" stuff?

To do this, it has to run another process on the Suggestions table, this time storing recommendations against a customer record, rather than a record of an item in its database. So, it might examine the stuff that I've bought over the past six months, selecting out all the suggestions that it would have made when I was placing those orders based on the suggestions it can now make. For example, it sees me buy the films Dead Man on Campus and Office Space and someone else buys Dead Man on Campus and Election. It knows that Election is a recommendation for people who've already bought Dead Man on Campus, which I've bought, and it also knows that I haven't bought Election from it, so that would be a good, general "Matthew Reynolds-specific recommendation". What's important to note here is that these kinds of systems are not dynamic – they prepare this information offline in batch processes, ready for my return visits to the store.

Summary

We started off this chapter by examining selling matrixes that can be used to define how you suggest other items when the customer is shopping around for items. We then saw how we can build database tables to store those matrixes in the database, how we can expand the WroxCommerce object model to let the administrator define them, and how to use them to present suggested sales to the user. We saw how suggestions work both when we're looking at an individual product, and when the user is looking at the basket.

We discussed the importance of featuring items on the home page that you particularly wanted to sell, or bring people's attention to. We then discussed how it is important that the front page is constantly changing, to keep people coming back. We then implemented an option in the administrative page that allows you to set whether a product is to be a featured product.

To round off the chapter, we looked at Amazon.com's unusual and highly sophisticated recommendation system, which is based on its extensive database of previous purchases.

Integration with Other Systems

Even in the time when the Internet was not as prevalent as it is today, it was usually a good idea to build a computer system that was able to communicate with the other systems that were around it. For example, it's always been a pain having to go through bank statements matching them up against entries in Microsoft Money or Intuit Quicken. Imagine a world where supermarket mainframes couldn't automatically order new cans of Coke in time to replenish inventory before anyone bought the last one on the shelves.

Integrating computer systems together has always been a tricky, non-trivial task, usually fraught with problems, and always involving great expense. Until recently **Electronic Data Interchange** (**EDI**) was the technology used by businesses that wanted their computer systems to work together. However, because EDI is so complex and the consultants that implement it are very highly trained (and hence expensive), it's so expensive to implement that only a tiny number of organizations can afford to realize EDI strategies.

Up to this point, we've successfully managed to create an e-commerce system that pretty much sits on an island all by itself without involvement with any other systems with which you may want to connect. You may well have suppliers e-mail their latest price and availability list each night, and you want your database to be dynamically updated to reflect any changes made in this list. On the other hand, perhaps you have an existing accounting system, and you want to pull orders from the Web site and enter them directly into that accounting system. How do you make all of the systems you use work together nicely, and how do you meet the looming e-business challenge of integrating your own systems with those of your partners?

The bad news is that there is no quick fix. There's no off-the-shelf solution for connecting your system with other systems that are out there (although some vendors offer toolkits that can make it easier to perform integration), so each time you do this you need to pull out your wrench, roll up your sleeves and prepare to get dirty. Each individual system is different and requires custom development time.

This will change, in time, as people start to develop suites of tools for connecting businesses together – effectively exposing sockets into an organization and inviting trusted partners to use those sockets as connection points through which to exchange information. As this happens, the sheer weight of interest from the Internet community, coupled with the inherent flexibility of the Internet, will mean that the cost of these tools will get driven right down. This will make it easy to deal with suppliers, customers, and other partners simply by asking if they support a certain commonly defined "socket". It's likely that the people who own the intellectual property behind this stuff will make so much money that Yahoo, Amazon, Excite and the rest of them will look like paupers.

Although no one's made any inroads into putting these things together, people do know that the most likely candidate for data interchange for the next decade is looking like XML, and it's primarily this technology that we'll be covering in this chapter.

We shall be discussing:

❑ What XML is

❑ How to publish data in XML

❑ The role of XML in merchant aggregation

❑ How to publish our product catalog in XML

❑ How to publish an order in XML

❑ How to use XML to update our product catalog

eXtensible Markup Language – XML

Let's begin by looking at **eXtensible Markup Language** (**XML**) in its historical context, before we start to see how we use it and what it looks like.

Markup Languages

A markup language is a set of rules, which you use to add special meanings or provide extra information to a document.

An example of a markup language that we are all familiar with is HTML. In HTML we define how a document should be rendered by adding tags such as <FONT>, <I>, and <DIV>. But in fact, another markup language, called SGML, defines HTML.

Standard Generalized Markup Language (**SGML**) is a markup language that is used to create other markup languages. It's been around since the 1960s and became an international standard in 1986 (ISO 8879). However, SGML is a very complex language and many of its features are rarely used.

HTML

HTML was originally created by Tim Berners-Lee in 1991 as a way of marking up technical papers so that they could easily be transferred across different platforms. He created a set of tags that he used to mark up a document so that it could be easily rendered by others into a usable format.

When HTML was used exclusively by the scientific community they were not concerned with how the documents looked, only that it be readable and usable. However, as Web browsers became increasingly popular with people who were not in the scientific community and they started to create their own Web pages, appearances became much more important. To meet the demand, the creators of Web browsers began to add their own tags that allowed users to display ever more appealing documents. This led to the inevitable drawback of Web pages being designed for one browser over the others, so that today we see signs on Web pages advising us to view them in Netscape Navigator or Internet Explorer.

What's Wrong with HTML?

As more and more users are getting onto the Internet, the inherent weaknesses of HTML are becoming increasingly apparent. The major failures being:

❑　　HTML does not allow you to define your own tags

❑　　HTML does not carry any information about the meaning of the content held within tags

❑　　A hierarchy of data cannot be defined as HTML

If we're to find a way to integrate our computer systems with our suppliers (and anyone else we might want to work with) we'll need to find a different tool than HTML, which makes it easier for humans to read a document, but not computers. If you receive an invoice as an HTML document it's fairly easy for a human to realize what it is and pull out the relevant information. If a computer is sent an invoice as an HTML document it has no way of recognizing its purpose or extracting the data it needs.

XML

To get around these problems SGML could be used, but as we discussed earlier, it's complex and not widely used. This is where XML comes in. XML is a simplified version of SGML, and is much easier to understand and write.

XML is not fixed like HTML. Users of XML can define their own tags, hence the name *eXtensible* Markup Language. These user-defined tags relate to the actual content of the document, not the way the document should appear.

> **In short, HTML is used to define how a document should be rendered, whereas XML is used to define the data contained within that document.**

The best way to learn what XML is and what is does is to actually see some, which is what we'll do now.

How Does It Work?

When people first started talking about XML about eighteen months ago, they said it would be the next big, important thing to happen to the Internet. Today, that's starting to become a truism as more and more vendors, developers, and consultants start believing XML is going to do the job it was designed for and start to make it happen.

As a side note, Bill Gates has strongly committed Microsoft to using XML wherever possible. XML is used heavily in Office 2000's file formats, and SQL Server 2000 will have native support for XML. Additionally, Windows DNA 2000 (the next revision of the Distributed interNet Architecture concept that the majority of the technology of this book borrows from) will make heavy use of XML.

Technically, XML is very simple. It comprises a set of nested tags and data, like this simple `<greeting>` tag that contains the word `Hello`:

```
<greeting>Hello!</greeting>
```

In HTML, we might want to define how we would like `Hello!` to be displayed, perhaps in bold or in a blue font. In XML, we define the content between the tags. `Hello!` is a greeting, so the tags state that.

XML is a very flexible language because its structure allows specific data format definitions. Imagine we wanted to describe a book; we might do it something like this:

```
<book>
    <author>Matthew Reynolds</author>
    <title>Beginning E-Commerce</title>
    <isbn>1861003986</isbn>
</book>
```

I can describe two books in a similar manner, although it's usually a good idea to enclose grouped items with some grouping tags, in this case the `<books>` tag:

```
<books>
    <book>
        <author>Matthew Reynolds</author>
        <title>Beginning E-Commerce</title>
        <isbn>1861003986</isbn>
    </book>
    <book>
        <author>David Siegel</author>
        <title>Futurize Your Enterprise</title>
        <isbn>0471357634</isbn>
    </book>
</books>
```

Unlike HTML, the hierarchical nature of these tags is not fixed to a specific standard. Contrast this to HTML where the well-known `<TR>` tag must go inside the well-known `<TABLE>` tag. As a developer working with XML, you can choose to structure the tags in whichever way suits your needs.

There are a few of gotchas, mainly to make the parsing of the files easier:

❑   Firstly, because each tag *has* to have an end tag, you can't do this:

```
<book>
    <author>Matthew Reynolds
</book>
```

If you want a tag that doesn't have an end tag, simply add a / to the end, like this:

```
<book>
    <author/>
</book>
```

As a side note, although you could do this with: `<author></author>`, `<author/>` takes up less space and can help on devices that don't have much space, like handheld computers or mobile phones.

❑   The second gotcha is that you have to close tags in the order in which they were opened. So, you can't do this:

```
<book>
    <author>Matthew Reynolds
</book>
</author>
```

❑   Thirdly, it's case sensitive. These two are *not* equivalent:

```
<AUTHOR>Matthew Reynolds</AUTHOR>
```

```
<author>Matthew Reynolds</author>
```

XML Standards

The fact that you can decide what tags you use in your XML documents on a completely arbitrary basis is also turning out to be the biggest problem of widespread acceptance of XML. As you can imagine, two people trying to communicate without knowledge of each other's tag meanings does not lead to productive communications. Several organizations are now trying to ratify standards for XML document interchange. The most notable of them out there right now are the Microsoft-led BizTalk (http://www.biztalk.org/), and cXML (http://www.cxml.org/). Their mandate is to put together definitions of what XML documents should look like, in order to help businesses communicate.

*If you do get to a point where your organization and another are sharing XML documents, you can use either **Data Type Documents (DTDs)** or **XML schemas** to make sure the documents you're sending and receiving fit the standards you and the other organization have negotiated. We won't be using either of these technologies here, as they're rather complicated, and I'd rather we concentrated on XML itself.*

Proven Use of XML

XML has been around long enough for people to prove that the technology actually works. Moreover (http://www.moreover.com/) is one company that's successfully utilized XML technology; Moreover is a news aggregator, meaning that it harvests a massive number of news sites each day and makes the headlines available to anyone who wants to use them on his or her site. You can choose from a number of different news categories.

As well as making its links available in the typical "JavaScript on home page" format, it also supplies its data in XML format. This extends the functionality of its service to anything you can think of. For example, you could examine each article for references to your own company and then e-mail a link to the article out to relevant staff members.

Here's an example of how Moreover describes an article:

```
<article id="4501930">
    <url>http://d.moreover.com/click/here.pl?x4501929</url>
    <headline_text>Vodafone Applies the Pressure</headline_text>
    <source>Wired News</source>
    <media_type>text</media_type>
    <cluster>UK business news</cluster>
    <tagline />
    <document_url>http://www.wired.com/news/</document_url>
    <harvest_time>Nov 19 1999 6:09PM</harvest_time>
    <access_registration />
    <access_status />
</article>
```

Note that the `<article>` tag at the beginning contains an attribute, much like the kind of attribute we'd see in HTML's `<IMG>` tag:

```
<IMG SRC="hello.gif">
```

In XML, the value of each attribute *must* be enclosed in quotes, whereas in HTML this isn't absolutely required.

Publishing Information in XML

Now let's see how we can publish information (to begin with, the version number of `WroxCommerce`) from our site in XML. If we were in a position where we wanted to share information on our system with another system (as is the goal of systems integration), the other system would be able to request data and we could return that format in XML, with that XML adhering to a format that the two parties agree on ahead of time.

To publish information as XML, we need to build:

❑ An object (`XML`) that can be called from an ASP page in response to a request for XML data coming from outside of the site

❑ A simple ASP page (`xmlquery.asp`) that generates an XML document showing the version of `WroxCommerce`

Let's begin by building the `XML` object in Visual Basic.

Try It Out – Creating the XML Object

1. For starters, create a new class module in the `WroxCommerce` project called `XML` and add this code:

```
Option Explicit

' Use IUtility to call back into the Visit and Database objects...
Private m_utility As IUtility

' Configure - set up IUtility...
Public Sub Configure(ByVal utility As IUtility)

    ' Hold the utility object...
    Set m_utility = utility

End Sub
```

2. Most of the time, we're going to want to push the XML down back to the caller through the `Response` object on the ASP page. However, for flexibility, we want to make sure we can redirect the stream to things like files, etc. Add this method to the `XML` object:

```
Option Explicit

' Use IUtility to call back into the Visit and Database objects...
Private m_utility As IUtility

' Where do we want to send the data...
Private m_response As Response

' Configure - set up IUtility...
Public Sub Configure(ByVal utility As IUtility)

    ' Hold the utility object...
    Set m_utility = utility

End Sub

' Stream - configure the output stream...
Public Property Set Stream(ByVal stream As Object)

    ' What type did we get?
    Select Case TypeName(stream)

        Case "IResponse"
            Set m_response = stream

    End Select

End Property
```

3. So that we can push the XML down the correct stream, add this method to the object:

```
' Add - sends data out to the stream...
Public Function Add(ByVal buf As String)

    ' Response?
    If Not m_response Is Nothing Then m_response.Write buf

End Function
```

4. We'll be putting a common header and footer on all our XML documents, so add these methods:

```
' StartXML - add a header to our XML document...
Public Function StartXML()

    ' Write out the header...
    Add "<?xml version=""1.0""?>"
    Add "<wroxcommerce>"
    Add "<site>"
    Add "<version>"
    Add "<string>" & m_utility.Visit.Version & "</string>"
    Add "<major>" & App.Major & "</major>"
    Add "<minor>" & App.Minor & "</minor>"
    Add "<revision>" & App.Revision & "</revision>"
    Add "</version>"
    Add "</site>"

End Function
```

```
' EndXML - add a footer to our XML document...
Public Function EndXML()

    ' write out the footer...
    Add "</wroxcommerce>"

End Function
```

As you can see, the StartXML and EndXML methods use the Add method to pump the XML-formatted data back down to the caller. We'll be creating similar methods as we work through this chapter.

5. Finally, we need to be able to create instances of the XML object. Add this method to the Visit object:

```
' CreateXMLPipe - creates an instance of an XML pipe...
Public Function CreateXMLPipe(ByVal stream As Object) As XML

    ' Create and configure...
    Set CreateXMLPipe = New XML
    CreateXMLPipe.Configure Me
    Set CreateXMLPipe.stream = stream

End Function
```

Creating an ASP Page that Generates XML Documents

In order to let people from outside the system make requests for information, we need to create an ASP page that is capable of generating the XML documents. These pages will be similar to the pages that we've been using to present the requests in HTML form. We call this page an **XML pipe**.

However, up to this point we've been using three template files – start.asp, end.asp, and site.asp – to manage the connections to the WroxCommerce objects and build navigation bars common to all pages. In xmlquery.asp, we won't be using this template, so we'll be closing the object model manually after the page has finished.

Try It Out – Creating xmlquery.asp

1. Create this ASP page and call it xmlquery.asp:

```
<%
    option explicit

    ' configure the ASP page to return XML data...
    Response.Buffer = true
    Response.ContentType = "text/xml"
%>
<!-- #include file="site.asp"-->
<%
    ' start xml...
    dim xml
    set xml = Visit.CreateXMLPipe(response)
    xml.StartXML

    ' stop xml...
    xml.EndXML

    ' close the site...
    Visit.Shutdown
    set m_visit = nothing
%>
```

2. When coding in HTML there are certain characters you're not supposed to use for fear of confusing the parser, and similarly there are some characters you're not supposed to use in XML, notably &, <, >, and ". This SafeXML method will replace any illegal characters with their legal equivalents and should be added to the XML object:

```
' EndXML - add a footer to our XML document...
Public Function EndXML()

    ' write out the footer...
    Add "</wroxcommerce>"

End Function
```

```
' SafeXML - converts text to safe XML...
Public Function SafeXML(ByVal buf As String) As String

    ' replace illegal characters...
    SafeXML = Replace(buf, "&", "&amp;")
    SafeXML = Replace(SafeXML, "<", "&lt;")
    SafeXML = Replace(SafeXML, ">", "&gt;")
    SafeXML = Replace(SafeXML, """", "&quot;")

End Function
```

How It Works

If you now run the VB project and browse to that ASP page, you'll be able to see something like this:

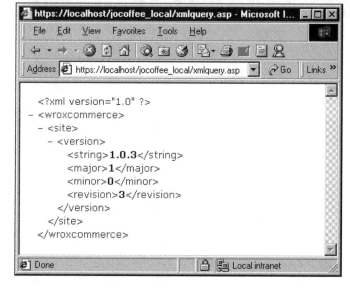

In this example, the `StartXML` and `EndXML` methods we created are being used to generate the basis of the XML document that you can see. In the remainder of this chapter, we'll learn how we can add more information to the document to create more useful results.

> **IE5 will kindly format XML information in a manner that can be easily read for debugging. However, you may discover that IE won't present this information in this neat format. To get around the problem, close the browser and reopen it directly to the URL of the XML page.**

Security

The XML pipe we're describing here creates a fairly obvious conduit for crackers and hackers to gain access directly into the e-commerce system. For this reason, it's a smart move to impose some kind of security on the pipe, and in this instance, we're going to use a combination of secure sockets (which we created back in Chapter 10), and a username and password.

1. To start with, we need a generalized way of returning errors back to the user of the XML pipe. Add this method to the XML object:

```
' AddError - adds an error to the results...
Public Function AddError(ByVal ErrorCode As Long, _
                         ByVal Description As String, _
                         Optional ByVal Data As String)

    ' pump out the error...
    Add "<error>"
    Add "<code>" & ErrorCode & "</code>"
    Add "<description>" & SafeXML(Description) & "</description>"
    Add "<data>" & SafeXML(Data) & "</data>"
    Add "</error>"

End Function
```

The AddError method uses the Add method to pump data back in the same manner that StartXML and EndXML employed earlier in the chapter. In this case, we're sending back an error code and message to the caller.

2. In Chapter 10, we talked about how we can use the Request.ServerVariables collection to determine if we are running on a secure page. Add this code to xmlquery.asp that will check to see if we are secure and, if not, call AddError to pump an error message back to the caller:

```
' start xml...
dim xml
set xml = Visit.CreateXMLPipe(response)
xml.StartXML

' are we running in a secure environment?
If Request.ServerVariables("https") = "on" Then
Else

    ' send back an error...
    xml.AddError 10001, _
        "This pipe is only accessible over a secure connection."

End If

' stop xml...
xml.EndXML
```

> If you do not have a secure server you can use for testing, simply change the If statement to check for **"off"** rather than **"on"**, but be careful to flip this back in a production environment.

3. As we discussed in Chapter 10, having a secure connection does not authenticate the person at the other end. We need to implement another level of security. For brevity, we're going to ask the user to supply a password using the query string. In this case, the password is `xmlpassword`:

```
' are we running in a secure environment?
If Request.ServerVariables("https") = "on" Then

    ' check the password...
    If Request("password") = "xmlpassword" Then

    Else

        ' send back an error...
        xml.AddError 10002, "The password supplied was invalid."

    End If

Else

    ' send back an error...
    xml.AddError 10001, _
        "This pipe is only accessible over a secure connection."

End If
```

> Obviously, the security scheme we're outlining here would not be sufficient for a line-of-business system placed in a production environment, and detailing such a scheme is beyond the scope of this book. You should make sure you design and implement your own scheme that fits the needs of your organization.

4. Finally, we're going to tell `xmlquery.asp` what kind of data we want back through another query string variable – this time it's called `action`. Add this code to `xmlquery.asp`:

```
' check the password...
If Request("password") = "xmlpassword" Then

    ' what do we want to do?
    Select Case Request("action")

        Case Else
            xml.AddError 10003, "Don't know what to do."
    End Select

Else
```

How It Works

If we try supplying an incorrect password, but over a secure connection using a URL like,

```
https://localhost/jocoffee_local/xmlquery.asp?password=wrong
```

here's what we get:

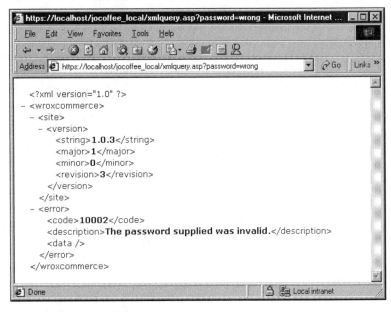

Now we can move on and see what we can do with that pipe...

Extracting Product Information

As e-commerce and e-business mature, you're likely to find yourself in a world where you no longer visit specific e-commerce sites to make purchases, but rather you'll employ software "agents" to do your shopping for you.

The concept of an agent has been banded around for some time, and we're starting to see some of this technology now become real. Specifically, the first step on the road to this agent-based shopping paradigm is already a popular and proven technology called **merchant aggregation**, and that's what we'll be looking at in this section.

Merchant Aggregation & Comparison Shopping

In the United States, one of the hottest growth areas of e-commerce is that of retailers selling computers and computer-related products. This growth is mainly because computer enthusiasts and professionals tend to understand how the Internet works and want to buy technology products.

Therefore, unlike books and CDs where there are a few major players, in the world of computer retail there are an incredible number of individual retailers. So many so in fact that it becomes impossible for people wanting to buy from these merchants to visit and examine the offerings of each retailer.

Merchant Aggregation is the concept of bringing all of the catalogs of all of the retailers together in one easy to search space, such that anyone wanting to buy a specific product can simply visit this aggregated site and find the product he or she wants. The success of these sites is further proof that people do not browse when shopping online – rather the average customer has a firm idea of exactly what they require and wishes to find the person most able to sell to them by comparing a number of factors such as price, availability and customer service.

One of the first movers in this space, PriceScan.com, has created a successful merchant aggregation site and has started to move away from dealing purely with computer products. Now, their site features books, CDs, and a host of other products. The huge CNet network has also identified merchant aggregation as an important space and offers similar services at Computers.com.

Merchant aggregators work by making, as the name suggests, a huge catalog of all the products available for sale and then inviting merchants to put their own price and terms of sale (the offer) against each product. In this section, we'll examine how we can generate XML that could be used by one of these aggregators to update their aggregated catalog. We won't be dealing with a specific aggregator, so this is more of a technology sampler than a specific solution.

As a side note, because XML is a relatively new technology, you may well find that an aggregator you try to deal with doesn't support XML – yet! They may well choose to hit every page on your site, harvesting the data off by reading the HTML and stripping out the offer information. However, as they evolve, every aggregator will start using XML.

DealTime.com

It's worth taking a moment to mention DealTime.com. This is another twist on merchant aggregation, but is actually another step closer to agent-based shopping. Rather than creating a big catalog of everything and having merchants update it, DealTime.com goes away and attempts to find offers matching the one you're look for. If you visit DealTime and search for Sony VAIO, DealTime will go away and try to find people selling Sony VAIOs. DealTime's model is also interesting because they will eventually deal with harvesting offers from auctions, traditional e-commerce, and any other way you can sell products.

R-U-Sure

One other shopping agent approach that's worth quickly mentioning is R-U-Sure (http://www.rusure.com/). R-U-Sure operates as a plug-in to Internet Explorer or Netscape Navigator. It monitors your visits to a number of shopping sites and waits for you to bring up information on a certain product. When you do this, it attempts to find other sites that sell the same item for less and pops up the results in a little window.

Publishing Your Product Catalog

If you have a large product catalog, it's unlikely you're going to want to publish the whole thing over the pipe in one lump. Instead, it's reasonable to expect people to ask for a specific department, or a specific manufacturer.

We're now going to extend the `XML` object and `xmlquery.asp` so that we can:

❑ Publish a list of departments

❑ Publish the details about a particular product

❑ Publish a list of all the products in a particular department

To start with, let's examine how you might publish a list of departments down to someone requesting that department list in XML format. All we have to do to make this happen is get a list of the departments and send them down the pipe one at a time.

Try It Out – Publishing a List of Departments

1. Add this method to the `XML` object:

```
' AddDepartment - adds a department to the results...
Public Function AddDepartment(ByVal DepartmentID As String)

    ' run...
    Dim department As Recordset
    Set department = m_utility.Visit.Catalog.GetDepartment(DepartmentID)
    If Not department.EOF Then

        ' Header...
        Add "<department>"

        ' Data...
        Add "<id>" & department("departmentid") & "</id>"
        Add "<idp>" & department("departmentidp") & "</idp>"
        Add "<name>" & SafeXML(department("name")) & "</name>"

        ' Footer...
        Add "</department>"

    End If
    department.Close
    Set department = Nothing

End Function
```

2. Now all we have to do is tweak `xmlquery.asp` to present a list of the departments to the caller. Remember, our department structure is hierarchical, so we'll need to build a **recursive function** (a function that is able to call back into itself to dig deeper into a set of values) that can walk down the department tree. This function is called `RecurseDepartments`, and we make the first call into it here:

```
' What do we want to do?
Select Case Request("action")

    Case "getdepartments"
```

```
        ' Header...
        xml.Add "<departments>"

        ' Call a helper function to get the departments...
        RecurseDepartments xml, ""

        ' Footer...
        xml.Add "</departments>"

    Case Else
        xml.AddError 10003, "Don't know what to do."

End Select
```

3. Next, add the `RecurseDepartments` function to the end of the ASP page so that we can query `WroxCommerce` to find the departments and call `AddDepartment` to pump them down to the caller:

```
' RecurseDepartments - finds and sends the departments...
Sub RecurseDepartments(xml, parent)

    ' Get the departments...
    Dim Depts
    If parent = "" then
        Set Depts = Visit.Catalog.GetDepartments
    Else
        Set Depts = Visit.Catalog.GetChildDepartments(parent)
    End If

    ' Loop and send...
    Do While Not Depts.EOF

        xml.AddDepartment Depts("departmentid")

        ' Recurse...
        xml.Add "<departments>"
        RecurseDepartments xml, Depts("departmentid")
        xml.Add "</departments>"

        ' Next
        Depts.MoveNext

    Loop

    ' Close...
    Depts.Close
    Set Depts = Nothing

End Sub
```

How It Works

The trick with all recursive operations is to call back into the same function with slightly different parameters.

In our case, we kick off `RecurseDepartments` by passing the `parent` parameter as an empty string, which tells the function to go away and find the root departments through the `GetDepartments` call:

```
If parent = "" then
    Set Depts = Visit.Catalog.GetDepartments
```

As each department is written out, the function is called again, but this time passing in the parent of the last "pumped" department through the `parent` parameter:

```
RecurseDepartments xml, Depts("departmentid")
```

So each time it's called after this, the function digs out the child departments and sends them down the pipe:

```
Set Depts = Visit.Catalog.GetChildDepartments(parent)
```

The only thing we have to remember is, each time we call into `RecurseDepartments`, we have to wrap `<departments>` and `</departments>` tags around the call so that the hierarchical relationships are passed down to the caller properly:

```
xml.Add "<departments>"
RecurseDepartments xml, Depts("departmentid")
xml.Add "</departments>"
```

If you were examining the results at the other end of the pipe, the first department you'd get (Coffee Consumables) would contain `<departments>` and `</departments>` tags, which in turn would contain the Coffee and Filter departments.

Now if we request the ASP page using:

```
xmlquery.asp?password=xmlpassword&action=getdepartments
```

We get this:

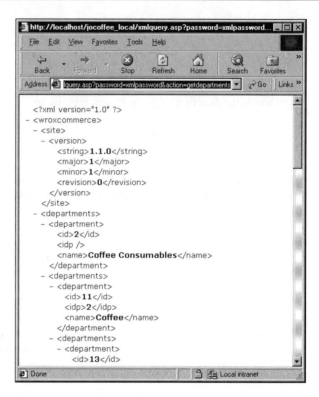

Returning products back down the pipe is more or less the same deal. However, this time we have a lot more information to send about a particular product, particularly manufacturer and type information.

Try It Out – Returning Individual Products

1. Add this method to the XML object:

```
' AddMfr - adds a manufacturer to the results...
Public Function AddMfr(ByVal MfrID As String)

    ' run...
    Dim Mfr As Recordset
    Set Mfr = m_utility.Visit.Catalog.GetMfr(MfrID)

    If Not Mfr.EOF Then

        ' Header...
        Add "<mfr>"

        ' Data...
        Add "<id>" & Mfr("mfrid") & "</id>"
        Add "<name>" & SafeXML(Mfr("name")) & "</name>"
        Add "<url>" & SafeXML(Mfr("url")) & "</url>"
```

```
      ' Footer...
      Add "</mfr>"

   End If
   Mfr.Close
   Set Mfr = Nothing

End Function
```

2.   The `AddMfr` method is virtually identical to the `AddDepartment` method. Now let's see how we can use both these methods in the `AddProduct` method of the `XML` object:

```
' AddProduct - adds a product to the results...
Public Function AddProduct(ByVal ProductID As String)

   ' get the product...
   Dim product As Recordset
   Set product = m_utility.Visit.Catalog.GetProduct(ProductID)

   If Not product.EOF Then

      ' Header...
      Add "<product>"

      ' Add the department...
      AddDepartment product("departmentid")

      ' Add the manufacturer details...
      AddMfr product("mfrid")

      ' Add the general details...
      Add "<id>" & product("productid") & "</id>"
      Add "<name>" & SafeXML(product("name")) & "</name>"
      Add "<details>" & SafeXML(product("details")) & "</details>"
      Add "<price>" & product("price") & "</price>"

      ' Footer...
      Add "</product>"

   End If
   product.Close
   Set product = Nothing

End Function
```

3.   However, `AddProduct` is useless unless we call it, so let's add some code to `xmlquery.asp`:

```
' What do we want to do?
Select Case Request("action")
```

```
' query a single product
Case "getproduct"
   xml.AddProduct Request("id")


Case "getdepartments"
```

This query makes the assumption that we want to pass down a single known product ID, and we supply this ID through a query string variable called id.

How It Works

Notice how AddProduct makes use of the previous methods we wrote for sending down departments and manufacturers. After we've sent both down, we simply send down the ID, name, short description, and price of the product:

```
' Add the department...
AddDepartment product("departmentid")

' Add the manufacturer details...
AddMfr product("mfrid")

' Add the general details...
Add "<id>" & product("productid") & "</id>"
Add "<name>" & SafeXML(product("name")) & "</name>"
Add "<details>" & SafeXML(product("details")) & "</details>"
Add "<price>" & product("price") & "</price>"
```

In the AddProduct method, we've made the assumption that we don't want to pass down sensitive information, such as cost and supplier, in order to make the pipe suitable for public consumption. If this pipe was designed to be used to integrate with existing internal systems we could create another method that would send this sensitive information down.

Now if we request the ASP page with this URL:

```
xmlquery.asp?password=xmlpassword&action=getproduct&id=1
```

We get something like this:

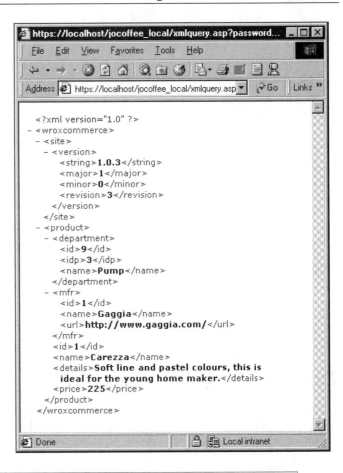

```
<?xml version="1.0" ?>
- <wroxcommerce>
  - <site>
    - <version>
        <string>1.0.3</string>
        <major>1</major>
        <minor>0</minor>
        <revision>3</revision>
      </version>
    </site>
  - <product>
    - <department>
        <id>9</id>
        <idp>3</idp>
        <name>Pump</name>
      </department>
    - <mfr>
        <id>1</id>
        <name>Gaggia</name>
        <url>http://www.gaggia.com/</url>
      </mfr>
        <id>1</id>
        <name>Carezza</name>
        <details>Soft line and pastel colours, this is
          ideal for the young home maker.</details>
        <price>225</price>
    </product>
  </wroxcommerce>
```

> Remember, because of the nature of **IDENTITY** columns in SQL Server, your Gaggia
> Carezza may not have an ID of 1.

In the example we just saw, we created code capable of sending down product information when we know the ID of the product that interests us. The last bit of code we meet in this section will be able to pass down a list of products when we know the department ID.

Try It Out – Sending Department Listings

1. Add this code to `xmlquery.asp`:

```
' What do we want to do?
Select Case Request("action")
```

```
' Query a single department...
Case "getdepartment"
```

```
    ' Add the department...
    xml.AddDepartment request("id")

    ' Add the products...
    xml.Add "<products>"
    Dim Products
    Set Products = Visit.Catalog.GetProductsInDepartment(request("id"))

    Do While Not Products.EOF

        ' Send...
        xml.AddProduct Products("productid")
        Products.MoveNext

    Loop

    Products.Close
    Set Products = Nothing
    xml.Add "</products>"
```

```
' query a single product
Case "getproduct"
   xml.AddProduct Request("id")
```

Downloading Orders

Another common request made of e-commerce systems is the integration of customer's orders with existing billing and ordering systems. An ideal way to do this is to simply ask the XML pipe to return the details of the orders that are in the system, much as we did in the last section.

In fact, because downloading orders is so similar to downloading department and product information, we're not going to cover it here in any detail. However, to make things clear, here is an example of what an XML document for an order might look like:

```
<?xml version="1.0" ?>
<wroxcommerce>
   <site>
      <version>
         <string>1.0.3</string>
         <major>1</major>
         <minor>0</minor>
         <revision>3</revision>
      </version>
   </site>
   <orders>
      <order>
         <id>25</id>
         <created>11/20/99 11:26:22 AM</created>
         <completed />
         <status>1</status>
```

```
<Customer>
    <id>5</id>
    <firstname>Matthew</firstname>
    <lastname>Reynolds</lastname>
    <email>matthew@bitsonthewire.com</email>
</Customer>
<billingaddress>
    <address>
        <id>5</id>
        <name>Matthew Reynolds</name>
        <company />
        <address1>1234 Nowhere St.</address1>
        <address2 />
        <city>St. Albans</city>
        <region>Herts</region>
        <postalcode>AL1 3MR</postalcode>
        <country>UK</country>
        <phone />
    </address>
</billingaddress>
<shippingaddress>
    <address>
        <id>5</id>
        <name>Matthew Reynolds</name>
        <company />
        <address1>1234 Nowhere St.</address1>
        <address2 />
        <city>St. Albans</city>
        <region>Herts</region>
        <postalcode>AL1 3MR</postalcode>
        <country>UK</country>
        <phone />
    </address>
</shippingaddress>
<parts>
    <orderpart>
        <id>25</id>
        <subtotal>225</subtotal>
        <shippingcharge>5</shippingcharge>
        <taxrate>0.175</taxrate>
        <taxcharge>39.375</taxcharge>
        <total>269.375</total>
        <status>0</status>
        <lines>
            <orderline>
                <id>20</id>
                <quantity>1</quantity>
                <priceeach>225</priceeach>
                <total>225</total>
                <product>
                    <department>
                        <id>9</id>
```

```
                                        <idp>3</idp>
                                        <name>Pump</name>
                                    </department>
                                    <mfr>
                                        <id>1</id>
                                        <name>Gaggia</name>
                                        <url>
                                        http://www.gaggia.com/
                                        </url>
                                    </mfr>
                                    <id>1</id>
                                    <name>Carezza</name>
                                    <details>Soft line and pastel
                                        colours, this is ideal
                                        for the young home
                                        maker.</details>
                                    <price>225</price>
                                </product>
                            </orderline>
                        </lines>
                    </orderpart>
                </parts>
            </order>
        </orders>
</wroxcommerce>
```

Updating the Catalog

Sending data down an XML pipe is only half the battle – you're likely to come across situations where you have to send data up the XML pipe as well. We describe this process as **pushing**. This is commonly required when you're in an environment where your supplier sends you updated price and availability information each day that you have to use in order to create an up-to-date catalog on the e-commerce site.

There are two ways you can do this:

❑   For simple changes to the database, there's no reason why you can't supply the data describing the change not as XML, but rather as variables on a query string. Here's an example:

```
xmlquery.asp?action=UpdateProductPrice&id=27&newprice=27.95
```

This actually has nothing to do with XML at all, but it does fall under the general "integration" umbrella. In fact, you can move this closer to an XML paradigm by getting an XML query to return a document describing the "before and after" state of the product in question.

❑   A more realistic solution is to physically send an XML document up to the server somehow, and then interpret the document on the server using the **Microsoft XML Parser**.

The Microsoft XML Parser is a technology you'll have to understand if you're using the data pulled from the XML pipe we've described thus far in other systems, and something we'll touch upon in a moment. It's included with IE4, so chances are you already have it on your system.

One potential issue with any system like this is abuse. When we were sending data down to someone who requested it, we used the secure layer of our site to stop the message being intercepted as it made its way through. Now we find that if we invite people to send data to us, we have to make sure it's legitimate.

The best way to do this is to encrypt the data using something like PGP, a product we met briefly back in Chapter 10. This guarantees that when it is time to process the data, we know that it is from a legitimate source. We won't be going into detail on how to decrypt these files before processing, so if you are going to develop a system like this, make sure you investigate ways to secure the transmission.

Physically uploading the XML to the server is actually quite a tricky problem. You have these options:

❑ Include the XML document as part of the query string. This will work, but the length of the XML document will be limited to the maximum possible length of the query string that the server and ASP can understand.

❑ Include the XML document as part of the extra form data. The tricky bit here is pushing the documents up. Traditionally, the only things capable of producing HTTP header requests are browsers, so if you were using HTTP, you'd need to write some software capable of doing this. As we're using HTTPS, this is even trickier.

❑ Create a folder on the server that contains a list of XML documents requiring parsing. Use FTP to push data into this folder, or allow partners to copy files to the folder using **Virtual Private Networking** (**VPN**). This is an easy solution, but it requires a separate batch process to trawl the directory and process the files.

❑ Use **Microsoft Message Queue** (**MSMQ**) configured in such a way that applications can post XML documents to the queue for processing. This is conceptually similar to creating a folder on the server, but more secure, more robust and a little more professional.

❑ Receive XML documents through e-mail. An alternative to the PGP encryption here would be to use S/MIME versions 2 or 3. Realistically, this would operate like a gateway, so you'd probably have a separate batch process that captured the e-mail and passed it to either the "folder on server" or message queue-based system.

In this section, we're going to use the "folder on server" approach, because it works and we can concentrate on getting the process working, rather than configuring a message queue. The components we build in this section will work in either.

In the rest of this chapter, we're going to update our product catalog by using:

❑ A text file containing XML (update.xml), which specifies the product we want to update and what we want to alter

❑ Two new functions of our XML object called ProcessXMLFile and ProcessXML, which take the XML document and use it to update our product catalog.

Try It Out – Creating an XML Update Document

1. We'll start off by creating a small document that can be used to update the price of an item in the product catalog. Save this file as a text file called `update.xml` somewhere on your computer:

```
<?xml version="1.0" ?>
<wroxupdate>

    <command>UpdateProduct</command>

    <data>
        <id>1</id>
        <price>190</price>
    </data>

</wroxupdate>
```

> In this sample, we have a product with an ID of 1 that refers to the Gaggia Carezza that's featured throughout this book. Check in your database to make sure you have a product with an ID of 1 and, if not, replace the ID specified here with one that exists in your database.

How It Works

We want to try to create an architecture that can be used for different types of "push" queries, which is why we've created a document that contains separate `<command>` and `<data>` tags. This lets us reuse the document by changing the `<command>` tag and adding different data to the `<data>` tag.

In the following Try It Out, we're going to imagine we have a way of trawling the update folder on the server and we're going to build a method on the XML object that can be instructed to process any one of those files. In our example, we're going to assume the XML document we described above is stored in `d:\XMLPush\update.xml`.

Try It Out – Reading the XML Document

1. In order to read the XML document from inside `WroxCommerce`, we need to include a reference to the Microsoft XML Parser. In the Visual Basic project, select Project | References from the menu and then locate and check on Microsoft XML 1.0:

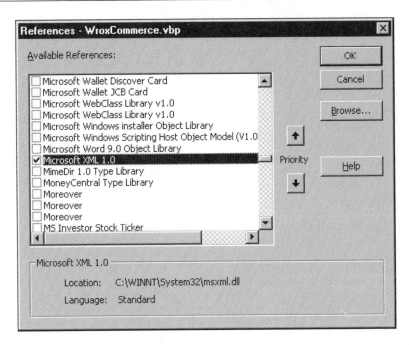

2. After you've included this reference, `WroxCommerce` will be able to access the Microsoft XML parser and use it to interpret any documents that are passed through. Add this method to the `XML` object:

```
' ProcessXMLFile - get a filename, extract the XML and pass it to
'                  another function...
Public Function ProcessXMLFile(ByVal FileName As String) As Long

   ' Pass the data over...
   ProcessXMLFile = ProcessXML("file:" & FileName)

End Function
```

For maximum flexibility, we want our XML push architecture to handle receiving documents from a number of sources. The Microsoft XML parser is able to receive data from a number of Internet-based resources, so in this case we take a file name and convert it to the `file:d:\XMLPush\update.xml` notation.

3. Let's build `ProcessXML` now:

```
' ProcessXML - process the supplied XML data...
Public Function ProcessXML(ByVal URL As String) As Long

   ' Open the XML parser...
   Dim Parser As New MSXML.XMLDocument

   ' It's better to be asynchronous on server-side stuff...
   Parser.async = False
```

```
' Give the parser our document...
Parser.URL = URL

' Somewhere to hold the command and the data...
Dim command As String
Dim data As IXMLElement2
Dim dataitem As IXMLElement2
Dim datascan As IXMLElement2

' Go through the document to find the nodes we want...
Dim n As Integer
Dim element As IXMLElement2

For n = 0 To Parser.root.children.length - 1

    ' Get the element...
    Set element = Parser.root.children.Item(n)

    ' What do we have?
    Select Case LCase(element.tagName)

        Case "command"
            command = LCase(element.Text)
        Case "data"
            Set data = element

    End Select

Next

' Did we get any data back?
If Not data Is Nothing Then

    ' Now that we have the command, do we understand it?
    Select Case LCase(command)

        Case "updateproduct"

            ' Use data to determine the id...
            For n = 0 To data.children.length - 1

                Set dataitem = data.children.Item(n)

                ' Got an ID?
                If LCase(dataitem.tagName) = "id" Then

                    ' Now, get the product row for updating...
                    Dim product As New Recordset
                    product.Open "select * from products where " & _
                            "productid=" & dataitem.Text, m_utility.DB.DB, _
                            adOpenKeyset, adLockOptimistic
```

```
                        ' loop the data tags again looking for changes...
                        Dim i As Integer

                        For i = 0 To data.children.length - 1

                            ' Get it...
                            Set datascan = data.children.Item(i)

                            ' Is this something we can understand and
                            ' use for updating?
                            Select Case LCase(datascan.tagName)

                                Case "mfrid"
                                    product("mfrid") = datascan.Text
                                Case "name"
                                    product("name") = datascan.Text
                                Case "departmentid"
                                    product("departmentid") = datascan.Text
                                Case "typeid"
                                    product("typeid") = datascan.Text
                                Case "details"
                                    product("details") = datascan.Text
                                Case "description"
                                    product("description") = datascan.Text
                                Case "supplierid"
                                    product("supplierid") = datascan.Text
                                Case "cost"
                                    product("cost") = datascan.Text
                                Case "price"
                                    product("price") = datascan.Text

                            End Select

                        Next

                        ' Finish
                        product.Update
                        product.Close
                        Set product = Nothing

                        ' Send the revised data back...
                        AddProduct dataitem.Text

                        ' Stop looping...
                        Exit For

                    End If

                Next

        Case Else
            AddError 10004, "Cannot understand push command", command
```

```
      End Select

   Else
      AddError 10005, "No data was supplied"
   End If

End Function
```

How It Works

That's quite a lengthy block of code, mainly because the XML parser requires you to work in quite a verbose fashion.

We start by creating the XML parser and instructing it to asynchronously load the XML document we require:

```
Dim Parser As New MSXML.XMLDocument

' It's better to be asynchronous on server-side stuff...
Parser.async = False

' Give the parser our document...
Parser.URL = URL
```

We then loop through all of the elements inside <wroxupdate>, searching for a tag called <command> and a tag called <data>:

```
For n = 0 To Parser.root.children.length - 1

   ' Get the element...
   Set element = Parser.root.children.Item(n)

   ' What do we have?
   Select Case LCase(element.tagName)

      Case "command"
         command = LCase(element.Text)
      Case "data"
         Set data = element

   End Select

Next
```

We don't have to tell the parser to explicitly find <wroxupdate> as XML documents can only have one root element and the parser automatically starts by examining tags inside this root by default.

After we've looped through looking for <command> and <data>, we check to see if we have reasonable values for each:

```
' Did we get any data back?
If Not data Is Nothing Then

    ' Now that we have the command, do we understand it?
    Select Case LCase(command)

        Case "updateproduct"
```

After we have <command>, we look to see what we want to do with it. If we choose to update a product, we have to determine which product we're talking about through the <id> tag contained within <data>:

```
' Use data to determine the id...
For n = 0 To data.children.length - 1

    Set dataitem = data.children.Item(n)

    ' Got an ID?
    If LCase(dataitem.tagName) = "id" Then
```

Again, we have to use this looping process to find the ID. Once we've found the ID, we ask ADO to return the relevant row back, but we configure the recordset such that it can be used for updating:

```
product.Open "select * from products where " & _
        "productid=" & dataitem.Text, m_utility.DB.DB, _
        adOpenKeyset, adLockOptimistic
```

We then loop through <data> one more time, this time searching for tags that describe the changes we want to make to the product. Our source XML document only contains instructions for updating the price, but you can see how in this function we can update the name, supplier, manufacturer, etc:

```
Select Case LCase(datascan.tagName)

    Case "mfrid"
        product("mfrid") = datascan.Text
    Case "name"
        product("name") = datascan.Text
    Case "departmentid"
        product("departmentid") = datascan.Text
    Case "typeid"
        product("typeid") = datascan.Text
    Case "details"
        product("details") = datascan.Text
    Case "description"
        product("description") = datascan.Text
    Case "supplierid"
        product("supplierid") = datascan.Text
    Case "cost"
        product("cost") = datascan.Text
    Case "price"
        product("price") = datascan.Text

End Select
```

We use the `AddError` and `AddProduct` methods in this process simply to provide a way of extracting error and status information out of any bulk process we perform. For example, in the code we build for the batch process that calls `ProcessXML`, we could configure an output stream that returned this status information back.

Try It Out – Testing the XML Document

1. As we've already said, you're most likely to use the `ProcessXML` function outside ASP, but for testing purposes, we can use the existing `xmlquery.asp` page. Add this code to the page:

```
' What do we want to do?
Select Case Request("action")
```

```
' Process a push file...
Case "processpushfile"

    ' tell the XML object to process the file we supplied...
    xml.ProcessXMLFile request("filename")
```

```
' Query a single department...
Case "getdepartment"
```

2. In order to use this, we need to request `xmlquery.asp` like this:

```
/xmlquery.asp?
password=xmlpassword&action=processpushfile&filename=d:\xmlpush\update.xml
```

How It Works

When we request this page, the logic we built into the `ProcessXML` method will affect the relevant changes. Now if we return to the main site and look at the Gaggia Carezza, we'll see this:

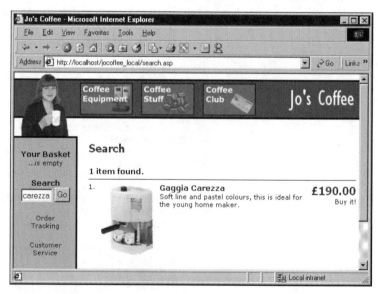

As you may recall from previous chapters and earlier in this chapter, the price of the Gaggia Carezza used to be £225. Now, our XML updating process has dynamically changed the price to £190.

Summary

We hope, now that you've worked through this chapter, you have an idea of some of the things you can do with the system integration possibilities afforded by XML. Although we didn't come up with any real world examples, the techniques seen here should help you build the tools and utilities you need to successfully perform these integrations.

We began the chapter by talking about why systems rarely stand alone in an organization of any kind and how effective integration is critically important to any e-business. We spoke about the existing, expensive solutions using EDI and hopefully whetted your appetite for the new breed of Internet-ready business interconnectivity services that will start to become available over the next year or two.

We then introduced you to the basics of XML and saw how you could create an XML pipe to publish product catalog and order information to any systems that required it. We then looked at how you could send data with other data – pushing XML documents containing update requests back to the site.

This chapter provided only a very brief introduction to XML; if you'd like to learn more then we recommend you refer to *Professional XML, ISBN 1861003110,* also by *Wrox Press.*

Marketing Your Site

Once your e-commerce site is ready to start selling, you're ready to start marketing the site to bring in new customers. Today, effectively marketing your Web site and attracting visitors and customers is one of the most challenging activities facing any Web site owners, especially the owners of e-commerce sites. There is no point having a great site if no one knows you're there and open for business.

The focus of this chapter is to detail some services you can use to help drive customers to your site, and keep them there once they've found it. Some of these services are either free or very low cost. In particular, we're going to discuss:

❑   Search engines

❑   Submission services

❑   Banner Advertising

❑   Associates programs

If you've got some money that you'd like to use for marketing (and, for an online retail strategy to be effective, you should be looking to spend at *least* as much on marketing as you did on engineering the site in the first place), you'll most likely need to look to a specialist marketing or consulting firm to help you spend your money wisely.

Tracking Success

In this chapter, we're going to talk about a few ways that you can market and promote your site. As a business owner, you're going to be interested in seeing which of the techniques you implement works to determine where you should make further investments.

The easiest way of doing this is to make a separate entry point for each possible referrer and track the results of each **click-through** (the process of entering a site by clicking on a link on another site) in a database table of some sort. You can then import the results into Microsoft Excel, or another decision support tool.

Logging Click-Throughs

How much data you capture when you detect a click-through is up to you. Some people like to collect a plethora of information containing source IPs, browser types, referral strings, etc. but this kind of information is better managed using a specialist tool such as WebTrends or Statistics Server (http://www.mediahouse.com/). In the system we're going to put together here, we're going to tally up how many referrals come from what place on which day. This technique is useful for links sent through e-mail, as well as links from directories and search engines.

Try It Out – Recording Click-Throughs

1. Create this table called `ClickThroughs` now:

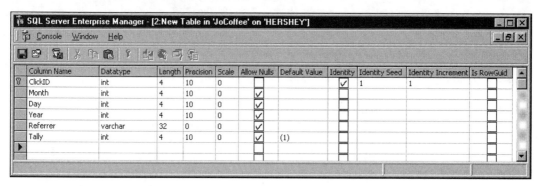

2. To record each click-through, we need to add a method to the `Visit` object. We'll call this method each time we detect an entry into the site:

```
' LogClickThrough - add a click-through to the database...
Public Function LogClickThrough(ByVal referrer As String) As Long

    ' Firstly, work out what day it is...
    Dim TheMonth As Integer, TheDay As Integer, TheYear As Integer
    TheMonth = Month(Now)
    TheDay = Day(Now)
    TheYear = Year(Now)

    ' Secondly, do we have a record for this day and this referrer?
    Dim CheckClick As Recordset
    Set CheckClick = IUtility_DB.DB.Execute("select * from " & _
                "clickthroughs where referrer='" & referrer & _
                "' and month=" & TheMonth & " and day=" & TheDay & _
                " and year=" & TheYear)

    If CheckClick.EOF Then

        ' Create a new record...
        Dim NewClick As New Recordset
        NewClick.Open "ClickThroughs", IUtility_DB.DB, _
                adOpenKeyset, adLockOptimistic
        NewClick.AddNew
```

```
      ' Add the details...
      NewClick("month") = TheMonth
      NewClick("day") = TheDay
      NewClick("year") = TheYear
      NewClick("referrer") = referrer
      NewClick("tally") = 1

      ' Save it...
      NewClick.Update
      LogClickThrough = NewClick("clickid")
      NewClick.Close
      Set NewClick = Nothing

   Else

      ' We need to increment the tally...
      CheckClick.Close
      IUtility_DB.DB.Execute "update ClickThroughs set " & _
               "Tally=Tally+1 where referrer='" & referrer & _
               "' and month=" & TheMonth & " and day=" & TheDay & _
               " and year=" & TheYear

   End If
   Set CheckClick = Nothing

End Function
```

How It Works

The first job of the `LogClickThrough` method is to determine the current month, day, and year in order to find the relevant row in the `ClickThroughs` table. The second job is to look to see if there is already a record for that referrer on that day. If there isn't, a new row is created; if there is, the `Tally` column is incremented.

Redirecting

There are two schools of thought to make this work. If we don't know who the referrer is, or we have a great many similar referrers, we can look at the request headers that come into the server and determine who the referrer is from that. We'll get a great deal of referrers when we register our site with the various search engines out there – a topic we also cover in this chapter. For now, we're going to look at a technique for grabbing click-through counts that works well when we have a small number of possible referrers. We'll look at a catch-all technique in the next section.

Imagine that we partner with a coffee information site called HappyCoffee.com and that we want to measure the clicks that come through from that site. To make this work, we will supply HappyCoffee.com with a specific URL that we would like them to use, rather than the default http://www.joscoffee.com/ URL we expect our customers to use. We will then redirect the visitor to our site's /default.asp, but only after we've made sure that we captured the referrer's details so that we can log it.

The easiest way to do this is to create a folder for each referrer and copy a new `default.asp` into each one that bounces the user back to the proper home page after it has recorded the link. We'll use short titles for our folder so that it's easy for the user to read and won't clog up e-mail clients if the links are sent through e-mail. For example, we might have our HappyCoffee.com listing pointing to this URL:

```
http://www.joscoffee.com/happycoffee/
```

Try It Out – Creating a default.asp for Referrals from HappyCoffee.com

1. We want to use the same alternative `default.asp` in all of the referrer folders that we have on the site. Create a new folder called `happycoffee` and create this `default.asp` inside it:

```
<%
    option explicit

    ' Work out the name of the folder...
    Dim url, n, found
    url = Request("script_name")

    ' Remove the "default.asp" from the script name...
    url = Left(url, Len(url) - len("default.asp"))

    ' Walk back through the URL until we get a slash...
    For n = Len(url) - 1 To 1 Step -1

        ' Found it?

        If Mid(url, n, 1) = "/" Then

            ' Store the URL...
            url = Mid(url, n + 1)
            url = Left(url, Len(url) - 1)

            ' Exit...
            Exit For

        End If

    Next

    ' Redirect the user to the parent, but log this clickthrough...
    Visit.LogClickThrough url

    ' Redirect the user...
    Response.Buffer = True
    Response.Clear
    Response.Redirect "../default.asp"
%>

<!-- #include file="../site.asp" -->

<html>
<head>
    <title><%=g_sitename%></title>
</head>
<body>
    Click <a href="../default.asp">here</a> to visit the site.
</body>

<%
    ' Close out the site...
    Visit.ShutDown
%>
```

How It Works

This snippet of code is a little complicated, simply because we want to reuse the same `default.asp` time and time again in different referrer folders. The bit of code at the top is used to examine the server variables to discover the name of the script:

```
url = Request("script_name")
```

Next, we need to extract the name of the folder. We begin by removing `default.asp` from the end of script name:

```
url = Left(url, Len(url) - len("default.asp"))
```

Then we walk backwards through what remains of the URL until we find a forward slash (taking care to avoid the one that was immediately before `default.asp`). When we've found the forward slash, we must have located the start of the folder name, which we can now extract:

```
' Remove the "default.asp" from the script name...
url = Left(url, Len(url) - len("default.asp"))

' Walk back through the URL until we get a slash...
For n = Len(url) - 1 To 1 Step -1

    ' Found it?

    If Mid(url, n, 1) = "/" Then

        ' Store the URL...
        url = Mid(url, n + 1)
        url = Left(url, Len(url) - 1)

        ' Exit...
        Exit For

    End If

Next
```

It's this folder name that we pass in as the referrer through to the `LogClickThrough` method:

```
Visit.LogClickThrough url
```

As we're accessing the database, we need to include the `site.asp` template file and make sure we call `ShutDown` when we're through in order to release the resources:

```
<!-- #include file="../site.asp" -->

<html>
<head>
    <title><%=g_sitename%></title>
</head>
<body>
    Click <a href="../default.asp">here</a> to visit the site.
</body>
```

```
<%
    ' Close out the site...
    Visit.ShutDown
%>
```

While this is easy to maintain when we're only expecting a few referrers, once we start to have more than a handful of them this method can start to become unmanageable.

Handling Many Different Referrers

If we submit our site to search engines, especially if we use a registration engine like the one we'll introduce later in this chapter, we will still want to keep track of the click-throughs, but we won't want to create a new folder for each one.

The HTTP protocol defines a technique for determining the URL of the page the user clicked on to get to your site. This URL is sent through in the request headers, and we can get at them through the `ServerVariables` collection of the `Request` object.

Try It Out – Handling Click-Throughs from a Large Number of Referrers

1. Add this code to the standard `default.asp`:

```
<% option explicit %>
```

```
<%' Are we being referred?
If Request.ServerVariables("http_referer") <> "" Then

    ' Get hold of where we're being referred from.
    ' This is always a full URL...
    Dim Referrer
    Referrer = Mid(Request("http_referer"), 8)
    Referrer = Left(Referrer, InStr(Referrer, "/") - 1)
    Referrer = LCase(Referrer)

    ' ignore it if we're from the local server...
    ' otherwise, add it to the log...
    If Referrer <> "localhost" And Referrer <> g_domainname Then
        Visit.LogClickThrough Referrer
    End If

End If %>

<HTML>
```

How It Works

The first thing we do is get hold of the referrer URL from the `ServerVariables` collection:

```
If Request.ServerVariables("http_referer") <> "" Then
```

For some reason, when the HTTP protocol standards were ratified, no one noticed that referrer had been spelt wrong, so make sure you don't include the other r, so that it reads `referer`.

Once we have the string, we assume it is a fully qualified URL, so we skip the first seven characters (as this contains the `http://` bit). Then we trim the string to get just the domain name by looking for the first forward-slash. We then set the string to lower-case:

```
Referrer = Mid(Request("http_referer"), 8)
Referrer = Left(Referrer, InStr(Referrer, "/") - 1)
Referrer = LCase(Referrer)
```

Finally, we check to make sure that we haven't been referred from ourselves. We test for both `localhost` and the domain name as defined in `site.asp` – in our example this is `jocoffee.com`:

```
If Referrer <> "localhost" And Referrer <> g_domainname Then
    Visit.LogClickThrough Referrer
End If
```

You'll get a referral URL even if the leading click was from the same domain as the page you're looking at, so we want to filter that from the results. If the URL is from another domain, we add it to the log using the same `LogClickThrough` method we used before.

Examining the Results

Obviously, data that you can't interpret has its limitations, but it's trivial to create a simple ASP page that can tell you all about the referrers for the month. What we will do is pump the results directly into an Excel workbook. To do this, all we have to do is tell ASP to return the content type in the headers as `application/x-msexcel` and return the data formatted as a normal HTML table – IE and Excel do the rest.

Try It Out – Displaying the Results as an Excel Workbook in an ASP Page

1. First of all, though, we have to ask the `Visit` object to return the referrers for a given period:

```
' GetClickThroughs - get the clickthroughs...
Public Function GetClickThroughs(ByVal TheMonth As Long, _
                                 ByVal TheYear As Long, _
                                 Optional ByVal TheDay As Long) As Recordset

    ' Return the stuff...
    Dim Where As String
    Where = "month=" & TheMonth & " and year=" & TheYear

    If TheDay <> 0 Then Where = Where & " and day=" & TheDay

    ' Run the query...
    Set GetClickThroughs = IUtility_DB.DB.Execute("select * from " & _
        "clickthroughs where " & Where & " order by month, day, year")

End Function
```

2. Secondly, create this simple ASP page called `referrerreport.asp`:

```
<%
    option explicit

    ' Tell it we're dealing with Excel...
    Response.Buffer = True
    Response.ContentType = "application/x-msexcel"

%>
<!-- #include file="site.asp" -->
<html>
<head>
</head>
<body>
    <table>
    <%

        ' Get the clicks...
        Dim clicks
        Set clicks = Visit.GetClickThroughs(Month(Now), Year(Now))

        Do While Not clicks.eof

            ' Draw it...
            response.write "<tr><td>"
            response.write clicks("Month") & "/" & clicks("Day") & _
                                        "/" & clicks("Year")
            response.write "</td><td>"
            response.write clicks("Referrer")
            response.write "</td><td>"
            response.write clicks("Tally")
            response.write "</td></tr>"

            ' Next
            clicks.MoveNext

        Loop

        clicks.Close
        Set clicks = Nothing

    %>
    </table>
</body>
<%
    ' Close out the site...
    Visit.ShutDown
%>
```

How It Works

The default activity of the `GetClickThroughs` function is to return all the records for a given month. What the function can also do is accept an optional "day" parameter that will zero the results in only on a given day:

```
Public Function GetClickThroughs(ByVal TheMonth As Long, _
                                 ByVal TheYear As Long, _
                                 Optional ByVal TheDay As Long) As Recordset
```

We also make sure that we return the results in date order:

```
Set GetClickThroughs = IUtility_DB.DB.Execute("select * from "+ & _
    "clickthroughs where " & Where & " order by month, day, year")
```

The first part of `referrerreport.asp` tells the browser that it's going to be returning a Microsoft Excel workbook:

```
Response.ContentType = "application/x-msexcel"
```

This gives Internet Explorer the opportunity to load an instance of Microsoft Excel into the browser and use it to present the report. Internet Explorer will create a temporary file on your computer whenever this happens.

We then grab the click-through details back through the `Visit` object and use them to generate a simple table:

```
Set clicks = Visit.GetClickThroughs(Month(Now), Year(Now))

    Do While Not clicks.eof

        ' Draw it...
        response.write "<tr><td>"
        response.write clicks("Month") & "/" & clicks("Day") & _
                                    "/" & clicks("Year")
        response.write "</td><td>"
        response.write clicks("Referrer")
        response.write "</td><td>"
        response.write clicks("Tally")
        response.write "</td></tr>"

        ' Next
        clicks.MoveNext

    Loop
```

Excel then takes that table and presents it like this:

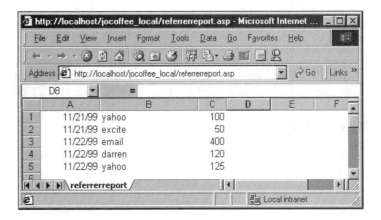

Traditional Marketing Media

If this book had been published eighteen months ago, probably the most significant difference would have been in the area of using traditional marketing media to promote Web sites.

Whereas eighteen months ago the typical ways to promote sites comprised of banner ads, sponsorship on other sites and direct e-mail, today we find Web sites being advertised on television, radio, newspapers, taxi-cabs, billboards, and magazines. In short, anywhere where non-Internet companies used to advertise is now fair game to **dot com** companies. Web sites, and particularly e-commerce sites, have become a fact of life for many people, and owners of these sites are finding that the best way to promote them is to leverage the same techniques they would have used 10 years ago to build their brand and share their 1-800 numbers.

There is one small caveat to this – promoting a Web site using traditional media costs plenty of money, so it's usually used by sites vying to own a particular high-profile space. Marketing of niche sites works in a completely different manner from marketing mainstream sites; niche sites might enjoy good returns from investing in print newspapers and magazines for their particular sector, such as trade journals and magazines. Nevertheless, don't forget that one of the important factors driving the growth of the Internet in our society as a whole is due to people wanting to learn more about specialist, niche subjects. You're likely to find more interest in niche markets in the form of online resource sites, meaning that online marketing may well be effective enough.

Search Engines

The first stop on our online site marketing travels involves registering our site with all the relevant search engines, like Yahoo, Excite, etc.

Search engines are often regarded as semi-evil in the eyes of Web site developers and owners, simply because getting your site to appear top of the rankings is an arduous and never-ending task. Although you might be lucky and get yours near the top for a while, the dynamic nature of the Web means that people continually submit their competing sites, pushing yours down the stack. Keeping the topmost listing on some search engines is virtually a full time job.

How important search engines are to you depends a lot on your kind of business. If you're competing in a high visibility space, like books or CDs, being in a search engine isn't going to help you much. Most people will use merchant aggregators (like those we met back in Chapter 17), or shopping portals like AltaVista, MSN, and Excite where you have to buy what are effectively "sponsorship slots". So, if you sold CDs, you'd have the option of buying a premium listing in their shopping directory under "Music & Video". If you're in a niche market, you may well get more benefit from being in search engines.

The Sites

As you're probably aware, there are a number of popular sites that are most likely the first in your potential customers' minds for their searching needs. A great site for helping you learn more about search engines is Search Engine Watch (http://www.searchenginewatch.com/).

Here are some popular sites. Please note, this section is not intended to be complete listing of all the possible engines out there, we're just trying to illustrate the different techniques search engines use.

Yahoo!

Yahoo is arguably the best-known search engine out there, and the best-known site, period! Perhaps because of its popularity, Yahoo is also the trickiest site to get listed in.

Unlike most search engines, Yahoo works by using a categorized tree of subjects, similar to the way we structured departments on Jo's Coffee. (This technically makes Yahoo an **index**.) Submitting your site to Yahoo and being listed effectively is one of the biggest black-art trick/techniques that you can pull off online. There are a number of great articles out there on sites like Search Engine Watch that can help you do this effectively. Most of the automated submission services, like the ones we'll be discussing later in the chapter, will *not* try to submit your site to Yahoo automatically because it's so tricky to get right.

Yahoo is very particular about the kinds of links they allow into their directory. Two basic rules are "wait until your site is finished, looking good and is fast to load" and "do not continually submit your site". Continual submissions to Yahoo will result in your site being blacklisted and you'll never achieve a listing. Human beings examine each submission and elect whether you deserve a listing in their index.

An interesting site to watch in the Yahoo-like index space is Netscape Open Directory (http://directory.netscape.com/). Originally, this site was called Newhoo and it was snapped up by Netscape as soon as it looked like it was going to be a success. From the users' perspective, it works in a similar fashion whereby it has a hierarchical category structure into which sites are placed. However, whereas Yahoo has 150 or so editors employed by Yahoo, inc. adding pages, Newhoo "hires" average Jo's and Joe's to help add the links to the catalog. Its new name comes from the Open Source Movement where people give up their time contributing to projects just to have the kudos of being involved with it.

Excite

Excite is one of many, many different search engines that work on the premise of trawling through your site indexing the text. They do this by setting a spider loose on your site that harvests all of the pages and pulls out relevant content and keywords.

Others in this category include InfoSeek, Lycos, AltaVista, and Google. Google deserves special mention because it's a "new kid on the block" and is actually backed by researchers at Stanford University who are basically thinking of neat new ways to search the Internet.

To submit your site to Excite and similar sites, all you have to do is prepare your site by placing keywords and descriptions in "hidden" areas of the site that the engines use to find out what the site is all about. We'll see how to add these keywords later in the chapter.

GoTo.com

GoTo is an interesting site, mainly because you have to pay to be listed. What happens is that you set up an account with them, give them some money, and you then supply a "bid" price for each keyword you want. When the user clicks through to your site, the bid price is deducted from your account. The more you pay, the higher in the listings you appear. So, for example, we might bid 1 cent to be listed against "espresso", but if one of our competitors bids 2 cents, he or she will appear above our listing. One of the neat things about GoTo is you get better control of your listings, and if you do the math, 1 cent per click-through can work out a lot cheaper than other promotion efforts. Some users are not keen on using sites where the listings are ordered based on the commercial contributions of the advertiser and so may well choose to boycott the site.

Preparing Your Site

The basic premise for preparing your site is adding tags to the top of each page called META tags, the purpose of which is to let the spider know what the site is about. This is done through two tags; one is a description, the other is a set of keywords. The spider will also take note of the <TITLE> tag on each page.

Try It Out – Adding META Tags to Our Site

1. We can easily add the META tags to our site by creating a separate include file containing them. First of all, create this file and call it meta.asp:

```
<META name="description" content="Selling the best coffee machines,
                        espresso machines and coffee equipment worldwide!">
<META name="keywords" content="coffee,espresso,filter,blend,bean,retail,
                        grinder,pos">
```

2. Then, add this line to any of the ASP pages in which you want to include the META tags. It's very important that you do this on default.asp as this is the page we will be submitting to the search engines:

```
<head>
    <!-- #include file="site.asp" -->
    <!-- #include file="meta.asp" -->
    <title><%=g_sitename%></title>
    <link rel="stylesheet" type="text/css" href="style.css">
</head>
```

3. To prevent spiders from indexing the admin pages of the site we need to add the following META tag to the HEAD section of admin/default.asp:

```
<META name="robots" content="noindex">
```

Note that spiders will not find our administration pages because there are no direct links to them from our site; this is merely a precautionary step.

How It Works

Now if you refresh the home page of Jo's Coffee and select View | Source from the menu, you'll see the META tags, and so will any spiders that visit your site.

Submission Services

There are two approaches you can take when submitting to search engines. You can either select a number of relevant engines and submit your site yourself, or you can get someone to submit them for you. Sites that offer a service where they try to get your site listed on your behalf are called **submission services**.

Submit It!

One of the most popular submission services is Submit It! (http://www.submitit.com/). This was originally an independent service but was snatched up by MSN and is now part of Microsoft bCentral (http://www.bcentral.com/).

You can find information on its current charges on the site, but at the time of going to press, it was charging $59 for a one-year license to publish up to two URLs. (For Jo's Coffee, we only need one URL, the root one.) It currently covers 400 search engines and one of its strengths is the fact that you can automatically resubmit your site throughout the year. This ability to resubmit is absolutely essential for making sure you stay near the top of the rankings.

SelfPromotion.com

The unsung hero in this drama is SelfPromotion.com. This is a service that has no specific fee. If you like the job it does, you're more than welcome to send it some money. This is an approach similar to shareware. SelfPromotion.com covers all of the major indexes and engines, and you can list as many URLs as you want in your account and continue to submit them throughout the year. They also have some excellent search engine information resources. Best of all, the way the site is constructed makes you believe that there's a gang of experts behind the scene making sure that you get the best listings you can.

Banner Advertising

Banner advertising is a curious beast. In the world of online marketing, there are two schools of thought. One dictates that banner advertising doesn't work and that eventually **conversions** (the percentage of customers coming to your site through a banner that subsequently make a purchase) are going to get so low that they disappear completely. The other dictates that banner advertising will be around forever and is the best way to build online branding.

The main issue people cite when attacking banner advertising is that the number of people clicking on banners is actually declining. However, an interesting comeback to this is that it's more likely that people's perception of banner advertising is actually maturing, bringing banners closer to the way that billboards and television adverts work. Consider this; when you see an advertisement for BMW on television, do you immediately phone up the 1-800 number on the screen to learn more about BMWs? Rather, do you find yourself thinking about BMWs – is the purpose of advertising to build brand awareness and make sure a particular company or offering is in the forefront of your mind? Banner advertising started off by enjoying excellent click-through rates because it was a new thing. Today we find that banners are probably just a good way of getting your name out there.

To determine if banner advertising is right for you, there's no alternative to just trying it to see if it works. There are, luckily, a number of ways to see if banner advertising does work.

Free Banner Exchanges

The easiest and quickest ways to get your banners on other sites is to join a banner exchange program. These programs allow you to put together banners that are then served on other sites, in exchange for which you have to put banners for other sites on your site. There's usually some form of ratio system in play, meaning that you have to show two or three **impressions** for other sites before yours is served on some other site.

The most popular is the LinkExchange Banner Network, which is now part of Microsoft's bCentral. LinkExchange offers you the ability to place a 468x60 pixel banner on your site and a 2:1 ratio, meaning you have to show two banners for each one of yours that is displayed. LinkExchange is currently the largest banner network with 450,000 members. It also offers targeting to specific industries and, starting soon, geographical areas.

> Remember, although we're talking specifically about LinkExchange here, there are a number of banner exchange programs out there that may better suit your needs. Make sure you research thoroughly before committing to a specific program.

The only caveat with these banner swap services is that they want to market their own service just as hard as they want to market yours. This means that each time you see one of their banners, you'll see an advertisement for their own service alongside. However, banner exchanges are usually very cheap (often free) and easy to set up, so they're usually worth trying in the first instance, unless you have cash and intentions for a larger strategy. Most services give you a simple snippet of HTML to add to the pages – LinkExchange's is just a few lines.

Here's the HTML code:

```
<!-- BEGIN LINKEXCHANGE CODE -->
<center>

<iframe src="http://leader.linkexchange.com/1/X1214362/showiframe?"
        width=468 height=60 marginwidth=0 marginheight=0 hspace=0
        vspace=0 frameborder=0 scrolling=no>
<a href="http://leader.linkexchange.com/1/X1214362/clickle" target="_top">
   <img width=468 height=60 border=0 ismap alt=""
        src="http://leader.linkexchange.com/1/X1214362/showle?">
</a>
</iframe>

<br>
<a href="http://leader.linkexchange.com/1/X1214362/clicklogo" target="_top">
<img src="http://leader.linkexchange.com/1/X1214362/showlogo?" width=468
     height=16 border=0 ismap alt="">
</a><br>

</center>
<!-- END LINKEXCHANGE CODE -->
```

Here's Jo's Coffee with a LinkExchange banner in place:

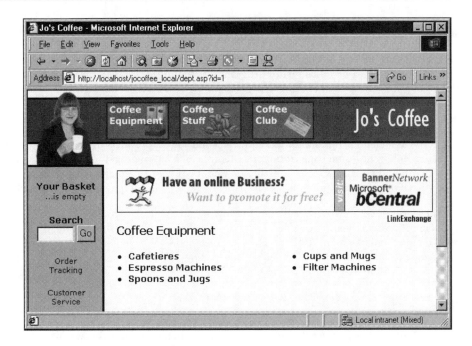

Major Banner Agencies

If you want something a little more professional than the free banner exchanges, the world of banner advertising starts to get a little more confusing.

The type of company you're looking for falls under the heading of **Ad Networks, Brokers, and Representatives**. These are organizations that buy, sell, and serve banners for people who either have advertising space to sell (such as an online magazine), or advertising space to buy (such as Jo's Coffee).

Some examples of banner agencies are DoubleClick (who we briefly met back in Chapter 13), HyperBanner (http://www.hyperbanner.com/), and FlyCast/CGMI (http://www.flycast.com).

Discussions on how to find the best deal with these organizations are way beyond the scope of this book (they would, in fact, fill another book of similar size), so there's nothing I can do here but suggest that you seek professional guidance for this.

AdAuction

One company that deserves special mention in this arena is AdAuction. AdAuction acts as a clearinghouse for companies that have unsold "advertising inventory" (space for banners). Again, this isn't a formal recommendation, but it's worth looking into if you want to buy advertising on the cheap.

Associates Programs

Associates programs are one of those things that came from nowhere, but are changing the world. Rumor has it that the idea of an associates program was first discussed at a dinner party the CEO of Amazon.com, Jeff Bezos, was attending. The principle behind an associates program is that you make it possible for anyone in the world to sell your company's goods and services, in return for which you give them a small cut of the action.

Amazon.com's associates program, for example, lets you sell its products in one of three ways. You can either create a link to its home page from your site, in which case you get 5% of anything that customer buys, or you can add a search box to your site that bounces over to Amazon to get the results (5% again), or you can list specific titles, in which case you get 15% of the purchase of that specific item.

Associates programs work *extremely* well and I highly recommend that you implement one on your own site. It's a fantastic way of getting members of the general public to sell your products. In addition, although you may balk at paying 10% of your sale to someone else, remember that's a fully qualified sale that's going to further motivate your new "salesperson". Compare that to other marketing techniques and it will most likely work out to be good value.

ClickTrade

Like most online activities, you can employ a company to handle your associates programs for you. ClickTrade (http://www.clicktrade.com/) is the most famous of these right now and simply lets you create an associates scheme where you define how much of each transaction (either a percentage or a fixed amount) you want to kick back to your associate when one of their referrals makes a purchase. ClickTrade is part of the Microsoft bCentral network.

To open an account with them, you have to deposit $100, which is used as a bond to ensure you're willing to actually pay the kickbacks. One of the big advantages to using them is that they have a directory where people can go to find associates schemes. So, if someone is putting together a site reviewing coffee shops in South London and decides to sell machines, he or she can visit ClickTrade's directory, look for "coffee" and may well choose to sell our stuff for a percentage of the profits.

Building an Associates Program

Rolling your own associates program is actually remarkably simple, so we're now going to see how we can build our own.

There are typically three parts to an associates program:

- ❏   Letting new associates opt into the program
- ❏   Capturing the relevant clicks and purchases that count towards associate purchases
- ❏   Figuring out how much to send to each associate

To keep this example brief, we're going to skip the bit that brings new associates on board and work under the assumption that anyone who has made a purchase on the site and is therefore a registered customer is able to participate in the scheme. In the real world, you'd most likely offer a sign up form of some sort, but still use the Customers table to keep track of the associates as well as the customers by adding an additional column indicating that they were a valid associate.

We can quickly get from here to the point where we can let our associate, Edward, create a link on his site to Jo's Coffee. We have to find some way to let Edward know what his associate ID is. As we mentioned before, in this example we're going to assume that his customer ID (6) will be his associate ID. Here's the link Edward places on his site:

```
http://www.joscoffee.com/default.asp?associateid=6
```

Tagging the Browser

Back in our chapter on privacy (Chapter 13), we spoke about how DoubleClick and Abacus were entering into a scheme to tag browsers so they could watch the user move from site to site. We need to do something similar here to tag the browser so that we know the customer came from Edward's site. Privacy advocates may well view this maneuver as taking liberties, so you might want to consider dropping a clause into your privacy statement so everyone knows what's going on.

To tag the browser, all we have to do is drop a cookie onto the machine containing the associate ID. When it comes time for the order to be processed, we can lookup this ID and store the appropriate kickback details. By using a cookie, we can let the new customer make the purchase anytime in the future after the browser has been tagged. It's unrealistic to expect that our new customer will make a purchase in the same browsing exercise that brought them over to the site, and seeing that the point of this technology is to make our associate want to sell more products, we want to make sure we keep track of their referrals.

The expected entry points into our site will be:

❑ The home page.

❑ The search results page. That way, we can let people add Jo's Coffee search boxes to their site wired into the `search.asp` we built in Chapter 11.

❑ The item information page. On this page, we also want to capture the ID of the product so, if we want, we can give people a large commission for specifying a particular product on their site.

Try It Out – Tagging the Visitors

1. Add this function to `site.asp`:

```
' SetAssociate - set an associate ID and related product...
Public Sub SetAssociate(AssociateID, ProductID)

    ' Set the cookies...
    Response.Cookies("AssociateID") = AssociateID
    Response.Cookies("AssociateID").Expires = DateAdd("y", 1, Now)
    Response.Cookies("AssociateProductID") = ProductID
    Response.Cookies("AssociateProductID").Expires = DateAdd("y", 1, Now)

End Sub
```

2. Now, add the following code to `default.asp`. Because we're going to be dropping cookies into the visitor's browser, we have to call the function before we send any HTML down. Make sure this code appears right at the top of the page:

```
' ignore it if we're from the local server...
        ' otherwise, add it to the log...
        If Referrer <> "localhost" And Referrer <> g_domainname Then
            Visit.LogClickThrough Referrer
        End If

    End If %>
```

```
    ' Do we have an associate?
    If Request("AssociateID") <> "" Then
        SetAssociate Request("AssociateID"), ""
    End If
%>
```

```
<HTML>
```

Now when the user clicks through from Edward's site, the `AssociateID` query string variable will be set and we can set the cookie using the `SetAssociate` function. To clarify, here's a reminder of the URL Edward will have on his site:

```
http://www.joscoffee.com/default.asp?associateid=6
```

3. To tag a particular product to an associate, we also have to capture the ID of that product. Add this code to `detail.asp`:

```
<% option explicit
    ' Do we have an associate? Tag the product ID if we do too...
    If Request("AssociateID") <> "" Then
        SetAssociate Request("AssociateID"), Request("ID")
    End If
%>
```

That way, Edward can add this link to his site:

```
http://www.joscoffee.com/detail.asp?id=1&associateid=6
```

...and if the new customer buys the item with an ID of 1, we know to credit him with more commission.

Tallying Associate Commissions

The next trick we have is keeping track of the associate's commission. This, obviously, has to be tied into the order processing system somehow. To do this we need to add a couple of columns to the `OrderLines` table to track the commissions, and provide a way of telling the `Orders` object that an associate's commission needs to be applied.

Our first step is to add columns to the `OrderLines` table that will track the associate and the relevant commission. What we will do here is store the actual percentage that we're going to kick back to the associate once the order has been confirmed (paid for and shipped). All we need to do then is build an accounting system capable of storing these kickbacks.

Try It Out – Keeping Track of an Associate's Commission

1. Add the `AssociateID` and `AssociateKickback` columns to the `OrderLines` table:

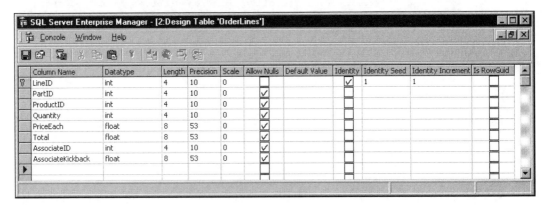

2. To tweak the `WroxCommerce` object model to work with the associates program, add these member variables to the `Orders` object to hold the details:

```
' Use IUtility to call back into the Visit and Database objects...
Private m_utility As IUtility
```

```
' Associate program details...
Public m_AssociateID As Long
Public m_AssociateProductID As Long
```

3. Next, add this method to the `Orders` object so we can tell WroxCommerce the ID of an associate, and any applicable product ID:

```
' SetAssociate - sets an associate's details...
Public Function SetAssociate(ByVal AssociateID As Long, _
                             ByVal AssociateProductID As Long)

    ' Set the values...
    m_AssociateID = AssociateID
    m_AssociateProductID = AssociateProductID

End Function
```

Now that we have methods in place to share the associate's details with the order processing components, we need to actually call them. Internally, we don't care about the associate until it becomes time to call the `SplitBasket` method on the `Orders` object, which if you remember is the method that populates the `Orders`, `OrderParts`, and `OrderLines` tables.

623

4. First off, we have to solve a small conundrum. The cookie containing the associate's details actually exists on the non-secure version of the site, so when we flip over to the secure site for checkout we won't be able to see the non-secure version's cookies. Therefore, we have to send over the associate details when we click the **Proceed to Checkout** button. Add this code to `basket.asp`:

```
' Add a form first...
Response.Write "<form action=" & _
               "https://127.0.0.1/jocoffee_local/checkout.asp"" method=post>"
Response.Write "<tr><td colspan=5 align=center>"
Response.Write "<input type=submit value=""Proceed to Checkout"">"
Response.Write "</td></tr>"
Response.Write "<tr><td><br></td></tr>"

' Add the basket ID to the form...
Response.Write "<input type=hidden name=basketid value=" & _
               Visit.Basket.ID & ">"
Response.write "<input type=hidden name=associateid value=" & _
               request.cookies("associateid") & ">"
Response.Write "<input type=hidden name=associateproductid value=" & _
               request.cookies("associateproductid") & ">"
```

5. We can then tweak `checkout.asp` in two ways. Firstly, we have to write the new associate details into a cookie on the secure site:

```
' Did we get given a basketid?
If Request.Form("BasketID") <> "" Then
   Visit.SetBasket Request("BasketID")
   SetAssociate Request("AssociateID"), Request("AssociateProductID")
End If
```

6. We then have to read the cookie details back and pass it over to the `SetAssociate` method we built earlier. These two bits of functionality make sure that the associate ID is traceable over the entire order process:

```
' Did we get given a basketid?
If Request.Form("BasketID") <> "" Then
   Visit.SetBasket Request("BasketID")
   SetAssociate Request("AssociateID"), Request("AssociateProductID")
End If

' Do we need to set associate details?
If Request.Cookies("AssociateID") <> "" Then
   Visit.Orders.SetAssociate Request.Cookies("AssociateID"), _
                             Request.Cookies("AssociateProductID")
End If
```

7. Assuming that we can now pass the associate ID around properly, we need to change the code on the `Orders` object's `SplitBasket` method to populate our new columns in the `OrderLines` table. Add this code to middle of the method:

```
' Copy the details from the basket
orderline("partid") = orderpart("partid")
orderline("productid") = Query("productid")
orderline("quantity") = Query("quantity")
orderline("priceeach") = Query("price")
orderline("total") = Query("lineprice")
```

```
' Any associates?
If m_AssociateID <> 0 Then
    orderline("associateid") = m_AssociateID

    ' If this is the specific product we were given,
    ' add a higher commission...
    If Query("productid") = m_AssociateProductID Then
        orderline("AssociateKickBack") = 15
    Else
        orderline("AssociateKickBack") = 5
    End If

End If
```

All that code has to do is look at the m_AssociateID member variable to determine if we're in an associate program "mode" and, if we are, add the ID of the associate into the column. We can then do a further check on the product we're actually adding to determine if it's the specific recommendation of the associate and, if it is, we can give them 15% commission, rather than the usual 5%.

Paying Associates

Obviously, we don't want to send money to an associate before we're confident that the sale has satisfactorily gone through the system, which is why we don't just dump the commission values down to a separate table but instead make sure we can calculate the commission they should earn in retrospect. We're not going to cover this topic in detail in this section, simply to keep the example brief, as there are implications as to what you do with the commissions once you've worked out who to pay them to. For example, do you want to create a Microsoft Excel spreadsheet containing the commissions and then pass them over to your accounts department, or do something else? Once the data is in the database, it's up to you how you deal with it.

The best way to do this is to run a batch process once a month that trawls the orders looking for commissions that need to be paid. It's a good idea to leave a month-long window in this process to make sure that you're happy with the order. (For example, don't pay October's commission until December 1st.) Then, simply select out the associates from the successful orders in that month with a SQL statement like this:

```
SELECT DISTINCT AssociateID
FROM OrderLines
WHERE PartID IN
        (SELECT PartID
     FROM OrderParts
     WHERE Status = 1 AND OrderID IN
             (SELECT OrderID
             FROM Orders
             WHERE Completed BETWEEN '10/1/1999' AND
                 '10/31/1999'))
```

With a list of the associates needing commission on hand, it's a simple task to loop through them and pull back the amount they are due:

```
SELECT total * (associatekickback / 100)
FROM OrderLines
WHERE PartID IN
        (SELECT PartID
    FROM OrderParts
    WHERE Status = 1 AND OrderID IN
            (SELECT OrderID
            FROM Orders
            WHERE Completed BETWEEN '10/1/1999' AND
                '10/31/1999'))
    AND associateid = 6
```

Other Marketing Opportunities

There's no end to the places where you can market yourself and your company online. Here are a few places worth mentioning...

Direct E-mail

Nothing has received more bad press in recent years than **spam**. Spam is the name given to unsolicited, junk e-mail that has no other purpose than to annoy, it is generally sent to large numbers of recipients whose names have been purchased by marketers. We spoke briefly about junk mail back in our chapter on privacy, Chapter 13.

However, direct, targeted e-mail is a very good way of keep in touch with customers and finding new ones. In Chapter 15, we saw how we could build a newsletter to keep our customers and potential customers in the loop about what was happening over at Jo's Coffee. Direct e-mailing through newsletters is a more than reasonable thing to do, providing that the person you're sending to has asked to be included, and that he or she has a way of getting off the list.

In the past few months, people have started to find that "opt-in" e-mail services are actually quite effective. What happens in these situations is people sign up to be told about products or services for a certain category or categories of products. For example, Jo herself might sign up for a "small online retailer" opt-in e-mail list and then her name is rented out to anyone who wants to target small online retailers. The idea behind it is that because Jo has explicitly stated she wants to be targeted, the messages she receives won't be perceived as spam.

One company that's been renting out opt-in e-mail addresses for a while now is BulletMail (http://www.bulletmail.com/). Another is PostMasterDirect (http://www.postmasterdirect.com/). You can find more companies like that through most of the major search engines. Most of the companies offer a service where they send out the e-mails on your behalf, so all you have to do is pay their invoice and give them the text of your message.

Merchant Aggregators and Comparison Shopping

In Chapter 17, we introduced the idea of merchant aggregation services that let people "comparison shop" between sites and their competitors easily.

It's worth saying that if, your industry has merchant aggregators, take steps to make sure you get involved. There is an old adage, which states "can you afford not to be in it?" and as these things become more and more popular, you're most likely going to end up shooting yourself in the foot by not competing in this way.

Directories and Catalogs

A big growth space right now is directories and catalogs that list companies, products or both. Their main motivation for this is to build their own brand and collect eyeballs, but you can benefit from the free advertising opportunities that these sites afford. Some also add additional benefits, such as BizRate, which we met back in Chapter 14. Some directories and catalog sites work on the basis that you pay them a **finders fee** if they direct new customers to you, so make sure you carefully examine each option.

Summary

The way you market your Web site determines its success. Simply, if a Web site owner does not get this right, the site will never receive any traffic, and never make any money. Frustratingly, this is the most difficult aspect of building a site's critical mass up to a point where it starts to become popular. Luckily, e-commerce is such a growth area that plenty of people are coming up with new, innovative ways to tell the general public where your site is.

We started out this chapter by looking at how, assuming we could get our message out there, we could log the links into our site using a simple database table and Microsoft Excel report. We then spoke about how, today, marketing through television, radio, and print is an effective means for advertising your mainstream site. We then touched on search engines and spoke a little about services that can help you register your site with search engines, and keep it listed effectively. Next, we moved on to the subject of banner advertising and described how, for an effective banner ad campaign, it's best to seek professional advice.

Finally, we showed you how you can build your own associates program to let anyone who's interested market products from your site on their own.

DataCash Component Reference

Detailed instructions on using the DataCash component can be found in Chapter 9.

> **A quick note to US readers: Switch cards are a form of debit card used in the UK. Also, as DataCash is a British company, they spell "authorize" with an "s", not a "z", and they also spell "check" as "cheque".**

To create the DataCash object, either put a reference to DataCash Payment Authorisation for Windows NT in your project and call:

```
Set DataCash = New DataCash
```

Or use CreateObject:

```
Set DataCash = CreateObject("MS.DataCash")
```

Authorise Method

The DataCash component has a very simple object model. The function used most often is the Authorise method, which we met in our above code sample. Here's a breakdown of the parameters on that method:

Authorize As Integer	Sends a payment request over to the DataCash server.
HostName As String	The name of the DataCash server to use. If omitted, new_auth.datacash.com is used.
HostPort As Long	The port on the server to use. If omitted, 9070 is used.
EncKey As String	The "Blowfish" key that should be used for encrypting the credit card number.

Table Continued on Following Page

`Request As String`	The type of transaction to perform. This can be authorization ("`auth`"), pre-authorization ("`pre`"), refund ("`refund`") or fulfillment notice ("`fulfill`"). (The different types of transaction are detailed below)
`CardNo As String`	The number of the card to authorize. There are a number of test numbers you can use, which are detailed below. `DataCash` will automatically strip out spaces and dashes.
`ExpMonth As Integer`	The month in which the card will expire.
`ExpYear As Integer`	The year in which the card will expire.
`SwitchIssue As String`	Either the Switch card issue number, or its start date in "mm/yy" format. (Note, Switch is not available in the US.)
`Reference As String`	The merchant's internal reference number. This must be between 6 and 12 digits.
`Client As String`	The `DataCash` "client" number (aka "username"). Issued when the account is opened. "`21859999`" is the test account.
`Password As String`	The password for the DataCash account. ("`Fred`" is the password for the test account.)
`Amount As Double`	The amount to authorize.
`Mode as Integer`	The operational mode of the module. This should be "`0`".
`LogFileName As String`	The name of a file to log the requests too. If omitted, no logging is performed.
`TimeOut As Integer`	The number of seconds to wait until canceling the connection.
`Currency As String`	The currency to use. If omitted, "`GBP`" (Great Britain Pounds) is used.
`AuthCode As String`	Reserved

"Authorise" Return Codes

The `Authorise` method is capable at returning a single integer representing the result of the operation. A value less than 0 indicates that something went wrong before the request got over to the DataCash servers. A value of 1 indicates that the transaction was a success. A value greater than 1 indicates something went wrong at the bank.

Here are the error codes that the `Authorise` method can return indicating a problem at our end:

Return Code	Meaning
-1	A connection to the DataCash host was not established.
-2	A connection to the DataCash host was established but no response was received to the transaction request.
-3	Some of the transaction details were omitted.
-4	Timeout occurred.
-5	The log file could not be opened.
-10	Card date is invalid. Date must be in the range now to 12/2030.
-11	Card number is invalid.
-20	Switch details are invalid. If an issue number was passed in, this must be in the range 1 to 29. If a start date was passed in, this must be in the range 01/1992 to now.
-30	Transaction reference is too short, too long or non-numeric. The transaction reference must be a number of 6-12 digits.
-31	Transaction amount was less than or equal to zero. Only positive, non-zero values will be passed to `DataCash`.
-40	Client identifier missing.
-41	Client password missing.
-42	Client encryption key missing.
-255	An internal error occurred in the module. If logging is being performed, check that the disk is not full and that security and file permissions for the logging file are appropriate.

Here are the codes that `Authorize` can return indicating an error at the bank:

Code	Name	Description
2	Socket write error	Communication was interrupted.
3	Timeout	A DataCash server did not respond.
5	Edit error	General Error.
6	Communications error	Error in communications link.

Table Continued on Following Page

631

Code	Name	Description
7	Not authorized	Transaction declined.
8	APACS-30 timeout	The bank's server did not respond.
9	Currency error	Currency not supported.
10	Security error	You specified an incorrect password and/or encryption key.
11	Pre-auth transaction error	General Error.
12	No authorization reference	General Error.
13	Initialization error	General Error.
14	Database server error	General Error.
15	Client error	General Error. (Password possibly wrong.)
16	Switch issue error	Issue number was not the correct length, or was not supplied.
17	Start date error	Start date was invalid, or was not supplied. (Switch cards only.)
18	No authorization code	No authorization code was supplied for a fulfillment request.
19	Cannot fulfill transaction	You attempted to fulfill a transaction that either could not be fulfilled (e.g. authorization, refund) or already has been.
20	Duplicate transaction reference	A successful transaction has already been sent using this reference number.
21	Invalid card type	The card requested cannot be used on this service.
22	Invalid reference	Reference numbers should be a numeric, non-zero value between 6 and 9 digits in length.
23	Date format invalid	Start and expiry dates should be specified as MM/YY, MMYY or MM-YY.
24	Card has already expired	The supplied expiry date is in the past.
25	Card number invalid	The card number does not pass the checksum test.
26	Card number wrong length	The card number does not have the expected number of digits.

Code	Name	Description
27	Issue number error	See 16.
28	Start date error	See 17.
29	Card is not valid yet	The supplied start date is in the future. (Switch cards only.)
30	Start date after expiry date	The supplied start date is after the expiry date. (Switch cards only.)
31	Two different start dates	Returned if there is two different start dates in the start date and issue number fields.
32	Issue number not needed	This card type does not require an issue number, but one was supplied. (May not be returned by some servers.)
33	Card number encrypted	The card number supplied was encrypted and could not be checked. If you get this error, you may be encrypting a credit card number with the wrong key.
34	Invalid amount	Amounts must be positive, non-zero values.
35	Couldn't allocate terminal	No TIDs were found for this vTID, using the supplied currency and card number combination. Typical reasons are: you don't take American Express; you don't take Switch in this currency; or the encryption key is wrong.
36	Card used recently	This credit card was used within the last 2 minutes.
40	Cheque request failed	You do not have authorization to process checks.
41	Cheque number wrong length	The supplied check number is too long.
42	Sort code wrong length	The sort code is too long. (US readers, a "sort code" is a "routing number".)
43	Cheque number and sort code wrong length	Both the check number and sort codes are wrong.
44	Invalid account number	The check's account number is wrong.
45	Cheque number wrong length and account number invalid	The check's number is too long and the account number is wrong.

Table Continued on Following Page

Code	Name	Description
46	Sort code wrong length and account number invalid	The sort code and account numbers are both wrong.
47	Cheque number and sort code wrong length, and account number invalid	None of the issues supplied for the check are correct!
52	No such vTID	General Error.
53	No free TIDs available for this vTID	General Error.
54	Incomprehensibl e vTID request	General Error.
55*	Could not release the given TID	General Error.
56	Card used too recently	See 36. (Also referred to as "speed limit")
57	Could not reload the database	General Error.
510	vTID table corrupt	General Error.

Once you have the code, you can use the `AuthCode` method to determine the result. If `Authorise` returns 1 then the transaction was authorized and `AuthCode` returns the actual authorization code the bank issues. Otherwise, `AuthCode` will return a string giving more information about the error.

`AuthCode As String`	Returns the result of a transaction. Returns the bank's authorization code if successful, otherwise it returns an error string.

Other Methods

Here are the other methods on the DataCash object:

`CardType As String`	Returns the type of the card, e.g. VISA, Mastercard, etc.
`Issuer As String`	Returns the name of the bank that issues the card, e.g. HSBC, Bank One, etc.
`Country As String`	Returns the country of the card issuer.
`TimeStamp As String`	Returns the date and time of the transaction. However, this is returned as a string of numbers, not as a VB `Date` data type.
`UniqueRef As String`	Returns a string that can uniquely identify the transaction anywhere in the DataCash system.

Magic Numbers

When testing your DataCash implementation, there is a set of card numbers called **magic numbers** you can pass through that are guaranteed certain results. So, if you want to test the component to see what happens when an authorization is successful, you can pass through any one of the numbers that will always return a positive result.

Here are the magic numbers:

Magic Number	`Authorise` Returns	`AuthCode` Returns
5473000000000015	1	Random authorization code
5473000000000023	1	Random authorization code
5473000000000031	1	Random authorization code
5473000000000049	1	Random authorization code
5473000000000056	1	Random authorization code
5473000000000064	1	Random authorization code
5473000000000072	1	Random authorization code
5473000000000098	1	Random authorization code
5473000000000106	7	"Declined"
5473000000000114	7	"Retain card"
5473000000000122	7	"Call Authorization Center"

Table Continued on Following Page

Magic Number	Authorise Returns	AuthCode Returns
5473000000000130	1	"123"
5473000000000205	2	"Socket write error"
5473000000000213	6	"Communications error"
5473000000000221	9	"Currency error"
5473000000000239	10	"Transaction error"
5473000000000247	11	"Pre-authorization failed"
5473000000000254	12	"No authorization reference"
5473000000000262	13	"Initialization error"
5473000000000270	14	"SQL server down"
5473000000000288	15	"Bad password"
5473000000000296	16	"Issue size error"
5473000000000304	17	"Switch standard error"
5473000000000312	20	"Duplicate"
5473000000000320	21	"Wrong card type"
5473000000000338	22	"Bad transaction reference"
5473000000000346	23	"Bad date"
5473000000000353	24	"Expired"
5473000000000361	25	"Invalid PAN"
5473000000000379	26	"Wrong length"
5473000000000387	27	"Bad issue number"
5473000000000395	28	"Missing start date"
5473000000000403	29	"Not valid yet"
5473000000000411	30	"Start greater than expiration"
5473000000000429	31	"Start equals expiration"
5473000000000437	32	"No issue number required"
5473000000000445	34	"Bad amount"

Getting Random Results

If you want to try the code with some numbers that don't always return the same thing, these numbers return a random result:

Card type	Card number	Extra information required
VISA	4444 3333 2222 1111	
	4242 4242 4242 4242	
	4444 2222 3333 1111	
Mastercard	5473 0000 0000 0007	
Switch/Solo	4936 0000 0000 0000 001	1-digit issue number
	6333 0000 0000 0005	Start date
American Express	3434 3434 3434 343	

American Express cards are handled as being only 15 digits long, not 16. There is no missing "4" from the above table.

Doug Dean's EZsite Forum 3 Component Reference

Detailed instructions on using the Doug Dean's EZsite Forum 3 component can be found in Chapter 15.

> **You can download evaluation copies of these components at**
> **http://www.dougdean.com/.**

The EZsite Forum components are typically used directly from ASP, rather than from within a Visual Basic component. Here's the code to create an instance of the component:

```
Set Forum = Server.CreateObject("EZsiteForum.Forum")
```

Creating the Database

Out of the box, EZsite Forum will attempt to use an Access database through a system data source name (DSN), although an OLEDB connection string may also be used, as described in Chapter 15. However, the components will easily upsize to MS SQL Server 7 and this can be achieved by running the EZsiteForumSchema.sql file that can be found in the Database folder. This script will create the appropriate schema, as well as inserting sample data.

Installing the Graphics

The EZsite Forum components manage their own presentation, meaning that they are able to send HTML content down through the Response object back to the browser. This makes them substantially easier to implement on a site, but less flexible in terms of customization.

The Graphics folder, installed along with the components, contains all of the graphics that are required by the components for presentation. This folder should be copied into the folder containing the site that uses the components. You can use the ImagePath property to set the graphics folder:

```
Forum.ImagePath = "graphics/"
```

Using the Forum Object

The Forum object, created with Server.CreateObject("EZsiteForum.Forum"), has a complex set of properties, the majority of which are concerned with customizing the graphics that are used in presentation.

Once you've configured the object, you can ask it to present the forum using the ShowForum method. You will need to use the administrative tools (covered later), to determine the ID of the forum you want to display. In this sample, we're asking the object to display forum ID "1":

```
Forum.ShowForum 1
```

General Properties

These are the general properties that control the way the Forum object behaves:

Property	Description	Type

DSN	Identifies the data source name to use, or identifies an OLE DB connection string.
	
	For example:
	`Forum.DSN = "DSN=JoCoffeeWeb;`
	`  UID=jocoffeeweb;PWD=eermlate"`
		String

ASPFileURL	Identifies the name of the page that called the forum.	String
ASPFrameSetURL	Identifies the name of the page that contains the FRAMESET tag used to create a forum that operates inside of a frame.	String

Property	Description	Type
ImagePath	Identifies the name of the folder that contains the images to be used when presenting the forum. For example: `Forum.ImagePath = "graphics/"`	String
SubmitAuthorMaxLength	Identifies the maximum length of the string that can be used to hold the name of the author in new postings.	Integer
SubmitAuthorSize	Identified the size of the `INPUT` tag that is used for the author name when presenting the posting form.	Integer
SubmitTitleMaxLength	Identifies the maximum length of the string that can be used to hold the title of a new posting.	Integer
SubmitTitleSize	Identifies the size of the `INPUT` tag that is used for the title when presenting the posting form.	Integer
SubmitResponseCols	Identifies the number of columns used on the `TEXTAREA` tag that captures the actual message.	Integer
SubmitResponseRows	Identifies the number of rows used on the `TEXTAREA` tag that captures the actual message.	Integer
SubmitResponseWrap	Identifies the wrapping mode for the `TEXTAREA` tag that captures the actual message.	String
ByPassNextLogon	Indicates whether or not the user should be asked to login when he or she posts again.	Boolean
ByPassPreview	Indicates whether the user should be asked to preview the posting before it is committed to the forum.	Boolean
ForumBorderSize	Identifies the size of the border that should be drawn around the Forum.	Integer

Table Continued on Following Page

Property	Description	Type
MsgAuthor	Identifies the name of the author that should be used on new postings. Can be used to integrate the Forum in with the personalization and membership functionality of the site itself. For example: `Forum.MsgAuthor = "Edward Behan"`	String
UseASPRedirection	Indicates whether to use ASP's `Response.Redirect` method or whether to use JavaScript redirection if the value is false.	Boolean
AlignCopyRight	Identifies the `ALIGN` attribute to be used when rendering the copyright message. The copyright message can be turned off in the registered version.	String

Interface Language Properties

These properties define the text that is used to display the forum to the user:

Property	Description	Default	Type
NextButton	Specifies the text on the Next button.	"Next"	String
EditButton	Specifies the text on the Edit button.	"Edit"	String
PostButton	Specifies the text on the Post button.	"Post"	String
PreviewButton	Specifies the text on the Preview button.	"Preview"	String
ButtonImageOn	Indicates whether or not to use graphical buttons, or typical form buttons.	False	Boolean
EditButtonImage	Specifies the image for the Edit button.	"ImageEditButton.gif"	String

Property	Description	Default	Type
PostButtonImage	Specifies the image for the Post button.	"ImagePostButton.gif"	String
NextButtonImage	Specifies the image for the Next button.	"ImageNextButton.gif"	String
SubmitButtonImage	Specifies the image for the Submit button.	"ImageSubmitButton.gif"	String
ResponseTo	Identifies the title for the response form.	"RESPOND TO:"	String
Your Name	Identifies the caption on the post message form that asks for the author's name.	"YOUR NAME:"	String
ResponseTitle	Identifies the caption on the post message form that asks for the message title.	"RESPONSE TITLE:"	String
ResponseText	Identifies the caption on the post message form that asks for the message body.	"RESPONSE TEXT:"	String
InvalidName	Identifies the text displayed when the author's name is invalid.	"You must enter your name."	String
InvalidTitle	Identifies the text displayed when the message title is invalid.	"You must enter your title."	String
InvalidResponse	Identifies the text displayed when the message text is invalid.	"You must enter a response."	String
BackFromInvalid	Identifies the message displayed when the author is asked to go back to the previous response.	"[Press your browsers back key to continue.]"	String
MemberName	Identifies the text displayed when author is being asked to log into their account.	"MEMBER NAME:"	String

Table Continued on Following Page

Property	Description	Default	Type
Password	Identifies the text displayed when author is being asked to supply their password.	"PASSWORD:"	String
Submit	Identifies the text for the submit button for the member login.	"Submit"	String
SavePassword	Identifies the text asking the user if their username/password should be saved.	"Save Password"	String
GetRegistered	Identifies the text prompting the user to register for a forum account.	"Get a password by completing the registration form."	String
NameDuplicationNotice	Identifies the text displayed when the new registration name conflicts with an existing one.	"- NAME DUPLICATION - The name you entered is already on file, use the back key to reenter a different name. "	String
ForumRegistrationTitle	Identifies the text displayed at the top of the registration form.	"FORUM REGISTRATION"	String
ReEnterPassword	Identifies the text for the password confirmation field.	"REENTER PASSWORD:"	String
Required	Identifies the text displayed next to required fields.	"REQUIRED"	String
PasswordUnmatched	Identifies the text displayed when the two passwords to not match.	"Your passwords do not match."	String
PasswordUnderFive	Identifies the text displayed when the password is less than five characters long.	"The 'Password' field must be at least 5 characters long."	String

Property	Description	Default	Type
MemberNameUnderFive	Identifies the text displayed when the member name is less than five characters long.	"The 'Member Name' field must be at least 5 characters long."	String
RequiredEmpty	Identifies the text displayed when a required field is missing.	"A required input field is empty."	String
MonitoredPostNotice	Identifies the text displayed when a post has been made to a moderated forum.	"Your post will be posted after it is reviewed"	String
MonitoredForumTitle	Identifies the text displayed at the top of a moderated forum.	"MONITORED FORUM"	String
MonitoredContinue	Identifies the text displayed for the Continue button on a moderated forum.	"Continue"	String
PasswordPageTitle	Identifies the text displayed on the password page.	"EZsite Forum"	String
InvalidPrivatePassword	Identifies the text displayed when the username/password combination is invalid.	"Invalid 'Member Name' and/or 'Password'"	String

Posts

When the Forum object has been asked to display the messages inside the forum using this command:

```
Forum.ShowForum 1
```

It will use a collection of properties to control the display. Here are those properties:

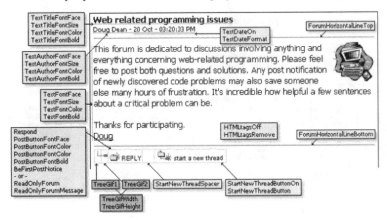

You can control whether or not messages are allowed to contain HTML formatting with these properties:

Property	Description	Default	Type
HTMLtagsOff	Indicates whether or not to allow HTML tags.	False	Boolean
HTMLtagsRemove	Indicates whether or not to remove HTML tags from the message body.	False	Boolean

You can control the appearance of the threads using these properties:

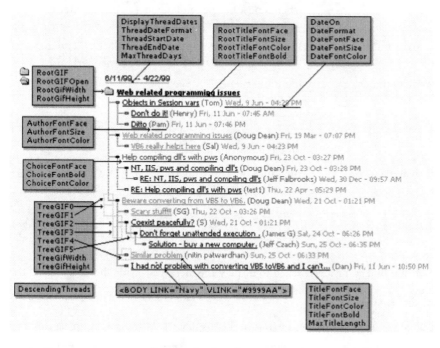

You can control how new posts are displayed using these properties:

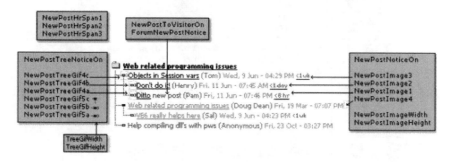

Collapsing Threads

You have the option when working with forums to see all of the threads expanded, or to expand and collapse threads at will. To turn on this functionality, use the `CollapseThreads` property:

```
Forum.CollapseThreads = True
```

These are the properties that control the graphics used for collapsing threads:

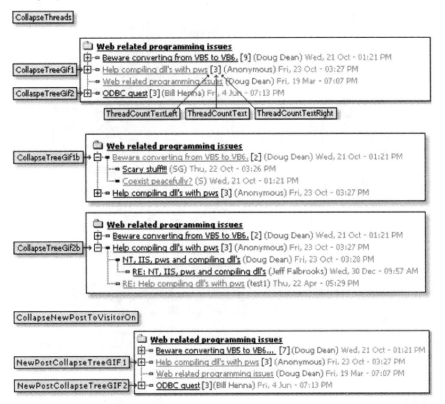

You can control the display of the number of posts inside each thread with these properties:

Property	Description	Default	Type
ThreadCountText	Specifies whether or not to include the thread count.	True	Boolean
ThreadCountTextLeft	Specifies the text to display to the left of the thread count.	"<FONT SIZE=""1"" FACE = ""Arial"" color=""MAROON"">"	String
ThreadCountTextRight	Specifies the text to the display to the right of the thread count.	" </FONT>"	String

Forum Search

It's possible to present a forum to the visitor that enabled him or her to search the contents of the forum.

```
Forum.ForumSearchOn = True
```

These are the properties that control display:

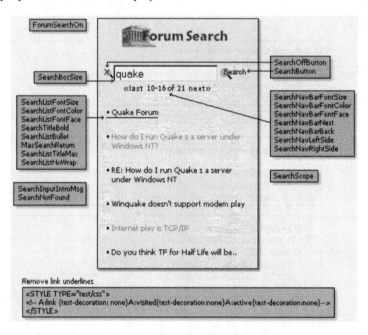

SearchScope	Specifies the level to perform the searching. Possible values are "Forum All", "Forum Default" and "Forum Site".	"Forum All"	String

Forum List

The Forum object is capable of displaying a list of forums in the database.

```
Forum.ListForums
```

These are the properties to control the appearance of the list:

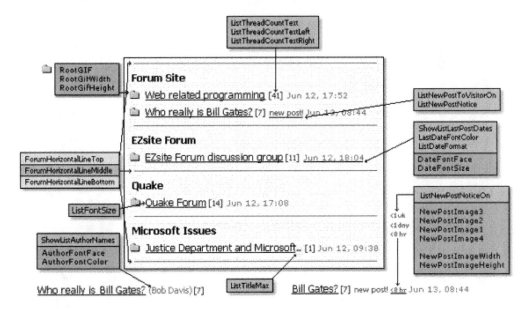

Using the Forum Manager

EZsite Forum is capable of presenting its own administration interface to the user. To do this, use this code:

```
<% Response.Buffer = true %>
<% Response.Expires = 0 %>

<HTML><HEAD><TITLE>EZsite Forum Manager</TITLE></HEAD>
<BODY>
<%
    ' create and configure the object...
    Set ObjForum = Server.CreateObject("EZsiteForum.ForumManager")
    ObjForum.DSN = "DSN=jocoffeeweb;UID=jocoffeeweb;PASSWORD=eermlate;"
    ObjForum.ShowForumID = true
    ObjForum.ShowAccountID = true
    ObjForum.ImagePath = "graphics/"


    ' run the manager...
    ObjForum.Manager
%>
</BODY>
</HTML>
```

ASP Quick Reference

ASP is a great tool for creating dynamic web pages. It is a Microsoft technology, which works by allowing us the functionality of a programming language, using the programming code to generate HTML for our web pages, dynamically. Using ASP you can do many things. You are able to draw upon the wealth of data available to you on the server and across the enterprise in various databases. You are able to customize pages to the needs of each different user that comes to your web site. In addition, by keeping your code on the server-side you can build a library of functionality. This library can be drawn from again and again to further enhance other web sites. Best of all, using server-side script libraries will allow your web sites to scale to multi-tier, or distributed, web applications.

To be able to do these things, you need a good understanding of the HTTP protocol, and how an HTTP server interacts with a browser. This model is important to understand when developing web applications that exist on the client and server side. We'll go through HTTP and give a simplified overview of how the protocol works. Then we'll give you a quick run through of Active Server Pages, or ASP. ASP is Microsoft's server-side scripting environment. It can be used to create everything from simple, static web pages, to database-aware dynamic sites, using HTML and scripting. Its other important use is as programming *glue*. Through the use of ASP, you can create and manipulate server-side components. These components can perhaps provide data to your application such as graphic image generation, or maybe link to a mainframe database. ASP does nothing but facilitate the use of these components on the Web. ASP comes with some built-in objects that are important to understand before their full potential can be unleashed. We will cover each of these objects in depth. Finally, we'll look at some real-world examples of using ASP on a web site.

The Anatomy of the HTTP Protocol

As you know, surfing the web is as simple as clicking a link on your browser. But do you know what really goes on beneath the hood of your web browser? It can be quite complex, but isn't too difficult to understand. More importantly, it will help you to understand the intricacies of client and server side scripting.

Overview

The **Hypertext Transfer Protocol**, or **HTTP**, is an *application level* TCP/IP protocol. An application level protocol is one that travels on top of another protocol. In this instance, HTTP travels on top of TCP, which is also a protocol. When two computers communicate over a TCP/IP connection, the data is formatted and processed in such a manner that it is guaranteed to arrive at its destination. This elaborate mechanism is the TCP/IP protocol.

HTTP takes for granted, and largely ignores, the entire TCP/IP protocol. It relies instead on text commands like GET and PUT. Application level protocols are implemented, usually, within an application (as opposed to at the driver level), hence the name. Some other examples of application level protocols are the **File Transfer Protocol** (FTP) and the mail protocols, **Standard Mail Transfer Protocol** (SMTP) and the **Post Office Protocol** (POP3). Pure binary data is rarely sent via these protocols, but when it is, it is encoded into an ASCII format. This is inefficient at best, and future versions of the HTTP protocol will rectify this problem. The most up-to-date version of HTTP is version 1.1, and almost all web servers available today support this version.

There is also a new HTTP protocol in the works called HTTP-NG, or HTTP-Next Generation. This newer, robust protocol will utilize bandwidth more efficiently and improve on many of the original HTTP's shortcomings. The biggest improvement in the new protocol is that data will be transferred in binary as opposed to text, thus making transactions quicker. More technical information about HTTP-NG is available from the W3C at http://www.w3.org/Protocols/HTTP-NG/Activity.html.

The HTTP Server

To carry out an HTTP request, there must be an HTTP or web server running on the target machine. This server is an application that listens for and responds to HTTP requests on a certain TCP port (by default, port 80). An HTTP request is for a single item from the web server. The item may be anything from a web page to a sound file. The server, upon receipt of the request, attempts to retrieve the data asked for. If the server finds the correct information, it formats and returns the data to the client. If the requested information could not be found, the server will return an error message.

Pulling up a single web page in your browser may cause dozens of HTTP transactions to occur. Each element on a web page that is not text needs to be requested from the HTTP server individually. The main point of all this is that each HTTP transaction consists of a request and a response:

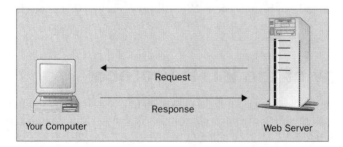

And it is in this transaction model that you must place yourself when you are programming web applications.

Protocol Basics

There are four basic states that make up a single HTTP transaction. They are:

❑ The Connection

❑ The Request

❑ The Response

❑ The Disconnection

A client connects to a server and issues the request. It waits for a response, then disconnects. A connection typically lasts only for a few seconds. On web sites like Yahoo where the data is not laden with graphics, and the information is fairly static, requests last less than one second.

The Connection

The client software, a web browser in this case, creates a TCP/IP connection to an HTTP server on a specific TCP/IP port. Port 80 is used if one is not specified. This is considered the default port for an HTTP server. A web server may, however, reside on any port allowed. It is completely up to the operator of the web server, and port numbers are often deliberately changed as a first line of defense against unauthorized users.

The Request

Once connected, the client sends a request to the server. This request is in ASCII, and must be terminated by a carriage-return/line-feed pair. Every request must specify a method, which tells the server what the client wants. In HTTP 1.1, there are eight methods: OPTIONS, GET, HEAD, POST, PUT, DELETE, TRACE, and CONNECT. For more information about the different methods and their use, please check out the HTTP specification on the W3C web site. For the purpose of this chapter, we are going to focus on the GET method.

The GET method asks the web server to return the specified page. The format of this request is as follows:

```
GET <URL> <HTTP Version>
```

You can make HTTP requests yourself with the **telnet** program. Telnet is a program that is available on most computer systems and it was originally designed for use on UNIX systems. Since basic UNIX is character-based, one could log in from a remote site and work with the operating system. Telnet is the program that allows you to connect to a remote machine and all versions of Windows come with a telnet program. The screenshot below shows what it looks like.

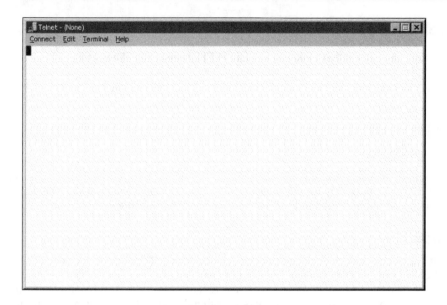

Microsoft's telnet leaves much to be desired. Thankfully, a company called Van Dyke Technologies (www.vandyke.com) created an excellent telnet program called CRT.

Telnet defaults to TCP/IP port 23. On UNIX systems, in order to telnet into a machine, that machine must be running a telnet server. This server listens for incoming telnet connections on port 23. However, almost all telnet programs allow you to specify the port on which to connect. It is this feature that we can utilize to examine HTTP running under the hood.

If you choose not to download the Van Dyke telnet client, you can test this by running Window's own telnet. Windows has no predefined menu item for this program, but it can usually be found at `C:\windows\telnet.exe`. To run it, press the **Start** button and select **Run**. Type in **telnet** and press ENTER. You should see a telnet window similar to the one above above.

Select **Remote System** from the **Connect** menu and you'll be presented with the following dialog:

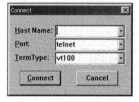

Type in the name of any web server; we chose http://www.mindbuilder.com. Then enter the web server's port. This is almost always 80.

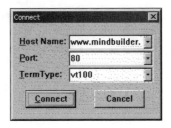

Once you are connected, the title bar will change to contain the name of the server to which you are connected. There is no other indication of connection. It is at this point that you need to type in your HTTP command. Type in the following, all in upper case:

```
GET / HTTP/1.0
```

Please note that unless you have turned on Local Echo in the Preferences, you will not see what you type. After you've entered the command you must send a carriage return (*Ctrl-M*) followed by a line feed (*Ctrl-J*). What is returned is shown as follows, and is the response to your HTTP request.

The Response

Upon receipt of the request, the web server will answer. This will most likely result in some sort of HTML data as shown previously. However, you may get an error as in the following example:

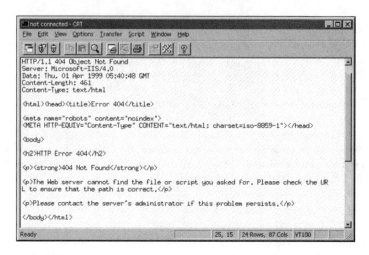

Again, the response is in HTML, but the code returned is an error code (404) instead of an OK (200).

HTTP Headers

What was actually returned is a two-part response. The first part consists of HTTP headers. These headers provide information about the actual response to the request, the most important header being the `status` header. In the listing above, it reads **HTTP/1.1 404 Object Not Found**. This indicates the actual status of the request.

The other headers that were returned with this request are `Server`, `Date`, `Content-Length`, and `Content-Type`. There are many different types of headers, and they are all designed to aid the browser in easily identifying the type of information that is being returned.

Disconnecting

After the server has responded to your request, it closes the connection thus disconnecting you. Subsequent requests require you to re-establish your connection with the server.

Introducing Active Server Pages

With the HTTP architecture laid out in the last section, you can clearly see that the real heart of the HTTP protocol lies in the request and the response. The client makes a request to the server, and the server provides the response to the client. What we're looking at here is really the foundations of client/server computing. A client makes a request from a server and the server fulfills that request. We see this pattern of behavior throughout the programming world today, not only in Web programming.

Microsoft recognized this pattern and developed a new technology that rendered web programming a much more accessible technique. This technology is Active Server Pages or ASP for short. ASP is a server-side scripting environment that comes with Microsoft's Internet Information Services. ASP allows you to embed scripting commands inside your HTML documents. The scripting commands are interpreted by the server and translated into the corresponding HTML and sent back to the server. This enables the web developer to create content that is dynamic and fresh. The beauty of this is that it does not matter which browser your web visitor is using, because the server returns only pure HTML. Sure you can extend your returned HTML with browser specific programming, but that is your prerogative. By no means is this all that ASP can do, but we'll cover more of its capabilities like form validation and data manipulation later on in this chapter.

Although you can use languages such as JavaScript or even Perl, by default the ASP scripting language is VBScript.

How the Server Recognizes ASPs

ASP pages do not have an .html or .htm extension; they have a .asp extension instead. The reason for this is twofold. First, in order for the web server to know to process the scripting in your web page, it needs to know that there is some in there. Well, by setting the extension of your web page to .asp, the server can assume that there are scripts in your page.

> *A nice side effect of naming your ASP pages with the* asp *extension is that the ASP processor knows that it does not need to process your HTML files. It used to be the case, as in ASP 2.0, that any page with the* .asp *extension, no matter whether it contained any server side scripting code or not, was automatically sent to the server, and would thereby take longer to process. With the introduction of ASP 3.0 in Windows 2000, the server is able to determine the presence of any server side code and process or not process the page accordingly. This increases the speed of your HTML file retrieval and makes your web server run more efficiently.*

Secondly, using an asp extension (forcing interpretation by the ASP processor every time your page is requested) hides your ASP scripts. If someone requests your .asp file from the web server, all he is going to get back is the resultant processed HTML. If you put your ASP code in a file called mycode.scr and requested it from the web server, you'll see all of the code inside.

ASP Basics

ASP files are really just HTML files with scripting embedded within them. When a browser requests an ASP file from the server, it is passed on to the ASP processing DLL for execution. After processing, the resulting file is then sent on to the requesting browser. Any scripting commands embedded from the original HTML file are executed and then removed from the results. This is excellent in that all of your scripting code is hidden from the person viewing your web pages. That is why it is so important that files that contain ASP scripts have a .asp extension.

The Tags of ASP

To distinguish the ASP code from the HTML inside your files, ASP code is placed between <% and %> tags. This convention should be familiar to you if you have ever worked with any kind of server-side commands before in HTML. The tag combination implies to the ASP processor that the code within should be executed by the server and removed from the results. Depending on the default scripting language of your web site, this code may be VBScript, JScript, or any other language you've installed.

Since the application in this book is written in VBScript, all of our ASP scripts will be in VBScript.

In the following snippet of HTML, you'll see an example of some ASP code between the <% and %> tags:

```
<TABLE>
<TR>
<TD>
<%
    x = x + 1
    y = y - 1
%>
</TD>
</TR>
</TABLE>
```

<SCRIPT> Blocks

You may also place your ASP code between <SCRIPT></SCRIPT> blocks. However, unless you direct the script to run at the server level, code placed between these tags will be executed at the client as normal client-side scripts. To direct your script block to execute on the server, use the RUNAT command within your <SCRIPT> block as follows:

```
<SCRIPT Language="VBScript" RUNAT="Server">
... Your Script ...
</SCRIPT>
```

The Default Scripting Language

As stated previously, the default scripting language used by ASP is VBScript. However, you may change it for your entire site, or just a single web page. Placing a special scripting tag at the beginning of your web page does this. This tag specifies the scripting language to use for this page only.

```
<%@ LANGUAGE=ScriptingLanguage%>
```

ScriptingLanguage can be any language for which you have the scripting engine installed. ASP comes with JScript, as well as VBScript.

You can set the default scripting language for the entire application by changing the Default ASP Language field in the Internet Service Manager on the App Options tab.

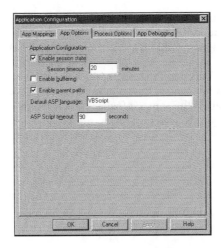

Mixing HTML and ASP

You've probably guessed by now that one can easily mix HTML code with ASP scripts. VBScript has all of the control flow mechanisms like If Then, For Next, and Do While loops. But with ASP you can selectively include HTML code based on the results of these operators. Let's look at an example.

Suppose you are creating a web page that greets the viewer with a "Good Morning", "Good Afternoon", or "Good Evening" depending on the time of day. This can be done as follows:

```
<HTML>
<BODY>
<P>The time is now <%=Time()%></P>
<%
  Dim iHour

  iHour = Hour(Time())

  If (iHour >= 0 And iHour < 12 ) Then
%>
Good Morning!
<%
  ElseIf (iHour > 11 And iHour < 5 ) Then
%>
Good Afternoon!
<%
  Else
%>
Good Evening!
<%
End If
%>
</BODY>
</HTML>
```

First we print out the current time. The <%= notation is shorthand to print out the value of an ASP variable or the result of a function call. We then move the hour of the current time into a variable called iHour. Based on the value of this variable we write our normal HTML text.

Notice how the HTML code is outside of the ASP script tags. When the ASP processor executes this page, the HTML that lies between control flow blocks that aren't executed is discarded, leaving you with only the correct code. Here is the source of what is returned from our web server after processing this page:

```
<HTML>
<BODY>
<P>The time is now 7:48:37 PM</P>

Good Evening!

</BODY>
</HTML>
```

As you can see, the scripting is completely removed leaving only the HTML and text.

The other way to output data to your web page viewer is using one of ASP's built-in objects called Response. We'll cover this approach in the next section as you learn about the ASP object model.

Commenting Your ASP Code

As with any programming language, it is of the utmost importance to comment your ASP code as much as possible. However, how many times have you come across a piece of code and said "eh?" Someone once told me that the only purpose comments served were to amuse the compiler. In some instances, he may have been correct. However, unclear comments are not worth putting in your code.

Comments in ASP are identical to comments in VBScript. When ASP comes across the single quote character it will graciously ignore the rest of the line:

```
<%
Dim iLumberJack

'I'm a comment and I'm O.K.
iLumberJack = iLumberJack + 1
%>
```

The Active Server Pages Object Model

ASP, like most Microsoft technologies, utilizes the Component Object Model or COM, to expose functionality to consumer applications. ASP is actually an extension to your web server that allows server-side scripting. At the same it also provides a compendium of objects and components, which manage interaction between the web server and the browser. These objects form the **Active Server Pages Object Model**. These 'objects' can be manipulated by scripting languages. Take a look at the following diagram:

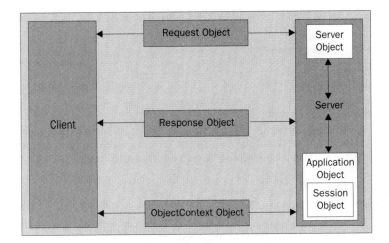

ASP 2.0 neatly divides up into six objects, which manage their own part of the interaction between client and server. As you can see in the diagram, at the heart of the interaction between client and server are the Request and Response objects, which deal with the HTTP request and response; but we will be taking a quick tour through all of the different objects and components that are part of ASP.

The object model consists of six core objects, each one with distinct properties and methods. The objects are:

❑   Request

❑   Response

❑   Application

❑   Session

❑   Server

❑   ObjectContext

Each of the objects, barring the Server and ObjectContext object, can use collections to store data. Before we look at each object in turn we need to take a quick overview of collections.

Collections

Collections in ASP are very similar to their VBScript namesakes. They act as data containers that store their data in a manner close to that of an array. The information is stored in the form of name/value pairs.

The Application and the Session object have a collection property called Contents. This collection of variants can hold any information you wish to place in it. Using these collections allow you to share information between web pages.

To place a value into the collection, simply assign it a key and then assign the value:

```
Application.Contents("Name") = "Evil Knievel"
```

Or:

```
Session.Contents("Age") = 25
```

Fortunately for us, Microsoft has made the Contents collection the default property for these two objects. Therefore the following shorthand usage is perfectly acceptable:

```
Application("Name") = "Evil Knievel"
Session("Age") = 25
```

To read values from the Contents collections, just reverse the call:

```
sName = Application("Name")
sAge = Session("Age")
```

Iterating the Contents Collection

Because the Contents collections work like regular VBScript collections, they are easily iterated. You can use the collections Count property, or use the For Each iteration method:

```
For x = 1 to Application.Contents.Count
 …
Next

For each item in Application.Contents
 …
Next
```

> Please note that the Contents collections are 1 based. That is to say that the first element in the collection is at position 1, not 0.

To illustrate this, the following ASP script will dump the current contents of the Application and Session objects' Contents collections:

```
<HTML>
<BODY>
<P>The Application.Contents</P>
<%
    Dim Item
```

```
        For Each Item In Application.Contents
          Response.Write Item & " = [" & Application(Item) & "]<BR>"
        Next
    %>
    <P>The Session.Contents</P>
    <%
        For Each Item In Session.Contents
          Response.Write Item & " = [" & Session(Item) & "]<BR>"
        Next
    %>
    </BODY>
    </HTML>
```

Removing an Item from the Contents Collection

The Application object's Contents collection contains two methods, and these are Remove and RemoveAll. These allow you to remove one or all of the items stored in the Application.Contents collection. At the time of writing, there is no method to remove an item from the Session.Contents collection.

Let's add an item to the Application.Contents collection, and then remove it.

```
    <%
        Application("MySign") = "Pisces"
        Application.Contents.Remove("MySign")
    %>
```

Or we can just get rid of everything...

```
    <%
        Application.Contents.RemoveAll
    %>
```

Not all of the collections of each object work in this way, but the principles remain the same and we will explain how each differs when we discuss each object.

The Request Object

When your web page is requested, much information is passed along with the HTTP request, such as the URL of the web page request and format of the data being passed. It can also contain feedback from the user such as the input from a text box or drop down list box. The Request object allows you to get at information passed along as part of the HTTP request. The corresponding output from the server is returned as part of the Response. The Request object has several collections to store information that warrant discussion.

The Request Object's Collections

The Request object has five collections. Interestingly, they all act as the default property for the object. That is to say, you may retrieve information from any of the five collections by using the abbreviated syntax:

```
    ClientIPAddress = Request("REMOTE_ADDR")
```

The REMOTE_ADDR value lies in the ServerVariables collection. However, through the use of the collection cascade, it can be retrieved with the above notation. Please note that for ASP to dig through each collection, especially if they have many values, to retrieve a value from the last collection is inefficient. It is always recommended to use the fully qualified collection name in your code. Not only is this faster, but it improves your code in that it is more specific, and less cryptic.

ASP searches through the collections in the following order:

- ❏ QueryString
- ❏ Form
- ❏ Cookies
- ❏ ClientCertificate
- ❏ ServerVariables

If there are variables with the same name, only the first is returned when you allow ASP to search. This is another good reason for you to fully qualify your collection.

QueryString

Contains a collection of all the information attached to the end of an URL. When you make an URL request, the additional information is passed along with the URL to the web page appended with a question mark. This information takes the following form: URL?item=data[&item=data][…]

The clue to the server is the question mark. When the server sees this, it knows that the URL has ended, and variables are starting. So an example of a URL with a query string might look like this:
http://www.buythisbook.com/book.asp?bookname=BeginningECommerce

We stated earlier that the collections store information in name/value pairs. Despite this slightly unusual method of creating the name/value pair, the principle remains the same. bookname is the name and BeginningECommerce is the value. When ASP gets hold of this URL request, it breaks apart all of the name/value pairs and places them into this collection for easy access. This is another excellent feature of ASP. Query strings are built up using ampersands to delimit each name/value pair so if you wished to pass the user information along with the book information, you could pass the following:
http://www.buythisbook.com/book.asp?bookname=BeginningECommerce
&buyer=MatthewReynolds

Query strings can be generated in one of three ways. The first is, as discussed, by a user typed URL. The second is as part of a URL specified in an Anchor tag.

```
<A HREF="book.asp?bookname=BeginningECommerce">Go to book buying page</A>
```

So when you click on the link, the name/value pair is passed along with the URL. The third and final method is via a form sent to the server with the GET method.

```
<FORM ACTION="book.asp" METHOD="GET">
Type your name: <INPUT TYPE="TEXT" NAME="buyer"><BR>
Type your requested book:  <INPUT TYPE="TEXT" NAME="bookname" SIZE=40><BR>
<INPUT TYPE=SUBMIT VALUE=Submit>
</FORM>
```

You input the information onto the text boxes on the form and the text is submitted when you click on Submit and two query strings are generated.

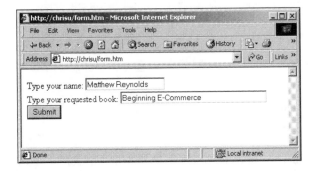

Next you need to be able to retrieve information, and you use this technique to retrieve from each of the three methods used to generate a query string.

```
Request.QueryString("buyer")
Request.QueryString("bookname")
```

Please note that these lines won't display anything by themselves, you need to add either the shorthand notation (equality operator) to display functions in front of a single statement, or when a number of values need displaying then use Response.Write to separately display each value in the collection.

e.g. <%=Request.QueryString("buyer")%> or
Response.Write(Request.QueryString("bookname"))

The first of the two Request object calls should return the name of Matthew Reynolds on the page and the second of the two should return Beginning E-Commerce. Of course you could always store this information in a variable for later access.

```
sBookName = Request.QueryString("bookname")
```

Form

Contains a collection of all the form variables posted to the HTTP request by an HTML form. Query strings aren't very private as they transmit information via a very visible method, the URL. If you want to transmit information from the form more privately then you can use the form collection to do so which sends its information as part of the HTTP Request body. The easy access to form variables is one of ASP's best features.

If we go back to our previous example, the only alteration we need to make to our HTML form code is to change the METHOD attribute. Forms using this collection must be sent with the POST method and not the GET method. It is actually this attribute that determines how the information is sent by the form. So if we change the method of the form as follows:

```
<FORM ACTION="book.asp" METHOD="POST">
Type your name: <INPUT TYPE="TEXT" NAME="buyer"><BR>
Type your requested book:  <INPUT TYPE="TEXT" NAME="bookname" SIZE=40><BR>
<INPUT TYPE=SUBMIT VALUE=Submit>
</FORM>
```

Once the form has been submitted in this style, then we can retrieve and display the information using the following:

```
<%=Request.Form("buyer")%>
```

Cookies

Contains a read-only collection of cookies sent by the client browser along with the request. Because the cookies were sent from the client, they cannot be changed here. You must change them using the `Response.Cookies` collection. A discussion of cookies can be found in the next topic.

ClientCertificate

When a client makes a connection with a server requiring a high degree of security, either party can confirm who the sender/receiver is by inspecting their digital certificate. A digital certificate contains a number of items of information about the sender, such as the holder's name, address and length of time the certificate is valid for. A third party, known as the Certificate Authority or CA, will have previously verified these details.

The `ClientCertificate` collection is used access details held in a client side digital certificate sent by the browser. This collection is only populated if you are running a secure server, and the request was via an https:// call instead of an http:// call. This is the preferred method to invoke a secure connection.

ServerVariables

When the client sends a request and information is passed across to the server, it's not just the page that is passed across, but information such as who created the page, the server name, and the port that the request was sent to. The HTTP header that is sent across together with the HTTP request also contains information of this nature such as the type of browser, and type of connection. This information is combined into a list of variables that are predefined by the server as environment variables. Most of them are static and never really change unless you change the configuration of your web server. The rest are based on the client browser.

These server variables can be accessed in the normal method. For instance, the server variable `HTTP_USER_AGENT`, which returns information about the type of browser being used to view the page, can be displayed as follows:

```
<%=Request.ServerVariables("HTTP_USER_AGENT")%>
```

Alternatively you can printout the whole list of server variables and their values with the following code:

```
For Each key in Request.ServerVariables
    Response.Write "<B>" & (key) & "</B> "
    Response.Write (Request.ServerVariables(key)) & "<BR>"
Next
```

This displays each of the `ServerVariables` collection in bold, and the contents of the key (if any) after it. The final product looks like this:

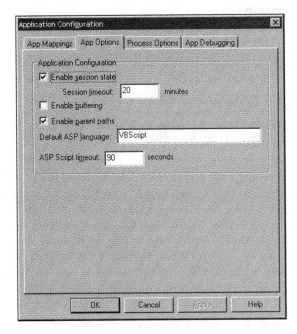

Server variables are merely informative, but they do give you the ability to customize page content for specific browsers, or to avoid script errors that might be generated.

Request Object Property and Method

The `Request` object contains a single property and a single method. They are used together to transfer files from the client to the server. Uploading is accomplished using HTML forms.

TotalBytes Property

When the request is processed, this property will hold the total number of bytes in the client browser request. Most likely you'd use it to return the number of bytes in the file you wish to transfer. This information is important to the `BinaryRead` method.

BinaryRead Method

This method retrieves the information sent to the web server by the client browser in a `POST` operation. When the browser issues a `POST`, the data is encoded and sent to the server. When the browser issues a `GET`, there is no data other than the URL. The `BinaryRead` method takes one parameter, the number of bytes to read. So if you want it to read a whole file, you pass it the total number of bytes in the file, generated by the `TotalBytes` property.

It's very rarely applied because `Request.QueryString` and `Request.Form` are much easier to use. That's because `BinaryRead` wraps its answer in a safe array of bytes. For a scripting language that essentially only handles variants, that makes life a little complicated. However this format is essential for file uploading when file contains something other than pure text. You can find full details on how to upload files and then decode a safe array of bytes in this excellent article at 15seconds.com: http://www.15seconds.com/Issue/981121.htm.

The Response Object

After you've processed the request information from the client browser, you'll need to be able to send information back. The `Response` object is just the ticket. It provides you with the tools necessary to send anything you need back to the client.

The Response Object's Collection

The `Response` object contains only one collection: `Cookies`. This is the version of the `Request` object's `Cookies` collection that can be written to.

If you've not come across them before, cookies are small (limited to 4kb of data) text files stored on the hard drive of the client that contain information about the user, such as whether they have visited the site before and what date they last visited the site on. There are lots of misapprehensions about cookies being intrusive as they allow servers to store information on the user's drive. However you need to remember that firstly the user has to voluntarily accept cookies or activate an Accept Cookies mechanism on the browser for them to work, secondly this information is completely benign and cannot be used to determine the user's e-mail address or such like. They are used to personalize pages that the user might have visited before. Examples of things to store in cookies are unique user ids, or user names; then, when the user returns to your web site, a quick check of cookies will let you know if this is a return visitor or not.

You can create a cookie on the user's machine as follows:

```
Response.Cookies("BookBought") = "Beginning E-Commerce"
```

You can also store multiple values in one cookie using an index value key. The cookie effectively contains a VBScript `Dictionary` object and using the key can retrieve individual items. Its functioning is very close to that of an array.

```
Response.Cookies("BookBought")("1") = "Beginning E-Commerce"
Response.Cookies("BookBought")("2") = "Instant HTML"
```

A cookie will automatically expire – disappear from the user's machine – the moment a user ends their session. To extend the cookie beyond this natural lifetime, you can specify a date with the `Expires` property. The date takes the following format *WEEKDAY DD-MON-YY HH:MM:SS*

```
Response.Cookies("BookBought").Expires = #31-Dec-99#
```

The # sign can be used to delimit dates in ASP (as in VBScript).

Other properties that can be used in conjunction with this collection are:

- ❑ Domain: a cookie is only sent to page requested within the domain from which it was created

- ❑ Path: a cookie is only sent to pages requested within this path

- ❑ HasKeys: specifies whether the cookie uses an index/Dictionary object or not

- ❑ Secure: specifies whether the cookie is secure. A cookie is only deemed secure if sent via the HTTPS protocol.

You can retrieve the cookies information using the Request object cookies collection, mentioned earlier. To do this you could do the following:

```
You purchased <%=Request.Cookies("BookBought")%> last time you visited the site.
```

If there were several cookies in the collection you could iterate through each cookie and display the contents as follows:

```
For Each cookie in Request.Cookies
    Response.Write (Request.Cookies(cookie))
Next
```

The Response Object's Methods

To understand what the Response object's methods and properties do, we need to examine the workings of how ASP sends a response in more detail. When an ASP script is run, an **HTML output stream** is created. This stream is a receptacle for the web server to store details and create the dynamic/interactive web page in. As mentioned before, the page has to be created entirely in HTML for the browser to understand it (excluding client-side scripting, which is ignored by the server).

The stream is initially empty when created. New information is added to the end. If any custom HTML headers are required then they have to be added at the beginning. Then the HTML contained in the ASP page is added next to the script, so anything not encompassed by <% %> tags is added. The Response object provides two ways of writing directly to the output stream, either using the Write method or it's shorthand technique.

Write

Probably the most used method of all the built-in objects, Write allows you to send information back to the client browser. You can write text directly to a web page by encasing the text in quotation marks:

```
Response.Write "Hello World!"
```

Or to display the contents of a variant you just drop the quotation marks:

```
sText = "Hello World!"
Response.Write sText
```

For single portions of dynamic information that only require adding into large portions of HTML, you can use the equality sign as shorthand for this method, as specified earlier, e.g.

```
My message is <% =sText %>
```

This technique reduces the amount of code needed, but at the expense of readability. There is nothing to choose between these techniques in terms of performance.

AddHeader

This method allows you to add custom headers to the HTTP response. For example, if you were to write a custom browser application that examined the headers of your HTTP requests for a certain value, you'd use this method to set that value. Usage is as follows:

```
Response.AddHeader "CustomServerApp", "BogiePicker/1.0"
```

This would add the header `CustomServerApp` to the response with the value of `BogiePicker/1.0`. There are no restrictions regarding headers and header value.

AppendToLog

Calling this method allows you to append a string to the web server log file entry for this particular request. This allows you to add custom log messages to the log file.

BinaryWrite

This method allows you to bypass the normal character conversion that takes place when data is sent back to the client. Usually, only text is returned, so the web server cleans it up. By calling `BinaryWrite` to send your data, the actual binary data is sent back, bypassing that cleaning process.

Clear

This method allows you to delete any data that has been buffered for this page so far. See discussion of the `Buffer` property for more details.

End

This method stops processing the ASP file and returns any currently buffered data to the client browser.

Flush

This method returns any currently buffered data to the client browser and then clears the buffer. See discussion of the `Buffer` property for more details.

Redirect

This method allows you to relinquish control of the current page to another web page entirely. For example, you can use this method to redirect users to a login page if they have not yet logged on to your web site:

```
<%
If (Not Session("LoggedOn") ) Then
    Response.Redirect "login.asp"
End If
%>
```

The Response Object's Properties

Buffer

You may optionally have ASP buffer your output for you. This property tells ASP whether or not to buffer output. Usually, output is sent to the client as it is generated. If you turn buffering on (by setting this property to `True`), output will not be sent until all scripts have been executed for the current page, or the `Flush` or `End` methods are called.

`Response.Buffer` has to be inserted after the language declaration, but before any HTML is used. If you insert it outside this scope you will most likely generate an error. A correct use of this method would look like:

```
<@ LANGUAGE = "VBSCRIPT">
<% Response.Buffer = True %>
<HTML>
...
```

The `Flush` method is used in conjunction with the `Buffer` property. To use it correctly you must set the `Buffer` property first and then at places within the script you can flush the buffer to the output stream, while continuing processing. This is useful for long queries, which might otherwise worry the user that nothing was being returned.

The `Clear` method erases everything in the buffer that has been added since the last `Response.Flush` call. It erases only the response body however and leaves intact the response header.

CacheControl

Generally when a proxy server retrieves an ASP web page, it does not place a copy of it into its cache. That is because by their very nature ASP pages are dynamic and, most likely, a page be stale the next time it is requested. You may override this feature by changing the value of this property to `Public`.

Charset

This property will append its contents to the HTTP content-type header that is sent back to the browser. Every HTTP response has a content-type header that defines the content of the response. Usually the content-type is "text/html". Setting this property will modify the type sent back to the browser.

ContentType

This property allows you to set the value of the content-type that is sent back to the client browser.

Expires

Most web browsers keep web pages in a local cache. The cache is usually as good as long as you keep your browser running. Setting this property allows you to limit the time the page stays in the local cache. The value of the `Expires` property specifies the length of time in minutes before the page will expire from the local cache. If you set this to zero, the page will not be cached.

ExpiresAbsolute

Just like the Expires property, this property allows you to specify the exact time and date on which the page will expire.

IsClientConnected

This read-only property indicates whether or not the client is still connected to the server. Remember that the client browser makes a request then waits for a response? Well, imagine you're running a lengthy script and during the middle of processing, the client disconnects because he was waiting too long. Reading this property will tell you if the client is still connected or not. Unfortunately in ASP 2.0, this property doesn't seem to function correctly, and has only been repaired within ASP 3.0 in Windows 2000.

Status

This property allows you to set the value returned on the status header with the HTTP response.

The Application and Session Objects

The Application and Session objects like Request and Response work very closely together. Application is used to tie all of the pages together into one consistent application, while the Session object is used to track and present a user's series of requests to the web site as a continuous action, rather than an arbitrary set of requests.

Scope Springs Eternal

Normally, you will declare a variable for use within your web page. You'll use it, manipulate it, then perhaps print out its value, or whatever. But when your page is reloaded, or the viewer moves to another page, the variable, with its value, is gone forever. By placing your variable within the Contents collection of the Application or Session objects, you can extend the life span of your variable!

Any variable or object that you declare has two potential scopes: procedure and page. When you declare a variable within a procedure, its life span is limited to that procedure. Once the procedure has executed, your variable is gone. You may also declare a variable at the web page level but like the procedure-defined variable, once the page is reloaded, the value is reset.

Enter the Application and Session objects. The Contents collections of these two objects allow you to extend the scope of your variables to session-wide, and application-wide. If you place a value in the Session object, it will be available to all web pages in your site for the life span of the current session (more on sessions later). Good session scope variables are user ids, user names, login time, etc, things that pertain only to the session. Likewise, if you place your value into the Application object, it will exist until the web site is restarted. This allows you to place application-wide settings into a conveniently accessible place. Good application scope variables are font names and sizes, table colors, system constants, etc; things that pertain to the application as a whole.

The global.asa File

Every ASP application may utilize a special script file. This file is named `global.asa` and it must reside in the root directory of your web application. It can contain script code that pertains to the application as a whole, or each session. You may also create ActiveX objects for later use in this scripting file.

The Application Object

ASP works on the concept that an entire web site is a single web application. Therefore, there is only one instance of the `Application` object available for your use in your scripting at all times. Please note that it is possible to divide up your web site into separate applications, but for the purposes of this discussion we'll assume there is only one application per web site.

Collections

The `Application` object contains two collections: `Contents` and `StaticObjects`. The `Contents` collection is discussed above. The StaticObjects collection is similar to `Contents`, but only contains the objects that were created with the `<OBJECT>` tag in the scope of your application. This collection can be iterated just like the `Contents` collection.

You cannot store references to ASP's built-in objects in `Application`*'s collections.*

Methods

The `Application` object contains two methods as detailed below.

Lock	The `Lock` method is used to "lock-down" the `Contents` collection so that it cannot be modified by other clients. This is useful if you are updating a counter, or perhaps grabbing a transaction number stored in the `Application`'s `Contents` collection.
Unlock	The `Unlock` method "unlocks" the `Application` object thus allowing others to modify the `Contents` collection.

Events

The `Application` object generates two events: `Application_OnStart` and `Application_OnEnd`. The `Application_OnStart` event is fired when the first view of your web page occurs. The `Application_OnEnd` event is fired when the web server is shut down. If you choose to write scripts for these events they must be placed in your `global.asa` file.

The most common use of these events is to initialize application-wide variables. Items such as font names, table colors, database connection strings, perhaps even writing information to a system log file. The following is an example `global.asa` file with script for these events:

```
<SCRIPT LANGUAGE=VBScript RUNAT=Server>
Sub Application_OnStart
    'Globals…
    Application("ErrorPage") = "handleError.asp"
```

```
        Application("SiteBanAttemptLimit") = 10
        Application("AccessErrorPage") = "handleError.asp"
        Application("RestrictAccess") = False

        'Keep track of visitors…
        Application("NumVisits") = Application("NumVisits") + 1
    End Sub
</SCRIPT>
```

The Session Object

Each time a visitor comes to your web site, a Session object is created for the visitor if the visitor does not already have one. Therefore, there is an instance of the Session object available to you in your scripting as well. The Session object is similar to the Application object in that it can contain values. However, the Session object's values are lost when your visitor leaves the site. The Session object is most useful for transferring information from web page to web page. Using the Session object, there is no need to pass information in the URL.

The most common use of the Session object is to store information in its Contents collection. This information would be session-specific in that it would pertain only to the current user.

Many web sites today offer a "user personalization" service, that is, to customize a web page to their preference. This is easily done with ASP and the Session object. The user variables are stored in the client browser for retrieval by the server later. Simply load the user's preferences at the start of the session and then, as the user browses your site, utilize the information regarding the user's preferences to display information.

Suppose your web site displays stock quotes for users. You could allow users to customize the start page to display their favorite stock quotes when they visit the site. By storing the stock symbols in your Session object, you can easily display the correct quotes when you render your web page.

This session management system relies on the use of browser cookies. The cookies allow the user information to be persisted even after a client leaves the site. Unfortunately, if a visitor to your web site does not allow cookies to be stored, you will be unable to pass information between web pages within the Session object.

Collections

The Session object contains two collections: Contents and StaticObjects. The Contents collection we discussed above. The StaticObjects collection is similar to Contents, but only contains the objects that were created with the <OBJECT> tag in your HTML page. This collection can be iterated just like the Contents collection.

Properties

Below are the properties that the Session object exposes for your use:

Property	Description
CodePage	Setting this property will allow you to change the character set used by ASP when it is creating output. This property could be used if you were creating a multi-national web site.
LCID	This property sets the internal locale value for the entire web application. By default, your application's locale is your server's locale. If you server is in the U.S., then your application will default to the U.S. Much of the formatting functionality of ASP utilizes this locale setting to display information correctly for the country in question. For example, the date is displayed differently in Europe versus the U.S. So based on the locale setting, the date formatting functions will output the date in the correct format.
	You can also change this property temporarily to output data in a different format. A good example is currency. Let's say your web site had a shopping cart and you wanted to display totals in U.S. dollars for U.S. customers, and Pounds Sterling for U.K. customers. To do this you'd change the LCID property to the British locale setting, and then call the currency formatting routine.
SessionID	Every session created by ASP has a unique identifier. This identifier is called the SessionID and is accessible through this property. It can be used for debugging ASP scripts.
Timeout	By default, ASP sessions will timeout after 20 minutes of inactivity. Every time a web page is requested or refreshed by a user, his internal ASP time clock starts ticking. When the time clock reaches the value set in this property, his session is automatically destroyed. You can set this property to reduce the timeout period if you wish.

Methods

The Session object contains a single method, Abandon. This instructs ASP to destroy the current Session object for this user. This method is what you would call when a user logs off your web site.

Events

The Session object generates two events: Session_OnStart and Session_OnEnd. The Session_OnStart event is fired when the first view of your web page occurs. The Session_OnEnd event is fired when the web server is shut down. If you choose to write scripts for these events they must be placed in your global.asa file.

The most common use of these events is to initialize session-wide variables. Items like usage counts, login names, real names, user preferences, etc. The following is an example global.asa file with script for these events:

```
<SCRIPT LANGUAGE=VBScript RUNAT=Server>
Sub Session_OnStart
    Session("LoginAttempts") = 0
    Session("LoggedOn") = False
End Sub
```

```
Sub Session_OnEnd
    Session("LoggedOn") = False
End Sub
</SCRIPT>
```

The Server Object

The next object in the ASP object model is the `Server` object. The `Server` object enables you to create and work with ActiveX controls in your web pages. In addition, the `Server` object exposes methods that help in the encoding of URLs and HTML text.

Properties

ScriptTimeout

This property sets the time in seconds that a script will be allowed to run. The default value for all scripts on the system is 90 seconds. Or, if a script has run for longer than 90 seconds, the web server will intervene and let the client browser know something is wrong. If you expect your scripts to run for a long time, you will want to use this property.

Methods

CreateObject

This method is the equivalent to VBScript's `CreateObject`, or using the `New` keyword – it instantiates a new instance of an object. The result can be placed into the `Application` or `Session Contents` collection to lengthen its life span.

Generally you'll create an object at the time the session is created and place it into the `Session.Contents` collection. For example, let's say you've created a killer ActiveX DLL with a really cool class that converts Fahrenheit to Celsius and vice versa. You could create an instance of this class with the `CreateObject` method and store it in the `Session.Contents` collection like this:

```
Set Session("MyConverter") = Server.CreateObject("KillerDLL.CDegreeConverter")
```

This object would be around as long as the session is and will be available for you to call. As you'll see in later chapters, this method is invaluable when working with database connections.

ASP comes with its own built in set of components that you can create instances of using the `CreateObject` method. These are:

❑ **AdRotator** – used to display a random graphic and link every time a user connects to the page.

❑ **Browser Capabilities** – manipulates a file `browscap.ini` contained on the server computer to determine the capabilities of a particular client's browser.

❑ **Content Linker** – provides a central repository file from where you manage a series of links and their URLs, and provide appropriate descriptions about them.

❑ **ContentRotator** – a cut down version of the Ad Rotator that provides the same function but without optional redirection.

❑ **PageCounter** – Counts the number of times a page has been hit.

❑ **PermissionChecker** – checks to see if a user has permissions before allowing them to access a given page.

❑ **Counters** – counts any value on an ASP page from anywhere within an ASP application

❑ **MyInfo** – can be used to store personal information about a user within an XML file.

❑ **Status** – used to collect server profile information.

❑ **Tools** – a set of miscellaneous methods that are grouped under the generic heading of Tools

❑ **IISLog** – allows you to create an object that allows your applications to write to and otherwise access the IIS log.

Execute

This method executes an ASP file and inserts the results into the response. You can use this call to include snippets of ASP code, like subroutines.

GetLastError

This method returns an ASPError object that contains all of the information about the last error that has occurred.

HTMLEncode

This method encodes a string for proper HTML usage. This is useful if you want to actually display HTML code on your web pages.

MapPath

This method returns a string that contains the actual physical path to the file in question. Subdirectories of your web site can be virtual. That is to say that they don't physically exist in the hierarchy of your web site. To find out the true whereabouts of a file, you can call this method.

Transfer

The Transfer method allows you to immediately transfer control of the executing page to another page. This is similar to the Response.Redirect method except for the fact that the Transfer method makes all variables and the Request collections available to the called page.

URLEncode

This method, as the title says, encodes a URL for transmission. This encoding includes replacing spaces with a plus sign (+) and replacing unprintable characters with hexadecimal values. You should always run your URLs through this method when redirecting.

The ObjectContext Object

The final object we shall consider is the `ObjectContext` object, which comes into play when you use transactions in your web page. When an ASP script has initiated a transaction, it can either be committed or aborted by this object. It has two methods to do this with.

SetAbort

`SetAbort` is called when the transaction has not been completed and you don't want resources updated.

SetComplete

`SetComplete` is called when there is no reason for the transaction to fail. If all of the components that form part of the transaction call `SetComplete`, then the transaction will complete.

Using Active Server Pages Effectively

Is it true that a little bit of knowledge is a bad thing? In the realm of ASP, I think not. A little bit of knowledge is probably just piquing your interest. For the final part of this appendix we're going to build a web site to demonstrate some of the features of ASP. This sample site will demonstrate many of the ASP features and principles described earlier in this chapter.

Designing the Site

Before we start creating our new web site, we should discuss the design. For your first ASP application, we'll keep it quite simple. What we want to create is an HTML form that accepts for input the following information: first name, last name, and email address. After the user submits the form, our ASP page will reformat the first and last name, and check the email address for proper syntax.

The user will be given three attempts to enter the information correctly or else a warning message will display at the bottom of the screen:

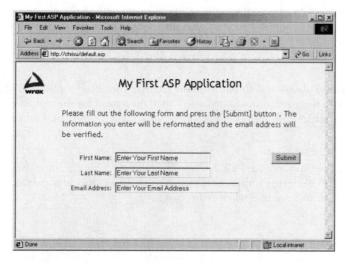

Creating the global.asa file

The first step in creating a new ASP application is to create your `global.asa` file. This is the file that houses your event handlers for the `Application` and `Session` objects. In addition, in this file you may set application, and session-wide variables to their default values. To create this file, in the root of your web server directory create a file called `global.asa`. Here is the content of our sample `global.asa`:

```
<SCRIPT LANGUAGE=VBScript RUNAT=Server>
Sub Application_OnStart
    Application("AllowedErrorsBeforeWarning") = 3
End Sub

Sub Session_OnStart
    Session("ErrorCount") = 0
End Sub

Sub Session_OnEnd
    'Nothing to do here...
End Sub

Sub Application_OnEnd
    'Nothing to do here...
End Sub
</SCRIPT>
```

Our file has handlers defined for `Application_OnStart`, `Application_OnEnd`, `Session_OnStart`, and `Session_OnEnd`. The `Application_OnEnd` and `Session_OnEnd` events are not used in this example, but shown above for completeness.

We want to set a limit on the number of submissions the user gets before a warning message is shown. Since this is a feature of the application and affects all users, we will store this constant in the `Application.Contents` collection. This is done in the `Application_OnStart` event. We add to the collection an item named `AllowedErrorsBeforeWarning` and set its value to 3.

Now that we know how many times a user can *try* to get it right, we need a place to store the number of times the user has *tried* to get it right. Since this counter is different for each user, we'll place this into the `Session.Contents` collection. We initialize our variable to 0. This is done in the `Session_OnStart` event. We add to the collection an item named, appropriately, `ErrorCount`, with a value of 0.

Creating our Main Page

Now that we've laid the groundwork for our ASP application, it's time to build the main page. Since this is a simple example, we will only utilize a single web page. Let's begin by creating this single page.

Create a new web page on your site and name it `default.asp`. This is the file name used by IIS as the default web page. The default web page is the page that is returned by a web server when no web page is specified. For example, when you call up http://www.wrox.com/, you aren't specifying a web page. The server looks through its list of default file names and finds the first match in the web site's root directory.

The following shows the contents of your `default.asp` page.

```
<%@ Language=VBScript %>
<%
Dim txtFirstName, txtLastName, txtEmailAddr
Dim sMessage

'*************************************************************************
'* Main
'*
'* The main subroutine for this page...
'*************************************************************************

Sub Main()
    'Was this page submitted?
    if ( Request("cmdSubmit") = "Submit" ) Then
        'Reformat the data into a more readable format...
        txtFirstName = InitCap(Request("txtFirstName"))
        txtLastName = InitCap(Request("txtLastName"))
        txtEmailAddr = LCase(Request("txtEmailAddr"))

        'Check the email address for the correct components...
        if ( Instr(1, txtEmailAddr, "@") = 0 or Instr(1, txtEmailAddr, ".") = 0 )
Then
          sMessage = "The email address you entered does not appear to be valid."
        Else
          'Make sure there is something after the period..
          if ( Instr(1, txtEmailAddr, ".") = Len(txtEmailAddr) _
          or Instr(1, txtEmailAddr, "@") = 1 or _
          (Instr(1, txtEmailAddr, ".") = Instr(1, txtEmailAddr, "@") + 1) ) Then
            sMessage = "You must enter a complete email address."
          end if
        End If

        'We passed our validation, show that all is good...
        if ( sMessage = "" ) Then
          sMessage = "Thank you for your input. All data has passed verification."
        else
          Session("ErrorCount") = Session("ErrorCount") + 1

          if ( Session("ErrorCount") > Application("AllowedErrorsBeforeWarning") )
then
            sMessage = sMessage & "<P><Font Size=1>You have exceeded the normal
number of times it takes to get this right!</Font>"
          end if
        End If
    Else
        'First time in here? Set some default values...
        txtFirstName = "Enter Your First Name"
        txtLastName = "Enter Your Last Name"
        txtEmailAddr = "Enter Your Email Address"
    End If
End Sub
```

```
'****************************************************************************
'* InitCap
'*
'* Capitalizes the first letter of the string
'****************************************************************************

Function InitCap(sStr)
    InitCap = UCase(Left(sStr, 1)) & LCase(Right(sStr, Len(sStr) - 1))
End Function

'****************************************************************************
'* Call our main subroutine
'****************************************************************************

Call Main()
%>

<html>
<head>
    <meta NAME="GENERATOR" Content="Microsoft FrontPage 3.0">
    <title>My First ASP Application</title>
</head>

<body>

<table border="0" cellPadding="0" cellSpacing="0" width="600">
<tbody>
    <tr>
      <td width="100"><a href="http://www.wrox.com" target="_blank" border=0
alt><img border=0 title="Check out the Wrox Press Web Site!"
src="images/wroxlogo.gif" WIDTH="56" HEIGHT="56"></a></td>
      <td width="500"><center><font size="5" face="Trebuchet MS">My First ASP
Application</font></center></td>
    </tr>

    <tr>
      <td width="100"> </td>
      <td width="500" align="1left"><font face="Trebuchet MS"><br>
      Please fill out the following form and press the [Submit] button. The
information you enter will be reformatted and the email address will be
verified.</font><form action="default.asp" id="FORM1" method="post"
name="frmMain">
        <table border="0" cellPadding="1" cellSpacing="5" width="100%">
        <tr>
          <td width="100" nowrap align="right"><font size="2" face="Trebuchet
MS">First Name:</font></td>
          <td width="350"><font size="2" face="Trebuchet MS">
            <input title="Enter your first name here" name="txtFirstName" size="30"
value="<%=txtFirstName%>" tabindex="1"></font></td>
          <td width="50"><div align="right"><font size="2" face="Trebuchet MS">
            <input type="submit" title="Submit this data for processing..."
value="Submit" name="cmdSubmit" tabindex="4"></font></td>
        </tr>
```

```
      <tr>
        <td width="100" nowrap align="right">
          <font size="2" face="Trebuchet MS">Last Name:</font></td>
        <td width="400" colspan="2">
          <font size="2" face="Trebuchet MS">
          <input title="Enter your last name here" name="txtLastName" size="30"
value="<%=txtLastName%>" tabindex="2"></font></td>
      </tr>

      <tr>
          <td width="100" nowrap align="right"><font size="2" face="Trebuchet
MS">Email Address:</font></td>
          <td width="400" colspan="2"><font size="2" face="Trebuchet MS"><input
title="Enter your valid email address here" name="txtEmailAddr"
          size="40" value="<%=txtEmailAddr%>" tabindex="3"></font></td>
        </tr>
        <tr>
          <td nowrap width=500 colspan="3" align="center"><font face="Trebuchet
MS"><br>
            <strong><%=sMessage%></strong> </font></td>
        </tr>
      </table>
    </form>
    <p> </td>
  </tr>
</tbody>
</table>
</body>
</html>
```

As you can see, the page is quite long. But it breaks logically into two distinct sections: the ASP/VBScript portion, and the HTML portion. Let's examine each section individually.

The ASP/VBScript Section

The top half of our file is where the ASP code lives. This is the code that is executed by the server before the page is returned to the browser that requested it. Any code, as you've seen, that is to be executed on the server before returning is enclosed in the special <% and %> tags.

For clarity (and sanity!), the ASP code has been divided into subroutines. This not only makes the code more readable, but also will aid in its reuse. Our code has two routines: Main, and InitCap.

Before we do anything else however, we declare some variables:

```
Dim txtFirstName, txtLastName, txtEmailAddr
Dim sMessage
```

When variables are declared outside of a subroutine in an ASP page, the variables retain their data until the page is completely processed. This allows you to pass information from your ASP code to your HTML code as you'll see.

After our variables have been declared, we have our `Main` routine. This is what is called by our ASP code every time a browser retrieves the page. The `Main` subroutine is not called automatically: we must explicitly call it ourselves.

```
'*********************************************************************
'* Main
'*
'* The main subroutine for this page...
'*********************************************************************

Sub Main()
   '  Was this page submitted?
  if ( Request("cmdSubmit") = "Submit" ) Then
    ' Reformat the data into a more readable format...
    txtFirstName = InitCap(Request("txtFirstName"))
    txtLastName = InitCap(Request("txtLastName"))
    txtEmailAddr = LCase(Request("txtEmailAddr"))
    ' Check the email address for the correct components...
    if ( Instr(1, txtEmailAddr, "@") = 0 or Instr(1, txtEmailAddr, ".") = 0 ) Then
      sMessage = "The email address you entered does not appear to be valid."
    Else
      '  Make sure there is something after the period..
      if ( Instr(1, txtEmailAddr, ".") = Len(txtEmailAddr) & _
          or Instr(1, txtEmailAddr, "@") = 1 or & _
          (Instr(1, txtEmailAddr, ".") = Instr(1, txtEmailAddr, "@") + 1) ) Then
        sMessage = "You must enter a complete email address."
      end if
    End If

    'We passed our validation, show that all is good...
    if ( sMessage = "" ) Then
      sMessage = "Thank you for your input. All data has passed verification."
    else
      Session("ErrorCount") = Session("ErrorCount") + 1

      if ( Session("ErrorCount") > Application("AllowedErrorsBeforeWarning") )
then
        sMessage = sMessage & "<P><Font Size=1>You have exceeded the normal number
of times it takes to get this right!</Font>"
      end if
    End If
  Else
    ' First time in here? Set some default values...
    txtFirstName = "Enter Your First Name"
    txtLastName = "Enter Your Last Name"
    txtEmailAddr = "Enter Your Email Address"
  End If
End Sub
```

First we see if the form was actually submitted by the user, otherwise we initialize our variables. To determine if the page has been submitted, we check the value of the cmdSubmit Request variable. This is the button on our form. When pressed, the form calls this page and sets the value of the cmdSubmit button to Submit. If a user just loads the page without pressing the button, the value of cmdSubmit is blank (""). There are other ways to determine if a web page was submitted, but this method is the simplest.

After we have determined that the page was in fact submitted, run the names through the second function on this page: InitCap. InitCap is a quick little function that will format a word to proper case. That is to say that the first letter will be capitalized, and the rest of the word will be lowercased. Here is the function:

```
'*******************************************************************
'* InitCap
'*
'* Capitalizes the first letter of the string
'*******************************************************************

Function InitCap(sStr)
    InitCap = UCase(Left(sStr, 1)) & LCase(Right(sStr, Len(sStr) - 1))
End Function
```

Now that we've cleaned up the names, we need to check the email address for validity. To do this we ensure that it contains an "@" sign and a period (.). Once past this check, we make sure that there is data after the period and that there is data before the "@" sign. This is 'quick and dirty' e-mail validity checking.

If either of these checks fail, we place a failure message into the string sMessage. This will be displayed in our HTML section after the page processing is complete.

Now, if our e-mail address has passed the test, we set the message (sMessage) to display a thank you note. If we failed our test, we increment our error counter that we set up in the global.asa file. Here we also check to see if we have exceeded our limit on errors. If we have, a sterner message is set for display.

Finally, the last thing in our ASP section is our call to Main. This is what is called when the page is loaded:

```
'*******************************************************************
'* Call our main subroutine
'*******************************************************************

Call Main()
```

The HTML Section

This section is a regular HTML form with a smattering of ASP thrown in for good measure. The ASP that we've embedded in the HTML sets default values for the input fields, and displays any messages that our server side code has generated.

The most important part of the HTML is where the ASP code is embedded. The following snippet illustrates this:

```
<input title="Enter your first name here" name="txtFirstName" size="30"
  value="<%=txtFirstName%>" tabindex="1">
```

Here we see a normal text input box. However, to set the value of the text box we use the `Response.Write` shortcut (`<%=`) to insert the value of the variable `txtFirstName`. Remember that we dimensioned this outside of our ASP functions so that it would have page scope. Now we utilize its value by inserting it into our HTML.

We do exactly the same thing with the Last Name and Email Address text boxes:

```
<input title="Enter your last name here" name="txtLastName" size="30"
  value="<%=txtLastName%>" tabindex="2">
<input title="Enter your valid email address here" name="txtEmailAddr"
  size="40" value="<%=txtEmailAddr%>" tabindex="3">
</tr>
```

The last trick in the HTML section is the display of our failure or success message. This message is stored in the variable called `sMessage`. At the bottom of the form, we display the contents of this variable like so:

```
<td nowrap width=500 colspan="3" align="center">
    <font face="Trebuchet MS">
    <br>
    <strong>
    <%=sMessage%>
    </strong>
    </font>
</td>
```

The beauty of this code is that if `sMessage` is blank then nothing is shown, otherwise the message is displayed.

Summary

In this reference we first looked at how HTTP is the transaction system that sends web pages to requesting clients. It is a very important piece of the puzzle. We then discussed Active Server Pages, or ASP. You learned how ASP pages are created, and what special HTML tags you need to include in your files to use ASP. We looked through the ASP object model and saw that the `Request` and `Response` objects are used to manage details of the HTTP request and responses. We saw that the `Application` object is used to group pages together into one application and we saw that the `Session` object is used to create the illusion that the interaction between user and site is one continuous action. Finally, we created a small application that demonstrates two uses for ASP: form validation and data manipulation.

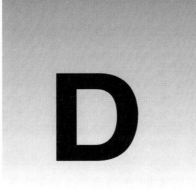

ASP Object Model

This appendix offers a handy reference to the Active Server Pages **object model**, and in each case provides the properties, methods, events and collections for its objects.

The Request Object

Together, the Request object and the Response object form the 'conversational mechanism' of ASP. The Request object is responsible for controlling how the user sends information to the server. Using the Request object, the server can obtain information about what the user wants – either explicitly (e.g. through programmed ASP code) or implicitly (e.g. through the HTTP headers).

Collections	Description
ClientCertificate	Client certificate values sent from the browser. Read Only
Cookies	Values of cookies sent from the browser. Read Only
Form	Values of form elements sent from the browser. Read Only
QueryString	Values of variables in the HTTP query string. Read Only
ServerVariables	Values of the HTTP and environment variables. Read Only

Property	Description
TotalBytes	Specifies the number of bytes the client is sending in the body of the request. Read Only

Method	Description
BinaryRead	Used to retrieve data sent to the server as part of the POST request

The Response Object

The Response object is responsible for sending the server's output to the client. In this sense, the Response object is the counterpart to the Request object: the Request object gathers information from both the client and the server, and the Response object sends, or resends, the information to the client by writing to the HTTP data stream.

Collection	Description
Cookies	Values of all the cookies to send to the browser.

Properties	Description
Buffer	Determines whether the page is to be buffered until complete
CacheControl	Determines whether proxy servers are allowed to cache the output generated by ASP
Charset	Appends the name of the character set to the content-type header
ContentType	HTTP content type (e.g. "Text/HTML") for the response
Expires	Number of minutes between caching and expiry, for a page cached on the browser
ExpiresAbsolute	Explicit date and/or time of expiry for a page cached on a browser
IsClientConnected	Indicates whether the client has disconnected from the server
PICS	Adds the value of a PICS label to the pics-label field of the response header
Status	Value of the HTTP status line returned by the server

Methods	Description
AddHeader	Adds or changes a value in the HTML header
AppendToLog	Adds text to the web server log entry for this request
BinaryWrite	Sends text to the browser without character-set conversion
Clear	Erases any buffered HTML output
End	Stops processing the page and returns the current result
Flush	Sends buffered output immediately
Redirect	Instructs the browser to connect to a different URL
Write	Writes variable values, strings etc. to the current page as a string

The `Response` interface elements can be divided into groups, like this:

Response Items	Description
`Write, BinaryWrite`	Inserts information into a page
`Cookies`	Sends cookies to the browser
`Redirect`	Redirects the browser
`Buffer, Flush, Clear, End`	Buffers the page as it is created
`Expires, ExpiresAbsolute, ContentType, AddHeader, Status, CacheContol, PICS, Charset`	Sets the properties of a page
`IsClientConnected`	Checks the client connection

The Application Object

Each application is represented by an instance of the `Application` object. This object stores variables and objects for application-scope usage. It also holds information about any currently-active sessions.

Collections	Description
`Contents`	Contains all of the items added to the application through script commands
`StaticObjects`	Contains all of the objects added to the application with the `<OBJECT>` tag

Methods	Description
`Lock`	Prevents other clients from modifying application properties
`Unlock`	Allows other clients to modify application properties

Events	Description
`OnStart`	Occurs when a page in the application is first referenced
`OnEnd`	Occurs when the application ends, i.e. when the web server is stopped

The Session Object

The Session object is used to keep track of an individual browser as it navigates through your web site.

Collections	Description
Contents	Contains all of the items added to the session through script commands
StaticObjects	Contains all of the objects added to the session with the <OBJECT> tag

Method	Description
Abandon	Destroys a Session object and releases its resources

Properties	Description
CodePage	Sets the codepage that will be used for symbol mapping
LCID	Sets the locale identifier
SessionID	Returns the session identification for this user
Timeout	Sets the timeout period for the session state for this application, in minutes

Events	Description
OnStart	Occurs when the server creates a new session
OnEnd	Occurs when a session is abandoned or times out

The Server Object

The main use of the Server object is to create components.

Property	Description
ScriptTimeout	Length of time a script can run before an error occurs

Methods	Description
CreateObject	Creates an instance of an object or server component
HTMLEncode	Applies HTML encoding to the specified string
MapPath	Converts a virtual path into a physical path
URLEncode	Applies URL encoding including escape chars to a string

The ObjectContext Object

When we use MTS (Microsoft Transaction Server) to manage a transaction, we have the functionality within our script to commit (or to abort) the transaction. This functionality is provided by the ObjectContext object.

Methods	Description
SetComplete	Declares that the script knows no reason for the transaction not to complete. If all participating components call SetComplete then the transaction will complete. SetComplete overrides any previous SetAbort method that has been called in the script
SetAbort	Aborts a transaction initiated by an ASP

Events	Description
OnTransactionCommit	Occurs after a transacted script's transaction commits
OnTransactionAbort	Occurs if the transaction is aborted

Microsoft ActiveX Data Objects 2.1 Library Reference

> All properties are read/write unless otherwise stated.

Objects and Collections

Name	Description
Command	A Command object is a definition of a specific command that you intend to execute against a data source.
Connection	A Connection object represents an open connection to a data store.
Error	An Error object contains the details about data access errors pertaining to a single operation involving the provider.
Errors	The Errors collection contains all of the Error objects created in response to a single failure involving the provider.
Field	A Field object represents a column of data within a common data type.
Fields	A Fields collection contains all of the Field objects of a Recordset object.
Parameter	A Parameter object represents a parameter or argument associated with a Command object based on a parameterized query or stored procedure.
Parameters	A Parameters collection contains all the Parameter objects of a Command object.
Properties	A Properties collection contains all the Property objects for a specific instance of an object.
Property	A Property object represents a dynamic characteristic of an ADO object that is defined by the provider.
Recordset	A Recordset object represents the entire set of records from a base table or the results of an executed command. At any time, the Recordset object only refers to a single record within the set as the current record.

Command Object

Methods

Name	Returns	Description
Cancel		Cancels execution of a pending Execute or Open call.
CreateParameter	Parameter	Creates a new Parameter object.
Execute	Recordset	Executes the query, SQL statement, or stored procedure specified in the CommandText property.

Properties

Name	Returns	Description
ActiveConnection	Variant	Indicates to which Connection object the command currently belongs.
CommandText	String	Contains the text of a command to be issued against a data provider.
CommandTimeout	Long	Indicates how long to wait, in seconds, while executing a command before terminating the command and generating an error. Default is 30.
CommandType	CommandTypeEnum	Indicates the type of Command object.
Name	String	Indicates the name of the Command object.
Prepared	Boolean	Indicates whether or not to save a compiled version of a command before execution.
State	Long	Describes whether the Command object is open or closed. Read only.

Connection Object

Methods

Name	Returns	Description
BeginTrans	Integer	Begins a new transaction.
Cancel		Cancels the execution of a pending, asynchronous Execute or Open operation.
Close		Closes an open connection and any dependant objects.
CommitTrans		Saves any changes and ends the current transaction.
Open		Opens a connection to a data source, so that commands can be executed against it.
RollbackTrans		Cancels any changes made during the current transaction and ends the transaction.

Properties

Name	Returns	Description
Attributes	Long	Indicates one or more characteristics of a Connection object. Default is 0.
CommandTimeout	Long	Indicates how long, in seconds, to wait while executing a command before terminating the command and generating an error. The default is 30.
ConnectionString	String	Contains the information used to establish a connection to a data source.
ConnectionTimeout	Long	Indicates how long, in seconds, to wait while establishing a connection before terminating the attempt and generating an error. Default is 15.
CursorLocation	CursorLocationEnum	Sets or returns the location of the cursor engine.

Table Continued on Following Page

Name	Returns	Description
DefaultDatabase	String	Indicates the default database for a Connection object.
IsolationLevel	IsolationLevelEnum	Indicates the level of transaction isolation for a Connection object. Write only.
Mode	ConnectModeEnum	Indicates the available permissions for modifying data in a Connection.
Provider	String	Indicates the name of the provider for a Connection object.
State	Long	Describes whether the Connection object is open or closed. Read only.
Version	String	Indicates the ADO version number. Read only.

Events

Name	Description
BeginTransComplete	Fired after a BeginTrans operation finishes executing.
CommitTrans	Fired after a CommitTrans operation finishes executing.
ConnectComplete	Fired after a connection starts.
Disconnect	Fired after a connection ends.
ExecuteComplete	Fired after a command has finished executing.
InfoMessage	Fired whenever a ConnectionEvent operation completes successfully and additional information is returned by the provider.
RollbackTransComplete	Fired after a RollbackTrans operation finished executing.
WillConnect	Fired before a connection starts.
WillExecute	Fired before a pending command executes on the connection.

Error Object

Properties

Name	Returns	Description
Description	String	A description string associated with the error. Read only.
HelpContext	Integer	Indicates the ContextID in the help file for the associated error. Read only.
HelpFile	String	Indicates the name of the help file. Read only.
NativeError	Long	Indicates the provider-specific error code for the associated error. Read only.
Number	Long	Indicates the number that uniquely identifies an Error object. Read only.
Source	String	Indicates the name of the object or application that originally generated the error. Read only.
SQLState	String	Indicates the SQL state for a given Error object. It is a five-character string that follows the ANSI SQL standard. Read only.

Errors Collection

Methods

Name	Returns	Description
Clear		Removes all of the Error objects from the Errors collection.

Properties

Name	Returns	Description
Count	Long	Indicates the number of Error objects in the Errors collection. Read only.

Field Object

Methods

Name	Returns	Description
AppendChunk		Appends data to a large or binary Field object.
GetChunk	Variant	Returns all or a portion of the contents of a large or binary Field object.

Properties

Name	Returns	Description
ActualSize	Long	Indicates the actual length of a field's value. Read only.
Attributes	Long	Indicates one or more characteristics of a Field object.
DefinedSize	Long	Indicates the defined size of the Field object. Write only.
Name	String	Indicates the name of the Field object. Read only
NumericScale	Byte	Indicates the scale of numeric values for the Field object. Write only.
OriginalValue	Variant	Indicates the value of a Field object that existed in the record before any changes were made. Read only.
Precision	Byte	Indicates the degree of precision for numeric values in the Field object. Read only.
Properties	Properties	Contains all of the Property objects for a Field object.
Type	DataTypeEnum	Indicates the data type of the Field object.
UnderlyingValue	Variant	Indicates a Field object's current value in the database. Read only.
Value	Variant	Indicates the value assigned to the Field object.

Fields Collection

Methods

Name	Returns	Description
Append		Appends a Field object to the Fields collection.
Delete		Deletes a Field object from the Fields collection.
Refresh		Updates the Field objects in the Fields collection.

Properties

Name	Returns	Description
Count	Long	Indicates the number of Field objects in the Fields collection. Read only.

Parameter Object

Methods

Name	Returns	Description
AppendChunk		Appends data to a large or binary Parameter object.

Properties

Name	Returns	Description
Attributes	Long	Indicates one or more characteristics of a Parameter object.
Direction	Parameter DirectionEnum	Indicates whether the Parameter object represents an input parameter, an output parameter, or both, or if the parameter is a return value from a stored procedure.
Name	String	Indicates the name of the Parameter object.

Table Continued on Following Page

Name	Returns	Description
NumericScale	Byte	Indicates the scale of numeric values for the Parameter object.
Precision	Byte	Indicates the degree of precision for numeric values in the Parameter object.
Type	DataTypeEnum	Indicates the data type of the Parameter object.
Value	Variant	Indicates the value assigned to the Parameter object.

Parameters Collection

Methods

Name	Returns	Description
Append		Appends a Parameter object to the Parameters collection.
Delete		Deletes a Parameter object from the Parameters collection.
Refresh		Updates the Parameter objects in the Parameters collection.

Properties

Name	Returns	Description
Count	Long	Indicates the number of Parameter objects in the Parameters collection. Read only.

Properties

Methods

Name	Returns	Description
Refresh		Updates the Property objects in the Properties collection with the details from the provider.

Properties

Name	Returns	Description
Count	Long	Indicates the number of Property objects in the Properties collection. Read only.

Property Object

Properties

Name	Returns	Description
Attributes	Long	Indicates one or more characteristics of a Property object.
Name	String	Indicates the name of the Property object. Read only.
Type	DataTypeEnum	Indicates the data type of the Property object.
Value	Variant	Indicates the value assigned to the Property object.

Recordset Object

Methods

Name	Returns	Description
AddNew		Creates a new record for an updateable Recordset object.
Cancel		Cancels execution of a pending asynchronous Open operation.
CancelBatch		Cancels a pending batch update.
CancelUpdate		Cancels any changes made to the current record, or to a new record prior to calling the Update method.

Table Continued on Following Page

Name	Returns	Description
Clone	Recordset	Creates a duplicate Recordset object from on existing Recordset object.
Close		Closes the Recordset object and any dependent objects.
CompareBookmarks	CompareEnum	Compares two bookmarks and returns an indication of the relative values.
Delete		Deletes the current record or group of records.
Find		Searches the Recordset for a record that matches the specified criteria.
GetRows	Variant	Retrieves multiple records of a Recordset object into an array.
GetString	String	Returns a Recordset as a string.
Move		Moves the position of the current record in a Recordset.
MoveFirst		Moves the position of the current record to the first record in the Recordset.
MoveLast		Moves the position of the current record to the last record in the Recordset.
MoveNext		Moves the position of the current record to the next record in the Recordset.
MovePrevious		Moves the position of the current record to the previous record in the Recordset.
NextRecordset	Recordset	Clears the current Recordset object and returns the next Recordset by advancing through a series of commands.
Open		Opens a Recordset.
Requery		Updates the data in a Recordset object by re-executing the query on which the object is based.
Resync		Refreshes the data in the current Recordset object from the underlying database.
Save		Saves the Recordset to a file.
Seek		Assuming the OLE DB provider supports indexes on recordsets, this method locates a row in a recordset based on key values.

Name	Returns	Description
Supports	Boolean	Determines whether a specified Recordset object supports particular functionality.
Update		Saves any changes made to the current Recordset object.
UpdateBatch		Writes all pending batch updates to disk.

Properties

Name	Returns	Description
AbsolutePage	PositionEnum	Specifies in which page the current record resides.
AbsolutePosition	PositionEnum	Specifies the ordinal position of a Recordset object's current record.
ActiveCommand	Object	Indicates the Command object that created the associated Recordset object. Read only.
ActiveConnection	Variant	Indicates to which Connection object the specified Recordset object currently belongs.
BOF	Boolean	Indicates whether the current record is before the first record in a Recordset object. Read only.
Bookmark	Variant	Returns a bookmark that uniquely identifies the current record in a Recordset object, or sets the current record to the record identified by a valid bookmark.
CacheSize	Long	Indicates the number of records from a Recordset object that are cached locally in memory.
CursorLocation	CursorLocationEnum	Sets or returns the location of the cursor engine.
CursorType	CursorTypeEnum	Indicates the type of cursor used in a Recordset object.
DataMember	String	Specifies the name of the data member to retrieve from the object referenced by the DataSource property. Write only.
DataSource	Object	Specifies an object containing data to be represented as a Recordset object. Write only.

Table Continued on Following Page

Name	Returns	Description
EditMode	EditModeEnum	Indicates the editing status of the current record. Read only.
EOF	Boolean	Indicates whether the current record is after the last record in a Recordset object. Read only.
Fields	Fields	Contains all of the Field objects for the current Recordset object.
Filter	Variant	Indicates a filter for data in the recordset.
Index	String	Indicates the name of the index currently in effect in the recordset.
LockType	LockTypeEnum	Indicates the type of locks placed on records during editing.
MarshalOptions	MarshalOptionsEnum	Indicates which records are to be marshaled back to the server.
MaxRecords	Long	Indicates the maximum number of records to return to a Recordset object from a query. Default is zero (no limit).
PageCount	Long	Indicates how many pages of data the Recordset object contains. Read only.
PageSize	Long	Indicates how many records constitute one page in the recordset.
Properties	Properties	Contains all of the Property objects for the current Recordset object.
RecordCount	Long	Indicates the current number of records in the Recordset object. Read only.
Sort	String	Specifies one or more field names the recordset is sorted on, and the direction of the sort.
Source	String	Indicates the source for the data in a Recordset object.
State	Long	Indicates whether the recordset is open, closed, or whether it is executing an asynchronous operation. Read only.
Status	Integer	Indicates the status of the current record with respect to match updates or other bulk operations. Read only.

Name	Returns	Description
StayInSync	Boolean	Indicates, in a hierarchical Recordset object, whether the parent row should change when the set of underlying child records changes. Read only.

Events

Name	Description
EndOfRecordset	Fired when there is an attempt to move to a row past the end of the recordset.
FetchComplete	Fired after all the records in an asynchronous operation have been retrieved into the Recordset.
FetchProgress	Fired periodically during a length asynchronous operation, to report how many rows have currently been retrieved.
FieldChangeComplete	Fired after the value of one or more Field object has been changed.
MoveComplete	Fired after the current position in the Recordset changes.
RecordChangeComplete	Fired after one or more records change.
RecordsetChangeComplete	Fired after the Recordset has changed.
WillChangeField	Fired before a pending operation changes the value of one or more Field objects.
WillChangeRecord	Fired before one or more rows in the Recordset change.
WillChangeRecordset	Fired before a pending operation changes the Recordset.
WillMove	Fired before a pending operation changes the current position in the Recordset.

Method Calls Quick Reference

Command

Command.Cancel
Parameter = Command.CreateParameter(Name As String, Type As DataTypeEnum, Recordset =
Command.Execute(RecordsAffected As Variant, Parameters As Variant, Options As Integer)

Connection

Integer = Connection.BeginTrans
Connection.Cancel
Connection.Close
Connection.CommitTrans
Recordset = Connection.Execute(CommandText As String, RecordsAffected As Variant, Options As Integer)
Connection.Open(ConnectionString As String, UserID As String, Password As String, Options As Integer)
Connection.RollbackTrans

Errors

Errors.Clear

Field

Field.AppendChunk(Data As Variant)
Variant = Field.GetChunk(Length As Integer)

Fields

Fields.Append(Name As String, Type As DataTypeEnum, DefinedSize As Integer, Attrib As FieldAttributeEnum)
Fields.Delete(Index As Variant)
Fields.Refresh

Parameter

Parameter.AppendChunk(Val As Variant)

Parameters

Parameters.Append(Object As Object)
Parameters.Delete(Index As Variant)
Parameters.Refresh

Properties

Properties.Refresh

Recordset

Recordset.AddNew([FieldList As Variant], [Values As Variant])

Recordset.Cancel

Recordset.CancelBatch(AffectRecords As AffectEnum)

Recordset.CancelUpdate

Recordset = Recordset.Clone(LockType As LockTypeEnum)

Recordset.Close

CompareEnum = Recordset.CompareBookmarks(Bookmark1 As Variant, Bookmark2 As Variant)

Recordset.Delete(AffectRecords As AffectEnum)

Recordset.Find(Criteria As String, SkipRecords As Integer, SearchDirection As SearchDirectionEnum, [Start As Variant])

Variant = Recordset.GetRows(Rows As Integer, [Start As Variant], [Fields As Variant])

String = Recordset.GetString(StringFormat As StringFormatEnum, NumRows As Integer, ColumnDelimeter As String, RowDelimeter As String, NullExpr As String)

Recordset.Move(NumRecords As Integer, [Start As Variant])

Recordset.MoveFirst

Recordset.MoveLast

Recordset.MoveNext

Recordset.MovePrevious

Recordset = Recordset.NextRecordset([RecordsAffected As Variant])

Recordset.Open(Source As Variant, ActiveConnection As Variant, CursorType As CursorTypeEnum, LockType As LockTypeEnum, Options As Integer)

Recordset.Requery(Options As Integer)

Recordset.Resync(AffectRecords As AffectEnum, ResyncValues As ResyncEnum)

Recordset.Save(FileName As String, PersistFormat As PersistFormatEnum)

Boolean = Recordset.Supports(CursorOptions As CursorOptionEnum)

Recordset.Update([Fields As Variant], [Values As Variant])

Recordset.UpdateBatch(AffectRecords As AffectEnum)

MTS Object Reference

Global Methods

Name	Description
GetObjectContext	Obtains a reference to the IObjectContext that's associated with the current MTS object
SafeRef	Used by an object to obtain a reference to itself that's safe to pass outside its context

Objects

Name	Description
ObjectContext	Provides access to the current object's context
SecurityProperty	Used to determine the current object's caller or creator
ObjectControl	Used to define context specific initialization and cleanup procedures and to specify whether or not the objects can be recycled

ObjectContext

Methods

Name	Returns	Description
CreateInstance	Variant	Creates an object using current object's context.
DisableCommit		Indicates that the object is not yet finished its work and any attempt to commit the transaction will force an abort.
EnableCommit		Indicates that the object is not yet finished its work but would allow the transaction to commit.
IsCallerInRole	Boolean	Returns TRUE if the caller's Userid is included in the identified role.
IsInTransaction	Boolean	Returns TRUE if this object context has an active transaction.
IsSecurityEnabled	Boolean	Returns TRUE if security is enabled.
SetAbort		Indicates that the object has completed its work and the transaction must be aborted.
SetComplete		Indicates that the object has completed its work and a transaction can be committed.

Properties

Name	Returns	Description	Type
Count	Integer	Get number of named properties	Read only
Item	Variant	Get a named property	Read only
Security	SecurityProperty	Returns the security object	Read only

SecurityProperty

Methods

Name	Returns	Description
GetDirectCallerName	String	Returns the Name of the direct caller
GetDirectCreatorName	String	Returns the Name of the direct creator
GetOriginalCallerName	String	Returns the Name of the original caller
GetOriginalCreatorName	String	Returns the Name of the original creator

Constants

Error_Constants

Name	Value	Description
mtsErrCtxAborted	-2147164158	The transaction was aborted
mtsErrCtxAborting	-2147164157	The transaction is aborting
mtsErrCtxActivityTimeout	-2147164154	The activity timed out
mtsErrCtxNoContext	-2147164156	There is no object context
mtsErrCtxNoSecurity	-2147164147	There is no security context
mtsErrCtxNotRegistered	-2147164155	The context is not registered
mtsErrCtxOldReference	-2147164153	The context has an old reference
mtsErrCtxRoleNotFound	-2147164148	The role was not found
mtsErrCtxTMNotAvailable	-2147164145	The Transaction Monitor is not available
mtsErrCtxWrongThread	-2147164146	Execution on wrong thread

XactAttributeEnum

Name	Value	Description
adXactAbortRetaining	262144	Performs retaining aborts, so calling Rollback automatically starts a new transaction
adXactCommitRetaining	131072	Performs retaining commits, thus calling CommitTrans automatically starts a new transaction. Provider dependant.

VBScript Language Reference

Array Handling

Dim – declares a variable. An array variable can be static, with a defined number of elements, or dynamic, and can have up to 60 dimensions.

ReDim – used to change the size of an array variable that has been declared as dynamic.

Preserve – keyword used to preserve the contents of an array being resized (otherwise data is lost when ReDim is used). If you need to use this then you can only re-dimension the rightmost index of the array.

Erase – reinitializes the elements of a fixed-size array or empties the contents of a dynamic array:

```
Dim arEmployees ()
ReDim arEmployees (9,1)

arEmployees (9,1) = "Phil"

ReDim arEmployees (9,2)              'loses the contents of element (9,1)
arEmployees (9,2) = "Paul"

ReDim Preserve arEmployees (9,3)   'preserves the contents of (9,2)
arEmployees (9,3) = "Smith"

Erase arEmployees              'now we are back to where we started - empty array
```

LBound – returns the smallest subscript for the dimension of an array. Note that arrays always start from the subscript zero so this function will always return the value zero.

UBound – used to determine the size of an array:

```
Dim strCustomers (10, 5)
intSizeFirst = UBound (strCustomers, 1)      'returns SizeFirst = 10
intSizeSecond = UBound (strCustomers, 2)     'returns SizeSecond = 5
```

> **The actual number of elements is always one greater than the value returned by** UBound **because the array starts from zero.**

Assignments

Let – used to assign values to variables (optional).
Set – used to assign an object reference to a variable.

```
Let intNumberOfDays = 365

Set txtMyTextBox = txtcontrol
txtMyTextBox.Value = "Hello World"
```

Constants

Empty – an empty variable is one that has been created, but has not yet been assigned a value.
Nothing – used to remove an object reference:

```
Set txtMyTextBox = txtATextBox      'assigns object reference
Set txtMyTextBox = Nothing          'removes object reference
```

Null – indicates that a variable is not valid. Note that this isn't the same as Empty.
True – indicates that an expression is true. Has numerical value –1.
False – indicates that an expression is false. Has numerical value 0.

Error constant

Constant	Value
vbObjectError	&h80040000

System Color constants

Constant	Value	Description
vbBlack	&h000000	Black
vbRed	&hFF0000	Red
vbGreen	&h00FF00	Green
vbYellow	&hFFFF00	Yellow
vbBlue	&h0000FF	Blue
vbMagenta	&hFF00FF	Magenta
vbCyan	&h00FFFF	Cyan
vbWhite	&hFFFFFF	White

Comparison constants

Constant	Value	Description
vbBinaryCompare	0	Perform a binary comparison.
vbTextCompare	1	Perform a textual comparison.

Date and Time constants

Constant	Value	Description
vbSunday	1	Sunday
vbMonday	2	Monday
vbTuesday	3	Tuesday
vbWednesday	4	Wednesday
vbThursday	5	Thursday
vbFriday	6	Friday
vbSaturday	7	Saturday
vbFirstJan1	1	Use the week in which January 1 occurs (default).
vbFirstFourDays	2	Use the first week that has at least four days in the new year.

Table Continued on Following Page

Constant	Value	Description
vbFirstFullWeek	3	Use the first full week of the year.
vbUseSystem	0	Use the format in the regional settings for the computer.
vbUseSystemDayOfWeek	0	Use the day in the system settings for the first weekday.

Date Format constants

Constant	Value	Description
vbGeneralDate	0	Display a date and/or time in the format set in the system settings. For real numbers display a date and time. For integer numbers display only a date. For numbers less than 1, display time only.
vbLongDate	1	Display a date using the long date format specified in the computer's regional settings.
vbShortDate	2	Display a date using the short date format specified in the computer's regional settings.
vbLongTime	3	Display a time using the long time format specified in the computer's regional settings.
vbShortTime	4	Display a time using the short time format specified in the computer's regional settings.

Message Box Constants

Constant	Value	Description
vbOKOnly	0	Display OK button only.
vbOKCancel	1	Display OK and Cancel buttons.
vbAbortRetryIgnore	2	Display Abort, Retry, and Ignore buttons.
vbYesNoCancel	3	Display Yes, No, and Cancel buttons.
vbYesNo	4	Display Yes and No buttons.
vbRetryCancel	5	Display Retry and Cancel buttons.
vbCritical	16	Display Critical Message icon.

Constant	Value	Description
vbQuestion	32	Display Warning Query icon.
vbExclamation	48	Display Warning Message icon.
vbInformation	64	Display Information Message icon.
vbDefaultButton1	0	First button is the default.
vbDefaultButton2	256	Second button is the default.
vbDefaultButton3	512	Third button is the default.
vbDefaultButton4	768	Fourth button is the default.
vbApplicationModal	0	Application modal.
vbSystemModal	4096	System modal.

String constants

Constant	Value	Description
vbCr	Chr(13)	Carriage return only
vbCrLf	Chr(13) & Chr(10)	Carriage return and linefeed (New line)
vbFormFeed	Chr(12)	Form feed only
vbLf	Chr(10)	Line feed only
vbNewLine	–	Newline character as appropriate to a specific platform
vbNullChar	Chr(0)	Character having the value 0
vbNullString	-	String having the value zero (not just an empty string)
vbTab	Chr(9)	Horizontal tab
vbVerticalTab	Chr(11)	Vertical tab

Tristate constants

Constant	Value	Description
TristateUseDefault	-2	Use default setting
TristateTrue	-1	True
TristateFalse	0	False

VarType constants

Constant	Value	Description
vbEmpty	0	Uninitialized (default)
vbNull	1	Contains no valid data
vbInteger	2	Integer subtype
vbLong	3	Long subtype
vbSingle	4	Single subtype
vbDouble	5	Double subtype
vbCurrency	6	Currency subtype
vbDate	7	Date subtype
vbString	8	String subtype
vbObject	9	Object
vbError	10	Error subtype
vbBoolean	11	Boolean subtype
vbVariant	12	Variant (used only for arrays of variants)
vbDataObject	13	Data access object
vbDecimal	14	Decimal subtype
vbByte	17	Byte subtype
vbArray	8192	Array

Control Flow

For...Next – executes a block of code a specified number of times:

```
Dim intSalary (10)
For intCounter = 0 to 10
    intSalary (intCounter) = 20000
Next
```

For Each...Next – repeats a block of code for each element in an array or collection:

```
For Each Item In Request.QueryString("MyControl")
    Response.Write Item & "<BR>"
Next
```

`Do...Loop` – executes a block of code while a condition is true or until a condition becomes true. Note that the condition can be checked either at the beginning or the end of the loop: the difference is that the code will be executed at least once if the condition is checked at the end.

```
Do While strDayOfWeek <> "Saturday" And strDayOfWeek <> "Sunday"
    MsgBox ("Get Up! Time for work")
    ...
Loop
```

```
Do
    MsgBox ("Get Up! Time for work")
    ...
Loop Until strDayOfWeek = "Saturday" Or strDayOfWeek = "Sunday"
```

We can also exit from a `Do...Loop` using `Exit Do`:

```
Do
    MsgBox ("Get Up! Time for work")
    ...
    If strDayOfWeek = "Sunday" Then
        Exit Do
    End If
Loop Until strDayOfWeek = "Saturday"
```

`If...Then...Else` – used to run various blocks of code depending on conditions:

```
If intAge < 20 Then
    MsgBox ("You're just a slip of a thing!")
ElseIf intAge < 40 Then
    MsgBox ("You're in your prime!")
Else
    MsgBox ("You're older and wiser")
End If
```

`Select Case` – used to replace `If...Then...Else` statements where there are many conditions:

```
Select Case intAge
Case 21,22,23,24,25,26
    MsgBox ("You're in your prime")
Case 40
    MsgBox ("You're fulfilling your dreams")
Case Else
    MsgBox ("Time for a new challenge")
End Select
```

`While...Wend` – executes a block of code while a condition is true:

```
While strDayOfWeek <> "Saturday" AND strDayOfWeek <> "Sunday"
    MsgBox ("Get Up! Time for work")
    ...
Wend
```

`With` – executes a series of statements for a single object:

```
With myDiv.style
    .posLeft = 200
    .posTop = 300
    .color = Red
End With
```

Functions

VBScript contains several inbuilt functions that can be used to manipulate and examine variables. These have been subdivided into these general categories:

❏   Conversion functions

❏   Date/time functions

❏   Math functions

❏   Object management functions

❏   Script engine identification functions

❏   String functions

❏   Variable testing functions

For a full description of each function and the parameters it requires, see the Microsoft web site at http://msdn.microsoft.com/scripting/.

Conversion Functions

These functions are used to convert values in variables between different types:

Function	Description
Abs	Returns the absolute value of a number.
Asc	Returns the numeric ANSI (or ASCII) code number of the first character in a string.
AscB	As above, but provided for use with byte data contained in a string. Returns result from the first byte only.
AscW	As above, but provided for Unicode characters. Returns the Wide character code, avoiding the conversion from Unicode to ANSI.
Chr	Returns a string made up of the ANSI character matching the number supplied.
ChrB	As above, but provided for use with byte data contained in a string. Always returns a single byte.

Function	Description
ChrW	As above, but provided for Unicode characters. Its argument is a Wide character code, thereby avoiding the conversion from ANSI to Unicode.
CBool	Returns the argument value converted to a Variant of subtype Boolean.
CByte	Returns the argument value converted to a Variant of subtype Byte.
CCur	Returns the argument value converted to a Variant of subtype Currency
CDate	Returns the argument value converted to a Variant of subtype Date.
CDbl	Returns the argument value converted to a Variant of subtype Double.
CInt	Returns the argument value converted to a Variant of subtype Integer.
CLng	Returns the argument value converted to a Variant of subtype Long
CSng	Returns the argument value converted to a Variant of subtype Single
CStr	Returns the argument value converted to a Variant of subtype String.
Fix	Returns the integer (whole) part of a number. If the number is negative, Fix returns the first negative integer greater than or equal to the number
Hex	Returns a string representing the hexadecimal value of a number.
Int	Returns the integer (whole) portion of a number. If the number is negative, Int returns the first negative integer less than or equal to the number.
Oct	Returns a string representing the octal value of a number.
Round	Returns a number rounded to a specified number of decimal places.
Sgn	Returns an integer indicating the sign of a number.

Date/Time Functions

These functions return date or time values from the computer's system clock, or manipulate existing values:

Function	Description
Date	Returns the current system date.
DateAdd	Returns a date to which a specified time interval has been added.
DateDiff	Returns the number of days, weeks, or years between two dates.
DatePart	Returns just the day, month or year of a given date.
DateSerial	Returns a Variant of subtype Date for a specified year, month and day.
DateValue	Returns a Variant of subtype Date.

Table Continued on Following Page

Function	Description
Day	Returns a number between 1 and 31 representing the day of the month.
Hour	Returns a number between 0 and 23 representing the hour of the day.
Minute	Returns a number between 0 and 59 representing the minute of the hour.
Month	Returns a number between 1 and 12 representing the month of the year.
MonthName	Returns the name of the specified month as a string.
Now	Returns the current date and time.
Second	Returns a number between 0 and 59 representing the second of the minute.
Time	Returns a Variant of subtype Date indicating the current system time.
TimeSerial	Returns a Variant of subtype Date for a specific hour, minute, and second.
TimeValue	Returns a Variant of subtype Date containing the time.
Weekday	Returns a number representing the day of the week.
WeekdayName	Returns the name of the specified day of the week as a string.
Year	Returns a number representing the year.

Math Functions

These functions perform mathematical operations on variables containing numerical values:

Function	Description
Atn	Returns the arctangent of a number.
Cos	Returns the cosine of an angle.
Exp	Returns e (the base of natural logarithms) raised to a power.
Log	Returns the natural logarithm of a number.
Randomize	Initializes the random-number generator.
Rnd	Returns a random number.
Sin	Returns the sine of an angle.
Sqr	Returns the square root of a number.
Tan	Returns the tangent of an angle.

Miscellaneous Functions

Function	Description
Eval	Evaluates an expression and returns a boolean result (e.g. treats x=y as an *expression* which is either true or false).
Execute	Executes one or more statements (e.g. treats x=y as a *statement* which assigns the value of y to x).
RGB	Returns a number representing an RGB color value

Object Management Functions

These functions are used to manipulate objects, where applicable:

Function	Description
CreateObject	Creates and returns a reference to an ActiveX or OLE Automation object.
GetObject	Returns a reference to an ActiveX or OLE Automation object.
LoadPicture	Returns a picture object.

Script Engine Identification

These functions return the version of the scripting engine:

Function	Description
ScriptEngine	A string containing the major, minor, and build version numbers of the scripting engine.
ScriptEngineMajorVersion	The major version of the scripting engine, as a number.
ScriptEngineMinorVersion	The minor version of the scripting engine, as a number.
ScriptEngineBuildVersion	The build version of the scripting engine, as a number.

String Functions

These functions are used to manipulate string values in variables:

Function	Description
Filter	Returns an array from a string array, based on specified filter criteria.
FormatCurrency	Returns a string formatted as currency value.
FormatDateTime	Returns a string formatted as a date or time.
FormatNumber	Returns a string formatted as a number.
FormatPercent	Returns a string formatted as a percentage.
InStr	Returns the position of the first occurrence of one string within another.
InStrB	As above, but provided for use with byte data contained in a string. Returns the byte position instead of the character position.
InstrRev	As InStr, but starts from the end of the string.
Join	Returns a string created by joining the strings contained in an array.
LCase	Returns a string that has been converted to lowercase.
Left	Returns a specified number of characters from the left end of a string.
LeftB	As above, but provided for use with byte data contained in a string. Uses that number of bytes instead of that number of characters.
Len	Returns the length of a string or the number of bytes needed for a variable.
LenB	As above, but is provided for use with byte data contained in a string. Returns the number of bytes in the string instead of characters.
LTrim	Returns a copy of a string without leading spaces.
Mid	Returns a specified number of characters from a string.
MidB	As above, but provided for use with byte data contained in a string. Uses that numbers of bytes instead of that number of characters.
Replace	Returns a string in which a specified substring has been replaced with another substring a specified number of times.
Right	Returns a specified number of characters from the right end of a string.
RightB	As above, but provided for use with byte data contained in a string. Uses that number of bytes instead of that number of characters.
RTrim	Returns a copy of a string without trailing spaces.

Function	Description
Space	Returns a string consisting of the specified number of spaces.
Split	Returns a one-dimensional array of a specified number of substrings.
StrComp	Returns a value indicating the result of a string comparison.
String	Returns a string of the length specified made up of a repeating character.
StrReverse	Returns a string in which the character order of a string is reversed.
Trim	Returns a copy of a string without leading or trailing spaces.
UCase	Returns a string that has been converted to uppercase.

Variable Testing Functions

These functions are used to determine the type of information stored in a variable:

Function	Description
IsArray	Returns a Boolean value indicating whether a variable is an array.
IsDate	Returns a Boolean value indicating whether an expression can be converted to a date.
IsEmpty	Returns a Boolean value indicating whether a variable has been initialized.
IsNull	Returns a Boolean value indicating whether an expression contains no valid data
IsNumeric	Returns a Boolean value indicating whether an expression can be evaluated as a number.
IsObject	Returns a Boolean value indicating whether an expression references a valid ActiveX or OLE Automation object.
TypeName	Returns a string that provides Variant subtype information about a variable.
VarType	Returns a number indicating the subtype of a variable.

Variable Declarations

Class – Declares the name of a class, as well as the variables, properties, and methods that comprise the class.

Const – Declares a constant to be used in place of literal values.

Dim – declares a variable.

Error Handling

On Error Resume Next – indicates that if an error occurs, control should continue at the next statement.

Err – this is the error object that provides information about run-time errors.

Error handling is very limited in VBScript and the Err object must be tested explicitly to determine if an error has occurred.

Input/Output

This consists of Msgbox for output and InputBox for input:

MsgBox

This displays a message, and can return a value indicating which button was clicked.

```
MsgBox "Hello There",20,"Hello Message","c:\windows\MyHelp.hlp",123
```

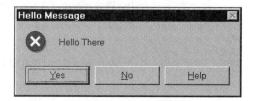

The parameters are:
"Hello There" – this contains the text of the message (the only obligatory parameter).

20 – this determines which icon and buttons appear on the message box.

"Hello Message" – this contains the text that will appear as the title of the message box.

"c:\windows\MyHelp.hlp" – this adds a Help button to the message box and determines the help file that is opened if the button is clicked.

123 – this is a reference to the particular help topic that will be displayed if the Help button is clicked.

The value of the icon and buttons parameter is determined using the following tables:

Constant	Value	Buttons
vbOKOnly	0	OK
vbOKCancel	1	OK Cancel
vbAbortRetryIngnore	2	Abort Retry Ignore
vbYesNoCancel	3	Yes No Cancel
vbYesNo	4	Yes No
vbRetryCancel	5	Retry Cancel

Constant	Value	Buttons
vbDefaultButton1	0	The first button from the left is the default.
vbDefaultButton2	256	The second button from the left is the default.
vbDefaultButton3	512	The third button from the left is the default.
vbDefaultButton4	768	The fourth button from the left is the default.

Constant	Value	Description	Icon
vbCritical	16	Critical Message	
vbQuestion	32	Questioning Message	

Table Continued on Following Page

Constant	Value	Description	Icon
vbExclamation	48	Warning Message	
vbInformation	64	Informational Message	

Constant	Value	Description
vbApplicationModal	0	Just the application stops until user clicks a button.
vbSystemModal	4096	On Win16 systems the whole system stops until user clicks a button. On Win32 systems the message box remains on top of any other programs.

To specify which buttons and icon are displayed you simply add the relevant values. So, in our example we add together 4 + 0 + 16 to display the Yes and No buttons, with Yes as the default, and the Critical icon. If we used 4 + 256 + 16 we could display the same buttons and icon, but have No as the default.

You can determine which button the user clicked by assigning the return code of the MsgBox function to a variable:

```
intButtonClicked = MsgBox ("Hello There",35,"Hello Message")
```

Notice that brackets enclose the MsgBox parameters when used in this format. The following table determines the value assigned to the variable intButtonClicked:

Constant	Value	Button Clicked
vbOK	1	OK
vbCancel	2	Cancel
vbAbort	3	Abort
vbRetry	4	Retry

Constant	Value	Button Clicked
vbIgnore	5	Ignore
vbYes	6	Yes
vbNo	7	No

InputBox

This accepts text entry from the user and returns it as a string.

```
strName = InputBox ("Please enter your name","Login","John Smith",500,500)
```

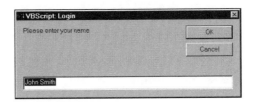

The parameters are:
"Please enter your name" – this is the prompt displayed in the input box.

"Login" – this is the text displayed as the title of the input box.

"John Smith" – this is the default value displayed in the input box.

500 – specifies the x position of the input box in relation to the screen.

500 – specifies the y position of the input box in relation to the screen.

As with the MsgBox function, you can also specify a help file and topic to add a <u>H</u>elp button to the input box.

Procedures

Call – optional method of calling a subroutine.

Function – used to declare a function.

Sub – used to declare a subroutine.

Other Keywords

Rem – old style method of adding comments to code (it's now more usual to use an apostrophe (').)

Option Explicit – forces you to declare a variable before it can be used (if used, it must appear before any other statements in a script).

Visual Basic Run-time Error Codes

The following error codes also apply to VBA code and many will not be appropriate to an application built completely around VBScript. However, if you have built your own components then these error codes may well be brought up when such components are used.

Code	Description
3	Return without `GoSub`
5	Invalid procedure call
6	Overflow
7	Out of memory
9	Subscript out of range
10	This array is fixed or temporarily locked
11	Division by zero
13	Type mismatch
14	Out of string space
16	Expression too complex
17	Can't perform requested operation
18	User interrupt occurred
20	Resume without error
28	Out of stack space
35	Sub or Function not defined
47	Too many DLL application clients
48	Error in loading DLL
49	Bad DLL calling convention
51	Internal error
52	Bad file name or number
53	File not found
54	Bad file mode
55	File already open
57	Device I/O error

Code	Description
58	File already exists
59	Bad record length
61	Disk full
62	Input past end of file
63	Bad record number
67	Too many files
68	Device unavailable
70	Permission denied
71	Disk not ready
74	Can't rename with different drive
75	Path/File access error
76	Path not found
91	Object variable not set
92	For loop not initialized
93	Invalid pattern string
94	Invalid use of Null
322	Can't create necessary temporary file
325	Invalid format in resource file
380	Invalid property value
423	Property or method not found
424	Object required
429	OLE Automation server can't create object
430	Class doesn't support OLE Automation
432	File name or class name not found during OLE Automation operation
438	Object doesn't support this property or method
440	OLE Automation error
442	Connection to type library or object library for remote process has been lost. Press OK for dialog to remove reference.

Table Continued on Following Page

Code	Description
443	OLE Automation object does not have a default value
445	Object doesn't support this action
446	Object doesn't support named arguments
447	Object doesn't support current locale setting
448	Named argument not found
449	Argument not optional
450	Wrong number of arguments or invalid property assignment
451	Object not a collection
452	Invalid ordinal
453	Specified DLL function not found
454	Code resource not found
455	Code resource lock error
457	This key is already associated with an element of this collection
458	Variable uses an OLE Automation type not supported in Visual Basic
462	The remote server machine does not exist or is unavailable
481	Invalid picture
500	Variable is undefined
501	Cannot assign to variable
502	Object not safe for scripting
503	Object not safe for initializing
504	Object not safe for creating
505	Invalid or unqualified reference
506	Class not defined
1001	Out of memory
1002	Syntax error
1003	Expected ':'
1004	Expected ';'
1005	Expected '('

Code	Description
1006	Expected ')'
1007	Expected ']'
1008	Expected '{'
1009	Expected '}'
1010	Expected identifier
1011	Expected '='
1012	Expected 'If'
1013	Expected 'To'
1014	Expected 'End'
1015	Expected 'Function'
1016	Expected 'Sub'
1017	Expected 'Then'
1018	Expected 'Wend'
1019	Expected 'Loop'
1020	Expected 'Next'
1021	Expected 'Case'
1022	Expected 'Select'
1023	Expected expression
1024	Expected statement
1025	Expected end of statement
1026	Expected integer constant
1027	Expected 'While' or 'Until'
1028	Expected 'While', 'Until' or end of statement
1029	Too many locals or arguments
1030	Identifier too long
1031	Invalid number
1032	Invalid character
1033	Un-terminated string constant

Table Continued on Following Page

Code	Description
1034	Un-terminated comment
1035	Nested comment
1036	'Me' cannot be used outside of a procedure
1037	Invalid use of 'Me' keyword
1038	'loop' without 'do'
1039	Invalid 'exit' statement
1040	Invalid 'for' loop control variable
1041	Variable redefinition
1042	Must be first statement on the line
1043	Cannot assign to non-ByVal argument
1044	Cannot use parentheses when calling a Sub
1045	Expected literal constant
1046	Expected 'In'
1047	Expected 'Class'
1048	Must be defined inside a Class
1049	Expected Let or Set or Get in property declaration
1050	Expected 'Property'
1051	Number of arguments must be consistent across properties specification
1052	Cannot have multiple default property/method in a Class
1053	Class initialize or terminate do not have arguments
1054	Property set or let must have at least one argument
1055	Unexpected 'Next'
1056	'Default' can be specified only on 'Property' or 'Function' or 'Sub'
1057	'Default' specification must also specify 'Public'
1058	'Default' specification can only be on Property Get
5016	Regular Expression object expected
5017	Syntax error in regular expression
5018	Unexpected quantifier

Code	Description
5019	Expected ']' in regular expression
5020	Expected ')' in regular expression
5021	Invalid range in character set
32811	Element not found

For more information about VBScript, visit Microsoft's Scripting site, at
http://msdn.microsoft.com/scripting.

Glossary

Although e-commerce is a relatively new thing, because it's based in the world of computing it already has a plethora of jargon associated with it. Here are some of the terms used in this book:

- **Banner ad** – the name given to a small advertisement that appears as a small rectangle somewhere on your site, usually at the top of the page. The industry standard size for a banner ad is 468x60 pixels.

- **Bricks and Mortar** – how we refer to the physical stores that people visit.

- **Brochureware** – the term given to Web sites that are effectively Web-based copies of a companies marketing information.

- **Business-to-Business E-commerce** (or **B2B**) – the term used when selling items to another business.

- **Business-to-Consumer E-commerce** (or **B2C**) – the term used when selling to members of the public.

- **Cart** – the name given to a software device which groups the items a visitor wants to buy.

- **Checkout** – the name given to the actual process of buying the items the visitor has in their cart.

- **Click-through** – the name given to a single click on a banner that takes the visitor over to the advertiser's site.

- **Community** – the name given to extended features in a site which attempt to group and coalesce people into groups or communities in the hope that they will buy products from you.

- **Credit Card Authentication** – how we authenticate the card once we've captured it.

- **Customer** – the name given to a visitor to the site that has purchased an item.

- **Customer Data Capture** – the process of safely and reliably capturing a customer's credit card, shipping, and billing information.

- **Department** – how we divide and arrange groups of products into common themes, like "espresso machines", "drip machines".

- **Drop shipping** – the process whereby suppliers and distributors ship packages to your customers, meaning you do not have to keep stock.

- **E-business** – the overall adoption of Internet based business practices.

- **E-commerce** – the process of selling goods and services over a Web site.

- **E-tailer** – a "cute" name for someone who sells products through e-commerce.

- **Firewall** – either a software, hardware, or hybrid device that controls traffic coming into and going out of a network. Your organization's network may have a firewall preventing access to certain game servers on the Internet, as well as preventing access to sensitive network resources to users outside of the network.

- **HTTPS** – the name given to the protocol which enables secure communication between a customer and the store.

- **Page view** – the name given to a single page requested by a visitor of the site. This is a factor for measuring site performance.

- **Portal** – A web site that presents a wide variety of resources and services.

- **Registration** – the process of capturing a visitor's information so they can be identified in community features.

- **Store** – the name given to the site that people visit and buy stuff from.

- **Visitor** – the name given to someone browsing our site that isn't known to have made a purchase.

Index

Index

Index